WELCOME TO PARIS

Paris is one of the most beautiful cities on earth, a truth easily appreciated on a stroll that could yield one stunning vista after another, from the epic Eiffel Tower to the regal Jardin des Tuileries to the petite cafés bursting onto the sidewalks. Beyond the city's visual appeal, the cultural riches of the French capital are unsurpassed. Whether you opt to explore the historic, fashion-conscious, bourgeois, or bohemian and arty sides of Paris, one thing is certain: the City of Light will always enthrall.

ASONS TO GO

★ **ndmarks:** From the Eiffel Tower to the Arc de Triomphe, Paris dazzles.

★ **Chic Shopping:** The Champs-Élysées and Rue St-Honoré are the ultimate shopaholic high.

★ **Heavenly Food:** Whether it's haute cuisine or baguettes, locals know how to eat.

★ **The Seine:** The river's bridges and islands reward exploration by foot or boat.

★ **Grand Museums:** From the mammoth Louvre to the petite Musée Rodin, art abounds.

★ **Majestic Churches:** Notre-Dame and Sacré-Coeur boldly mark the city's skyline.

Fodor's PARIS

Design: Tina Malaney, *Associate Art Director*; Erica Cuoco, *Production Designer*

Photography: Jennifer Arnow, *Senior Photo Editor*; Mary Robnett, *Photo Researcher*

Maps: Rebecca Baer, *Senior Map Editor*; Mark Stroud, Henry Colomb (Moon Street Cartography), David Lindroth, *Cartographers*

Production: Angela L. McLean, *Senior Production Manager*; Jennifer DePrima, *Editorial Production Manager*

Sales: Jacqueline Lebow, *Sales Director*

Business & Operations: Chuck Hoover, *Chief Marketing Officer*; Joy Lai, *Vice President and General Manager*; Stephen Horowitz, *Head of Business Development and Partnerships*

Writers: Nancy Heslin, Linda Hervieux, Jennifer Ladonne, Virginia Power, Jack Vermee

Editors: Amanda Sadlowski, Sue MacCallum-Whitcomb

Production Editor: Carrie Parker

32nd Edition

ISBN 978-1-101-87993-1

ISSN 0149–1288

PRINTED IN THE UNITED STATES OF AMERICA

10 9 8 7 6 5 4 3 2 1

Fodor's

PARIS

Oct 2016

CONTENTS

CONTENTS

ABOUT THIS GUIDE

Fodor's Recommendations

Everything in this guide is worth doing—we don't cover what isn't—but exceptional sights, hotels, and restaurants are recognized with additional accolades. Fodor's Choice ★ indicates our top recommendations, and **Best Bets** call attention to notable hotels and restaurants in various categories. Care to nominate a new place? Visit Fodors.com/contact-us.

Trip Costs

We list prices wherever possible to help you budget well. Hotel and restaurant price categories from **$** to **$$$$** are noted alongside each recommendation. For hotels, we include the lowest cost of a standard double room in high season. For restaurants, we cite the average price of a main course at dinner or, if dinner isn't served, at lunch. For attractions, we always list adult admission fees; discounts are usually available for children, students, and senior citizens.

Hotels

Our local writers vet every hotel to recommend the best overnights in each price category, from budget to expensive. Unless otherwise specified, you can expect private bath, phone, and TV in your room. *For expanded hotel reviews, facilities, and deals, visit Fodors.com.*

Restaurants

Unless we state otherwise, restaurants are open for lunch and dinner daily. We mention dress code only when there's a specific requirement and reservations only when they're essential or not accepted.

Credit Cards

The hotels and restaurants in this guide typically accept credit cards. If not, we'll say so.

Top Picks	Hotels & Restaurants
★ Fodor's Choice	⊡ Hotel
	↵ Number of rooms
Listings	
⊠ Address	❍ Meal plans
⊠ Branch address	✕ Restaurant
☎ Telephone	⚓ Reservations
🖷 Fax	🏛 Dress code
⊕ Website	▭ No credit cards
✉ E-mail	$ Price
✈ Admission fee	
⊙ Open/closed times	**Other**
Ⓜ Subway	⇨ See also
✛ Directions or Map coordinates	☞ Take note
	🏌 Golf facilities

EUGENE FODOR

Hungarian-born Eugene Fodor (1905–91) began his travel career as an interpreter on a French cruise ship. The experience inspired him to write *On the Continent* (1936), the first guidebook to receive annual updates and discuss a country's way of life as well as its sights. Fodor later joined the U.S. Army and worked for the OSS in World War II. After the war, he kept up his intelligence work while expanding his guidebook series. During the Cold War, many guides were written by fellow agents who understood the value of insider information. Today's guides continue Fodor's legacy by providing travelers with timely coverage, insider tips, and cultural context.

EXPERIENCE PARIS

PARIS TODAY

Bienvenue à Paris! Or, welcome to Paris! Although it may seem as if time stands still in this city—with its romantic buildings, elegant parks, and sublime squares—there's an undercurrent of small but significant changes happening here that might not be immediately obvious.

The Environment

Despite the pall cast by severe smog in recent years, Parisians are breathing a little easier these days as the city becomes more environmentally aware. Emission-free buses and the first hydrogen-powered riverboat are making the capital more eco-friendly. The popular Vélib' bike program and the Autolib' car-sharing service are further helping to reduce Paris's carbon footprint. In addition to the gradual replacement of paved streets with more aesthetically pleasing cobblestones and the widening of tree-lined sidewalks, the city is slowly implementing an ambitious project to permanently pedestrianize expressways along the Seine, following the success of Paris Plage, the yearly beach party. In September 2015, vehicles were banned from the city center from 11 am to 7 pm, an unprecedented car-free day that was heralded by strolling locals and tourists alike, and starting in spring 2016, the Champs-Élysées was completely pedestrianized once a month. There are also plans in the works to have half the city's parks open 24/7 from mid-April through mid-September.

Healthy Eating

You'll always find foie gras, steak frites, and *macarons* in this gastonomic mecca (though a poll confirms 29% of the population forgo the former for "ethical reasons"). Yet Parisians are opening up to more diverse dining options and healthier lifestyles, causing a massive boom in vegetarian restaurants. There are now some 220 eateries listed in Paris serving non-meat dishes, including the new Wild and the Moon in the Marais district, which serves a 100% vegan and gluten-free menu. Parisians are also moving their bodies, and ever-expanding fitness facilities are making exercising more culturally acceptable than ever before.

Tech-Savvy Citizens

France has one of the highest smartphone usages in Europe, and new gadgets are popping up everywhere since an ongoing government program began encouraging innovation. Centers like the Gaîté Lyrique mix technology with art on a daily basis. Google opened the Google Cultural

WHAT'S HOT

In a major campaign to clean up its act, Paris's deputy mayor in charge of cleanliness has upped the ante against environmental pollution, so in 2017 you'll be fined for littering (including gum), not scooping after pooping (for Fido, that is), and for throwing away your cigarette butt in the street (for that, it's a €68 ticket).

After eight years, the reopening of the Musée de l'Homme brings with it exceptional views of the Eiffel Tower and the Seine while over at the French mint, La Monnaie de Paris, a Zen garden and Guy Savoy café have set up shop. By the end of 2016, the restoration at the Grand Palais will be complete, including the addition of an entrance court and new passageways. Visitors can also now discover the roof of the 1900 World Fair building.

Institute, which includes a permanent exhibit at the Pavillon de l'Arsenal. Versailles enlists the latest technology to engage visitors, and the Louvre uses Nintendo 3DS systems as its audioguides. Bakeries are giving a nod to the future by letting you pay at automated machines while the revolutionary Smarter Paris app updates continuously (and offline) in real-time everything from bus info to maps and restaurant reviews, avoiding roaming charges.

Culture

Music lovers and architecture buffs alike rejoiced when the curtain rose at La Philharmonie de Paris in the Parc de la Villette in 2015. Designed by Jean Nouvel, the striking new home of the Orchestre de Paris seats 2,400 and cost a whopping €381 million. Makeovers of existing venues (most notably the Musée Rodin's Hôtel Biron) are also cause for celebration. In fact, culture vultures are still buzzing about the reopening of the Musée Picasso Paris after extensive renovation work—including the installation of bullet-proof windows at €12,000 a pop—as well as the eight-year, €96 million overhaul of the Musée de l'Homme, where Picasso himself used to go to admire African art.

Safety

The year 2015 changed Paris forever, with the Charlie Hebdo attack in January and the Bataclan massacre in November leaving the capital wondering how life could ever return to normal. But rather than shuttering up their apartments and cowering to threats, Parisians took to the streets, filled café seats, and lived their lives with the usual *joie de vivre*. While tourism did understandably see a decline during the weeks immediately following the November attacks, public security in Paris, and all other cities in France, continues to be the government's number one priority. You'll notice longer lines for airport security checks, see yellow, orange, or red colored signs for "Vigipirate," the national security alert system, and, on the streets, an increased presence of police and soldiers. Despite the events of 2015, Paris remains one of the world's safest cities, and travelers shouldn't feel discouraged from experiencing the culture and beauty the city has to offer.

After a four-year, multimillion dollar renovation, famed Paris hotel The Ritz finally reopened its doors in 2016. Aside from luxurious rooms, there are also three restaurants, three bars (including the famous Bar Hemingway), and a signature spa that will be devoted exclusively to Chanel products.

Fondation Galeries Lafayette has found a new home in the Marais: 25,000 square feet over five stories of a 17th-century historic building, designed by Dutch architect Rem Koolhaas. In addition, the 18th-century Hôtel de la Marine at Place de la Concorde is now open to the public.

WHAT'S WHERE

The numbers refer to chapters.

2 Ile de la Cité and Ile St-Louis. Just a few steps from the "mainland," these small islands in the Seine are the heart of Paris. This is where you'll find Notre-Dame and Sainte-Chapelle.

3 Around the Eiffel Tower. With the Champ de Mars, Les Invalides, and the Seine nearby, many lovely strolls give you camera-ready views of Paris's ultimate monument.

4 Champs-Élysées. The Champs-Élysées and Arc de Triomphe are obvious stops for visitors, but several excellent museums here are also well worth checking out.

5 Around the Louvre. Anchored by the renowned museum, this neighborhood has ultra-chic streets and *passages couverts* that attract shoppers as well as art lovers.

6 The Grands Boulevards. Use the Opéra Garnier as your landmark and set out to do some power shopping. There are some good, small museums in the area, too.

7 Montmartre. Like a village within a city, Montmartre feels separate from the rest of Paris—but it's prime tourist territory, with Sacré-Coeur as its main attraction.

8 The Marais. Paris's old Jewish neighborhood is now one of the city's hippest hoods. While here, visit the renovated Picasso Museum and linger at lovely Place des Vosges.

9 Eastern Paris. If it's new and happening, you'll find it out here. Neighborhoods like Canal St-Martin are full of trendy eateries, funky galleries, and edgy boutiques.

10 The Latin Quarter. Built around the fabled Sorbonne, the Latin Quarter has been the center of student life since 1257. It's also home to the Panthéon and Musée de Cluny.

11 St-Germain-des-Prés. The Musée d'Orsay is a must-see for fans of Impressionism, but make sure you leave time to amble through the charming Jardin du Luxembourg.

12 Montparnasse. Once the haunt of creative souls—Picasso and Hemingway included—Montparnasse is now known for its contemporary-art scene, as well as the Catacombs.

13 Western Paris. The Bois de Boulogne is one great reason to trek here. The popular park contains the kid-friendly Jardin d'Acclimatation and art-filled Fondation Louis Vuitton.

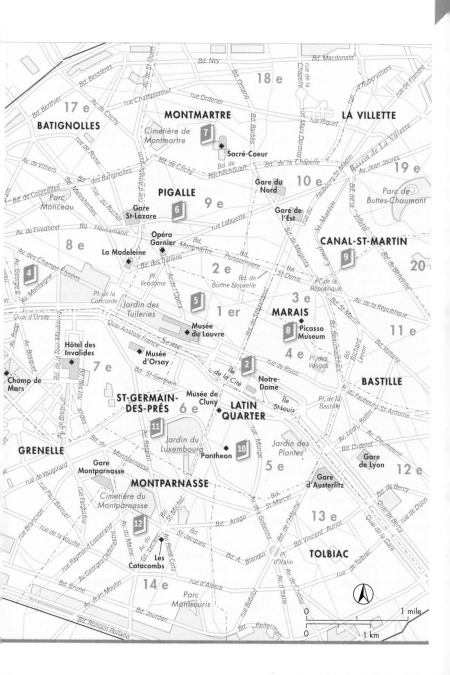

PARIS PLANNER

When to Go

Although the City of Light is magical all year round, summer is the most popular (and priciest) time to go. As recently as 2011, Paris was largely deserted in August when locals fled to the coast or country-side, leaving a wake of closed shops and restaurants. But today it remains very much alive throughout the summer, with outdoor music festivals, open-air movie screenings, and fun activities like those available at the popular Paris Plage, the "beach" on the Right Bank of the Seine.

Nevertheless, the city is perhaps most appealing in late spring and early fall. June, when long, warm days translate into extended hours of sightseeing (the sun doesn't set until 10 pm), is particularly gorgeous. Ditto for September, which promises temperate weather, saner rates, and cultural events timed for the *rentrée* (or return), signifying the end of summer vacation. In the third weekend in September, scores of national buildings that are normally closed to the public open for visits during the annual Journées du Pat-rimoine (Patrimony Days).

Winter can be dark and cold, but it's also the best time to find cheap airfares and hotel deals. Spring tends to remain damp and chilly into May, when prices start rising in synch with the mercury in local thermometers.

Getting Around

Thanks to Baron Haussmann's mid-19th-century redesign, Paris is a compact won-der of wide boulevards, gracious parks, and leafy squares; and, without question, the best way to explore it is on foot.

When you want a lift, though, public transportation is easy and inexpensive. The *métro* (subway) will get you just about anywhere you want to go for €1.80 a ride (a *carnet,* or "pack" of 10 tickets, is €14.10); tickets also work on buses, trams, and the RER train line within Paris.

If you're sticking to sites on or near the river, Batobus offers a convenient on-the-water alternative. A ticket for one day of unlimited hop-on/hop-off boat travel costs €16.

Paris is divided into 20 *arrondissements* (neighborhoods) spiraling out from the center of the city. The numbers reveal the neighborhood's location and its age, the 1er arrondissement at the city's heart being the oldest. The arrondissements in central Paris—the 1er to 8e—are the most visited. It's worth picking up a copy of *Paris Pratique Par Arrondissement,* the essential map guide, available at news-stands and bookstores.

Saving Time and Money

Paris is one of the world's most visited cities—with the crowds to prove it—so it pays to be prepared. Buy tickets online when you can: most cultural centers and museums offer advance-ticket sales, and the small service fee you'll pay might be worth the time saved waiting in line. Investigate alternative entrances at pop-ular sites (there are three at the Louvre, for example), and check when rates are reduced, often during once-a-week eve-ning openings. Also note that national museums are free the first Sunday of each month; this includes the Louvre, Musée d'Orsay, and Centre Pompidou.

A Paris Museum Pass (⊕ *www.paris museumpass.com*) can save you money if you're planning on serious sightseeing, but it might be even more valuable because it allows you to bypass the lines. It's sold at the destinations it covers as well as at air-ports, major métro stations, and the tour-ism office in the Carrousel du Louvre. The two-, four-, and six-day passes cost €42, €56, and €69, respectively.

Stick to the omnipresent ATMs (but try to use indoor machines) for the best exchange rates; exchanging cash at your hotel or in a store is never going to be to your advantage.

Hours

Paris is by no means a 24/7 city, so planning your days beforehand can save you aggravation. Museums are closed one day a week (usually Monday or Tuesday), and most stay open late at least one night each week, which is also the least crowded time to visit. Store hours are generally 9:30 or 10 am to 7 or 8 pm, Monday through Saturday, though smaller shops may close for several hours during the afternoon. For the past few years, "Yes Weekend" demonstrations by workers have encouraged the government to relax laws banning stores from opening on Sunday; shops are now permitted to open 12 Sundays per year at the owner's discretion rather than the previous five. Stores in tourist areas are exempt from these restrictions, so the best spots for Sunday shopping are the Champs-Élysées and the Marais where most retailers open around 2 pm.

Eating Out

Restaurants follow French mealtimes, serving lunch from noon to 2:30 pm and dinner from 7:30 or 8 pm. Some cafés serve food all day long. If you have your heart set on a specific restaurant, it's wise to reserve a table for dinner; top choices book up months in advance. When you're ready for the check, you must ask for it (it's considered rude to bring a bill unbidden). In cafés you'll get a register receipt with your order. *Service* (gratuity) is always included, but it's good form to leave something extra if you're satisfied with the service: a few cents for drinks, €1 for lunch, €3 at dinner. Leave 5% of the bill only in higher-end restaurants.

What to Wear

When it comes to clothing, the standard French look is dressier than the American equivalent. Athletic clothes are reserved for sports. Sneakers are not usually worn by adults, but if you pack yours, keep them for daytime only. Neat jeans are acceptable everywhere except at more chic restaurants; check to see whether there's a dress code.

Paris Etiquette

The Parisian reputation for rudeness is undeserved. In fact, Parisians are sticklers for politeness and exchanging formal greetings is the rule. Informal American-style manners are considered impolite. Beginning an exchange with a simple "Do you speak English?" will get you on the right foot. Learning a few key French words will take you far. Offer a hearty *bonjour* (bohn-zhoor) when walking into a shop or café and an *au revoir* (o ruh-vwahr) when leaving, even if nobody seems to be listening (a chorus may reply). When speaking to a woman over age 16, use *madame* (ma-dam), literally "my lady." For a young woman or girl, use *mademoiselle* (mad-mwa-zel). A man of any age goes by *monsieur* (murh-syur). Always say please, *s'il vous plaît* (seel-voo-play), and thank you, *merci* (mehr-see).

PARIS
TOP ATTRACTIONS

Eiffel Tower

(A) No monument symbolizes Paris better than Gustave Eiffel's iconic Iron Lady, a "temporary" structure that opened in 1889. It's breathtaking, whether you join the millions of visitors taking selfies from the top or see it sparkling from your hotel window after dark. Check out the glass floor on the first level.

Notre-Dame

(B) It took almost 200 years to finish this cathedral, but it was well worth the wait. Immortalized by Victor Hugo and his fictional hunchback, the Dame is a Gothic masterpiece. In 2013 she celebrated her 850th birthday with a bang—or at least a clang: nine new bells now reproduce the sounds of yesteryear.

Jardin du Luxembourg

(C) Beloved by urban-weary Parisians, this is one of the Left Bank's prime leisure spots. Relax in a reclining park chair with a picnic or a book, watch a game of *boules* while the kids enjoy a marionette show, or visit an exhibition at the Musée du Luxembourg in the 17th-century Palais de Luxembourg.

Jardin des Tuileries

(D) This formal, oh-so-French garden stretches between the Louvre and Place de la Concorde. Originally laid out in the 16th century, it's punctuated by contemporary sculptures and includes two noteworthy museums: the Jeu de Paume and the Musée de l'Orangerie. In summer, there's a small amusement park, too.

Arc de Triomphe

(E) The 164-foot-tall Arc de Triomphe has served as the backdrop for official military parades since its completion in 1836. Use the underground passageway to reach the monument, where you can visit the Tomb of the Unknown Soldier beneath the arch or mount the stairs for amazing panoramic views.

Musée d'Orsay

(F) Built as a train station for the 1900 World's Fair, this beautiful Belle Époque building is now filled with Art Nouveau objects, Impressionist paintings, vintage photography, and realist sculptures. Be sure to drink in the Seine views from the grand ballroom, which today houses a restaurant.

Opéra Garnier

(G) Magnificently over the top, Charles Garnier's opera house is a Second Empire jewel. Its marble staircase and ruby-red box seats have been featured in films from *Dangerous Liaisons* to *Marie-Antoinette*, and its backstage corridors are famously haunted by the Phantom of the Opera.

Centre Pompidou

(H) Renzo Piano and Richard Rogers's groundbreaking "inside-out" design delivered a visual shock when Centre Pompidou opened back in 1977—and it's still an eye-popper. The galleries (including one aimed at kids) make it a top destination for connoisseurs of modern and contemporary art.

Sacré-Coeur

(I) Poised at the highest point in the city, this white wedding cake of a basilica dominates Montmartre's hilltop. Most visitors are content with the views overlooking Paris from Sacré-Coeur's stairs, but ambitious sightseekers can ascend to the top of its 271-foot dome for an even better perspective.

Musée du Louvre

(J) The grandest museum in the world began as a medieval fortress and morphed into a sumptuous royal palace before the French Revolution gave it a new lease on life as home to the Republic's art collection. Don't miss the art lover's "holy trinity"—*Mona Lisa*, Winged Victory, and Venus de Milo.

PARIS LIKE A LOCAL

To appreciate the City of Light as the locals do, start by learning some of the daily rituals of Parisian life. These simple pleasures will quickly get you into the swing of things.

Shopping

Hit the markets. Parisians prefer the boisterous atmosphere of bustling street markets to the drab *supermarchés* (supermarkets). Even if you're just buying picnic fixings, you can follow suit. The city's website (⊕ *www.paris.fr/english*) has a full listing of Paris's markets (many of which are closed Mondays), but a few of our faves include Le Marché d'Aligre, just off Rue du Faubourg St-Antoine beyond the Opéra Bastille, a food market which dates back to the 18th century. Le Marché Mouffetard, between the Panthéon and the Jardin des Plantes, is a combination of stands and food shops that spills out onto Rue Mouffetard, a cobbled pedestrian street crammed with restaurants, cafés, and tempting little stores. You might not need to buy a bouquet, but the flower markets are lovely for wandering.

Go on a shopping spree. You can't avoid the fact that Parisians dress spectacularly and would not be caught dashing to the *boulangerie* for a morning croissant in sweatpants, if they even own a pair. A pair of belted jeans, a black tee with a navy boyfriend blazer, leather ballet flats (or 6-inch heels, depending on the mood), and a designer handbag draped over an arm is more likely the look you need to go for to fit in. Yet few do their shopping on the Champs-Élysées, which these days is littered with chain stores. The Marais district is a safe bet for one-off shops, but for prestigious brands head to Avenue Montaigne or Faubourg St-Honoré.

Getting Around

Ride the métro. Taxis in France are pretty expensive (and there's a war against Uber) so the métro is a practical and often economical way to buzz around the city. Trains start running at 5:30 am with the last train pulling into the station at around 12:30 am weekdays (and 1:30 to 2 am on weekends). Tickets can be purchased at the green machines in stations with bills or coins, and chip-based credit cards; remember to validate your ticket at the turnstile and hold on to it in case an inspector asks to see it, otherwise you could be fined. Except for new trains, you'll have to open the doors by button or handle. Use the train number as your guide, not the color, and if you go the wrong direction, get off at the next stop and turn around; you don't have to buy a new ticket. There's the Visiter Paris en Métro app to help guide you.

Take a blue bike. The city's bike plan Vélib' has 20,000 bikes across the city at your disposal 24/7. It's a convenient way to get around with the added advantage of discovering off-the-beaten-path routes. You can buy a 1-day pass (€1.70) or a 7-day ticket (€8) online or at any Vélib' station, which includes the first 30 minutes free. If you keep it for more than 30 minutes you pay an additional €1, then €2 for the next 30 minutes, and €4 for each half hour on top of that.

Food and Drink

Soak in the coffee culture. *Le café* in Paris isn't simply a drink that begins the day: it's a way of life. Though Parisians do stop at the counter to order a quick *café expresse, bien serré, s'il vous plaît* ("good and strong, please"), more often people treat the café as an extension of their home or office, with laptops precariously balanced, cell phones ringing, gossip being shared, and business being done at any time of the day. Choose one with a patio or good windows for people-watching, or pause at the nearest counter, and you're in for a dose of Parisian café culture. There's no rush to leave and it's fine to request a glass of water. Just one caveat: don't complicate your coffee order. Other than at a trickle of places, cafés don't serve low-fat or soy milk, even if they say they do.

Chomp down on a baguette. The Eiffel Tower might be the most famous symbol of Paris, but perhaps the true banner of France is the baguette, the long, caramel-color bread offered at every meal. Locals take inordinate pride at finding the best baguette in the neighborhood. To locate a worthy *boulangerie*—a bakery that specializes in bread, as opposed to a *pâtisserie*, one specializing in pastries—look for a line outside on weekend mornings. Also look for places labeled *artisan* to ensure that you're getting the genuine creation, not a less-tasty industrial version. A tip: if you see little raised dots on the underside, it means the baguette was made by a machine instead of by hand. True Parisians know that all baguettes are not created equal and will order one *bien cuit* (well-done) to get the crispiest of the batch. After buying yours, do what many locals do: nibble the end of the crust while it's still warm.

Indulge in some pastries. High prices are making luxury all the more elusive in Paris, but there's one indulgence most people can still afford, at least occasionally: fine pastries. As you can see when you stop in at any of Paris's extraordinary *pâtisseries* (pastry shops), a wonderful array of French treats awaits those with a sweet tooth. Be sure to try the deliciously airy and intense *macarons*—which have nothing in common with the heavy American shredded-coconut macaroons you might be familiar with. Another traditional sweet is the *mont-blanc*, a mini-mountain of chestnut puree capped with whipped cream.

PARIS WITH KIDS

Paris is often promoted as an adult destination, but there's no shortage of children's activities to keep the young ones busy—even many of the city's top attractions have carousels parked outside them in summer. Make sure to buy a *Pariscope* (found at most newsstands) and check the *enfants* section for current children's events.

Museums

Paris has a number of museums that cater to the young and young at heart. They're great places to occupy restless minds, especially if the weather is bad. The Parc de la Villette's **Cité des Sciences et de l'Industrie** is an enormous science center with a kids' area that's divided into two main sections: one for 2- to 7-year-olds, another for the 5 to 12 set. Interactive exhibits let inquisitive young visitors do everything from building a house to learning about communications through the ages. The **Musée de la Musique,** also in the Parc de la Villette, will appeal to more arts-minded children. The **Musée de la Poupée,** a cozy museum in the heart of the Marais, has a collection of 500-plus dolls dating back to the 1800s, complete with costumes, furniture, accessories, and even a "hospital," where "sick" dolls and plush toys come to be repaired. Labels might be in French, but they're not really the point anyway. The whole family can spend hours ogling exhibits about the natural world at the **Grande Galerie de l'Évolution**; its hands-on Galerie des Enfants, for children aged 6 to 12, is an added bonus. The **Palais de la Découverte** has high-definition, 3-D exhibits covering subjects like chemistry, biology, meteorology, and physics, so there's bound to be some interesting dinner conversation when the day is done. Many of the displays are in French, but that doesn't stop most kids from having a blast—the choice between this and the Louvre is a no-brainer. The **Musée de l'Homme** is a bit more of a grown-up museum, but the collection of 120 mummies will certainly wow kids.

Zoos

Visiting a zoo is usually a good way to get kids' attention, although you might want to keep in mind that most European ones aren't as spacious as their American counterparts. A part of the **Muséum National d'Histoire Naturelle** (with its own exceptional butterfly collection and Gallery of Paleontology and Comparative Anatomy with too many bones on display to count), the **Ménagerie** at the Jardin des Plantes is an urban zoo dating from 1794 and is home to more than 240 mammals, nearly 400 birds, 210 reptiles, and 900 insects. The country's largest zoo, the **Parc Zoologique** in the Bois de Vincennes, lets you observe animals in realistic-looking habitats. The **Musée de la Chasse et de la Nature** in the Marais is another place to get up close and personal with ferocious lions, tigers, and one in-your-face polar bear—these critters just aren't alive. The impressive collection of taxidermy trophies takes children on a safari to discover man's relationship with animals.

Shows

What child could pass up the circus? There are several in the city, including the **Espaces Chapiteaux** at the Parc de la Villette. **Pinderland,** an attraction south of Paris, promises an interactive experience: the first European theme park dedicated entirely to the circus comes complete with a circus academy and themed museum. For traditional entertainment, try **Les Guignols,** French puppet shows. The original Guignol was a marionette character created by Laurent Mourguet, supposedly in his own likeness, celebrating life, love, and wine; today, shows are primarily aimed at children, and are found in open-air theaters throughout the city in the warmer months. Check out the Marionettes des Champs-Élysées, Champ de Mars, Parc Montsouris, Parc des Buttes-Chaumont, Jardin du Luxembourg, and the Parc Floral in the Bois de Vincennes. Even if they don't understand French, kids are usually riveted.

Underground Paris

There's something about exploring underground that seems to fascinate kids, at least the older ones. **Les Égouts,** the Paris sewer system, has a certain gross factor but isn't actually that disgusting. It's worth noting, though, that the smell is definitely ranker in the summer months. At the redesigned **Catacombs,** in Montparnasse, dark tunnels filled with skulls and skeletons of 6 million Parisians are spookily titillating—provided you're not prone to nightmares. For some cheap underground entertainment without the ick factor, the **métro** itself can be its own sort of adventure, complete with fascinating station art such as the submarine decor at Arts-et-Metiers, the colorful Parisian timeline murals at Tuileries, or the Egyptian statues of the Louvre–Rivoli station. A good tip: métro Lines 1 and 14 feature conductorless trains that let you sit at the very front, and kids love the sensation that they're driving.

Active Options

Many kids are oddly thrilled at the prospect of climbing countless stairs just to get a cool view. The **Eiffel Tower** is the quintessential Paris climb (especially now that the first level boasts a dizzying glass floor), but **Notre-Dame** gets extra points for the gargoyles, and the **Arc de Triomphe** is a good bet, since it's at the end of the

Champs-Élysées. Parks offer other opportunities for expending energy. In summer, kids can work off steam on trampolines or ride ponies at the **Jardin des Tuileries;** the **Jardin du Luxembourg** has a playground and a pond where they can rent miniature boats; and the **Bois de Boulogne** has real rowboats, bumper cars, plus lots of wide-open spaces. For rainy-day rescues, La Galerie des Enfants at the **Pompidou Centre** has an indoor playground, as well as art exhibitions. In winter, consider ice-skating. From mid-December through February several outdoor sites transform into spectacular rinks with twinkling lights, music, and rental skates available; the main one is at **Place de l'Hôtel de Ville,** in front of City Hall.

Sweet Treats

All that activity will no doubt make kids hungry, and luckily there's no shortage of special places to stop for a snack. Crêperies always aim to please and you'll find plenty along the main tourist streets. Also be on the look-out for hot chocolate—the French version is deliciously thick and yummy, unlike what American children are usually used to. You'll also find plenty of places offering decadent ice cream. French children adore the pastel clouds of meringue that decorate almost every pâtisserie window—and, when in need, a chocolate croissant is never hard to find. After filling up, you can cap the day with perhaps the best treat of all, a **boat ride on the Seine.** It's the perfect way to see the sights while resting weary feet.

GREAT ITINERARIES

Paris is a treasure of neighborhoods and history, and a visit to this glorious city is never quite as simple as a quick look at a few landmarks. But if you only have a day to take it all in, there are some icons that you just can't miss. Over five days, you'll have the luxury to truly take in the sites and museums while leaving time for random exploring including sampling the foods and beverages that have put the capital on the gastronomic world map.

PARIS IN 1 DAY

Begin your day at the Trocadéro métro, where you can get the best views of the **Eiffel Tower** from the esplanade of the Palais de Chaillot. If you want to ride to the top, now is the best time to get in line (it opens at 9 am). Afterward, take a walk along the Seine, stopping to visit the sculpture gardens of the **Musée Rodin** (entrance to the gardens €2), and continuing on to the **Musée d'Orsay** to tackle the late-19th-century works of art and admire the gorgeous former train station.

If your feet are still happy, cross the gilded Pont Tsar Alexandre III to the **Champs-Élysées**, passing the Belle Époque art palaces known as the **Grand Palais** and **Petit Palais.** You can take Bus 73 (€1.80) from the **Assemblée Nationale** across the bridge to **Place de la Concorde** and all the way up **Avenue des Champs-Élysées** to the **Arc de Triomphe.** Open until 10:30 pm (11 pm from May to September), its panoramic viewing platform is ideal for admiring the City of Light.

Next, head to the most famous art museum in the world, the **Louvre**. With just one day in the city, you'll have to limit your time here, but grab a museum guide and hit up the Big Three: the *Mona Lisa,* Venus de Milo, and Winged Victory Of Samothrace. There should still be time to see **Notre-Dame Cathedral,** and, if it's before 6 pm, get a glimpse inside.

PARIS IN 5 DAYS

Day 1: Notre-Dame and the Latin Quarter

Start your day at Pont Neuf for excellent views off the western tip of Ile de la Cité, then explore the island's magnificent architectural heritage, including the **Conciergerie, Sainte-Chapelle,** and **Notre-Dame.** The brave can climb the corkscrew staircase to the towers for a gargoyle's-eye view of the city.

Take a detour to neighboring Ile St-Louis for lunch before heading into the medieval labyrinth of the **Latin Quarter;** its most valuable treasures are preserved in the **Musée de Cluny,** including the reconstructed ruins of 2nd-century Gallo-Roman steam baths. At the summit of the hill above the Sorbonne University is the imposing **Panthéon,** a monument (and mausoleum) of French heroes. Follow Rue Descartes to Rue Mouffetard for a café crème on one of the oldest market streets in Paris.

Day 2: Jardin des Tuileries, the Louvre, and the Musée d'Orsay

Begin at **Place de la Concorde,** where an Egyptian obelisk replaces the guillotine where Louis XVI and Marie-Antoinette met their bloody fate during the French Revolution, then escape the traffic in the formal **Jardin des Tuileries,** which once belonged to the 16th-century Tuileries Palace, destroyed during the Paris Commune of 1871. Pass through the small Arc du Carrousel to the modern glass pyramid that serves as the main entrance to the **Louvre,** the world's grandest museum, once a 12th-century fortress. You'll never be able to see it all, but take a few hours to explore and make sure you hit up all the essentials.

The **Musée d'Orsay** merits an afternoon gander and the short post-Louvre stroll to this museum on the Left Bank is just long enough to get some fresh air before feasting your eyes on the world's biggest collection of Impressionist and Postimpressionist masterpieces, housed in a building that's equally magnificent visually.

Day 3: Eiffel Tower, Champs-Élysées, and Arc de Triomphe

Begin your day at the Trocadéro métro, where you can get the best views of the **Eiffel Tower** from the esplanade of the Palais de Chaillot. Visit the newly reopened **Musée de l'Homme,** with 120 mummies among its 30,000 prehistoric artifacts, and take advantage of the spectacular selfie ops of both the Tour Eiffel and the Seine.

Then meander over to Quai d'Orsay, near Invalides, stopping for a *plat du jour* along the way before crossing the Alexandre III bridge to the Grand Palais, where you can now sneak some rooftop peeks, and then visit its sister, the Petit Palais. From here, you can walk all the way up **Avenue des Champs-Élysées** (focus on the prize and not the chain stores that line the avenue) to the **Arc de Triomphe**. Open until 10:30 pm (11 pm from May to September), its panoramic viewing platform is ideal for admiring the City of Light.

Day 4: The Marais

In the 4th arrondissement, the hip Marais district just keeps getting hipper, and is the perfect neighborhood to spend a relaxing day filled with culture, food, and fashion. To the south you can find the **Hôtel de Sens,** home to King Henry IV's feisty ex-wife Queen Marguerite, and one of the few surviving examples of late-medieval

architecture. Around the corner on Rue Charlemagne is a preserved section of the city's 12th-century fortifications built by King Philippe-Augustus. Cross busy Rue St-Antoine to Le Marais and enter the **Hôtel de Sully,** a fine example of the elegant private mansions built here by aristocrats in the early 17th century. Stop by any of the old aristocratic mansions in Le Marais that have been turned into museums, including the **Musée Carnavalet** and the newly renovated **Musée Picasso**.

Day 5: Versailles

On Day 5, head 20 km (12½ miles) southwest of Paris to the gilded palace and reminder of pre-Revolution indulgence that is **Versailles**. The estate is divided into four sections: the Palace with the King's Grand Apartments and the famous Hall of Mirrors, the Grand Trianon, Marie-Antoinette's Estate, and, of, course, the spectacular gardens. Book an English tour, which includes the King's Apartments, Royal Chapel, and Opera, and make sure you get there by 9 am so you can be sure to see everything. The easiest (and least expensive) way to visit Versailles is by the 45-minute Paris RER train serviced from St-Michel–Notre-Dame, Musée d'Orsay, Invalides, and Tour Eiffel stations. Buy tickets (destination: Versailles Rive G) directly from the automatic ticket machines or from the booth.

FREE AND CHEAP

It's easy to break the bank in Paris, but those acquainted with the city know where to find the free (or almost free) stuff. Here are some tips.

Free Exhibits

Thanks to the city of Paris's dedication to promoting culture, access to the permanent collections in municipal museums is free, so you can learn about the city's rich history and revel in artworks without dropping a dime. The **Hôtel de Ville** (City Hall) in the Marais regularly runs several expositions at a time, most of which focus on French artists. Past expos have included the "Life of Edith Piaf" and the works of photographers Wally Ronis and Robert Doisneau. The **Maison Européene de la Photographie,** also in the Marais, is a favorite among flashbulb-poppers and amateur-photography buffs alike—and Wednesdays from 5 to 8 this museum opens its doors free of charge. Expositions can cover everything from the history of the camera and the evolution of printing to selections from some of the world's most famous photographers. Near Place des Vosges, the **Musée Carnavalet**—yup, this is in the Marais, too—puts Paris's past on display with a collection of old signs, keepsakes, relics from bars and cafés, plus paintings of what the city looked like before it was fully developed. It's an excellent place to get a feel for Paris then and now (a €5 donation is appreciated). Other free museums include **Maison de Balzac, Maison de Victor Hugo, Musée Cognacq-Jay, Musée d'Art Moderne de la Ville de Paris,** and the **Petit Palais,** also known as **Musée des Beaux Arts de la Ville de Paris.** And while it's not necessarily an exhibition, there's a free fashion show every Friday at 3 pm on the 4th floor of **Galleries Lafayette;** reserve your place by emailing *fashionshow@galerieslafayette.com.*

Free Music

Many of Paris's churches host free or almost-free concerts at lunchtime and in the evening, allowing you to enjoy fine classical music in an ethereal setting. Look for flyers posted around the city and outside the churches, or check weekly events listings. There are free organ recitals on Sunday at **Notre-Dame** and **Église St-Eustache,** both in the 1er arrondissement, at 4:30 and 5:30 pm respectively. Free concerts at **Église de la Madeleine** (*8e*), **Église St-Roch** (*1er*), the **American Church in Paris** (*7e*), **Église St-Merry** (*4e*), and **Église de la Trinité** (*9e*) are music to frugal ears, too. You can watch up-and-coming students perform in 300 concerts *entrée libre* at the **Conservatoire Nationale Supérieur de Musique. Radio France** also sponsors about 180 free concerts throughout the year (usually at 7:30 on Tuesday, with tickets given out 60 minutes beforehand in Hall B at the studio). In summer and fall there are free concerts in the city's parks, including the **Jardin des Luxembourg** (classical music), the **Parc de la Villette** (world music, pop, and jazz), and the **Parc Floral** in the Bois de Vincennes (classical and jazz). During **Paris Plage,** in late summer, there are free nightly pop and rock concerts on the quays of the Seine. When the weather's nice you're also likely to find musicians along the quai of the **Canal St-Martin,** or in **Place des Vosges,** guitars in hand for spontaneous song.

Parks

If the hustle and bustle of Paris is getting to you, there are plenty of parks where you can kick back for free. Some host no- or low-cost activities and events: the **Parc de la Villette,** for one, shows free open-air movies in July and August as part of the Cinéma en Plein Air Festival. Parisians also like to recharge their batteries with an afternoon catnap in one of the handy reclined chairs scattered throughout the city's gardens. This is the cheapest option for relaxation, reading, and postcard writing—just make sure your possessions are secure if you're actually going to grab some shut-eye. Perennial favorites for parking yourself are the **Jardin du Luxembourg** and the **Jardin des Tuileries**, but one of the most serene venues, buffered from the traffic by the arcaded shops, is the garden at the **Palais Royal,** not far from the Louvre. Any perch along the Seine will also do in a pinch if the busy streets start to feel overwhelming: it's amazing how tranquil a spot by the water can be, so close to the frenetic workings of the city, especially if you find yourself on the incomparably charming **Ile de la Cité.**

Cheap Souvenirs

What souvenir retails for about €0.10 and makes a perfect memento for friends back home? The postcard, of course. Go retro and send some quintessential scenery home with a "J'aime Paris" scribbled on the back, or just bring back a little packet of choice images. For the best prices, check out the news kiosks along Rue de Rivoli and the Grands Boulevards. Keep an eye out for vintage postcards sold by the *bouquinistes* along the Seine and by collectors inside Passage des Panoramas. You can buy stamps at any *tabac* as well as at post offices. Alternatively, you can pop into a French pharmacy where you'll find more than a few products that are cheaper than back home, including some unique French beauty products.

(Almost) Free Sightseeing Tours

Some of the city's public bus routes are fantastically scenic; hop on the right one and you can get a great tour for just €1.80—sans squawking commentary. The **No. 29** route reaches from Gare St-Lazare,

past the Opéra Garnier, to the heart of the Marais, crossing Place des Vosges before ending up at the Bastille. This is one of the few lines that runs primarily on small streets, not major arteries. Hop the **No. 69** bus at Champ de Mars (by the Tour Eiffel) and ride through parts of the Quartier Latin, across the bridge to the Rive Droite near the Louvre, and on to the Bastille. The **No. 72** bus follows the Seine from the Hôtel de Ville west past the Louvre and most of the big-name Rive Droite sights, also giving you views of the Rive Gauche, including the Tour Eiffel. Bus **No. 73** is the only line that goes along Avenue des Champs-Élysées, from the Arc de Triomphe through Place de la Concorde and ending at Musée d'Orsay. You can also take walking tours with the enthusiastic guides from **Paris Greeters** (⊕ *www.greeters.paris*), **Sandemans** (⊕ *www.newparistours.com*), or **City Free Tour** (⊕ *cityfreetour.com*)—all are free, though tips are appreciated.

Free Wine Tastings

Here's a tip for getting tipsy: wine stores sometimes offer free or inexpensive wine tastings, generally on the weekends. Check out **La Derniere Goutte** (*6 rue de Bourbon le Château, 6e, 01–43–29–11–62*) on Saturday from 11 to 7:30, and the prestigious **Caves Taillevent** (*199 rue du Faubourg St-Honoré, 8e, 01–45–61–14–09*) on Saturday from 10:30 to 6. Paris in spring becomes even more enticing with tastings at **Caves Augé** (*116 bd. Haussmann, 8e, 01–45–22–16–97*) each Saturday from 11 to 6 in April and May. **La Cave du Panthéon** (*174 rue St-Jacques, 5e, 01–46–33–90–35*), touted for its conviviality, is another destination where wine lovers congregate on Saturday afternoon to learn about—and indulge in—their favorite beverage.

PARIS MUSEUMS, AN OVERVIEW

There's no shortage of museums in Paris, so it's a good idea to make a plan. This overview includes all of those listed elsewhere in the book; check the index for full listings.

The Big Names

Ambitious art lovers will focus on the Big Three—the **Louvre**, the **Musée d'Orsay**, and **Centre Georges Pompidou.** The Louvre's collection spans from about 7000 BC until 1848, and has its own Big Three: the *Mona Lisa*, the Venus de Milo, and Winged Victory. The d'Orsay's collection picks up where the Louvre's leaves off and continues until 1914. The Pompidou has art from the early 20th century to the present. Of course, smaller spots can have a big impact, too: the **Musée de l'Orangerie** provides a stunning setting for Monet's *Water Lilies*, while the underrated **Musée des Beaux-Arts de la Ville de Paris** in the Petit Palais has an excellent collection of art and *objets*.

One-Man Shows

Three major must-sees are **Musée Rodin**, with its lovely sculpture garden and Hôtel Biron, a listed monument since 1926; **Musée Picasso Paris** (which recently underwent a massive redo); and **Musée Marmottan Monet**, which boasts the single largest collection of works by Claude Monet. Other options include the **Musée Delacroix, Espace Dalí, Musée Gustave Moreau,** and **Musée Zadkine,** all of which are devoted to works by the titular artist. French chanson fans shouldn't miss the one-woman show at the tiny **Edith Piaf Museum.**

House Museums

A house museum is doubly appealing because it offers two treats in one: the art or exhibits and the actual abode. **Maison de Victor Hugo** and **Maison de Balzac** are the former homes of renowned writers.

Musée Jacquemart-André has an intriguing collection of Italian art, and **Musée Nissim de Camondo** has decorative art, mostly from the 18th century. **Musée de la Vie Romantique,** celebrating the novelist George Sand, was the elegant town house of Dutch-born painter Ary Scheffer, and **Musée Cognacq-Jay** was the residence of Ernest Cognacq, founder of the now closed La Samaritaine department store. The small **Musée Baccarat** displays some crystal masterpieces in the former mansion of Marie-Laure de Noailles, patron of the Surrealist circle.

Contemporary Art

Excellent venues for modern art include the **Palais de Tokyo** and **Musée d'Art Moderne de la Ville de Paris.** There's also **Fondation Cartier pour l'Art Contemporain** for emerging artists' work, and **La Maison Rouge,** which shows private collections. The **Pinacothèque de Paris** is a private museum dedicated solely to temporary exhibits, while **Halle St-Pierre** has exhibits of outsider and folk art. **Le 104** is an offbeat option with artist studios, boutiques, and performance spaces. For something new and noteworthy, see **Fondation Louis Vuitton** in the Bois de Boulogne; designed by Franky Gehry, the stunning structure displays a stellar private collection and hosts top-notch temporary exhibitions.

African, Asian, and Islamic Art

There are two superlative places in Paris to see Asian art: **Musée Guimet,** where you'll find a massive collection that spans seven millennia, and **Musée Cernuschi,** a small house museum that holds the personal Asian art collection of Enrico Cernuschi. For Arab and Islamic art and architecture, visit the impressive **Institut du Monde Arabe;** for African art, head instead to **Musée Dapper.** If you have trouble choosing, try the

Musée du Quai Branly: it turns the spotlight on pieces from Africa, Asia, and Oceania.

Photography and Design

For a mix of photographs from different artists, your best bet is the **Maison Européenne de la Photographie. Fondation Henri Cartier-Bresson** features works by the well-known French photographer in a building that was also his atelier. The **Jeu de Paume,** in the Tuileries, showcases modern photography. For modern design, **Fondation Le Corbusier** is well worth the trip to the city's western edge. **Fondation Pierre Bergé-Yves Saint Laurent** is the designer's atelier as well as an archive and gallery of his work. Late 2014 saw the unveiling of another venue honoring a fashion giant: the **Musée Pierre Cardin** in the Marais. The **Musée de la Mode** in Palais Galliera hosts temporary exhibits about fashion in an ornate palace. Offering a different take on textiles, the **Manufacture des Gobelins** traces the history of weaving and tapestry. And don't miss **Les Arts Décoratifs,** which includes the **Musée de la Mode et du Textile** and **Musée de la Publicité,** plus the **Musée des Arts Decoratifs,** featuring one of the world's great decorative-art collections.

French History

Musée de Cluny, home to the well-known *Lady and the Unicorn* tapestry, recalls the Middle Ages. Beginning in that same period, the **Musée d'Art et d'Histoire du Judaïsme** documents Jewish history in France. For Parisian history, don't miss **Musée Carnavalet.** Montmartre has its own museum, **Musée de Montmartre.** The **Cité de l'Architecture et du Patrimoine** presents a history of French architecture, and Google's permanent exhibit in association with **Pavillon de l'Arsenal** traces the history of the city—and envisions its future—through the lens of urban planning.

Maritime history is the subject of the **Musée National de la Marine** in the Palais Chaillot. The **Musée de la Légion d'Honneur** showcases French and foreign military decoration; the phenomenal collection at the **Musée de l'Armée** includes everything from antique weapons to Napoléon's trademark hat; and the **Musée Jean Moulin,** in the Jardin Atlantique, focuses on the life of the famous leader of the French Resistance.

Etc.

Some museums aren't easily classifiable. Anthropology and prehistory of human evolution can be discovered at the **Musée de l'Homme** (the Museum of Mankind), which reopened with great anticipation in October 2015 after a six-year renovation. The **Musée de l'Erotisme** is a seven-story building that explores erotic fantasy. The **Musée du Vin** details the history of wine making and also stages wine tastings.

Art Galleries

The city's hottest avant-garde art scene is on and around Rue Vieille du Temple in the north Marais. Around St-Germain and Place des Vosges the galleries are more traditional; works by old masters and established modern artists dominate the galleries around Rue du Faubourg St-Honoré and Avenue Matignon. Carré Rive Gauche, around Rue du Bac in St-Germain, has dozens of art and antiques galleries on its narrow streets.

The **Association des Galeries** (⊕ *www.associationdesgaleries.org*) lists exhibits in more than 125 galleries through the city. **Paris-art.com** (⊕ *www.paris-art.com*) focuses on contemporary art, with reviews, exhibition calendars, and interviews, in French only.

BEST TOURS IN PARIS

Sometimes a guided tour is the way to go, even if you usually prefer to fly solo while traveling. Tours can be a great way to explore out-of-the-way neighborhoods, to get an insider's perspective on where locals eat and play, and to learn about interesting aspects of the city's history, inhabitants, or architecture. Whether you want a boat tour along the Seine or a more personal, interest-specific walk, you'll find it here.

Boat Tours

Batobus. Hop on and off at one of Batobus's nine stops, which include the Eiffel Tower, Musée d'Orsay, Notre-Dame, and the Champs-Élysées. A one-day pass for unlimited travel—boats are heated and have panoramic views but offer no commentary—is €16; a two-day pass is only €19. ⊠ *Port de la Bourdonnais, Around the Eiffel Tower* ☎ *33/08–25–05–01–01* ⊕ *www.batobus.com* ✉ *From €16.*

Green River Cruises. Whether it's a Sunday cruise or a candlelight happy hour along the Seine, the boat outings offered by Green River Cruises last from one to three hours. They're limited to 11 people maximum, providing a more intimate tour of the city. Champagne is included in some options, but you are welcome to bring your own wine and snacks. ⊠ *Play Time Boat, 34 Quait d'Austerlitz, Montparnasse* ☎ *33/06–50–22–90–65* ⊕ *www.greenriver-paris.fr/en* ✉ *From €34 per person.*

Walking Tours

Sight Seeker's Delight. This company's unique 2½- to 3-hour walking tours bring the city's various quarters to life with engaging infomation and personal insight from English-speaking guides. ⊠ *Paris* ☎ *33/07–82–86–42–89* ⊕ *www. sightseekersdelight.com* ✉ *From €95.*

Wego Walking Paris. These 3½-hour walking tours are in English and begin next to Notre-Dame or at the Eiffel Tower, covering 25 attractions with lots of history and fun anecdotes. Often called the most entertaining tour in Paris, it's pay what you wish, or more accurately, you pay your guide what you think he or she deserves. ⊠ *1 Pont au Double, Ile de la Cité* ⊕ *www.wegowalking.com.*

Speciality Tours

Better Travel Photos Paris. Discover the City of Light through your camera lens while learning how to take skilled snaps under the advice of professional (and English-speaking) photographers. Itineraries range from 3½-hour to multiday tours, covering the Marais, Montmartre, and other classic Paris locations. ⊠ *Paris* ⊕ *www.bettertravelphotos.com* ✉ *From €95.*

Culinary Tours of Paris. Spend over three hours discovering French food, wine, and culture with a French-American tour guide who has lived in Paris for nearly a decade. During the English-speaking tours, you'll dine at two or three different restaurants, with digestive walks of the neighborhoods in between destinations. Tour options focus on the Latin Quarter, Montmartre, or the French countryside (45 minutes east of the city). ⊠ *Paris* ⊕ *www.culinarytoursofparis.com* ✉ *From €80.*

Midnight In Paris On Wheels. Take in the city's main monuments in a nocturnal escapade in a classic 2CV car. The tour guide will tailor the ride to your tastes, whether it be history or a desire to discover new areas. ⊠ *Paris* ☎ *33/06–51–19–24–88* ⊕ *www.midnightinparisonwheels.com/en* ✉ *From €90.*

ILE DE LA CITÉ
AND ILE ST-LOUIS

GETTING ORIENTED

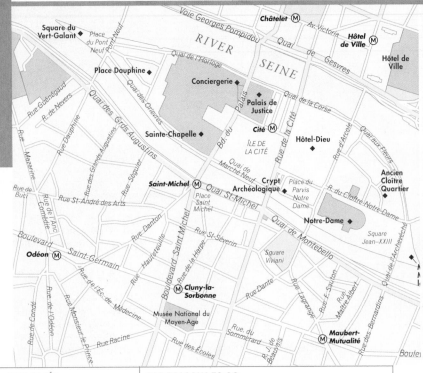

La Charlotte de l'Isle. Sip tea (or lusciously thick hot chocolate) and sample tasty cakes at this atmospheric salon. ⊠ *24 rue St-Louis-en-l'Ile, Ile St-Louis* ☎ *01-43-54-25-83* ⊕ *www. lacharlottedelisle.fr* ⊗ *Closed Tues.* Ⓜ *Pont Marie.*

Le Saint-Régis. Wondering where locals take their coffee on touristy Ile St-Louis? Try this old-timer—it's open until 2 am daily. ⊠ *6 rue Jean de Bellay, Ile St-Louis* ☎ *01-43-54-59-41* ⊕ *www.cafesaintregisparis.com* Ⓜ *Pont Marie.*

Notre-Dame. This gorgeous Gothic cathedral has welcomed visitors to Paris for centuries. Gaze at its famed rose windows, climb the bell tower to mingle with gargoyles, or amble around back to contemplate the awe-inspiring flying buttresses from Square Jean-XXIII. At the end of the plaza in front of the cathedral, down the stairs, is the interesting Crypte Archéologique, a museum that showcases the city's Roman ruins.

Sainte-Chapelle. Visit on a sunny day to best appreciate the exquisite stained glass in this 13th-century chapel built for King Louis IX.

Strolling the islands. Ile de la Cité is where Paris began. Start with the city's oldest bridge, the Pont Neuf (incongruously called the "new bridge") and give a nod to the statue of Henry IV, who once proudly said, "I make love, I make war, and I build." From here, cross to Place Dauphine and make your way to Ile St-Louis, one of the city's most exclusive enclaves.

2

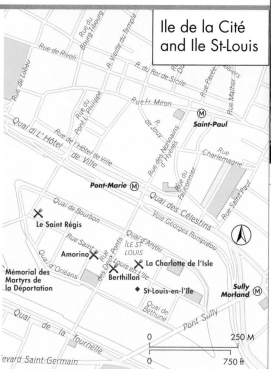

Ile de la Cité and Ile St-Louis

Rue du Bourg l'Abbé
Rue de Rivoli
R. Vieille du Temple
R. du Roi de Sicile
Rue des Rosiers
Rue Pavée
Rue de Lobau
Rue Mahler
Quai de L'Hôtel
Rue Fr. Miron
Ⓜ **Saint-Paul**
Rue du Pont L. Philippe
Rue de l'Hôtel de Ville
R. de Jouy
Rue Charlemagne
Rue des Nonnains d'Hyères
Rue du Fauconnier
Rue Saint-Paul

Pont-Marie Ⓜ
Quai des Célestins
Quai de Bourbon
✕ **Le Saint Régis**
Voie Georges Rompidou
Rue Saint
ILE ST-LOUIS
Quai d'Anjou
✕ **Amorino**
Rue des Deux Ponts
✕ **La Charlotte de l'Isle**
Quai d'Orléans
Rue St-Louis en l'Ile
Berthillon ✕
Mémorial des Martyrs de la Déportation
♦ **St-Louis-en-l'Ile**
Sully Morland Ⓜ
Quai de Béthune
Quai de la Tournelle
Pont Sully
'evard Saint-Germain

0   250 M
0   750 ft

MAKING THE MOST OF YOUR TIME

This little area of Paris is easily walkable and packed with sights and stunning views, so give yourself as much time as possible to explore. With Notre-Dame, the Conciergerie, and Sainte-Chapelle, you could spend a day wandering, but the islands are easily combined with the St-Germain quarter. On warmer days, Rue de Buci is an ideal place to pick up a picnic lunch to enjoy in leafy Square du Vert-Galant at the tip of Ile de la Cité. If you have limited time in the area, make sure you visit Notre-Dame and go for a stroll.

GETTING HERE

Ile de la Cité and Ile St-Louis are in the 1er and 4e arrondissements (Boulevard du Palais is the dividing line between the 1er and 4e arrondissements on Ile de la Cité). If you're too far away to get here on foot, take the métro to St-Michel station or La Cité.

ICE CREAM VS. GELATO

Amorino. Popping up all over—and winning converts faster than you can finish a double scoop—is the Amorino chain of gelaterias, which serves inventive frozen concoctions in the shape of a flower blossom. Popular flavors include rich *bacio* (dark chocolate with hazelnuts) and mascarpone with figs. ✉ *47 rue St-Louis-en-l'Ile, Ile St-Louis* ☎ *01-44-07-48-08* ⊕ *www.amorino.com* Ⓜ *Pont-Marie.*

Berthillon. Parisian ice cream is served at cafés all over town, but it's worth making a pilgrimage to the mecca of artisanal *crèmes glacées* to understand what all the fuss is about. The family-owned Berthillon shop features more than 30 flavors that change with the seasons, from mouth-puckering *cassis* (black currant) in summer to nutty *marron* (candied chestnut) in winter. Expect to wait in a lengthy line for a tiny scoop. ✉ *31 rue St-Louis-en-l'Ile, Ile St-Louis* ☎ *01-43-54-31-61* ⊕ *www.berthillon.fr* ⊙ *Closed Mon. and Tues.* Ⓜ *Pont-Marie.*

Sightseeing
★★★★
Dining
★★
Lodging
★★★
Shopping
★★
Nightlife
★

At the heart of Paris, linked to the banks of the Seine by a series of bridges, are two small islands: Ile St-Louis and Ile de la Cité. They're the perfect places to begin your visit, with postcard-worthy views all around. The Ile de la Cité is anchored by mighty Notre-Dame; farther east, the atmospheric Ile St-Louis is dotted with charming hotels, cozy restaurants, and small specialty shops.

ILE DE LA CITÉ

Updated by
Jack Vermee

At the western tip of Ile de la Cité is regal **Place Dauphine,** one of Paris's oldest squares. The impressive Palais de Justice (courthouse) sits between **Sainte-Chapelle,** the exquisite medieval chapel of saintly King Louis IX, and the **Conciergerie,** the prison where Marie-Antoinette and other bluebloods awaited their slice of history at the guillotine.

The Gothic powerhouse that is **Notre-Dame** originally loomed over a medieval huddle of buildings that were later ordered razed by Baron Georges-Eugène Haussmann, the 19th-century urban planner who transformed Paris into the city we see today. In front of the cathedral is Place du Parvis, the point from which all roads in France are measured. On the north side of the square is the **Hôtel-Dieu** (roughly translated as "general hospital"): it was immortalized by Balzac as the squalid last stop for the city's most unfortunate, but today houses a modern hospital. Just behind the cathedral lies Rue du Cloître-Notre-Dame, which cuts through the **Ancien Cloître Quartier,** on whose narrow streets you can imagine the medieval quarter as it once was, densely packed and teeming with activity. At 9–11 quai aux Fleurs, a plaque commemorates the abode that was the setting of the tragic, 12th-century love affair between the philosopher Peter Abélard and his young conquest, Héloïse.

At the eastern tip of Ile de la Cité is the **Mémorial des Martyrs de la Déportation,** all but hidden in a pocket-size park. A set of stairs leads down to this impressive and moving memorial, which commemorates the French citizens who died in Nazi concentration camps.

TOP ATTRACTIONS

FAMILY **Conciergerie.** Most of the Ile de la Cité's medieval structures fell victim to wunderkind urban planner Baron Haussmann's ambitious rebuilding program of the 1860s. Among the rare survivors are the jewel-like Sainte-Chapelle, a vision of shimmering stained glass, and the Conciergerie, the cavernous former prison where Marie-Antoinette and other victims of the French Revolution spent their final days.

> ### MONSIEUR GUILLOTIN
>
> Beheading by means of an ax or sword was a popular form of punishment long before the French Revolution, but it was Dr. Joseph-Ignace Guillotin who suggested there was a more humane way of decapitating prisoners. Not surprisingly, Dr. Guillotin's descendants changed their surname.

Constructed by Philip IV in the late 13th and early 14th centuries, the Conciergerie—which takes its name from the building's concierge or keeper—was part of the original palace of the kings of France before the royals moved into the Louvre around 1364. In 1391, it became a prison. During the French Revolution, Marie-Antoinette languished 76 days here awaiting her date with the guillotine. There is a re-creation of the doomed queen's sad little cell—plus others that are far smaller—complete with wax figures behind bars. In the chapel, stained glass, commissioned after the queen's death by her daughter, is emblazoned with the initials M. A. Outside you can see the small courtyard where women prisoners took meals and washed their clothes in the fountain (men enjoyed no similar respite). Well-done temporary exhibitions on the ground floor aim to please kids and adults alike; themes have included enchanted forests and Gothic castles. There are free guided tours (in French only) most days at 11 and 3. ⊠ *2 bd. du Palais, Ile de la Cité* ☎ *01–53–40–60–80* ⊕ *www.conciergerie.monuments-nationaux.fr* 🎫 *€8.50; €13.50 with joint ticket to Sainte-Chapelle* ⊗ *Daily 9:30–6* ☞ *Ticket window closes at 5:30* Ⓜ *Cité.*

Mémorial des Martyrs de la Déportation (*Memorial of the Deportation*). On the east end of Ile de la Cité lies this stark monument to the more than 200,000 French men, women, and children who died in Nazi concentration camps during World War II. The evocative memorial, inaugurated by Charles de Gaulle in 1962, was intentionally designed to be claustrophobic. Concrete blocks mark the narrow entrance to the crypt, which contains the tomb of an unknown deportee killed at the Neustadt camp. A dimly lit narrow gallery studded with 200,000 pieces of glass symbolizes the lives lost, while urns at the lateral ends contain ashes from the camps. ⊠ *Square de l'Île de France, 7 quai de l'Archevêché, Ile de la Cité* 🎫 *Free* ⊗ *Oct.–Mar., Tues.–Sun. 10–5; Apr.–Sept., Tues.–Sun. 10–7* Ⓜ *Cité, St-Michel.*

Fodor's Choice ★ **Notre-Dame.** Looming above Place du Parvis, this Gothic sanctuary is the symbolic heart of Paris and, for many, of France itself. Napoléon was crowned here, and kings and queens exchanged marriage vows before its altar. Begun in 1163, completed in 1345, badly damaged during the Revolution, and restored in the 19th century by Eugène Viollet-le-Duc,

Notre-Dame may not be the country's oldest or largest cathedral, but in beauty and architectural harmony it has few peers—as you can see by studying the front facade. Its ornate doors seem like hands joined in prayer, the sculpted kings above them form a noble procession, and the west rose window gleams with what seems like divine light.

The front facade has three main entrances: the Portal of the Virgin (left); the Portal of the Last Judgment (center); and the Portal of St. Anne (right). As you enter the nave, the faith of the early builders permeates the interior: the soft glow of the windows contrasts with the exterior's triumphant glory. At the entrance are the massive 12th-century columns supporting the towers. Look down the nave to the transepts—the arms of the church—where, at the south entrance to the choir, you'll glimpse the haunting 12th-century statue of Notre-Dame de Paris, *Our Lady of Paris*, for whom the cathedral is named. On the choir's south side is the Treasury, with its small collection of religious artifacts. On the north side is the north rose window, one of the cathedral's original stained-glass panels; at the center is an image of Mary holding a young Jesus. Biblical scenes on the choir's north and south screens depict the life of Christ and apparitions of him after the Resurrection. Behind the choir is the Pietà, representing the Virgin Mary mourning over the dead body of Christ.

The best time to visit is early morning, when the cathedral is brightest and least crowded. Audioguides are available at the entrance (€5); free guided tours in English run Wednesday and Thursday at 2, and Saturday at 2:30. A separate entrance, to the left of the front facade, provides access to the towers via 387 stone steps. These wind up to the bell tolled by the fictional Quasimodo in Victor Hugo's 1831 *Notre-Dame de Paris*. The famed gargoyles (technically chimeras since they lack functioning waterspouts) were 19th-century additions. Lines to climb the tower are shortest on weekday mornings. Down the stairs in front of the cathedral is the Crypte Archéologique, an archaeological museum offering a fascinating subterranean view of this area from the 1st century, when Paris was a Roman city called Lutetia, through medieval times. Note that Notre-Dame was one of the first buildings to make use of flying buttresses—exterior supports that spread the weight of the building and roof. People first thought they looked like scaffolding that hadn't been removed. By day, the most tranquil place to appreciate these and other architectural elements is Square Jean-XXIII, the lovely garden behind the cathedral. By night, Seine boat rides promise stellar views. ⊠ *Pl. du Parvis, Ile de la Cité* 🕾 *01–42–34–56–10* ⊕ *www.notredameateparis.fr* 🖃 *Cathedral free; towers €8.50; crypt €7; treasury €4* ☾ *Cathedral weekdays 8–6:45, weekends 8–7:15. Towers Apr.–June and Sept., daily 10–6:30; July and Aug., Sun.–Thurs. 10–6:30, Fri. and Sat. 10 am–11 pm; Oct.–Mar., daily 10–5:30. Crypt Tues. and Sun. 10–6. Treasury daily 9:30–6* ☞ *Towers close early when overcrowded* Ⓜ *Cité*.

Fodor's Choice **Sainte-Chapelle.** Built by the obsessively pious Louis IX (1214–70), this
★ Gothic jewel is home to the oldest stained-glass windows in Paris. The chapel was constructed over three years, at phenomenal expense, to house the king's collection of relics acquired from the impoverished

emperor of Constantinople. These included Christ's Crown of Thorns, fragments of the Cross, and drops of Christ's blood—though even in Louis's time these were considered of questionable authenticity. Some of the relics have survived and can be seen in the treasury of Notre-Dame, but most were lost during the Revolution.

The narrow spiral staircase by the entrance takes you to the upper chapel where the famed beauty of Sainte-Chapelle comes alive: 6,458 square feet of stained glass are delicately supported by painted stonework that seems to disappear in the colorful light streaming through the windows. Deep reds and blues dominate the background, noticeably different from later, lighter medieval styles such as those of Notre-Dame's rose windows.

THE FLOWER MARKET

Every day of the week, you can find the Marché aux Fleurs (flower market) facing the entrance to the imposing Palais de Justice on Boulevard du Palais. It's a fragrant detour from the Ile de la Cité, and the Guimard-designed entrance to the Cité métro station seems to blend beautifully with the potted plants on display in open-air and covered pavilions. On Sunday, the place is chirping with birds and other small pets for sale.

The chapel is essentially an enormous magic lantern illuminating 1,130 biblical figures. Its 15 windows—each 50 feet high—were dismantled and cleaned with laser technology during a 40-year restoration, completed in 2014 to coincide with the 800th anniversary of St. Louis's birth. Besides the dazzling glass, observe the detailed carvings on the columns and the statues of the apostles. The lower chapel is gloomy and plain, but take note of the low, vaulted ceiling decorated with fleurs-de-lis and cleverly arranged Ls for Louis.

Sunset is the optimal time to see the rose window; however, to avoid waiting in killer lines, plan your visit for a weekday morning, the earlier the better. Come on a sunny day to appreciate the full effect of the light filtering through all that glorious stained glass.

You can buy a joint ticket with the Conciergerie: lines are shorter if you purchase it there or online, though you'll still have to go through a longish metal-detector line to get into Sainte-Chapelle itself.

The chapel makes a divine setting for classical concerts; check the schedule at ⊕ www.infoconcert.com. ⊠ 4 bd. du Palais, Ile de la Cité ☎ 01–53–40–60–97 ⊕ www.sainte-chapelle.monuments-nationaux.fr ⬛ €8.50; €13.50 with joint ticket to Conciergerie ⊙ Mar.–mid-May and mid-Sept.–Oct., daily 9:30–6; mid-May–mid-Sept., Thurs.–Tues. 9:30–6, Wed. 9:30 am–9:30 pm; Nov.–Feb., daily 9–5 ⬟ Ticket window closes 30 mins before closing Ⓜ Cité.

WORTH NOTING

Fodor's Choice ★ **Ancien Cloître Quartier.** Hidden in the shadows of Notre-Dame is an evocative, often-overlooked tangle of medieval streets. Through the years lucky folks, including Ludwig Bemelmans (who created the beloved *Madeleine* books) and the Aga Khan have called this area home, but back in the Middle Ages it was the domain of cathedral seminary students. One of them was the celebrated Peter Abélard (1079–1142)—philosopher, questioner of the faith, and renowned declaimer of love poems. Abélard boarded with Notre-Dame's clergyman, Fulbert, whose 17-year-old niece, Héloïse, was seduced by the compelling Abélard, 39 years her senior. She became pregnant and the vengeful clergyman had Abélard castrated; amazingly, he survived and fled to a monastery, while Héloïse took refuge in a nunnery. The poetic, passionate letters between the two cemented their fame as thwarted lovers, and their story inspired a devoted following during the romantic 19th century. They still draw admirers to the Père-Lachaise Cemetery, where they're interred *ensemble*. The clergyman's house at 10 rue Chanoinesse was redone in 1849; a plaque at the back of the building at 9–11 quai aux Fleurs commemorates the lovers. ⊠ *Rue du Cloître-Notre-Dame north to Quai des Fleurs, Ile de la Cité* Ⓜ *Cité.*

Palais de Justice. This 19th-century neoclassical courthouse complex occupies the site of the former royal palace of St-Louis that later housed Parliament until the French Revolution. It is recognizable from afar with the tower of Sainte-Chapelle, tucked inside the courtyard, peeking out. Some 4,000 magistrates, lawyers, state *fonctionnaires*, and police officials work on the property. Black-frocked judges can often be spotted taking a cigarette break on the majestic rear staircase facing Rue du Harlay. ⊠ *4 bd. du Palais, Ile de la Cité* ⊕ *www.ca-paris.justice.fr* 🎫 *Free* ⊙ *Weekdays 8:30–6:30* Ⓜ *Cité.*

Place Dauphine. The Surrealists called Place Dauphine "le sexe de Paris" because of its suggestive V shape; however, its origins were much more proper. The pretty square on the western side of Pont Neuf was built by Henry IV, who named it as a homage to his son the crown prince (or dauphin) who became Louis XIII when Henry was assassinated. In warmer weather, treat yourself to a romantic meal on a restaurant terrace here—the square is one of the best places in Paris to dine *en plein air*. ⊠ *Ile de la Cité* Ⓜ *Cité.*

Square du Vert-Galant. The equestrian statue of the Vert Galant himself—amorous adventurer Henry IV—keeps a vigilant watch over this leafy square at the western end of the Ile de la Cité. The dashing but ruthless Henry, king of France from 1589 until his assassination in 1610, was a stern upholder of the absolute rights of monarchy and a notorious womanizer. He is probably best remembered for his cynical remark that *"Paris vaut bien une messe"* ("Paris is worth a Mass"), a reference to his readiness to renounce Protestantism to gain the throne of predominantly Catholic France. To ease his conscience, he issued the Edict of Nantes in 1598, according French Protestants (almost) equal rights with their Catholic countrymen. The square is a great place for a quai-side picnic. It's also the departure point for Vedette Pont Neuf tour boats (at the bottom of the steps to the right). ⊠ *Ile de la Cité* Ⓜ *Pont Neuf.*

ILE ST-LOUIS

Nearby Pont St-Louis, which always seems to be occupied by street performers, leads to the Ile St-Louis, one of the city's best places to wander. There are no cultural hot spots, just a few narrow streets that comprise one of the most privileged areas in Paris. Small hotels, eateries, art galleries, and shops selling everything from chocolate and cheese to silk scarves line the main street, Rue St-Louis-en-L'Ile. There were once two islands here, Ile Notre-Dame and Ile aux Vaches ("Cow Island," an erstwhile grazing pasture), both owned by the Church. Speculators bought the islands, joined them, and sold the plots to builders who created what is today some of the city's most elegant and expensive real estate. Baroque architect Louis Le Vau (who later worked on Versailles) designed fabulous private mansions for aristocrats, including the majestic Hôtel de Lauzun on lovely Quai d'Anjou.

St-Louis-en-L'Ile. You can't miss the unusual lacy spire of this church as you approach the Ile St-Louis; it's the only church on the island and there are no other steeples to compete with it. It was built from 1652 to 1765 according to the Baroque designs of architect François Le Vau, brother of the more famous Louis, who designed several mansions nearby—as well as the Palace of Versailles. St-Louis's interior was essentially stripped during the Revolution, as were so many French churches, but look for the odd outdoor iron clock, which dates from 1741. Check the church website for upcoming classical music events. ⊠ *19 bis, rue St-Louis-en-L'Ile, Ile St-Louis* ☎ *01–46–34–11–60* ⊕ *www.saintlouisenlile. catholique.fr* ⊙ *Mon.–Sat. 9:30–1 and 2–7:30, Sun. 9:30–1 and 2–7* Ⓜ *Pont Marie.*

AROUND THE EIFFEL TOWER

GETTING ORIENTED

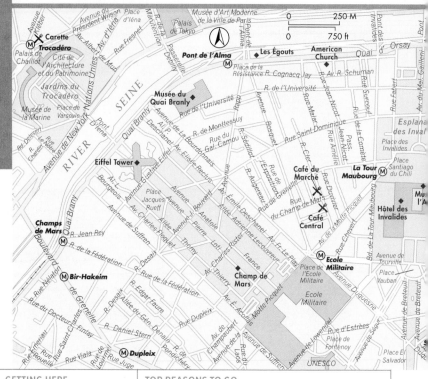

GETTING HERE	TOP REASONS TO GO
This neighborhood includes the 7e, 15e, and 16e arrondissements. The most romantic way to reach the Eiffel Tower is by boat. Alternately, you can head for RER C: Champs de Mars/ Tour Eiffel. For the best view, get off at the Trocadéro station (métro Line 9 or 6) and make the short walk over the Pont (bridge) d'Iéna to the tower. For the Musée Rodin, get off at Varenne (Line 13). Use this stop, or La Tour-Maubourg (Line 8), for Napoléon's Tomb and Hôtel des Invalides.	**Eiffel Tower.** No question, the ultimate symbol of France is worth a visit at least once in your life. **Musée Rodin.** A must-see for fans of the master sculptor, this magnificent 18th-century *hôtel particulier* (private mansion) was Rodin's former workshop. The manicured garden is a perfect setting for his timeless works. **Napoléon's Tomb.** The golden-domed Hôtel des Invalides is a fitting place for Napoléon's remains. Military history buffs will appreciate the impressive display of weaponry and armor in the adjoining Musée de l'Armée. **A boat ride.** Whether you choose a guided Bateaux Mouche tour or a Batobus (water bus) trip, cruising the Seine is a relaxing way to see city highlights without traffic or crowds. Book a ride after dark when all of Paris is aglow.

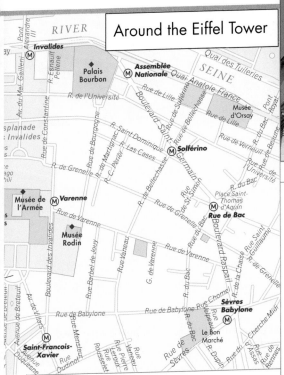

Around the Eiffel Tower

3

BEST CAFÉS

Café Central. If it's apéritif time, this is the place to be. With soft lighting, loungy music, plus a generous selection of wines, cocktails, and beers, Café Central makes an ideal spot for an end-of-the-afternoon drink. ⊠ *40 rue Cler, Around the Eiffel Tower* ☎ *01–47–05–00–53* ⊕ *www. cafecentralparis.com* ▭ *No credit cards* Ⓜ *École Militaire.*

Café du Marché. On the quaint Rue Cler, this small but busy café is popular with residents. Savor your morning café and croissant here, or enjoy an inexpensive prix-fixe lunch on the popular *terrasse.* ⊠ *38 rue Cler, Around the Eiffel Tower* ☎ *01–47–05–51–27* ▭ *No credit cards* Ⓜ *La Tour-Maubourg, École Militaire.*

Carette. Serving chic Parisians since 1927, this Art Deco tea salon on Place du Trocadéro is a hot spot for lunch or afternoon tea. ⊠ *4 pl. du Trocadero, Around the Eiffel Tower* ☎ *01–47–27–98–85* Ⓜ *Trocadéro.*

MAKING THE MOST OF YOUR TIME

This neighborhood is home to one of the world's most iconic sites, the Eiffel Tower. Depending on the time of year, you can wait hours to ascend La Tour (it helps to buy your ticket online or come at night, when lines are shorter), but even if you stay firmly on the ground, it's worth a trip to see the landmark up close. Afterward, explore Rue St-Dominique's shops, bakeries, and restaurants. If you're up for a picnic, grab fixings on Rue Cler (between Rue de Grenelle and Avenue de La Motte Piquet), a pedestrian-only market street; then head back to the park at the foot of the tower.

If you have a day to spare, visit the Musée Rodin. If you're pressed for time, do a quick tour of the garden, where some of the best-known sculptures can be seen. From here it's a short walk to Napoléon's over-the-top tomb at the Hôtel des Invalides, which also houses the Musée de l'Armée devoted to military history. To appreciate art from Asia, Africa, and Oceania, spend an hour or two in the Musée du Quai Branly.

Sightseeing
★★★★★

Dining
★★★

Lodging
★★★★★

Shopping
★★★★

Nightlife
★★★

One of Paris's most upscale neighborhoods, the posh 7e arrondissement (where nearly every block affords a view of La Tour Eiffel) is home to the French *bourgeoisie* and well-heeled expats. Commanding the southwestern end of Paris, the Eiffel Tower was considered an iron-latticed monstrosity when it opened in 1889. Today it is a beloved icon, especially at night when thousands of twinkling lights sparkle at the top of every hour.

Updated by
Jack Vermee

There are other monumental sights here, too, notably the **Hôtel des Invalides**, a sprawling Baroque complex with a towering golden dome under which lies the enormous tomb of the pint-size dictator, Napoléon. Along the river, the **Palais Bourbon**, seat of the French Parliament, is an 18th-century homage to ancient Greek architecture. Nearby is the modern **Musée du Quai Branly**, built by star architect Jean Nouvel. Don't miss the **Musée Rodin**, where the master's sculptures ooze sensuality both outside in the garden and inside the elegant Hôtel Biron.

From the Eiffel Tower east, the walkway along the Seine will take you past **Les Égouts** (where you can embark on a subterranean tour of actual working sewers) and the **American Church**. For one of the best views in Paris, cross **Pont Alexandre III**, the city's most ornate bridge spanning the Seine from Invalides to the Grand Palais. Named for the Russian czar to celebrate Franco-Russian friendship, it was built between 1896 and 1900 and is bedecked with gilded sculptures, cherubs, and Art Nouveau lamps.

TOP ATTRACTIONS

FAMILY

Fodor'sChoice

★

Eiffel Tower (*Tour Eiffel*). The Eiffel Tower is to Paris what the Statue of Liberty is to New York and what Big Ben is to London: the ultimate civic emblem. French engineer Gustave Eiffel—already famous for building viaducts and bridges—spent two years working to erect this iconic monument for the World Exhibition of 1889.

Because its colossal bulk exudes such a feeling of permanence, you may have trouble believing that the tower nearly became 7,000 tons of scrap (it contains 12,000 pieces of metal and 2,500,000 rivets) when the concession expired in 1909. Only its potential use as a radio antenna saved the day; and it still bristles with a forest of radio and television transmitters. Given La Tour's landmark status, it is equally hard to believe that so many Parisians—including arbiters of taste like Guy de Maupassant and Alexandre Dumas—initially derided the 1,063-foot structure. (De Maupassant reputedly had lunch in the tower's restaurant every day because it was the only place in Paris from which the tower wasn't visible.)

Gradually, though, the Tour Eiffel became part of the city's topography, entering the hearts and souls of residents and visitors alike. Today it is most breathtaking at night, when every girder is highlighted in a sparkling display originally conceived to celebrate the turn of the millennium. The glittering light show was so popular that the 20,000 lights were reinstalled for permanent use in 2003. The tower does its electric dance for five minutes every hour on the hour until 1 am.

More recent enhancements are also noteworthy. A two-year, €30 million renovation of the first level, completed in 2014, added a vertigo-inducing "transparent" floor 187 feet above the esplanade, plus a pair of glass-facade pavilions that hug the side of the tower and house interactive educational areas. A new mini-turbine plant, four vertical-turbine windmills, and eco-friendly solar panels will minimize the tower's carbon footprint over time, too.

You can stride up 704 steps as far as the second level, but if you want to go to the top you'll have to take the elevator. (Be sure to look closely at the fantastic ironwork.) Although the view of the flat sweep of Paris at 1,000 feet may not beat the one from the Tour Montparnasse skyscraper, the setting makes it considerably more romantic—especially if you come in the late evening, after the crowds have dispersed. Beat the crushing lines by reserving your ticket online. You can also book a guided tour (€25). ⌧ *Quai Branly, Around the Eiffel Tower* ☎ *08–92–70–12–39 €0.34 per min* ⊕ *www.toureiffel.paris* ✉ *By elevator: 1st and 2nd levels €11; top €17. By stairs: 1st and 2nd levels only, €7* ☾ *Mid-June–early Sept., daily 9 am–12:45 am (11 pm for summit); early Sept.–mid-June, daily 9:30 am–11:45 pm (10:30 pm for summit)* ☞ *Stairs close at 6 pm in off-season* Ⓜ *Trocadéro, Bir-Hakeim, École Militaire; RER: Champ de Mars–Tour Eiffel.*

Fodor's Choice ★ **Hôtel des Invalides.** The Baroque complex known as Les Invalides (pronounced lehz-ahn-vah- *leed*) is the eternal home of Napoléon Bonaparte (1769–1821) or, more precisely, the little dictator's remains, which lie entombed under the towering golden dome.

Louis XIV ordered the facility built in 1670 to house disabled soldiers (hence the name), and at one time 4,000 military men lived here. Today, a portion of it still serves as a veterans' residence and hospital. The Musée de l'Armée, containing an exhaustive collection of military artifacts from antique armor to weapons, is also here.

If you see only a single sight, make it the Église du Dome (one of Les Invalides' two churches) at the back of the complex. Napoléon's tomb was moved here in 1840 from the island of Saint Helena, where he died in forced exile. The emperor's body is protected by a series of no fewer than six coffins—one set inside the next, sort of like a Russian nesting doll—which are then encased in a sarcophagus of red quartzite. The bombastic tribute is ringed by statues symbolizing Napoléon's campaigns of conquest. To see more Napoléoniana, check out the collection in the Musée de l'Armée featuring his trademark gray frock coat and huge bicorne hat. Look for the figurines reenacting the famous coronation scene when Napoléon crowns his empress, Josephine. You can see a grander version of this scene by the painter David hanging in the Louvre.

The Esplanade des Invalides, the great lawns in front of the building, are favorite spots for pickup soccer, Frisbee games, sunbathing, and dog walking—despite signs asking you to stay off the grass. ■ TIP→ The best entrance to use is at the southern end, on Place Vauban (Avenue de Tourville). The ticket office is here, as is Napoléon's Tomb. There are automatic ticket machines at the main entrance on Place des Invalides. ⊠ *Pl. des Invalides, Around the Eiffel Tower* ☎ *01–44–42–38–77* ⊕ *www.musee-armee.fr* 🔲 *€11 (€9 after 5 Apr.–Oct., and after 4 Nov.– Mar.)* ☉ *Église du Dôme and museums Apr.–Oct., daily 10–6; Nov.– Mar., daily 10–5; closed 1st Mon. of every month Oct.–June* ☞ *Last admission 30 min. before closing* Ⓜ *La Tour–Maubourg, Varenne.*

FAMILY **Musée du Quai Branly.** This eye-catching museum overlooking the Seine was built by star architect Jean Nouvel to house the state-owned collection of "non-Western" art, culled from the Musée National des Arts d'Afrique et d'Océanie and the Musée de l'Homme. Exhibits mix artifacts from antiquity to the modern age, such as funeral masks from Melanesia, Siberian shaman drums, Indonesian textiles, and African statuary. A corkscrew ramp leads from the lobby to a cavernous exhibition space, which is color coded to designate sections from Asia, Africa, and Oceania. The lighting is dim—sometimes too dim to read the information panels (which makes investing in the €5 audioguide a good idea).

Renowned for his bold modern designs, Nouvel has said he wanted the museum to follow no rules; however, many critics gave his vision a thumbs-down when it was unveiled in 2006. The exterior resembles a massive, rust-color rectangle suspended on stilts, with geometric shapes cantilevered to the facade facing the Seine and louvered panels on the opposite side. The colors (dark reds, oranges, and yellows) are meant to evoke the tribal art within. A "living wall" comprised of some 150 species of exotic plants grows on the exterior, which is surrounded by a wild jungle garden with swampy patches—an impressive sight after dark when scores of cylindrical colored lights are illuminated. The trendy Les Ombres restaurant on the museum's fifth floor (separate entrance) has prime views of the Tour Eiffel—and prices to match. The budget-conscious can enjoy the garden at Le Café Branly on the ground floor. ⊠ *37 quai Branly, Around the Eiffel Tower* ☎ *01–56– 61–70–00* ⊕ *www.quaibranly.fr* 🔲 *€9; €11 with temporary exhibits* ☉ *Tues., Wed., and Sun. 11–7; Thurs.–Sat. 11–9* ☞ *Ticket office closes 1 hr before museum* Ⓜ *Alma-Marceau.*

FAMILY

Fodor's Choice

★

Musée Rodin. Auguste Rodin (1840–1917) briefly made his home and studio in the Hôtel Biron, a grand 18th-century mansion that now houses a museum dedicated to his work. He died rich and famous, but many of the sculptures that earned him a place in art history were originally greeted with contempt by the general public, which was unprepared for his powerful brand of sexuality and raw physicality. The reaction to this museum's new look is markedly different. It's finally emerged from a three-year, tiptoe renovation that has seen everything from the building and grounds to Rodin's sculptures themselves restored and re-presented. The reputed cost was €16 million; the overall effect is nothing short of dazzling.

Most of Rodin's best-known sculptures are in the gardens. The front one is dominated by *The Gates of Hell* (circa 1880). Inspired by the monumental bronze doors of Italian Renaissance churches, Rodin set out to illustrate stories from Dante's *Divine Comedy*. He worked on the sculpture for more than 30 years, and it served as a "sketch pad" for many of his later works. Look carefully and you can see miniature versions of *The Kiss* (bottom right), *The Thinker* (top center), and *The Three Shades* (top center). Inside, look for *The Bronze Age*, which was inspired by the sculptures of Michelangelo: this piece was so realistic that critics accused Rodin of having cast a real body in plaster. In addition, the museum now showcases long-neglected models, plasters, and paintings, which offer insight into Rodin's creative process. Pieces by other artists, gleaned from his personal collection, are on display as well—including paintings by van Gogh, Renoir, and Monet. Antiquities Rodin collected (and was inspired by) have been removed from storage and given their own room. There's also a room devoted to works by Camille Claudel (1864–1943), his student and longtime mistress, who was a remarkable sculptor in her own right. Her torturous relationship with Rodin eventually drove her out of his studio—and out of her mind. In 1913 she was packed off to an asylum, where she remained until her death. An English audio guide (€6) is available for the permanent collection and for temporary exhibitions. Tickets can be purchased online for priority access (€1.30 service fee). If you wish to linger, the lovely Café du Musée Rodin serves meals and snacks in the shade of the garden's linden trees. ✉ *77 rue de Varenne, Around the Eiffel Tower* ☎ *01-44-18-61-10* ⊕ *www.musee-rodin.fr* 🖃 *€10; €4 gardens only (free 1st Sun. of month)* ⊗ *Tues. and Thurs.–Sun. 10–5:45, Wed. 10–8:45* ⏱ *Last admission 30 min. before closing* Ⓜ *Varenne.*

WORTH NOTING

American Church. Not to be confused with the American Cathedral, across the river at 23 avenue George V, this pretty neo-Gothic Protestant church was built between 1927 and 1931. It features a pair of Tiffany stained-glass windows—a rare find in Europe. Besides ecumenical services, the church hosts architectural tours, free classical and acoustic concerts, plus popular exercise classes (including yoga). You can check event listings and download a self-guided PDF tour at the church website. ✉ *65 quai d'Orsay, Around the Eiffel Tower* ☎ *01-40-62-05-00* ⊕ *www.acparis.org* ⊗ *Mon.–Sat. 9–noon and 1–10:30, Sun. 3–7:30* Ⓜ *Alma-Marceau; RER: Pont de l'Alma.*

FAMILY **Champ de Mars.** Flanked by tree-lined paths, this long expanse of grass lies between the Eiffel Tower and École Militaire. It was previously used as a parade ground and was the site of the world exhibitions in 1867, 1889 (when the tower was built), and 1900. Today the park, landscaped at the start of the 20th century, is a great spot for temporary art exhibits, picnics, pickup soccer games, and outdoor concerts. You can also just sprawl on the center span of grass, which is unusual for Paris. There's a playground where kids can let off steam, too. Visiting during Bastille Day? If you can brave the crowds, arrive early to get a premier viewing position for the spectacular July 14th fireworks display, with the Eiffel Tower as a backdrop. Be vigilant at night. ⊠ *Around the Eiffel Tower* Ⓜ *École Militaire; RER: Champ de Mars–Tour Eiffel.*

FAMILY **Les Égouts** (*The Sewers*). Leave it to the French to make even sewers seem romantic. Part exhibit but mostly, well, sewer, the 1,650-foot stretch of tunnels provides a fascinating—and not too smelly—look at the underbelly of Paris. Visitors can stroll the so-called galleries of this city beneath the city, which comes complete with street signs mirroring those aboveground. Walkways flank tunnels of whooshing wastewater wide enough to allow narrow barges to dredge sand and sediment. Lighted panels, photos, and explanations in English detail the workings of the system. Immortalized as the escape routes of the Phantom of the Opera and Jean Valjean in *Les Misérables*, the 19th-century sewers have a florid real-life history. Since Napoléon ordered the underground network built to clean up the squalid streets, they have played a role in every war, secreting revolutionaries and spies and their stockpiles of weapons. Grenades from World War II were recovered not far from where the gift shop now sits. The display cases of stuffed toy rats and "Eau de Paris" glass carafes fold into the walls when the water rises after heavy rains. Buy your ticket at the kiosk on the Left Bank side of the Pont de l'Alma. Guided one-hour tours by friendly *égoutiers* (sewer workers) are available in French only; call or email ahead for details. ⊠ *Opposite 93 quai d'Orsay, Around the Eiffel Tower* ☎ *01–53–68– 27–81* ✉ *visite-des-egouts@paris.fr* ⊕ *www.paris.fr* 🎫 *€4.40* ☉ *May– Sept., Sat.–Wed. 11–5; Oct.–Apr., Sat.–Wed. 11–4; closed 2 wks in Jan.* Ⓜ *Alma-Marceau; RER: Pont de l'Alma.*

Palais Bourbon. The most prominent feature of the Palais Bourbon— home of the Assemblée Nationale (or French Parliament) since 1798—is its colonnaded facade, commissioned by Napoléon to match that of the Madeleine, across the Seine. Jean-Pierre Cortot's sculpted pediment portrays France holding the tablets of Law, flanked by Force and Justice. Inside is an exquisite library with a soaring ceiling of cupolas painted by Delacroix. Unfortunately, guided tours have been discontinued; however, you can still watch political debates when the assembly is in session. ⊠ *33 quai d'Orsay, Around the Eiffel Tower* ☎ *01–40–63–60–00* ⊕ *www.assemblee-nationale.fr* 🎫 *Free* Ⓜ *Assemblée Nationale.*

THE CHAMPS-ÉLYSÉES

GETTING ORIENTED

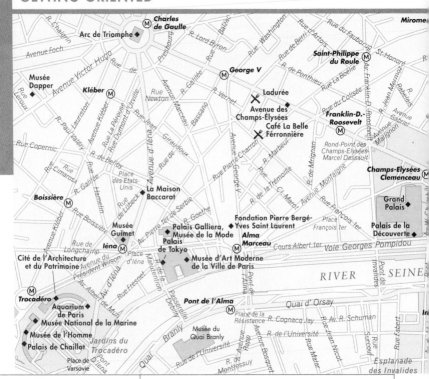

GETTING HERE	TOP REASONS TO GO
This neighborhood includes the 8e and 16e arrondissements. For the top of the Champs-Élysées/Arc de Triomphe, take métro Line 1, 2, or 6, or the RER A, to Charles-de-Gaulle–Étoile. For the bottom of the avenue, near the Grand Palais, go to the Champs-Élysées–Clemenceau métro station on Line 1. For the Palais de Chaillot, use the Trocadéro métro station on Lines 6 and 9.	**Avenue des Champs-Élysées.** Splurge in the upscale boutiques on and around this fabled avenue, or simply practice the fine art of *lèche-vitrines* (literally "window licking," the French term for window-shopping).
	Palais de Chaillot. A favorite of fashion photographers, this statue-lined plaza-terrace at Place du Trocadéro boasts the city's best view of the Eiffel Tower.
	Musée Guimet. One of Paris's finest smaller museums has a world-class collection of art from all over Asia. Don't miss the rare Khmer sculptures from Cambodia.
	Macarons **from Ladurée.** Is it worth lining up for 30 minutes to get a little taste of heaven? You decide. But rest assured: the round meringue cookies made by this famous pâtissier since 1862 are as scrumptious as ever.

The Champs-Élysées

BEST CAFÉS

Café La Belle Férronnière. A favorite of Parisians for morning *noisettes*, business lunches, and after-work *apéros*, this popular spot is a short walk from the Champs-Élysées. Settle in at a sidewalk table or retreat to the quieter interior. The enigmatic painting for which the café is named—da Vinci's *Portrait of an Unknown Woman*—hangs in the Louvre. ⊠ *53 rue Pierre Charron, Champs-Élysées* ☎ *01-42-25-03-82* Ⓜ *George V.*

Ladurée. With 50-plus locations worldwide, the most opulent branch of the Ladurée tea salon empire is worth the splurge. Reserve a table upstairs or grab a bite in the Art Nouveau bar in the back. The menu promises generous salads and flavorful *plats du jour*. Sweets are a house specialty. In addition to more than a dozen flavors of *macarons*, it has assorted cakes, pastries, and beautifully boxed treats ideal for gift-giving. ⊠ *75 av. des Champs-Élysées, Champs-Élysées* ☎ *01-40-75-08-75* ⊕ *www.laduree.com* Ⓜ *George V.*

MAKING THE MOST OF YOUR TIME

This neighborhood is an essential stop for every first-time visitor to Paris, and returning travelers will find plenty to do, too. Leave yourself a full day to tour some of the museums around Place du Trocadéro before heading to the Champs-Élysées, worth a walk from end to end. Stop for lunch or dessert at one of the cafés or tea salons en route; then detour down Avenue Montaigne, Paris's answer to Rodeo Drive.

If your time is limited, you can just come for a stroll at night, when the Champs is alight: there are bars and nightclubs for all tastes, plus movie houses showing French films and English-language blockbusters (look for v.o., meaning *version originale*, if you prefer to see an undubbed one).

Make no mistake: the Champs-Élysées, while ceding some of its elegance in recent times, remains the most famous avenue in Paris—and, perhaps, the world. Like New York's Times Square or London's Piccadilly Circus, it is a mecca for travelers and locals alike. Some Parisians complain that fast-food joints and chain stores have cheapened Avenue des Champs-Élysées, but others are more philosophical, noting that there is something here for everyone. If you can't afford lunch at Ladurée, there's always McDonald's (and the view from its second floor is terrific).

Updated by
Jack Vermee

Anchoring the Champs is the **Arc de Triomphe,** Napoléon's monument to himself. At the other end, the exquisitely restored **Grand Palais** plays host to some of the city's grandest art exhibitions. Across the street, the permanent art collection is free at the **Petit Palais,** and there's also a quiet garden café. Between here and **Place du Trocadéro,** a busy traffic circle, you can find several museums housed in some of Paris's most impressive buildings. The **Palais de Chaillot** complex includes the **Cité de l'Architecture et du Patrimoine,** a must for architecture buffs, along with the nautical-themed **Musée National de la Marine** and the anthropology-oriented **Musée de l'Homme.** Farther on, the **Musée Guimet** has a superlative Asian art collection. The **Musée d'Art Moderne de la Ville de Paris,** on Avenue du Président Wilson, contains a free permanent collection of 20th-century pieces. Contemporary-art lovers should also check out what's showing next door at the trendy **Palais de Tokyo.** These twin Art Nouveau buildings, constructed for the 1937 World's Fair, are notable for their monumental facades. Across the street is the **Palais Galliera:** framed by a lovely garden outside, it has a museum inside that focuses on fashion.

TOP ATTRACTIONS

Fodor'sChoice
★
Arc de Triomphe. Inspired by Rome's Arch of Titus, this colossal, 164-foot triumphal arch was ordered by Napoléon—who liked to consider himself the heir to Roman emperors—to celebrate his military successes. Unfortunately, Napoléon's strategic and architectural visions were not entirely on the same plane, and the Arc de Triomphe proved something of an embarrassment. Although the emperor wanted the monument completed in time for an 1810 parade in honor of his new bride, Marie-Louise, it was still only a few feet high, and a dummy arch of painted canvas was strung up to save face. Empires come and go, but Napoléon's had been gone for more than 20 years before the Arc was finally finished in 1836. A small museum halfway up recounts its history.

The Arc de Triomphe is notable for magnificent sculptures by François Rude, including *The Departure of the Volunteers in 1792*, better known as *La Marseillaise*, to the right of the arch when viewed from the Champs-Élysées. Names of Napoléon's generals are inscribed on the stone facades—the underlined names identify the hallowed figures who fell in battle.

The traffic circle around the Arc is named for Charles de Gaulle, but it's known to Parisians as "L'Étoile," or the Star—a reference to the streets that fan out from it. Climb the stairs to the top of the arch and you can see the star effect of the 12 radiating avenues and the vista down the Champs-Élysées toward Place de la Concorde and the distant Musée du Louvre.

■ TIP→ **France's Unknown Soldier is buried beneath the arch, and a commemorative flame is rekindled every evening at 6:30. That's the most atmospheric time to visit, but, to beat the crowds, come early in the morning or buy your ticket online (€1.60 service fee).** ⊠ *Pl. Charles-de-Gaulle, Champs-Élysées* ☎ *01–55–37–73–77* ⊕ *arc-de-triomphe. monuments-nationaux.fr* ⊠ *€9.50* ⊙ *Apr.–Sept., daily 10 am–11 pm; Oct.–Mar., daily 10 am–10:30 pm* ☞ *Last admission 45 min before closing* Ⓜ *Métro or RER: Charles-de-Gaulle–Étoile.*

FAMILY
Avenue des Champs-Élysées. Marcel Proust lovingly described the genteel elegance of the storied Champs-Élysées (pronounced chahnz- *eleezay,* with an "n" sound instead of "m" and no "p") during its Belle Époque heyday, when its cobblestones resounded with the clatter of horses and carriages. Today, despite unrelenting traffic and the intrusion of chain stores and fast-food franchises, the avenue still sparkles. There's always something happening here: stores are open late (and many are open on Sunday, a rarity in Paris); nightclubs remain top destinations; and cafés offer prime people-watching, though you'll pay for the privilege—after all, this is Europe's most expensive piece of real estate. Along the 2-km (1¼-mile) stretch, you can find marquee names in French luxury, like Cartier, Guerlain, and Louis Vuitton. Car manufacturers lure international visitors with space-age showrooms. Old stalwarts, meanwhile, are still going strong—including the Lido cabaret and Fouquet's, whose celebrity clientele extends back to James Joyce. The avenue is also the setting for the last leg of the Tour de France bicycle race (the third or

fourth Sunday in July), as well as Bastille Day (July 14) and Armistice Day (November 11) ceremonies. The Champs-Élysées, which translates to "Elysian Fields" (the resting place of the blessed in Greek mythology), began life as a cow pasture and in 1666 was transformed into a park by the royal landscape architect André Le Nôtre. Traces of its green origins are visible towards the Concorde, where elegant 19th-century park pavilions house the historic restaurants Ledoyen, Laurent, and the more recent Lenôtre. ✉ *Champs-Élysées* Ⓜ *Champs-Élysées–Clemenceau, Franklin-D.-Roosevelt, George V, Charles-de-Gaulle–Étoile.*

NEED A BREAK?

Publicis Drugstore. A stone's throw from the Arc de Triomphe, this trendy spot—part mini department store, part brasserie—is stocked with an ever-changing array of upscale wares from designer handbags and diamond bracelets to fine wine and cigars. When you're done browsing, enjoy a quick bite at the on-site eatery (a prix-fixe menu is available) or stop by the bakery for food to take away. ✉ *133 av. des Champs-Élysées, Champs-Élysées* ☎ *01–44–43–75–07* ⊕ *www.publicisdrugstore.com* Ⓜ *Charles-de-Gaulle–Étoile.*

Cité de l'Architecture et du Patrimoine. The greatest gems of French architecture are represented at the City of Architecture and Heritage, which occupies the east wing of the Palais de Chaillot. Reopened in 2007 after an €84 million renovation, the former French Monuments Museum contains some 350 plaster-cast reproductions spread out over 86,000 square feet. While it may seem odd to see a collection comprised entirely of copies, these are no ordinary ones: they include partial facades from some of the most important Gothic churches, a gallery of frescoes and windows (among them a stained-glass stunner from the famous Chartres cathedral), plus an assembly of gargoyles practically leaping off the back wall of the soaring first-floor gallery. Video monitors with joysticks allow a 360-degree view of some of the grandest cathedrals. The upper-floor gallery is devoted to architecture since 1851, with a life-size replica of a postwar apartment in Marseille designed by the urban-planning pioneer Le Corbusier. It's well worth picking up the free English audiovisual guide. When you're ready for a break, the museum's small café offers a great view of the Eiffel Tower. ✉ *Palais de Chaillot, 1 pl. du Trocadéro, Champs-Élysées* ☎ *01–58–51–52–00* ⊕ *www.citechaillot.fr* ⛟ *€8; €12 with temporary exhibits* ☉ *Fri.–Mon. and Wed. 11–7, Thurs. 11–9* Ⓜ *Trocadéro.*

Grand Palais. With its curved-glass roof and gorgeously restored Belle Époque ornamentation, you can't miss the Grand Palais whether you're approaching from the Seine or the Champs-Élysées. It forms an elegant duo with the Petit Palais across Avenue Winston Churchill: both stone buildings, adorned with mosaics and sculpted friezes, were built for the 1900 World's Fair, and, like the Eiffel Tower, were not intended to be permanent. The exquisite main exhibition space called le Nef (or nave) plays host to large-scale shows that might focus on anything from jewelry to cars. The art-oriented shows staged here—including the annual FIAC, Paris's contemporary-art fair—are some of the hottest tickets in town. Previous must-sees included an Edward Hopper retrospective

and *Picasso and the Masters*. To skip the long queue, booking an advance ticket online for an extra euro is strongly advised. ✉ *Av. Winston Churchill, Champs-Élysées* 🕾 *01–40–13–48–00* ⊕ *www.grandpalais.fr* 🎫 *Around €14 (exhibits vary)* ☉ *Wed.–Mon. 10–8 or 10–10, depending on exhibit* Ⓜ *Champs-Élysées–Clemenceau.*

Musée d'Art Moderne de la Ville de Paris (*Paris Museum of Modern Art*). Although the city's modern art museum hasn't generated a buzz comparable to that of the Centre Georges Pompidou, visiting can be a more pleasant experience because it draws fewer crowds. The Art Nouveau building's vast, white-walled galleries make an ideal backdrop for temporary exhibitions of 20th-century art and postmodern installation projects. The permanent collection on the lower floor takes over where the Musée d'Orsay leaves off, chronologically speaking: among the earliest works are Fauvist paintings by Maurice Vlaminck and André Derain, followed by Pablo Picasso's early experiments in Cubism. Other highlights include works by Robert and Sonia Delaunay, Chagall, Matisse, Rothko, and Modigliani. ✉ *11 av. du Président Wilson, Champs-Élysées* 🕾 *01–53–67–40–00* ⊕ *www.mam.paris.fr* 🎫 *Free; up to €12 for temporary exhibitions* ☉ *Tues.–Sun. 10–6 (Thurs. until 10 for some temporary exhibitions)* Ⓜ *Alma-Marceau, Iéna.*

FAMILY **Musée de l'Homme.** After a *raison d'être* revamp and six years of renovation, Paris's storied anthropology museum, located in the west wing of the Palais de Chaillot, reopened its doors in late 2015. When President Jacques Chirac's legacy project (the Musée du Quai Branly, dedicated to the world's indigenous arts and cultures) pilfered half of this museum's pieces, few thought the rest would survive. But now it has come roaring back to life. Focused now on "science and human societies," the Musée de l'Homme has 33,368 square feet of sparkling exhibition space, where it displays more than 700,000 prehistoric artifacts and art objects. And it now does so using the most modern of museum tricks—including interactive displays, 3-D projections, and educational games—to help visitors understand the history of the human species. While you're admiring the 23,000-year-old Venus of Lespugue or comparing the skull of Cro-Magnon man with that of René Descartes, don't forget to look out the window: the view from the upper floors across to the Eiffel Tower and southern Paris is spectacular. ✉ *Palais de Chaillot, 17 Pl. du Trocadéro, Champs-Élysées* 🕾 *01–44–05–72–72* ⊕ *www.museedelhomme.fr* 🎫 *€10* ☉ *Thurs.–Mon. 10–6, Wed. 10–9* Ⓜ *Trocadéro.*

Fodor's Choice **Musée Guimet.** The outstanding Musée Guimet boasts the western
★ world's biggest collection of Asian art, thanks to the 19th-century wan-
derings of Lyonnaise industrialist Émile Guimet. Exhibits, enriched by
the state's vast holdings, are laid out geographically in airy, light-filled
rooms. Just past the entry, you can find the largest assemblage of Khmer
sculpture outside Cambodia. The second floor has statuary and masks
from Nepal, ritual funerary art from Tibet, and jewelry and fabrics
from India. Peek into the library rotunda, where Monsieur Guimet once
entertained the city's notables under the gaze of eight caryatids atop
Ionic columns; Mata Hari danced here in 1905. The much-heralded
Chinese collection, made up of 20,000-odd objects, covers seven millennia. Grab a free English-language audioguide and brochure at the
entrance. If you need a pick-me-up, stop at the Salon des Porcelaines
café on the lower level for a ginger milk shake. Don't miss the Guimet's
impressive Buddhist Pantheon, with two floors of Buddhas from China
and Japan, and a Japanese garden; it's just up the street at 19 avenue
d'Iéna, and admission is free with a Musée Guimet ticket. ⊠ 6 pl. d'Iéna,
Champs-Élysées ☎ 01–56–52–53–00 ⊕ www.guimet.fr ⊠ €7.50; €9.50
with temporary exhibition ⊘ Wed.–Mon. 10–6 Ⓜ Iéna, Boissiére.

FAMILY **Palais de Chaillot.** This honey-color Art Deco cultural center on Place
du Trocadéro was built in the 1930s to replace a Moorish-style building constructed for the 1878 World's Fair. Its esplanade is a top draw
for camera-toting visitors intent on snapping the perfect shot of the
Eiffel Tower. In the building to the left is the Cité de l'Architecture
et du Patrimoine—billed as the largest architectural museum in the
world—and the Théâtre National de Chaillot, which occasionally stages
plays in English. Also here is the Institut Français d'Architecture, an
organization and school. The twin building to the right contains the
Musée National de la Marine, an engaging museum showcasing nautical history, as well as the newly renovated Musée de l'Homme, a
thoroughly modern anthropology museum. Sculptures and fountains
adorn the garden leading to the Seine. ⊠ Pl. du Trocadéro, Champs-
Élysées Ⓜ Trocadéro.

Palais de Tokyo. The go-to address for some of the city's funkiest exhibitions, the Palais de Tokyo is a stripped-down venue that spotlights provocative, ambitious contemporary art. There is no permanent collection:
instead, cutting-edge temporary shows are staged in a cavernous space
reminiscent of a light-filled industrial loft. The programming extends
to performance art, concerts, readings, and fashion shows. Night owls
will appreciate the midnight closing. The museum's Tokyo Eat restaurant—serving an affordable French–Asian-fusion menu—is a haunt of
hip locals, especially at lunch. Visit the offbeat gift shop for souvenirs
that are as edgy and subversive as the exhibits. ⊠ 13 av. du Président
Wilson, Champs-Élysées ☎ 01–81–97–35–88 ⊕ www.palaisdetokyo.
com ⊠ €10 ⊘ Wed.–Mon. noon–midnight Ⓜ Iéna.

Fodor's Choice **Palais Galliera, Musée de la Mode.** The city's Museum of Fashion occu-
★ pies a suitably fashionable mansion—the 19th-century residence of
Marie Brignole-Sale, Duchess of Galliera; and, having emerged from
an extensive makeover in 2013, it is now more stylish than ever.
Inside, temporary exhibitions focus on costume and clothing design (a

reopening retrospective, for instance, honored the visionary Azzedine Alaïa). Covering key moments in fashion history and showcasing iconic French designers, the museum's collection includes 100,000 dresses and accessories that run the gamut from basic streetwear to haute couture. Details on shows (there are no permanent displays) are available on the museum website. Don't miss the lovely 19th-century garden that encircles the palace. ⊠ *10 av. Pierre-1er-de-Serbie, Champs-Élysées* ☎ *01–56–52–86–00* ⊕ *palaisgalliera.paris.fr* 🔳 *€8 and up, depending on the exhibition* ⊙ *Tues., Wed., and Fri.–Sun. 10–6, Thurs. 10–9 during temporary exhibitions only* Ⓜ *Iéna.*

Petit Palais, Musée des Beaux-Arts de la Ville de Paris. The "little" palace has a small, overlooked collection of excellent paintings, sculpture, and objets d'art, with works by Monet, Gauguin, and Courbet, among others. Temporary exhibitions, beefed up in recent years (and occasionally free), are particularly good—especially those dedicated to photography. The building, like the Grand Palais across the street, is an architectural marvel of marble, glass, and gilt built for the 1900 World's Fair, with impressive entry doors and huge windows overlooking the river. Search directly above the main galleries for 16 plaster busts set into the wall representing famous artists. Outside, note two eye-catching sculptures: French World War I hero Georges Clemenceau faces the Champs-Élysées, while a resolute Winston Churchill faces the Seine. In warmer weather, head to the garden café with terrace seating. ⊠ *Av. Winston Churchill, Champs-Élysées* ☎ *01–53–43–40–00* ⊕ *www.petitpalais. paris.fr* 🔳 *Free; €5–€12 for temporary exhibitions* ⊙ *Tues.–Sun. 10–6 (Fri. until 9 for temporary exhibitions)* Ⓜ *Champs-Élysées–Clemenceau.*

NEED A BREAK? ✕ **Le Jardin du Petit Palais.** The quiet little café hidden in the lush garden inside the Petit Palais is one of this quarter's best-kept secrets. ⊠ *Av. Winston Churchill, Champs-Élysées* ☎ *01–53–43–40–00* ⊕ *www.petitpalais. paris.fr* Ⓜ *Champs-Élysées–Clemenceau.*

WORTH NOTING

FAMILY **Aquarium de Paris.** An aquarium and cinema may seem like a strange combination, but the two coexist nicely in this attractive space beneath the Trocadéro gardens. In addition to 10,000 fish and a giant tank of small sharks, it promises puppet and magic shows, along with workshops for children in animation, art, and dance (these are offered in French, but the staff speaks English). There are also kid-oriented films showing on one big screen and, for the grown-ups, feature films playing on a second. Check the website for times and activities. Book tickets online to avoid lines. ⊠ *5 av. Albert De Mun, Champs-Élysées* ☎ *01–40–69–23–23* ⊕ *www.cineaqua.com* 🔳 *€20.50* ⊙ *Daily 10–7* ☞ *Last entry 1 hr before closing* Ⓜ *Trocadéro.*

Fondation Pierre Bergé–Yves Saint Laurent. With his longtime business and life partner Pierre Bergé, the late fashion designer Yves Saint Laurent reopened his former atelier as a gallery and archive of his work in 2004. Unfortunately, YSL's private collection of dresses can be viewed only on private group tours booked in advance. What you can see here are exhibitions staged three times a year. Themes include painting, photography, and, of course, fashion—such as a retrospective on couture maven Nan Kempner. ✉ *3 rue Léonce Reynaud, Champs-Élysées* ☎ *01-44-31-64-00* ⊕ *www.fondation-pb-ysl.net* 💶 *€7* 🕐 *Tues.–Sun. 11–6 during temporary exhibitions only* ☞ *Last entry at 5:15* Ⓜ *Alma-Marceau.*

La Maison Baccarat. Playing on the building's Surrealist legacy, designer Philippe Starck brought an irreverent *Alice in Wonderland* approach to the HQ and museum of the venerable Baccarat crystal firm: Cocteau, Dalí, Buñuel, and Man Ray were all frequent guests of the mansion's onetime owner, Countess Marie-Laure de Noailles. At the entrance, talking heads are projected onto giant crystal urns, and a lighted chandelier is submerged in an aquarium. Upstairs, the museum features masterworks created by Baccarat since 1764, including soaring candlesticks made for Czar Nicholas II and the perfume flacon Dalí designed for Schiaparelli. Don't miss the rotunda's "Alchemy" section by Gérard Garouste, showcasing the technical history of cutting, wheel engraving, enamelling, and gilding. If you're in the mood for shopping, contemporary crystal by top-name designers as well as stemware, vases, tableware, jewelry, chandeliers, and even furniture are sold in the onsite shop. Set aside a few moments to enjoy the little park just outside in the Place des États-Unis with impressive statues of Washington and Lafayette. ✉ *11 pl. des États-Unis, Champs-Élysées* ☎ *01-40-22-11-00* ⊕ *www.baccarat.fr* 💶 *€10* 🕐 *Mon. and Wed.–Sat. 10–6* Ⓜ *Iéna.*

Musée Dapper. Dedicated to the art of Africa and the African diaspora, the Dapper Museum showcases an ever-changing selection of impressive temporary exhibitions, ranging from elaborate masks, traditional sculptures, and ceremonial jewelry to contemporary African designs. Opened in 1986 as a museum and cultural space by Christiane Falgayrettes-Leveau (a native of French Guyana) and her husband, Michel Leveau, the museum relocated to its current modern-design building in 2000. A visit to the Dapper makes a good pairing with a stop at the nearby Musée Guimet. Most of the visitor information is in French, but the website usually has English descriptions of current exhibitions. ✉ *35 bis, rue Paul Valéry, Champs-Élysées* ☎ *01-45-00-91-75* ⊕ *www.dapper.fr* 💶 *€6* 🕐 *Mon., Wed., and Fri.–Sun. 11–7 during exhibitions only* Ⓜ *Charles-de-Gaulle–Étoile.*

FAMILY **Musée National de la Marine** (*Maritime Museum*). Perfect for naval and history buffs, this underrated museum in the west wing of the Palais de Chaillot has a treasure trove of art and artifacts documenting maritime development pertinent to France over the centuries. It's one of five national museums dedicated to all things nautical (other locations are in Brest, Port-Louis, Rochefort, and Toulon). Inside you'll see impressive models of vessels from 17th-century flagships to modern warships. Kids can climb a step to get a closer look at a model aircraft carrier, cut in half to expose its decks. The main gallery displays several figureheads recovered from sunken ships, including a giant Henri IV, with hand on heart, miraculously saved from a shipwreck in 1854 during the Crimean War. Another enormous representation of Napoléon, in his favored guise as a Roman emperor, was taken from the prow of the frigate *Iéna* in 1846. There is also a metal diving suit from 1882 and the menu from a 1935 voyage of the SS *Normandie* cruise ship. Free English audioguides are available. ✉ *Palais de Chaillot, 17 pl. du Trocadéro, Champs-Élysées* ☎ *01–53–65–69–53* ⊕ *www.musee-marine.fr* ✆€8.50; €10 *with temporary exhibits* ☉ *Wed.–Mon. 10–6* Ⓜ *Trocadéro.*

FAMILY **Palais de la Découverte** (*Palace of Discovery*). The Palace of Discovery, a popular science museum in the rear of the Grand Palais complex, has a wide variety of exhibits spread out over two floors under an elegant glass-and-iron roof. Subjects include astronomy, chemistry, biology, physics, and earth sciences. Although most information is in French, there are plenty of buttons and levers to press and pull to keep little (and not so little) hands busy. This fun facility—a smaller cousin of the Cité des Sciences et de l'Industrie in Parc de la Villette—also features regularly scheduled demos and 3-D films, along with daily planetarium shows (in French only). ✉ *Av. Franklin-D.-Roosevelt, Champs-Élysées* ☎ *01–56–43–20–20* ⊕ *www.palais-decouverte.fr* ✆€9; €12 *with planetarium* ☉ *Tues.–Fri. 9:30–6, Sat. 9:30–7, Sun. 10–7* Ⓜ *Champs-Élysées–Clemenceau.*

5

AROUND THE
LOUVRE

GETTING ORIENTED

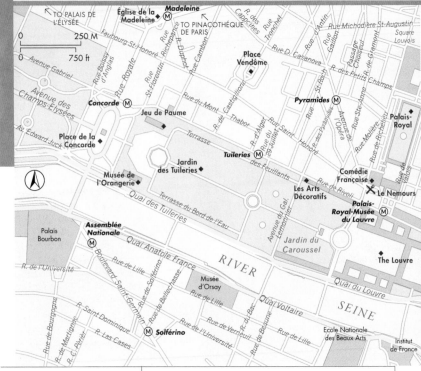

GETTING HERE	TOP REASONS TO GO
The neighborhoods in this chapter include the 1er and 2e arrondissements, from the Faubourg St-Honoré to Les Halles. If you're heading to the Louvre, take the métro Line 1 to the Palais-Royal–Musée du Louvre or Louvre–Rivoli stop. For the Tuileries, use the Tuileries stop on the same line. For Place de la Concorde, use the Concorde stop on Line 1, 8, or 12. This is a good starting point for a walk on Rue St-Honoré. If you're going to Les Halles, take Line 4 to Les Halles or Line 1 to Châtelet.	**Musée du Louvre.** The world's first great art museum—which displays such renowned works as the serenely smirking *Mona Lisa* and the statuesque Venus de Milo—deserves a long visit.
	Tuileries to Place de la Concorde. For centuries, Parisians and visitors alike have strolled the length of this magnificent garden to the gold-tipped obelisk at Place de la Concorde.
	Galerie Vivienne. The prettiest 19th-century glass-roofed shopping arcade left in Paris, this *passage* is worth a stop for shopping, lunch, or afternoon tea.
	Palais-Royal. Visit these arcades and the romantic garden to understand why the French writer Colette called the view from her window "a little corner of the country."
	Rue Montorgueil. This historic market street, lined with food shops and cafés, is at the heart of one of the city's trendiest neighborhoods.

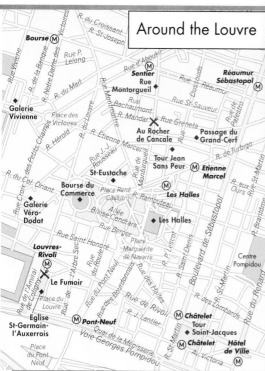

Around the Louvre

BEST CAFÉS

Au Rocher de Cancale. As its impressive facade attests, this café has a special history. It opened in 1846, when Balzac was a regular and Rue Montorgueil was the place to buy oysters. ⊠ *78 rue Montorgueil, Around the Louvre* ☏ *01–42–33–50–29* Ⓜ *Les Halles.*

Le Fumoir. Equal parts café, bar, and restaurant, Le Fumoir is a timelessly popular place to sip coffee and read the paper, or enjoy an after-dinner drink. Reservations are recommended for dinner and Sunday brunch. ⊠ *Pl. du Louvre, 6 rue de l'Amiral-Coligny, Around the Louvre* ☏ *01–42–92–00–24* ⊕ *www.lefumoir.com* Ⓜ *Louvre-Rivoli.*

Le Nemours. Plan your day over a croissant and a *café crème* at this classic café with two long rows of tables overlooking lively Place Colette, just steps from the Palais-Royal and the Musée du Louvre. ⊠ *2 pl. Colette, Around the Louvre* ☏ *01–42–61–34–14* Ⓜ *Palais-Royal–Louvre.*

MAKING THE MOST OF YOUR TIME

Try to devote two days or more—one alone for the Louvre—to these vastly different neighborhoods. Along the narrow sidewalks of the Faubourg St-Honoré you'll find some of the finest Parisian boutiques. Place de la Concorde is the gateway to the Tuileries garden. At the eastern end, Les Halles (the old market district) is booming with shops and eateries popping up around cobbled Rue Montorgueil, where traffic is mercifully restricted.

If you're headed to the mammoth Musée du Louvre, it's best to have a game plan in mind. First step: buy your ticket online at ⊕ *www.louvre.fr.* If there is a crowd waiting to enter the Pyramide, use the entrance in the underground mall, the Carrousel du Louvre, 99 rue de Rivoli.

Sightseeing
★★★★
Dining
★★
Lodging
★★★★
Shopping
★★★★★
Nightlife
★★

The neighborhoods from the très chic Faubourg St-Honoré to trendy Les Halles are a study in contrasts, with the Louvre in the midst of the bustle. The posh Rue Faubourg St-Honoré, once the stomping ground of kings and queens, is now home to the French president and assorted foreign ambassadors. Beloved by fashionistas for three centuries, it is as popular today as it was when royal mistresses shopped here—which explains the plethora of high-end stores (almost every luxury brand is represented). Not surprisingly, ritzy restaurants and haute hotels are located here as well.

Updated by
Linda Hervieux

To the east, **Les Halles** (pronounced leh- *ahl*) has risen from its roots as a down-and-out market district to become one of the city's hottest, hippest neighborhoods. Vermin-infested cobbled streets have given way to trendy shops, cafés, and bars, centered on Rue Montorgueil; and a sweeping multiyear renovation of the former wholesale food market (which closed in 1969) is giving a much-needed face-lift to the plaza aboveground and the vast shopping mall below.

Between Faubourg St-Honoré and Les Halles, you can find some of Paris's top draws—namely the mighty **Musée du Louvre** and, next door, the majestic **Jardin des Tuileries.** The garden is home to the **Musée de l'Orangerie,** with its curved galleries showcasing Monet's *Water Lilies,* while nearby **Les Arts Décoratifs** is a must for design buffs. In Place Colette, the stately theater, the **Comédie Française,** is still going strong after 400 years, and at the edge of the square is the psychedelic sculpture—doubling as a métro entrance—of the *kiosque des noctambules* (kiosk of the nightcrawlers), designed by artist Jean-Michel Othoniel. Hidden just off Place Colette is the **Palais-Royal,** a romantic garden ringed by arcades with boutiques selling everything from old-fashioned music boxes to fashion-forward frocks. A stone's throw away is **Galerie Vivienne,** an exquisitely restored 19th-century shopping arcade.

TOP ATTRACTIONS

Galerie Véro-Dodat. A lovely 19th-century passage that's been gorgeously restored, the Véro-Dodat has a dozen artsy boutiques selling objets d'art, textiles, furniture, and accessories. The headliner tenant is Christian Louboutin, at Rue Jean-Jacques Rousseau, whose red-soled stilettos are favored by Angelina, Madonna, and other members of the red-carpet set. On the opposite end, at the Rue du Bouloi entrance, star cosmetics-maker Terry De Gunzburg has a boutique, By Terry. ⊠ *Main entrance at 19 rue Jean-Jacques Rousseau, Around the Louvre* Ⓜ *Palais-Royal–Louvre.*

Galerie Vivienne. Considered the grande dame of Paris's 19th-century *passages couverts*—the world's first shopping malls—this graceful covered arcade evokes an age of gaslights and horse-drawn carriages. Once Parisians came to passages like this one to tred tiled floors instead of muddy streets and to see and be seen browsing boutiques under the glass-and-iron roofs. Today, the Galerie Vivienne still attracts unique retailers selling clothing, accessories, and housewares. La Marelle (No. 21) stocks second-hand designer labels, and wine merchant Legrand Filles & Fils (1 rue de la Banque) is the place for an upscale wine tasting. The Place des Victoires, a few steps away, is one of Paris's most picturesque squares. In the center is a statue of an outsized Louis XIV (1643–1715), the Sun King, who appears almost as large as his horse. ⊠ *Main entrance at 4 rue des Petits-Champs, Around the Louvre* Ⓜ *Palais-Royal–Louvre, Bourse.*

NEED A BREAK?

A Priori Thé. American Peggy Hancock opened A Priori Thé in 1980. She—and her delicious scones and cakes—have been comforting travelers ever since. Come for lunch, afternoon tea, or weekend brunch. ⊠ *35 Galerie Vivienne, Around the Louvre* ☎ *01–42–97–48–75* ⊕ *www.apriorithe.com* Ⓜ *Palais-Royal–Louvre, Bourse.*

FAMILY

Fodor's Choice

★

Jardin des Tuileries. The quintessential French garden, with its verdant lawns, manicured rows of trees, and gravel paths, was designed by André Le Nôtre for Louis XIV. After the king moved his court to Versailles in 1682, the Tuileries became *the* place for stylish Parisians to stroll. (Ironically, the name derives from the decidedly unstylish factories which once occupied this area: they produced *tuiles,* or roof tiles, fired in kilns called *tuileries.*) Monet and Renoir captured the garden with paint and brush, and it's no wonder the Impressionists loved it—the gray, austere light of Paris's famously overcast days make the green trees appear even greener.

The garden still serves as a setting for one of the city's loveliest walks. Laid out before you is a vista of must-see monuments, with the Louvre at one end and the Place de la Concorde at the other. The Eiffel Tower is on the Seine side, along with the Musée d'Orsay, reachable across a footbridge in the center of the garden. A good place to begin is at the Louvre end, at the Arc du Carrousel, a stone-and-marble arch ordered by Napoléon to showcase the bronze horses he stole from St. Mark's Cathedral in Venice. The horses were eventually returned and replaced here with a statue of a *quadriga,* a four-horse chariot. On the Place

de la Concorde end, twin buildings bookend the garden. On the Seine side, the former royal greenhouse is now the exceptional Musée de l'Orangerie, home to the largest display of Monet's lovely *Water Lilies* series, as well as a sizable collection of early-20th-century paintings. On the opposite end is the Jeu de Paume, which has some of the city's best temporary photography exhibits.

Garden buffs will enjoy the small bookstore at the Place de la Concorde entrance, open 10 am to 7 pm. Aside from volumes on gardening and plants (including some titles in English), it has gift items, knickknacks, and toys for the junior gardener.

Note that the Tuileries is one of the best places in Paris to take kids if they're itching to run around. There's a carousel (€2.50), trampolines (€2.50), and, in summer, an amusement park.

If you're hungry, look for carts serving gelato from Amorino or sandwiches from the chain bakery Paul at the eastern end near the Louvre. Within the gated part of the gardens are four cafés with terraces. Le Médicis near Place de la Concorde is a good place to stop for late-afternoon tea or apéritifs. ⊠ *Bordered by Quai des Tuileries, Pl. de la Concorde, Rue de Rivoli, and the Louvre, Around the Louvre* ☎ *01–40–20–90–43* 🖥 *Free* ☉ *June–Aug., daily 7 am–11 pm; Apr., May, and Sept., daily 7:30 am–9 pm; Oct.–Mar., daily 7:30–7:30* Ⓜ *Tuileries or Concorde.*

Fodor'sChoice
★

Les Arts Décoratifs. Sharing a wing of the Musée du Louvre, but with a separate entrance and admission charge, Les Arts Décoratifs is actually three museums in one. Spread across nine floors, it showcases a stellar array of decorative arts, design and fashion, and graphics. The collection includes altarpieces from the Middle Ages and furnishings from the Italian Renaissance to the present day. There are period rooms reflecting the ages, such as the early 1820s salon of the Duchesse de Berry (who actually lived in the building), plus several rooms reproduced from designer Jeanne Lanvin's 1920s apartment. Don't miss the gilt-and-green-velvet bed of the Parisian courtesan who inspired the boudoir in Émile Zola's novel *Nana*; you can hear Zola's description of it on the free English audioguide, which is highly recommended. The second-floor jewelry gallery is another must-see.

The museum is also home to an exceptional collection of textiles, advertising posters, films, and related objects that are shown in rotating temporary exhibitions. Before leaving, take a break at the museum's restaurant (the outdoor terrace is an ideal spot for lunch or afternoon tea). Shoppers should browse through the on-site boutique as well. Stocked with an interesting collection of books, paper products, toys, tableware, accessories, and jewelry, it is one of the city's best museum shops. If you're combining a visit here with the Musée du Louvre, note that the two close on different days, so don't come on Monday or Tuesday. If you're pairing it with the exquisite Nissim de Camondo, joint tickets are available at a reduced cost. ⊠ *107 rue de Rivoli, Around the Louvre* ☎ *01–44–55–57–50* ⊕ *www.lesartsdecoratifs.fr* 🖥 *€11; €15 with temporary exhibits; €13 joint ticket with Musée Nissim de Camondo* ☉ *Tues.–Sun. 11–6 (Thurs. until 9 during exhibits)* Ⓜ *Palais-Royal–Louvre.*

Les Halles. For 800 years, Paris was fed by the acres of food halls over-flowing with meats, fish, and vegetables that made up this district. Sensuously described in Émile Zola's novel *The Belly of Paris,* Les Halles was teeming with life—though not all of it good. Hucksters and the homeless shared these streets with prostitutes (who still ply their trade in diminishing numbers on nearby Rue St-Denis); and the plague of cat-size rats didn't cease until the market moved to the suburbs in 1969. Today, you can still see stuffed pests hanging by their tails in the windows of the circa-1872 shop Julien Aurouze (8 rue des Halles) whose sign, *Destruction des Animaux Nuisibles* (in other words, vermin extermination), says it all. All that remains of the 19th-century iron-and-glass market buildings, designed by architect Victor Baltard, is a portion of the superstructure on the southern edge of the Jardins des Halles. The Fontaine des Innocents, from 1550, at Rues Berger and Pierre Lescot, marks the site of what was once a vast cemetery before the bones were moved to the Catacombs.

After years of delays, Les Halles is undergoing one of the city's most ambitious public works projects: a sweeping €500 million renovation intended to transform the plaza, and the much-maligned underground concrete mall called the Forum des Halles, into a must-go destination. While the project was not without opponents, even famously grumpy Parisians are finally happy about the prospect of a prettier Les Halles—especially now that the end is in sight. In an echo of the past, a 48-foot iron-and-glass rippling canopy has been suspended over the entrance, flooding light into the caverns below. Renovations of the underground mall and bustling train station, taking place in stages, are on track to be completed by 2018. Aboveground, a 10-acre park called the Jardin Nelson Mandela is dotted with trees, decorative pools, and play areas for kids. On the northern end, a redesigned Place René Cassin has tiered steps centered around *L'Ecoute*, Henri de Miller's giant head and hand sculpture. Looming behind is the magnificent church of St-Eustache, a Gothic gem. Film buffs with time to spare can stop by the Forum des Images, with some 7,000 films available for viewing on individual screens. To find it, enter the mall on the side of the church at the Porte St-Eustache.

The streets surrounding Les Halles have boomed in recent years with boutiques, bars, and restaurants galore that have sent rents skyrocketing. Historic Rue Montorgueil is home to food shops and cafés. Running parallel, Rue Montmartre, near the church, still has a few specialty shops selling foie gras and other delicacies, though these merchants, like the butchers and bakers before them, are slowly being pushed out by trendy clothing boutiques. ⊠ *Garden entrances on Rues Coquillière, Berger, and Rambuteau. Mall entrances on Rues Pierre Lescot, Berger, and Rambuteau, Around the Louvre* ⊕ *www.forumdeshalles.com* ⊙ *Mall Mon.–Sat. 10–8* Ⓜ *Les Halles; RER: Châtelet–Les Halles.*

Fodor'sChoice **The Louvre.** Simply put, the Louvre is the world's greatest art museum—
★ and the largest, with 675,000 square feet of works from almost every civilization on earth. The *Mona Lisa* is, of course, a top draw, along with the Venus de Milo and Winged Victory. These and many more of the globe's most coveted treasures are displayed in three wings—the

It would take decades to see every piece of art within the Louvre, but most visitors make it a priority to see what are called "The Big Three": Venus de Milo, Winged Victory, and *Mona Lisa*.

Richelieu, the Sully, and the Denon—which are arranged like a horseshoe. Nestled in the middle is I.M. Pei's Pyramide, the giant glass pyramid surrounded by a trio of smaller ones that opened in 1989 over the new entrance in the Cour Napoléon. To plot your course through the complex, grab a color-coded map at the information desk. For an excellent overview, book a 90-minute English-language tour (€12, daily at 11:30 and 2); slick Nintendo 3DS multimedia guides (€5), available at the entrance to each wing, offer a self-guided alternative.

Having been first a fortress and later a royal residence, the Louvre represents a saga that spans nine centuries. Its medieval roots are on display below ground in the Sully wing, where vestiges of the foundation and moat remain. Elsewhere in this wing you can ogle the largest display of Egyptian antiques outside of Cairo, most notably the magnificent statue of Ramses II (salle 12). Upstairs is the armless Venus de Milo, a 2nd-century representation of Aphrodite (salle 16). Highlights of the wing's collection of French paintings from the 17th century onward include the *Turkish Bath* by Jean-August-Dominique Ingres (salle 60). American Cy Twombly's contemporary ceiling in salle 32 adds a 21st-century twist. In the Denon wing, climb the sweeping marble staircase (Escalier Daru) to see the sublime Winged Victory of Samothrace, carved in 305 BC. This wing is also home to the iconic, enigmatic *Mona Lisa* (salle 6); two other da Vinci masterpieces hang in the adjacent Grand Galerie. The museum's latest architectural wonder is here as well—the 30,000-square-foot Arts of Islam exhibition space, which debuted in 2012. Topped with an undulating golden roof evoking a flowing veil, its two-level galleries contain one of the largest collections of art from the Islamic world. After admiring it, be sure to visit the Richelieu wing and the Cour Marly, with its quartet of horses carved for Louis XIV and Louis XV. On the ground floor, the centerpiece of the Near East Antiquities Collection is the Lamassu, carved 8th-century winged beasts (salle 4). The elaborately decorated Royal Apartments of Napoléon III are on the first floor. On the second floor, French and Northern School paintings include Vermeer's *The Lacemaker* (salle 38). Note that crowds are thinner on Wednesday and Friday nights, when the museum is open late. Save queue time by purchasing online tickets; the €15 fee includes temporary exhibitions and same-day entry to the charming Musée Eugène-Delacroix. If you arrive without a ticket, use the automatic machines below the Pyramide entrance or head for the entrance at the end of the underground mall, Carrousel du Louvre. ⊠ *Palais du Louvre, Around the Louvre* ☎ *01–40–20–53–17 information* ⊕ *www. louvre.fr* ✉ *€15, includes same-day entry to Musée Eugène Delacroix (free 1st Sun. of month, Oct.–Mar.)* ⊗ *Mon., Thurs., and weekends 9–6, Wed. and Fri. 9 am–9:45 pm* Ⓜ *Palais-Royal–Louvre, Louvre-Rivoli.*

Musée de l'Orangerie. The lines can be long to see Claude Monet's huge, meditative *Water Lilies (Les Nymphéas)*, displayed in two curved galleries designed in 1914 by the master himself. But they are well worth the wait. These works are the highlight of the Orangerie Museum's small but excellent collection, which also features early-20th-century paintings by Renoir, Cézanne, and Matisse. Many hail from the private holdings of art dealer Paul Guillaume (1891–1934), among them Guillaume's portrait by Modigliani; entitled *Novo Pilota,* or "New Pilot," it signals Guillaume's status as an important presence in the arts world. Built in 1852 to shelter orange trees, the museum includes a portion of the city's 16th-century wall (you can see remnants on the lower floor). You'll find a small café and gift shop here, too. ⊠ *Jardin des Tuileries at Pl. de la Concorde, Around the Louvre* ☎ *01–44–77–80–07* ⊕ *www. musee-orangerie.fr* ✉ *€9 (€6.50 after 5); €14 joint ticket with Musée d'Orsay; €18.50 joint ticket with Giverney valid for one year* ⊗ *Wed.– Mon. 9–6* Ⓜ *Concorde.*

Fodor's Choice ★ **Palais-Royal.** The quietest, most romantic Parisian garden is enclosed within the former home of Cardinal Richelieu (1585–1642). It's the perfect place to while away an afternoon, cuddling with your sweetheart on a bench under the trees, soaking up the sunshine beside the fountain, or browsing the 400-year-old arcades that are now home to boutiques ranging from quirky (picture Anna Joliet's music boxes) to chic (think designs by Stella McCartney). One of the city's oldest restaurants is here, the haute-cuisine Le Grand Véfour, where brass plaques recall regulars like Napoléon and Victor Hugo. Built in 1629, the *palais* became royal when Richelieu bequeathed it to Louis XIII. Other famous residents include Jean Cocteau and Colette, who wrote of her pleasurable "country" view of the *province à Paris*. Today, the garden often plays host to giant-size temporary art installations sponsored by another tenant, the Ministry of Culture. The courtyard off Place Colette is outfitted with an eye-catching collection of squat black-and-white columns created in 1986 by artist Daniel Buren. ⊠ *Pl. du Palais-Royal, Around the Louvre* Ⓜ *Palais-Royal–Louvre.*

Place de la Concorde. This square at the foot of the Champs-Élysées was originally named after Louis XV. It later became the Place de la Révolution, where crowds cheered as Louis XVI, Marie-Antoinette, and some 2,500 others lost their heads to the guillotine. Renamed Concorde in 1836, it got a new centerpiece: the 75-foot granite Obelisk of Luxor, a gift from Egypt quarried in the 8th century BC. Among the handsome 18th-century buildings facing the square is the Hôtel Crillon, which was originally built as a private home by Gabriel, the architect of Versailles's Petit Trianon. ⊠ *Rue Royale, Around the Louvre* Ⓜ *Concorde.*

Place Vendôme. Jules-Hardouin Mansart, an architect of Versailles, designed this perfectly proportioned octagonal plaza near the Tuileries in 1702; and, to maintain a uniform appearance, he gave the surrounding *hôtels particuliers* (private mansions) identical facades. It was originally called Place des Conquêtes to extoll the military conquests of Louis XIV, whose statue on horseback graced the center until Revolutionaries destroyed it in 1792. Later, Napoléon ordered his likeness erected atop a 144-foot column modestly modeled after Rome's Trajan Column. But that, too, was toppled in 1871 by painter Gustave Courbet and his band of radicals. The Third Republic raised a new column and sent Courbet the bill, though he died in exile before paying it. The Ritz, a longtime tenant, picked up the tab for a 2016 renovation teamed with the hotel's own four-year clean-up. Chopin lived and died at No. 12, which is also where Napoléon III enjoyed trysts with his mistress; since 1902 it has been home to the high-end jeweler Chaumet. ⊠ *Pl. Vendôme, Around the Louvre* Ⓜ *Tuileries.*

Fodor'sChoice ★ **Rue Montorgueil.** Rue Montorgueil was once the gritty oyster hub of Les Halles. Now lined with food shops and cafés, the cobbled street whose name translates to Mount Pride is the heart of one of the city's trendiest neighborhoods. History runs deep here. Monet captured the scene in 1878 when Montorgueil was ablaze with tricolor flags during the World's Fair (see it in the Musée d'Orsay). Honoré de Balzac and his 19th-century band of scribes frequented Au Rocher de Cancale at No. 78, whose famously crumbling facade has been painstakingly restored with gilt panache. Other addresses have been around for centuries: Stohrer at No. 58 has been baking elaborate pastries since 1730; and L'Escargot Montorgueil at No. 38, a favorite of Charlie Chaplin, is still graced by a giant golden snail. Relative newcomers include the luxury Nuxe spa at Nos. 32 and 34. Browse the boutiques on Rue Montmartre, which runs parallel, or shop for cookware at Julia Child's old haunt, E. Dehillerin, still in business at 18–20 rue Coquillière. Rue Tiquetonne is rife with bistros, and once-sleepy Rue St-Sauveur became a destination when the Experimental Cocktail Club (No. 37) moved in, joined by other trendy eating and drinking spots. Even Rue St-Denis, once a scruffy red-light district, is now a hipster fave with bar-restaurants like Le Pas Sage at the entrance of the lovely covered arcade, Passage du Grand Cerf. ⊠ *Rue Montorgueil, off Rue de Turbigo, Around the Louvre* Ⓜ *Sentier, Les Halles.*

St-Eustache. Built as the market neighborhood's answer to Notre-Dame, this massive church is decidedly squeezed into its surroundings. Constructed between 1532 and 1640 with foundations dating to 1200, the church mixes a Gothic exterior, complete with impressive flying buttresses, and a Renaissance interior. On the east end (Rue Montmartre), Dutch master Rubens's *Pilgrims of Emmaus* (1611) hangs in a small chapel. Two chapels to the left is Keith Haring's *The Life of Christ*, a triptych in bronze and white-gold patina: it was given to the church after the artist's death in 1990, in recognition of the parish's efforts to help people with AIDS. On the Rue Montmartre side of the church, look for the small door to

> **DID YOU KNOW?**
>
> Place de la Madeleine has what may be Paris's nicest public toilet. Opened in 1905, the free Art Nouveau loo features colorful tiles and cubicle doors of stained glass and carved wood. There's an attentive attendant. Look for the underground entrance on the southeast corner near the flower market on Rue du Surène. It's open 10–noon and 1–6:15.

Saint Agnes's crypt, topped with a stone plaque noting the date, 1213, below a curled fish, an indication the patron made his fortune in fish. ⊠ *2 impasse St-Eustache, Around the Louvre* ⊕ *www.saint-eustache. org for concert info* ⊗ *Weekdays 9:30–7, weekends 9–7* Ⓜ *Les Halles; RER: Châtelet–Les Halles.*

WORTH NOTING

Bourse du Commerce. Best approached from the rear, the old Commerce Exchange looks like a giant spaceship. Now home to the International Chamber of Commerce, it's worth a stop inside to see the beautifully restored iron-and-glass dome, which Victor Hugo dismissively likened to a jockey's cap. Built in 1809, this was the first iron structure in France. Behind it, the 100-foot-tall Colonne Medicis is a remnant of a mansion constructed in 1572 for Catherine de Medici. The column, which miraculously escaped destruction through the ages, was used as a platform for stargazing by her powerful astrologer, Cosimo Ruggieri. Legend has it that on stormy nights, a silhouetted figure can be seen in the metal cage at the top. To learn more about the building of the dome, check out the short video of its construction in the Musée des Arts et Métiers. ⊠ *2 rue de Viarmes, Around the Louvre* Ⓜ *Les Halles; RER: Châtelet–Les Halles.*

Comédie Française. Refined productions by Molière and Racine are staged regularly (though only in French) at the vintage venue where actress Sarah Bernhardt began her career. Founded in 1680 by Louis XIV, the theater finally opened its doors to the public in 1799. It nearly burned to the ground a hundred years later. The current building dates from 1900. ⊠ *Salle Richelieu, 1 pl. Colette, Around the Louvre* ☎ *08–25–10–16–80* €*0.18 per minute* ⊕ *www.comedie-francaise.fr* Ⓜ *Palais-Royal–Louvre.*

Église de la Madeleine. With its rows of uncompromising columns, this enormous neoclassical edifice in the center of Place de la Madeleine was consecrated as a church in 1842, nearly 78 years after construction began. Initially planned as a Baroque building, it was later razed and begun anew by an architect who had the Roman Pantheon in mind. Interrupted by the Revolution, the site was razed yet again when

Napoléon decided to make it into a Greek temple dedicated to the glory of his army. Those plans changed when the army was defeated and the emperor deposed. Other ideas for the building included making it into a train station, a market, and a library. Finally, Louis XVIII decided to make it a church, which it still is today. Classical concerts are held here regularly, some of them free. ⊠ *Pl. de la Madeleine, Around the Louvre* ☎ *01–44–51–69–00* ⊕ *www.eglise-lamadeleine.com* ⊙ *Daily 9:30–7* Ⓜ *Madeleine*.

NEED A BREAK?

✕ **Foyer de la Madeleine.** A cheap meal in the Madeleine? Even most Parisians don't know it's possible to find one in this posh *place*, yet a reasonable option awaits in the basement of the eponymous Église. On the Rue de Surène side of the church is the entrance to the Foyer, where friendly church ladies provide a three-course lunch for €15.50 (€8.50 plus €7 for a one-year membership card). The fare—served buffet style on weekdays, from 11:45 to 2—is solid, if not gourmet, and the wine is a great deal at €7 a bottle. Best to go early when the food is freshest. ⊠ *Pl. de la Madeleine, Around the Louvre* ☎ *01–47–42–39–84* Ⓜ *Madeleine*.

Église St-Germain-l'Auxerrois. Founded in 500 AD, this grand church across from the Louvre's eastern end is one of the city's oldest. It was destroyed during the Norman siege in 885–886, rebuilt in the 11th century, and subsequently expanded until the current edifice was finished in 1580. The bell, named Marie, dates from 1527. ⊠ *2 pl. du Louvre, Around the Louvre* ☎ *01–42–60–13–96* ⊕ *www.saintgermainauxerrois. fr* ⊙ *Tues.–Sat. 9–7, Sun. 9:30–8:30* Ⓜ *Louvre-Rivoli*.

Jeu de Paume. This Napoléon III–era building at the north entrance of the Jardin des Tuileries began life in 1861 as a place to play *jeu de paume* (or "palm game"), a forerunner of tennis. It later served as a transfer point for art looted by the Germans during World War II. Now it displays some of the city's best photography, serving as an ultramodern, white-walled showcase for up-and-comers as well as icons such as Diane Arbus, Richard Avedon, Cindy Sherman, and Robert Frank. ⊠ *1 pl. de la Concorde, Around the Louvre* ☎ *01–47–03–12–50* ⊕ *www. jeudepaume.org* ▱ *€10* ⊙ *Tues. 11–9, Wed.–Sun. 11–7* Ⓜ *Concorde*.

Passage du Grand-Cerf. This stately glass-roofed arcade was built in 1825 and expertly renovated in 1988. Today it's home to about 20 shops, many of them small designers selling original jewelry, accessories, and housewares. If it's apéritif time, stop by the popular Le Pas Sage, with a wine bar and a restaurant flanking either side of the entrance at Rue St-Denis. ⊠ *Entrances at 145 rue St-Denis and 8 rue Dussoubs, Around the Louvre* Ⓜ *Étienne Marcel*.

FAMILY **Tour Jean Sans Peur.** This fascinating little tower is the only remnant of a sprawling complex built on the edge of the original city walls in 1369. It is named for Jean Sans Peur (John the Fearless), the Duke of Burgundy, who gained power in 1407 after ordering the assassination of his rival, the king's brother. In 1409, as civil war raged, he had the tower erected and put his bedroom on a high floor with a bird's-eye view of approaching enemies. Carved into the vaulted second-floor ceiling—a masterwork of medieval architecture—is an ornate sculpture of an oak tree entwined with plants representing the duke's family. Children will enjoy the climb up to see the restored red-velvet-lined latrine, a state-of-the-art comfort in its time. Costumed mannequins and medieval-themed exhibits covering subjects from food to furniture give the tower added kid appeal. Be sure to ask for English information at the entry. ⊠ *20 rue Étienne Marcel, Around the Louvre* ☎ *01–40–26–20–28* ⊕ *www.tourjeansanspeur.com* ✉ *€5* ⊗ *Wed.–Sun. 1:30–6* Ⓜ *Étienne Marcel.*

Tour Saint-Jacques. For centuries, this 170-foot bell tower guided pilgrims to a starting point of the Chemin de Saint Jacques (the Way of Saint James). Built in 1508 in the Flamboyant Gothic style, it's all that remains of the Église Saint-Jacques-de-la-Boucherie, which was destroyed in the French Revolution. Purchased by the city in 1836, the tower languished until a three-year renovation, completed in 2009, restored 660 tons of stone and statues, including the gargoyles hanging from the upper reaches and the figure of Saint Jacques gracing the top. Blaise Pascal was among the medieval scientists who conducted experiments here (his involved gravity), which is why his statue sits at the base. If you wish to enter the tower, guided tours are given in the summer by reservation only; make yours online at ⊕ *www.desmotsetdesarts.com.* ⊠ *39 rue de Rivoli, Around the Louvre* ⊕ *www.tour-saint-jacques-paris.com* ✉ *Tours €10* ⊗ *Jun.–Sept., Fri.–Sun. 10–5* Ⓜ *Châtelet.*

6

LES GRANDS
BOULEVARDS

GETTING ORIENTED

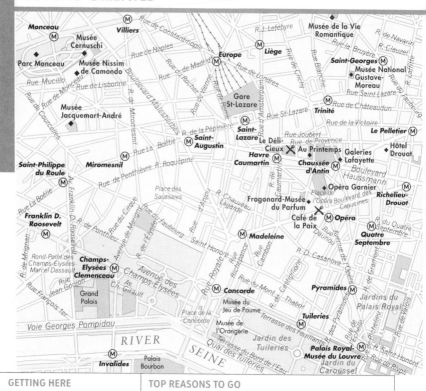

This neighborhood covers parts of the 2e, 3e, 8e, and 9e arrondissements. Take the métro to the Opéra station, named for the opulent opera house. Just behind it, you can find the department stores Galeries Lafayette and Au Printemps, each with three buildings (women's, men's, home) along Baron Haussmann's wide avenues known as the Grands Boulevards. If you're planning to visit the numerous small museums, take the métro to Parc Monceau.

Les Grands Magasins. Sample a new perfume under the magnificent dome at Galeries Lafayette; update your look, wander the sumptuous food halls, or gaze at Parisian rooftops from the outdoor café at Au Printemps.

Opéra Garnier. It may not be haunted by the Phantom, but this 19th-century opera house still dazzles. Enjoy a ballet or an opera, take the guided tour, or simply ogle the halls bedecked in marble and gold leaf.

Musée Jacquemart-André. Peruse the private collection of Italian Renaissance masterpieces and admire the elegant furnishings in one of the city's grandest mansions.

Parc Monceau. Join the well-dressed children of well-heeled Parisians and frolic on some of the prettiest lawns in the city.

Les Passages Couverts. Stroll the passages Jouffroy, Verdeau, and Panoramas to experience what the original shopping malls were like 200 years ago.

Les Grands Boulevards

BEST CAFÉS

Café de la Paix. Once described as the "center of the civilized world," this grand café was a meeting place for the Belle Époque's glitterati. It's an elegant spot to enjoy a drink (or meal) in the shadow of the Opéra Garnier. ⊠ *5 pl. de l'Opéra, Les Grands Boulevards* ☎ *01–40–07–36–36* ⊕ *www. cafedelapaix.fr* Ⓜ *Opéra.*

Delaville Café. This edgy café is a favorite with locals. Open late, it's best for an evening apéritif and snack. A DJ spins tunes at night, Thursday through Saturday. ⊠ *34 bd. de Bonne Nouvelle, Les Grands Boulevards* ☎ *01–48–24–48–09* ⊕ *www.delavillecafe.com* Ⓜ *Bonne Nouvelle.*

Le Déli-Cieux. Perched on the top floor of Printemps Maison, Déli-Cieux serves sandwiches, salads, and burgers. It's not expensive, and the view from the outdoor terrace is priceless. ⊠ *Au Printemps, Bd. Haussmann and Rue du Havre, 9th fl., Les Grands Boulevards* ☎ *01–42–82–62–76* ⊘ *Closed Sun.* Ⓜ *Havre–Caumartin, St-Lazare.*

MAKING THE MOST OF YOUR TIME

If you're a serious shopper, plan on a day-long visit to this neighborhood, beginning with the department stores near the Opéra métro stop. Nearly every French chain has a shop dotting the boulevard, which changes names several times (Boulevard Haussmann, Montmartre, Poissonnière, de Bonne Nouvelle, etc.) as it stretches from west to east.

If shopping isn't your bag, plan on a long afternoon's visit: tour the Opéra Garnier and one or two museums, or bring a picnic lunch to lovely Parc Monceau on the western edge.

Sightseeing
★★★

Dining
★★★

Lodging
★★★★★

Shopping
★★★★★

Nightlife
★★★★★

In Belle Époque Paris, the Grands Boulevards were the place to see and be seen: in the cafés, at the opera, or in the ornate *passages couverts* (glass-roofed arcades that served as the world's first malls). If you close your eyes, you can almost imagine the Grands Boulevards immortalized on canvas by the Impressionists, with well-attired Parisians strolling wide avenues dotted with shops, cafés, and horse-drawn carriages—all set against a backdrop of stately Haussmannian buildings. Today, despite the chain stores, sidewalk vendors, and fast-food joints, the Grands Boulevards remain the city's shopping epicenter, home to the most popular department stores, Galeries Lafayette and Au Printemps, near Place de l'Opéra.

Updated by
Jack Vermee

Shopping aside, the Grands Boulevards are a cultural destination anchored by the magnificent **Opéra Garnier,** commissioned by Napoléon III. The neighborhood is also home to some of the city's best small museums, all former private collections housed in 19th-century *hôtels particuliers* (mansions) that alone are worth the trip. The exquisite **Musée Jacquemart-André** displays an impressive collection of Italian Renaissance art, while the jewel-box **Musée Nissim de Camondo** remembers one family's tragic end. The **Musée Cernuschi** has a dazzling array of Asian art, and the **Musée National Gustave-Moreau** is an offbeat tribute to the Symbolist master.

TOP ATTRACTIONS

Au Printemps. Encompassing a trio of upscale department stores (Printemps Mode, Printemps Maison, and Printemps Homme), this vast, venerable retailer has been luring shoppers since 1865. Besides the clothes, shoes, housewares, and everything else, there are appealing lunch options here. You can admire the Belle Époque green-and-gold dome in Brasserie Printemps on the sixth floor of the main store; Le World Bar on the fifth floor of the men's store is a cozy pub with a cool vibe; and Le Déli-Cieux, the ninth-floor cafeteria-style restaurant at Printemps Maison, has a large outdoor terrace with a great view. ⊠ *64 bd. Haussmann, Les Grands Boulevards* ☏ *01–42–82–50–00* ⊕ *www. printemps.com* ⊙ *Mon.–Wed., Fri., and Sat. 9:35–8, Thurs. 9:35–8:45* Ⓜ *Havre-Caumartin, St-Lazare.*

FAMILY **Chocostory: Le Musée Gourmand du Chocolat.** Considering that a daily dose of chocolate is practically obligatory in Paris, it's hard to believe that this spot (opened in 2010) is the city's first museum dedicated to the sweet stuff. Exhibits on three floors tell the story of chocolate from the earliest traces of the "divine nectar" in Mayan and Aztec cultures, through to its introduction in Europe by the Spanish, who added milk and sugar to the spicy dark brew and launched a Continental craze. There are detailed explanations in English, with many for the kids. While the production of chocolate is a major topic, there is also a respectable collection of some 1,000 chocolate-related artifacts, such as terra-cotta Mayan sipping vessels (they blew into straws to create foam) and delicate chocolate pots in fine porcelain that were favored by the French royal court. Frequent chocolate-making demonstrations finish with a free tasting. ⊠ *28 bd. de Bonne Nouvelle, Les Grands Boulevards* ☏ *01–42–29–68–60* ⊕ *www.museeduchocolat.fr* ☏ *€11; €14 with a cup of hot chocolate* ⊙ *Daily 10–6* ☞ *Last entry at 5* Ⓜ *Bonne-Nouvelle, Strasbourg, St-Denis.*

Galeries Lafayette. The stunning Byzantine glass *coupole* (dome) of the city's most famous department store is not to be missed. Amble to the center of the main store, amid the perfumes and cosmetics, and look up. If you're not in the mood for shopping, sip a glass of Champagne at the Bar à Bulles at the top of the first-floor escalator; or have lunch at one of the restaurants, including a rooftop café in the main store (open in spring and summer). On your way down, the top floor of the main store is a good place to pick up interesting Parisian souvenirs. Next door, the excellent Lafayette Gourmet food hall, on the second floor of the men's store, has one of the city's best selections of delicacies. Try a green-tea éclair from Japanese–French baker Sadaharu Aoki. ⊠ *35–40 bd. Haussmann, Les Grands Boulevards* ☏ *01–42–82–34–56* ⊕ *www. galerieslafayette.com* ⊙ *Mon.–Wed., Fri., and Sat. 9:30–8, Thurs. 9:30–9* Ⓜ *Chaussée d'Antin, Havre-Caumartin.*

Fodor'sChoice ★ **Musée Cernuschi.** Wealthy Milanese banker and patriot Enrico (Henri) Cernuschi fled to Paris in 1850 after the new Italian government collapsed, only to be arrested during the 1871 Paris Commune. He subsequently decided to wait out the unrest by traveling and collecting Asian art. Upon his return 18 months later, he had a special mansion built on the edge of Parc Monceau to house his treasures, notably a two-story bronze Buddha from Japan. Today, this well-appointed museum contains France's second-most-important collection of Asian art, after the Musée Guimet. Cernuschi had an eye not only for the bronze pieces he adored but also for Neolithic pottery (8000 BC), *mingqi* tomb figures

(300–900 AD), and an impressive array of terra-cotta figures from various dynasties. A collection highlight is La Tigresse, a bronze wine vessel in the shape of a roaring feline (11th century BC) purchased after Cernuschi's death. Although the museum is free, there is a charge for temporary exhibitions: previous shows have featured Japanese drawings, Iranian sculpture, and Imperial Chinese bronzes. ⊠ *7 av. Velasquez, Les Grands Boulevards* ☎ *01–53–96–21–50* ⊕ *www. cernuschi.paris.fr* ⊡ *Free; €8 for temporary exhibitions* ☺ *Tues.– Sun. 10–6* Ⓜ *Monceau.*

Fodor'sChoice   **Musée Jacquemart-André.** Perhaps
★   the city's best small museum, the opulent Musée Jacquemart-André is home to a huge collection of art and furnishings lovingly assembled in the late 19th century by banking

heir Edouard André and his artist wife, Nélie Jacquemart. Their midlife marriage in 1881 raised eyebrows—he was a dashing bachelor and a Protestant, and she, no great beauty, hailed from a modest Catholic family. Still, theirs was a happy union fused by a common passion for art. For six months every year, the couple traveled, most often to Italy, where they hunted down works from the Renaissance, their preferred period. Their collection also includes French painters Fragonard, Jacques-Louis David, and François Boucher, plus Dutch masters Van Dyke and Rembrandt. The Belle Époque mansion itself is a major attraction. The elegant ballroom, equipped with collapsible walls operated by then-state-of-the-art hydraulics, could hold 1,000 guests. The winter garden was a wonder of its day, spilling into the *fumoir,* where André would share cigars with the *grands hommes* (important men) of the day. You can tour the separate bedrooms—his in dusty pink, hers in pale yellow. The former dining room, now an elegant café, features a ceiling by Tiepolo. Don't forget to pick up the free audioguide in English, and do inquire about the current temporary exhibition (two per year), which is usually top-notch. Plan on a Sunday visit and enjoy the popular brunch (€29.30) in the café from 11 to 2:30. Reservations are not accepted, so come early or late to avoid waiting in line. ⊠ *158 bd. Haussmann, Les Grands Boulevards* ☎ *01–45–62–16–32* ⊕ *www. musee-jacquemart-andre.com* ⊡ *€14* ☺ *Daily 10–6 (until 8:30 Mon. and Sat. during exhibitions)* Ⓜ *St-Philippe-du-Roule, Miromesnil.*

OFF THE BEATEN PATH

Musée National Gustave-Moreau. Visiting the quirky town house and studio of painter Gustave Moreau (1826–98) is well worth your time. With an eye on his legacy, Moreau—a high priest of the Symbolist movement—created an enchanting gallery to showcase his dark paintings,

Paris's Covered Arcades

Before there were the *grands magasins,* there were the *passages couverts,* covered arcades that offered the early-19th-century Parisian shopper a hodgepodge of shops under one roof and a respite from the mud and grit of streets that did not have sidewalks. Until the rise of department stores in the latter part of the century, they would rule as the top places to wander, as well as shop. Technical and architectural wonders of the time, the vaulting structures of iron and frosted glass inspired artists and writers such as Émile Zola.

Of the 150 arcades built around Paris in the early 1800s, only about a dozen are still in business today, mostly in the 2e and 9e arrondissements. Two arcades still going strong are the fabulously restored **Galerie Vivienne** (*4 rue Petits Champs, 2e*) and the **Galerie Véro-Dodat** (*19 rue Jean-Jacques Rousseau, 1er*), both lined with unique and glamorous boutiques.

Three other modest passages enjoying a renaissance can be found end to end off the Grands Boulevards, east of Place de l'Opéra. Begin with the most refined, the **Passage Jouffroy** (*10–12 bd. Montmartre, 9e*), which is home to the Musée Grévin and the well-regarded, budget-friendly Hotel Chopin. There's an eclectic array of shops such as M.G.W. Segas at No. 34, where the three Segas brothers sell a wildly eccentric collection of furnishings and canes capped with animal heads and whatnot. You can outfit your dollhouse at Pain D'épices (No. 29), which stocks thousands of miniatures. Pop out at the northern end of Passage Jouffroy and cross Rue de la Grange-Batelière into the **Passage Verdeau** (*9e*), where you can pick up some antique candlesticks—or a cow skull—at the quirky, red-walled Valence gallery at No. 22. On the southern end of the Passage Jouffroy, across Boulevard Montmartre, is the **Passage des Panoramas** (*2e*). The granddaddy of the arcades, opened in 1800, became the first public space in Paris equipped with gaslights in 1817. A few philatelist shops remain, though the arcade is now dominated by restaurants, including two popular wine bar–bistros (Racines at No. 8 and Coinstot Vino at No. 26, bis), as well as Paris's original gluten-free restaurant (Noglu, at No. 16).

drawings, and sculpture. The recently refurbished first-floor rooms, closed to the public for more than a decade, now trace Moreau's "sentimental journey"; their walls are festooned with family portraits and works offered by close friends and allies like Chassériau, Fromentin, and Degas. The two light-flooded top floors house Moreau's vast workshops, where hundreds of paintings, watercolors, and more than 4,000 drawings give a broad overview of his techniques and subjects. Some of the pieces appear unfinished, such as *Unicorns* (No. 213) inspired by the medieval tapestries in the Musée de Cluny: Moreau refused to work on it further, spurning the wishes of a wealthy would-be patron. His interpretation of Biblical scenes and Greek mythology combine flights of fantasy with a keen use of color, shadow, and tracings influenced by Persian and Indian miniatures. There are wax sculptures and cupboards with sliding vertical doors containing small-format paintings. The Symbolists loved objects, and Moreau was no different. His cramped private apartment on the second floor is jam-packed with bric-a-brac, and artworks cover every inch of the walls. ✉ *14 rue de la Rochefoucauld, Les Grands Boulevards* ☎ *01–48–74–38–50* ⊕ *www.musee-moreau.fr* 🖾 *€6* ☉ *Mon., Wed., and Thurs. 10–12:45 and 2–5:15, Fri.–Sun. 10–5:15* Ⓜ *Trinité, St-Georges.*

Fodor's Choice **Opéra Garnier.** Haunt of the Phantom of the Opera and the real-life
★ inspiration for Edgar Degas's dancer paintings, the gorgeous Opéra Garnier is one of two homes of the National Opera of Paris. The building, the Palais Garnier, was begun in 1860 by then-unknown architect Charles Garnier, who finished his masterwork 15 long years later, way over budget. Festooned with (real) gold leaf, colored marble, paintings, and sculpture from the top artists of the day, the opera house was about as subtle as Versailles and sparked controversy in post-Revolutionary France. The sweeping marble staircase, in particular, drew criticism from a public skeptical of its extravagance. But Garnier, determined to make a landmark that would last forever, spared no expense. The magnificent grand foyer is one of the most exquisite salons in France. In its heyday, the cream of Paris society strolled all 59 yards of the vast hall at intermission, admiring themselves in the towering mirrors. To see the opera house, buy a ticket for an unguided visit, which allows access to most parts of the building, including a peek into the auditorium. There is also a small ballet museum with a few works by Degas and the tutu worn by prima ballerina Anna Pavlova when she danced her epic Dying Swan in 1905. To get to it, pass through the unfinished entrance built for Napoléon III and his carriage (construction was abruptly halted when the emperor abdicated in 1870). On the upper level, you can see a sample of the auditorium's original classical ceiling, which was later replaced with a modern version painted by a septuagenarian Marc Chagall. His trademark willowy figures encircling the dazzling crystal chandelier—today the world's third largest—shocked an unappreciative public upon its debut in 1964. Critics who fret that Chagall's masterpiece clashes with the fussy crimson-and-gilt decor can take some comfort in knowing that the original ceiling is preserved underneath, encased in a plastic dome.

The Opéra Garnier plays host to the Paris Ballet as well as a few operas each season (most are performed at the Opéra Bastille). If you're planning to see a performance, tickets cost €10–€230 and should be reserved as soon as they go on sale—typically a month ahead at the box office, earlier by phone or online; otherwise, try your luck last minute. To learn about the building's history, and get a taste of aristocratic life during the Second Empire, take an entertaining English-language tour. They're offered most months at 11:30 and 3:30 on Wednesday, Saturday, and Sunday; tours go at the same times daily in summer, with an extra one added at 2. To complete the experience, dine at L'Opéra, the contemporary on-site restaurant run by chef Stéphane Bidi; or browse through the Palais Garnier gift shop for ballet-inspired wares, fine Bernardaud porcelain depicting the famous Chagall ceiling, and an exceptional selection of themed DVDs and books. ✉ *Pl. de l'Opéra, Les Grands Boulevards* ☎ *08–92–89–90–90 €0.34 per min, 01–71–25–24–23 from outside France* ⊕ *www.operadeparis.*

fr ☕ *€11; €14.50 for tours* ⊘ *Building Sept.–mid-July, daily 10–5; mid-July–Aug., daily 10–6. Box office Mon.–Sat. 11:30–6:30* ☞ *last admission 30 mins before closing* Ⓜ *Opéra.*

FAMILY **Parc Monceau.** This exquisitely landscaped park began in 1778 as the Duc de Chartres's private garden. Though some of the land was sold off under the Second Empire (creating the exclusive real estate that now borders the park), the refined atmosphere and some of the fanciful faux ruins have survived. Immaculately dressed children play under the watchful eye of their nannies, while lovers cuddle on the benches. In 1797 André Garnerin, the world's first-recorded parachutist, staged a landing in the park. The rotunda—known as the Chartres Pavilion—is surely the city's grandest public restroom: it started life as a tollhouse. ✉ *Entrances on Bd. de Courcelles, Av. Velasquez, Av. Ruysdaël, Av. van Dyck, Les Grands Boulevards* ⊘ *May–Aug., daily 7 am–10 pm; Sept., daily 7 am–9 pm; Oct.–May, 7 am–8 pm* Ⓜ *Monceau.*

WORTH NOTING

Fragonard Musée du Parfum. More of a showroom than a museum, the small exhibit run by *parfumier* Fragonard above its boutique on Rue Scribe is heavy on decorative objects associated with perfume, including crystal bottles, gloves, and assorted bibelots. The shop is a good place to find gifts, like body lotion made with royal jelly, myriad soaps, and, of course, perfume. True fragrance aficionados can double their pleasure by visiting the Théâtre Musée des Capucines-Fragonard, another mini-museum nearby at 39 boulevard des Capucines. ✉ *9 rue Scribe, Les Grands Boulevards* ☎ *01–47–42–04–56* ⊕ *www.fragonard.com* 🎫 *Free* ⊘ *Mon.–Sat. 9–6, Sun. 9–5* Ⓜ *Opéra.*

Hôtel Drouot. Hidden away in a small antiques district, not far from the Opéra Garnier, is Paris's central auction house. With everything from old clothes to haute-couture gowns and from tchotchkes to ornate Chinese lacquered boxes, rare books, and wine, Drouot sells it all. Anyone can attend the sales and viewings, which draw a mix of art dealers, ladies who lunch, and art amateurs hoping to discover an unknown masterpiece. Check the website to see what's on the block. Don't miss the small galleries and antiques dealers in the Quartier Drouot, a warren of small streets around the auction house, notably on Rues Rossini and de la Grange-Batelière. ✉ *9 rue Drouot, Les Grands Boulevards* ☎ *01–48–00–20–20* ⊕ *www.drouot.com* 🎫 *Free* ⊘ *Viewings of merchandise Mon.–Sat. 11–6; auctions usually begin at 2* Ⓜ *Richelieu-Drouot.*

NEED A BREAK? **J'go.** Steps from the Drouot auction house, J'go, one of two Paris outposts of the Toulouse wine bar/restaurant, is perfect for an apéritif or light dinner. The cozy bar serves impressive *grignotages* (tapas) from France's southwest. ✉ *4 rue Drouot, Les Grands Boulevards* ☎ *01–40–22–09–09* ⊕ *www.lejgo.com* Ⓜ *Richelieu-Drouot.*

Musée de la Vie Romantique. A visit to the charming Museum of Romantic Life, dedicated to novelist George Sand (1804–76), will transport you to the countryside. Occupying a pretty 1830s mansion in a tree-lined courtyard, the small permanent collection features drawings by Delacroix and Ingres, among others, though Sand is the undisputed star. Displays include glass cases stuffed with her jewelry and even a mold of the hand of composer Frédéric Chopin—one of her many lovers. The museum, about a five-minute walk from the Musée National Gustave-Moreau, is in a picturesque neighborhood once called New Athens, a reflection of the architectural tastes of the writers and artists who lived there. There is usually an interesting temporary exhibit here, too. The garden café (open mid-March to mid-October) is a lovely spot for lunch or afternoon tea. ✉ *16 rue Chaptal, Les Grands Boulevards* ☎ *01–55–31–95–67* ⊕ *parismusees.paris.fr/en/museum-romantics* 🖭 *Free; €5 temporary exhibits* 🕙 *Tues.–Sun. 10–6* Ⓜ *Blanche, Pigalle, St-Georges.*

FAMILY **Musée Grévin.** If you like wax museums, this one founded in 1882 ranks among the best. Pay the steep entry price and ascend a grand Phantom-of-the-Opera–like staircase into the Palais des Mirages, a mirrored salon from the 1900 Paris Exposition that transforms into a hokey light-and-sound show the kids will love (it was a childhood favorite of designer Jean-Paul Gaultier). From there, get set for a cavalcade of nearly 300 statues, from Elvis to Ernest Hemingway, Picasso to Barack Obama. Every king of France is here, along with Michael Jackson and George Clooney, plus scores of French singers and celebrities. ✉ *Passage Jouffroy, 10 bd. Montmartre, Les Grands Boulevards* ☎ *01–47–70–85–05* ⊕ *www.grevin-paris.com/fr* 🖭 *From €17* 🕙 *Usually weekdays 10–6, weekends 9:30–7 (hrs vary, check website for details)* Ⓜ *Grands Boulevards.*

Musée Nissim de Camondo. The story of the Camondo family is steeped in tragedy, and it's all recorded within the walls of this superb museum. Patriarch Moïse de Camondo, born in Istanbul to a successful banking family, built his showpiece mansion in 1911 in the style of the Petit Trianon at Versailles and stocked it with some of the most exquisite furniture, wainscoting, and bibelots of the mid-to-late 18th century. Despite his vast wealth and purported charm, his wife left him five years after their marriage. Then his son, Nissim, was killed in World War I. Upon Moïse's death in 1935, the house and its contents were left to the state as a museum named for his lost son. A few years later, daughter Béatrice, her husband, and two children were murdered at Auschwitz. No heirs remained and the Camondo name died out. Today, the house remains an impeccable tribute to Moïse's life. ✉ *63 rue de Monceau, Les Grands Boulevards* ☎ *01–53–89–06–50* ⊕ *www.lesartsdecoratifs.fr* 🖭 *€9; €13 joint ticket with Les Arts Décoratifs* 🕙 *Wed.–Sun. 10–5:30* Ⓜ *Villiers, Monceau.*

MONTMARTRE

GETTING ORIENTED

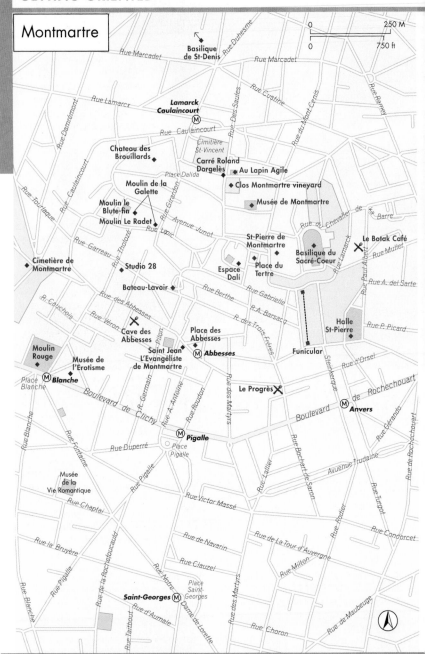

Montmartre

0 ——— 250 M
0 ——— 750 ft

Rue Marcadet
Basilique de St-Denis
Rue Marcadet
Rue Duhesme
Rue Ramey
Rue Lamarcx
Rue Custine
Rue Des Saules
Rue du Mont-Cens
Lamarck Caulaincourt Ⓜ
Rue Caulaincourt
Cimitière St-Vincent
Chateau des Brouillards
Carré Roland Dorgelès
Place Dalida
Au Lapin Agile
Clos Montmartre vineyard
Moulin de la Galette
Musée de Montmartre
Moulin le Blute-fin
Moulin Le Radet
Avenue Junot
Rue Lepic
Rue Girardon
Rue du Chevalier de
la Barre
Le Botak Café
Rue Tourlaque
Rue Caulaincourt
Rue Garreau
Rue Tholoze
St-Pierre de Montmartre
Basilique du Sacré-Coeur
Rue Lamarck
Rue Paul Albert
Rue Muller
Rue A. del Sarte
Cimetière de Montmartre
Studio 28
Espace Dalí
Place du Tertre
Bateau-Lavoir
Rue des Abbesses
Rue Berthe
Rue Gabrielle
R.A. Barsacq
Halle St-Pierre
Rue P. Picard
R. Cauchois
Rue Véron
Cave des Abbesses
R. Piron
Place des Abbesses
R. des Trois Frères
Funicular
Rue d'Orsel
Moulin Rouge
Musée de l'Erotisme
Saint Jean L'Evangéliste de Montmartre
Ⓜ Abbesses
Rue des Martyrs
Rue d'Antoine
Rue Roudon
Le Progrès ✕
Steinkerque
Place Blanche
Ⓜ Blanche
Boulevard de Clichy
R. St-Germain
Boulevard de Rochechouart
Ⓜ Anvers
Rue Gérando
Rue de Rochechouart
Rue Blanche
Rue Fontaine
Ⓜ Pigalle
Rue Duperré
Place Pigalle
Rue Pigalle
Rue Lallier
Rue Bochart de Saron
Avenue Trudaine
Rue Turgot
Musée de la Vie Romantique
Rue Chaptal
Rue Victor Massé
Rue de La Tour d'Auvergne
Rue Condorcet
Rue Rodier
Rue la Bruyère
Rue de Navarin
Rue Milton
Rue Pigalle
Rue Clauzel
Place Saint-Georges
Saint-Georges Ⓜ
Rue Notre Dame de Lorette
Rue des Martyrs
Rue Choron
Rue de Maubeuge
Rue Taitbout
Rue d'Aumale
Rue Blanche
Rue de la Rochefoucauld

MOULIN ROUGE

TOP REASONS TO GO

Basilique du Sacré-Coeur. The best view of Paris is worth the climb—or the funicular ride—especially at twilight when the city lights create a magnificent panorama below the hill of Montmartre.

Place du Tertre. This bustling square behind Sacré-Coeur teems with crowds of tourists and hordes of street artists clamoring to paint them.

Place des Abbesses. Capture the village ambience that makes Montmartre special by exploring the tiny streets branching out from this picturesque square.

Carré Roland Dorgelès. Bring your camera to this little square overlooking a pair of classic Montmartre sights: the city's only vineyard and the famous Au Lapin Agile cabaret.

MAKING THE MOST OF YOUR TIME

Devote a day to this neighborhood if you want to see more than the obligatory Sacré-Coeur Basilica. If possible, avoid weekends, when the narrow—and extremely hilly—streets are jam-packed.

GETTING HERE

Montmartre is in the 18e arrondissement. Take Line 2 to Anvers métro station, and then take the funicular (one métro ticket) up to Sacré-Coeur. Or take Line 12 to Abbesses station and take your time wandering the cobbled streets and staircases that lead up to the basilica. For a scenic tour, hop the public bus, Montmartrobus (one métro ticket). An easy starting point is the métro station Jules-Joffrin (Line 12): the bus winds up the hilly streets, with a convenient stop at Sacré-Coeur. Alternatively, pile the kids onto Le Petit Train de Montmartre (€4.50–€6.50), a bus disguised as a mini train that runs a circuit every 30 minutes (45 in winter) from Place Blanche.

BEST CAFÉS

Cave des Abbesses. Locals head to this charming retro-looking *caviste* (wineshop) and wine bar for a glass of something special with a side of oysters, or perhaps La Grande Mixte, a platter of charcuterie, terrine, and cheese (€14). ⊠ *43 rue des Abbesses, Montmartre* ☎ *01–42–52–81–54* Ⓜ *Abbesses.*

Le Botak Café. On the eastern side of Sacré-Coeur, at the bottom of the stairs, you'll find the leafy Square Louise Marie and this little café, which serves a small, ever-changing menu of French home cooking. The daily lunch specials (€14) are a great deal, but service can sometimes be slow when it's busy. ⊠ *1 rue Paul Albert, Montmartre* ☎ *01–46–06–98–30* Ⓜ *Anvers, Château Rouge.*

Le Progrès. This photo op-ready corner café draws a quirky mix of hipsters, artists, and discriminating tourists. The food is good and includes classics like steak tartare. For a weekday lunch, try the two-course menu du jour (€18.50). If you're craving a taste of home, the excellent cheeseburger comes with a heap of crispy fries. ⊠ *7 rue des Trois Frères, Montmartre* ☎ *01–42–64–07–37* Ⓜ *Abbesses.*

Sightseeing
★★★★

Dining
★★★

Lodging
★★

Shopping
★★★

Nightlife
★

Montmartre has become almost too charming for its own good. Yes, it feels like a village (if you wander off the beaten path); yes, there are working artists here (though far fewer than there used to be); and yes, the best view of Paris is yours for free from the top of the hill (if there's no haze). That's why on any weekend day, year-round, you can find scores of visitors crowding these cobbled alleys, scaling the staircases that pass for streets, and queuing to see Sacré-Coeur, the "sculpted cloud," at the summit.

Updated by
Jack Vermee

If you're lucky enough to have a little corner of Montmartre to yourself, you'll understand why locals love it so. Come at nonpeak times, on a weekday, or in the morning or later in the evening. Stroll around **Place des Abbesses,** where the rustic houses and narrow streets escaped the heavy hand of urban planner Baron Haussmann. Until 1860 the area was, in fact, a separate village, dotted with windmills. Always a draw for bohemians and artists, many of whom had studios at what is now the **Musée de Montmartre** and **Bateau-Lavoir,** Montmartre has been home to such painters as Suzanne Valadon and her son Maurice Utrillo, Picasso, van Gogh, Géricault, Renoir, and, of course, Henri de Toulouse-Lautrec, whose iconic paintings of the cancan dancers at the **Moulin Rouge** are now souvenir-shop fixtures. While you can still see shows at the Moulin Rouge in **Place Blanche** and the pocket-size cabaret **Au Lapin Agile,** much of the entertainment here is on the seedier side—the area around Pigalle is the city's largest red-light district, though it's far tamer than it used to be. **Boulevard de Clichy** was virtually an artists' highway at the turn of the 20th century: Degas lived and died at No. 6, and Picasso lived at No. 11. The *quartier* is a favorite of filmmakers (the blockbuster *Moulin Rouge* was inspired by it), and visitors still seek out Café des Deux Moulins at 15 rue Lepic, the real-life café (unfortunately with a remodeled look) where Audrey Tautou waited tables in 2001's *Amélie*. In 1928 **Studio 28** opened as the world's first cinema for experimental films.

TOP ATTRACTIONS

Fodors'Choice **Basilique du Sacré-Coeur.** It's hard to not feel as though you're ascend-
★ ing to heaven when you visit Sacred Heart Basilica, the white castle
in the sky, perched atop Montmartre. The French government commissioned it in 1873 to symbolize the return of self-confidence after
the devastating years of the Commune and Franco-Prussian War, and
architect Paul Abadie employed elements from Romanesque and Byzantine styles when designing it—a mélange many critics dismissed as
gaudy. Construction lasted until World War I, and the church was finally
consecrated in 1919.

Many people now come to Sacré-Coeur to admire the superlative view
from the top of its 271-foot-high dome. But if you opt to skip the climb
up the spiral staircase, the view from the front steps is still ample com-
pensation for the trip.

Inside, expect another visual treat—namely the massive golden mosaic
set high above the choir. Created in 1922 by Luc-Olivier Merson, *Christ
in Majesty* depicts Christ with a golden heart and outstretched arms,
surrounded by various figures, including the Virgin Mary and Joan of
Arc. It remains one of the largest mosaics of its kind. Also worth noting are the portico's bronze doors, decorated with biblical scenes; and
the stained-glass windows, which were installed in 1922, destroyed by
a bombing during World War II (there were miraculously no deaths),
and rebuilt in 1946. In the basilica's 262-foot-high campanile hangs La
Savoyarde, one of the world's heaviest bells, weighing about 19 tons.

The best time to visit Sacré-Coeur is early morning or early evening, and
preferably not on a Sunday, when the crowds are thick. Photographers
angling for the perfect shot of the church should aim for a clear blue-
sky day or arrive at dusk, when the pink sky plays nicely with the lights
of the basilica. If you're coming to worship, there are daily Masses.

■ TIP→ To avoid the steps, take the funicular, which costs one métro
ticket each way. ⊠ *Pl. du Parvis-du-Sacré-Coeur, Montmartre* ☎ *01–53–
41–89–00* ⊕ *www.sacre-coeur-montmartre.com* 🕿 *Basilica free; dome
€6* 🕙 *Basilica daily 6 am–10:30 pm; dome Oct.–Apr., daily 9–5 and
May.–Sept., daily 8:30–8* Ⓜ *Anvers, plus funicular; Jules Joffrin plus
Montmartrobus.*

Bateau-Lavoir (*Wash-barge*). The birthplace of Cubism isn't open to the
public, but a display in the front window details this unimposing spot's
rich history. Montmartre poet Max Jacob coined the name because the
original structure here reminded him of the laundry boats that used to
float in the Seine, and he joked that the warren of paint-splattered artists' studios needed a good hosing down (wishful thinking, since the
building had only one water tap). It was in the Bateau-Lavoir that, early
in the 20th century, Pablo Picasso, Georges Braque, and Juan Gris made
their first bold stabs at Cubism, and Picasso painted the groundbreaking
Les Demoiselles d'Avignon in 1906–07. The experimental works of the
artists weren't met with open arms, even in liberal Montmartre. All but
the facade was rebuilt after a fire in 1970. Like the original building,
though, the current incarnation houses artists and their studios. ⊠ *13
pl. Émile-Goudeau, Montmartre* Ⓜ *Abbesses.*

Carré Roland Dorgelès. This unassuming square is a perfect place to take in two of Montmartre's most photographed sites: the pink-and-green Au Lapin Agile cabaret and Clos Montmartre, Paris's only working vineyard. While the former, famously painted by Camille Pissarro, still welcomes revelers after 150 years, the latter is closed to visits except during the annual Fête de Jardins (Garden Festival) weekend in September. The stone wall on the northwestern edge of the square borders the peaceful Cimetière St-Vincent, one of the neighborhood's three atmospheric cemeteries. ⊠ *Corner of Rue des Saulnes and Rue St-Vincent, Montmartre* Ⓜ *Lamarck-Caulaincourt.*

Halle St-Pierre. The elegant iron-and-glass 19th-century market hall at the foot of Sacré-Coeur stages dynamic exhibitions of *art brut* (raw art), or outsider and folk art. The international artists featured are contemporary in style and out of the mainstream. There's also a good bookstore and a café serving light, well-prepared dishes, such as savory tarts and quiches with salad on the side, plus homemade desserts. ⊠ *2 rue Ronsard, Montmartre* ☏ *01–42–58–72–89* ⊕ *www.hallesaintpierre. org* 🖼 *Museum €8.50* ⊙ *Sept.–July, weekdays 11–6, Sat. 11–7, Sun. noon–6; Aug., weekdays noon–6* Ⓜ *Anvers.*

Moulin de la Galette. Of the 14 windmills (*moulins*) that used to sit atop this hill, only two remain. They're known collectively as Moulin de la Galette—the name being taken from the bread that the owners used to produce. The more storied of the two is Le Blute-Fin. In the late 1800s there was a dance hall on the site, famously captured by Renoir (you can see the painting in the Musée d'Orsay). A facelift restored the windmill to its 19th-century glory; however, it is on private land and can't be visited. Down the street is the other moulin, Le Radet. ⊠ *Le Blute-Fin, corner of Rue Lepic and Rue Tholozé, Montmartre* Ⓜ *Abbesses.*

Place des Abbesses. This triangular square is typical of the countrified style that has made Montmartre famous. Now a hub for shopping and people-watching, the *place* is surrounded by hip boutiques, sidewalk cafés, and shabby-chic restaurants—a prime habitat for the young, neo-bohemian crowd and a sprinkling of expats. Trendy streets like Rue Houdon and Rue des Martyrs have attracted small designer shops, an international beer seller, and even a cupcake shop. Many retailers remain open on Sunday afternoon. ⊠ *Intersection of Rue des Abbesses and Rue la Vieuville, Montmartre* Ⓜ *Abbesses.*

Place du Tertre. Artists have peddled their wares in this square for centuries. Busloads of tourists have changed the atmosphere, but if you come off-season—when the air is chilly and the streets are bare—you can almost feel what is was like when up-and-coming Picassos lived in the houses that today are given over to souvenir shops and cafés. ⊠ *East end of Rue Norvin, Place du Tertre, Montmartre* Ⓜ *Abbesses.*

WORTH NOTING

▌ OFF THE
BEATEN
PATH

Basilique de St-Denis. Built between 1136 and 1286, St-Denis Basilica is one of the most important Gothic churches in France. It was here, under dynamic prelate Abbé Suger, that Gothic architecture (typified by pointed arches and rib vaults) was said to have made its first

appearance. The kings of France soon chose St-Denis as their final resting place, and their richly sculpted tombs—along with what remains of Suger's church—can be seen in the choir area at the east end. The basilica was battered during the Revolution; afterward, however, Louis XVIII reestablished it as the royal burial site by moving the remains of Louis XVI and Marie-Antoinette here to join centuries' worth of monarchial bones. The vast 13th-century nave is a brilliant example of structural logic; its columns, capitals, and vault are a model of architectural harmony. The facade, retaining the rounded arches of the Romanesque that preceded the Gothic period, is set off by a small rose window, reputedly the oldest in France. Check out the extensive archaeological finds, such as a Merovingian queen's grave goods. Guided tours in English are available by reservation; if you'd rather explore on your own, audioguides are available for €4.50. ⊠ *1 rue de la Légion d'Honneur, St-Denis* ☏ *01–48–09–83–54* ⊕ *www.saint-denis.monuments-nationaux.fr* ⛟ *€8.50* ◷ *Apr.–Sept., Mon.–Sat. 10–6:15, Sun. noon–6:15; Oct.–Mar., Mon.–Sat. 10–5:15, Sun. noon–5:15* Ⓜ *Basilique de St-Denis.*

Cimetière de Montmartre. Overshadowed by better-known Père-Lachaise, this cemetery is just as picturesque. It's the final resting place of a host of luminaries, including painters Degas and Fragonard; Adolphe Sax, inventor of the saxophone; dancer Vaslav Nijinsky; filmmaker François Truffaut; and composers Hector Berlioz and Jacques Offenbach. The Art Nouveau tomb of novelist Émile Zola (1840–1902) lords over a lawn near the entrance—though Zola's remains were removed to the Panthéon in 1908. ⊠ *20 av. Rachel, Montmartre* ◷ *Mar. 16–Nov. 5, weekdays 8–6, Sat. 8:30–5:30, Sun. 9–6; Nov. 6–Mar. 15, weekdays 8–5:30, Sat. 8:30–5:30, Sun. 9–5:30* Ⓜ *Blanche.*

Espace Dalí (*Dalí Center*). One of several museums dedicated to the Surrealist master, the permanent collection in this black-walled exhibition space includes about 300 works, mostly etchings and lithographs. Among the two dozen sculptures are versions of Dalí's melting bronze clock and variations on the Venus de Milo. Since he was a multimedia pioneer ahead of his time, there are videos with Dalí's voice, and temporary exhibits have included the mustachioed man's foray into holograms. There's plenty of information in English, and audioguides can be rented for €3.50. ⊠ *11 rue Poulbot, Montmartre* ☏ *01–42–64–40–10* ⊕ *www.daliparis.com* ⛟ *€11.50* ◷ *Sept.–June, daily 10–6; July and Aug., daily 10–8* Ⓜ *Abbesses.*

Moulin Rouge. When this world-famous cabaret opened in 1889, aristocrats, professionals, and the working classes all flocked in to ogle the scandalous performers (the cancan was considerably more kinky in Toulouse-Lautrec's day, when girls kicked off their knickers). There's not much to see from the outside except for tourist buses and sex shops; if you want to catch a show inside, ticket prices start at €112. Souvenir seekers should check out the Moulin Rouge gift shop (around the corner at 11 rue Lepic), which sells official merchandise, from jewelry to sculpture, by reputable French makers. ⊠ *82 bd. de Clichy, Montmartre* ☏ *01–53–09–82–82* ⊕ *www.moulinrouge.fr* Ⓜ *Blanche.*

Musée de l'Érotisme. What better place for the Museum of Erotic Art than smack in the heart of the city's red-light district? Though the subject matter is rather limited, the collection features a respectable mix of world art (think carvings from Africa, Indonesia, and Peru, plus Chinese ivories and Japanese prints). It also has racy cartoons by Robert Crumb and photographs of Pigalle prostitutes and bordellos, some quite chic, from the 1930s and 1940s. Three floors are dedicated to temporary exhibits by contemporary artists and photographers. ⊠ *72 bd. de Clichy, Montmartre* ☎ *01–42–58–28–73* ⊕ *www.musee-erotisme.com* 🎫 *€10; €8 per person or €14 per couple if purchased online* ⊗ *Daily 10 am–2 am* Ⓜ *Blanche.*

Musée de Montmartre. During its turn-of-the-20th-century heyday, this building—now home to Montmartre's historical museum—was occupied by painters, writers, and cabaret artists. Foremost among them was Pierre-Auguste Renoir, who painted *Le Moulin de la Galette* (an archetypal scene of sun-drenched revelers) while living here. Recapping the area's colorful past, the museum has a charming permanent collection, which includes many Toulouse-Lautrec posters and original Eric Satie scores. An ambitious renovation, completed in 2014, doubled its space by incorporating both the studio-apartment once shared by mother-and-son duo Suzanne Valadon and Maurice Utrillo (now fully restored) and the adjoining Demarne Hotel (which has been redesigned to house temporary exhibitions). The lovely surrounding gardens—named in honor of Renoir—have also been revitalized. An audioguide is included in the ticket price. ⊠ *12 rue Cortot, Montmartre* ☎ *01–49–25–89–39* ⊕ *www.museedemontmartre.fr* 🎫 *€9.50* ⊗ *Daily 10–6 (until 7 in summer)* Ⓜ *Lamarck–Caulaincourt.*

Saint Jean L'Evangéliste de Montmartre. This eye-catching church with a compact Art Nouveau interior was the first modern house of worship built in Paris (1897–1904) and the first to be constructed of reinforced cement. Architect Anatole de Baudot's revolutionary technique defied the accepted rules at the time with its use of unsupported masonry; critics, who failed to stop construction, feared the building would crumble under its own weight. Today the church attracts a steady flow of visitors curious about its unusual Moorish-inspired facade of redbrick and curved arches. Note the tiny clock at the top left of the bell tower and the handsome stained-glass windows. Free concerts and art exhibitions are staged in the church from time to time. ⊠ *19 rue des Abbesses, Montmartre* ☎ *01–46–06–43–96* ⊕ *www.saintjeandemontmartre.com* ⊗ *Mon.–Sat. 9–7, Sun. 9:30–6 (until 7 in summer)* Ⓜ *Abbesses.*

St-Pierre de Montmartre. Tucked in the shadow of mighty Sacré-Coeur is one of the oldest churches in Paris. Built in 1147 on the site of a 5th-century temple to the god Mars, this small sanctuary with its impressive sculpted metal doors was once part of a substantial Benedictine abbey. Besides the church, all that remains is a small cemetery, now closed (you can see it through the ornate metal door on the left as you enter the courtyard). Renovated multiple times through the ages, St-Pierre combines various styles. Interior elements, such as the columns in the nave, are medieval; the facade dates to the 18th century, with renovations in the 19th century; and the stained-glass windows are 20th century. Maurice Utrillo's 1914

A Scenic Walk in Montmartre

One of Paris's most charming walks begins at the Abbesses métro station (Line 12), which has one of only two remaining iron-and-glass Art Nouveau canopies designed by famed architect Hector Guimard. Explore the streets ringing **Place des Abbesses,** or begin the walk immediately by heading west along Rue des Abbesses. Turn right on Rue Tholozé and note the historic movie house, **Studio 28,** at No. 10. At the top of the street is **Le Blute-Fin,** a windmill portrayed in a well-known work by Renoir. A right on Rue Lepic takes you past the only other windmill still standing, **Le Radet.** Take a left here onto Rue Girardon, to **Place Dalida,** marked with a voluptuous bust of the beloved French singer who popularized disco. (Yolanda Gigliotti, aka Dalida, lived until her death in 1987 at 11 bis, rue d'Orchampt, one of the city's narrowest streets, opposite Le Radet.)

The stone house behind Dalida's bust is the 18th-century **Château des Brouillards,** whose name, Castle of the Mists, is taken from the light fog that used to cloak this former farmland. Detour down the romantic alley of the same name. Renoir is said to have lived in the château before moving to the small house across the way at No. 8. From Place Dalida, head down winding Rue de l'Abreuvoir, one of the most photographed streets in Paris. Residents used to walk their horses to the *abreuvoir,* or watering trough, at No. 15. Pissarro kept a pied-à-terre at No. 12. The stone-and-wood-beam house at No. 4 was once home to a historian of the Napoleonic wars whose family symbol was an eagle. Notice the wooden sundial with a rooster and the inscription:

"When you chime, I'll sing." At the pink-and-green **Maison Rose** restaurant, committed to canvas by resident artist Maurice Utrillo, turn left on Rue des Saules where you'll find Paris's only working vineyard, **Clos de Montmartre.**

Across the street is the famous cabaret **Au Lapin Agile,** still going strong. On the opposite corner, a stone wall rings the **Cimetière Saint-Vincent,** one of the city's smallest cemeteries, where Utrillo is buried (to see it, walk west along Rue St-Vincent, take a right, then another quick right). Backtrack up Rue des Saules and take the first left onto Rue Cortot to the **Musée de Montmartre,** once home to a bevy of artists. Renoir rented a studio here to store his painting of Le Blute-Fin. A few doors down, at No. 6, the composer Erik Satie, piano player at Le Chat Noir nightclub, lived during a penniless period in a 6-by-4-foot flat with a 9-foot ceiling (plus skylight). At the corner of Rue Mont-Cenis, the white water tower Château d'Eau still services the neighborhood. Turn right to reach **Place du Tertre,** a lively square packed with tourists and street artists. Easily overlooked is **St-Pierre de Montmartre,** one of the city's oldest churches, founded in 1147. End your walk at the basilica **Sacré-Coeur,** and enjoy one of the best views of Paris from the city's highest point. This *butte,* or hilltop, has been famous since the 3rd century: St-Denis (the first bishop of Paris) was martyred here, and after his decapitation he was said to have walked miles while holding his own head. For an easy descent, take the funicular, which has been ferrying people up and down since 1900.

7

painting of the titular saint hangs in the Musée de l'Orangerie. ✉ *2 rue du Mont Cenis, off Pl. du Tertre, Montmartre* ☎ *01–46–06–57–63* ⊕ *www. saintpierredemontmartre.net* ⊘ *Sat.– Thurs. 9–7:30, Fri. 9–6* Ⓜ *Anvers.*

Studio 28. This little movie house has a distinguished history: when it opened in 1928, it was the first theater in the world purposely built for *art et essai,* or experimental film (Luis Buñuel and Salvador Dalí's *L'Age d'Or* caused a riot when it premiered here). Through the years artists and writers came to see "seventh art" creations by directors such as Jean Cocteau, François Truffaut, and Orson Welles. Today it's a repertory cinema, showing first-runs, just-runs, and previews—usually in their original language. Movies are screened from 3 pm daily, and tickets cost €9. In the back of the movie house is a cozy bar and café that has a quiet outdoor terrace decorated with murals of film stars. Oh, and those charmingly bizarre chandeliers in the *salle?* Cocteau designed them. ✉ *10 rue Tholozé, Montmartre* ☎ *01–46–06–47–45* ⊕ *www.cinema-studio28.fr/en* 🎟 *Movie tickets €9* ⊘ *Movies from 3 pm daily* Ⓜ *Abbesses.*

THE MARAIS

GETTING ORIENTED

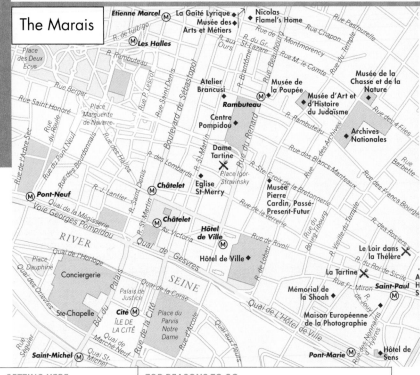

The Marais

Place des Deux Ecus

Rue Saint Honoré

Place Marguerite de Navarre

Rue de l'Arbre Sec

Rue du Pont Neuf

Rue des Bourdonnais

Rue du Roule

Pont-Neuf Ⓜ

Quai de la Mégisserie

Voie Georges Pompidou

RIVER

Quai de l'Horloge

Place Dauphiné

Quai des Orfèvres

Conciergerie

Palais de Justice

Ste-Chapelle

Cité Ⓜ
ÎLE DE
LA CITÉ

Place du Parvis Notre Dame

Quai de Marché Neuf

Rue Séguier

Saint-Michel Ⓜ Quai St. Michel

Etienne Marcel Ⓜ

R. de Turbigo

Ⓜ**Les Halles**

R. Rambuteau

Rue Berger

R. P. Lescot

Rue Saint Denis

Boulevard de Sébastopol

La Gaîté Lyrique◆
Musée des◆
Arts et Métiers

R. aux Ours

R. du Gr. St-Lazare

Rue M. le Comte

◆ *Nicolas Flamel's Home*

Rue de Montmorency

Rue Chapon

R. Beaubourg

R. Brantôme

Atelier Brancusi ◆

Rambuteau Ⓜ

Centre Pompidou ◆

Musée de la Poupée ◆

R. du Renard

R. des Lombards

R. St-Martin

Dame Tartine ✕

Place Igor Stravinsky

Châtelet Ⓜ Eglise St-Merry

Rue de la Verrerie

Ⓜ *Châtelet*

Av. Victoria

Hôtel de Ville

Quai de Gesvres

SEINE

Quai de la Corse

Quai d'Arcole

Quai aux Fleurs

Rue Pastourelle

Rue du Temple

R. du Temple

Musée de la Chasse et de la Nature

Musée d'Art et ◆ d'Histoire du Judaïsme

R. Rambuteau

Rue des 4 Files

Archives Nationales ◆

Rue Barbette

Rue des Blancs Manteaux

Rue des Francs Bourgeois

Musée ◆ Pierre Cardin, Passé-Present-Futur

R. Ste-Croix-de-la-Bretonnerie

Ⓜ Hôtel de Ville

Rue de Rivoli

R. du Bourg Tibourg

Rue Vieille-du-Temple

R. de Lobau

Hôtel de Ville ◆

La Tartine ✕

Quai de L'Hôtel de Ville

Mémorial de ◆ la Shoah

Maison Européenne de la Photographie

Le Loir dans ✕ la Thélère

R. du Roi de Sicile

Rue Fr. Miron **Saint-Paul** Ⓜ

Rue des Rosiers

R. Vieille-du-Temple

R. du Roi de Sicile

R. de Jouy

Pont-Marie Ⓜ

◆ Hôtel de Sens

R. des Nonnains d'Hyères

GETTING HERE	TOP REASONS TO GO
The Marais includes the 3e and 4e arrondissements. It's a pleasant walk from the Beaubourg—the area around Centre Pompidou—into the heart of the Marais. Rue Rambuteau turns into Rue des Francs-Bourgeois, which runs right into Place des Vosges. If you're going by métro, the most central stop is St-Paul on Line 1. If you're going to the Pompidou, take Line 11 to Rambuteau. For the Musée Picasso, the closest stop is St-Sébastien–Froissart on Line 8. For the 3e arrondissement, get off at Arts et Métiers on Line 3 or 11, or Filles du Calvaire on Line 8.	**Centre Pompidou.** Paris's leading modern art museum is also a vast (and architecturally ambitious) arts center that presents films, theater, and dance performances. **Place des Vosges.** The prettiest square in the French capital surrounds a manicured park, where inviting patches of grass are accessible to those needing a siesta. **Musée Picasso.** Spectacularly renovated, this museum is a must-see for fans of the Spanish master, who painted some of his best work while living in the city. **Jewish history tour.** The old Jewish quarter has two world-class sites: Mémorial de la Shoah (the Holocaust Memorial) and the Musée d'Art et d'Histoire du Judaïsme. **No reason at all.** Lose yourself in simple pleasures, like exploring the tiny streets near the Centre Pompidou or people-watching in a café on Rue Vieille du Temple.

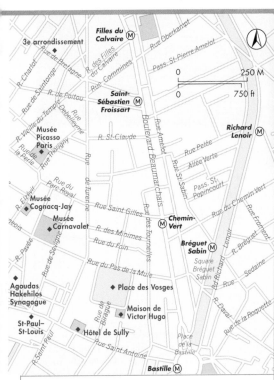

3e arrondissement

Filles du Calvaire Ⓜ

Rue Oberkampf

Rue Chariot

Rue de Bretagne

R. des Filles du Calvaire

Pass. St-Pierre Amelot

Rue de Saintonge

Rue de Poitou

Rue Commines

Saint-Sébastien Froissart Ⓜ

R. Vieille du Temple

Rue Debelleyme

Rue Charlot

Musée Picasso Paris

Rue Thorigny

R. St-Claude

Boulevard Beaumarchais

Rue Amelot

Richard Lenoir Ⓜ

Rue Pelée

Rue de la Perle

Rue du Parc Royal

Allée Verte

Rue St-Sabin

Musée Cognacq-Jay

Rue Elzévir

Rue Saint-Gilles

Rue de Turenne

Pass. St-Popincourt

Rue du Chemin Vert

Chemin-Vert Ⓜ

Musée Carnavalet

R. des Minimes

Rue Froment

Rue de Sévigné

Rue Payee

Rue du Foin

Bréguet Sabin Ⓜ

R. Bréguet

Rue du Pas-de-la-Mule

Square Bréguet Sabin

Rue Sedaine

Agoudas Hakehilos Synagogue

Place des Vosges

Rue

St-Paul–St-Louis

Rue de Birague

Maison de Victor Hugo

Rue Daval

Rue de la Roquette

R. St-Paul

Hôtel de Sully

Rue Saint-Antoine

Place de la Bastille

Bastille Ⓜ

0 — 250 M

0 — 750 ft

MAKING THE MOST OF YOUR TIME

The Marais has something for everyone, and how much time you spend here depends on how much time you have in Paris. One day seems painfully short, but it would allow you to take a do-it-yourself walking tour, peeking into private courtyards and picnicking in the Place des Vosges as you proceed. Leave at least two days if your itinerary includes the Centre Pompidou and the Musée Picasso. In three days you could cover some of the smaller museums, which are well worth visiting as many are housed in exquisite mansions. If time permits, wander to the 3e arrondissement to see the charming streets, away from the crowds, or drop into the quirky science-centric Musée des Arts et Métiers. Sunday afternoon is a lively time to come because many shops are open, notably on Rue des Francs-Bourgeois. This neighborhood thrives after dark as well; business is brisk at cafés and bars—particularly those aimed at the gay community.

BEST CAFÉS

Dame Tartine. Cafés abound around the Centre Pompidou, but this one—overlooking the Stravinsky fountain—is a good choice. You won't go wrong with any of the many *tartines*, toasts topped with delicious ingredients. ⊠ *2 rue Brisemiche, Marais* ☎ *01-42-77-32-22* Ⓜ *Rambuteau.*

La Tartine. This calm café on busy Rue de Rivoli is a local favorite with an impressive wine list. Try the €8 French onion soup or indulge in classic French dishes like *steak frites* or escargots. ⊠ *24 rue de Rivoli, Marais* ☎ *01-42-72-76-85* ⊕ *www.latartineparis.fr* Ⓜ *St-Paul.*

Le Loir dans la Théière. Sink into a shabby armchair at this popular tearoom, whose name translates to "the Dormouse in the Teapot" (from *Alice in Wonderland*). The savory tarts are stellar, but the real stars are desserts like the decadent chocolate crumble tart. ⊠ *3 rue des Rosiers, Marais* ☎ *01-42-72-90-61* Ⓜ *St-Paul.*

8

Sightseeing
★★★★★

Dining
★★★★

Lodging
★★★★

Shopping
★★★★★

Nightlife
★★★★

From swampy to swanky, the Marais has a fascinating history. Like an aging pop star, the *quartier* has remade itself many times, and today retains several identities. It's the city's epicenter of cool with hip boutiques, designer hotels, and art galleries galore; the hub of Paris's gay community; and, though fading, the nucleus of Jewish life. You could easily spend your entire visit to Paris in this neighborhood—there is that much to do.

Updated by
Jack Vermee

"Marais" means marsh, and that is exactly what this area was until the 12th century, when it was converted to farmland. In 1605 Henri IV began building the Place Royale (today's Place des Vosges, the oldest square in Paris), which touched off a building boom, and the wealthy and fabulous moved in. Despite the odors—the area was one of the city's smelliest—it remained the chic quarter until Louis XIV transferred his court to Versailles, trailed by dispirited aristocrats unhappy to decamp to the country. Merchants moved into their exquisite *hôtels particuliers* (private mansions), which are some of the city's best surviving examples of Baroque architecture. Here you can see the hodgepodge of narrow streets that so vexed Louis Napoléon and his sidekick, Baron Haussmann, who feared a redux of the famous *barricades* that Revolutionaries threw up to thwart the monarchy. Haussmann leveled scores of blocks like these, creating the wide, arrow-straight avenues that are a hallmark of modern Paris. Miraculously, the Marais escaped destruction, though much of it fell victim to neglect and ruin. Thanks to restoration efforts over the past half century, the district is enjoying its latest era of greatness, and the apartments here—among the city's oldest—are also the most in demand, with *beaucoup* charm, exposed beams, and steep crooked staircases barely wide enough for a supermodel. (Should you be lucky enough to find an elevator, don't expect it to fit your suitcase.) Notice the impressive *portes cochères*, the huge doors built to accommodate aristocratic carriages that today open into many sublime courtyards and hidden gardens.

The 4e arrondissement, the Marais's glitzier half, is sandwiched between two opposite poles—the regal **Place des Vosges** in the east and the eye-teasing modern masterpiece **Centre Pompidou** in the west. Between these points you'll find most of the main sites, including the **Musée Picasso**, the **Maison Européenne de la Photographie**, and the **Musée Carnavalet**, which is the best place to see how the city evolved through the ages. To tour an exquisitely restored 17th-century hôtel particulier, visit the excellent **Musée Cognacq-Jay** or wander into the manicured back garden of the magnificent **Hôtel de Sully.** The quieter 3e arrondissement half of the Marais, around Rue de Bretagne, has become one of Paris's most in-demand areas to live—and one of the most interesting to explore. Here you'll find intriguing, off-the-tourist-track boutiques, bars, and galleries, plus sites such as the **Musée des Arts and Métiers**, Europe's oldest science museum.

Paris's **Jewish quarter** (the Pletzl, Yiddish for "little place") has existed in the Marais in some form since the 13th century, and it still thrives around Rue des Rosiers, even as hipster hangouts encroach on the traditional bakeries and delis. Not far away is the beating heart of the **gay Marais**, radiating out from Rue Vieille du Temple, along Rue St-Croix de la Bretonnerie to Rue du Temple; it's filled with trendy shops, cool cafés, and lively nightspots aimed at gays but welcoming to all.

TOP ATTRACTIONS

FAMILY
Fodor's Choice
★

Centre Pompidou. Love it or hate it, the Pompidou is certainly a unique-looking building. Most Parisians have warmed to the industrial, Lego-like exterior that caused a scandal when it opened in 1977. Named after French president Georges Pompidou (1911–74), it was designed by then-unknowns Renzo Piano and Richard Rogers. The architects' claim to fame was putting the building's guts on the outside and color-coding them: water pipes are green, air ducts are blue, electrics are yellow, and things like elevators and escalators are red. Art from the 20th century to the present day is what you can find inside.

The Musée National d'Art Moderne (Modern Art Museum, entrance on Level 4) occupies the top two levels. Level 5 is devoted to modern art from 1905 to 1960, including major works by Matisse, Modigliani, Marcel Duchamp, and Picasso; Level 4 is dedicated to contemporary art from the '60s on, including video installations. The Galerie d'Enfants

(Children's Gallery) on the mezzanine level has interactive exhibits designed to keep the kids busy. Outside, next to the museum's sloping plaza—where throngs of teenagers hang out (and where there's free Wi-Fi)—is the Atelier Brancusi. This small, airy museum contains four rooms reconstituting Brancusi's Montparnasse studios with works from all periods of his career. On the opposite side, in Place Igor-Stravinsky, is the Stravinsky fountain, which has 16 gyrating mechanical figures in primary colors, including a giant pair of ruby red lips. On the opposite side of Rue Rambuteau, on the wall at the corner of Rue Clairvaux and Passage Brantôme, is the appealingly bizarre mechanical brass-and-steel clock, *Le Défenseur du Temps*.

The Pompidou's permanent collection takes up a relatively small amount of the space when you consider this massive building's other features: temporary exhibition galleries, with a special wing for design and architecture; a highly regarded free reference library (there's often a queue of university students on Rue Renard waiting to get in); and the basement, which includes two cinemas, a theater, a dance space, and a small, free exhibition space.

On your way up the escalator, you'll have spectacular views of Paris, ranging from Tour Montparnasse, to the left, around to the hilltop Sacré-Coeur on the right. The rooftop restaurant, Georges, is a romantic spot for dinner. Be sure to reserve a table near the window. ⊠ *Pl. Georges-Pompidou, Marais* ☎ *01–44–78–12–33* ⊕ *www.centrepompidou.fr* ⊒ *Centre access free; Atelier Brancusi free; museum and exhibits €14 (free 1st Sun. of month)* ⊙ *Centre Wed.–Mon. 11–10; Atelier Brancusi Wed.–Mon. 2–6; museum and exhibits Wed.–Mon. 11–9* Ⓜ *Rambuteau.*

Église St-Merry. This impressive Gothic church, in the shadow of the Centre Pompidou, was completed in 1550. Notable features include the turret (it contains the oldest bell in Paris, cast in 1331) and an 18th-century pulpit supported on carved palm trees. There are free concerts here Saturday at 8 pm and Sunday at 4 pm. See the website for more information. ⊠ *76 rue de la Verrerie, Marais* ☎ *01–42–71–93–93* ⊕ *www.saintmerry.org* ⊙ *Mon.–Sat. 9–6* Ⓜ *Hôtel de Ville.*

Maison de Victor Hugo. France's most famous scribe lived in this house on the northeast corner of Place des Vosges between 1832 and 1848. It's now a museum dedicated to the multitalented author. In Hugo's apartment on the second floor, you can see the tall desk, next to the short bed, where he began writing his masterwork *Les Misérables* (as always, standing up). There are manuscripts and early editions of the novel on display, as well as others such as *Notre-Dame de Paris*, known to English readers as *The Hunchback of Notre-Dame*. You can see illustrations of Hugo's writings, including Bayard's rendering of the impish Cosette holding her giant broom (which has graced countless *Les Miz* T-shirts). The collection includes many of Hugo's own, sometimes macabre, ink drawings (he was a fine artist) and furniture from several of his homes. Particularly impressive is the room of carved and painted Chinese-style wooden panels that Hugo designed for the house of his mistress, Juliet Drouet, on the island of Guernsey, when he was exiled there for agitating against Napoléon III. Try to spot the intertwined Vs and Js (hint: look for the angel's trumpet in the left corner). The first floor is dedicated to temporary exhibitions that often have modern ties to Hugo's work. ✉ *6 pl. des Vosges, Marais* ☎ *01–42–72–10–16* ⊕ *www.maisonsvictorhugo.paris.fr* 🖃 *Free; €5–€7 for temporary exhibitions* ⊙ *Tues.–Sun. 10–6* Ⓜ *St-Paul, Bastille.*

Maison Européenne de la Photographie (*Center for European Photography*). Much of the credit for the city's ascendancy as a hub of international photography goes to MEP and its director, Jean-Luc Monterosso, who also founded Paris's hugely successful Mois de la Photo festival (a biennial event held in November of even-numbered years). The MEP hosts up to four simultaneous exhibitions, changing about every three months. Shows feature an international crop of photographers and video artists. Works by superstar Annie Leibovitz or designer-photographer Karl Lagerfeld may overlap with a collection of self-portraits by an up-and-coming artist. MEP often stages retrospectives of the classics (by Doisneau, Cartier-Bresson, Man Ray, and others) from its vast private collection. Programs are available in English, and English-language tours are sometimes given; check the website for details. ✉ *5/7 rue de Fourcy, Marais* ☎ *01–44–78–75–00* ⊕ *www.mep-fr.org* 🖃 *€8, free Wed. after 5* ⊙ *Wed.–Sun. 11–7:45* Ⓜ *St-Paul.*

Mémorial de la Shoah (*Memorial to the Holocaust*). The first installation in this compelling memorial and museum is the deeply moving Wall of Names, tall plinths honoring the 76,000 French Jews deported from France to Nazi concentration camps, of whom only 2,500 survived. Opened in 2005, the center has an archive on the victims, a library, and a gallery hosting temporary exhibitions. The permanent collection includes riveting artifacts and photographs from the camps, along with video testimony from survivors. The children's memorial is particularly poignant and not for the faint of heart—scores of back-lighted photographs show the faces of many of the 11,000 murdered French children. The crypt, a giant black marble Star of David, contains ashes recovered from the camps and the Warsaw ghetto. You can see the orderly drawers containing small files on Jews kept by the French police. (France only officially acknowledged the Vichy government's role in 1995.) The history of anti-Semitic persecution in the world is revisited as well as the rebounding state of Jewry today. There is a free guided tour in English the second Sunday of every month at 3. ✉ *17 rue Geoffroy l'Asnier, Marais* ☎ *01–42–77–44–72* ⊕ *www.memorialdelashoah.org* 🖃 *Free* ⊙ *Sun.–Wed. and Fri. 10–6, Thurs. 10–10* Ⓜ *Pont Marie, St-Paul.*

Fodor's Choice ★ **Musée Carnavalet.** If it has to do with Parisian history, it's here. A fascinating hodgepodge of artifacts and art, the collection ranges from the prehistoric canoes used by Parisii tribes to the furniture of the cork-lined bedroom where Marcel Proust labored over his evocative novels. Thanks to scores of paintings, nowhere else in Paris can you get such a precise picture of the city's evolution through the ages. The museum fills two adjacent mansions, the Hôtel Le Peletier de St-Fargeau and the Hôtel Carnavalet. The latter is a Renaissance jewel that in the mid-1600s became the home of writer Madame de Sévigné. Throughout her long life, Sévigné wrote hundreds of frank and funny letters to her daughter, giving an incomparable view of both public and private life

8

during the time of Louis XIV. The museum offers a glimpse into her world, but the collection covers far more than just the 17th century. The exhibits on the Revolution are especially interesting, with scale models of guillotines and a replica of the Bastille prison carved from one of its stones. Louis XVI's prison cell is reconstructed along with mementos of his life, even medallions containing locks of his family's hair. Other impressive interiors are reconstructed from the Middle Ages through the rococo period and into Art Nouveau—showstoppers include the Fouquet jewelry shop and the Café de Paris's original furnishings. The sculpted garden at 16 rue des Francs-Bourgeois is open from April to the end of October. Extensive renovations, begun in 2013, are ongoing; check the website for room closures. ⊠ *16 rue des Francs-Bourgeois, Marais* ☎ *01–44–59–58–58* ⊕ *www.carnavalet.paris.fr* ⊠ *Free; around €7 for temporary exhibitions* ⊙ *Tues.–Sun. 10–6* Ⓜ *St-Paul.*

NEED A BREAK?

L'As du Falafel. Jewish food is tops in the Marais, where you can get a falafel sandwich to go, loaded with salad and sauce, for €7. You'll find one of the best versions here. ⊠ *34 rue des Rosiers, Marais* ☎ *01–48–87–63–60* ⊙ *Closed Fri. after sundown and Sat.* Ⓜ *St-Paul.*

Musée Cognacq-Jay. One of the loveliest museums in Paris, this 16th-century rococo-style mansion contains an outstanding collection of mostly 18th-century artwork in its rooms of *boiserie* (intricately carved wood paneling). A tour through them allows a rare glimpse into the lifestyle of wealthy 19th-century Parisians. Ernest Cognacq, founder of the now closed department store La Samaritaine, and his wife, Louise Jay, amassed furniture, porcelain, and paintings—notably by Fragonard, Watteau, François Boucher, and Tiepolo—to create one of the world's finest private collections of this period. Some of the best displays are also the smallest, like the tiny enamel medallion portraits showcased on the second floor; or, on the third floor, the glass cases filled with exquisite inlaid snuff boxes, sewing cases, pocket watches, perfume bottles, and cigar cutters. Exhibits are labeled in French only, but free pamphlets and €5 audioguides are available in English. ⊠ *8 rue Elzévir, Marais* ☎ *01–40–27–07–21* ⊕ *www.museecognacqjay.paris.fr* ⊠ *Free; €6–€8 for temporary exhibitions* ⊙ *Tues.–Sun. 10–6* Ⓜ *St-Paul.*

Musée d'Art et d'Histoire du Judaïsme. This excellent museum traces the tempestuous history of French and European Jews through art and history. Housed in the refined 17th-century Hôtel St-Aignan, exhibits have good explanatory texts in English, but the free English audioguide adds another layer of insight; guided tours in English are also available on request. Highlights include 13th-century tombstones excavated in Paris; a wooden model of a destroyed Eastern European synagogue; a roomful of early paintings by Marc Chagall; and Christian Boltanski's stark, two-part tribute to Shoah (Holocaust) victims in the form of plaques on an outer wall naming the (mainly Jewish) inhabitants of the Hôtel St-Aignan in 1939, and canvas hangings with the personal data of the 13 residents who were deported and died in concentration camps. The rear-facing windows offer a view of the Jardin Anne Frank. To visit it, use the entrance on Impasse Berthaud, off Rue Beaubourg, just north of Rue Rambuteau. ☒ *71 rue du Temple, Marais* ☎ *01–53–01–86–53* ⊕ *www.mahj.org* ⊒ *€8; €10 with temporary exhibitions* ☉ *Weekdays 11–6, Sun. 10–6* Ⓜ *Rambuteau, Hôtel de Ville.*

FAMILY **Musée des Arts et Métiers.** Science buffs should not miss this cavernous museum, Europe's oldest dedicated to invention and technology. It's a treasure trove of wonkiness with 80,000 instruments, machines, and gadgets—including 16th-century astrolabes, Pascal's first mechanical calculator, and film-camera prototypes by the Frères Lumière. You can watch video simulations of groundbreaking architectural achievements, like the cast-iron dome, or see how Jacquard's mechanical loom revolutionized clothmaking. Kids will love the flying machines (among them the first plane to cross the English Channel), and the impressive display of old automobiles in the high-ceilinged chapel of St-Martin-des-Champs. Also in the chapel is a copy of Foucault's Pendulum, which proved to the world in 1851 that the Earth rotated (demonstrations are staged daily at noon and 5). The building, erected between the 11th and 13th centuries, was a church and priory. It was confiscated during the Revolution, and, after incarnations as a school and a weapons factory, became a museum in 1799. Most displays have information in English, but renting an English audioguide (€5) helps. There is a quiet café on the first floor. If you're taking the subway here, check out the platform of métro Line 11 in the Arts and Métiers station—one of the city's most elaborate—made to look like the inside of a Jules Verne-style machine, complete with copper-color metal walls, giant bolts, and faux gears. ☒ *60 rue Réaumur, Marais* ☎ *01–53–01–82–00* ⊕ *www.arts-et-metiers. net* ⊒ *€8; €9 with temporary exhibitions* ☉ *Tues., Wed., and Fri.–Sun. 10–6, Thurs. 10–9:30* Ⓜ *Arts et Métiers.*

Fodor'sChoice **Musée Picasso Paris.** This immensely popular museum rose phoenix-like
★ in late 2014, when it finally reopened after an ambitious (and often controversial) five-year makeover that cost an estimated €52 million. Home to the world's largest public collection of Picasso's inimitable oeuvre, it now covers almost 54,000 square feet in two buildings: the regal 17th-century Hôtel Salé and a sprawling new structure in the back garden that's dedicated to temporary exhibitions. Diego Giacometti's exclusively designed furnishings in the former are an added bonus.

The collection of 200,000-plus paintings, sculptures, drawings, documents, and other archival materials (much of it previously in storage for lack of space) spans the artist's entire career; and while it doesn't include his most recognizable works, it does contain many of the pieces treasured most by Picasso himself. The renovated museum (which now has more than double the dedicated public space) is split into three distinct areas. The first two floors cover Picasso's work from 1895 to 1972. The top floor illustrates his relationship to his favorite artists; landscapes, nudes, portraits, and still lifes taken from his private collection detail his "artistic dialogue" with Cézanne, Gauguin, Degas, Rousseau, Matisse, Braque, Renoir, Modigliani, Miró, and others. The basement centers around Picasso's workshops, with photographs and engravings, paintings, and sculptures that document or evoke key pieces created at the Bateau Lavoir, Château de Boisgeloup, Grands-Augustins, the Villa La Californie, and his farmhouse, Notre-Dame-de-Vie, in Mougins. With

8

The Musée Picasso Paris highlights various works from Pablo Picasso, including his longtime devotion to sculpture.

plenty of multimedia components and special activities that cater to kids, this is ideal for both children and adult art lovers alike.

It's worth paying the extra €1 to buy tickets online well in advance of your planned visit; if possible, it's also wise to avoid coming on weekends, when the crowds are thickest. ⊠ *5 rue de Thorigny, Marais* 🕿 *01–85–56–00–36* ⊕ *www.museepicassoparis.fr* 🎟 *€12.50 (free 1st Sun. of month)* 🕙 *Tues.–Fri. 11:30–6 (until 9 every 3rd Fri.), weekends 9:30–6* Ⓜ *St-Sébastien–Froissart.*

NEED A BREAK?

Jardin des Rosiers–Joseph-Migneret. Tucked behind the Maison de l'Europe, the Jardin Francs-Bourgeois-Rosiers is a Zen gem in the heart of the bustling Marais. Bring a snack to enjoy in this quiet garden amid the roses and little trees. ⊠ *35–37 rue des Francs-Bourgeois or 10 rue des Rosiers (wheelchair access), Marais* 🕙 *Oct.–Feb., daily 8–5; Mar., daily 8–6; Apr.–Sept., daily 8–7* Ⓜ *St-Paul.*

FAMILY
Fodor'sChoice
★

Place des Vosges. The oldest square in Paris and—dare we say it?—the most beautiful, Place des Vosges represents an early stab at urban planning. The precise proportions offer a placid symmetry, but things weren't always so calm here. Four centuries ago this was the site of the Palais des Tournelles, home to King Henry II and Queen Catherine de Medici. The couple staged regular jousting tournaments, and Henry was fatally lanced in the eye during one of them in 1559. Catherine fled to the Louvre, abandoning her palace and ordering it destroyed. In 1612 the square became Place Royale on the occasion of Louis XIII's engagement to Anne of Austria. Napoléon renamed it Place des Vosges to honor the northeast region of Vosges, the first in the country to pony up taxes to the Revolutionary government.

At the base of the 36 redbrick-and-stone houses—nine on each side of the square—is an arcaded, covered walkway lined with art galleries, shops, and cafés. There's also an elementary school, a synagogue (whose barrel roof was designed by Gustav Eiffel), and several chic hotels. The formal, gated garden's perimeter is lined with chestnut trees; inside are a children's play area and a fountain.

Aside from hanging out in the park, people come here to see the house of the man who once lived at No. 6—Victor Hugo, the author of *Les Misérables* and *Notre-Dame de Paris* (aka *The Hunchback of Notre-Dame*).

■TIP➔ **One of the best things about this park is that you're actually allowed to sit—or snooze or snack—on the grass during spring and summer.** There is no better spot in the Marais for a picnic: you can pick up fixings at the nearby street market on Thursday and Saturday mornings (it's on Boulevard Richard Lenoir between Rues Amelot and St-Sabin). The most likely approach to Place des Vosges is from Rue de Francs-Bourgeois, the main shopping street. However, for a grander entrance walk along Rue St-Antoine until you get to Rue de Birague, which leads directly into the square. ⊠ *Off Rue des Francs-Bourgeois, near Rue de Turenne, Marais* ⊙ *Gated garden weekdays 8–8:30, weekends 9–8:30* Ⓜ *Bastille, St-Paul.*

3e arrondissement. The thick crowds that flock to Place des Vosges rarely venture to the other side of the Marais: the 3e arrondissement, which has morphed into one of the hottest neighborhoods in Paris. Good luck finding an apartment to rent here—most are small walk-ups with exposed wooden beams and lots of charm. But even if you can't move in, you can enjoy this trendy quartier like a local. First, head to Rue de Bretagne, the main drag. Stop for lunch at one of the food stalls in the Marché des Enfants Rouges (No. 39, open Tuesday through Sunday): it's the oldest covered market in Paris. Next, explore narrow side streets, like Rues Charlot, Debelleyme, and Poitou, lined with art galleries and small boutiques. Stop for a real English scone at the Marais outpost of the popular Rose Bakery (30 rue Debelleyme); try a cup of Joe and a croissant at Poilâne (38 rue Debelleyme); or treat yourself to a gelato at Mary's (1 rue Charles-Francois Dupuis). Across the street is the 19th-century iron-and-glass Carreau du Temple, which, after a long-overdue renovation, reopened as a locally driven arts and sports community center. This is the site of the former Templar Tower, where Louis XIV and Marie-Antoinette were imprisoned before the king's date with the guillotine (Napoléon later razed it). For your evening apéritif, make a beeline for the buzzy Café Charlot, at 38 rue de Bretagne. If you're in the mood for couscous, try Chez Omar, a neighborhood institution at No. 47. ⊠ *Marais* Ⓜ *Arts et Métiers, Filles du Calvaire.*

WORTH NOTING

Agoudas Hakehilos Synagogue. Art Nouveau genius Hector Guimard built this unique synagogue (also called Synagogue de la Rue Pavée) in 1913 for a Polish-Russian Orthodox association. The facade resembles an open book: Guimard used the motif of the Ten Commandments to inspire the building's shape and its interior, which can only rarely be visited. Knock on the door and see if the caretaker will let you upstairs to the balcony, where you can admire Guimard's well-preserved decor. Like other Parisian synagogues, its front door was dynamited by Nazis on Yom Kippur, 1941. The Star of David over the door was added after the building was restored. ⊠ *10 rue Pavé, Marais* ☎ *01–48–87–21–54* Ⓜ *St-Paul.*

Archives Nationales. Thousands of important historical documents are preserved inside the Hôtel de Soubise and Hôtel de Rohan—a pair of spectacular buildings constructed in 1705 as private homes. Fans of the decorative arts will appreciate a visit to the former, where the well-preserved private apartments of the Prince and Princess de Soubise are among the first examples of the rococo style, which preceded the more somber Baroque opulence of Louis XIV. The Hôtel de Soubise also has a museum that displays documents dating from 625 to the 20th century. Highlights include the Edict of Nantes (1598), the Treaty of Westphalia (1648), the wills of Louis XIV and Napoléon, and the Declaration of Human Rights (1789). Louis XVI's diary is also here, containing his sadly clueless entry for July 14, 1789—the day the Bastille was stormed and the French Revolution was launched. The Hôtel de Rohan, open to the public only during Patrimony Weekend in September, was built for Soubise's son, Cardinal Rohan. Before you leave, notice the medieval turrets in the courtyard: this is the Porte de Clisson, all that remains of a stately 14th-century mansion. ⊠ *60 rue des Francs-Bourgeois, Marais* ☎ *01–40–27–60–96* ⊕ *www.archives-nationales.culture.gouv.fr* ✉ *Hôtel de Soubise €3 (free 1st Sun. of month); €6 for temporary exhibitions* ☉ *Hôtel de Soubise Mon. and Wed.–Fri. 10–5:30, weekends 2–5:30* Ⓜ *Rambuteau.*

Hôtel de Sens. One of the few remaining structures in Paris from the Middle Ages, this little castle was most famously the home of Queen Margot, who took up residence here in 1605 after her marriage to Henry IV was annulled. Margot was known for her many lovers (she supposedly wore wigs made from locks of their hair) and reputedly ordered a servant beheaded in the courtyard after he ridiculed one of her companions. The street is said to be named after a fig tree she ordered cut down because it was inconveniencing her carriage. Perhaps for that reason there's a fig tree planted in the elegant rear garden, which is open to the public. Notice the cannonball lodged in the front facade commemorating a battle here during the three-day revolution in July 1830. Built for the archbishop of Sens in 1475, the castle was extensively renovated in the 20th century and is today home to the Bibliothèque Forney, a library that also stages temporary exhibitions drawn from its extensive collection of fine and graphic arts. ⊠ *1 rue du Figuier, Marais* ☎ *01–42–78–14–60* ⊕ *equipement.paris.fr/bibliotheque-forney-18* ✉ *Library* *free; €6 for exhibitions* ⊙ *Library Tues., Fri., and Sat. 1–7:30, Wed. and Thurs. 10–7:30; exhibitions Tues.–Sat. 1–7* Ⓜ *Pont Marie.*

Hôtel de Sully (*Hôtel de Béthune-Sully*). This early Baroque gem, built in 1624, is one of the city's loveliest *hôtels particuliers*. Like much of the area, it fell into ruin until the 1950s, when it was rescued by the institute for French historic monuments (the Centre des Monuments Nationaux), which is based here. The recently renovated headquarters aren't open to the public; however, you are welcome to enjoy the equally lovely garden. Stroll through it, past the Orangerie, to find a small passage into nearby Place des Vosges: Sully's best buddy, King Henri IV, would have lived there had he not been assassinated in 1610. An on-site bookstore (with a 17th-century ceiling of exposed wooden beams) sells specialized English-language guides to Paris. ⊠ *62 rue St-Antoine, Marais* ☎ *01–44–61–21–50* ⊕ *www.sully. monuments-nationaux.fr* ⊙ *Garden and bookstore daily 9–7* Ⓜ *St-Paul.*

Hôtel de Ville. Overlooking the Seine, City Hall contains the residence and offices of the mayor. Reconstructed in 1873 after an attack by rioting crowds, it is one of Paris's most stunning buildings, made all the more dramatic by elaborate nighttime lighting. The adjoining public library stages frequent free exhibits celebrating famous photographers like Doisneau or Atget and their notable subjects, often the city herself (the entrance is on the side across from the department store BHV). Alas, the impressive interior of the main administrative building, with its lavish reception halls and staircases, is only open for independent visits during Patrimony Weekend in September. If your French is good, however, free guided tours are given biweekly in summer, weekly in other seasons: call ahead for further information and reservations. The grand public square out front is always lively, playing host to events and temporary exhibitions. There's a carousel and a beach volleyball court (or similar) in summer, and an ice-skating rink (with skate rental available) in winter. ⊠ *Pl. de l'Hôtel-de-Ville, Marais* ☎ *01–42–76–43–43 for tours* ⊕ *www.paris.fr* ⊡ *Free* ⊙ *Library weekdays 9:30–6* ☞ *Access for visits at 5 rue Lobau* Ⓜ *Hôtel de Ville.*

La Gaîté Lyrique. One of Paris's newest contemporary-art venues combines innovative exhibits with live musical performances and a multimedia space that features a library, movies, and free video games. Think of it as a smaller, more interactive Centre Pompidou. La Gaîté Lyrique occupies three floors of a 19th-century theater—remnants of which are visible in the café upstairs. ⊠ *3 bis, rue Papin, Marais* ☎ *01–53–01–52–00* ⊕ *www. gaite-lyrique.net* ⊡ *Free; €5–€7 for temporary exhibitions; concert prices vary* ⊙ *Tues.–Fri. 2–8, weekends 11–7* Ⓜ *Réaumur-Sébastopol.*

FAMILY **Musée de la Chasse et de la Nature.** Mark this down as one of Paris's most bizarre—and fascinating—collections. The museum, housed in the gorgeous 17th-century Hôtel de Guénégaud, features lavishly appointed rooms stocked with animal- and hunt-themed art by the likes of Rubens and Gentileschi, plus antique weaponry and taxidermy animals. In a tribute to Art Nouveau, the decor includes chandeliers curled like antlers and matching railings. Older kids will appreciate the jaw-dropping Trophy Room with an impressive menagerie of beasts, not to mention the huge polar bear stationed outside. There is a lovely multimedia exhibit on the myth of the unicorn, as well as an interactive display of bird calls. Temporary exhibits and silent auctions take place on the first floor. ⊠ *62 rue des Archives, Marais* ☎ *01–53–01–92–40* ⊕ *www.chassenature.org* 🎫 *€8* ⏲ *Tues. and Thurs.–Sun. 11–6, Wed. 11–9:30* Ⓜ *Rambuteau.*

FAMILY **Musée de la Poupée** (*Doll Museum*). Providing an impressive overview of dolls through the ages, this charming museum is a little girl's dream. Here you'll see dolls made from Bisque porcelain, sturdy wood, soft cotton, delicate papier-mâché, plus the first plastic dolls from the early 20th century. Some play music, others make tea. Cases lining the walls are stocked with baby dolls, minidolls (*mignonettes*), and grown-up lady dolls in satin dresses—the foremothers of Barbie. There are also antique toy strollers, high chairs, and tattered teddy bears in need of a hug. Too extensive to show at one time, the permanent collection changes frequently and can be arranged by period or theme. Temporary exhibitions might focus on Barbie's evolution or offer a classic look at postwar French dolls. Workshops allow kids to make a doll to take home (they're in French, but the mostly bilingual staff is happy to speak English; check the website for details). There's also an on-site doll hospital and a well-stocked gift shop. ⊠ *Impasse Berthaud, Marais* ☎ *01–42–72–73–11* ⊕ *www.museedelapoupeeparis.com* 🎫 *€8; €14 with workshop* ⏲ *Tues.–Sat. 1–6* Ⓜ *Rambuteau.*

Musée Pierre Cardin, Passé-Présent-Futur. Housed, appropriately, in a former necktie factory, this museum was opened in late 2014 by Cardin himself (then age 92). Covering three levels and six decades, it serves up the forward-thinking couturier's most memorable fashion statements. You'll see 200-plus designs—including the iconic "bubble dress"—as well as assorted accessories. ⊠ *5 rue St-Merri, 4e, Marais* ☎ *01–42–76– 00–57* ⊕ *www.pierrecardin.com* 🎫 *€25* ⏲ *Wed.–Fri. 11–6, weekends 1–6* Ⓜ *Hotel de Ville, Rambuteau.*

OFF THE
BEATEN
PATH

Nicolas Flamel's Home. Built in 1407 and reputed to be the oldest house in Paris (though other buildings also claim that title), this abode has a mystical history. Harry Potter fans should take note: this was the real-life residence of Nicolas Flamel, the alchemist whose sorcerer's stone is the source of immortality in the popular book series. A wealthy scribe, merchant, and dabbler in the mystical arts, Flamel willed his home to the city as a dormitory for the poor, on the condition that boarders pray daily for his soul. Today, the building contains apartments and a restaurant. ⊠ *52 rue Montmorency, Marais* Ⓜ *Rambuteau.*

St-Paul–St-Louis. The leading Baroque church in the Marais, its dome rising 180 feet above the crossing, was begun in 1627 by the Jesuits, who modeled it after their Gesù church in Rome. Recently cleaned on the outside but dark and brooding inside, it contains Delacroix's *Christ on the Mount of Olives* in the transept and a shell-shape holy-water font at the entrance, which was donated by Victor Hugo. Hugo lived in nearby Place des Vosges, and his beloved daughter Léopoldine was married here in 1843—though she met a tragic end less than seven months later, when she fell into the Seine and drowned, along with her husband Charles, who tried to save her. ⊠ *99 rue St-Antoine, Marais* ☎ *01–42–72–30–32* ⊕ *www.spsl.fr* ⏲ *Daily 8–8* Ⓜ *St-Paul.*

EASTERN PARIS

with Bastille, Canal St-Martin,
République, and Belleville

GETTING ORIENTED

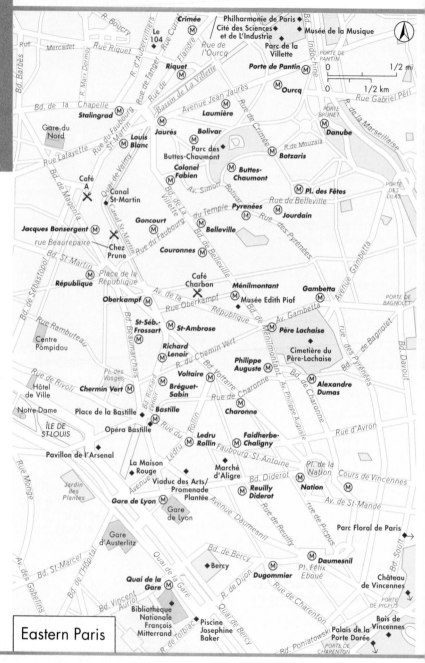

Crimée Ⓜ

Philharmonie de Paris ◆
Cité des Sciences ◆
et de L'Industrie

◆ Musée de la Musique

Le 104

Parc de la
Villette

Rue de
l'Ourcq

R. Boucry

R. Mercadet

Rue

Rue Riquet

R. d'Aubervilliers

R. Max Dormoy

Rue de Tanger

Rue Curial

Rue de Flandre

Riquet Ⓜ

Porte de Pantin Ⓜ

PORTE DE
PANTIN

0   1/2 mi

0   1/2 km

Bassin de La Villette

Ⓜ Ourcq

Rue Gabriel Péri

Bd. Barbès

Bd. de la Chapelle

Avenue Jean Jaurès

Rue de Crimée

Rue de la Marseillaise

PORTE
BRUNET

Stalingrad Ⓜ

Laumière Ⓜ

Gare du
Nord

Rue du Faubourg
St-Martin

Jaurès Ⓜ

Bolivar Ⓜ

Danube Ⓜ

Louis
Blanc Ⓜ

Parc des
Buttes-Chaumont

R. de Mouzaïa

Botzaris Ⓜ

Rue Lafayette

Quai de Valmy

Colonel
Fabien Ⓜ

Buttes-
Chaumont Ⓜ

Pl. des Fêtes Ⓜ

PORTE
DES
LILAS

Café
A

Canal
St-Martin Ⓜ

Bd. de Magenta

Av. Simon Bolivar

Canal St-Martin

Rue de la Villette

Pyrénées Ⓜ

Rue de Belleville

Goncourt Ⓜ

du Temple

Belleville Ⓜ

Ⓜ Jourdain

Rue des Pyrénées

Jacques Bonsergent Ⓜ

rue Beaurepaire

Bd. du Faubourg

Bd. de Belleville

Chez
Prune

Bd. St-Martin

Couronnes Ⓜ

Avenue Gambetta

Bd. de Sébastopol

Place de la
République Ⓜ

République

Av. de la

Café
Charbon

Ménilmontant Ⓜ

Gambetta Ⓜ

PORTE DE
BAGNOLET

Rue Rambuteau

Oberkampf Ⓜ

Rue Oberkampf

Ⓜ Musée Edith Piaf

République

Av. Gambetta

Centre
Pompidou

Bd. Beaumarchais

St-Séb.-
Frossart Ⓜ

St-Ambrose Ⓜ

Père Lachaise Ⓜ

Rue des de Bagnolet

Bd. Davout

Richard
Lenoir Ⓜ

R. du Chemin Vert

Philippe
Auguste Ⓜ

Cimetière du
Père-Lachaise ◆

Rue des Pyrénées

Hôtel
de Ville

Rue de Rivoli

Pl. des
Vosges

Chermin Vert Ⓜ

Voltaire Ⓜ

Bd. Voltaire

Av. Ménilmontant

Alexandre
Dumas Ⓜ

Notre-Dame

Bréguet-
Sabin Ⓜ

Rue de Charonne

Rue de Bagnolet

ÎLE DE
ST-LOUIS

Place de la Bastille Ⓜ

Bastille Ⓜ

Charonne Ⓜ

Bd. Richard Lenoir

Pavillon de l'Arsenal ◆

Opéra Bastille

Rue du

Ledru
Rollin Ⓜ

Faidherbe-
Chaligny Ⓜ

Rue d'Avron

Av. Philippe Auguste

Rue de Charonne

Jardin
des
Plantes

La Maison
Rouge ◆

Marché
d'Aligre ◆

Faubourg-St-Antoine

Pl. de la
Nation Ⓜ

Cours de Vincennes

Rue Monge

Avenue

Viaduc des Arts/
Promenade
Plantée

Bd. Diderot

Reuilly
Diderot Ⓜ

Nation Ⓜ

Av. de St-Mandé

Gare de Lyon Ⓜ

Gare
de Lyon

Avenue Daumesnil

Rue de Reuilly

Rue de Picpus

Parc Floral de Paris

Gare
d'Austerlitz

Bd. de Bercy

Parc Floral de Paris →

Av. des Gobelins

Bd. St-Marcel

Bd. de l'Hôpital

Quai de la Gare

Rue de Dijon

◆ Bercy

Pl. Félix
Eboué

Dugommier Ⓜ

Daumesnil Ⓜ

Bd. Soult

Château
de Vincennes

PORTE
DE PICPUS

Quai de la
Gare Ⓜ

Bd. Vincent Auriol

Bibliothèque
Nationale
François
Mitterrand

◆ Piscine
Josephine
Baker

Quai de Bercy

Rue de Charenton

Bois de
Vincennes

Palais de la
Porte Dorée ◆

PORTE
DE CHARENTON

R. de Tolbiac

Bd. Poniatowski

Eastern Paris

TOP REASONS TO GO

Canal St-Martin. This scenic canal is now one of the city's hottest, hippest hangouts—it's great for strolling, with plenty of galleries, shops, and cafés en route.

Place de la Bastille. The flashpoint of the French Revolution still draws agitators and their frequent, noisy demonstrations. It's also a nightlife hub and home to the Opéra Bastille.

Cimetière du Père-Lachaise. Fans of celebrities, from Frédéric Chopin to Oscar Wilde to Jim Morrison, come to pay tribute at their final resting place.

Parc de la Villette. As the site of the city's well-regarded science museum and planetarium, this is a good destination for both curious kids and grown-up science buffs.

Viaduc des Arts/Promenade Plantée. An abandoned rail line has been turned into a tree-fringed walkway perched atop a brick viaduct that's bursting with boutiques.

BEST CAFÉS

Café A. The Maison de l'Architecture—a center for architectural advancement—occupies a onetime monastery near the Canal St-Martin. Inside its Renaissance courtyard, Café A offers a seasonal menu at prices that are reasonable for this ever-gentrifying area. ⊠ *148 rue du Faubourg St-Martin, Canal St-Martin* ☎ *09–81–29–83–38* ▭ *No credit cards* Ⓜ *Gare de l'Est.*

Café Charbon. This ultracool café is a neighborhood institution that stays open late every night of the week. ⊠ *109 rue Oberkampf, Oberkampf* ☎ *01–43–57–55–13* ▭ *No credit cards* Ⓜ *Parmentier, Menilmontant.*

Chez Prune. Grab an outdoor table at this hot spot on the Canal St-Martin and watch the world go by. ⊠ *36 rue Beaurepaire, Canal St-Martin* ☎ *01–42–41–30–47* ▭ *No credit cards* Ⓜ *Jacques Bonsergent, République.*

GETTING HERE

Eastern Paris includes the 10e, 11e, 12e, 19e, and 20e arrondissements. The Bastille métro stop, on Lines 1, 5, and 8, is a good place to start. For the Canal St-Martin, use the Place de la République stop (Lines 3, 5, 8, 9, 11) and walk along Rue Faubourg du Temple; use the Gare de l'Est stop (Lines 4, 5, 7) and walk along Rue des Récollets; or choose the Jaurès stop (Lines 2, 5, and 7bis), take the Boulevard de Villette exit, and walk a mere 80 feet south. For Oberkampf, go to the Parmentier stop on Line 3 or the Oberkampf stop on Line 9. For the Cimetière du Père-Lachaise, take Line 2 or 3 to the eponymous stop.

MAKING THE MOST OF YOUR TIME

The Canal St-Martin is one of the most popular places in the city, particularly on Sunday afternoon, when the streets are closed to cars. Have lunch in a café, grab a Vélib' rental bike, and head to Parc de la Villette. A Sunday morning trip to the picturesque Marché d'Aligre is also recommended, even if you're not buying. The heaps of fresh produce and colorful flowers hawked by spirited vendors are worth seeing. On any day Place de la Bastille is a lively spot to stop for drinks or lunch; if time is limited, reserve this neighborhood for after dark, when the streets around Place de la Bastille and Oberkampf really come to life.

9

Sightseeing
★★
Dining
★★★★
Lodging
★★
Shopping
★★★★
Nightlife
★★★★★

Updated by
Jack Vermee

The Bastille used to be the star of this area, and a stop here—at the epicenter of the French Revolution—was obligatory. The small streets forking off Place de la Bastille still buzz at night, thanks to bars, music clubs, and the top-flight Opéra Bastille.

There are also noteworthy attractions, like the nearby **Viaduc des Arts**, an urban-renewal project that transformed an old elevated rail line into arcaded, design-focused studios and shops. Along the top, the Promenade Plantée makes for a lovely stroll through the 12e arrondissement, which includes stately apartment buildings and pretty Square Trousseau, gateway to the **Marché d'Aligre**. But today the neighborhoods farther afield are the real draw, having evolved into some of Paris's top destinations.

The **Canal St-Martin,** once the down-and-out cousin on the northern border, is now trend-spotting central, brimming with funky bars, cafés, art galleries, and boutiques. The scene is similar on Rues Oberkampf, St-Maur, and Jean-Pierre-Timbaud, where artists and small designers have set up shop, and where a substantial slice of the city's *bobo* (bourgeois-bohemian) contingent is buying up the no-longer-so-affordable apartments.

Continuing east, you'll find the city's largest cemetery, **Père-Lachaise,** with a roster of famous tenants. Not far away is the impressively wild **Parc Buttes-Chaumont,** with grassy fields, a small Greek-style temple, and sweeping hilltop views of Paris. It's the perfect place to eat a picnic lunch and let museum-weary kids blow off some steam. The eastern section is also home to two other popular parks: the **Parc de la Villette,** which contains a pair of engaging museums, and the **Bois de Vincennes,** home to the city's largest zoo.

To the south of the Bastille, the old wine warehouses at **Bercy** have become a veritable village of shops and restaurants bordering Parc de Bercy. Directly across the Seine is the **Bibliothéque Nationale François Mitterrand,** the National Library of France, a sprawling complex of modern glass towers opened in 1998.

TOP ATTRACTIONS

FAMILY **Bercy.** Tucked away south of the Gare de Lyon in the 12e arrondissement, blocks of stone warehouses that once stored wine are now home to Bercy Village, a collection of boutiques and eateries that stay open unusually late for Paris—many shops until 9 pm, Monday to Saturday; some restaurants until 2 am daily (⊠ *28 rue François Truffaut* ☎ *08–25–16–60–75* ⊕ *www.bercyvillage.com*). You can still see the old train tracks used to transport the wine barrels from the provinces. Adjacent to the shops is the tranquil Parc de Bercy, with lawns, ponds, and flower beds crisscrossed by gravel paths, and the Jardin Yitzhak Rabin, a garden named for the late Nobel peace prize winner. Nearby, at 51 rue de Bercy, a Cubist building by Frank Gehry houses the Cinémathèque Française, a film buff's paradise, showing classic films, many in English; there are frequent homages to directors and actors, plus a cinema library and museum. ⊠ *Eastern Paris* Ⓜ *Cour St-Emilion, Bercy.*

NEED A BREAK?

Pink Flamingo. This American-owned pizzeria will deliver your pie directly to the banks of the canal—they spot you thanks to the pink balloon you're holding. ⊠ **67 rue Bichat, Canal St-Martin** ☎ **01–42–02–31–70** ⊕ **www. pinkflamingopizza.com** Ⓜ **Jacques Bonsergent, Colonel Fabien.**

Fodor'sChoice **Canal St-Martin.** This once-forgotten canal has morphed into one of
★ the city's trendiest places to wander. A good time to come is Sunday afternoon, when the Quai de Valmy is closed to cars and some of the shops are open. Rent a bike at any of the many Vélib' stations, stroll along the banks, or go native and cuddle quai-side in the sunshine with someone special.

In 1802 Napoléon ordered the 4.3-km (2.7-mile) canal dug as a source of clean drinking water after cholera and other epidemics swept the city. When it finally opened 23 years later, it extended north from the Seine at Place de la Bastille to the Canal de l'Ourcq, near La Villette. Baron Haussmann later covered a 1.6-km (1-mile) stretch of it, along today's Boulevard Richard Lenoir. It nearly became a highway in the 1970s, before the city's urban planners regained their senses. These days you can take a boat tour from end to end through the canal's nine locks: along the way, the bridges swing or lift open. The drawbridge with four giant pulleys at Rue de Crimée, near La Villette, was a technological marvel when it debuted in 1885.

In recent years gentrification has transformed the once-dodgy canal, with artists taking over former industrial spaces and creating studios and galleries. The bar and restaurant scene is hipster central, and small designers have arrived, fleeing expensive rents in the Marais. To explore this evolving *quartier,* set out on foot. Start on the Quai de Valmy at Rue Faubourg du Temple (use the République métro stop). Here, at Square Frédéric Lemaître facing north, there is a good view of one of the locks (behind you the canal disappears underground). As you head north, detour onto side streets like Rue Beaurepaire, a fashionista destination with several "stock" (or surplus) shops for popular brands, some open on Sunday. Rues Lancry and Vinaigriers are lined with bars, restaurants, and small shops.

A swing bridge across the canal connects Lancry to the Rue de la Grange aux Belles, where you'll find the entrance to the massive Hôpital Saint-Louis, built in 1607 to accommodate plague victims and still a working hospital today. In front of you is the entrance to the chapel, which held its first Mass in July 1610, two months after the assassination of the hospital's patron, Henry IV. Stroll the grounds, flanked by the original brick-and-stone buildings with steeply sloping roofs. The peaceful courtyard garden is a neighborhood secret.

Back on Quai Valmy, browse more shops near the Rue des Récollets. Nearby is the Jardin Villemin, the 10e arrondissement's largest park (4.5 acres) on the former site of another hospital. The nighttime scene, especially in summer, is hopping with twentysomethings spilling out of cafés and bars and onto the canal banks. If you've made it this far, reward yourself with a fresh taco or burrito at the tiny and authentically Mexican El Nopal taqueria at 3 rue Eugène Varlin. Farther up, just past Place Stalingrad, is the Rotonde de la Villette, a lively square with restaurants and twin MK2 cinemas on either side of the canal, plus a boat to ferry ticket holders across. Canauxrama (⊕ *www.canauxrama. com*) offers 2½-hour boat cruises through the locks (€18). Embarkation is at each end of the canal: at Bassin de la Villette (*13 quai de la Loire, La Villette*) or Marina Arsenal (*50 bd. de la Bastille, Bastille*). ⊠ *Canal St-Martin* Ⓜ *Jaurès (north end), République (south end), Gare de l'Est (middle)*.

NEED A BREAK?

Hôtel du Nord. With a retro white facade, the Hôtel du Nord looks like a movie set—and indeed, it was famously used by Marcel Carné in his 1938 namesake film. The star, actress-icon Arletty, claimed to be unmoved by the romantic canal-side setting, uttering the memorable line "Atmosphere, atmosphere, I've had it with atmosphere!" Today the restaurant, beautifully restored, is a hipster favorite, though the food is not as fabulous as the ambience. ⊠ *102 quai de Jemmappes, Canal St-Martin* ☎ *01-40-40-78-78* ⊕ *www.hoteldunord.org* Ⓜ *Jacques Bonsergent.*

Fodor's Choice ★ **Cimetière du Père-Lachaise.** Bring a red rose for "the Little Sparrow" Edith Piaf when you visit the cobblestone avenues and towering trees that make this 118-acre oasis of green perhaps the world's most famous cemetery. Named for Père François de la Chaise, Louis XIV's confessor, Père-Lachaise is more than just a who's who of celebrities. The Paris Commune's final battle took place here on May 28, 1871, when 147 rebels were lined up and shot against the Mur des Fédérés (Federalists' Wall) in the southeast corner. Aside from the sheer aesthetic beauty of the cemetery, the main attraction is what (or who, more accurately) is below ground.

Two of the biggest draws are Jim Morrison's grave (with its own guard to keep Doors fans under control) and the life-size bronze figure of French journalist Victor Noir, whose alleged fertility-enhancing power accounts for the patches rubbed smooth by hopeful hands. Other significant grave sites include those of 12th-century French philosopher Pierre Abélard and his lover Héloïse; French writers Colette, Honoré de Balzac, and Marcel Proust; American writers Richard Wright, Gertrude

DID YOU KNOW?

Many people take boat rides on the Seine, but there are also several companies that offer trips along the Canal St-Martin. Check out 🌐 *en. pariscanal.com* or 🌐 *www. canauxrama.com* for more information.

Famed cemetery Père-Lachaise is the final resting place for artists like Edith Piaf, Jim Morrison, Marcel Proust, Oscar Wilde, and many more.

Stein, and Alice B. Toklas; Irish writer Oscar Wilde; French actress Sarah Bernhardt; French composer Georges Bizet; Greek-American opera singer Maria Callas; Franco-Polish composer Frédéric Chopin; painters of various nationalities including Georges-Pierre Seurat, Camille Pissaro, Jean-Auguste-Dominique Ingres, Jacques-Louis David, Eugène Delacroix, Théodore Géricault, Amedeo Clemente Modigliani, and Max Ernst; French jazz violinist Stephane Grappelli; French civic planner Baron Haussmann; French playwright and actor Molière; and French singer Edith Piaf.

■TIP→ Pinpoint grave sites on the website before you come, but buy a map anyway outside the entrances—you'll still get lost, but that's part of the fun. One of the best days to visit is on All Saints' Day (November 1), when Parisians bring flowers to adorn the graves of loved ones or favorite celebrities. ✉ *Entrances on Rue des Rondeaux, Bd. de Ménilmontant, and Rue de la Réunion, Eastern Paris* ☎ *01–55–25–82–10* ⊕ *www.pere-lachaise.com* ✉ *Free* ☽ *Weekdays 8–6, Sat. 8:30–6, Sun. 9–6 (closes at 5:30 in winter)* Ⓜ *Gambetta, Philippe-Auguste, Père-Lachaise.*

FAMILY **Cité des Sciences et de l'Industrie** (*Museum of Science and Industry*). Occupying a colorful three-story industrial space that recalls the Pompidou Center, this ambitious science museum in Parc de la Villette is packed with things to do—all of them accessible to English speakers. Scores of exhibits focus on subjects like space, transportation, and technology. Hands-on workshops keep the kids entertained, and the planetarium is invariably a hit. Temporary exhibitions, like a recent exploration of the human voice, are always multilingual and usually interactive. ✉ *Parc de* *la Villette, 30 av. Corentin-Cariou, Eastern Paris* ☎ *01–40–05–70–00, 01–40–05–80–00 Interactive Voice response* ⊕ *www.cite-sciences.fr* 🎟 *€9; €12 for the permanent exhibition and one temporary exhibition* ⊙ *Tues.–Sat. 10–6, Sun. 10–7* Ⓜ *Porte de la Villette.*

La Maison Rouge. One of the city's premier spaces for contemporary art, La Maison Rouge art foundation was established by former gallery owner Antoine de Galbert to fill a hole in the Parisian art world. Always edgy, often provocative, the foundation stages several temporary exhibitions each year in a cleverly renovated industrial space anchored by a central courtyard building that's painted bright red on the outside (hence the name). Past shows have included *Tous Cannibales*, themed around cannibalism, and *Memories of the Future*, a death-obsessed display featuring artists from Hieronymus Bosch to Damien Hirst. Check the website to see what's on. Stop by the Rose Bakery near the entrance: it's the latest Parisian outpost of the popular English café. ✉ *10 bd. de la Bastille, Bastille* ☎ *01–40–01–08–81* ⊕ *www.lamaisonrouge.org* 🎟 *€9* ⊙ *Wed. and Fri.–Sun. 11–7, Thurs. 11–9* Ⓜ *Quai de la Rapée, Bastille.*

Marché d'Aligre. Place d'Aligre boasts two of Paris's best markets: the lively outdoor Marché d'Aligre and the covered Marché Beauvau. Open every day but Monday, both are great places to pick up picnic essentials, which you can enjoy nearby in the small park at Square Trousseau or on the Promenade Plantée. The picturesque outdoor market has dozens of boisterous vendors, their stands laden with fresh fruits and vegetables, flower bouquets, and regional products such as jam, honey, and dried sausage. The best bargains are had just before closing time, and many vendors are happy to give you a taste of whatever they're selling. The covered market stocks everything from meats and cheeses to Belgian beer. Sunday morning, when the accompanying flea market is in full swing, is the liveliest time to visit. Don't forget your camera. Stop for a plate of *saucisse* and a glass of *rouge* (even on Sunday morning) at one of the city's quirkiest wine bars, Le Baron Rouge, 1 rue Théophile Roussel. ✉ *Pl. d'Aligre, Bastille* ⊕ *www.equipement.paris.fr/marche-couvert-beauvau-marche-d-aligre-5480* ⊙ *Marché d'Aligre Tues.–Fri. 7:30–1:30, weekends 7:30–2:30. Marché Beauvau Tues.–Fri. 9–1 and 4–7:30, Sat. 9–1 and 3:30–7:30, Sun. 9–1:30* Ⓜ *Ledru-Rollin, Bastille.*

FAMILY **Musée de la Musique.** Parc de la Villette's music museum contains four centuries' worth of instruments from around the world—about 1,000 in total, many of them exquisite works of art. Their sounds and stories are evoked on numerous video screens and via commentary you can follow on headphones (ask for a free audioguide in English). Leave time for the excellent temporary exhibitions, like the recent one on the marriage between cinema and music. On the plaza, adjacent to the museum, the outdoor terrace at Café des Concerts (☎ *01–42–49–74–74* ⊕ *www. cafedesconcerts.com*) is an inviting place to have a drink on a sunny day. ✉ *Parc de la Villette, 221 av. Jean-Jaurès, Eastern Paris* ☎ *01–44–84–44–84* ⊕ *www.philharmoniedeparis.fr* 🎟 *€7; €10 with temporary exhibits* ⊙ *Tues.–Fri. noon–6, weekends 10–6* Ⓜ *Porte de Pantin.*

Opéra Bastille. Paris's main opera house opened its doors on July 14, 1989 to mark the bicentennial of the French Revolution. The fabulous acoustics of the steeply sloping, stylish auditorium have earned more plaudits than the modern facade designed by Uruguay-born architect Carlos Ott. If you want to see a show, reserve your ticket well in advance, or take your chances snagging a same-day seat just prior to the performance. Once the doors open, 32 standing-room-only tickets also go on sale for €5. Tickets for a 90-minute guided tour (in French only) cost €15. ⊠ *Pl. de la Bastille, Bastille* ☎ *08–92–89–90–90 for tickets (€0.34 per minute), 01–71–25–24–23 from outside of France, 01–40–01–19–70 for tours* ⊕ *www.operadeparis.fr* ☉ *Box office Mon.– Sat. 11:30–6:30 and one hr before curtain call* Ⓜ *Bastille.*

FAMILY **Parc de la Villette.** This former abattoir is now an ultramodern, 130-acre park. With lawns and play areas, an excellent science museum, a music complex, and a cinema, it's also the perfect place to entertain exhausted kids. You could easily spend a whole day here.

The park itself was designed in the 1980s by postmodern architecture star Bernard Tschumi, who melded industrial elements, children's games (don't miss the dragon slide), ample green spaces, and funky sculptures along the canal into one vast yet unified playground. Loved by picnickers, the lawns also attract rehearsing samba bands and pickup soccer players. In summer there are outdoor festivals and a free open-air cinema, where people gather at dusk to watch movies on a huge inflatable screen.

In cold weather you can visit an authentic submarine and the Espace Chapiteaux (a circus tent featuring contemporary acrobatic theater performances) before hitting the museums. The hands-on one at the Cité des Sciences et de l'Industrie is a favorite stop for families and a must for science fans; its 3-D Omnimax cinema (La Géode) is housed in a giant mirrored ball. Arts-oriented visitors of all ages will marvel at the excellent, instrument-filled Musée de la Musique. The park has even more in store for music lovers now that the curtain has risen on the new Philharmonie de Paris, a striking 2,400-seat concert hall designed by Jean Nouvel.

As for the abattoir that once stood here, all that's left of the slaughterhouse is La Grande Halle, a magnificent iron-and-glass building currently used for exhibitions, performances, and trade shows. ⊠ *Parc de la Villette, 211 ave. Jean Jaurès, Eastern Paris* ☎ *01–40–03–75–75* ⊕ *www.lavillette.com* Ⓜ *Porte de Pantin, Porte de la Villette.*

FAMILY **Parc des Buttes-Chaumont.** If you're tired of perfectly manicured Parisian parks with lawns that are off-limits to your weary feet, this place is for you. Built in 1863 on abandoned gypsum quarries and a former gallows, it was northern Paris's first park, part of Napoléon III's planned greening of the city (the emperor had spent years in exile in London, where he fell in love with the public parks). Today the lovely 61-acre hilltop expanse in the untouristy 19e arrondissement has grassy fields, shady walkways, waterfalls, and a picturesque lake dotted with swans. Rising from the lake is a rocky cliff you can climb to find a mini Greek-style temple and a commanding view of Sacré-Coeur Basilica. A favorite of families, the park also has pony rides and an open-air puppet theater—Guignol de Paris (€4.50; shows at 3 pm and 4 pm Wednesday and at 4 pm and 5 pm weekends, year-round)—not far from the entrance at the Buttes-Chaumont métro stop. When you've worked up an appetite, grab a snack at the Rosa Bonheur café (⊕ *www.rosabonheur.fr*), or reserve a table for weekend lunch at Le Pavillon du Lac restaurant (⊕ *www.lepavillondulac.fr*). Major renovation work through 2017 will mean some unsightly construction and limited access to certain areas; however, the park will remain open. ⊠ *Entrances on Rue Botzaris or Rue Manin, Belleville* ⊗ *May–Aug., daily 7 am–10 pm; Apr. and Sept., daily 7 am–9 pm; Oct.–Mar., daily 7 am–8 pm* Ⓜ *Buttes-Chaumont, Botzaris, Laumière.*

Place de la Bastille. Almost nothing remains of the infamous Bastille prison, destroyed more than 225 years ago, though tourists still ask bemused Parisians where to find it. Until the late 1980s, there was little more to see here than a busy traffic circle ringing the Colonne de Juillet (July Column), a memorial to the victims of later uprisings in 1830 and 1848. The opening of the Opéra Bastille in 1989 rejuvenated the area, however, drawing art galleries, bars, and restaurants to the narrow streets, notably along Rue de Lappe—once a haunt of Edith Piaf—and Rue de la Roquette.

Before it became a prison, the Bastille St-Antoine was a defensive fortress with eight immense towers and a wide moat. It was built by Charles V in the late 14th century and transformed into a prison during the reign of Louis XIII (1610–43). Famous occupants included Voltaire, the Marquis de Sade, and the Man in the Iron Mask. On July 14, 1789, it was stormed by an angry mob that dramatically freed all of the remaining prisoners (there were only seven), thereby launching the French Revolution. The roots of the revolt ran deep. Resentment toward Louis XVI and Marie-Antoinette had been building amid a severe financial crisis. There was a crippling bread shortage, and the free-spending monarch was blamed. When the king dismissed the popular finance minister, Jacques Necker, enraged Parisians took to the streets. They marched to Les Invalides, helping themselves to stocks of arms, then continued on to the Bastille. A few months later, what was left of the prison was razed—and 83 of its stones were carved into miniature Bastilles and sent to the provinces as a memento (you can see one of them in the Musée Carnavalet). The key to the prison was given to George Washington by Lafayette and has remained at Mount Vernon ever since. Today, nearly every major street demonstration in Paris—and there are many—passes through this square. ⊠ *Bastille* Ⓜ *Bastille.*

Viaduc des Arts/Promenade Plantée (*La Coulée Verte*). Once a train line from the Paris suburbs to Bastille, this redbrick viaduct is now the green heart of the unpretentious 12e arrondissement. The rails have been transformed into a 4.5-km (2.8-mile) walkway lined with trees, bamboo, and flowers, offering a bird's-eye view of the stately Haussmannian buildings along Avenue Daumesnil. Below, the *voûtes* (arcades) have been transformed by the city into artisan boutiques, many focused on decor and design. All tenants are hand-picked. There are also temporary galleries showcasing art and photography. The Promenade, which gained fame as a setting in the 2004 film *Before Sunset,* was the inspiration for New York's High Line. It ends at the Jardin de Reuilly. From here you can continue your walk to the Bois de Vincennes. If you're hungry, grab a bite at L'Arrosoir, a cozy café under the viaduct at 75 avenue Daumesnil. ⊠ *Av. Daumesnil, Bastille* ☎ *01–71–18–75–68* ⊕ *www. leviaducdesarts.com* Ⓜ *Bastille, Gare de Lyon.*

WORTH NOTING

Bibliothèque Nationale François Mitterrand. The National Library of France, across the sleek Simone de Beauvoir footbridge from Bercy Park, is a stark complex comprised of four 22-story L-shaped buildings representing open books. Commissioned by President Mitterrand, the €1 billion library was said to be the world's most modern when it opened in 1998—a reputation quickly sullied when it was discovered that miles of books and rare documents were baking in the glass towers, unprotected from the sun (movable shutters were eventually installed). Some of the most important printed treasures of France are stored here, though the majority of them are available only to researchers. Visitors can see the impressive 17th-century Globes of Coronelli, a pair of 2-ton orbs made for Louis XIV. There's a sunken center garden with tall trees (open to the public the first weekend in June) ringed by low-ceilinged reading rooms, which are nothing special. A first-floor gallery hosts popular temporary exhibitions on subjects such as the life of Casanova. Enter through the easternmost tower. ⊠ *Quai François Mauriac, Eastern Paris* ☎ *01–53–79–59–59* ⊕ *www.bnf.fr* ⊠ *Globes gallery free; reading rooms €3.50; exhibitions €9 (€11 for two)* ☉ *Tues.–Sat. 10–8, Sun. 1–7* Ⓜ *Bibliothèque, Quai de la Gare.*

FAMILY **Bois de Vincennes.** Like the Bois de Boulogne to the west, this much-loved retreat on the city's eastern border was landscaped by Napoléon III. Its roots, however, reach back to the 13th century, when Philippe Auguste created a hunting preserve in the shadow of the royal Château de Vincennes, which once ranked as the largest château in Europe. In 1731 Louis XV created a public park here, and the bois (or wood) now features lush lawns, a flower garden, and summertime jazz concerts. Rowboats are for hire at a pair of lakes: Lac Daumesnil, which has two islands, and Lac des Minimes, which has three. Here, too, you'll find the stunning Palais de la Porte Dorée (home to an immigration museum and a tropical aquarium), the Parc Zoologique, the Hippodrome de Vincennes racetrack, two cafés, and, in spring, an amusement park. Bikes can be rented at the Château de Vincennes métro stop. ⊠ *Bois de Vincennes, Eastern Paris* Ⓜ *Château de Vincennes, Porte Dorée.*

Château de Vincennes. This imposing high-walled château, on the northern edge of the Bois de Vincennes, was France's medieval answer to Versailles. Built and expanded by various kings between the 12th and 14th centuries, it is now surrounded by a dry moat and dominated by a 170-foot keep (the last of nine original towers). The royal residence eventually became a prison holding convicts, notably of both sexes—and "the doors did not always remain closed between them," as one tour guide coyly put it. Inmates included the philosopher Diderot and the Marquis de Sade. Both the château and its cathedral, Sainte-Chapelle (designed in the style of the Paris church of the same name) have undergone a spectacular restoration, returning them to their previous glory. If you speak French, the free 90-minute tour is worthwhile; otherwise, consider spending €4.50 for the English audioguide. ✉ *Av. de Paris, Eastern Paris* ☎ *01–48–08–31–20* ⊕ *www.chateau-vincennes.fr* 🎟 *€8.50* ☉ *Mid-May–mid-Sept., daily 10–6; mid-Sept.–mid-May, daily 10–5* Ⓜ *Château de Vincennes.*

OFF THE
BEATEN
PATH

Le 104. Le Cent Quatre takes its name from its address in a rough-around-the-edges corner of the 19e arrondissement, not far from the top of the Canal St-Martin. The former site of the city morgue, this cavernous art hub is home to an offbeat collection of performance venues, shops, and studios (artists of all genres compete for free studio space, and sometimes you can get a sneak peek of them at work). Contemporary art exhibits, some of which charge admission, are staged here, as are concerts. On-site you'll also find a restaurant, a café, a bookstore, a natural-clothing boutique, a secondhand shop, and a play area for children. Check the website before going to see what's on. ✉ *104 rue d'Aubervilliers, Eastern Paris* ☎ *01–53–35–50–00* ⊕ *www.104. fr* 🎟 *Free; prices for exhibits and concerts vary* ☉ *Tues.–Fri. noon–7, weekends 11–7* Ⓜ *Stalingrad.*

OFF THE
BEATEN
PATH

Musée Edith Piaf. Devotees will appreciate the tiny two-room apartment where the "little sparrow" lived for a year, when she was 28 years old and sang in the working-class cafés on Rue Oberkampf. The flat was obtained by Les Amis d'Edith Piaf in 1978 and is now a shrine to the petite crooner, whose life-size photo (she was just 4 feet, 9 inches tall) greets visitors at the door. The red walls are covered with portraits of Piaf done by her many artist friends, and her personal letters are framed. On display, you'll see her books and handbags, as well as a few dresses, her size 4 shoes, and a touching pair of old boxing gloves belonging to one of her great loves—champion pugilist Marcel Cerdan. ✉ *5 rue Crespin du Gast, Oberkampf* ☎ *01–43–55–52–72* 🎟 *Free, donations strongly encouraged* ☉ *July, Aug., and Oct.–May, Mon.–Wed. 1–6, by reservation only (no English spoken)* Ⓜ *Ménilmontant.*

9

FAMILY

Palais de la Porte Dorée. If you're bound for the Bois de Vincennes, pay a visit to the Palais de la Porte Dorée. Built for the 1931 Colonial Exhibition, it's one of the best examples of Art Deco architecture in Paris. The ornate facade features bas-relief sculptures representing France's erstwhile empire. Inside, the elaborate marble, ornate metalwork, and original lighting are all beautifully maintained. Entry to the ground floor is free. On either end are furnished salons, one representing Asia, the other Africa (a Gucci commercial was filmed in the latter); peek into the central room, called the Forum, where restored Africa-inspired mosaics line the walls. The upper floors are occupied by the Cité Nationale de l'Historie de l'Immigration, a well-executed modern museum tracing the history of immigration in France. The basement contains L'Aquarium Tropical, a small but engaging aquarium with a pair of rare albino alligators plus many types of exotic marine life. ⊠ *293 av. Daumesnil, Eastern Paris* ☎ *01–53–59–58–60* ⊕ *www.histoire-immigration. fr; www.aquarium-portedoree.fr* ◱ *Ground floor free; museum €4.50; aquarium €5; combined ticket €8* ۞ *Tues.–Fri. 10–5:30, weekends 10–7* Ⓜ *Porte Dorée.*

FAMILY **Parc Floral de Paris.** A lake, a butterfly garden, and seasonal displays of blooms make the Bois de Vincennes's 70-acre floral park a lovely place to spend a summer afternoon. Kids will also enjoy the miniature train, paddleboats, ponies, pool, and game area, among other attractions (most of which cost extra). The park hosts jazz concerts most weekends from April through September, but other months many attractions are closed. ⊠ *Rte. de la Pyramide, Eastern Paris* ☎ *01–43–28–41–59* ◱ *€5.50 Wed., weekends, days of concerts or events, and June–Sept.; free other days in season and every day off-season* ۞ *Apr.–Sept., daily 9:30–8; Oct.–Mar., daily 9:30–5* Ⓜ *Château de Vincennes.*

FAMILY **Pavillon de l'Arsenal.** If your knowledge of Paris history is *nul* (nil), stop here for an entertaining free tutorial. Built in 1879 as a private museum, the Pavillon today is a restored structure of glass and iron that showcases the city's urban development through the ages. A giant model of Paris traces its evolution (with information in English). There are photos, maps, and videos, plus a giant digital interactive model detailing what Paris is predicted to look like in 2020. The standout, created in partnership with Google, is a floor mosaic made up of 48 LED screens that allows visitors at stationary consoles to explore the city via Google Maps. The Pavillon also has a café-bookstore and hosts frequent architecture-themed temporary exhibits. ⊠ *21 bd. Morland, Bastille* ☎ *01–42–76–33–97* ⊕ *www.pavillon-arsenal.com* ◱ *Free* ۞ *Tues.–Sat. 10:30–6:30, Sun. 11–7* Ⓜ *Sully-Morland, Bastille.*

FAMILY **Piscine Josephine Baker.** This modern floating aquatic center, named after the much-beloved American entertainer, features a pool with a retractable glass roof, two solariums, a steam room, Jacuzzis, and a gym. Check the opening hours and schedule of classes online. ⊠ *Porte de la Gare, 21 quai François Mauriac, Eastern Paris* ☎ *01–56–61–96–50* ⊕ *www.carilis.fr/centre/piscine-josephine-baker* ◱ *€3.60 for pool (€5 in summer); fees may apply for other activities* ۞ *Weekdays 7–8:30 am and 1–9 pm (Tues. until 10 pm, Thurs. until 11 pm), weekends 11–7; extended hrs during school vacations* Ⓜ *Quai de la Gare, Bibilothèque.*

THE LATIN
QUARTER

GETTING ORIENTED

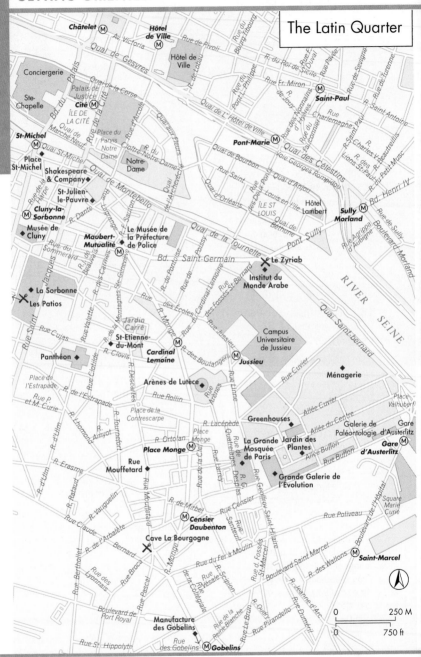

The Latin Quarter

TOP REASONS TO GO

Musée de Cluny. On the site of an ancient Roman bath, this former abbey is home to the famous *Lady and the Unicorn* tapestries; the building, tranquil garden, and extensive collection have the hush of a medieval monastery.

Shakespeare & Company. This legendary English-language bookstore is more than a shopping destination; it's a meeting place for young expats and literature-loving travelers alike.

Rue Mouffetard. Whether you're a gastronome or just plain hungry, you'll be enthralled by the array of characteristically French edibles sold on this winding market street.

Jardin des Plantes. This garden is a great spot to enjoy a picnic or to rest your tired feet on one of the many shaded benches.

La Grande Mosquée de Paris. Relax with a little glass of mint tea in the leafy courtyard café at Paris's most beautiful mosque.

MAKING THE MOST OF YOUR TIME

The Quartier Latin is the perfect place to wander sans itinerary, though there is no shortage of sites worth seeing. Shopping here is generally more affordable (but less original) than in other neighborhoods, and there are lots of new- and used-book stores, many of which stock English-language titles. Pick up picnic supplies in the food shops along Rue Mouffetard or the open-air market at Place Monge (Wednesday, Friday, and Sunday morning), then savor your booty on a bench at the Jardin des Plantes. Linger over mint tea at the lovely Grande Mosquée de Paris or take in a terrific view from the roof of the Institut du Monde Arabe. Stroll the hilly streets around the Panthéon on your way to see the treasures at the Musée de Cluny. Finish with a sunset apéritif on one of the barge cafés (open spring to fall) along the Seine, across from Notre-Dame.

GETTING HERE

The Quartier Latin is in the 5e arrondissement. Take métro Line 4 to St-Michel to start exploring at the Lucifer-slaying fountain near Shakespeare & Company, across the Seine from Notre-Dame. Go to the Cluny stop on Line 10 if you're heading to the Musée de Cluny. The Place Monge stop on Line 7 puts you near the Panthéon and Rue Mouffetard, the Mosquée de Paris, and the Jardin des Plantes. Les Gobelins neighborhood straddles the 5e, 13e, and 14e arrondissements, but is considered part of the 5e because of the Manufacture des Gobelins.

BEST CAFÉS

Cave La Bourgogne. Settle in on the terrace of this old-school bistro for lunch, or join the locals at the zinc bar. ✉ *144 rue Mouffetard, Latin Quarter* ☎ *01–47–07–82–80* ⊘ *Closed Mon.* Ⓜ *Censier-Daubenton.*

Les Patios. If you're young—or young at heart—come here to hang with the Sorbonne crowd. ✉ *5 pl. de la Sorbonne, Latin Quarter* ☎ *01–43–54–34–43* Ⓜ *Cluny–La Sorbonne.*

Le Zyriab. This café with an outdoor terrace on the top floor of the Institut du Monde Arabe has a fantastic view. ✉ *Institut du Monde Arabe, 1 rue des Fossés-St-Bernard, Latin Quarter* ☎ *01–55–42–55–42* ⊕ *www.noura.com* Ⓜ *Jussieu.*

10

Sightseeing
★★★★
Dining
★★★
Lodging
★★★★
Shopping
★★★
Nightlife
★★★

The Quartier Latin is the heart of student Paris—and has been for more than 800 years. France's oldest university, La Sorbonne, was founded here in 1257, and the neighborhood takes its name from the fact that Latin was the common language of the students, who came from all over Europe. Today the area is full of cheap and cheerful cafés, bars, and shops.

Updated by
Jack Vermee

The main drag, **Boulevard St-Michel,** is a busy street where bookshops have given way to chain clothing stores and fast-food joints—but don't let that stop you! There are (almost) as many French people wandering the streets here as there are tourists. At **Place St-Michel,** the symbolic gateway to the *quartier,* notice the 19th-century fountain depicting Saint Michael slaying the "great dragon," Satan—a symbolic warning to rebellious locals from Napoléon III. Today the fountain serves as a meeting spot and makes a rather fine metaphor for the boulevard it anchors: a bit grimy but extremely popular.

When you've had enough of the crowds, turn off the boulevard and explore the side streets, where you can find quirky boutiques and intimate bistros. Or stop for a *demi* (a half pint of draft beer) at one of the cafés on **Place de la Sorbonne,** ground zero for students (and their many noisy demonstrations). Around the winding streets behind the **Panthéon,** where French luminaries are laid to rest, you can still encounter plenty of academics arguing philosophy while sipping espresso, but today the 5e arrondissement is also one of Paris's most charming and sought-after (read: expensive) places to live.

Shop along **Rue Mouffetard** as Parisians do—all the while complaining about the high prices—for one of the best selections of runny cheeses, fresh breads, and charcuterie. Grab a seat in a bustling café, or follow the locals' lead and stand at the bar, where drinks are always cheaper. Film buffs won't have to look far to find one of the small cinema revival houses showing old American films in English (look for v.o., for *version originale*). Not far from le Mouffe is the gorgeous white **Grande**

Mosquée de Paris with its impressive minaret. Just beyond the mosque is the **Jardin des Plantes**—a large, if somewhat bland, botanical garden that is home to three natural history museums, most notably the **Grande Galerie de l'Évolution.** Inside, kids can marvel at enormous whale skeletons, along with all sorts of taxidermy. Some of Paris's most intriguing sites are in this neighborhood, including the **Musée de Cluny** and the innovative **Institut du Monde Arabe.** See ancient history mingle with modern life at the **Arènes de Lutèce,** a Roman amphitheater and favorite soccer pitch for neighborhood kids.

TOP ATTRACTIONS

FAMILY **Grande Galerie de l'Évolution** (*Great Hall of Evolution*). With a parade of taxidermied animals ranging from the tiniest dung beetle to the tallest giraffe, this four-story natural history museum in the Jardin des Plantes will perk up otherwise museum-weary kids. The flagship of three natural history museums in the garden, this restored 1889 building has a ceiling that changes color to suggest storms, twilight, or the hot savanna sun. Other must-sees are the gigantic skeleton of a blue whale and the stuffed royal rhino (he came from the menagerie at Versailles, where he was a pet of Louis XV). Kids 6 to 12 will enjoy La Galerie d'Enfants (The Children's Gallery): opened in 2010, it has bilingual interactive exhibits about the natural world. A lab stocked with microscopes often offers free workshops, and most of the staff speaks some English. Hang on to your ticket; it will get you a discount at the other museums within the Jardin des Plantes. ✉ *36 rue Geoffroy-St-Hilaire, Latin Quarter* ☎ *01–40–79–54–79* ⊕ *www.grandegaleriedelevolution. fr* 🎫 *€9; €11 combined with Children's Gallery* ☉ *Wed.–Mon. 10–6* Ⓜ *Place Monge, Censier-Daubenton.*

FAMILY **Institut du Monde Arabe.** This eye-catching metal-and-glass tower by architect Jean Nouvel cleverly uses metal diaphragms in the shape of square Arabic-style screens to work like a camera lens, opening and closing to control the flow of sunlight. The vast cultural center's layout is intended to reinterpret the traditional enclosed Arab courtyard. Inside, there are various spaces—among them a museum that explores the culture and religion of the 22 Arab League member nations. With the addition of elements from the Louvre's holdings and private donors, the museum's impressive collection includes Islamic art, artifacts, ceramics, and textiles, which are displayed on four floors. There is also a performance space, a sound-and-image center, a library, and a bookstore. Temporary exhibitions usually have information and an audioguide in English. Glass elevators whisk you to the ninth floor, where you can

10

sip mint tea in the rooftop café, Le Zyriab, while feasting on one of the best views in Paris. ⊠ *1 rue des Fossés-St-Bernard, Latin Quarter* ☎ *01–40–51–38–38* ⊕ *www.imarabe.org* 💲*€8* ⊗ *Tues.–Thurs. 10–6, Fri. 10–9:30, weekends 10–7* Ⓜ *Jussieu.*

FAMILY

Fodor's Choice

★

Jardin des Plantes (*Botanical Gardens*). Opened in 1640 and once known as the Jardin du Roi (or King's Garden), this sprawling patch of greenery is a neighborhood gem. It's home to several gardens and various museums, all housed in 19th-century buildings whose original architecture blends glass with ornate ironwork. If you have kids, take them to the excellent Grande Galerie de l'Évolution or one of the other natural history museums here: the Galerie de Paléontologie, stocked with dinosaur and other skeletons, and the recently renovated, rock-laden Galerie de Minéralogie. The botanical and rose gardens are impressive, and plant lovers won't want to miss the towering greenhouses (*serre* in French)— they are filled with one of the world's most extensive collections of tropical and desert flora. If the kids prefer fauna, visit the Ménagerie, a small zoo founded in 1794 whose animals once fed Parisians during the 1870 Prussian siege. The star attractions are Nénette, the grande-dame orangutan from Borneo, and her swinging friends in the monkey and ape house. If you need a break, there are three kiosk cafés in the Jardin. ⊠ *Entrances on Rue Geoffroy-St-Hilaire, Rue Cuvier, Rue de Buffon, and Quai St-Bernard, Latin Quarter* ☎ *01–40–79–56–01* ⊕ *www.jardindesplantes.net; www.mnhn.fr* 💲 *Museums €6–€11; zoo €13; greenhouses €6; gardens free* ⊗ *Museums Wed.–Mon. 10–5 or 6; zoo daily 9–5; gardens daily, hrs vary (check website for details)* Ⓜ *Gare d'Austerlitz, Jussieu; Place Monge, Censier-Daubenton for Grande Galerie de l'Évolution.*

Fodor's Choice

★

Musée de Cluny (*Musée National du Moyen-Age [National Museum of the Middle Ages]*). Built on the ruins of Roman baths, the Hôtel de Cluny has been a museum since medievalist Alexandre Du Sommerard established his collection here in 1844. The ornate 15th-century mansion was created for the abbot of Cluny, leader of the mightiest monastery in France. Symbols of the abbot's power surround the building, from the crenellated walls that proclaimed his independence from the king, to the carved Burgundian grapes twining up the entrance that symbolize his valuable vineyards. The scallop shells (*coquilles St-Jacques*) covering the facade are a symbol of religious pilgrimage, another important source of income for the abbot; the well-traveled pilgrimage route to Spain once ran around the corner along Rue St-Jacques. The highlight of the museum's collection is the world-famous *Dame à la Licorne* (*Lady and the Unicorn*) tapestry series, woven in the 16th century, probably in Belgium, and now presented in refurbished surroundings. The vermillion tapestries (Room 13) are an allegorical representation of the five senses. In each, a unicorn and a lion surround an elegant young woman against an elaborate *millefleur* (literally, "1,000 flowers") background. The enigmatic sixth tapestry is thought to be either a tribute to a sixth sense, perhaps intelligence, or a renouncement of the other senses. "To my only desire" is inscribed at the top. The collection also includes the original sculpted heads of the *Kings of Israel and Judah* from Notre-Dame, decapitated during the Revolution and discovered

CLOSE UP

Literary Lion

The English-language bookstore **Shakespeare & Company** (*37 rue de la Bûcherie, 01–43–25–40–93* ⊕ *www.shakespeareandcompany. com*) is one of Paris's most eccentric and lovable literary institutions. Founded by George Whitman, the maze of new and used books has offered a sense of community (and often a bed) to wandering writers since the 1950s. The store takes its name from Sylvia Beach's original Shakespeare & Co., which opened in 1919 at 12 rue d'Odéon, welcoming the likes of Ernest Hemingway, James Baldwin, and James Joyce. Beach famously bucked the system when she published Joyce's *Ulysses* in 1922, but her original store closed in 1941. After the war Whitman picked up the gauntlet, naming his own bookstore after its famous predecessor.

When Whitman passed away in 2011, heavy-hearted locals left candles and flowers in front of his iconic storefront. He is buried in the literati-laden Père-Lachaise cemetery; however, his legacy lives on through his daughter Sylvia, who runs the shop and welcomes a new generation of Paris dreamers. Walk up the almost impossibly narrow stairs to the second floor and you'll still see laptops and sleeping bags tucked between the aging volumes and under dusty daybeds; it's sort of like a hippie commune. A revolving cast of characters helps out in the shop or cooks meals for fellow residents. They're in good company; Henry Miller, Samuel Beckett, and William Burroughs are among the famous writers to benefit from the Whitman family hospitality.

in 1977 in the basement of a French bank. The *frigidarium* (Room 9) is a stunning reminder of the city's cold-water Roman baths; the soaring space, painstakingly renovated, houses temporary exhibits. Also notable is the pocket-size chapel (Room 20) with its elaborate Gothic ceiling. Outside, in Place Paul Painlevé, is a charming medieval-style garden where you can see flora depicted in the unicorn tapestries. The free audio guide in English is highly recommended. For a different kind of auditory experience, check the event listings; concerts of medieval music are often staged Sunday afternoon and Monday at lunchtime (€6).

Note that extensive renovations, intended to vastly improve accessibility and transform the museum experience, are under way. They are slated to be complete sometime in 2020; in the interim, check the website for select exhibit closures. ⊠ *6 pl. Paul-Painlevé, Latin Quarter* ☎ *01–53–73–78–00* ⊕ *www.musee-moyenage.fr* 🎫 *€8 (free 1st Sun. of month); €9 during temporary exhibitions* ☉ *Wed.–Mon. 9:15–5:45* Ⓜ *Cluny–La Sorbonne.*

NEED A BREAK? **Place de la Contrescarpe.** This popular square behind the Panthéon attracts locals, students, and Hemingway enthusiasts (he once lived around the corner). It has a small-town feel during the day and a lively atmosphere after dusk when the bars and eateries fill up. Try Café Delmas (*2 pl. de la Contrescarpe, 01–43–26–51–26*), which features a large terrace and serves food daily until 2 am; there's a diner-style restaurant next door for more relaxed meals. ⊠ *Latin Quarter* Ⓜ *Place Monge.*

Panthéon. Rome has St. Peter's, London has St. Paul's, and Paris has the Panthéon, whose enormous dome dominates the Left Bank. Built as the church of Ste-Geneviève, the patron saint of Paris, it was later converted to an all-star mausoleum for some of France's biggest names, including Voltaire, Zola, Dumas, Rousseau, and Hugo. Pierre and Marie Curie were reinterred here together in 1995. Begun in 1764,

> **THE 13E ARRONDISSEMENT**
>
> The village-like neighborhood of La Butte aux Cailles (in the 13e arrondissement, south of Place d'Italie) is a fun destination with a hip crowd, not far from the Quartier Latin if you want a break from the tourists.

the building was almost complete when the French Revolution erupted. By then, architect Jacques-German Soufflot had died—supposedly from worrying that the 220-foot-high dome would collapse. He needn't have fretted: the dome was so perfect that Foucault used it in his famous pendulum test to prove the Earth rotates on its axis. Time has taken its toll on the Panthéon, and the structure is now in the midst of an extensive, multiyear overhaul; however, the crypt and nave remain accessible to the public, and the famous pendulum has been returned to its place of honor. ⊠ *Pl. du Panthéon, Latin Quarter* ☎ *01–44–32–18–00* ⊕ *www. paris-pantheon.fr* ⊠ *€7.50* ☉ *Apr.–Sept., daily 10–6:30; Oct.–Mar., daily 10–6* Ⓜ *Cardinal Lemoine; RER: Luxembourg.*

Fodor'sChoice ★ **Rue Mouffetard.** This winding cobblestone street is one of the city's oldest and was once a Roman road leading south from Lutetia (the Roman name for Paris) to Italy. The upper half is dotted with restaurants and bars that cater to tourists and students; the lower half is the setting of a lively morning market, Tuesday through Sunday. The highlight of le Mouffe, though, is the stretch in between where the shops spill into the street with luscious offerings such as roasting chickens and potatoes, rustic *saucisson,* pâtés, and pungent cheeses, especially at Androuët (No. 134). If you're here in the morning, Le Mouffetard Café (No. 116) is a good place to stop for a Continental breakfast (about €10). If it's apéritif time, head to Place de la Contrescarpe for a cocktail, or enjoy a glass of wine at Cave La Bourgogne (No. 144). Prefer to just do a little noshing? Sample the chocolates at de Neuville (No. 108) and Mococha (No. 89). For one of the best baguettes in Paris and other delicious organic offerings, detour to nearby Boulanger de Monge, at 123 rue Monge. Note that most shops are closed Monday. ⊠ *Latin Quarter* Ⓜ *Place Monge, Censier-Daubenton.*

WORTH NOTING

FAMILY **Arènes de Lutèce** (*Lutetia Amphitheater*). This Roman amphitheater, designed as a theater and circus, was almost completely destroyed by barbarians in AD 280. The site was rediscovered in 1869, and you can still see part of the stage and tiered seating. Along with the remains of the baths at Cluny, the arena constitutes rare evidence of the powerful Roman city of Lutetia that flourished on the Rive Gauche in the 3rd century. It's a favorite spot for picnicking, pickup soccer, or *boules.*

Hemingway's Paris

There is a saying: "Everyone has two countries, his or her own—and France." For the Lost Generation after World War I, these words rang particularly true. Lured by favorable exchange rates, free-flowing alcohol, and a booming arts scene, many American writers, composers, and painters moved to Paris in the 1920s and 1930s, Ernest Hemingway among them. He arrived in Paris with his first wife, Hadley, in December 1921 and headed for the Rive Gauche—the Hôtel de l'Angleterre, to be exact (still operating at 44 rue Jacob). To celebrate their arrival the couple went to the Café de la Paix for a meal they nearly couldn't afford.

Hemingway worked as a journalist and quickly made friends with expat writers such as Gertrude Stein and Ezra Pound. In 1922 the Hemingways moved to 74 rue du Cardinal Lemoine, a bare-bones apartment with no running water (his writing studio was around the corner, on the top floor of 39 rue Descartes). Then, in 1924, they and their baby son settled at 113 rue Notre-Dame des Champs. Much of *The Sun Also Rises,* Hemingway's first serious novel, was written at nearby café La Closerie des Lilas. These were the years in which he forged his writing style, paring his sentences down to the pith—as he noted in *A Moveable Feast,* "hunger was good discipline." There were some especially hungry months when Hemingway gave up journalism for short-story writing, and the family was "very poor and very happy."

They weren't happy for long: in 1926, as *The Sun Also Rises* made him famous, Hemingway left Hadley. The next year, he wed his mistress, Pauline Pfeiffer, and moved to 6 rue Férou, near the Musée du Luxembourg.

For gossip and books, and to pick up his mail, Papa would visit Shakespeare & Company (then at 12 rue de l'Odéon). For cash and cocktails, Hemingway usually headed to the upscale Rive Droite. He collected the former at the Guaranty Trust Company, at 1 rue des Italiens. He found the latter, when he was flush, at the bar of the landmark Hôtel de Crillon, on Place de la Concorde next to the American Embassy, or, when poor, at the Caves Mura, at 19 rue d'Antin, or Harry's Bar, still in brisk business at 5 rue Daunou. Hemingway's loyal and legendary association with the Hôtel Ritz was sealed during the Liberation in 1944, when he strode in at the head of his platoon and "liberated" the joint by ordering martinis all around. Here Hemingway asked Mary Welsh to become his fourth wife, and here also, the story goes, a trunk full of notes regarding his first years in Paris turned up in the 1950s, giving him the raw material for writing *A Moveable Feast.*

✉ *Entrances on Rues Monge, de Navarre, and des Arènes, Latin Quarter* ☎ *01–45–35–02–56* 🎟 *Free* ⏱ *Mar., daily 8–7; Apr. and Sept., daily 8 am–8:30 pm; May–Aug., daily 8 am–9:30 pm; Oct.–Feb., daily 8–5:45* Ⓜ *Place Monge, Cardinal Lemoine, Jussieu.*

La Grande Mosquée de Paris. This awe-inspiring white mosque, built between 1922 and 1926, has tranquil arcades and a minaret decorated in the style of Moorish Spain. Enjoy sweet mint tea and an exotic pastry in the charming courtyard tea salon or tuck into some couscous in the restaurant. Prayer rooms are not open to sightseers, but there are inexpensive—and quite rustic—hammams, or Turkish steam baths, with scrubs and massages offered to women and men on separate days (check website for times and prices). ✉ *2 bis, pl. du Puits de l'Ermite, entrance to tea salon and restaurant at 39 rue Geoffroy St-Hillaire, Latin Quarter* ☎ *01–45–35–97–33,* ⊕ *www.mosqueedeparis.net* 💲 *€3* ⊙ *Sat.–Thurs. 9–noon and 2–7 (until 6 in winter); open Fri. for worship only* Ⓜ *Place Monge.*

La Sorbonne *(Paris IV)*. Unless your French is good enough to justify joining a 90-minute group tour (€9, by reservation only), you can't get into the city's most famous university without a student ID—but it's still fun to hang out with the young scholars. Although La Sorbonne remains the soul of the Quartier Latin, it is only one of several campuses that make up the public Université de Paris. ✉ *1 rue Victor Cousin, Latin Quarter* 📧 *visites.sorbonne@ac-paris.fr for tour reservations* ⊕ *www. sorbonne.fr* Ⓜ *Cluny–La Sorbonne.*

OFF THE BEATEN PATH

Le Musée de la Préfecture de Police. Crime buffs will enjoy this museum hidden on the second floor of the 5e arrondissement's police station. Although the exhibits are in French only, the photographs, letters, drawings, and memorabilia pertaining to some of the city's most sensational crimes are easy enough to follow. Among the 2,000-odd relics you'll find a guillotine, old uniforms, and remnants of the World War II occupation—including what's left of a firing post, German machine guns, and the star insignias worn by Jews. ✉ *4 rue de la Montagne Ste-Geneviève, Latin Quarter* ☎ *01–44–41–52–50* 💲 *Free* ⊙ *Weekdays 9–5:30* Ⓜ *Maubert-Mutualité.*

Manufacture des Gobelins. Tapestries have been woven at this spot in southeastern Paris, on the banks of the long-covered Bièvre River, since 1662. The Galerie des Gobelins stages exhibitions on two light-flooded floors, highlighting tapestries, furnishings, timepieces, and other treasures mostly drawn from the state collection. Guided visits to the Manufacture (in French, by reservation only) allow a fascinating look at weavers—from students to accomplished veterans—as they work on tapestries and rugs that take years to complete. Also on-site is a highly selective school that teaches weaving, plus a workshop charged with repairing and restoring furnishings belonging to the French government, which are also stored here in a vast concrete warehouse. ✉ *42 av. des Gobelins, Latin Quarter* ☎ *01–44–08–53–49* ⊕ *www.mobiliernational. culture.gouv.fr* 💲 *€6 temporary exhibits (free last Sun. of month); €9 workshop; €11 workshop and exhibits* ⊙ *Galerie Tues.–Sun. 11–6; workshop tours Sat. at 2:30 and 4* ☞ *Come early as workshop tour places are limited* Ⓜ *Gobelins.*

Place St-Michel. This square was named for Gabriel Davioud's grandiose 1860 fountain sculpture of St. Michael vanquishing Satan—a loaded political gesture from Napoléon III's go-to guy, Baron Haussmann, who hoped St-Michel would quell the Revolutionary fervor of the neighborhood. The fountain is often used as a meeting point for both local students and young tourists. ✉ *Latin Quarter* Ⓜ *Métro or RER: St-Michel.*

St-Étienne-du-Mont. This jewel box of a church has been visited by several popes, owing to the fact that Ste-Geneviève (the patron saint of Paris) was buried here before Revolutionaries burned her remains. Built on the ruins of a 6th-century abbey founded by Clovis, the first King of the Franks, it has a unique combination of Gothic, Renaissance, and early Baroque elements, which adds a certain warmth that is lacking in other Parisian churches of pure Gothic style. Here you'll find the only rood screen left in the city—an ornate 16th-century masterwork of carved wood spanning the nave like a bridge, with a spiral staircase on either side. Observe the organ (dating from 1631, it is the city's oldest) and the marker in the floor near the entrance that commemorates an archbishop of Paris who was stabbed to death here by a defrocked priest in 1857. Guided tours are free, but a small offering is appreciated; call for times. ⊠ *Pl. Ste-Geneviève, 30 rue Descartes, Latin Quarter* ☎ *01–43–54–11–79* ⊕ *www.saintetiennedumont.fr* ۞ *Tues.–Fri. 8:45–7:45, Sat. 8:45–12 and 2–7:45, Sun. 8:45–12:15 and 2:30–7:45* Ⓜ *Cardinal Lemoine.*

St-Julien-le-Pauvre. This tiny shrine in the shadow of Notre-Dame is one of the three oldest churches in Paris. Founded in 1045, it became a meeting place for university students in the 12th century and was Dante's church of choice when he was in town writing his *Divine Comedy.* Today's structure dates mostly from the 1600s, but keep an eye out for older pillars, which crawl with carvings of demons. You can maximize your time inside by attending one of the classical or gospel concerts held here. Alternately, go outside and simply perch on a bench in the garden to relish the view of Notre-Dame. ⊠ *1 rue St-Julien-le-Pauvre, Latin Quarter* ☎ *01–43–54–52–16* ⊕ *www.sjlpmelkites.fr* ۞ *Mon. and Wed. 9–noon; Tues., Thurs., and Fri. 9–4* Ⓜ *St-Michel.*

ST-GERMAIN-DES-PRÉS

GETTING ORIENTED

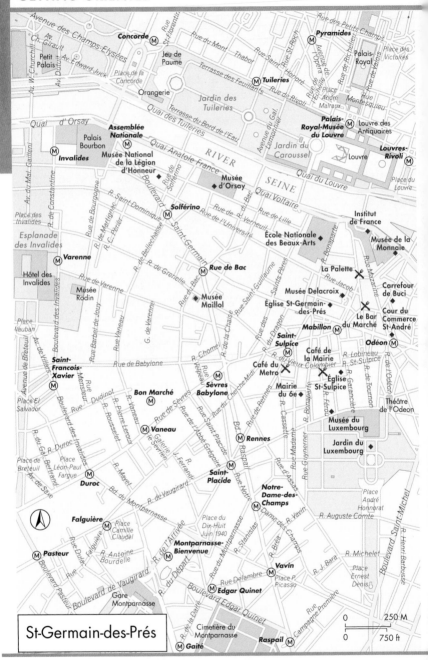

St-Germain-des-Prés

TOP REASONS TO GO

Musée d'Orsay. The magnificent vaulted ceiling and abundant natural light inside this train station–turned–art museum are reminders of why the Impressionist painters thought *les gares* were the cathedrals of the 19th century.

Jardin du Luxembourg. Take in a puppet show, wander the tree-lined gravel paths, or simply laze by the fountain in one of the city's most elegant gardens.

Boulevard St-Germain. The main artery of this chic neighborhood is edged with shops and galleries. The top boutiques are clustered around Rue de Rennes.

Café life. This is prime people-watching territory. So pull up a seat at a comfy café, order a coffee, beer, or *boisson*, and prepare to watch the world go by.

MAKING THE MOST OF YOUR TIME

Aim for an early start—savor a *café crème* at a café along the river and get to the Musée d'Orsay early, when crowds are thinner. Leave some time for window-shopping around Boulevard St-Germain and Rue de Rennes on your way to the Jardin du Luxembourg. You might want to plan your visit on a day other than Monday, when the Orsay, many of the art galleries, and even some shops are closed.

GETTING HERE

The St-Germain neighborhood is in the 6e arrondissement and a bit of the 7e. To get to the heart of this area, take the Line 4 métro to St-Germain-des-Prés. For shopping, use this station or St-Sulpice. It's a short walk to the Jardin du Luxembourg, or take the RER B line to the Luxembourg station. For the Musée d'Orsay, take the Line 12 métro to Solferino or the RER C line to the Musée d'Orsay.

BEST CAFÉS

Café de la Mairie. Overlooking the St-Sulpice church, this retro café recalls the Latin Quarter of yesteryear before the proliferation of luxury boutiques and trendy eateries. ✉ 8 pl. St-Sulpice, St-Germain-des-Prés ☎ 01–43–26–67–82 Ⓜ St-Sulpice.

Café du Métro. You can refuel at this friendly café-brasserie after a shopping spree around Rue de Rennes. Main menu items are pricey, but the free Wi-Fi compensates. Closed Sunday. ✉ 67 rue de Rennes, St-Germain-des-Prés ☎ 01–45–48–58–56 ⊕ www.cafedumetro.com Ⓜ St-Sulpice.

La Palette. The terrace of this corner café, opened in 1902, is a favorite haunt of local gallery owners and Beaux Arts students. Light fare is available throughout the day. ✉ 43 rue de Seine, St-Germain-des-Prés ☎ 01–43–26–68–15 ⊕ www.cafelapaletteparis.com Ⓜ Mabillon, Odéon.

Le Bar du Marché. Grab a sidewalk table—if you're lucky—or stand at the bar, skip the food, and order an apéritif at this constantly packed little place. The feel is classic French with a splash of kitsch, right down to the waiters in overalls and berets. ✉ 75 rue de Seine, St-Germain-des-Prés ☎ 01–43–26–55–15 Ⓜ Mabillon.

Sightseeing
★★★★★
Dining
★★★
Lodging
★★★★★
Shopping
★★★★★
Nightlife
★★

If you had to choose the most classically Parisian neighborhood, this would be it. St-Germain-des-Prés has it all: genteel blocks lined with upscale art galleries, storied cafés, designer boutiques, atmospheric restaurants, and a fine selection of museums. Cast your eyes upward after dark and you may spy a frescoed ceiling in a tony apartment. These historic streets can get quite crowded, especially in summer, so mind your elbows and plunge in.

Updated by
Virginia Power

This *quartier* is named for the oldest church in Paris, **St-Germain-des-Prés**, and it's become a prized address for Parisians and expats alike. Despite its pristine facade, though, this wasn't always silver-spoon territory. Claude Monet and Auguste Renoir shared a cramped studio at 20 rue Visconti, and the young Picasso barely eked out an existence in a room on Rue de Seine. By the 1950s St-Germain bars bopped with jazz, and the likes of Albert Camus, Jean-Paul Sartre, and Simone de Beauvoir puffed away on Gauloises while discussing the meaninglessness of life at Café Flore. Nearby in the 7e arrondissement, the star attraction is the **Musée d'Orsay,** home to a world-class collection of Impressionist paintings in a converted Belle Époque railway station on the Seine. It's famous for having some of Paris's longest lines, so a visit to the Orsay should be planned with care. There are also several smaller museums worth a stop, including the impressive **Musée Maillol,** a private collection in an elegant mansion dedicated to the work of sculptor Aristide Maillol. The **Musée Delacroix,** in lovely Place Furstenberg, is home to a small collection of the Romantic master's works. Not far away is the stately **Église St-Sulpice,** where you can see two impressive Delacroix frescoes.

Paris is a city for walking, and St-Germain is one of the most enjoyable places to practice the art of the *flâneur,* or stroll. Make your way to the busy crossroads of **Carrefour de Buci,** dotted with cafés, flower markets, and shops. Rue de l'Ancienne Comédie is so named because it was the first home of the legendary Comédie Française; it cuts through to busy Place de l'Odéon and Rue St-André des Arts. Along the latter you can find the historic **Cour du Commerce St-André** (opposite No. 66), a charming cobbled passageway filled with cafés—including, halfway down on the left, Paris's oldest, Le Procope.

Make sure you save some energy for the exquisite **Jardin du Luxembourg,** a vintage French garden whose tree-lined paths have attracted fashionable fresh-air fans through the ages.

TOP ATTRACTIONS

FAMILY
Fodor's Choice
★

Carrefour de Buci. Just behind the neighborhood's namesake St-Germain church, this colorful crossroads (*carrefour* means "intersection") was once a notorious Rive Gauche landmark. During the French Revolution, the army enrolled its first volunteers here. It was also here that thousands of royalists and priests lost their heads during the 10-month wave of public executions known as the Reign of Terror. There's certainly nothing sinister about the area today, though; brightly colored flowers are for sale alongside take-out ice cream and other sweet treats. Devotees of the superb, traditional bakery Carton (at 6 rue de Buci) line up for fresh breads and pastries (try the *pain aux raisins, tuiles* cookies, and *tarte au citron*). ⊠ *Intersection of Rues Mazarine, Dauphine, and de Buci, St-Germain-des-Prés* Ⓜ *Mabillon.*

Église St-Germain-des-Prés. Paris's oldest church was built to shelter a simple shard of wood, said to be a relic of Jesus' cross brought back from Spain in AD 542. Vikings came down the Seine and sacked the sanctuary, and Revolutionaries used it to store gunpowder. Yet the elegant building has defied history's abuses: its 11th-century Romanesque tower continues to be the central symbol of the neighborhood. The colorful 19th-century frescoes in the nave are by Hippolyte Flandrin, a pupil of the classical master Ingres; and the Saint Benoit chapel contains the tomb of philosopher René Descartes. Step inside for spiritual nourishment, or pause in the square to people-watch—there's usually a street musician tucked against the church wall, out of the wind. The church stages superb organ concerts and recitals. See the website for details. ⊠ *Pl. St-Germain-des-Prés, St-Germain-des-Prés* ☎ *01–55–42–81–10* ⊕ *www.eglise-sgp.org* ⊘ *Daily 8–7:45* Ⓜ *St-Germain-des-Prés.*

Fodor's Choice
★

Église St-Sulpice. Dubbed the Cathedral of the Rive Gauche, this enormous 17th-century Baroque church has entertained some unlikely christenings—among them those of the Marquis de Sade and Charles Baudelaire—as well as the nuptials of novelist Victor Hugo. More recently, the church played a supporting role in the best-selling novel *The Da Vinci Code,* and it now draws scores of tourists to its obelisk (part of a *gnomon,* a device used to determine exact time and the equinoxes, built in the 1730s). Other notable features include the exterior's asymmetrical towers and two magnificent Delacroix frescoes, which can be seen in a chapel to the right of the entrance. In the square just in front, view Visconti's magnificent 19th-century fountain. It's especially beautiful at night. ⊠ *Pl. St-Sulpice, 2 rue Palatine, St-Germain-des-Prés* ☎ *01–42–34–59–60* ⊕ *www.paris.catholique.fr/-saint-sulpice* ⊘ *Daily 8–7:30* Ⓜ *St-Sulpice, St-Germain-des-Pres, Mabillon.*

The cafés in St-Germain-des-Prés are perfect for people-watching along with coffee, dinner, or an apéro (cocktail).

QUICK BITES

Les Editeurs. Once favored by the Parisian publishing set, Les Editeurs is a casual, occasionally noisy café where you can sip a *kir* (white wine with black-currant syrup) from a perch on the skinny sidewalk or at an inside table shadowed by book-lined walls. The menu offers a twist on French classics. ⊠ *4 carrefour de l'Odéon, St-Germain-des-Prés* ☎ *01–43–26–67–76* ⊕ *www.lesediteurs.fr* Ⓜ *Odéon.*

FAMILY
Fodor'sChoice
★

Jardin du Luxembourg. Everything that is charming, unique, and befuddling about Parisian parks can be found in the Luxembourg Gardens: cookie-cutter trees, ironed-and-pressed walkways, sculpted flower beds, and immaculate emerald lawns meant for admiring, not necessarily for lounging. The tree- and bench-lined paths are a marvelous reprieve from the bustle of the two neighborhoods it borders: the Quartier Latin and St-Germain-des-Prés. Beautifully austere during the winter months, the garden grows intoxicating as spring brings blooming beds of daffodils, tulips, and hyacinths, and the circular pool teems with wooden sailboats nudged along by children. The park's northern boundary is dominated by the Palais du Luxembourg, which houses the Sénat (Senate), one of two chambers that make up the Parliament. The original inspiration for the gardens came from Marie de Medici, nostalgic for the Boboli Gardens of her native Florence. She is commemorated by the Fontaine de Medicis.

As you stroll the paths, you might be surprised by a familiar sight: one of the original (miniature) casts of the Statue of Liberty was installed in the gardens in 1906. Check out the rotating photography exhibits hanging on the perimeter fence near the entrance on Boulevard St-Michel and Rue de Vaugirard. If you want to burn off that breakfast *pain au chocolat*, there's a well-maintained trail around the perimeter that is frequented by gentrified joggers. Gendarmes regularly walk the grounds to ensure park rules are enforced; follow guidelines posted on entry gates. ⊠ *Bordered by Bd. St-Michel and Rues de Vaugirard, de Medicis, Guynemer, Auguste-Comte, and d'Assas, St-Germain-des-Prés* ⊕ *www.senat.fr/visite/jardin* ⊠ *Free* ⊙ *Daily 7:30–dusk (depending on season)* Ⓜ *Odéon; RER: B Luxembourg.*

FAMILY **Musée d'Orsay.** Opened in 1986, this gorgeously renovated Belle Époque
Fodor's Choice train station displays a world-famous collection of Impressionist and
★ Postimpressionist paintings on three floors. To visit the exhibits in a roughly chronologic manner, start on the first floor, take the escalators to the top, and end on the second. If you came to see the biggest names here, head straight for the top floor and work your way down. English audio guides and free color-coded museum maps (both available just past the ticket booths) will help you plot your route.

■ TIP→ Lines here are among the worst in Paris. Book ahead online or buy a Museum Pass, then go directly to entrance C. Otherwise, go early. Thursday evening the museum is open until 9:45 pm and less crowded. Don't miss the views of Sacré-Coeur from the balcony—this is the Paris that inspired the Impressionists. The Musée d'Orsay is closed Monday, unlike the Pompidou and the Louvre, which are closed Tuesday. ⊠ *1 rue de la Légion d'Honneur, St-Germain-des-Prés* ☎ *01–40–49–48–14* ⊕ *www.musee-orsay.fr* ⊠ *€11; €8.50 after 4:30, except Thurs. after 6; free the first Sun. of every month* ⊙ *Tues., Wed., Fri. and weekends 9:30–6, Thurs. 9:30 am–9:45 pm* Ⓜ *Solférino; RER: Musée d'Orsay.*

Musée du Luxembourg. Located in the northwestern corner of the Luxembourg Gardens, this former orangery for the Palais du Luxembourg became the city's first public painting gallery in 1884. It now features excellent temporary exhibits that are well worth a visit. ⊠ *19 rue de Vaugirard, St-Germain-des-Prés* ☎ *01–40–13–62–00* ⊕ *www.museeduluxembourg.fr* ⊠ *€12* ⊙ *Mon. and Fri. 10–9:30; Tues.–Thurs. and weekends 10–7. Last entry 45 min before closing* Ⓜ *Rennes, St-Sulpice.*

WORTH NOTING

Cour du Commerce St-André. Like an 18th-century engraving come to life, this charming street arcade is a remnant of *ancien* Paris with its uneven cobblestones, antique roofs, and old-world facades. Famed for its rabble-rousing inhabitants—journalist Jean-Paul Marat ran the Revolutionary newspaper *L'Ami du Peuple* at No. 8, and the agitator Georges Danton lived at No. 20—it is also home to Le Procope, Paris's oldest café. The passageway contains a turret from the 12th-century wall of Philippe-Auguste, which is visible through the windows of Un Dimanche à Paris, a chocolate shop–pastry atelier at No. 4. ⊠ *Linking Bd. St-Germain and Rue St-André-des-Arts, St-Germain-des-Prés* Ⓜ *Odéon.*

École Nationale des Beaux-Arts. Occupying three large mansions near the Seine, the national fine arts school—today the breeding ground for

painters, sculptors, and architects—was once the site of a convent founded in 1608 by Marguerite de Valois, the first wife of Henri IV. After the Revolution the convent was turned into a museum for works of art salvaged from buildings attacked by the rampaging French mobs. In 1816 the museum was turned into a school. Today its peaceful courtyards host contemporary installations and exhibits. The courtyard and school galleries are accessible on 90-minute guided tours. ⊠ *14 rue Bonaparte, St-Germain-des-Prés* ☎ *01–47–03–50–00* ⊕ *www.beauxartsparis. com* ▦ *€7.50* ⊗ *Tues.–Sun. 1–7* Ⓜ *St-Germain-des-Prés.*

Institut de France. The Institut de France is one of the country's most revered cultural institutions, and its golden dome is one of the Rive Gauche's most impressive landmarks. The site was once punctuated by the Tour de Nesle (forming part of Philippe-Auguste's medieval fortification wall, the tower had many royal occupants—including Henry V of England). Then, in 1661, wealthy Cardinal Mazarin willed 2 million French *livres* (pounds) for the construction of a college here. It's also home to the Académie Française: the protectors of the French language. The edicts issued by this esoteric group of 40 *perpétuel* (lifelong) members are happily ignored by the French public. The interior is off-limits to visitors. ⊠ *Pl. de l'Institut, St-Germain-des-Prés* ⊕ *www.institut-de-france.fr* Ⓜ *Pont Neuf.*

Mairie du 6e. The *mairie* (town hall) of the 6e arrondissement often stages impressive free art exhibitions and other cultural offerings. Stop by the *accueil* (reception desk) on the ground floor to see what's on or to pick up information on other timely happenings around this artsy district. ⊠ *78 rue Bonaparte, St-Germain-des-Prés* ☎ *01–40–46–75–06* ⊕ *www.mairie6.paris.fr* ▦ *Free* ⊗ *Weekdays 8:30–5, Sat. 9–12:30* Ⓜ *Saint-Sulpice.*

Musée Delacroix. The final home of artist Eugène Delacroix (1798–1863) contains only a small collection of his sketches and drawings. But you can check out the lovely studio he had built in the large garden at the back to work on frescoes he created for St-Sulpice Church, where they remain on display today. The museum also plays host to temporary exhibitions, such as Delacroix's experiments with photography. France's foremost Romantic painter had the good luck to live on Place Furstenberg, one of the smallest, most romantic squares in Paris: seeing it is reason enough to come. ⊠ *6 rue Furstenberg, St-Germain-des-Prés* ☎ *01–44–41–86–50* ⊕ *www.musee-delacroix.fr* ▦ *€7; €15 with same-day admission to the Louvre* ⊗ *Wed.–Mon. 9:30–5* Ⓜ *St-Germain-des-Prés.*

CLOSE UP

Dueling Cafés

Les Deux Magots (*6 pl. St-Germain-des-Prés*) and the neighboring **Café de Flore** (*172 bd. St-Germain*) have been duking it out on this bustling corner in St-Germain for more than a century. Les Deux Magots, the snootier of the two, is named for the two Chinese figurines, or *magots,* inside, and has hosted the likes of Oscar Wilde, Hemingway, James Joyce, and Richard Wright. Jean-Paul Sartre and Simone du Beauvoir frequented both establishments, though they are claimed by the Flore. The two cafés remain packed, but these days you're more likely to rub shoulders with tourists than with philosophers. Still, if you're in search of that certain je ne sais quoi of the Rive Gauche, you can do no better than to station yourself at one of the sidewalk tables—or at a window table on a wintry day—to watch the passing parade. Stick to a croissant and an overpriced coffee, or enjoy an early-evening apéritif; the food is expensive and nothing special.

Musée de la Monnaie. Louis XVI transferred the royal mint to this imposing mansion in the late 18th century. It was moved again (to Pessac, near Bordeaux) in 1973; however, weights and measures, medals, and limited-edition coins are still made here, and the site houses a museum devoted to currency. The Musée de la Monnaie has an extensive collection of coins and related artifacts, plus workshops where you can watch artisans in action as they mint, mold, sculpt, polish, and engrave using century-old techniques. Refreshed public spaces host cultural programs and temporary contemporary art exhibitions. ⊠ *11 quai de Conti, St-Germain-des-Prés* 🕾 *01–40–46–56–66* ⊕ *www.monnaiedeparis.fr* 🖃 *€12* ⊗ *Mon.–Sat. 11–7* Ⓜ *Pont Neuf, Odéon.*

Musée Maillol. Bronzes by Art Deco sculptor Aristide Maillol (1861–1944), whose voluptuous, stylized nudes adorn the Tuileries Gardens, can be admired at this handsome mansion lovingly restored by his former model and muse, Dina Vierny. The museum is particularly moving because it's Vierny's personal collection. She met Maillol when she was a teenager and he was already an old man. The stunning life-size drawings upstairs are both erotic and tender—age gazing on youth with fondness and longing. The museum often stages temporary exhibits that are worth the visit. ⊠ *61 rue de Grenelle, St-Germain-des-Prés* 🕾 *01–42–22–59–58* ⊕ *www.museemaillol.com* ⊗ *Daily 10:30–7* Ⓜ *Rue du Bac.*

Musée National de la Légion d'Honneur (*Hôtel de Salm*). A must for military-history buffs, the National Museum of the Legion of Honor is dedicated to French and foreign military leaders. Housed in an elegant mansion just across from the Musée d'Orsay, it features a broad collection of military decorations, themed paintings, and video tributes to various luminaries—including U.S. general Dwight Eisenhower, a Légion member who led the Allied liberation of France in 1944. The palatial complex was completed in 1788 and acquired by the Legion of Honor in 1804. Admission includes an English audioguide. ⊠ *2 rue de la Légion d'Honneur, St-Germain-des-Prés* 🕾 *01–40–62–84–25* ⊕ *www.legiondhonneur.fr* 🖃 *Free* ⊗ *Wed.–Sun. 1–6* Ⓜ *Solférino; RER: Musée d'Orsay.*

12

MONTPARNASSE

GETTING ORIENTED

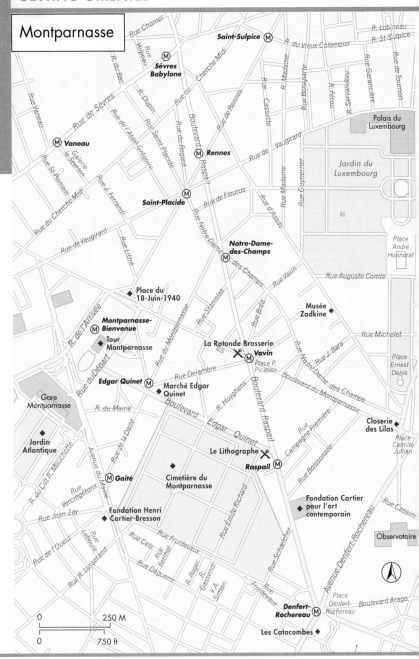

Montparnasse

Rue Chomel
Rue Velpeau
Rue du Bac
Saint-Sulpice Ⓜ
R. du Vieux Colombier
R. St-Sulpice
R. Lobineau
Ⓜ Sèvres Babylone
Rue du Cherche-Midi
Rue de Sèvres
R. Dupin
R. de l'Abbé Grégoire
Rue-Saint-Placide
Rue du Regard
Boulevard Raspail
Rue de Rennes
Rue Cassette
R. Madame
R. Bonaparte
R. Férou
R. Servandoni
Hugomès
Rue Garancière
Rue de Tournon

Palais du Luxembourg

Rue Vaneau
Ⓜ **Vaneau**
Galerie le Seurlen
Rue St-Romain
Rue du Cherche Midi
Rue J. Ferrandi
Rue de Vaugirard
Rue Littré
Rue de Vaugirard
Rue du Montparnasse
Rue du Départ
R. de l'Arrivée

Ⓜ **Rennes**
Rue de Vaugirard
Rue de Fleurus
Rue Notre-Dame-des-Champs
Rue d'Assas
Rue Madame
Rue Guynemer

Jardin du Luxembourg

Saint-Placide
Ⓜ

Notre-Dame-des-Champs
Ⓜ

Place André Honnorat

Rue Auguste Comte

◆ Place du 18-Juin-1940
Rue Stanislas
Rue Bréa
Rue Vavin

Rue Michelet

Place Ernest Denis

Montparnasse-Bienvenue
Ⓜ
◆ Tour Montparnasse

Gare Montparnasse

La Rotonde Brasserie
✕ Ⓜ **Vavin**
Place P. Picasso
Rue Delambre
Rue Notre-Dame-des-Champs
Rue J.-Bara

Edgar Quinet Ⓜ
◆ Marché Edgar Quinet
R. du Maine
R. Huyghens
Boulevard Raspail
Boulevard du Montparnasse

Closerie des Lilas ◆
Place Camille Jullian

Jardin Atlantique ◆
R. de la Gaîté
Avenue du Maine
Boulevard Edgar Quinet
Rue Campagne-Première
Rue Boissonade

Ⓜ **Gaîté**
◆ Cimetière du Montparnasse
Le Lithographe ✕
Raspail Ⓜ

R. du Cdt. R. Mouchotte
Rue Vercingétorix
Rue Jean Zay
Rue de l'Ouest
Rue Ledoux
Rue R. Losserand
Rue Cels
Rue Ferrat
Rue Froidevaux
Rue Émile Richard
Rue Daguerre
R. Roger
Gassendi
V.A. Simon
Rue Schoelcher
Rue Froidevaux

Fondation Henri Cartier-Bresson ◆

Fondation Cartier pour l'art contemporain ◆
Rue Cassini

Observatoire

Avenue Denfert-Rochereau

Denfert-Rochereau Ⓜ
Place Denfert-Rochereau
Boulevard Arago

Les Catacombes ◆

0 —— 250 M
0 —— 750 ft

TOP REASONS TO GO

Catacombs. History buffs, lovers of the macabre, and the just plain curious can make an unforgettable descent into Paris's underground bastion of bones. Claustrophobic folks, however, need not apply.

Fondation Cartier pour l'art contemporain. Connoisseurs of cutting-edge art will appreciate what's on view here. The building itself was designed by Jean Nouvel, the avant-garde darling of Paris architecture.

Fondation Henri Cartier-Bresson. Photography fans shouldn't miss the chance to see Cartier-Bresson's restored atelier, featuring a small collection of his work plus photographs from young artists.

The Tour Montparnasse. Even though this 680-foot black behemoth of a skyscraper is considered one of the biggest eyesores in Paris, its open-air roof terrace is still one of the best spots to see the City of Light.

BEST CAFÉS

La Rotonde Brasserie. A second home to foreign artists and political exiles in the '20s and '30s, La Rotonde has a less exotic but faithful clientele today. It's still a very pleasant place to have coffee or a quick bite on the sunny terrace. If you want a heartier meal, head inside for a traditional French dining experience. ⊠ *105 bd. Montparnasse, Montparnasse* ☎ *01–43–26–48–26* ⊕ *www.rotondemontparnasse.com* Ⓜ *Vavin.*

Le Lithographe. With its Art Nouveau decor, friendly waitstaff, and menu of fresh bistro food, this is the perfect place for a drink or meal after visiting the nearby Montparnasse Cemetery or Fondation Cartier. Homemade tapenade and toasted baguettes are served with drinks. ⊠ *234 bd. Raspail, Montparnasse* ☎ *01–77–13–26–08* ⊕ *www. lelithographe.fr* Ⓜ *Raspail.*

GETTING HERE

Montparnasse includes the 14e and 15e arrondissements. Take Line 4, 6, 12, or 13 to Montparnasse–Bienvenue for the Tour Montparnasse; walk along Boulevard du Montparnasse to reach the cafés. Take Line 4 or 6 to the Raspail métro stop for the Cimetière du Montparnasse or the Fondation Cartier. To visit the Catacombs, take the 4 or 6 line to Denfert-Rochereau. Other nearby métro stops include the Edgar Quinet stop on the 6 line and the Gaîté stop on the 13 line for the Fondation Henri Cartier-Bresson.

MAKING THE MOST OF YOUR TIME

If you can get to the top of the Tour Montparnasse on a clear day, you'll be rewarded with a vista unmatched in all of Paris. The viewing deck is open until 10:30 pm (11:30 on Friday and Saturday), so you can watch the lights sparkle on the Eiffel Tower at the top of the hour. The Catacombs and the Fondation Henri Cartier-Bresson are closed Monday. The Cimetière du Montparnasse is open daily.

Sightseeing
★★★
Dining
★★★
Lodging
★★
Shopping
★
Nightlife
★★

Once a warren of artists' studios and swinging cafés, much of Montparnasse was leveled in the 1960s to make way for a gritty train station and the Tour Montparnasse, Paris's only—and much maligned—skyscraper. Nevertheless, the neighborhood has maintained its reputation as a hub for its lively cafés and the kind of real-life vibe lost in some of the trendier sections of the city.

Updated by
Virginia Power

Despite its soulless modern architecture, the **Tour Montparnasse** has an upside—after all, the rooftop terrace provides a prime panoramic view of Paris. It's okay to feel smug during your ascent as you consider how savvy you've been to avoid the long lines at the Tour Eiffel; afterward, congratulate yourself with a fancy cocktail at Le Bar Américain on the 56th floor.

The other star attraction of Montparnasse is underground. The labyrinthine tunnels of the Paris **Catacombs** contain the bones of centuries' worth of Parisians, moved here when disease, spread by rotting corpses, threatened the city center.

The café society that flourished in the early 20th century—Picasso, Modigliani, Hemingway, Man Ray, and even Trotsky raised a glass here—is still evident along Boulevard du Montparnasse. The Art Deco interior of **La Coupole** attracts diners seeking piles of golden choucroute.

Along Boulevard Raspail you can see today's art stars at the **Fondation Henri Cartier-Bresson** and the **Fondation Cartier pour l'art contemporain,** or pay your respects to Baudelaire, Alfred Dreyfus, or Simone de Beauvoir in the **Cimetière du Montparnasse.**

TOP ATTRACTIONS

Cimetière du Montparnasse. Many of the neighborhood's most illustrious residents rest here, a stone's throw from where they lived and loved: Charles Baudelaire, Frédéric Bartholdi (who designed the Statue of Liberty), Alfred Dreyfus, Guy de Maupassant, and, more recently, photographer Man Ray, playwright Samuel Beckett, writers Marguerite Duras, Jean-Paul Sartre, and Simone de Beauvoir, actress Jean Seberg, and singer-songwriter Serge Gainsbourg. Opened in 1824 and spread over 47 acres, the ancient farmland is the second-largest burial ground in Paris. ⊠ *Entrances on Rue Froidevaux, Bd. Edgar Quinet, Montparnasse* ⊙ *Mid-Mar.–early Nov., weekdays 8–6, Sat. 8:30–6, Sun. 9–6; early Nov.–mid-Mar., weekdays 8–5:30, Sat. 8:30–5:30, Sun. 9–5:30* Ⓜ *Raspail, Edgar Quinet, Gaîté.*

FAMILY
FodorśChoice
★

Fondation Cartier pour l'art contemporain. There's no shortage of museums in Paris, but this eye-catching gallery may be the city's premier place to view cutting-edge art. Funded by luxury giant Cartier, the foundation is at once an architectural landmark, a corporate collection, and an exhibition space. Architect Jean Nouvel's 1993 building is a glass house of cards layered seamlessly between the boulevard and the garden. The foundation regularly hosts *Soirées Nomades* (Nomadic Nights) featuring lectures, dance, music, film, or fashion on Thursday evenings. Some are in English. Family tours and creative workshops for children ages 9 to 13 are available. ⊠ *261 bd. Raspail, Montparnasse* ☎ *01–42–18–56–50* ⊕ *www.fondation.cartier.com* ⊡ *€10.50* ⊙ *Tues. 11–10, Wed.–Sun. 11–8* Ⓜ *Raspail.*

FodorśChoice
★

Fondation Henri Cartier-Bresson. Photography has deep roots in Montparnasse, as great experimenters like Louis Daguerre and Man Ray lived and worked here. In keeping with this spirit of innovation, Henri Cartier-Bresson, legendary photographer and creator of the Magnum photo agency, launched this foundation with Martine Franck and their daughter Melanie. The restored 1913 artists' atelier holds three temporary exhibitions of contemporary photography each year. Be sure to go to the top floor to see a small gallery of Cartier-Bresson's own work. ⊠ *2 impasse Lebouis, Montparnasse* ☎ *01–56–80–27–00* ⊕ *www.henricartierbresson.org* ⊡ *€7; free on Wed. 6:30 pm–8:30 pm* ⊙ *Tues., Thurs., Fri., and Sun. 1–6:30, Wed. 1–8:30, Sat. 11–6:45* Ⓜ *Gaîté, Edgar Quinet.*

FodorśChoice
★

Les Catacombes. This is just the thing for anyone with morbid interests: a descent through dark, clammy passages brings you to Paris's principal ossuary, which also once served as a hideout maze for the French Resistance. Bones from the defunct Cimetière des Innocents were the first to arrive in 1786, when decomposing bodies started seeping into the cellars of the market at Les Halles, drawing swarms of ravenous rats. The legions of bones dumped here are stacked not by owner but by type—rows of skulls, packs of tibias, and piles of spinal disks, often rather artfully arranged. Among the nameless 6 million or so are the bones of Madame de Pompadour (1721–64), laid to rest with the riffraff after a lifetime spent as the mistress of Louis XV. Unfortunately, one of the most interesting aspects of the catacombs is one you probably won't see: *cataphiles,* mostly art students, have found alternate entrances into its 300 km (186 miles) of tunnels and here they make art, party, and purportedly raise hell. Arrive early as the line can get long and only 200 people can descend at a time. Audioguides are available for €5. Not recommended for claustrophobes or young children. ⊠ *1 ave. du Colonel Henri Roi-Tanguy, Montparnasse* ☎ *01–43–22–47–63* ⊕ *www.*

catacombes.paris.fr 🖾 *€10* ⊙ *Tues.–Sun. 10–8 (last entry at 7)* Ⓜ *Métro or RER: Denfert-Rochereau.*

Musée Zadkine. Sculptor Ossip Zadkine spent nearly four decades living in this bucolic retreat near the Jardin du Luxembourg, creating graceful, elongated figures known for their clean lines and simplified features. Zadkine, a Russian-Jewish émigré, moved to Paris in 1910 and fell into a circle of avant-garde artists. His early works, influenced by African, Greek, and Roman art, later took a Cubist turn, no doubt under the influence of his friend, the founder of the Cubist movement: Pablo Picasso. The museum displays a substantial portion of the 400 sculptures and 300 drawings bequeathed to the city by his wife, artist Valentine Prax. There are busts in bronze and stone reflecting the range of Zadkine's style, and an airy back room filled with lithe female nudes in polished wood. The leafy garden is worth the trip alone: it contains a dozen statues nestled in the trees, including *The Destroyed City,* a memorial to the Dutch city of Rotterdam, destroyed by the Germans in 1940. ⊠ *100 bis, rue d'Assas, Montparnasse* ☏ *01–55–42–77–20* ⊕ *www.zadkine.paris.fr* 🖾 *Free; fee for temporary exhibitions* ⊙ *Tues.–Sun. 10–6* Ⓜ *Vavin, Notre-Dame-des-Champs; RER: Port Royal.*

Tour Montparnasse. A 40-second elevator ride gets you to the top of one of continental Europe's tallest skyscrapers, where you can take in the stupendous panoramic view of Paris and beyond from the glass-enclosed observation deck on the 56th floor. On a clear day, you can see for 40 km (25 miles). The more adventurous can climb another three flights to the open-air roof terrace, complete with a champagne bar so you can really celebrate the occasion. Built in 1973, the 680-foot building attracts approximately one million gawkers each year. Café 360 serves light refreshments while bragging about its status as the highest panoramic bar in Europe. Purchase tickets in advance to avoid lines. ⊠ *Rue de L'Arrivee, Montparnasse* ☏ *01–45–38–52–56, 01–40–64–77–64 Le Ciel de Paris* ⊕ *www.tourmontparnasse56.com* 🖾 *€15* ⊙ *Apr.–Sept., daily 9:30 am–11:30 pm; Oct.–Mar., Sun.–Thurs. 9:30 am–10:30 pm, Fri. and Sat. 9:30 am–11 pm; last elevator 30 mins before closing* Ⓜ *Montparnasse–Bienvenüe.*

WORTH NOTING

Closerie des Lilas. Now a popular and pricey bar-restaurant, the Closerie remains a staple of all Parisian literary tours. Commemorative plaques are bolted to the bar as if they were still saving seats for their former clientele: an impressive list of literati including Zola, Baudelaire, Rimbaud, Apollinaire, Beckett, and, of course, Hemingway. ("Papa" wrote pages of *The Sun Also Rises* here and lived around the corner at 115 rue Notre-Dame-des-Champs.) Although the lilacs that once graced the garden—and shaded such habitués as Ingres, Whistler, and Cézanne—are gone, the terrace still opens onto a garden wall of luxuriant foliage. There is live music in the piano bar. ⊠ *171 bd. du Montparnasse, Montparnasse* ☏ *01–40–51–34–50* ⊕ *www.closeriedeslilas.fr* ⊙ *Daily noon–midnight* Ⓜ *Vavin; RER: Port Royal.*

Artists, Writers, and Exiles

Paris became a magnet for the international avant-garde in the mid-1800s and remained Europe's creative capital until the 1950s. It all began south of **Montmartre**, when Romantics, including writers Charles Baudelaire and George Sand (with her lover, Polish composer Frédéric Chopin), moved into the streets below Boulevard de Clichy. Impressionist painters Claude Monet, Edouard Manet, and Mary Cassatt had studios here, near Gare St-Lazare, so they could commute to the countryside. In the 1880s the neighborhood dance halls had a new attraction: the cancan, and in 1889 the **Moulin Rouge** cabaret was opened.

The artistic maelstrom continued through the Belle Époque and beyond. In the early 1900s Picasso and Braque launched Cubism from a ramshackle hillside studio, the **Bateau-Lavoir,** and a similar beehive of activity was established at the south end of the city in a curious studio building called La Ruche (the beehive, at the Convention métro stop). Artists from different disciplines worked together on experimental productions. In 1917 the modernist ballet *Parade* hit the stage, danced by impresario Sergei Diaghilev's Ballets Russes, with music by Erik Satie and costumes by Picasso—everyone involved was hauled off to court, accused of being cultural anarchists.

World War I shattered this creative frenzy, and when peace returned, the artists had moved. The narrow streets of **Montparnasse** had old buildings suitable for studios, and the area hummed with a wide, new, café-filled boulevard. At 27 rue Fleurus, Gertrude Stein held court with her partner, Alice B. Toklas. Picasso drew admirers to **La Rotonde,** and F. Scott Fitzgerald drank at the now-defunct Dingo.

The Spanish Civil War and World War II brought an end to carefree Montparnasse. But the literati reconvened in **St-Germain-des-Prés.** Café de Flore and **Deux Magots** had long been popular with an alternative crowd. Expat writers Samuel Beckett and Richard Wright joined existentialists Jean-Paul Sartre, Simone de Beauvoir, and Albert Camus in the neighborhood, drawn into the orbit of literary magazines and publishing houses.

Although Paris can no longer claim to be the epicenter of Western artistic innovation, pockets of outrageous creativity still bubble up. The galleries on Rue Louise Weiss in **Tolbiac** and the open-studio weekends in **Belleville** and **Oberkampf,** for instance, reveal the city's continuing artistic spirit; and the Ménilmontant district, where past arts icons rest in peace at the Père-Lachaise Cemetery, is considered a new mecca for creative souls.

Jardin Atlantique. Built above the tracks of Gare Montparnasse, this park nestled among tall modern buildings is named for its assortment of trees and plants typically found in coastal regions near the Atlantic Ocean. At the far end of the garden are small twin museums devoted to World War II: the **Mémorial du Maréchal-Leclerc,** named for the liberator of Paris, and the adjacent **Musée Jean-Moulin,** devoted to the leader of the French Resistance. Both feature memorabilia and share a common second floor showing photos and video footage (with English subtitles) of the final days of the war. Admission is free, though temporary exhibitions cost a few euros. In the center of the park, what looks like a quirky piece of metallic sculpture is actually a meteorological center, with a battery of flickering lights reflecting temperature, wind speed, and monthly rainfall. ⊠ *1 pl. des Cinq-Martyrs-du-Lycée-Buffon, Montparnasse* ☎ *01–40–64–39–44* ⊕ *www.equipement.paris.fr* ☉ *Jardin weekdays 8–dusk, weekends 9–dusk; museums Tues.–Sun. 10–6* Ⓜ *Montparnasse–Bienvenüe.*

Marché Edgar Quinet. To experience local living in one of the best ways, visit this excellent street market that sells everything from fresh fruit to wool shawls on Wednesday and Saturday. On Wednesdays there are produce stands, but also inexpensive clothing, jewelry, and knick-knacks. Saturdays are a food lover's delight with multiple stands selling spices, olives, fish, cheese, meat, and other gastronomic delights. It's a good place to pick up lunch on the go before paying your respects at Cimetière du Montparnasse across the street. ⊠ *Bd. du Edgar Quinet at métro Edgar Quinet, Montparnasse* ☉ *Wed. and Sat. 8–2* Ⓜ *Edgar Quinet.*

Place du 18-Juin-1940. At the busy intersection of Rue de Rennes and Boulevard du Montparnasse, this square commemorates an impassioned radio broadcast Charles de Gaulle made from London on June 18, 1940. In it he urged the French to resist Nazi occupiers (who had invaded the month prior), thereby launching the French Resistance Movement. It was also here that German military governor Dietrich von Choltitz surrendered to the Allies in August 1944, ignoring Hitler's orders to destroy the city as he withdrew. The square (in fact, a triangle) has been restored and is now a small but proper plaza, with a bench and fountain. ⊠ *Montparnasse* Ⓜ *Montparnasse–Bienvenüe.*

WESTERN PARIS

GETTING ORIENTED

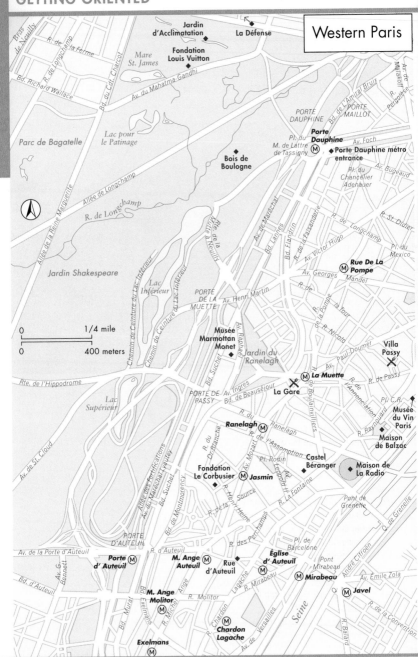

Western Paris

Jardin
d'Acclimatation

La Défense

Fondation
Louis Vuitton

Bras
de Neuilly

R. de la Ferme

R. de Longchamp

Bd. Richard Wallace

Mare
St. James

Av. du Mahatma-Gandhi

Bd. du Cdt. Charcot

PORTE
DAUPHINE

Bd. de l'Amiral Bruix

PORTE
MAILLOT

R. Pereire

Av. de
Malakoff

Pl. du
M. de Lattre
de Tassigny

Porte
Dauphine

Ⓜ

Av. Foch

Porte Dauphine métro
entrance

Parc de Bagatelle

Lac pour
le Patinage

Bois de
Boulogne

Pl. du
Chancelier
Adenauer

Av. Bugeaud

Allée de Longchamp

R. de Longchamp

Rte. de la
à Neuilly

Av. du Maréchal

Bd. Lannes

Bd. Flandrin

R. de la Faisanderie

R. de Longchamp

Av. Victor Hugo

R. St.-Didier

Jardin Shakespeare

Allée de la Reine Marguerite

Lac
Inférieur

PORTE
DE LA
MUETTE

Av. Henri Martin

Chemin de Ceinture du Lac Inférieur

Chemin de Ceinture du Lac Intérieur

Rue De La
Pompe

Ⓜ

Av. Georges
Mandel

Pl. du
Mexico

R. de

R. de la Tour

R. de la Pompe

R. Nicolo

0   1/4 mile
0   400 meters

Rte. de l'Hippodrome

Lac
Supérieur

Musée
Marmottan
Monet

Av. Raphaël

Jardin du
Ranelagh

Bd. Suchet

Av. Ingres

Av. de Beauséjour

PORTE DE
PASSY

La Gare

Ⓜ La Muette

Av. Paul-Doumer

R. de l'Annonciation

R. de Passy

Villa
Passy

Pl. C.R.

Musée
du Vin
Paris

R. Raynouard

Maison
de Balzac

Av. de St.-Cloud

Allée des fortifications

Av. du Maréchal Lyautey

Bu. Suchet

R. du
Dr.-Blanche

Ranelagh

Ⓜ

R. du

R. Ranelagh

Pl. Rodin

Av. Mozart

R. de l'Assomption

Castel
Béranger

R. Leopold II

R. La Fontaine

Maison de
La Radio

R. de Boulainvilliers

Pont de
Grenelle

Q. de Grenelle

Fondation
Le Corbusier

Ⓜ Jasmin

R. Henri Heine

R. de la Source

R. des Perchamps

PORTE
D'AUTEUIL

Av. de la Porte d'Auteuil

Bd. de Montmorency

Pl. de
Barcelone

Église
d'Auteuil

Pont
Mirabeau

André Citroën

Av. d'Auteuil

Av. G.
Bennett

Bd. d'Auteuil

Porte
d' Auteuil

Ⓜ

R. d'Auteuil

R. Michel Ange

M. Ange
Auteuil

Ⓜ

Rue
d'Auteuil

R. La Fontaine

Lagache

R. Mirabeau

Ⓜ Mirabeau

Av. Émile Zola

Ⓜ Javel

Bd. Murat

Bd. Exelmans

M. Ange
Molitor

Ⓜ

R. Michel Ange

R. Molitor

Chardon

Av. de Versailles

Seine

R. de la Convention

R. Balard

Exelmans

Ⓜ

Chardon
Lagache

Ⓜ

Seine

TOP REASONS TO GO

Fondation Louis Vuitton. Contemporary art meets iconoclastic architecture at this new museum designed by Frank Gehry in a sculptural mix of wood, steel, and glass.

Musée Marmottan Monet. If you're a fan of Claude Monet, don't miss this gem of a museum tucked away deep in the 16e near the Jardin du Ranelagh.

Bois de Boulogne. Whether you spend your afternoon in a rowboat or wandering gardens filled with foliage, the Bois is a perfect escape from the city.

Jardin d'Acclimatation. There's not a child under the age of five who won't love this amusement park on the northern edge of the Bois de Boulogne.

MAKING THE MOST OF YOUR TIME

If this isn't your first time in Paris, or even if it is and you've had enough of the touristy central part of the city, this neighborhood is a great choice and can be treated like a day trip. Spend the morning admiring the Monets at the uncrowded Musée Marmottan Monet, then take in the Art Nouveau architecture on Rue Jean de la Fontaine; or while away the day in the leafy Bois de Boulogne.

GETTING HERE

Western Paris includes the 16e and 17e arrondissements. Take Line 9 to La Muette métro stop for the Musée Marmottan Monet, or to the Jasmin stop (also Line 9) to explore Rue Jean de la Fontaine. Take Line 6 to the Passy stop for the Musée du Vin or to reach the main drag, Rue de Passy; alternately, take Bus 72 from the Hôtel de Ville or 63 from St. Sulpice. For the main entrance of the Bois de Boulogne, take Line 2 to the Porte Dauphine stop or RER C to Avenue Foch. For the Jardin d'Acclimatation, enter the park from the Les Sablons or Porte Maillot métro stops on Line 1. If you're heading out to La Défense, it's the terminus of Line 1.

BEST CAFÉS

La Gare. Housed in a former train station, this restaurant-lounge is frequented by business types and chic youth alike. Sit on the large terrace or descend the wide staircase to a room bathed in natural light by day and warm golden tones at night. Reasonable set menus feature traditional and inventive French cuisine. ⊠ *19 chausée de la Muette, Western Paris* ☎ *01–42–15–15–31* ⊕ *restaurantlagare.com* Ⓜ *La Muette.*

Villa Passy. The courtyard of this bucolic café just off Rue de Passy may make you think you've stumbled into a small village. Sit outside on a cushioned banquette shaded by ivy and order the plat du jour, prepared with fresh market ingredients. On Sunday, a €25 brunch is served from noon to 3:45 pm. ⊠ *4 impasse des Carrières, opposite 31 rue de Passy, Western Paris* ☎ *01–45–27–68–76* ☺ *Closed Mon.* Ⓜ *Passy.*

13

Sightseeing
★★
Dining
★
Lodging
★
Shopping
★
Nightlife
—

Meet Paris at its most prim and proper. This genteel area is a study in smart urban planning, with classical architecture and newer construction cohabiting as easily as the haute bourgeoisie inhabitants mix with their expat neighbors. There's no shortage of celebrities seeking some peace and quiet here, but you're just as likely to find well-heeled families who decamped from the center of the city in search of a spacious apartment. Passy, once a separate village and home to American ambassadors Benjamin Franklin and Thomas Jefferson, was incorporated into the city in 1860 under Napoléon III.

Updated by
Jack Vermee

A walk along the main avenues gives you a sense of Paris's finest Art Nouveau and Modernist buildings, including **Castel-Béranger,** by Hector Guimard, and the **Fondation Le Corbusier** museum, a prime example of the titular architect's pioneering style (it was one of Le Corbusier's first Paris commissions). This neighborhood is also home to one of the city's best and most overlooked museums—the **Musée Marmottan Monet**—which has an astonishing collection of Impressionist art. Enjoy a *dégustation* (tasting) at the **Musée du Vin** or simply find a café on Rue de Passy and savor a moment in one of the city's most exclusive enclaves. For outdoor adventures, the **Bois de Boulogne** is the place to be, especially if you have kids in tow. At *le Bois,* you can explore the Pré Catelan and peacock-filled Bagatelle gardens, both meticulously landscaped and surrounded by woods. You can also admire contemporary art in the new **Fondation Louis Vuitton,** head to the old-fashioned amusement park at the Jardin d'Acclimatation, take a rowboat out on one of the park's two bucolic lakes, or rent a bike and hit 14 km (9 miles) of marked trails.

TOP ATTRACTIONS

FAMILY
Fodor'sChoice
★
Bois de Boulogne. When Parisians want to experience the great outdoors without going too far from home, they head to the Bois de Boulogne. Once a royal hunting ground, the Bois is not a park in the traditional sense—more like a vast tamed forest where romantic lakes and wooded paths are complemented by formal gardens and family-friendly amusements. On nice days, it's filled with cyclists, rowers, rollerbladers, joggers, pétanque players, picnickers, and hordes of preschoolers. Art lovers are also flocking here thanks to the opening of the Louis Vuitton Foundation, a stunning exhibition space dedicated to contemporary art near the Jardin d'Acclimatation.

The Parc de Bagatelle is a floral garden with irises, roses, tulips, water lilies, and roaming peacocks that is at its most colorful between April and June. Pré Catelan contains one of Paris's largest trees: a copper beech more than 200 years old. Romantic Le Pré Catelan restaurant, where *le tout Paris* used to dine on the elegant terrace during the Belle Époque, still draws diners and wedding parties—especially on weekends. The Jardin Shakespeare inside the Pré Catelan has a sampling of the flowers, herbs, and trees mentioned in Shakespeare's plays, and it becomes an open-air theater for the Bard's works in spring. The Jardin d'Acclimatation, on the northern edge of the Bois, is an amusement park that attracts seemingly every local preschooler on summer Sunday afternoons. Boats or bikes can be rented for a few euros at Lac Inférieur. You can row or take a quick "ferry" to the island restaurant, Le Chalet des Iles. Two popular horse-racing tracks are also in the park: the Hippodrome de Longchamp and the Hippodrome d'Auteuil. Fans of the French Open can visit its home base, Stade Roland-Garros.

The main entrance to the Bois is off Avenue Foch near the Porte Dauphine métro stop on Line 2; it is best for accessing the Pré Catelan and Jardin Shakespeare, both located off the Route de la Grande-Cascade by the lake. For the Jardin d'Acclimatation, off Boulevard des Sablons, take Line 1 to Les Sablons or Porte Maillot, where you can walk or ride the Petit Train to the amusement park. The Parc de Bagatelle, off Route de Sèvres-à-Neuilly, can be accessed from either Porte Dauphine or Porte Maillot, though it's a bit of a hike. You'll want to leave the park by dusk, as the Bois—seedy and potentially dangerous after dark—turns into a distinctly "adult" playground. ⊠ *Western Paris* ☎ *01–53–64–53– 80 Parc de Bagatelle, 01–40–67–90–85 Jardin d'Acclimatation ⊕ www. jardindacclimatation.fr* 🖾 *Parc de Bagatelle free except during exhibitions, otherwise €6; Jardin Shakespeare free; Jardin d'Acclimatation €3 entry, €2.90 per person for rides* ☉ *Daily, hrs vary according to time of yr but are generally around 10–dusk* Ⓜ *Porte Dauphine for main entrance; Porte Maillot or Les Sablons for northern end; Porte d'Auteuil for southern end.*

Fodor'sChoice
★
Castel Béranger. It's a shame you can't go inside this house, which is considered the city's first Art Nouveau structure. Dreamed up in 1898 by Hector Guimard, the wild combination of materials and the grimacing grillwork led neighbors to call it Castle *Dérangé* (Deranged). Yet the project catapulted the 27-year-old Guimard into the public eye, leading

to his famous métro commission. After ogling the sea-inspired front entrance, go partway down the alley to admire the inventive treatment of the traditional Parisian courtyard, complete with a melting water fountain. A few blocks up the road at No. 60 is the Hotel Mezzara, designed by Guimard in 1911 for textile designer Paul Mezzara. You can trace Guimard's evolution by walking to the subtler Agar complex at the end of the block. Tucked beside the stone entrance at the corner of Rue Jean de la Fontaine and Rue Gros is a tiny café-bar with an Art Nouveau glass front and furnishings. ⊠ *14 rue Jean de la Fontaine, Western Paris* Ⓜ *Ranelagh; RER: Maison de Radio France.*

Fondation Le Corbusier (*Le Corbusier Foundation*). Maison La Roche is a must-see for architecture and design lovers. Built as a private residence in 1923, it's a stellar example of Swiss architect Le Corbusier's innovative construction techniques based on geometric forms, recherché color schemes, and a visionary use of iron and concrete. The sloping ramp that replaces the traditional staircase is one of the most eye-catching features. Free, hour-long English tours are available at 2 pm every Tuesday and must be reserved online. ⊠ *8–10 sq. du Docteur Blanche, Western Paris* ☎ *01–42–88–75–72 Maison La Roche* ⊕ *www. fondationlecorbusier.fr* ⤳ *€8; €12 for combined visit with Le Corbusier's studio-apartment* ⊙ *Mon. 1:30–6, Tues.–Sat. 10–6* Ⓜ *Jasmin, Michel-Ange–Auteuil.*

Fodor's Choice ★ **Fondation Louis Vuitton.** Rising up out of the Bois de Boulogne like a magnificent ship sporting billowing crystal sails, Frank Gehry's new contemporary-art museum and cultural center is the most captivating addition to the Parisian skyline since the unveiling of the Centre Pompidou in 1977. Commissioned by Bernard Arnault (chairman and CEO of luxury-goods conglomerate LVMH), it houses Arnault's substantial private collection, including pieces by Pierre Huyghe, Gerhard Richter, Thomas Schütte, Ellsworth Kelly, Bertrand Lavier, Taryn Simon, Sarah Morris, and Christian Boltanski, among others. La Fondation Louis Vuitton also hosts extensive temporary exhibitions, like the mesmerizing light installations of Danish-Icelandic artist Olafur Eliasson. Le Frank, the pricey on-site restaurant overseen by Michelin-starred chef Jean-Louis Nomicos, is rapidly gaining fans for its mix of French and international cuisine. The museum is a 12-minute walk from Les Sablons métro on Line 1; alternatively, you can catch the Fondation shuttle (€1), which leaves every 10 to 15 minutes from Avenue de Friedland at Place de l'Étoile. ⊠ *8 av. du Mahatma Gandhi, Western Paris* ☎ *01–40–69–96–00* ⊕ *www.fondationlouisvuitton.fr* ⤳ *€14, includes entrance to Jardin d'Acclimatation* ⊙ *Mon., Wed., and Thurs. noon–7, Fri. noon–11, weekends 11–8* Ⓜ *Les Sablons.*

Fodor's Choice ★ **Musée Marmottan Monet.** This underrated museum boasts the largest collection of Monet's work anywhere. More than 100 pieces, donated by his son Michel, occupy a specially built basement gallery in an elegant 19th-century mansion, which was once the hunting lodge of the Duke de Valmy. Among them you can find such works as the *Cathédrale de Rouen* series (1892–96) and *Impression: Soleil Levant* (*Impression: Sunrise*, 1872), the painting that helped give the Impressionist movement its name. Other exhibits include letters exchanged by

Impressionist painters Berthe Morisot and Mary Cassatt. Upstairs, the mansion still feels like a graciously decorated private home. Empire furnishings fill the salons overlooking the Jardin du Ranelagh on one side and the private yard on the other. There's also a captivating room of illuminated medieval manuscripts. To best understand the collection's context, buy an English-language catalog in the museum shop on your way in. ⊠ *2 rue Louis-Boilly, Western Paris* ☎ *01–44–96–50–33* ⊕ *www.marmottan.fr* ▦ *€11* ⊗ *Wed. and Fri.–Sun. 10–6, Thurs. 10–9* Ⓜ *La Muette.*

WORTH NOTING

OFF THE BEATEN PATH

La Défense. First conceived in 1958, this Modernist suburb just west of Paris was inspired by Le Corbusier's dream of high-rise buildings, pedestrian walkways, and sunken vehicle circulation. Built as an experiment to keep high-rises out of the historic downtown, the Parisian business hub has survived economic uncertainty to become the city's prime financial district. Visiting La Défense gives you a crash course in contemporary skyscraper evolution, from the solid blocks of the 1960s and '70s to the curvy fins of the '90s and beyond. Today 20,000 people live in the suburb, but 180,000 people work here, and many more come to shop in its enormous mall. Arriving via métro Line 1, you'll get a view of the Seine, then emerge at a pedestrian plaza studded with some great public art, including César's giant thumb, Joan Miró's colorful figures, and one of Calder's great red "stabiles." The Grande Arche de La Défense dominates the area: it was designed as a controversial closure to the historic axis of Paris (an imaginary line that runs through the Arc de Triomphe, the Arc du Carrousel, and the Louvre Pyramide). Glass-bubble elevators in a metal-frame tower whisk you a heart-jolting 360 feet to the viewing platform. At the end of June, La Defense hosts an annual weeklong jazz festival with free concerts and events; click ⊕ *www.ladefense.fr* and follow the links to the festival for further information. ⊠ *Parvis de La Défense, Western Paris* ☎ *01–46–93–19–00* ⊕ *www.grandearche.com* ▦ *Grande Arche €10* ⊗ *Apr.–Aug., daily 10–8; Sept.–Mar., daily 10–7* Ⓜ *Métro or RER: Grande Arche de La Défense.*

Maison de Balzac. Literature aficionados can visit the modest home of the great French 19th-century novelist Honoré de Balzac (1799–1850), which contains exhibits charting his tempestuous yet prolific career. Balzac penned nearly 100 novels and stories known collectively as *The Human Comedy,* many of them set in Paris. You can still feel his presence in his study and pay homage to his favorite coffeepot—his working hours were fueled by a tremendous consumption of the "black ink." He would escape his creditors by exiting the flat through a secret passage that led down to what is now the Musée du Vin. ⊠ *47 rue Raynouard, Western Paris* ☎ *01–55–74–41–80* ⊕ *en.parisinfo.com/paris-museum-monument/71078/Maison-de-Balzac* ▦ *Free; around €4 for temporary exhibitions* ⊗ *Tues.–Sun. 10–6; last entry at 5:30* Ⓜ *Passy, La Muette.*

Maison de la Radio. Headquarters to France's state broadcasting company, this imposing 1963 circular building is more than 500 yards in circumference. It's said to have more floor space than any other building in the country and features a 200-foot tower that overlooks the Seine. Radio France sponsors 100-plus concerts a year, including performances by its own Orchestre Philharmonique de Radio France and the Orchestre National de France. Though they take place at venues throughout the city, a great number are held here, and they're generally either free of charge or inexpensive. French-only building tours are offered Saturday at 2:30. ✉ *116 av. du Président-Kennedy, Western Paris* ☎ *01–56–40–15–16 for tour reservations* ⊕ *www.maisondelaradio.fr* 💶 *€10 for tours* 🕐 *Mon.–Sat. 11–6* Ⓜ *Ranelagh; RER: Maison de Radio France; Bus 22, 52, 72.*

Musée du Vin Paris. Oenophiles with some spare time will enjoy this quirky museum housed in a 15th-century abbey, a reminder of Passy's roots as a pastoral village. Though hardly exhaustive and geared to beginners, the small collection contains old wine bottles, glassware, and ancient wine-related pottery excavated in Paris. Wine-making paraphernalia shares the grotto-like space with hokey figures retired from the city's wax museum, including Napoléon appraising a glass of Burgundy. But you can partake in a thoroughly nonhokey wine tasting, or bring home one of the 200-plus bottles for sale in the tiny gift shop. Check online for a calendar of wine tastings and classes offered in English. You can book ahead for a casual lunch, too (restaurant open Tuesday through Saturday, noon to 3, reservations required). ✉ *Rue des Eaux/5 sq. Charles Dickens, Western Paris* ☎ *01–45–25–63–26* ⊕ *www.museeduvinparis.com* 💶 *€10; €15 with a glass of wine; €25 with 3 wine tastings and lecture* 🕐 *Tues.–Sat. 10–6* Ⓜ *Passy.*

Porte Dauphine Métro Entrance. Visitors come here to snap pictures of the queen of subway entrances—one of the city's two remaining Art Nouveau canopied originals designed by Hector Guimard (the other is at the Abbesses stop on Line 12). A flamboyant scalloped "crown" of patina-painted panels and runaway metal struts adorns this whimsical 1900 creation. Porte Dauphine is the terminus of Line 2. The entrance is on the Bois de Boulogne side of Avenue Foch, so take the Boulevard de l'Amiral Bruix exit. ✉ *Av. Foch, Western Paris* Ⓜ *Porte Dauphine.*

Rue d'Auteuil. This narrow shopping street escaped Haussmann's urban renovations and today still retains the country feel of old Auteuil, a sedate bourgeois enclave. Molière once lived on the site of No. 2, while Racine was on nearby Rue du Buis: the pair met up to clink glasses and exchange drama notes at the Mouton Blanc Inn, now a traditional brasserie, at No. 40. Numbers 19–25 and 29 are an interesting combination of 17th- and 18th-century buildings. At the foot of the street, the scaly dome of the Église Notre-Dame d'Auteuil (built in the 1880s) is an unmistakable small-time cousin of Sacré-Coeur in Montmartre. Rue d'Auteuil is at its liveliest on Wednesday and Saturday mornings, when a much-loved street market crams onto Place Jean-Lorraine. ✉ *Western Paris* Ⓜ *Michel-Ange–Auteuil, Église d'Auteuil.*

14

WHERE TO EAT

EAT LIKE A LOCAL

Parisians are many things, but above all, they are great eaters, and social ones at that. After that first flaky croissant and frothy café crème, the day revolves around what, when, and with whom the next meal will be. Given that Parisians are spoiled for choice, this is no surprise.

BREAD

One of the great mainstays of French food, not all bread in Paris is created equal. Many boulangeries still offer industrial baguettes (made from frozen dough) that go hard within the hour. Others offer traditional crusty loaves so glorious you will happily travel across town to get one. If you don't have the time to experiment, a good compromise is to buy at a reputable *épicerie* (grocery store).

PASTRY

What would Paris be without pastries, and what would a pastry be without Paris? The two go hand in hand, but like bread, the quality varies from indifferent to sublime. Pierre Hermé, the father of Paris's new wave pastry, is a great place to start, but you can't go wrong with any of the following: Sébastien Gaudard (whose shop, on the fabulous Rue des Martyrs, is a dream), Jean-Paul Hévin, Jacques Genin (to be eaten only in the elegant tea salon on the premises), Eric Kayser, Pain de Sucre, and Blé Sucré. Several have multiple locations, making a stop easy.

CHEESE

No visit to France is complete without sampling a few of the country's some 625 unpasteurized cheeses, made from either sheep, goat, or cow's milk and best paired simply with a crusty baguette and a fresh green salad. Made in specific regions, often in optimal conditions for a very specific microbe (like the caves of Roquefort), you won't find their equivalent anywhere else.

CRÊPES

Paris's first street food, the humble crêpe, which hails from Brittany and Normandy, can still be found on city corners. There are two kinds: the savory *galette,* made with buckwheat flour and filled with cheese, egg, veggies, and other hearty ingredients, and the sweet crêpe, made with white flour and filled with nutella, jam, caramel, or simply lemon with a dusting of sugar.

CHOCOLATE

In the last few years, Paris has surpassed both Zurich and Brussels as the chocolate center of Europe. And Paris's 6e arrondissement has emerged as the epicenter, with no less than 15 truly world-class *chocolatiers* (many also *pâtissiers*) plying their yummy trade.

CHARCUTERIE

A meat-based art form, charcuterie encompasses all those pâtés (including the controversial aristocrat *fois gras*) and cured meats and sausages perfected by the great *bouchers* (butchers) of Lyon. France is enjoying a much-needed renaissance of the genre, and now artisanal charcuterie can be found in all

the best épiceries, including the melt-in-your-mouth *jambon de Paris* made right here.

GOURMET ÉPICERIES

Derived from the disappearing local mom-and-pop shops where you could pick up anything from a variety of homemade cold salads and pâtés to a goose breast stuffed with chestnuts, gourmet grocers are a fairly recent trend in Paris. From the chic new Maison Plisson in the Marais to the Bon Marché's exceptional La Grande Épicerie, these are a great introduction to a wide range of top-quality French artisanal foods.

Updated
by Jennifer
Ladonne

A new wave of culinary confidence has been running through one of the world's great food cities and spilling over both banks of the Seine. Whether cooking up *grand-mère*'s roast chicken and *riz au lait* or placing a whimsical hat of cotton candy atop wild-strawberry-and-rose ice cream, Paris chefs—established and up-and-coming, native and foreign—have been breaking free from the tyranny of tradition and following their passion.

Emblematic of the "bistronomy" movement is the proliferation of "gastrobistros"—often in far-flung or newly chic neighborhoods—helmed by established chefs fleeing the constraints of the star system or passionate young chefs unfettered by overblown expectations. Among the seasoned stars and exciting newcomers to the scene are Yannick Alléno, who left behind two Michelin stars at Le Meurice to open his locavore bistro Terroir Parisien at the Palais Brogniart and earned three stars at the storied Pavillon Ledoyen within his first year at the helm; David Toutain at the exceptional Restaurant David Toutain; Sylvestre Wahid at Brasserie Thoumieux; and Katsuaki Okiyama's Abri.

But self-expression is not the only driving force behind the current trend. A traditional high-end restaurant can be prohibitively expensive to operate. As a result, more casual bistros and cafés, which reflect the growing allure of less formal dining and often have lower operating costs and higher profit margins, have become attractive opportunities for even top chefs.

For tourists, this development can only be good news, because it makes the cooking of geniuses such as Joël Robuchon, Guy Savoy, Eric Frechon, and Pierre Gagnaire a bit more accessible (even if these star chefs rarely cook in their lower-price restaurants) and opens up a vast range of new possibilities for exciting dining.

Like the chefs themselves, Paris diners are breaking away from tradition with renewed enthusiasm. New restaurants, wine bars, and rapidly

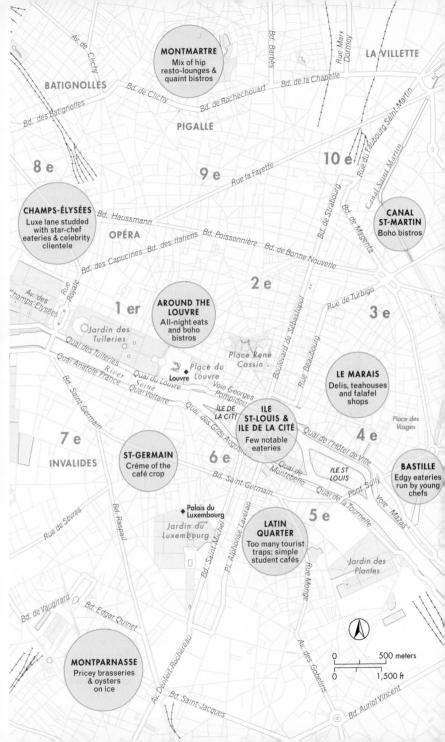

multiplying *épicieries* (gourmet grocers) and sandwich shops recognize that not everyone wants a three-course blowout every time they dine out. And because Parisians are more widely traveled than in the past, many ethnic restaurants—notably the best North African, Vietnamese–Laotian, Chinese, Spanish, and Japanese spots—are making fewer concessions to French tastes, resulting in far better food.

PLANNING

WINE BARS

For tantalizing wines, good food, and great value, look no farther than one of Paris's many wine bars. The past 10 years have seen an explosion of a new kind of *bar à vins,* or, more accurately, *cave à manger*—essentially amplified wineshops with a few tables, which serve a plate or two of regional cheeses or artisanal charcuterie to complement the wines. The new generation of *cavistes* stood apart as champions of natural wines, which are unfiltered, contain minimal or no added sulfites, and are often *bio* (organic) or grown biodynamically, that is, according to a specific set of agricultural guidelines. As the natural-wine movement dovetailed with the crusade toward simply prepared foods made from quality seasonal ingredients, the contemporary wine bar was born. Indeed, the food in a handful of wine bars now rivals that in the best Paris bistros—and can be a lot more affordable. Whatever the emphasis, the upward trajectory of the wine bar has had a major hand in reinvigorating Paris's wine-and-food scene.

Wine bars usually keep restaurant hours (noon to 2 pm and 7:30 to 11 pm); some combine with an épicerie, stay open all day, and close earlier in the evening; others offer a late-night scene. Although casual, most wine bars nowadays require reservations, so call in advance, especially if Sunday brunch is available—still a rarity in Paris. Look for the "wine bar" designation in our restaurant listings.

CHILDREN

Some restaurants provide booster seats, but don't count on them: be sure to ask when you confirm your reservation.

HOURS

Paris restaurants generally serve food from noon to 2 pm and from 7:30 or 8 pm to about 11 pm. Brasseries have longer hours and often serve all day and late into the evening; some are open 24 hours. Surprisingly, many restaurants close on Saturday as well as Sunday, and Monday closings are also not uncommon. July and August are common months for annual closings, but restaurants may also close for a week in February, around Easter, or at Christmas.

MENUS

All establishments must post menus outside so they're available to look over before you enter. Most have two basic types of menu: à la carte and fixed price (*prix fixe, le menu,* or *la formule*). Although it limits your choices, the prix fixe is usually the best value. If you feel like indulging, the *menu dégustation* (tasting menu), consisting of numerous small courses, lets you sample the chef's offerings. ⇨ *See the Menu Guide in the Understanding Paris section at the back of this book for guidance about common French menu items.*

ORDERING WINE

Most sommeliers are knowledgeable about their lists and can make appropriate suggestions after you've made your tastes and budget known. Simpler spots serve wine in carafes (*en carafe*, or *en pichet*). All restaurants sell wine by the glass, but prices can be steep; be sure to do the math.

RESERVATIONS

Restaurant staff will nearly always greet you with the phrase "*Avez-vous réservé?*" (Have you reserved?), and a confident "*Oui*" is the best answer, even in a neighborhood bistro. Although some wine bars do not take reservations—or take them online only—many do, so call and check.

SMOKING

Many Parisians are accustomed to smoking before, during, and after meals, but since 2008, the national smoking ban was extended to restaurants, bars, and cafés. Many establishments have compensated by adding covered terraces for smokers, but you'll be happy to know that inside, the air is much clearer.

TIPPING AND TAXES

According to French law, prices must include tax and tip (*service compris* or *prix nets*), but pocket change left on the table in cafés, or an additional 5% in better restaurants, is always appreciated. Beware of bills stamped "Service Not Included" in English or restaurants slyly using American-style credit-card slips, hoping that you'll be confused and add the habitual 15% tip.

WHAT IT COSTS

You'll be lucky to find a good bistro meal for €25 or less, even at lunch, so consider economizing on some meals to have more to spend on the others. Slurping inexpensive Japanese noodles on Rue Ste-Anne, grabbing a sandwich at a casual eatery, or having a picnic in a park will save euros for dinner. And, of course, if you've rented an apartment, you can shop at the city's wonderful markets and cook a few meals at "home."

WHAT IT COSTS				
	$	$$	$$$	$$$$
AT DINNER	under €18	€18–€24	€25–€32	over €32

Price per person for a main course at dinner, or if dinner is not served, at lunch, including tax (19.6%) and service.

WHAT TO WEAR

Casual dress is acceptable at all but the fanciest restaurants—this usually means stylish sportswear, which might be a bit dressier than in the United States. When in doubt, leave the T-shirts and sneakers behind. If an establishment requires jacket and tie, it's noted in our review.

RESTAURANT REVIEWS

In alphabetical order by neighborhood. Use the coordinates (✥ 1:B2) at the end of each review to locate a property on the corresponding map at the end of the chapter.

ILE DE LA CITÉ AND ILE ST-LOUIS

Ile de la Cité and Ile St-Louis are great for sightseeing, which is why much of the dining scene on these islands revolves around fast food and tourist traps. Luckily, a few long-established brasseries and inspired bistros on elegant Ile St-Louis—not to mention the legendary Berthillon, the city's great *glacier* (ice-cream maker)—more than compensate. Among the shops, épiceries, and ancient bookstores of Rue St-Louis en l'Ile, the island's central spine, you'll find enough quality dining to keep you satisfied at any time of the day.

ILE ST-LOUIS

$$ BRASSERIE

🍴 **Brasserie de l'Isle Saint-Louis.** With its dream location on the tip of Ile St-Louis overlooking the Seine and Notre-Dame, you'd think this charming brasserie, like so many before it, would have succumbed to its own success. Yet it remains exactly what a decent neighborhood brasserie should be, with an authentic decor, efficiently friendly service, and solid brassiere fare—classic leeks vinaigrette, country terrine, and a savory onion tarte *à la maison* for starters, followed by tender sole meunière, classic choucroute, or buttered entrecôte. The outdoor terrace simply can't be beat. [$] *Average main: €20* ✉ *55 quai de Bourbon, 4e, Ile St-Louis* ☎ *01–43–54–02–59* 🌐 *www.labrasserie-isl.fr* 🕓 *Closed Wed.* ✍ *Reservations not accepted* [M] *Pont Marie, Maubert-Mutualité, Sully-Morland* ✥ *4:E3.*

$$ MODERN FRENCH Fodor's Choice ★

🍴 **Mon Vieil Ami.** "Modern Alsatian" might sound like an oxymoron, but once you've tasted the food here, you'll understand. The updated medieval dining room—stone walls and dark-wood tables—provides a stylish milieu for the inventive cooking, which showcases heirloom vegetables such as yellow carrots and pink-and-white beets. Pâté *en croûte* (wrapped in pastry) with a knob of foie gras is hard to resist among the starters. Among the mains, red mullet might come in a bouillabaisse sauce with sautéed baby artichokes, and the shoulder of lamb with white beans, preserved lemon, and cilantro has become a classic. This is not necessarily the place for a romantic dinner, since seating is a little tight, but the quality of the food never falters, and the portions are quite generous. [$] *Average main: €24* ✉ *69 rue St-Louis-en-l'Ile, 4e, Ile St-Louis* ☎ *01–40–46–01–35* 🌐 *www.mon-vieil-ami.com* [M] *Pont Marie* ✥ *4:E3.*

AROUND THE EIFFEL TOWER

Lively bistros and daring contemporary restaurants bring unexpected exuberance to the otherwise sedate streets around the Eiffel Tower. Because money is rarely an object in this area, you can find everything from top-notch contemporary restaurants that draw foodies to nostalgic bistros that appeal to aristocratic residents with comfort-food cravings.

$$ BISTRO 🍴 **Afaria.** This otherwise unexciting arrondissement has become home to yet another promising young chef: Ludivine Merlin. Basque cooking is known for its bold flavors and generosity, and the choices at Afaria are no exception: crisp-skinned duck breast with balsamic-fig vinegar (for two) is served dramatically, inside a ceramic roof tile, with the accompanying potato gratin perched on a bed of twigs; and big chunks of spoon-tender, slow-cooked pork from Gascony come in an earthenware dish with cubes of roasted celery root. Tapas are served at a high table near the entrance, and there's a large-screen TV for rugby matches. [$] *Average main: €20* ✉ *15 rue Desnouettes, 15e, Around the Eiffel Tower* ☎ *01–48–42–95–90* 🌐 *www.restaurant-afaria.fr* ⏲ *Closed Sun. and Mon., 3 wks in Aug.* [M] *Convention* ✣ *3:C6.*

$$$$ BISTRO 🍴 **Au Bon Accueil.** To see what well-heeled Parisians like to eat these days, book a table at this chic little bistro run by Jacques Lacipière as soon as you get to town. The contemporary dining room is unusually comfortable, and the sidewalk tables have an Eiffel Tower view, but it's the excellent, well-priced *cuisine du marché* that has made this spot a hit. The sophisticated fare sometimes features Salers beef and green asparagus, roast lobster with mushroom risotto, and game in season. House-made desserts could include citrus terrine with passion-fruit sorbet or caramelized apple mille-feuille with hazelnut ice cream. The €35 prix-fixe menu for lunch or dinner, featuring dishes with a distinct haute-cuisine touch, is one of the city's great bargains. [$] *Average main: €39* ✉ *14 rue de Monttessuy, 7e, Around the Eiffel Tower* ☎ *01–47–05–46–11* 🌐 *www.aubonaccueilparis.com* ⏲ *Closed weekends and 3 wks in Aug.* ✍ *Reservations essential* [M] *Métro or RER: Pont de l'Alma* ✣ *3:D1.*

$ CAFÉ FAMILY 🍴 **Café Coutume.** A lofty space between the Musée Rodin and the Bon Marché makes this the perfect pit stop between museum going and shopping. Look for healthy salads, sandwiches, snacks, desserts, and a delicious cup of any kind of coffee drink that takes your fancy. The meticulously sourced artisanal beans are freshly and lovingly roasted on the premises. [$] *Average main: €8* ✉ *47 rue de Babylone, 7e, Around the Eiffel Tower* ☎ *01–45–51–50–47* ⏲ *No dinner* ✍ *Reservations not accepted* [M] *Saint-François Xavier, Sèvres-Babylone* ✣ *3:G3.*

$$$ BISTRO 🍴 **D'Chez Eux.** The red-checked tablecloths and jovial maître d'hôtel at this authentic southwestern French bistro near the École Militaire might seem like a tourist cliché—until you realize that the boisterous dining room is just as popular with food-loving locals and French politicians as it is with foreigners. The best way to start a meal here is with the "chariot" of starters, everything from lentil salad to ratatouille; just point to the ones you want. Classics among the main courses are duck confit with sautéed garlic potatoes, cassoulet, and game dishes in winter. Everything is hearty and delicious, if not especially refined—don't miss the gooey help-yourself chocolate mousse. Best value is the weekday lunch *tradition gourmande* set menu for €34, which brings you the hors d'oeuvres spread, a main course, and three desserts (you can try them all). [$] *Average main: €30* ✉ *2 av. de Lowendal, 7e, Around the Eiffel Tower* ☎ *01–47–05–52–55* 🌐 *www.chezeux.com* ⏲ *Closed Aug.* [M] *Varenne, École Militaire* ✣ *3:E3.*

BEST BETS FOR PARIS DINING

With thousands of restaurants to choose from, how will you decide where to eat? Fodor's writers and editors have selected their favorite restaurants by price, cuisine, and experience below. You can also search by neighborhood for excellent eating experiences—peruse the following pages.

Fodor's Choice ★

Abri, $$
Alain Ducasse at the Plaza Athénée, $$$$
Bal Café, $
Breizh Café, $
Café Lomi, $
Fish la Boissonerie, $$
Frenchie, $$$
Frenchie Bar à Vins, $
Guy Savoy, $$$$
Hiramatsu, $$$$
Holybelly, $
Jacques Genin Salon de Thé, $
Juvéniles, $$
L'Abeille, $$$$
L'Ardoise, $$$
L'Arpège, $$$$
L'Astrance, $$$$
La Bourse et La Vie, $$$$
La Régalade St. Honoré, $$$
La Table d'Akihiro, $$$
Le Baratin, $$
Le Bistrot Paul Bert, $$
Le Cinq, $$$$
Le Galopin, $$
Le Servan, $$
Mon Vieil Ami, $$
Pavillon Ledoyen, $$$$
Rech, $$$$
Restaurant David Toutain, $$$$
Saturne, $$$$
Semilla, $$$
Soul Kitchen, $
Spring, $$$$
Télescope, $
Terroir Parisien–Palais Brongniart, $$
Yam'Tcha, $$$$
Ze Kitchen Galerie, $$$$

By Price

$

Au Passage
Bal Café
Breizh Café
Café des Musées
Café Lomi
Dong Huong
Frenchie Bar à Vins
Frenchie To Go
Higuma
Holybelly
Jacques Genin Salon de Thé
Jeanne A
L'As du Fallafel
La Crêperie Josselin
Le Café Constant
Rose Bakery
Soul Kitchen
Télescope
Verjus Bar à Vins

$$

Abri
Fish la Boissonérie
Juvéniles
La Bourse et la Vie
Lazare
Le Baratin
Le Bistrot Paul Bert
Le Galopin
Le Servan
Le Verre Volé
Les Papilles
Mon Vieil Ami
Philou
Septime
Terroir Parisien–Palais Brongniart

$$$

Drouant
Frenchie
Guilo Guilo
L'Ardoise
La Régalade St. Honoré
La Table Lauriston
Saturne
Semilla

$$$$

Alain Ducasse at the Plaza Athénée
Guy Savoy
Hiramatsu
Il Vino
L'Abeille
L'Arpège
L'Astrance
L'Atelier de Joël Robuchon
La Bourse et La Vie
La Table d'Akihiro
Le Chateaubriand
Le Cinq
Pavillon Ledoyen
Pierre Gagnaire
Rech
Restaurant David Toutain
Saturne
Spring
Yam'Tcha
Ze Kitchen Galerie

By Type

BISTRO

Benoît, $$$$
Frenchie, $$$
Jadis, $$
Juvéniles, $$
Le Café Constant, $

BRASSERIE

Brasserie de l'Isle Saint-Louis, $$
Lazare, $$
Le Dôme, $$$$

CAFÉ

Bal Café, $
Café Coutume, $
Café de Flore, $$
Café Lomi, $
Holybelly, $
La Caféothèque, $
Soul Kitchen, $
Télescope, $

FRENCH FUSION

Hiramatsu, $$$$
Il Vino, $$$$
Restaurant David Toutain, $$$$
Sola, $$$$
Yam'Tcha, $$$$

JAPANESE

Guilo Guilo, $$$
Higuma, $
Kifune, $$$$
Yen, $$$
Zen, $

MODERN

Drouant, $$$
Hélène Darroze, $$$$
KGB, $$$
L'Atelier de Joël Robuchon, $$$$
Le Chateaubriand, $$$$
Le Servan, $$
Saturne, $$$$
Ze Kitchen Galerie, $$$$

SEAFOOD

Huîtrerie Régis, $$
L'Huîtrier, $$$
Rech, $$$

VEGETARIAN

Alain Ducasse at the Plaza Athénée, $$$$
Cantine Merci, $
L'Arpège, $$$$
L'As du Fallafel, $
La Bastide Odéon, $$
Macéo, $$$
Rose Bakery, $

By Experience

CHILD-FRIENDLY

Bofinger, $$
Breizh Café, $
Drouant, $$$
L'Avant-Goût, $$
La Coupole, $$$
La Crêperie Josselin, $
Le Troquet, $$
Rose Bakery, $
Soul Kitchen, $

DINING ALONE

Breizh Café, $
Cantine Merci, $
Jeanne A, $
L'Ambassade d'Auvergne, $$
Rose Bakery, $

DINNER PRIX FIXE

Le Troquet, $$
Philou, $$
Ribouldingue, $$
Semilla, $$$
Spring, $$$$

GREAT VIEW

La Tour d'Argent, $$$$
Lapérouse, $$$$
Le Georges, $$$
Le Jules Verne, $$$$

HOT SPOT

Abri, $$
L'Atelier de Joël Robuchon, $$$$
Lazare, $$
Le Dauphin, $$
Mini Palais, $$$
Saturne, $$$$
Thoumieux, $$$$

LATE-NIGHT

Au Pied de Cochon, $$
Bofinger, $$
Julien, $$$
La Coupole, $$$
Le Vaudeville, $$$

LOTS OF LOCALS

Josephine Chez Dumonet, $$$$
La Ferrandaise, $$
Le Petit Rétro, $$$

LUNCH PRIX FIXE

Au Passage, $
Café des Musées, $
La Boulangerie, $$
Lazare, $$
Le Pré Verre, $$
Le Repaire de Cartouche, $$
Les Papilles, $$
Taillevent, $$$$
Willi's Wine Bar, $$

MOST ROMANTIC

La Tour d'Argent, $$$$
Lapérouse, $$$$
Le Grand Véfour, $$$$
Le Pré Catelan, $$$$
Pavillon Ledoyen, $$

OUTDOOR DINING

Au Bourguignon du Marais, $$
Brasserie de l'Isle Saint-Louis, $$
Le Georges, $$$
Le Pré Catelan, $$$$
Mini Palais, $$$
Philou, $$

$$$$ FRENCH FUSION Fodor's Choice ★

🍴 **Hiramatsu.** In this Art Deco dining room near Trocadéro, Takashi Nakagawa continues his variations on the subtly Japanese-inspired French cuisine of restaurant namesake Hiroyuki Hiramatsu, who still sometimes works the kitchen. Luxury ingredients feature prominently in dishes such as thin slices of lamb with onion jam and thyme-and-truffle-spiked jus, or an unusual pot-au-feu of oysters with foie gras and black truffle. For dessert, a mille-feuille of caramelized apples comes with rosemary sorbet. Helpful sommeliers will guide you through the staggering wine list, with more than 1,000 different bottles to choose from. There's no way to get away cheaply, so save this for a special occasion, when you might be tempted to order a carte-blanche menu for €115 (lunch menus at €48). [$] *Average main: €50* ✉ *52 rue de Longchamp, 16e, Around the Eiffel Tower* ☎ *01–56–81–08–80* 🌐 *www.hiramatsu.co.jp/fr* ⏲ *Closed weekends, Aug., and 1 wk at Christmas* ✍ *Reservations essential* [M] *Trocadéro* ✥ *1:B6.*

$$$$ FRENCH FUSION

🍴 **Il Vino.** It might seem audacious to present hungry diners with nothing more than a wine list, but the gamble is paying off at this wine-centric restaurant with a branch in Courchevel, in the French Alps. The hip decor—plum-color banquettes, body-hugging white chairs, a few high tables—attracts a mostly young clientele that's happy to play the game by ordering one of the blind, multicourse tasting menus. The €95 menu, with four dishes and four wines, is a good compromise that might bring you a white Mâcon with saffron risotto, a full-bodied red from Puglia with Provençal-style lamb, sherry-like *vin jaune* d'Arbois with aged Comté cheese, and sweet Jurançon with berry crumble. You can also order individual wine-food combinations à la carte or pick a bottle straight from the cellar and ask for a meal to match. [$] *Average main: €40* ✉ *13 bd. de la Tour-Maubourg, 7e, Around the Eiffel Tower* ☎ *01–44–11–72–00* 🌐 *www.ilvinobyenricobernardo.com* ⏲ *Closed Sun. and Mon. No lunch Sat.* ✍ *Reservations essential* [M] *Invalides* ✥ *3:F1.*

$$ BISTRO

🍴 **Jadis.** There's something very grown-up about the cooking of young chef Guillaume Delage, which isn't a surprise when you learn that he trained with the likes of Michel Bras, Frédéric Anton (of Le Pré Catelan), and Pierre Gagnaire. It's worth making your way to what seems like the middle of nowhere to taste his nostalgic bistro cooking with a modern touch: you might find pâté en croûte among the chef's suggestions, but there are also dishes like the shrimp with saté spices, creamed black rice, and spinach. Though simple, the gray-and-burgundy dining room decorated with mirrors and vintage posters has charm. [$] *Average main: €23* ✉ *208 rue de la Croix-Nivert, 15e, Around the Eiffel Tower* ☎ *01–45–57–73–20* 🌐 *www.bistrotjadisparis.com* ⏲ *Closed weekends and 1 wk at Christmas* ✍ *Reservations essential* [M] *Convention, Porte de Versailles* ✥ *3:B6.*

$$$$ MODERN FRENCH Fodor's Choice ★

🍴 **L'Abeille.** Everything here, from the dove-gray decor to the sparkling silver, speaks of quiet elegance—all the better to savor the restaurant's masterful cuisine. Choices include a "harlequin" of yellow, red, and white beets with a ginger-tinged yogurt and aloe vera emulsion; Breton langoustine in a cinnamon-perfumed gelée, with grapefruit pulp and a ginger- and Tahitian vanilla–infused mayonnaise; and lightly caramelized scallops in an ethereal cloud of white-chocolate foam. Desserts are subtle and surprising, like the apple Reinette, paired with fennel and candied lemon zest. Service is friendly, discrete, devoid of snobbery, and includes all the flourishes that make a dining experience unforgettable, from the first flute of Champagne to the parting gift of—like the name suggests—a jar of honey. [$] *Average main: €100* ✉ *Paris Shangri-La Hotel, 10 av. d'Iéna, 16e, Around the Eiffel Tower* ☎ *01–53–67–19–90* 🌐 *www.shangri-la.com* 🕓 *Closed Sun. and Mon. No lunch Sat.–Wed.* ✍ *Reservations essential* [M] *Iéna* ✣ *1:B6.*

$$$$
BASQUE

🍴 **L'Ami Jean.** If you love Yves Camdeborde's southwestern France–inflected cooking at Le Comptoir but can't get a table for dinner, head to this tavern-like Basque restaurant run by his longtime second-in-command, Stéphane Jégo. Jégo's style is remarkably similar to Camdeborde's because he uses the same suppliers and shares his knack for injecting basic ingredients with sophistication reminiscent of haute cuisine. You can go hearty with Spanish *piquillo* peppers stuffed with salt-cod paste or *poulet basquaise* (chicken stewed with peppers), or lighter with seasonal dishes that change weekly. The restaurant is popular with rugby fans (a sport beloved of Basques), who create a festive mood. Reserve at least a week ahead for dinner. [$] *Average main: €39* ✉ *27 rue Malar, 7e, Around the Eiffel Tower* ☎ *01–47–05–86–89* 🌐 *www.lamijean.fr* 🕓 *Closed Sun., Mon., and Aug.* ✍ *Reservations essential* [M] *Invalides* ✣ *3:E1.*

$$$$
MODERN FRENCH
Fodor's Choice ★

🍴 **L'Arpège.** Breton-born Alain Passard, one of the most respected chefs in Paris, famously shocked the French culinary world by declaring that he was bored with meat. Though his vegetarianism is more theoretical than practical—L'Arpège still caters to fish and poultry eaters—he does cultivate his own vegetables outside Paris, which are then zipped into the city twice a day by high-speed train. His dishes elevate the humblest vegetables to sublime heights: salt-roasted beets with aged balsamic vinegar, leeks with black truffles, black radishes, and *cardon,* a kind of thistle related to the artichoke, with Parmigiano Reggiano. The understated decor places the emphasis firmly on the food, but try to avoid the gloomy cellar room. [$] *Average main: €100* ✉ *84 rue de Varenne, 7e, Around the Eiffel Tower* ☎ *01–47–05–09–06* 🌐 *www.alain-passard.com* 🕓 *Closed weekends* [M] *Varenne* ✣ *3:G2.*

$$$$
MODERN FRENCH
Fodor's Choice ★

🍴 **L'Astrance.** Pascal Barbot rose to fame thanks to his restaurant's reasonable prices and casual atmosphere, but after the passage of several years, Astrance has become resolutely haute. There's no à la carte; you can choose from a lunch menu for €70, a seasonal menu for €150, or the full tasting menu for €230 (this is what most people come for). His dishes often draw on Asian ingredients, as in grilled lamb with miso-lacquered eggplant and a palate-cleansing white sorbet spiked with chili pepper and lemongrass. Each menu also comes at a (significantly) higher price with wines to match each course. Barbot's cooking has such an ethereal quality that it's worth the considerable effort of booking a table—you should start trying at least two months in advance. [$] *Average main: €120* ✉ *4 rue Beethoven, 16e, Around the Eiffel Tower* ☎ *01–40–50–84–40* 🕓 *Closed weekends and Mon., 1 wk in Nov., 1 wk at Christmas, and Aug.* ✍ *Reservations essential* [M] *Passy* ✣ *1:B6.*

CLOSE UP

French Restaurant Types

Bistro: The broadest category, a bistro can be a simple, relaxed restaurant serving traditional fare, one of the new "bistronomic" eateries, or a chic hot spot where dinner costs more than €50 per person. The bistro menu is fairly limited and usually changes with the season.

Brasserie: More informal than a bistro, the brasserie is large, lively, and always has a bar. Ideal for relatively quick meals, it often specializes in Alsatian fare, like *choucroute garnie* (a mixed meat dish with sauerkraut and potatoes) or seafood platters. With flexible hours (usually open all day and well into the night) and diverse menus, brasseries are an excellent choice if you're traveling with kids.

Café: Often an informal neighborhood hangout, the café may also be a showplace attracting a well-heeled crowd or one of the newer barista cafés serving up a virtuosic brew to a much more exacting standard. A limited menu of sandwiches, simple dishes, and classic desserts is usually available throughout the day. Beware of the prices: a half bottle of mineral water can cost €5 or more.

French Fusion: The French fusion restaurant has discernable influences of French cuisine and the cuisine of another region or country.

Haute French: Ambitious and expensive, the haute French restaurant is helmed by a pedigreed chef who prepares multicourse meals to be remembered.

Modern French: Although not necessarily super expensive or pretentious, the modern French restaurant boasts a creative menu showcasing a variety of culinary influences.

Wine Bar: A more recent phenomenon, the wine bar serves more than the usual three or four wines by the glass—and often with an emphasis on natural wines—along with traditional charcuterie or cheese, small dishes, or, more often nowadays, a full gourmet meal.

$$$$ MODERN FRENCH Fodor's Choice ★

🍴 **La Table d'Akihiro.** Did the stars align during our meal, or could it be that La Table d'Akihiro actually *is* the most perfect restaurant in Paris? Set in a quiet, aristocratic *quartier* near the Musée Rodin, its pale celadon walls, crisp white linen, and restrained lighting add up to a simple elegance, all the better to highlight the thrilling cuisine centered on the sea. The chef works all alone in an open kitchen while 16 lucky diners await the next course: lush, simple dishes like plump langoustine shimmering in a silky shallot-fennel sauce, or delicate medallions of sole in a mellow red-wine-and-leek reduction. [$] *Average main: €40* ✉ *49 rue Vaneau, 7e, Around the Eiffel Tower* ☎ *01–45–44–43–48* ⏲ *Closed Sun., Mon., 2 wks in Feb., and Aug.* ✍ *Reservations essential* [M] *Saint-François-Xavier* ✣ *3:G3.*

$$$ BISTRO

🍴 **La Table Lauriston.** This chic bistro near the Trocadéro has a winning formula: top-notch ingredients, simply prepared and generously served. To start, you can't go wrong with the silky foie gras *au torchon*—the liver is poached in a flavorful bouillon—or one of the seasonal salads, such as white asparagus in herb vinaigrette. The trademark dish, a

VEGETARIAN PARIS

Vegetarianism was so uncommon in Paris that star chef Alain Passard caused a sensation when he declared a few years ago that he was bored with red meat and would be focusing on vegetables and fish. True to his word, Passard established a small farm outside Paris where he grows heirloom vegetables that are whizzed to his restaurant **L'Arpège** (*84 rue Varenne, 01–45–51–47–33*) by high-speed train. Customers pay the price; a simple yet sensational beet dish costs €45. Though Paris is hardly a vegetarian paradise, Passard's initiative seems to have rubbed off on other chefs in the

7e. **Le Violon d'Ingres** (*135 rue St-Dominique, 01–45–55–15–05*) and **L'Atelier de Joël Robuchon** (*5 rue Montalembert, 01–42–22–56–56*) both cater, with imagination, to vegetarians. Next door, in the 8e, Alain Ducasse's splendid dining room in the newly spiffed up Plaza Athénée (**Alain Ducasse at the Plaza Athénée**, *25 av. Montaigne, 01–53–67–65–00*) gives Arpège its first real Paris competition. The superstar-chef's stellar new menu puts grains, vegetables—sourced from Versailles's *jardin de la reine*—and fish front and center.

gargantuan rib steak, is big enough to silence even the hungriest Texan. Given the neighborhood you might expect a business-like setting, but the dining room feels cheerful, with vividly colored walls and velvet-upholstered chairs, and there is a 16-seat terrace. Don't miss the giant *baba au rhum*, which the waiters will douse with a choice of three rums. $ *Average main: €26* ⊠ *129 rue de Lauriston, 16e, Around the Eiffel Tower* ☎ *01–47–27–00–07* ⊕ *www.restaurantlatablelauriston. com* ☉ *Closed Sun. and 4 wks in Aug. No lunch Sat.* ⊴ *Reservations essential* Ⓜ *Trocadéro* ✛ *1:A6.*

$ ✕ **Le Café Constant.** Parisians are a nostalgic bunch, which explains
BISTRO   the popularity of this down-to-earth venue, a relatively humble bistro with cream-color walls, red banquettes, and wooden tables. The menu reads like a French cookbook from the 1970s—who cooks veal *cordon bleu* these days?—but the dishes taste even better than before. There's delicious and creamy lentil soup with morsels of foie gras, and the artichoke salad comes with fresh—not bottled or frozen—hearts. A towering *vacherin* (meringue layered with ice cream) might bring this delightfully retro meal to a close. On weekdays there is a bargain lunch menu for €16 (two courses) or €23 (three courses). $ *Average main: €16* ⊠ *139 rue St-Dominique, 7e, Around the Eiffel Tower* ☎ *01–47–53–73–34* ⊕ *www.maisonconstant.com* ⊴ *Reservations not accepted* Ⓜ *École Militaire; Métro or RER: Pont de l'Alma* ✛ *3:D2.*

$$$$ ✕ **Le Jules Verne.** Alain Ducasse doesn't set his sights low, so it was no
MODERN FRENCH   real surprise when he took over this prestigious dining room on the second floor of the Eiffel Tower and had designer Patrick Jouin give the room a neo-futuristic look in shades of brown. Most accessible is the €105 lunch menu (weekdays only), which brings you à la carte dishes in slightly smaller portions. Spend more (about €200 to €250 per person without drinks) and you'll be entitled to lavish dishes such as lobster with celery root and black truffle, and fricassee of Bresse chicken with

crayfish. For dessert the kitchen reinterprets French classics, as in an unsinkable pink grapefruit soufflé with grapefruit sorbet. Book months ahead or try your luck at the last minute. $ *Average main: €90* ✉ *Tour Eiffel, south pillar, Av. Gustave Eiffel, 7e, Around the Eiffel Tower* ☎ *01–45–55–61–44* ⊕ *www.lejulesverne-paris.com* ✍ *Reservations essential* ⌂ *Jacket and tie* Ⓜ *Bir-Hakeim* ✛ *3:C2.*

$$
MODERN FRENCH
FAMILY

✕ **Le Troquet.** A quiet residential street shelters one of the best-value bistros around: prix-fixe menus start at €30 at lunch and rise to €41 for a six-course tasting menu (there are also à la carte selections), but it's the quality, not quantity, that counts. A changing roster of dishes from the Basque and Béarn regions of southwestern France are available, and a typical meal might include vegetable soup with foie gras and cream, panfried scallops in crab sauce or *axoa de veau* (a Basque veal sauté), and a vanilla soufflé with cherry jam. Béarn red wine fills the glasses and happy regulars fill the dining room. $ *Average main: €21* ✉ *21 rue François-Bonvin, 15e, Around the Eiffel Tower* ☎ *01–45–66–89–00* ⊘ *Closed Sun., Mon., 3 wks in Aug., 1 wk in May, and 1 wk at Christmas* Ⓜ *Ségur* ✛ *3:E5.*

$$$$
MODERN FRENCH

✕ **Le Violon d'Ingres.** Following in the footsteps of Joël Robuchon and Alain Senderens, Christian Constant gave up the Michelin-star chase in favor of relatively accessible prices and a packed dining room (book at least a week ahead). Here, the food is sophisticated and the atmosphere is lively; you can find signature dishes like the almond-crusted sea bass with rémoulade (a buttery caper sauce), alongside game and scallops (in season), and comforting desserts like *pots de crème* and chocolate tart. With wines starting at around €40 (and a €45 lunch menu on weekdays), this is a wonderful place for a classic yet informal French meal. $ *Average main: €36* ✉ *135 rue St-Dominique, 7e, Around the Eiffel Tower* ☎ *01–45–55–15–05* ⊕ *www.maisonconstant.com* ✍ *Reservations essential* Ⓜ *École Militaire* ✛ *3:D2.*

$$
MODERN FRENCH

✕ **Les Cocottes de Christian Constant.** Chef Christian Constant has an unfailing sense of how Parisians want to eat these days, as proved by this third addition to his mini restaurant empire near the Eiffel Tower. At Les Cocottes he's shifted the normally leisurely bistro experience into high gear, which allows him to keep prices moderate. Seated at a long counter on slightly uncomfortable stools that discourage lingering, diners can mix and match from a menu of soups, salads, *cocottes* (dishes served in cast-iron pots), *verrines* (starters presented in tapas-style glasses), and comforting desserts, all made from fresh, seasonal ingredients. $ *Average main: €19* ✉ *135 rue St-Dominique, 7e, Around the Eiffel Tower* ⊕ *www.maisonconstant.com* ✍ *Reservations not accepted* Ⓜ *École Militaire; Métro or RER: Pont de l'Alma* ✛ *3:D2.*

$$$$
CANTONESE

✕ **LiLi.** The operatically beautiful LiLi, in the Peninsula Hotel, places sophisticated Cantonese cuisine in its rightful place—the gastronomic center of the world. Sheathed in cascades of red silk, the glamorous dining room, especially romantic in the evening, shimmers with ebony and gold damask under indigo-blue chandeliers. The menu features all the classics, raised to the status of haute cuisine: small plates of dim sum (seafood, vegetable, or pork dumplings) alongside more substantial fare like fried rice studded with market-fresh vegetables, succulent

Sichuan shrimp, and barbecued suckling pig. The chef's signature *crème de mangue* laced with pomelo pearls is an ethereal ending to an exceptional meal. At €68, the prix-fixe lunch menu is a wonderful introduction to this timeless cuisine. Ⓢ *Average main: €36* ⊠ *The Peninsula Paris, 19 rue Kléber, 16e, Around the Eiffel Tower* ☎ *01–58–12–67–50* ⊕ *paris.peninsula.com* ⌲ *Reservations essential* Ⓜ *Kléber, Charles de Gaulle–Étoile* ✛ *1:B5.*

$$$$
FRENCH FUSION
Fodor's Choice
★

✕ **Restaurant David Toutain.** Youthful David Toutain is often called a prodigy, a status applied sparingly in Paris and in this case well deserved. Although his approach may be exasperatingly conceptual for some, others find his earthy, surprising, and inspired concoctions utterly thrilling. Each dish is a lesson in contrasts—of temperature, texture, and flavor—as well as a feat of composition: briny oysters, brussels sprouts, and foie gras in a warm potato consommé; creamy raw oysters with tart kiwi and yuzu; crispy pork chips alongside velvety smoked potato puree. Toutain has a particular soft spot for root vegetables and truffles, which he sprinkles liberally throughout dishes like salsify broth with lardo and black truffle. The €45 lunch menu is a great way to sample a unique and challenging cuisine that changes daily. Ⓢ *Average main: €40* ⊠ *29 rue Surcouf, 7e, Around the Eiffel Tower* ☎ *01–45–50–11–10* ⊕ *www.davidtoutain.com* ☾ *Closed weekends* ⌲ *Reservations essential* Ⓜ *Invalides, La Tour–Maubourg* ✛ *3:E1.*

$$$$
BRASSERIE

✕ **Thoumieux.** When this old-world bistro was revived, much of its vintage character was thankfully preserved, with globe lights and etched mirrors. Despite its location in the sedate 7e arrondissement, this has quickly become the place to be seen eating thrilling dishes a good notch above brasserie fare. A juicy Angus beef hamburger comes with a superfluous shower of Parmesan and ultraskinny fries, while the more sophisticated slow-cooked salmon is accompanied by vegetables from star market gardener Joël Thiébault. For dessert, try the piping-hot churros with chocolate sauce. The restaurant *gastronomique* upstairs is ever so chic and a good bit pricier, yet proffers an experience commensurate with the top bistros in town (there's a €154 set menu at lunch and dinner and a €75 three-course menu at lunch). Reservations are taken exactly six days ahead. Ⓢ *Average main: €40* ⊠ *79 rue St-Dominique, 7e, Around the Eiffel Tower* ☎ *01–47–05–49–75* ⊕ *www.thoumieux.fr* ⌲ *Reservations essential* Ⓜ *La Tour–Maubourg* ✛ *3:E1.*

THE CHAMPS-ÉLYSÉES

Style often wins out over substance around the Champs-Élysées, but a handful of restaurants continue to defy fashion. This part of Paris is home to many of the city's most ambitious chefs, whose restaurants are surrounded by palatial hotels, bourgeois apartments, embassies, and luxury boutiques. Some, such as Eric Frechon at Le Bristol's Epicure, offer sophisticated updates of French classics, whereas others, like Pierre Gagnaire, constantly push culinary boundaries in the manner of a mad scientist. A few solid bistros survive here, notably the Art Deco Savy.

A Cheese Primer

Their cuisine might be getting lighter, but the French aren't ready to relinquish their cheese. Some restaurants present a single, lovingly selected slice, whereas the more prestigious restaurants wheel in a trolley of specimens aged on the premises. Cheese always comes after the main course and before—or instead of—dessert.

Among the best bistros for cheese are **Astier,** where a giant basket of oozy wonders is brought to the table, and **Le Comptoir,** where a dazzling cheese platter is part of the five-course prix-fixe dinner, or **Le Bistro Paul Bert,** where an overflowing cheese board is left on your table for you to help yourself. A few *bars à fromages* are springing up, too: devoted to cheese the way *bars à vins* are dedicated to wine. **Fromagerie Cantin** (*12 rue du Champ de Mars, 01–45–50–43–94* ⊕ *www.cantin.fr*) is a terrific example.

Armed with these phrases, you can wow the waiter and work your way through the most generous platter.

Avez-vous le Beaufort d'été? Do you have summer Beaufort?

Beaufort is similar to Gruyère, and the best Beaufort is made with milk produced in summer, when cows eat fresh grass. Aged Beaufort is even more reminiscent of a mountain hike.

Je voudrais un chèvre bien frais/bien sec. I'd like a goat cheese that's nice and fresh/nice and dry.

France produces many goat cheeses, some so fresh they can be scooped with a spoon, some tough enough to use as doorstops. It's a matter of taste, but hard-core cheese eaters favor drier specimens, which stick to the roof of the mouth and have a frankly goaty aroma.

C'est un St-Marcellin de vache ou de chèvre? Is this St-Marcellin made with cow's or goat's milk?

St-Marcellin is a more original choice than the ubiquitous *crottin de chèvre* (poetically named after goats' turds). Originally a goat cheese, today it's more often made with cow's milk. The best have an oozy center, though some like it dry as a hockey puck.

C'est un Brie de Meaux ou de Melun? Is this Brie from Meaux or Melun?

There are many kinds of Brie. Brie de Meaux is the best known, with a smooth flavor and runny center; the much rarer Brie de Melun is more pungent and saltier.

Je n'aime pas le Camembert industriel! I don't like industrial Camembert!

Camembert might be a national treasure, but most of it is industrial. Real Camembert has a white rind with rust-color streaks and a yellow center.

Avez-vous de la confiture pour accompagner ce brebis? Do you have any jam to go with this sheep's cheese?

In the Basque region berry jam is the traditional accompaniment for sharp sheep's-milk cheeses like Ossau-Iraty.

C'est la saison du Mont d'Or. It's Mont d'Or season.

This potent mountain cheese, also known as Vacherin, is produced only from September to March. It's so runny, it's eaten with a spoon.

$$$$ ✕**Alain Ducasse at the Plaza Athénée.** Set within the Plaza Athénée hotel,
MODERN FRENCH Alain Ducasse's three-star Paris flagship totally redefines French haute
Fodor's Choice cuisine. Arguably the world's most visible chef, Ducasse surprises here,
★ devoting himself entirely to vegetables, grains, and fish. From the moment you enter the glittering dining room, alight with thousands of crystals reflected in sinuous mirrored banquettes, you know you've entered a parallel universe entirely devoted to sybaritic pleasure. Chef Romain Meder executes Ducasse's recipes, which mix the most luxe with the humblest ingredients, to sublime effect: caviar over tender langoustine in a lemongrass-infused broth; a stack of lacy buckwheat blini accompanied by lentils and caviar in a smoked gelée topped with ethereal truffle cream. Desserts like lemon ice with candied lemon and silky kombu seaweed take the notion of dining for pleasure and health to vertiginous new heights. $ *Average main: €120* ⊠ *Hôtel Plaza Athénée, 25 av. Montaigne, 8e, Champs-Élysées* ☎ *01–53–67–65–00* ⊕ *www.alain-ducasse.com* ☉ *Closed weekends. No lunch Mon.–Wed.* ⌣ *Reservations essential* 𝄐 *Jacket required* Ⓜ *Alma-Marceau* ✛ *1:D6.*

$$$$ ✕**Alléno Paris au Pavillon Ledoyen.** Tucked away in a quiet garden across
MODERN FRENCH from the Petit Palais, Ledoyen—open since 1779—is a study in Empire-
Fodor's Choice style elegance. Star chef Yannick Alléno injects the three-star dining
★ room with a frisson of modernity by putting fresh farmhouse ingredients front and center. At €295, the 10-course tasting extravaganza may seem *de trop*, but in Alléno's hands dishes like smoked eel soufflé with watercress coulis and candied onion, tender mussels with tart green apple and caviar, or artichoke-and-Parmesan gratin are rendered as light as a feather. The desserts are tiny masterpieces. For a purely Parisian splurge, the five-course €135 lunch menu is worth every cent. $ *Average main: €120* ⊠ *1 av. Dutuit, on Carré des Champs-Élysées, 8e, Champs-Élysées* ☎ *01–53–05–10–01* ⊕ *www.yannick-alleno.com/ restaurant/le-pavillon-ledoyen* ☉ *Closed Sun. and Aug.* ⌣ *Reservations essential* 𝄐 *Jacket required* Ⓜ *Concorde, Champs-Élysées–Clemenceau* ✛ *1:F6.*

$$$ ✕**Chez Savy.** Just off the glitzy Avenue Montaigne, Chez Savy occupies
BISTRO its own circa-1930s dimension, oblivious to the area's fashionization. The Art Deco cream-and-burgundy interior is blissfully intact (avoid the back room unless you're in a large group), and the waiters show not a trace of attitude. Fill up on rib-sticking specialties from the Aveyron region of central France—lentil salad with bacon, foie gras (prepared on the premises), perfectly charred lamb with featherlight shoestring frites, and pedigreed Charolais beef. Order a celebratory bottle of Mercurey with your meal and feel smug that you've found this place. $ *Average main: €29* ⊠ *23 rue Bayard, 8e, Champs-Élysées* ☎ *01–47–23–46–98* ⊕ *www.chezsavy.com* ☉ *Closed weekends and Aug.* Ⓜ *Franklin-D.- Roosevelt* ✛ *1:E5.*

$$$$ ✕**Dominique Bouchet.** To taste the cooking of one of the city's great
BISTRO chefs, head to Dominique Bouchet's elegant bistro, where contemporary art brightens cream-painted walls. On the menu, refined French technique meets country-style cooking, as in leg of lamb braised in wine with roasted cocoa bean and potato puree, or a chocolate éclair with black cherries and ice cream. Sometimes the dishes can get a touch

too complicated, but the warm and very professional service makes up for it. If you're feeling indecisive, you might treat yourself to the €105 dinner tasting menu: a succession of six small plates followed by a dessert. [$] *Average main: €35* ✉ *11 rue Treilhard, 8e, Champs-Élysées* ☎ *01–45–61–09–46* 🌐 *www.dominique-bouchet.com* 🕒 *Closed weekends and 3 wks in Aug.* ✍ *Reservations essential* [M] *Miromesnil* ✣ *1:F3.*

$$$$ MODERN FRENCH Fodor's Choice ★

🍴 **Guy Savoy.** Within the beautifully restored La Monnaie (the old Paris mint), you'll find star chef Guy Savoy's newest spot. The revamped menu retains the master's classics—artichoke soup with black truffles—with some new dishes like oysters pot-au-feu and sweet, bitter, and peppery roasted duck *paletot* that reveal the magnitude of his talent. If the waiters see you're relishing a dish, they won't hesitate to offer second helpings. Generous half portions allow you to graze your way through the menu—unless you choose a blowout feast with set menus ranging from €360 to €490 for the 18-course option—and reasonably priced wines are available (though beware the cost of wines by the glass). [$] *Average main: €120* ✉ *18 rue Troyon, 17e, Champs-Élysées* ☎ *01–43–80–40–61* 🌐 *www.guysavoy.com* 🕒 *Closed Sun., Mon., and 1 wk at Christmas. No lunch Sat.* ✍ *Reservations essential* 👔 *Jacket required* [M] *Charles-de-Gaulle–Étoile* ✣ *1:C3.*

$$$$ JAPANESE

🍴 **Kifune.** Some Japanese expats say you won't find anything closer to authentic Japanese cooking in Paris than the kitchen in Kifune. Sit at the bar to admire the sushi chef's lightning-quick skills or opt for a more intimate table. The crab-and-shrimp salad is a sublime starter, and the miso soup with clams is deeply flavored. To follow, you can't go wrong with the sashimi. A meal here will leave a dent in your wallet (though there is a €33 set menu at lunch), but for fans of Japanese cuisine, the meals are worth it. With only 20 seats, it often turns away would-be customers, so be sure to book in advance. [$] *Average main: €35* ✉ *44 rue St-Ferdinand, 17e, Champs-Élysées* ☎ *01–45–72–11–19* 🕒 *Closed Sun. and Mon., 3 wks in Aug., and 1 wk in Dec.* ✍ *Reservations essential* [M] *Argentine* ✣ *1:A3.*

$$$$ MODERN FRENCH

🍴 **L'Arôme.** Eric Martins ran a popular bistro in the far reaches of the 15e arrondissement before opening this contemporary restaurant off the Champs-Élysées, and his background in haute cuisine makes this ambitious restaurant an easy transition. The spot turns out seasonal dishes with a touch of finesse from the open kitchen; foie gras confit with rosemary-poached quince and wild-rose jam, or scallops *à la plancha* (from the grill) with vanilla and spaghetti squash might be featured. There is no à la carte, and if the dinner menus seem steep at €99 (€159 with wine pairing), try the lunch menu for €79. Watch out for the pricey wines by the glass. [$] *Average main: €45* ✉ *3 rue St-Philippe du Roule, 8e, Champs-Élysées* ☎ *01–42–25–55–98* 🌐 *www.larome.fr* 🕒 *Closed weekends and Aug.* ✍ *Reservations essential* [M] *St-Philippe du Roule* ✣ *1:E4.*

$$$ SEAFOOD

🍴 **L'Huîtrier.** If you have a single-minded craving for oysters, this is the place for you. The friendly owner will describe the many different kinds available, and you can follow with any of several daily fish specials—or opt for a full seafood platter for around €50. Mood lighting, blond wood, and cream tones create a tranquil, stylish atmosphere. [$] *Average* *main: €27* ⊠ *16 rue Saussier-Leroy, 17e, Champs-Élysées* ☎ *01–40–54–83–44* ⊕ *www.huitrier.fr* ⊗ *Closed Aug.* Ⓜ *Ternes* ✛ *1:C2.*

$$$$ ✕ **La Cristal Room.** The success of this restaurant in the Baccarat museum-
MODERN FRENCH boutique stems not only from the stunning decor by Philippe Starck—mirrors, patches of exposed-brick wall, and a black chandelier—but also from the culinary stylings of chef Guy Martin, also of Le Grand Véfour. The menu provides a taste of his ultrarefined style with dishes such as green asparagus soup with a lemon-poached egg, and sole meunière with grapefruit and an arugula flan. Plan on reserving a week or two ahead for dinner; lunch requires little advance notice and is a reasonable €36. Ⓢ *Average main: €42* ⊠ *11 pl. des États-Unis, 16e, Champs-Élysées* ☎ *01–40–22–11–10* ⊕ *www.baccarat.fr* ⊗ *Closed Sun.* ⌓ *Reservations essential* Ⓜ *Kléber* ✛ *1:C5.*

$$$$ ✕ **La Table du Lancaster.** Operated by one of the most enduring families
MODERN FRENCH in French gastronomy (the Troisgros clan has run a world-famous restaurant in Roanne for three generations), this stylish, two-Michelin-star boutique-hotel restaurant is the perfect setting for stellar cosmopolitan cuisine; try to sit in the gorgeous Asian-inspired courtyard with its red walls and bamboo. Often drawing on humble ingredients such as eel or pigs' ears, the food reveals fascinating flavor and texture contrasts, like silky sardines on crunchy melba toast or tangy frogs' legs in tamarind; the salmon with sorrel sauce is a classic Troisgros dish. Ⓢ *Average main: €55* ⊠ *Hotel Lancaster, 7 rue de Berri, 8e, Champs-Élysées* ☎ *01–40–76–40–18* ⊕ *www.hotel-lancaster.fr* ⊗ *Closed weekends* ⌓ *Reservations essential* Ⓜ *George V* ✛ *1:D4.*

$$$$ ✕ **Le Cinq.** Christian Le Squer is not the most famous chef in Paris
MODERN FRENCH but he *is* one of the best, as proved by his turn here at one of the
Fodor's Choice city's most deluxe dining rooms. You'll find all the luxury products
★ you might expect—caviar, truffles, game in season—but treated with a light touch that often draws on Breton ingredients such as oysters or lamb. A perfect example would be his famous Ile de Chausey lobster marinated in citrus and served in a heart of caramelized romaine with a featherlight beurre blanc mousseux. Desserts are ethereal and service is unfailingly thoughtful. Ⓢ *Average main: €110* ⊠ *Hôtel Four Seasons George V, 31 av. George V, 8e, Champs-Élysées* ☎ *01–49–52–70–00* ⊕ *www.fourseasons.com/paris* ⌓ *Reservations essential* 🏛 *Jacket and tie* Ⓜ *George V* ✛ *1:D5.*

$$ ✕ **Le Hide.** Hide Kobayashi, known as "Koba," is one of several Japanese
BISTRO chefs in Paris who trained with some of the biggest names in French cuisine before opening their own restaurants. Not surprisingly, this great-value bistro near the Arc de Triomphe (the three-course prix fixe is €36) became instantly popular with locals as well as visiting Japanese and Americans who follow the food scene. Generosity is the key to the cooking here, which steers clear of haute-cuisine flourishes: both the monkfish fricassee with anchovy-rich tapenade and a classic veal kidney in mustard sauce, for instance, come with a heap of mashed potatoes. For dessert try the stunning *île flottante* (floating island), made with oven-baked meringue. Wines by the glass start at €5—unheard-of in this area. Ⓢ *Average main: €20* ⊠ *10 rue du Général Lanzerac, 8e, Champs-Élysées* ☎ *01–45–74–15–81* ⊕ *www.lehide.fr* ⊗ *Closed Sun.,*

2 wks in May, and 3 wks in Aug. ⟨ *Reservations essential* Ⓜ *Charles de Gaulle–Étoile* ✛ *1:B3.*

$$ ✕ **Le Petit Verdot du 17e.** Sandwich bars might be threatening the tradi-
BISTRO   tional two-hour lunch, but that doesn't stop this old-fashioned neigh-
borhood bistro with its painted facade and wine-theme dining room
from flourishing. Business executives loosen their neckties to feast on
homemade pâté, plate-engulfing steak for two, or guinea hen with cab-
bage, along with one of 50 or so small-producer wines. Ⓢ *Average
main: €18* ⊠ *9 rue Fourcroy, 17e, Champs-Élysées* ☎ *01–42–27–47–42*
⊘ *Closed Sun. No lunch Sat.* Ⓜ *Charles de Gaulle–Étoile* ✛ *1:C2.*

$$$$ ✕ **Le Relais Plaza.** Parisian to its core, the Hotel Plaza Athénée's Art Deco
FRENCH   dining room—think 1930s Lalique glass, black-lacquer furnishings, and
a mural that's a registered historic landmark—is a cherished neighbor-
hood stalwart. Masterful updates of French classics include dishes like
warm salad of delicate greens, thin-sliced artichokes, and Parmesan,
flecked with shaved black truffles; house-made foie gras with slices
of fresh figs and a rich dried-fruit chutney; and sole meunière served
with a light lemon butter to highlight the freshness and delicacy of the
perfectly cooked fish. Go on the last Wednesday of the month, when
the dining room is transported to the 1940s with live jazz and an audi-
ence primed for a rollicking good time. Ⓢ *Average main: €50* ⊠ *Plaza
Athénée, 21 av. Montaigne, 8e, Champs-Élysées* ☎ *01–53–67–64–00*
⊕ *www.alain-ducasse.com/en/restaurant/le-relais-plaza* ⟨ *Reservations
essential* Ⓜ *Alma-Marceau, Franklin D. Roosevelt* ✛ *1:D6.*

$$$ ✕ **Mini Palais.** Inside the Grand Palais, Mini Palais has gotten things
MODERN FRENCH   smashingly right. With silvery ceilings, dark wood, and faux classical
marble, it's among Paris's most stylish dining rooms, but the menu is
the real draw. The burger *de magret et foie gras,* a flavorful mélange
of tender duckling breast and duck foie gras drizzled with truffled jus
on a buttery brioche bun, underscores what's best about this place: a
thoroughly modern cuisine with an old-fashioned extravagance. For a
summer meal or a cocktail, the majestically pillared terrace overlooking Pont d'Alexandre III must be the most beautiful in Paris. Ⓢ *Average
main: €25* ⊠ *3 av. Winston Churchill, 8e, Champs-Élysées* ☎ *01–42–
56–42–42* ⊕ *www.minipalais.com* ⟨ *Reservations essential* Ⓜ *Champs-
Élysées–Clemenceau* ✛ *1:F6.*

$$$$ ✕ **Pierre Gagnaire.** If you want to venture to the frontier of contemporary
MODERN FRENCH   cooking—and if money is no object—dinner here is a must. Chef Pierre
Gagnaire's work is at once intellectual and poetic, often blending three
or four unexpected tastes and textures in a single dish. Just taking in
the menu requires concentration (ask the waiters for help), so complex
are the multiline descriptions about each dish's six or seven ingredients.
The Grand Dessert, a seven-dessert marathon, will leave you breathless,
though it's not as overwhelming as it sounds. The uninspiring prix-fixe
lunch (€155) and occasional ill-judged dishes linger as drawbacks, and
prices keep shooting skyward, so Pierre Gagnaire is an experience best
saved for the financial elite. Ⓢ *Average main: €130* ⊠ *6 rue de Balzac,
8e, Champs-Élysées* ☎ *01–58–36–12–50* ⊕ *www.pierre-gagnaire.com*
⊘ *Closed weekends, Aug., and at Christmas* ⟨ *Reservations essential*
Ⓜ *Charles de Gaulle–Étoile* ✛ *1:D4.*

$$$$
SEAFOOD
Fodor's Choice
★

✕ **Rech.** Having restored the historic Paris bistros Aux Lyonnais and Benoît to their former glory, star chef Alain Ducasse turned his piercing attention to this seafood brasserie founded in 1925. His wisdom lies in knowing what not to change: the original Art Deco chairs in the main-floor dining room; seafood shucker Malec, who has been a fixture on this chic stretch of sidewalk since 1982; and the XL éclair (it's supersize) that's drawn in locals for decades. There are also many Med-inspired dishes such as tomato cream with crayfish and fresh almonds or Niçoise-style sea bass with thyme fritters. A great-value €44 menu is available at lunch; the dinner menu is €54. $ *Average main: €33* ⊠ *62 av. des Ternes, 17e, Champs-Élysées* ☎ *01–45–72–29–47* ⊕ *www. restaurant-rech.fr* ⊗ *Closed Sun., Mon., late July–late Aug., and 1 wk at Christmas* ⌦ *Reservations essential* Ⓜ *Ternes* ✣ *1:B3.*

$$$$
MODERN FRENCH

✕ **Taillevent.** Perhaps the most traditional—for many diners this is only high praise—of all Paris luxury restaurants, this grande dame basks in renewed freshness under brilliant chef Alain Solivérès, who draws inspiration from the Basque country, Bordeaux, and Languedoc for his daily menu. Traditional dishes such as scallops meunière (with butter and lemon) are matched with contemporary choices like a splendid spelt risotto with truffles and frogs' legs or panfried duck liver with caramelized fruits and vegetables. One of the 19th-century paneled salons has been turned into a winter garden, and contemporary paintings adorn the walls. The service is flawless, and the exemplary wine list is well priced. $ *Average main: €110* ⊠ *15 rue Lamennais, 8e, Champs-Élysées* ☎ *01–44–95–15–01* ⊕ *www.taillevent.com* ⊗ *Closed weekends and Aug.* ⌦ *Reservations essential* 🎩 *Jacket and tie* Ⓜ *Charles de Gaulle–Étoile* ✣ *1:D4.*

AROUND THE LOUVRE

Home to the city's wholesale food market until the 1960s, Les Halles is still the place to go for late-night onion soup or steak frites, washed back with gulps of cheap and tasty red wine. The streets grow more subdued around the Louvre and Palais Royal, where you can slurp oysters at a classic brasserie or indulge in the more experimental haute cuisine at a foodie hangout.

$$
BRASSERIE

✕ **Au Pied de Cochon.** One of the few remnants of Les Halles's raucous all-night past is this brasserie, which has been open every day since 1946. Now run by the Frères Blanc group, it still draws both a French and a foreign crowd with round-the-clock hours and trademark traditional fare such as seafood platters, breaded pigs' trotters, beer-braised pork knuckle with sauerkraut, and cheese-crusted onion soup. It's perfect stick-to-your-rib fare for a winter's day or to finish off a bar crawl. The dining room, with its white tablecloths and little piggy details, feels resolutely cheerful, and it's open 24/7. $ *Average main: €22* ⊠ *6 rue Coquillière, 1er* ☎ *01–40–13–77–00* ⊕ *www.pieddecochon.com* Ⓜ *Les Halles* ✣ *2:C6.*

$$$
CAFÉ

✕ **Café Marly.** Run by the Costes brothers, this café overlooking the main courtyard of the Louvre and I.M. Pei's glass pyramid is one of the more stylish places in Paris to meet for a drink or a coffee, whether in the stunning jewel-toned dining rooms with their molded ceilings or on the Louvre's long, sheltered terrace. Regular café service shuts down during meal hours, when fashion-conscious folks dig into Asian-inspired salads and pseudo-Italian pasta dishes. [$] *Average main: €30* ✉ *Cour Napoléon du Louvre, enter from Louvre courtyard, 93 rue de Rivoli, 1er, Around the Louvre* ☎ *01–49–26–06–60* 🌐 *www.beaumarly.com* [M] *Palais-Royal* ✥ *4:B1.*

$$$ BISTRO

🍴 **Chez Georges.** If you were to ask Parisian bankers, aristocrats, or antiques dealers to name their favorite bistro for a three-hour weekday lunch, many would choose Georges. The traditional fare is very good—chicken-liver terrine, curly endive salad with bacon and a poached egg, steak with béarnaise—and the atmosphere is better, compensating for the steep prices. Order one of the wines indicated in colored ink on the menu and you can drink as much or as little of it as you want (and be charged accordingly); there's also another wine list with grander bottles. [$] *Average main: €32* ✉ *1 rue du Mail, 2e, Around the Louvre* ☎ *01–42–60–07–11* 🕓 *Closed weekends, Aug., and 1 wk at Christmas* [M] *Sentier* ✥ *2:C5.*

$$$ BISTRO Fodor's Choice ★

🍴 **Frenchie.** The prodigiously talented Grégory Marchand worked with Jamie Oliver in London before opening this brick-and-stone-walled bistro on a pedestrian street near Rue Montorgueil. It quickly became one of the most packed bistros in town, with tables booked months in advance, despite two seatings each evening. Marchand owes a large part of his success to the good-value €68 five-course menu at dinner (prix fixe only)—boldly flavored dishes such as calamari gazpacho with squash blossoms, and melt-in-the-mouth braised lamb with roasted eggplant and spinach are excellent options. Service can be, shall we say, a tad brusque, but for some that's a small price to pay for food this good. [$] *Average main: €32* ✉ *5 rue du Nil, 2e, Around the Louvre* ☎ *01–40–39–96–19* 🌐 *www.frenchie-restaurant.com* 🕓 *Closed weekends, 2 wks in Aug., and 10 days at Christmas. No lunch* ✍ *Reservations essential* [M] *Sentier* ✥ *2:D5.*

$ WINE BAR Fodor's Choice ★

🍴 **Frenchie Bar à Vins.** If this weren't one of Paris's outstanding wine bars, the wait, attitude, and metal tractor seats might be a deterrent. Yet wine lovers would be hard-pressed to find a better venue for sampling a great list of French wines and inspired selections from Italy and Spain—all sold by the bottle or glass, with suberb cuisine to match. Feast on masterful small dishes like the "coleslaw" of citrusy calamari, black-olive coulis, and a sprinkling of pine nuts; bresaola with apples, spicy mizuna leaves, and dollops of creamy horseradish; and a wedge of Stilton served atop a paste of Speculoos biscuits with poached pears and smoked walnuts. [$] *Average main: €17* ✉ *6 rue du Nil, 2e, Around the Louvre* ☎ *No phone* 🌐 *www.frenchie-restaurant.com* 🕓 *Closed weekends. No lunch* ✍ *Reservations not accepted* [M] *Sentier* ✥ *2:D5.*

$ MODERN FRENCH FAMILY

🍴 **Frenchie To Go.** The third outpost in Frenchie's Rue du Nil empire, Frenchie To Go capitalizes on three of the latest Paris food trends: breakfast, fast food, and takeaway, but with a spin that's totally Frenchie. The hot dogs and tasty pastrami (almost unheard of in Paris) are meticulously sourced, as is pretty much everything else—Brittany lobster for the lobster rolls and line-caught hake for the scrumptious fish-and-chips. A cheerful, modern space invites lingering if you're lucky enough to snag a table—more likely for breakfast (which is served all day) or during the off-hours, when a cup of hot chocolate, a home-made ginger beer, or a good cup of coffee and a doughnut are just the thing. The price-to-value quotient is excellent. $ *Average main: €10* ✉ *9 rue du Nil, 2e, Around the Louvre* ☎ *01–40–39–96–19* ⊕ *www. frenchietogo.com* ≋ *Reservations not accepted* Ⓜ *Sentier* ✛ *2:D5.*

$$
WINE BAR
Fodor's Choice
★
✕ **Juvéniles.** An address we'd keep to ourselves if everyone weren't talking about it, Juvéniles is the ideal kind of neighborhood outpost that mixes seriously good dining with an inspired wine list, all at affordable prices. The €16.50 lunch menu might start with velvety foie gras *maison* (paired with a crisp Riesling), followed by slow-braised beef with a tangy tarragon-and-dill sauce *ravigote*. Finish with verbena-infused panna cotta or rhubarb compote with juicy Plougastel strawberries. This petit bistro's off-the-tourist-trail location close to the Palais Royal gardens and the Louvre is an extra bonus. $ *Average main: €20* ✉ *47 rue de Richelieu, 1er, Around the Louvre* ☎ *01–42–97–46–49* ⊘ *Closed Sun. No lunch Mon.* ≋ *Reservations essential* Ⓜ *Bourse, Pyramides* ✛ *2:B6.*

$$$
BISTRO
Fodor's Choice
★
✕ **L'Ardoise.** A minuscule storefront decorated with enlargements of old sepia postcards of Paris, L'Ardoise is a model of the kind of contemporary bistro making waves in Paris. The first-rate three-course dinner menu for €38 tempts with such original dishes as mushroom-and-foie-gras ravioli with smoked duck; farmer's pork with porcini mushrooms; and red mullet with creole sauce (you can also order à la carte, but it's less of a bargain). Just as enticing are the desserts, such as a superb *feuillantine au citron*—caramelized pastry leaves filled with lemon cream and lemon slices—and a boozy baba au rhum. With friendly waiters and a small but well-chosen wine list, L'Ardoise would be perfect if it weren't so popular (meaning noisy and crowded). $ *Average main: €27* ✉ *28 rue du Mont Thabor, 1er* ☎ *01–42–96–28–18* ⊕ *www.lardoise-paris. com* ⊘ *No lunch Sun.* ≋ *Reservations essential* Ⓜ *Concorde* ✛ *1:H6.*

$$$$
BISTRO
Fodor's Choice
★
✕ **La Bourse et La Vie.** After a takeover by the French-trained American chef Daniel Rose, this bistro stalwart transformed from a duckling to a swan, with elegant revamps of its bistro decor and an upgrade on those deeply satisfying French comfort-food classics. The humble steak frites is a buttery, melt-in-the-mouth slab of beef ringed by a halo of perfectly crisp golden frites. Start with the exceptional house fois gras with artichokes, followed by a splendid *pot à feu* (veal and vegetables in broth). All meals begin with superb *gougère* (a warm cheesy bread), and, if you're wise, will end with dessert, which might be a classic mousse au chocolat, apricot and almond tart, or the best tarte tatin in Paris. $ *Average main: €35* ✉ *12 rue Vivienne, 2e, Around the Louvre* ☎ *01–42–60–08–83* ⊕ *www.labourselavie.com* ⊘ *Closed weekends and Aug.* ≋ *Reservations essential* Ⓜ *Bourse* ✛ *2:C5.*

$$$
MODERN FRENCH
Fodor's Choice
★
✕ **La Régalade Saint-Honoré.** When Bruno Doucet bought the original La Régalade from bistro-wizard Yves Camdeborde, some feared the end of an era. How wrong they were. While Doucet kept some of what made the old dining room so popular (country terrines, reasonably priced wines, convivial atmosphere), he had a few tricks under his toque,

creating a brilliantly successful haute-cuisine-meets-comfort-food destination with dishes like earthy morel mushrooms in a frothy cream for a starter, followed by the chef's signature succulent caramelized pork belly over tender Puy lentils. For dessert, don't skip the updated take on grand-mère's creamy rice pudding or the house Grand Marnier soufflé. With an excellent price-to-value ratio (€39 for the prix-fixe menu at lunch and dinner), this chic bistro has evolved into a Paris gastronome staple. $ *Average main: €25* ⊠ *123 rue Saint-Honoré, 1er, Around the Louvre* ☎ *01–42–21–92–40* ⌕ *Reservations essential* Ⓜ *Louvre–Rivoli* ⊹ *4:C1.*

$$ ✕ **La Robe et le Palais.** Come here for the more than 120 French wines
WINE BAR served *au compteur* (according to the amount consumed), and a good selection of bistro-style food in a congenial atmosphere for lunch or dinner. Although a tad pricier than other *bistrots à vins*, the food is reliably good. $ *Average main: €22* ⊠ *13 rue des Lavandières-Ste-Opportune, 1er, Around the Louvre* ☎ *01–45–08–07–41* ⊘ *Closed Sun.* Ⓜ *Châtelet–Les Halles* ⊹ *4:D1.*

$$$ ✕ **Le Georges.** One of those rooftop show-stopping venues so popular in
MODERN FRENCH Paris, Le Georges preens atop the Centre Georges Pompidou, accessed by its own entrance to the left of the main doors. The staff is as streamlined and angular as the furniture, and about as responsive. Come snappily dressed or you may be relegated to something resembling a dentist's waiting room. Part of the Costes brothers' empire, the establishment trots out fashionable dishes such as sesame-crusted tuna and coriander-spiced beef fillet flambéed with cognac. It's all considerably less dazzling than the view, except for the suitably decadent desserts (indulge in the Cracker's cheesecake with yogurt sorbet). $ *Average main: €32* ⊠ *Centre Pompidou, 6th fl., 19 rue Beaubourg, 4e, Around the Louvre* ☎ *01–44–78–47–99* ⊕ *www.restaurantgeorgesparis.com* ⊘ *Closed Tues.* ⌕ *Reservations essential* Ⓜ *Rambuteau* ⊹ *4:E1.*

$$$$ ✕ **Le Grand Véfour.** Victor Hugo could stride in and still recognize this
MODERN FRENCH restaurant, which was in his day, as now, a contender for the title of most beautiful restaurant in Paris. Originally built in 1784, it has welcomed everyone from Napoléon to Colette to Jean Cocteau under its mirrored ceiling, and amid the early-19th-century glass paintings of goddesses and muses that create an air of restrained seduction. The rich and fashionable gather here to enjoy the unique blend of sophistication and rusticity, as seen in dishes such as frogs' legs with sorrel sauce, and oxtail *parmentier* (a kind of shepherd's pie) with truffles. There's an outstanding cheese trolley, and for dessert try the house specialty, *palet aux noisettes* (meringue cake with chocolate mousse, hazelnuts, and salted caramel ice cream). $ *Average main: €130* ⊠ *17 rue de Beaujolais, 1er, Around the Louvre* ☎ *01–42–96–56–27* ⊕ *www.grand-vefour. com* ⊘ *Closed weekends, Aug., and Christmas holidays* ⌕ *Reservations essential* Ⓜ *Palais-Royal* ⊹ *2:B6.*

$$ ✕ **Les Fines Gueules.** Invest in good ingredients and most of the work is
BISTRO done: that's the principle of this wine bar–bistro that's developed a loyal following. The products are treated simply, often serving high-quality meats and vegetables raw alongside a salad or sautéed potatoes; the steak tartare with mesclun salad dressed in truffle oil is unparalleled.

CLOSE UP

Museum Dining

Most Paris museums offer a passable café, but sometimes a top-notch lunch, teatime, or even dinner is just the thing after a few hours of museum going. For a good meal in a superb environment, these spots can't be beat, even if you don't buy a ticket.

Les Arts Décoratifs, Le Saut du Loup: The menu here reflects the decor—elegant and contemporary. A sleek upstairs lounge has great views of the Eiffel Tower and the Louvre, and the outdoor terrace, part of the Tuileries gardens, is one of the nicest in Paris. Best for a snack or afternoon tea. Museum entrance not necessary, but a slight discount is offered on prix-fixe menus with a ticket. ✉ *107 rue de Rivoli, 1er* ☎ *01–44–55–57–50, Palais-Royal.*

Musée Jacquemart-André Café: Housed in the mansion's original dining room—with marble-topped tables, painted ceilings, and murals—the excellent salads and daily plat du jour make this lovely café a favorite with Parisian ladies who lunch, whether they've seen the exhibit or not. Wonderful for teatime or a copious prix-fixe brunch on weekends. ✉ *158 bd. Haussmann, 8e* ☎ *01–45–62–11–59* 🌐 *musee-jacquemart-andre.com, Miromesnil.*

Musée du Quai Branly, Les Ombres: The magnificent glass-ceilinged dining room, designed by museum architect Jean Nouvel, is perched atop the museum and boasts a *gastronomique* restaurant with some of the best views of Paris and the Eiffel Tower. Good prix-fixe deals on lunch, dinner, and teatime, and a roomy outdoor terrace. ✉ *27 quai Branly, 7e* ☎ *01–47–53–68–00* 🌐 *lesombres-restaurant.com, Alma-Marceau.*

Musee d'Orsay: In a classified historic monument, the soaring ceilings, chandeliers, gilding, and murals are part of the original train station's dining room. Open for lunch every day, and dinner on Thursday, the classic French fare is punctuated by a special dish inspired by the museum program. ✉ *1 rue de la Légion d'Honneur, 7e* ☎ *01–45–49–47–03* 🌐 *musee-orsay.fr, Solférino.*

Beyond the tiny café-like area downstairs is a staircase leading to a cozy upstairs dining room, which is invariably lively. In keeping with the theme, wines are organic or natural and many are available by the glass. [$] *Average main: €20* ✉ *43 rue Croix des Petits Champs, 1er, Around the Louvre* ☎ *01–42–61–35–41* 🌐 *www.lesfinesgueules.fr* ✍ *Reservations essential* [M] *Palais-Royal* ✥ *2:C6.*

$$$ MODERN FRENCH

✕ **Macéo.** With a reasonably priced set menu, this is an ideal spot for a relaxed meal after the Louvre. Natural light streams through the restaurant, and a broad, curved staircase leads to a spacious upstairs salon. It's also a hit with vegetarians: there's a meatless prix-fixe menu with two starter and two main-course options—perhaps summer vegetables with Mimolette cheese, followed by pasta with wild mushrooms, herbs, and artichokes. Meat lovers might sink their teeth into farmer's lamb with confit vegetables and mousseline potatoes. [$] *Average main: €28* ✉ *15 rue des Petits-Champs, 1er, Around the Louvre* ☎ *01–42–97–53–85* 🌐 *www.maceorestaurant.com* ⏲ *Closed Sun. and 3 wks in Aug. No lunch Sat.* [M] *Palais-Royal* ✥ *2:B5.*

$$$$
MODERN FRENCH
Fodor'sChoice
★

✕ **Spring.** The private-party atmosphere in this intimate, elegantly modern space may be exuberance at having finally snagged a table, but most likely it's the inspired cuisine. Two different menus are improvised each day, one for lunch and one for dinner. Fresh, top-quality ingredients are sourced from every corner of France, creating dishes that are both refined and deeply satisfying: you might have an updated parmentier with a velvety layer of deboned pig's foot topped with lemon-infused whipped potatoes or buttery venison with tart-sweet candied kumquats. A four-course dinner menu will run you €84. $ *Average main: €45* ✉ *6 rue Bailleul, 1er, Around the Louvre* ☎ *01–45–96–05–72* ⊕ *www.springparis.fr* ☾ *Closed Sun. and Mon. No lunch* ⇗ *Reservations essential* Ⓜ *Louvre–Rivoli* ✛ *4:C1.*

$
CAFÉ
Fodor'sChoice
★

✕ **Télescope.** This warm, elegant space near the Palais Royal gardens is the perfect spot to savor an expertly prepared cup of coffee accompanied by just the right gourmet sweet. Strike up a conversation with the passionate barista and you may end up sampling several of the velvety artisanal brews from carefully sourced beans hand-roasted by the owners. Here, true love and coffee go hand in hand. $ *Average main: €7* ✉ *5 rue Villedo, 1e, Around the Louvre* ☎ *01–42–61–33–14* ⊕ *www.telescopecafe.com* ⇗ *Reservations not accepted* Ⓜ *Palais Royal–Musée du Louvre, Pyramides* ✛ *2:B6.*

$
WINE BAR

✕ **Verjus Bar à Vins.** On an atmospheric street behind the Palais Royal gardens, this tiny wine bar allows customers to perch on metal stools at a narrow bar and enjoy a small but choice selection of wines by the glass and some very good nibbles. Although not a substitute for dinner—portions are minuscule, with three to five bite-size morsels—for a drink and a nosh on your way to or from somewhere else, including the excellent restaurant upstairs, it's ideal. The most plentiful dish is an assortment of artisanal cheeses, and the scrumptious butterscotch pudding flecked with toffee and topped with crème Chantilly is a toothsome finale. $ *Average main: €10* ✉ *47 rue Montpensier, 1e, Around the Louvre* ☎ *01–42–97–54–40* ⊕ *verjusparis.com* ☾ *Closed weekends. No lunch* ⇗ *Reservations not accepted* Ⓜ *Palais Royal–Musée du Louvre* ✛ *2:B6.*

$$
MODERN FRENCH

✕ **Willi's Wine Bar.** More a restaurant than a wine bar, this British-owned spot is a stylish haunt for Parisian and visiting gourmands who might stop in for a glass of wine at the oak bar or settle into the wood-beamed dining room. The selection of reinvented classic dishes changes daily and might include roast cod with artichokes and asparagus in spring, venison in wine sauce with roasted pears and celery-root chips in fall, and mango candied with orange and served with vanilla cream in winter. The restaurant is prix fixe only, but you can order appetizers at the bar. $ *Average main: €20* ✉ *13 rue des Petits-Champs, 1er, Around the Louvre* ☎ *01–42–61–05–09* ⊕ *www.williswinebar.com* ☾ *Closed Mon. in Aug and Sun. year-round* Ⓜ *Bourse* ✛ *2:B6.*

$$$$
FRENCH FUSION
Fodor'sChoice
★

✕ **Yam'Tcha.** Inspired by Chinese cooking, many of the dishes here rely on brilliant flavor combinations and very precise cooking, like the roasted Challans duck (a cross between wild and domestic) with Sichuan-style eggplant; two elements that create magic together. There's also a tea sommelier, who introduces diners to earthy or grassy flavors that complement the food (Yam'Tcha means "to eat small steamed dishes while sipping tea"), though alcohol is also available. Menus are prix fixe only (€120 at lunch and dinner), but the €60 "discovery" lunch menu is a nice introduction. $ *Average main: €100* ✉ *121 rue St. Honoré, 1er, Around the Louvre* ☏ *01–40–26–08–07* ⊕ *www.yamtcha.com* ☽ *Closed Sun., Mon., Christmas, and Aug. No lunch Tues.* ⟵ *Reservations essential* Ⓜ *Louvre–Rivoli, Les Halles* ✛ *4:C1.*

$ ✕ **Zen.** There's no shortage of Japanese restaurants around the Louvre,
JAPANESE but this one is a cut above much of the competition. The white-and-lime-green space feels refreshingly bright and modern, and you can perch at one of the curvy counters for a quick bite or settle in at a table. The menu has something for every taste, from warming ramen soups (part of a €12 lunch menu that includes five pork dumplings) to sushi and sashimi prepared with particular care. The *donburi*—rice topped with meat or fish—and the Japanese curry with breaded pork or shrimp are also very good. $ *Average main: €17* ✉ *8 rue de l'Echelle, 1er, Around the Louvre* ☏ *01–42–61–93–99* ☽ *Closed 10 days in mid-Aug.* Ⓜ *Pyramides, Palais-Royal* ✛ *2:B6.*

LES GRANDS BOULEVARDS

One of Paris's most atmospheric, and up-and-coming, neighborhoods, it's also a culinary melting pot, with everything from the minuscule Japanese noodle shops lining Rue St-Anne, authentic 19th-century brasseries that evoke the old working-class *bouillons*, and Art Nouveau–style Belle Époque dining rooms, to a new generation of young, talented chefs cooking up some of the city's most exciting cuisine.

$$$ ✕ **Aux Lyonnais.** With a passion for the old-fashioned bistro, Alain
BISTRO Ducasse resurrected this 1890s gem by appointing a terrific young chef to oversee the short, frequently changing, and reliably delicious menu of Lyonnais specialties. Dandelion salad with crisp potatoes, bacon, and a poached egg; watercress soup poured over parsleyed frogs' legs; and fluffy *quenelles de brochet* (pike-perch dumplings) show he is no bistro dilettante. The decor hews to tradition, too, with a zinc bar, an antique coffee machine, and original turn-of-the-20th-century woodwork. $ *Average main: €26* ✉ *32 rue St-Marc, 2e, Les Grands Boulevards* ☏ *01–42–96–65–04* ⊕ *www.auxlyonnais.com* ☽ *Closed Sun., Mon., 1 wk at Christmas, and 3 wks in Aug. No lunch Sat.* ⟵ *Reservations essential* Ⓜ *Bourse* ✛ *2:B4.*

$ ✕ **Chartier.** This classic *bouillon* (a term referring to the Parisian soup
BISTRO restaurants popular among workers in the early 20th century) is a part
FAMILY of the Gérard Joulie group of bistros and brasseries, which discreetly updated the menu without changing the fundamentals. People come here more for the bonhomie and the stunning 1896 interior than the cooking, which could be politely described as unambitious—then again, where else can you find a plate of foie gras for €7? This cavernous restaurant— the only original fin-de-siécle bouillon to remain true to its mission of serving cheap, sustaining food to the masses—enjoys a huge following, including one regular who has come for lunch nearly every day since 1946. $ *Average main: €12* ✉ *7 rue du Faubourg-Montmartre, 9e, Les*

Grands Boulevards ☎ *01–47–70–86–29* 🌐 *www.bouillon-chartier.com* ✍ *Reservations not accepted* [M] *Montmartre* ✣ *2:C4.*

$$ BISTRO
🍴 **Chez Casimir.** This bright, easygoing bistro is popular with polished Parisian professionals, for whom it serves as a sort of canteen—why cook when you can eat this well so affordably? The €32 dinner menu (€24 for two courses at lunch) covers lentil soup with fresh croutons, braised endive and andouille salad, and roast lamb on a bed of Paimpol beans, and there are 12 cheeses to choose from. Drop in at lunchtime on the weekend for the great-value €28 buffet. There is no à la carte. [$] *Average main: €19* ✉ *6 rue de Belzunce, 10e* ☎ *01–48–78–28–80* ⏲ *No dinner weekends* [M] *Gare du Nord* ✣ *2:E2.*

$$$ MODERN FRENCH FAMILY
🍴 **Drouant.** Best known for the literary prizes awarded here since 1914, Drouant has shed its dusty image to become a forward-thinking restaurant. The playful menu revisits the French hors d'oeuvres tradition with starters that come as a series of four plates. Diners can pick from themes such as French classics (like a deconstructed leek salad) or convincing mini-takes on Thai and Moroccan dishes. Main courses similarly encourage grazing, with accompaniments in little cast-iron pots and white porcelain dishes. Even desserts take the form of several tasting plates. Pace yourself, since the portions are generous and the cost of a meal quickly adds up. This is the place to bring adventurous young eaters, thanks to the €15 children's menu. [$] *Average main: €25* ✉ *16–18 pl. Gaillon, 2e, Les Grands Boulevards* ☎ *01–42–65–15–16* 🌐 *www.drouant.com* [M] *Pyramides* ✣ *2:B5.*

$$$ BISTRO
🍴 **Goupil le Bistro.** The best Paris bistros emit an air of quiet confidence, and this is certainly the case with Goupil, a triumph despite its out-of-the-way location not far from the Porte Maillot conference center. The dining room attracts dark suits at lunch and a festive crowd in the evenings, with a few well-informed English speakers sprinkled into the mix. The tiny open kitchen works miracles with seasonal ingredients, transforming mackerel into luxury food (on buttery puff pastry with mustard sauce) and panfrying monkfish to perfection with artichokes and chanterelles. [$] *Average main: €26* ✉ *4 rue Claude Debussy, 17e, Les Grands Boulevards* ☎ *01–45–74–83–25* ⏲ *Closed weekends and 3 wks in Aug.* ✍ *Reservations essential* [M] *Porte de Champerret* ✣ *1:B1.*

$ JAPANESE
🍴 **Higuma.** When it comes to steaming bowls of noodles, this no-frills dining room divided into three sections beats its many neighboring competitors. Behind the counter—an entertaining spot for solo diners—cooks toil over giant flames, tossing strips of meat and quick-fried vegetables, then ladling noodles and broth into giant bowls. A choice of *formules* (fixed-price menu options) allows you to pair various soups and stir-fried noodle dishes with six delicious *gyoza* (Japanese dumplings), and the stir-fried dishes are excellent, too. Don't expect much in the way of service, but it's hard to find a more generous meal in Paris at this price. There is a more subdued annex (without the open kitchen) at 163 rue St-Honoré, near the Louvre. [$] *Average main: €13* ✉ *32 bis, rue Ste-Anne, 1er* ☎ *01–47–03–38–59* 🌐 *www.higuma.fr* [M] *Pyramides* ✣ *2:B5.*

$$$ MODERN FRENCH
🍴 **Julien.** Famed for its 1879 decor—think Art Nouveau stained glass and *La Bohème*–style street lamps hung with vintage hats—this Belle Époque dazzler in the up-and-coming neighborhood near Gare de l'Est

certainly lives up to its oft-quoted moniker, "the poor man's Maxim's." Look for smoked salmon, stuffed roast lamb, cassoulet, and, to finish, profiteroles or the *coupe Julien* (ice cream with cherries). The scene here is lots of fun, and the restaurant has a strong following with the fashion crowd, so it's mobbed during the biannual fashion and fabric shows. [$] *Average main: €27* ✉ *16 rue du Faubourg St-Denis, 10e* ☎ *01–47–70–12–06* 🌐 *www.julienparis.com* [M] *Strasbourg St-Denis* ✥ *2:E4.*

$$ BRASSERIE

🍴 **Lazare.** With so many of Paris's fabled brasseries becoming parts of upscale chains, the news that this place was opening at the St-Lazare train station was met with a mix of curiosity and joy. Bright and loft-like, dazzling Lazare riffs on familiar brasserie themes—think marble-top tables, globe lights, chalkboard menus, and mosaic floors. Meat dishes, like slow-cooked lamb with lemon confit and olives, or crispy grilled pork on a bed of turnip kraut, are tender and comforting (just like grand-mère used to make). And chef Eric Frechon doesn't forget the classics: steak tartare, escargots, and charcuterie make memorable appearances. [$] *Average main: €24* ✉ *108 rue Saint-Lazare, 8e* ☎ *01–45–23–42–06* 🌐 *www.lazare-paris.fr* ✍ *Reservations essential* [M] *St-Lazare* ✥ *1:H3.*

14

$$$ BRASSERIE

🍴 **Le Vaudeville.** Part of the Flo group of historic brasseries, Le Vaudeville tends to fill with journalists, bankers, and locals *d'un certain âge* who come for the good-value assortment of prix-fixe menus, starting at €25, and highly professional service. Shellfish, house-smoked salmon, foie gras with raisins, slow-braised lamb, and desserts like the floating island topped with pralines are particularly enticing. Enjoy the graceful 1920s decor—almost the entire interior of this intimate dining room is done in real or faux marble—and lively dining until midnight (except Sunday and Monday, when the kitchen closes at 11 pm). [$] *Average main: €25* ✉ *29 rue Vivienne, 2e* ☎ *01–40–20–04–62* 🌐 *www.vaudevilleparis.com* [M] *Bourse* ✥ *2:C5.*

$$$ WINE BAR

🍴 **Racines.** The secret of the deceptively simple yet hearty food served here is top-quality ingredients and expert preparation. The wines are all natural—sulfite-free, hand-harvested, and unfiltered—so it's a great place to try out unusual, hard-to-find wines. The old tile floors, wood tables, and location in the atmospheric Passage des Panoramas, Paris's oldest covered arcade, only add to the ambience. It's packed at mealtimes, so be sure to reserve. [$] *Average main: €26* ✉ *8 passage des Panoramas, 2e* ☎ *01–40–13–06–41* 🌐 *www.racinesparis.com* ⏲ *Closed weekends, 3 wks in Aug., and at Christmas* ✍ *Reservations essential* [M] *Grands Boulevards, La Bourse* ✥ *2:C4.*

$$$$ MODERN FRENCH Fodor's Choice ★

🍴 **Saturne.** It's no surprise that chef Sven Chartier, a veteran of famous produce-centric restaurants L'Arpège and Racines, would focus his restaurant around seasonal, locally sourced veggies, along with the freshest seafood and pedigreed meats. The luminous dining room, with a huge central skylight, pale wood, and industrial details, is as contemporary and devoid of ostentation as the food. Dishes tend to be fresh and minimally cooked, featuring unusual pairings of vegetables and greens that are sophisticated almost to the point of cerebral. Desserts are equally original, and a superb roster of natural wines insures that diners who care to broaden their horizons won't be disappointed. It's prix fixe only.

$ *Average main: €33* ✉ *17 rue Notre-Dame des Victoires, 2e* ☎ *01–42–60–31–90* 🌐 *www.saturne-paris.fr* ⏲ *Closed weekends* ✍ *Reservations essential* [M] *Bourse* ✣ *2:C5.*

$$ BISTRO Fodor's Choice ★ 🍴 **Terroir Parisien–Palais Brongniart.** Yannick Alléno's departure from Le Meurice, where he'd earned three Michelin stars, may have stunned the culinary world, but it's good news for diners. Now Alléno presides over this warm, modern space under the Paris Bourse, the city's stock exchange. The star chef's dishes achieve an ephemeral balance, allowing top-notch ingredients to shine through while combining flavors and textures in unexpected and delightful ways. Tender roasted leeks are sprinkled with eggs, shallots, chives, and sprigs of chervil. A perfectly prepared steak with crispy matchstick fries and tender boudin blanc sausage with truffled celery root puree are comfort food at its best. There's also a "rillette bar," where you can take out traditional French charcuterie: *rillettes de lapin* (rabbit terrine) and *pâté de campagne* (country terrine). $ *Average main: €23* ✉ *28 pl. de la Bourse, 2e* ☎ *01–83–92–20–30* 🌐 *www.yannick-alleno.com/restaurant/paris-terroir-parisien-palais-brongniart* ⏲ *Closed Sun. No lunch Sat.* ✍ *Reservations essential* [M] *Bourse* ✣ *2:C5.*

MONTMARTRE

Perched above central Paris, Montmartre is buzzing with a hip vibe. Idyllic as the portrayal of Montmartre might seem in Jean-Pierre Jeunet's film *Amélie,* it's surprisingly close to reality. Though decidedly out of the way, Montmartre is still one of the most desirable areas in Paris, seamlessly blending the trendy and the traditional. The less picturesque neighborhood around Gare du Nord and Gare de l'Est is making its mark on the culinary scene: besides classic brasseries, tucked-away bistros, and the city's most authentic Indian restaurants, you'll find a new generation of cafés and gastrobistros exploding onto the scene.

$ CAFÉ FAMILY Fodor's Choice ★ 🍴 **Bal Café.** Set in a bright, modern space on a tiny street at the lower reaches of Montmartre, the popular Bal Café caters to a diverse clientele that comes for the great coffee, excellent food, lively and diverse crowd, and the art gallery–bookstore. Weekend brunch is an event, with artists, hipsters, expats, and young families enthusiastically enjoying all of the above. British–French-inspired cuisine with far-flung influences (like kedgeree, a Scottish–Indian rice-and-smoked-haddock dish), tender pancakes, fried eggs with ham and roasted tomatoes, and buttery scones with jam represent some the best comfort food in town. $ *Average main: €12* ✉ *6 impasse de la Défense, 18e, Montmartre* ☎ *01–44–70–75–51* 🌐 *www.le-bal.fr* ⏲ *Closed Mon. and Tues. No dinner Sun.* ✍ *Reservations essential* [M] *Place de Clichy* ✣ *2:A1.*

$$ BISTRO 🍴 **Bistrot des Deux Théâtres.** This theater lover's bistro with red-velour banquettes, black-and-white photos of actors, and a giant oil painting depicting celebrities, is always packed, and with good reason. The great-value prix-fixe menu for €41 (there's no à la carte option) includes three courses, a bottle of unpretentious wine, and coffee. This isn't a place for modest eaters, so have foie gras or escargots to start, a meaty main such as the crackly crusted rack of lamb, and a potent baba au rhum or rustic

lemon meringue tart for dessert. Waiters are jokey, English-speaking, and efficient. $ *Average main: €22* ✉ *18 rue Blanche, 9e, Montmartre* ☏ *01–45–26–41–43* ⊕ *www.lesdeuxtheatres.com* ⚱ *Reservations essential* Ⓜ *Trinité* ✛ *2:A2.*

$

CAFÉ

Fodor's Choice

★

✕ **Café Lomi.** A trailblazer on the Paris gastro-coffee scene, Café Lomi first supplied expertly roasted single-origin coffees to the first wave of barista cafés and top restaurants. Now Lomi's industrial-chic loft is equal parts roaster, café, workshop, and pilgrimage stop for hard-core coffee lovers, serving up a range of splendid brews along with a tidy menu of warm and cold dishes—wild-mushroom risotto with chorizo, leek and eggplant tarts, and a range of healthy salads—and a hearty brunch on weekends. $ *Average main: €8* ✉ *3 ter rue Marcadet, 18e, Montmartre* ☏ *09–80–39–56–24* ⊕ *www.cafelomi.com* ⊗ *Closed 3 wks in Aug.* ⚱ *Reservations not accepted* Ⓜ *Marcadet-Poissonière* ✛ *2:E1.*

$$$

JAPANESE

✕ **Guilo Guilo.** Already a star in Kyoto, Eiichi Edakuni created a sensation with his first Parisian restaurant, where 20 diners seated around the black bar can watch him at work each night. The €49 set menu is a bargain given the quality and sophistication of the food. It changes every month, but you might come across dishes such as sea bream and Wagyu beef on shiso leaves with ponzu sauce, or the chef's signature foie-gras sushi, an idea that could easily fall flat but instead soars. If you can afford it, complement your meal with exceptional sakes by the glass, one of which is sparkling. Beware: the first seating gets very rushed; reserve the 9:30 seating if you want to linger. $ *Average main: €26* ✉ *8 rue Garreau, 18e, Montmartre* ☏ *01–42–54–23–92* ⊗ *Closed Sun. and Mon. No lunch* ⚱ *Reservations essential* Ⓜ *Abbesses* ✛ *2:B1.*

$$$

BRASSERIE

✕ **La Mascotte.** Though everyone talks about the "new Montmartre," exemplified by a wave of chic residents and throbbingly cool cafés and bars, it's good to know that the old Montmartre is alive and well at the untrendy-and-proud-of-it Mascotte. This old-fashioned café-brasserie—which dates from 1889, the same year that saw the opening of the Tour Eiffel and the Moulin Rouge—is where you can find neighborhood fixtures such as the drag queen Michou (of the nearby club Chez Michou), who always wears blue. Loyalists come for the seafood platters, the excellent steak tartare, the warming *potée auvergnate* (pork stew) in winter, and the gossip around the *comptoir* (bar) up front. $ *Average main: €26* ✉ *52 rue des Abbesses, 18e, Montmartre* ☏ *01–46–06–28–15* ⊕ *www.la-mascotte-montmartre.com* Ⓜ *Abbesses* ✛ *2:B1.*

$$

BISTRO

FAMILY

✕ **Le Miroir.** Residents of Montmartre are breathing a sigh of relief: they no longer have to leave the neighborhood to find a good-value bistro. A meal might start with a plate of *cochonailles* (pâté, cured sausage, and deboned pig's trotter with onion jam) or perhaps a salad of whelks and white beans, before hearty main courses such as a stunning beef rib for two with sautéed potatoes or duck breast with chanterelle mushrooms and a slice of panfried foie gras. To finish, it's hard to choose between the aged Beaufort cheese or the vanilla pot de crème, served with shortbread and chocolate *financiers* (almond cakes). $ *Average main: €22* ✉ *94 rue des Martyrs, 18e, Montmartre* ☏ *01–46–06–50–73* ⊕ *www.restaurantmiroir.com* ⊗ *Closed 3 wks in Aug.* ⚱ *Reservations essential* Ⓜ *Abbesses* ✛ *2:B1.*

14

$ BRITISH FAMILY 🍴 **Rose Bakery.** On a street lined with French food shops selling produce, fish, bread, and cheeses, this British-run café-restaurant might easily go unnoticed—if it weren't for the frequent line out the door. Whitewashed walls, naive art, and concrete floors provide the decor, and organic producers supply the ingredients for food so fresh and tasty it draws crowds to feast on fresh juices, salads, soups, and hot dishes, such as delicious risotto, followed by carrot cake, sticky toffee pudding, or lemon tarts. Rose Bakery also has branches at 30 rue Debelleyme in the Marais and a spot in the Bastille, inside the Galerie Maison Rouge, at 10 boulevard de la Bastille. [$] *Average main: €15* ✉ *46 rue des Martyrs, 9e, Montmartre* ☎ *01–42–82–12–80* 🕒 *Closed Mon. and 2 wks in Aug. No dinner* ✍ *Reservations not accepted* [M] *Notre-Dame-de-Lorette* ✥ *2:C2.*

$ CAFÉ FAMILY Fodor's Choice ★ 🍴 **Soul Kitchen.** Montmartre finally has a café equal to its charm. Run by three friendly young women, the snug Soul Kitchen unites a pleasantly homey decor and welcoming atmosphere with the kind of Anglo-French all-organic comfort food that soothes body and soul: Gruyère mac and cheese, chevre and leek tarts, house-made foie gras, and a pastry counter laden with treats like homemade scones, cheesecake, tiramisu, and rich mousse au chocolat. The ladies also know their beverages: good, well-priced wines by the glass, fresh fruit and vegetable juices, and some serious coffee. [$] *Average main: €12* ✉ *33 rue Lamarck, 18e, Montmartre* ☎ *01–71–37–99–95* 🕒 *Closed Mon.* ✍ *Reservations not accepted* [M] *Lamarck-Caulaincourt* ✥ *2:C1.*

THE MARAIS

The once-run-down Marais is now the epitome of chic, but you can still find reminders of its down-to-earth past along Rue des Rosiers, where falafel shops and Eastern European delis jostle with designer boutiques. Truly ambitious restaurants are few and far between in the Marais, but picturesque old bistros, like Benoît and the wonderful Café des Musées, and smaller veggie-centric eateries are popping up all over. A brand-new generation of barista cafés serving gourmet snacks for breakfast and lunch have created their own niche, answering a need for better coffee and faster sit-down dining. The popular Breizh Café attracts young and old alike with its inexpensive and authentic *galettes* (buckwheat crêpes) made with quality ingredients and served with a crisp, delicious *cidre* from Normandy or Brittany.

$$ BISTRO 🍴 **Au Bourguignon du Marais.** The handsome, contemporary look of this Marais bistro and wine bar is the perfect backdrop for traditional fare and excellent Burgundies served by the glass and bottle. Unusual for Paris, food is served nonstop from noon to 11 pm, and you can drop by just for a glass of wine in the afternoon. Always on the menu are Burgundian classics such as *jambon persillé* (ham in parsleyed aspic jelly), escargots, and *boeuf bourguignon* (beef stewed in red wine). More up-to-date picks include a cèpe-mushroom velouté with poached oysters, though the fancier dishes are generally less successful. [$] *Average main: €22* ✉ *52 rue François-Miron, 3e, Marais* ☎ *01–48–87–15–40* [M] *St-Paul* ✥ *4:F2.*

$$$$
BISTRO

× **Benoît.** Without changing the vintage 1912 setting, superchef Alain Ducasse and Thierry de la Brosse of L'Ami Louis have subtly improved the menu here, with dishes such as marinated salmon, frogs' legs in a morel-mushroom cream sauce, and an outstanding cassoulet served in a cast-iron pot. It's a splurge to be here, so go all the way and top off your meal with the caramelized tarte tatin or a rum-doused baba. $ Average main: €35 ⊠ 20 rue St-Martin, 4e, Marais ☎ 01–42–72–25–76 ⊕ www.benoit-paris.com ⊗ Closed Aug. and 1 wk in Feb. Ⓜ Châtelet ✛ 4:D1.

$
FRENCH
FAMILY
Fodor's Choice
★

× **Breizh Café.** Eating a crêpe in Paris might seem a bit clichéd, until you venture into this modern offshoot of a Breton crêperie. The pale-wood, almost Japanese-style decor is refreshing, but what really makes the difference are the ingredients—farmers' eggs, unpasteurized Gruyère, shiitake mushrooms, Valrhona chocolate, homemade caramel, and extraordinary butter from a Breton dairy farmer. You'll find all the classics among the galettes, but it's worth choosing something more adventurous like the *cancalaise* (traditionally smoked herring, potato, crème fraîche, and herring roe). You might also slurp a few Cancale oysters, a rarity in Paris, and try one of the 20 artisanal ciders on offer. $ Average main: €12 ⊠ 109 rue Vieille du Temple, 3e, Marais ☎ 01–42–72–13–77 ⊕ www.breizhcafe.com ⊗ Closed Mon., Tues., and Aug. ⌖ Reservations essential Ⓜ St-Sébastien–Froissart ✛ 4:F1.

$
WINE BAR

× **Bubar.** In summer look for the hip crowd spilling out the front of this signless wine bar in the Marais. It's named for Jean-Louis, the bartender (*bubar* or *barbu* is French slang for "bearded"). The wine menu—with many selections available by the glass—features French wines and small-batch vintages from South Africa, Chile, and Argentina. Try the small dishes and some lovely *tartines* (toasted bread with various toppings) or bring in whatever noshes suit your fancy from the neighborhood—the owner encourages it! $ Average main: €12 ⊠ 3 rue des Tournelles, 4e, Marais ☎ 01–40–29–97–72 ⊗ No lunch Ⓜ Bastille ✛ 4:G2.

$
BISTRO

× **Café des Musées.** Warm and authentic, this bustling little bistro near the Musée Picasso offers a convivial slice of Parisian life—and excellent value. Here traditional French bistro fare is adapted to a modern audience, and the best choices are the old tried-and-trues: hand-cut *tartare de boeuf*; rare entrecôte served with a side of golden-crisp frites and homemade béarnaise; and the classic parmentier with pheasant instead of the usual ground beef. $ Average main: €17 ⊠ 49 rue de Turenne, 3e, Marais ☎ 01–42–72–96–17 ⊕ www.lecafedesmusees.fr ⌖ Reservations essential Ⓜ St-Paul ✛ 4:G1.

$
MODERN FRENCH

× **Cantine Merci.** Deep inside this concept store, whose proceeds go to charities for women in India and Madagascar, lurks the perfect spot for a quick and healthy lunch between bouts of shopping. The brief menu of soups, salads, risottos, and a daily hot dish is more than slightly reminiscent of another city lunch spot, Rose Bakery—salads such as fava beans with radish and lemon wedges or melon, cherry tomato, and arugula are bright, lively, and crunchy, and you can order a freshly squeezed juice or iced tea with fresh mint to wash it all down. $ Average main: €17 ⊠ 111 bd. Beaumarchais, 3e, Marais ☎ 01–42–77–79–28 ⊕ www.merci-merci.com ⊗ Closed Sun. No dinner Ⓜ St-Sébastien–Froissart ✛ 4:G1.

14

$$$ ✕**Chez Julien.** This charming vintage bistro next to the Seine was easy
BISTRO to overlook until the Costes brothers—famous for stylish brasseries
such as Café Marly and Georges—worked their magic on it. With a
terrace that extends across the cobbled pedestrian street and a few mod-
ish touches in the turn-of-the-20th-century dining room that was once
a boulangerie, Chez Julien is now one of the Marais's hippest spots.
The steep prices for rather ordinary food reflect this transformation,
so you might decide to skip the starters, linger over a thick steak with
crisp shoestring fries or roast farmer's chicken with baby potatoes, then
head into the Marais for ice cream or gelato. Ⓢ*Average main: €30* ⊠ *1
rue du Pont Louis-Philippe, 4e, Marais* ☎*01–42–78–31–64* ⊕*www.
chezjulien.paris* ⌂*Reservations essential* Ⓜ*Pont Marie* ✛ *4:E2.*

$ ✕**Chez Marianne.** You'll know you've found Marianne's when you see
MIDDLE EASTERN the line of people reading the bits of wisdom and poetry painted across
the windows. This restaurant-deli serves Middle Eastern and Jewish
specialties like hummus, fried eggplant, and soul-warming chopped
liver, which you can match with one of the affordable wines or a steam-
ing glass of sweetened mint tea. The sampler platter lets you try four,
five, or six items, and even the smallest plate is a feast, to be enjoyed
on the scenic stone terrace overlooking the church and the Seine on
warm days. Falafel sandwiches are available at the takeout window.
Ⓢ*Average main: €14* ⊠ *2 rue des Hospitalières-St-Gervais, 4e, Marais*
☎*01–42–72–18–86* Ⓜ*St-Paul* ✛ *4:F2.*

$$ ✕**L'Ambassade d'Auvergne.** A rare authentic Parisian bistro that refuses
BISTRO to change, the Ambassade claims one of the city's great restaurant char-
acters: the maître d' Francis Panek, with his handlebar mustache and
gravelly voice. Settle into the dining room in this ancient Marais house
to try rich dishes from the Auvergne, a sparsely populated region in
central France. Indulge in a heaping serving of the superb lentils in
goose fat with bacon or the Salers beef in red wine sauce with *aligot*
(mashed potatoes with cheese). You might want to loosen your belt for
the astonishingly dense chocolate mousse, served in a giant bowl that
allows you to decide the quantity. Ⓢ*Average main: €20* ⊠ *22 rue du
Grenier St-Lazare, 3e, Marais* ☎*01–42–72–31–22* ⊕*www.ambassade-
auvergne.com* Ⓜ*Rambuteau* ✛ *4:E1.*

$ ✕**L'As du Falafel.** Look no further than the fantastic falafel stands on the
MIDDLE EASTERN pedestrian Rue de Rosiers for some of the cheapest and tastiest meals in
FAMILY Paris. L'As (the Ace) is widely considered the best of the bunch, which
accounts for the lunchtime line that extends down the street. A falafel
sandwich costs €6 to go, €8 in the dining room, and comes heaped with
grilled eggplant, cabbage, hummus, tahini, and hot sauce. The sha-
warma (grilled, skewered meat) sandwich, made with chicken or lamb,
is also one of the finest in town. Though takeout is popular, it can be
more fun (and not as messy) to eat off a plastic plate in one of the two
frenzied dining rooms. Fresh lemonade is the falafel's best match. Ⓢ*Average main: €10* ⊠ *34 rue des Rosiers, 4e, Marais* ☎*01–48–87–63–60*
☉*Closed Sat. No dinner Fri.* Ⓜ*St-Paul* ✛ *4:F2.*

$ ✕**La Caféothèque.** Paris's first and most famous coffee bar, founded by
CAFÉ former Guatemalan ambassador to France Gloria Montenegro, La
Caféothèque is where the city's initial wave of baristas came to worship

TARTE TATIN

A development in the land of the long lunch is the new focus on fast food. No, not those pernicious chains found the world over, but one-of-a-kind eateries, often associated with a well-known bistro or wine bar, where you can grab a sandwich at a small table or go when a full day of sightseeing doesn't allow for lingering over a many-course lunch. These three standouts are the newest examples of a trend that's caught on like wildfire. **L'Epicerie le Verre Volé** (✉ *54 rue la Folie Méricourt* ☎ *01-48-05-36-55*), an offshoot of the beloved *cave à manger,* offers cheese, olive oil, charcuterie, and lovingly prepared gourmet sandwiches. **Verjus Bar à Vins** (✉ *5 rue Montpensier* ☎ *01-42-97-54-40*), behind the Palais Royal gardens, offers superb sandwiches and some toothsome salads, including one with shaved Brussels sprouts, fennel, dill, and red onions. **Frenchie To Go** (✉ *9 rue du Nil* ☎ *01-40-39-96-19*) serves a tempting array of breakfast noshes, such as scones, sticky buns, and smoked bacon on English muffins. Stop in for a pastrami on rye, classic fish-and-chips, or something a little more unusual, like a French take on the lobster roll. And don't say no to dessert.

and train. With three spacious rooms, any coffee preparation under the sun, and a daily special brew chosen from among dozens of varieties of meticulously sourced beans from plantations around the globe, this place is a Paris institution. [$] *Average main: €4* ✉ *52 rue de l'Hotel de Ville, 4e, Marais* ☎ *01–53–01–83–84* 🌐 *www.lacafeotheque.com* [M] *Pont Marie, St-Paul* ✣ *4:E2.*

EASTERN PARIS

Head over to the up-and-coming Canal St-Martin to watch Parisian *bobos,* or bohemian bourgeois, in action. The area is home to fashion designers, artists, and media folk who make the most of the waterside cafés on sunny days. The bistro scene gets interesting east of the Bastille, where lower rents have encouraged young chefs to set up shop. Around Père Lachaise the selection thins, but wander a little farther to multicultural Belleville to find an intriguing mix of Chinese and North African eateries alongside some superb gastrobistros from a handful of gifted young chefs.

BASTILLE

$$$$ BISTRO ✕ **Au Trou Gascon.** This elegant establishment off Place Daumesnil—well off the beaten tourist track but worth the trip—does a refined take on the cuisine of Gascony, a region renowned for its ham, foie gras, lamb, and duck. Most popular with the regulars are the surprisingly light cassoulet (all the meats are grilled before going into the pot) with big white Tarbais beans and a superb duck or goose confit. There is an ethereal dessert of raspberries, ice cream, and meringue. Prices are steep, but there is a limited-choice lunch menu for €42 and a seven-course tasting menu at dinner for €68. With some 1,100 wines and 130 Armagnacs to choose from, this is the place to splurge on vintage. [$] *Average main:*

€35 ✉ 40 rue Taine, 12e ☎ 01–43–44–34–26 🌐 www.autrougascon.com ⏲ Closed weekends, Aug., and 1 wk in Jan. [M] Daumesnil ⊕ 4:H4.

$ WINE BAR 🍴 **Bistrot Mélac.** In the same family since 1938, this wine bar is named after the jolly second-generation owner who harvests grapes from the vine outside and bottles his own wines. Cheese is hacked from a giant hunk of Cantal, and much of the hearty bistro fare hearkens back to the Aveyron, a notable gastronomic region of France whence the Mélac family proudly hails. [$] *Average main: €17 ✉ 42 rue Léon-Frot, 11e ☎ 01–43–70–59–27 🌐 www.bistrot-melac.fr ⏲ Closed Sun., Mon., and 2 wks in Aug. [M] Charonne ⊕ 4:H2.*

$$ BRASSERIE FAMILY 🍴 **Bofinger.** One of the oldest, loveliest, and most popular brasseries in Paris has improved in recent years, so stake out one of the tables, which are dressed in crisp white linen under a glowing Art Nouveau glass cupola, and enjoy classic brasserie fare. Stick to trademark dishes such as the seafood, choucroute, steak tartare, or smoked haddock with spinach, as the seasonal specials can be hit-or-miss. Take advantage of the prix-fixe menus for €31 (two courses) and €38 (three courses) and all-day service beginning at noon on Sunday. [$] *Average main: €21 ✉ 5–7 rue de la Bastille, 4e ☎ 01–42–72–87–82 🌐 www.bofingerparis.com [M] Bastille ⊕ 4:H2.*

$$$ BRASSERIE 🍴 **Café Français.** This is one of Paris's largest bar-restaurant-clubs and a welcome contrast to the Bastille's somewhat tatty café scene. This luxe design-lover's paradise has a vast terrace with panoramic views of Place de la Bastille, an oasis of red- and blue-leather banquettes, expressive black-and-white marble floors, mirrors, and gilded embellishments. Classics like steak tartare and steak with béarnaise sauce are several steps above your average brasserie fare. [$] *Average main: €27 ✉ 1 pl. de la Bastille, 4e, Bastille ☎ 01–40–29–04–02 🌐 www.cafe-francais.fr ✍ Reservations essential [M] Bastille ⊕ 4:H3.*

$ FRENCH Fodor's Choice ★ 🍴 **Jacques Genin Salon de Thé.** Master chocolatier-pâtissier Jacques Genin deserves the Legion d'honneur for his efforts to restore great traditional French pastries to their classic form, particularly the august mille-feuille. Genin's stripped-down version disposes with the usual bells and whistles—fresh fruit, custard, chocolate—to achieve a scintillating clarity: layers of lightly caramelized *pâte feuilletée,* a buttery puff pastry, and an ethereal, barely sweet pastry cream in either vanilla, caramel, or praline. The glorious pastries in this tearoom, chocolate boutique, and pastry shop (probably the most beautiful in Paris, by the way) are no longer available for takeaway, but are assembled to order to be eaten fresh on the premises. Along with a cup of Genin's bittersweet hot chocolate—well, you get the picture. Oh, yes, and then there are the chocolates, some of Paris's finest. [$] *Average main: €8 ✉ 133 rue de Turenne, 3e ☎ 01–45–77–29–01 🌐 jacquesgenin.fr ⏲ Closed Mon. [M] Filles du Calvaire ⊕ 2:G6.*

$ WINE BAR 🍴 **Le Baron Rouge.** This proletarian wine bar near the Place d'Aligre market is a throwback to another era, with a few tables and giant barrels along the walls for filling and refilling your take-home bottles. A fun time to come is Sunday morning (yes, morning) when it's packed with locals who have just been to the market, or on a winter's day when oysters are shucked and slurped curbside. $ *Average main: €11* ✉ *1 rue Théophile Roussel, 12e* ☎ *01–43–43–14–32* Ⓜ *Ledru-Rollin* ✛ *4:H3.*

$$ ✕ **Le Bistrot Paul Bert.** Faded 1930s decor: check. Boisterous crowd:
BISTRO check. Thick steak with real frites: check. Good value: check. The Paul
Fodor'sChoice Bert delivers everything you could want from a traditional Paris bistro,
★ so it's no wonder its two dining rooms fill every night with a cosmo-
politan crowd. The impressively stocked wine cellar helps, as does the
cheese cart, the laid-back yet efficient staff, and hearty dishes such as
monkfish with white beans and duck with pears. The reasonable prix
fixe is three courses for €41, or you can order à la carte. $ *Average
main: €25* ✉ *18 rue Paul Bert, 11e* ☎ *01–43–72–24–01* ⊘ *Closed Sun.
and Mon.* ⌲ *Reservations essential* Ⓜ *Rue des Boulets* ✛ *4:H3.*

$$ ✕ **Le Repaire de Cartouche.** In this split-level, dark-wood bistro between
BISTRO Bastille and République, disciplined creativity is applied to earthy
French regional dishes. The menu changes regularly, but typical options
are a salad of haricots verts topped with tender slices of squid; scallops on a bed of diced pumpkin; juicy lamb with white beans; game
dishes in winter; and old-fashioned desserts like baked custard with
tiny shell-shaped madeleines. In keeping with cost-conscious times,
there is a bargain three-course lunch menu for €20 that doesn't skimp
on ingredients. $ *Average main: €24* ✉ *99 rue Amelot, 11e, Bastille*
☎ *01–47–00–25–86* ⊘ *Closed Sun., Mon., and Aug.* ⌲ *Reservations
essential* Ⓜ *Filles du Calvaire* ✛ *4:G1.*

$$$ ✕ **Sardegna a Tavola.** Paris might have more Italian restaurants than you
ITALIAN can shake a noodle at, but few smack of authenticity like this out-of-
the-way Sardinian spot with peppers, braids of garlic, and cured hams
hanging from the ceiling. Dishes are listed in Sardinian with French
translation—*malloredus* is a gnocchi-like pasta; Sardinian ravioli are
stuffed with cheese and mint. Perhaps best of all are the clams in a spicy
broth with tiny pasta and the orange-scented prawns with tagliatelle,
though the choice of dishes changes with the seasons and the chef's
imagination. $ *Average main: €30* ✉ *1 rue de Cotte, 12e* ☎ *01–44–75–
03–28* ⊘ *Closed Sun. and Aug. No lunch Mon.* Ⓜ *Ledru-Rollin* ✛ *4:H4.*

$$ ✕ **Septime.** This is the kind of bistro we'd all love in our neighborhood—
BISTRO good food and a convivial atmosphere where diners crane to admire
each other's plates. Seasonal ingredients, inventive pairings, excellent
natural wines, plus dishes like creamy gnochetti in an orange-rind-
flecked Gouda sauce sprinkled with coriander flowers; tender fillet of
Landes hen in a mustard-peanut sauce, with braised endive and cabbage
perfumed with lemon; and fresh white asparagus with raspberries and
blanched almonds are sophisticated and satisfying. $ *Average main:
€22* ✉ *80 rue de Charonne, 11e* ☎ *01–43–67–38–29* ⊕ *www.septime-
charonne.fr* ⊘ *Closed weekends. No lunch Mon.* ⌲ *Reservations essential* Ⓜ *Ledru Rollin, Charonne* ✛ *4:H3.*

$$$ ✕ **Unico.** An architect and a photographer, both Parisians born in Argen-
MODERN tina, teamed up to open one of Bastille's hottest restaurants—literally
ARGENTINE hot, too, since the Argentinean meat served here is grilled over char-
coal—and good-looking young locals pile into the orange-tiled, vin-
tage 1970s dining room or the covered terrace to soak up the party
vibe. Whichever cut of beef you choose (the ultimate being *lomo,* or

14

fillet), it's so melt-in-your-mouth that the sauces served on the side seem almost superfluous. [$] *Average main: €29* ✉ *15 rue Paul-Bert, 11e* ☎ *01–43–67–68–08* 🌐 *www.resto-unico.com* 🕐 *Closed Sun. No lunch Mon.* [M] *Faidherbe–Chaligny* ✥ *4:H3.*

BELLEVILLE

$ VIETNAMESE

🍴 **Dong Huong.** Dong Huong isn't a secret, but you wouldn't find it by accident. These two undecorated dining rooms on a Belleville side street are where the local Chinese and Vietnamese come for a reassuring bowl of *pho* (noodle soup) or plate of grilled lemongrass-scented meat with rice. Spicy, peanut-y *saté* soup is a favorite, and at this price (€8) you can also spring for a plate of crunchy imperial rolls, to be wrapped in accompanying lettuce and mint. Try one of the lurid nonalcoholic drinks; they're surprisingly tasty. [$] *Average main: €11* ✉ *14 rue Louis-Bonnet, 11e, Belleville* ☎ *01–43–32–25–74* 🕐 *Closed Tues. and 3 wks in Aug.* [M] *Belleville* ✥ *2:H4.*

$$ BISTRO FAMILY Fodor's Choice ★

🍴 **Le Baratin.** This place has been around for more than 20 years, but that hasn't stopped it from recently becoming one of the most fashionable out-of-the-way bistros in Paris. The key to its success is the combination of inventive yet comforting cooking and a lovingly selected list of organic and natural wines from small producers. The chef learned the art of making bouillons from none other than star Breton chef Olivier Roellinger, and uses them to bring out the best in any ingredient from fish to foie gras. [$] *Average main: €23* ✉ *3 rue Jouye Rouve, 20e* ☎ *01–43–49–39–70* 🕐 *No lunch Sat. Closed Sun., Mon., and Aug.* ✍ *Reservations essential* [M] *Pyrénées, Belleville* ✥ *2:H3.*

CANAL ST-MARTIN

$$ MODERN FRENCH Fodor's Choice ★

🍴 **Abri.** This tiny storefront restaurant's well-deserved popularity has much to do with the fresh and imaginative food, the friendly servers, and great prices. The chef works from a small open kitchen behind a zinc bar, putting forth skillfully prepared dishes, like lemon-marinated mackeral topped with micro-thin slices of beet with honey vinaigrette, succulent duck breast with vegetables au jus, or a scrumptious pumpkin soup with fragrant coffee cream. With food this good, and prices to match (€26 at lunch, €48 for a four-course dinner) be sure to reserve early. [$] *Average main: €23* ✉ *92 rue du Faubourg-Poissonnière, 10e, Canal St-Martin* ☎ *01–83–97–00–00* 🕐 *Closed Sun., Mon., 1 wk at Christmas, and Aug.* ✍ *Reservations essential* [M] *Poissonnière, Cadet* ✥ *2:D3.*

$ CAFÉ FAMILY Fodor's Choice ★

🍴 **Holybelly.** A welcome addition to the Canal St-Martin area, this spacious, modern coffee bar caters to Paris's blossoming breakfast scene with a menu of classics: homemade granola, pancakes topped with fruit, and eggs and bacon served up all day long, accompanied by hearty sandwiches, healthy salads (with kale!), and sinful desserts. And, of course, there's the wonderful coffee—all you'd expect from baristas trained in the ways of the good brew. [$] *Average main: €12* ✉ *19 rue Lucien Sampaix, 10e, Canal St-Martin* ☎ *09–73–60–13–64* 🕐 *Closed Tues. and Wed. No dinner* ✍ *Reservations not accepted* [M] *Jacques Bonsergent* ✥ *2:F4.*

$ WINE BAR 🍴 **Jeanne A.** This six-table épicerie-bistro–wine bar–traiteur on a pretty cobbled street is just the thing for an uncomplicated lunch, dinner, or afternoon snack. Whether you desire a great glass of wine and a plate of charcuterie and cheese or a full meal, the classic French fare is always excellent. Tasty rotisserie chicken is served daily, along with another main, like *gigot d'agneau* (leg of lamb), rabbit, or duck fresh from the kitchen next door, along with a creamy potato gratin, side salad, or soup of the day, with a dense almond financier for dessert. All this comes for under €17 for a two-course lunch and €27 for a three-course dinner. [$] *Average main: €14* ✉ *42 rue Jean-Pierre-Timbaud, 11e, Canal St-Martin* ☎ *01–43–55–09–49* [M] *Parmentier, Oberkampf* ✣ *2:H5.*

$$$$ MODERN FRENCH 🍴 **Le Chateaubriand.** A chef who once presented a single, peeled apple pip (really) on a plate (at the museum restaurant Le Transversal outside Paris) has no ordinary approach to food. Self-taught Basque cook Inaki Aizpitarte is undeniably provocative, but he gets away with it because (a) he's young and extremely cool and (b) he has an uncanny sense of which unexpected ingredients go together, as in a combination of oysters and lime zest in chicken stock. The €65 set-dinner menu is modern and deconstructed, and the vintage dining room buzzes with an artsy, black-dressed crowd. [$] *Average main: €40* ✉ *129 av. Parmentier, 11e, Canal St-Martin* ☎ *01–43–57–45–95* 🌐 *www.lechateaubriand.net* ⏲ *Closed Sun., Mon., and 1 wk at Christmas. No lunch* ✍ *Reservations essential* [M] *Goncourt* ✣ *2:H5.*

$$ WINE BAR 🍴 **Le Dauphin.** Avant-garde chef Inaki Aizpitarte transformed a dowdy café into a sleek, if chilly, all-marble watering hole for late-night cuisinistas. Honing his ever-iconoclastic take on tapas, the dishes served here are a great way to get an idea of what all the fuss is about. Offerings like sweetly delicate crabmeat punctuated with tart marinated radish and avocado puree, or a well-prepared lemon sole drizzled with hazelnut butter highlight what this chef can do with quality ingredients. Dishes are small, well priced, and meant to be shared to maximize exposure to the food. [$] *Average main: €20* ✉ *131 av. Parmentier, 11e, Canal St-Martin* ☎ *01–55–28–78–88* 🌐 *www.restaurantledauphin.net* ⏲ *Closed Sun., Mon. and 1 wk at Christmas. No lunch Sat.* ✍ *Reservations essential* [M] *Parmentier* ✣ *2:H5.*

$$ BISTRO Fodor's Choice ★ 🍴 **Le Galopin.** Across from a pretty square on the border of two up-and-coming neighborhoods, this light-drenched spot is one of Paris's better bistros. By adhering to a tried-and-true formula—meticulously sourced produce, natural wines, open kitchen—dishes here are small wonders of texture and flavor, like velvety Basque pork with razor-thin slices of cauliflower, briny olives, and crunchy pumpkin seeds; or crisp-moist sea bass with spring-fresh asparagus and mint. This is a great choice for diners eager to experience what this scene's all about in a hip, off-the-beaten-path locale. [$] *Average main: €22* ✉ *34 rue Sainte-Marthe, 10e, Canal St-Martin* ☎ *01–42–06–05–03* 🌐 *www.le-galopin.com* ⏲ *Closed weekends. No lunch Mon.–Wed.* ✍ *Reservations essential* [M] *Goncourt, Belleville, Colonel Fabien* ✣ *2:H3.*

$$ MODERN FRENCH Fodor's Choice ★ 🍴 **Le Servan.** This stylish, pared-down dining room became an instant sensation when young chef Tatiana Levha, a veteran of two three-star Paris kitchens, including Alain Passard's brilliant Arpège, opened her doors in late 2014. Levha's skilled but unfussy gastronomic menu

14

features a concise offering of Asian-inflected dishes that express the food's far-flung influences: a starter of "zakouskis," several small dishes that may include deep-fried giblets, fresh radishes with anchovy butter, or herb-infused cockles, warms you up for a sublime entrée of whole lacquered quail, cod with spicy black-bean reduction, or crispy melt-in-your mouth pork on a bed of braised leeks. Deliciously nuanced desserts, a good selection of all-natural wines, and an unbeatable three-course, €25 lunch menu add up to an essential Paris dining experience. $ *Average main: €20* ✉ *32 rue Saint-Maur, 11e, Canal St-Martin* ☎ *01–55–28–51–82* ⊕ *www.leservan.com* ⊘ *Closed weekends. No lunch Mon.* ⚼ *Reservations essential* Ⓜ *Voltaire, Rue Saint-Maur, Parmentier* ✛ *4:H2.*

$$
WINE BAR
✕ **Le Verre Volé.** Cyril Bordarier blazed a path with this small bar à vins, which quickly became the ticket for hipsters seeking out exceptional, good-value natural wines with food to match. Nowadays you're as likely to be seated next to a table of American tourists or expats as a bunch of French wine aficionados. This is not so much due to the chic factor as to Bordarier's insistence on top-quality products. Wines are mostly organic, the charcuterie hails from top artisan producers, and the variety of small dishes alongside a few hearty main courses works just as well for lunch on the fly as for a leisurely dinner. This is a popular spot, so reserve ahead. $ *Average main: €24* ✉ *67 rue de Lancry, 10e, Canal St-Martin* ☎ *01–48–03–17–34* ⊕ *www.leverrevole.fr* ⚼ *Reservations essential* Ⓜ *République* ✛ *2:G4.*

$$
BISTRO
✕ **Philou.** On a quiet street between Canal St-Martin and the historic Hôpital Saint-Louis, few places could be more pleasant than a sidewalk table at this most welcome addition to Paris's thriving bistro scene. On a cool day the red banquettes and Ingo Maurer chandelier cast a cozy glow, all the better to enjoy a hearty, well-priced selection of dishes, like slices of foie gras served atop *crème de lentilles* and sprinkled with garlicky croutons, or a rosy beef entrecôte with roasted baby Yukon gold potatoes and mushrooms *de Paris*. In springtime, fat white asparagus is nicely paired with salty smoked haddock and spring peas. $ *Average main: €22* ✉ *12 av. Richerand, 10e, Canal St-Martin* ☎ *01–42–38–00–13* ⊕ *www.restophilou.com* ⊘ *Closed Sun. and Mon.* ⚼ *Reservations essential* Ⓜ *Jacques Bonsergent* ✛ *2:G4.*

$
CAFÉ
✕ **Ten Belles.** Canal St-Martin's first seriously good coffee bar, Ten Belles is where pedigreed baristas cater to a hip crowd of connoisseurs of the good brew. Sandwiches, soups, and an irresistable assortment of snacks and sweets all come from the ladies at the Bal Café. $ *Average main: €6* ✉ *10 rue de la Grange aux Belles, 10e, Canal St-Martin* ☎ *01–42–40–90–78* ⊕ *www.tenbelles.com* ⊘ *No dinner* ⚼ *Reservations not accepted* Ⓜ *Jacques Bonsergent, République* ✛ *2:G4.*

$
BAKERY
✕ **Véronique Mauclerc.** To really know Paris is to know her great boulangeries, a tradition in free fall since the advent of that notorious cricket bat, the industrial baguette. Thankfully there's an ever-growing group of bakers carrying the flame, literally. Véronique Mauclerc, one of the best, makes her breads, classic *viennoiserie* (croissants, turnovers, pain au chocolat), and savory tarts on the premises in a traditional wood-fired oven using only organic flour and natural ferments

for leavening. As if this weren't enough, her pastries are a triumph. The fine traditional Paris Brest—a slightly sweet, hazelnut-cream-filled pâte à choux sprinkled with slivered almonds—sells out quickly, as do the excellent mini chocolate cakes and fruit strudels. [$] *Average main: €5* ✉ *83 rue de Crimée, 19e, Canal St-Martin* ☎ *01–42–40–64–55* [M] *Botzaris* ✣ *2:H1.*

RÉPUBLIQUE

$$ BISTRO FAMILY 🍴 **Astier.** There are three good reasons to go to Astier: the generous cheese platter plunked on your table atop a help-yourself wicker tray, the exceptional wine cellar with bottles dating back to the 1970s, and the French bistro fare (even if portions seem to have diminished over the years). Dishes like marinated herring with warm potato salad, sausage with lentils, and baba au rhum are classics on the frequently changing set menu for €45, which includes a selection of no less than 20 cheeses. The vintage 1950s wood-panel dining room attracts plenty of locals and remains a fairly sure bet in the area, especially because it's open every day. [$] *Average main: €21* ✉ *44 rue Jean-Pierre Timbaud, 11e, République* ☎ *01–43–57–16–35* 🌐 *www.restaurant-astier.com* ✍ *Reservations essential* [M] *Parmentier* ✣ *2:H5.*

$ WINE BAR 🍴 **Au Passage.** This *bistrot à vins* has the lived-in look of a longtime neighborhood favorite—which it was until two veterans of the raging Paris wine-bar scene reinvented the place, keeping the laid-back atmosphere and adding a serious foodie menu that's one of the best deals in town. A blackboard lists a selection of small €5 to €13 tapas dishes—including several house-made pâtés, fresh tomato or beet salad, a superb seafood carpaccio, and artisanal charcuterie and cheeses. Four or more diners can hack away at a crispy-succulent roasted lamb haunch. [$] *Average main: €15* ✉ *1 bis, passage Saint-Sébastien, 11e, République* ☎ *01–43–55–07–52* 🌐 *www.restaurant-aupassage.fr* ⏲ *Closed Sun. No lunch* ✍ *Reservations essential* [M] *Saint-Ambroise, Saint-Sebastien–Froissart, Richard Lenoir* ✣ *2:H6.*

$$ MOROCCAN 🍴 **Le Martel.** Of the scads of neighborhood couscous joints in Paris, a few have become fashionable thanks to their host's magnetic personality and their stylish setting—and this converted bistro ranks among the best. It's crowded, but the clientele of fashion designers, photographers, models, and media folk are as cool as it gets in this up-and-coming quartier. Everyone digs in to a mix of French standbys (such as artichokes with vinaigrette) and more exotic fare like lamb tagine with almonds, prunes, and dried apricots. [$] *Average main: €18* ✉ *3 rue Martel, 10e, République* ☎ *01–47–70–67–56* [M] *Château d'Eau* ✣ *2:E4.*

LATIN QUARTER

Thanks to its student population, the Latin Quarter caters to those on a budget with kebab shops, crêpe stands, fast-food joints, and no-nonsense bistros. Look beyond the pedestrian streets such as Rue de la Huchette and Rue Mouffetard for less touristy eateries preferred by locals. As you might expect in an area known for its *gauche caviar* (wealthy intellectuals who vote Socialist), the Latin Quarter brims with atmospheric places to linger over a tiny cup of black coffee.

$$$
SPANISH
✕**Fogón St-Julien.** The most ambitious Spanish restaurant in Paris, this spot occupies an airy Seineside space, avoiding tapas-bar clichés. The seasonal all-tapas menu, at €51 per person, is the most creative choice, but that would mean missing out on the seven different takes on paella that are available daily: perhaps saffron with seafood (which could be a bit more generous), inky squid, vegetable, or Valencia-style with rabbit, chicken, and vegetables. Finish up with custardy crème Catalan and a glass of Muscatel. $ *Average main: €26* ✉ *45 quai des Grands-Augustins, 6e, Latin Quarter* ☎ *01–43–54–31–33* ⊕ *www.restaurantfogon.com* ☢ *Closed Mon., 2 wks in Aug., and 1 wk at Christmas* ⚞ *Reservations essential* Ⓜ *St-Michel* ✛ *4:C2.*

PARIS CAFÉ CULTURE

The café capital of the world is making room for the new barista cafés sweeping cities across the globe. For discerning coffee lovers this is good news indeed. Scattered throughout Paris's most compelling neighborhoods, most of the new cafés have a character all their own and, alongside superb gastronomic coffee, offer a selection of top-notch snacks or even meals.

Some of the very best include Bal Café, Café Coutume, Holybelly, La Caféothèque, Télescope, and Ten Belles.

$$$
BISTRO
✕**Itinéraires.** In the spacious former premises of the noted Chez Toutoune, the once-faded surroundings have been revitalized here with taupe walls, a long *table d'hôte* (shared table), and a bar for solo meals or tapas-style snacks. The cooking, meanwhile, is as inspired as ever with highlights including a tart of foie gras, duck confit, and nutmeg; cod poached in a vegetable and sage bouillon; and a deconstructed lemon tart with a touch of celery. Prices run the gamut from a €49 four-course lunch to a €90 degustation menu at dinner. $ *Average main: €27* ✉ *5 rue de Pontoise, 5e, Latin Quarter* ☎ *01–46–33–60–11* ☢ *Closed Sun., Mon., and 2 wks in Aug. No lunch Sat.* ⚞ *Reservations essential* Ⓜ *Maubert-Mutualité* ✛ *4:E4.*

$$
BISTRO
FAMILY
✕**L'Avant-Goût.** Christophe Beaufront belongs to a generation of gifted bistro chefs who have rejected the pressure-cooker world of haute cuisine in favor of something more personal and democratic. The result: delighted and loyal customers. Typical of his market-inspired cooking is his signature pot-au-feu *de cochon aux épices,* in which spiced pork stands in for the usual beef, and the bouillon is served separately. Children get an especially warm welcome here. $ *Average main: €21* ✉ *26 rue Bobillot, 13e* ☎ *01–53–80–24–00* ⊕ *www.lavantgout.com* ☢ *Closed Sun. and Mon.* ⚞ *Reservations essential* Ⓜ *Place d'Italie* ✛ *4:G6.*

$$
BISTRO
✕**L'Ourcine.** Sylvain Danière knows just what it takes to open a wildly popular bistro: choose an obscure location in a residential neighborhood, decorate it simply but cheerfully, work extremely hard, set competitive prices (€38 for three courses at dinner, €28 for two courses at lunch), and constantly reinvent your menu. The real key ingredient is talent, though, and Danière has plenty of it, as demonstrated by his updated duckling *au sang* (in blood sauce) with celery-root puree, and a popular *crémeux au chocolat* (chocolate pudding) to finish things off.

Locals mingle with well-informed tourists from Texas or Toulouse in the red-and-cream dining room, and you can watch the chef hard at work in his small kitchen. [$] *Average main: €20* ✉ *92 rue Broca, 13e, Latin Quarter* ☎ *01–47–07–13–65* 🌐 *www.restaurant-lourcine.fr* ⏲ *Closed Sun., Mon., 3 wks in Aug., 1 wk at Christmas, and 1 wk in Feb.* [M] *Les Gobelins* ✥ *4:G6.*

$ CHINESE FAMILY 🍴 **La Chine Massena.** With wonderfully overwrought rooms that seem draped in a whole restaurant-supply catalog's worth of Asiana (plus four monitors showing the very latest in Hong Kong music videos), this is a fun place. Not only is the pan-Asian food good and moderately priced, but the restaurant itself has lots of entertainment value—wedding parties often provide a free floor show, and on weekends Asian disco follows variety shows. Steamed dumplings, lacquered duck, and the fish and seafood you'll see swimming in the tanks are specialties, and the oyster bar serves heaping seafood platters. [$] *Average main: €13* ✉ *Centre Commercial Masséna, 96 bd. Masséna, 13e, Latin Quarter* ☎ *01–45–83–98–88* 🌐 *www.chinemassena.fr* [M] *Porte de Choisy* ✥ *4:G6.*

$$$$ MODERN FRENCH 🍴 **La Tour d'Argent.** You can't deny the splendor of this restaurant's setting overlooking the Seine; if you don't want to splash out on dinner, treat yourself to the three-course lunch menu for a reduced price of €85. This entitles you to succulent slices of one of the restaurant's numbered ducks (the great duck slaughter began in 1919 and is now well past the millionth mallard, as your numbered certificate will attest). Don't be too daunted by the vast wine list—with the aid of the sommelier you can splurge a little (about €85) and perhaps taste a rare vintage Burgundy from the extraordinary cellars, which survived World War II. [$] *Average main: €105* ✉ *15–17 quai de la Tournelle, 5e, Latin Quarter* ☎ *01–43–54–23–31* 🌐 *www.latourdargent.com* ⏲ *Closed Sun., Mon., and Aug.* ✍ *Reservations essential* 👔 *Jacket and tie* [M] *Cardinal Lemoine* ✥ *4:E4.*

$$ BRASSERIE FAMILY 🍴 **Le Balzar.** Regulars grumble about the uneven cooking at Le Balzar, but they continue to come back because they can't resist the waiters' wry humor and the dining room's amazing people-watching possibilities (you can also drop in for a drink on the terrace). The restaurant attracts politicians, writers, tourists, and local eccentrics—and remains one of the city's classic brasseries: the perfect stop before or after a film in a local art-house cinema. Don't expect miracles from the kitchen, but stick to evergreens like snails in garlic butter, onion soup, panfried veal liver with sautéed potatoes, and baba au rhum for dessert. [$] *Average main: €23* ✉ *49 rue des Écoles, 5e, Latin Quarter* ☎ *01–43–54–13–67* 🌐 *www.brasseriebalzar.com* ✍ *Reservations essential* [M] *Cluny–La Sorbonne* ✥ *4:C4.*

$ VIETNAMESE 🍴 **Le Bambou.** The line outside this restaurant anytime after 7 pm is a sure sign that something exciting is going on in the kitchen. Its small dining room is crowded and noisy, and service is more than brisk—the only thing missing is an eject button on your seat—but it's well worth it for some of the cheapest and most authentic Vietnamese food in town. If you find yourself in doubt about how to eat some of the dishes that involve wrapping meat and herbs in transparent rice paper or lettuce leaves, just spy on the regulars, many of them Vietnamese. Otherwise, go for one of the huge bowls of soup: tripe is popular, though there are plenty of other meat and seafood variations. $ *Average main: €12* ⊠ *70 rue Baudincourt, 13e, Latin Quarter* ☎ *01–45–70–91–75* ⊘ *Closed Mon. and 3 wks in Aug.* Ⓜ *Tolbiac, Olympiades* ✛ *4:G6.*

$$$ ✕ **Le Buisson Ardent.** This charming Quartier Latin bistro with wood-
BISTRO work and murals dating from 1925 is always packed and boisterous. A glance at the €39.90 set menu—a bargain €28 at lunch for three courses—makes it easy to understand why. Dishes such as chestnut soup with spice bread, squid with chorizo and creamy quinoa, and quince Tatin (upside-down tart) with mascarpone and pink pralines put a fresh twist on French classics, and service is reliably courteous. If you don't finish your bottle of wine, you can take it with you to savor the last drops. $ *Average main: €26* ⊠ *25 rue Jussieu, 5e, Latin Quarter* ☎ *01–43–54–93–02* ⊕ *www.lebuissonardent.fr* ⌲ *Reservations essential* Ⓜ *Jussieu* ✛ *4:E4.*

$$ ✕ **Le Pré Verre.** Chef Jean-François Paris knows his cassia bark from his
MODERN FRENCH cinnamon thanks to a long stint in Asia. He opened this lively bistro with its purple-gray walls and photos of jazz musicians to showcase his culinary style, rejuvenating archetypal French dishes with Asian and Mediterranean spices. His bargain prix-fixe menus (€14.50 at lunch, €32 at dinner) change constantly, but his trademark spiced suckling pig with crisp cabbage is always a winner, as is his rhubarb compote with gingered white-chocolate mousse. $ *Average main: €20* ⊠ *8 rue Thénard, 5e, Latin Quarter* ☎ *01–43–54–59–47* ⊕ *www.lepreverre.com* ⊘ *Closed Sun., Mon., and 1 wk at Christmas* ⌲ *Reservations essential* Ⓜ *Maubert–Mutualité* ✛ *4:D4.*

$$ ✕ **Les Papilles.** Part wineshop and épicerie, part restaurant, Les Papilles
WINE BAR has a winning formula—pick any bottle off the well-stocked shelf and pay a €7 corkage fee to drink it with your meal. You can also savor one of several superb wines by the glass at your table or around the classic zinc bar. The excellent set menu—made with top-notch, sea-sonal ingredients—usually begins with a luscious velouté, a velvety soup served from a large tureen, and proceeds with a hearty-yet-tender meat dish alongside perfectly cooked vegetables—well worth spending a little extra time for lunch or dinner. $ *Average main: €18* ⊠ *30 rue Gay-Lussac, 5e, Latin Quarter* ☎ *01–43–25–20–79* ⊕ *www.lespapillesparis.fr* ⊘ *Closed Sun., Mon., last wk of July, and 2 wks in Aug.* ⌲ *Reservations essential* Ⓜ *Cluny–La Sorbonne* ✛ *4:C5.*

$$$$ ✕ **Sola.** Here, dishes like miso-lacquered foie gras or sake-glazed suck-
ECLECTIC ling pig—perfectly crisp on the outside and melting inside—pair tra-ditional Japanese and French ingredients to wondrous effect. Costing €48, the three-course set weekday lunch menu offers a choice of fish or meat and finishes with some stunning confections. Shoes stay on in the tranquil half-timbered dining room upstairs, but the vaulted room downstairs is totally traditional—and one of the loveliest in Paris. $ *Average main: €35* ⊠ *12 rue de l'Hôtel Colbert, 5e, Latin Quarter* ☎ *01–43–29–59–04* ⊕ *www.restaurant-sola.com* ⊘ *Closed Sun. and Mon.* ⌲ *Reservations essential* Ⓜ *Maubert–Mutualité* ✛ *4:D3.*

$$$$ ✕ Ze Kitchen Galerie. The name of this contemporary bistro might not
MODERN FRENCH be inspired, but the cooking shows creativity and a sense of fun: from
Fodor'sChoice a deliberately deconstructed menu featuring raw fish, soups, pastas,
★ and à la plancha (grilled) plates, consider the roast and confit duck
with a tamarind-and-sesame condiment and foie gras, or lobster with
mussels, white beans, and Thai herbs. A tireless experimenter, the chef
buys heirloom vegetables direct from farmers and tracks down herbs
and spices in Asian supermarkets. $ *Average main: €39* ✉ *4 rue des
Grands-Augustins, 6e, Latin Quarter* ☎ *01–44–32–00–32* ⊕ *www.
zekitchengalerie.fr* ⊘ *Closed weekends* ⚑ *Reservations essential* Ⓜ *St-
Michel* ✛ *4:C2.*

ST-GERMAIN-DES-PRÉS

St-Germain is enjoying a revival as a foodie haunt, with Yves Camdeborde's Le Comptoir du Relais Saint-Germain the perfect example of
the kind of market-inspired bistro that Parisians (and foreigners) adore.
The neighborhood's old leftist roots and new bobo sensibility blend
together nicely in eateries that are not too upscale yet reflect a discerning
touch. You'll find everything from top Paris chefs (Darroze, Robuchon)
to neighborhood favorites so good (Semilla, Fish) that they draw Parisians from bordering arrondissements—and that's saying a lot.

$$$ ✕ Alcazar. When Sir Terence Conran opened this impressive 300-seat
BRASSERIE restaurant, he promised to reinvent the Parisian brasserie, and he's come
close. Alcazar's mezzanine bar is famed for its DJ, and with its slick
decor and skylight roof, it feels more like London than the Rive Gauche.
The food is resolutely French with the occasional Mediterranean touch,
plus the house classic fish-and-chips. The chef seems to have found his
groove with dishes such as salmon with ginger and veal braised with
morels. For dessert, it's hard to pass up the profiteroles, mille-feuille,
or baba au rhum. Sunday brunch is popular, and the restaurant is now
the Paris venue for the TV show *Top Chef.* $ *Average main: €26* ✉ *62
rue Mazarine, 6e, St-Germain-des-Prés* ☎ *01–53–10–19–99* ⊕ *www.
alcazar.fr* Ⓜ *Odéon* ✛ *4:B2.*

$ ✕ Au Sauvignon. Edge your way in among the students and lively tipplers
WINE BAR at this homey, old-fashioned spot—one of Paris's oldest wine bars—with
antique tiles and a covered terrace. The basic menu, which includes
several small dishes, like charcuterie, terrine, or regional cheeses, makes
ordering the right glass a breeze. $ *Average main: €15* ✉ *80 rue des Sts-
Pères, 7e, St-Germain-des-Prés* ☎ *01–45–48–49–02* Ⓜ *Sèvres-Babylone*
✛ *4:A3.*

$$ ✕ Boucherie Roulière. If it's steak you're craving, put your faith in Jean-
BISTRO Luc Roulière, a fifth-generation butcher who opened this long, nar-
row bistro near St-Sulpice church. Partner Franck Pinturier is from
the Auvergne region, which is also known for its melt-in-the-mouth
meat, so start with truffle-scented ravioli or a rich marrow bone before
indulging in a generous slab of Limousin or Salers beef, excellent veal
kidney, or, for the meat-shy, perhaps lobster or sea bass. The minimalist cream-and-brown dining room with checkerboard floor tiles and
black-and-white photos on the walls keeps the focus on the food, and

waiters are of the professional Parisian breed. $ *Average main: €23* ✉ *24 rue des Canettes, 6e, St-Germain-des-Prés* ☎ *01–43–26–25–70* ⊕ *www.boucherie-rouliere.com* ☉ *Closed Aug.* Ⓜ *Mabillon* ✛ *4:B3.*

$$$$
BRASSERIE

✕ **Brasserie Lipp.** Step through the antique revolving door of this landmark brasserie for a blast from the past. These are the same tables where Hemingway penned pre-war notes, Proust ordered Alsatian beer, and intellectuals like Camus rubbed elbows with artists like Chagall. Maintaining its original 1926 decor (think paneled wood, mirrors, and tiled floors), the eatery serves hearty dishes, such as *choucroute* with sausages and *confit de canard* with sautéed potatoes. Expect a convivial atmosphere and friendly service from traditionally dressed waiters. $ *Average main: €35* ✉ *151 bd. St-Germain, 6e, St-Germain-des-Prés* ☎ *01–45–48–53–91* ⊕ *www.ila-chateau.com/lipp* Ⓜ *St-Germain-des-Pres, St-Sulpice, Mabillon* ✛ *4:A3.*

$$
CAFÉ

✕ **Café de Flore.** Picasso, Chagall, Sartre, and de Beauvoir, attracted by the luxury of a heated café, worked and wrote here in the early 20th century. Today you'll find more tourists than intellectuals, and prices are hardly aimed at struggling artists, but the outdoor terrace is great for people-watching and popular with Parisians. The service is brisk and the food is fine, but nothing special. $ *Average main: €22* ✉ *172 bd. St-Germain, 6e, St-Germain-des-Prés* ☎ *01–45–48–55–26* Ⓜ *St-Germain-des-Pres* ✛ *4:A3.*

$
BISTRO

✕ **Eggs & Co.** With a cheerfully bright and tiny, wood-beamed dining room—there's more space in the loftlike upstairs—this spot is devoted to the egg in all its forms, and whether you like yours baked with smoked salmon, whisked into an omelet with truffle shavings, or beaten into fluffy pancakes, there will be something for you on the blackboard menu. It's perfect for a late breakfast or light lunch on weekdays (it opens at 10 am), though rather mobbed for weekend brunch (10 am to 6 pm). $ *Average main: €12* ✉ *11 rue Bernard Palissy, 6e, St-Germain-des-Prés* ☎ *01–45–44–02–52* ⊕ *www.eggsandco.fr* Ⓜ *St-Germain-des-Prés* ✛ *4:A3.*

$$
BISTRO
Fodor's Choice
★

✕ **Fish La Boissonerie.** A perennial favorite, expats and locals prize this lively, unpretentious bistro for its friendly atmosphere, consistently good food, solid wine list, and English-speaking staff—a quartet sorely lacking in the neighborhood. Dishes like velvety black squid-ink risotto, roasted cod with tender braised fennel, and crispy pumpkin tempura always hit the spot, especially when followed by decadent molten chocolate cake, honey-roasted figs, or banana-bread pudding. $ *Average main: €22* ✉ *69 rue de Seine, 6e, St-Germain-des-Prés* ☎ *01–43–54–34–69* ⌔ *Reservations essential* Ⓜ *St-Germain-des-Prés, Odéon* ✛ *4:B3.*

$$$$
MODERN FRENCH

✕ **Gaya Rive Gauche.** If you can't fathom paying upward of €200 per person to taste the cooking of Pierre Gagnaire (the city's most avant-garde chef) at his eponymous restaurant, book a table at his fashionable fish restaurant. At Gaya Rive Gauche, Gagnaire uses seafood as a palette for his creative impulses: expect small portions of artfully presented food, as in a seafood gelée encircled by white beans and draped with Spanish ham, or cod "petals" in a martini glass with soba noodles, mango, and grapefruit. $ *Average main: €38* ✉ *44 rue du Bac, 7e, St-Germain-des-Prés* ☎ *01–45–44–73–73* ⊕ *www.pierre-gagnaire.com* ☉ *Closed Sun. and Mon.* ⌔ *Reservations essential* Ⓜ *Rue du Bac* ✛ *3:H2.*

$$$$ MODERN FRENCH 🍴 **Hélène Darroze.** The most celebrated female chef in Paris is now cooking at the Connaught in London, but her St-Germain dining room is an exclusive setting for her sophisticated take on southwestern French food. Darroze's intriguingly modern touch comes through in such dishes as a sublime duck-foie-gras confit served with an exotic-fruit chutney or a blowout of roast wild duck stuffed with foie gras and truffles. At its best, the food lives up to the very high prices, but for a sampling without the wallet shock, her €28 eight-course tapas lunch menu, served in the plush red salon, is one of the best deals in town. [$] *Average main: €65* ✉ *4 rue d'Assas, 6e, St-Germain-des-Prés* ☎ *01–42–22–00–11* 🌐 *www.helenedarroze.com* 🕓 *Closed Sun. and Mon.* ✍ *Reservations essential* [M] *Sèvres-Babylone* ✥ *4:A4.*

$$ SEAFOOD 🍴 **Huîtrerie Régis.** When the oysters are this fresh, who needs anything else? That's the philosophy of this bright 14-seat restaurant with crisp white tablecloths and pleasant service, popular with the area's glitterati. If you find yourself puzzling over the relative merits of *fines de claires, spéciales,* and *pousses en claires,* you can always go with the €30 prix fixe that includes a glass of Charentais, a dozen No. 3 (medium) oysters, and coffee—or ask the knowledgeable waiters for advice. You can supplement this simplest of meals with shrimp and perhaps a slice of freshly made fruit pie. [$] *Average main: €24* ✉ *3 rue de Montfaucon, 6e, St-Germain-des-Prés* ☎ *01–44–41–10–07* 🌐 *www.huitrerieregis.com* 🕓 *Closed early July–early Sept.* [M] *Mabillon* ✥ *4:B3.*

$$$$ BISTRO 🍴 **Josephine Chez Dumonet.** Theater types, politicos, and locals fill the moleskin banquettes of this venerable bistro, where the frosted-glass lamps and amber walls put everyone in a good light. Unlike most bistros, Josephine caters to the indecisive, since generous half portions allow you to graze your way through the temptingly retro menu. Try the excellent boeuf bourguignon, roasted saddle of lamb with artichokes, top-notch steak tartare prepared table-side, or anything with truffles in season; game is also a specialty in fall and winter. [$] *Average main: €35* ✉ *117 rue du Cherche-Midi, 6e, St-Germain-des-Prés* ☎ *01–45–48–52–40* 🕓 *Closed weekends* ✍ *Reservations essential* [M] *Duroc* ✥ *3:G5.*

$$$ MODERN FRENCH 🍴 **KGB.** After extravagant success with his Asian-infused cuisine at Ze Kitchen Galerie, master-chef William Ledeuil extended his artistry to annex KGB (Kitchen Galerie Bis) just down the street, this time with a different focus and gentler prices. For starters, the "zors-d'oeuvres" of two, four, or six mini-dishes—think cubes of foie gras *mi-cuit* (half-cooked) in duck consommé, tender pork wontons in coconut milk with a hint of galanga—allow for a deeper exploration of what makes Ledeuil's cooking so alluring. Main courses, like roasted monkfish with a prune-lemongrass relish or the superb braised veal cheek in teriyaki jus, showcase his wizardry. [$] *Average main: €29* ✉ *25 rue des Grands Augustins, 6e, St-Germain-des-Prés* ☎ *01–46–33–00–85* 🌐 *www.zekitchengalerie.fr* 🕓 *Closed Sun., Mon., and Aug.* ✍ *Reservations essential* [M] *Odéon, St-Michel* ✥ *4:C3.*

$$$$ MODERN FRENCH 🍴 **L'Atelier de Joël Robuchon.** Worldwide phenomenon Joël Robuchon retired from the restaurant business for several years before opening this red-and-black-lacquer space with a bento-box-meets-tapas aesthetic. Robuchon's devoted kitchen staff whip up small plates for grazing as

well as full portions, which can turn out to be the better bargain. Highlights from the oft-changing menu have included an intense tomato jelly topped with avocado puree and the thin-crusted mackerel tart, although his inauthentic (but who's complaining?) take on carbonara with cream and Alsatian bacon, and the *merlan* Colbert (fried herb butter) remain signature dishes. Reservations are taken for the first sittings only at lunch and dinner. $ *Average main: €40* ✉ *5 rue Montalembert, 7e, St-Germain-des-Prés* ☎ *01–42–22–56–56* ⊕ *www.atelier-robuchon-saint-germain.com* Ⓜ *Rue du Bac* ✛ *4:A2.*

$$ ✕ **L'Epigramme.** Great bistro food is not so hard to find in Paris, but
BISTRO   only rarely does it come in a comfortable setting. At L'Epigramme,
FAMILY   the striped orange-and-yellow chairs are softly padded, there's space between you and your neighbors, and a big glass pane lets in plenty of light from the courtyard. The kitchen has an almost magical touch with meat: try the stuffed suckling pig with turnip choucroute, or seared slices of pink lamb with root vegetables in a glossy reduced sauce. $ *Average main: €22* ✉ *9 rue de l'Eperon, 6e, St-Germain-des-Prés* ☎ *01–44–41–00–09* ☾ *Closed Sun., Mon., 3 wks in Aug., and 1 wk in Jan.* ⟐ *Reservations essential* Ⓜ *Odéon* ✛ *4:C3.*

$$ ✕ **La Bastide Odéon.** The open kitchen of this popular Provençal bistro
BISTRO   allows you to watch the cooks demonstrate a creative hand with Mediterranean cuisine. Expect unusual dishes such as aged Spanish ham with a grilled pepper pipérade and artichokes; mushroom-and-pea risotto with arugula; and duck breast with orange sauce, date puree, polenta, and wild asparagus. Unusual for Paris, an entire section of the menu is devoted to vegetarian dishes. $ *Average main: €20* ✉ *7 rue Corneille, 6e, St-Germain-des-Prés* ☎ *01–43–26–03–65* ⊕ *www.bastideodeon. com* Ⓜ *Odéon; RER: Luxembourg* ✛ *4:C4.*

$$ ✕ **La Ferrandaise.** Portraits of cows adorn the stone walls of this bistro
BISTRO   near the Luxembourg Gardens, hinting at the kitchen's penchant for meaty cooking (Ferrandaise is a breed of cattle). Still, there's something for every taste on the market-inspired menu, which always lists three meat and three fish mains. Dill-marinated salmon with sweet mustard sauce is a typical starter, and a thick, milk-fed veal chop might come with a squash pancake and spinach. The dining room buzzes with locals who appreciate the good-value €37 prix fixe—there is no à la carte—and the brilliant bento box–style €16 lunch menu, in which three courses are served all at once. $ *Average main: €24* ✉ *8 rue de Vaugirard, 6e, St-Germain-des-Prés* ☎ *01–43–26–36–36* ⊕ *www. laferrandaise.com* ☾ *Closed Sun. and 3 wks in Aug. No lunch Mon. and Sat.* Ⓜ *Odéon; RER: Luxembourg* ✛ *4:C4.*

$$$$ ✕ **Lapérouse.** Émile Zola, George Sand, and Victor Hugo were regulars
BISTRO   here, and the restaurant's mirrors still bear diamond scratches from the days when mistresses would double-check their jewels' value. It's hard not to fall in love with this storied 17th-century Seine-side town house with a warren of woodwork-graced salons. The cuisine seeks a balance between traditional and modern, often drawing on Mediterranean inspirations. For a truly intimate meal, reserve one of the legendary private *salons* where anything can happen (and probably has). $ *Average main: €50* ✉ *51 quai des Grands Augustins, 6e, St-Germain-des-Prés*

☏ *01–43–26–68–04* ⊕ *www.laperouse.com* ⊘ *Closed Sun. No lunch.* ⌂ *Reservations essential* Ⓜ *St-Michel* ✛ *4:C2.*

$$　✕ **Le Bouillon Racine.** Originally a *bouillon*—one of the Parisian soup res-
BRASSERIE taurants popular at the turn of the 20th century—this two-story restau-
rant is now a lushly renovated Belle Époque haven with a casual setting
downstairs and a lavish room upstairs. The menu changes seasonally:
lamb knuckle with licorice, wild boar *parmentier* (like shepherd's pie,
with mashed potatoes on top and meat underneath), and roast suckling
pig are warming winter dishes. For dessert, dig into crème brûlée with
maple syrup or the *café liégeois* (coffee-flavored custard topped with
whipped cream), which comes in a jug. Ⓢ *Average main: €22* ⊠ *3 rue
Racine, 6e, St-Germain-des-Prés* ☏ *01–44–32–15–60* ⊕ *www.bouillon-
racine.com* Ⓜ *Odéon* ✛ *4:C4.*

$$　✕ **Le Comptoir du Relais Saint-Germain.** Run by legendary bistro chef Yves
BISTRO Camdeborde, this tiny Art Deco hotel restaurant is booked up well in
advance for the single dinner sitting featuring five courses of haute-
cuisine fare. On weekdays from noon to 6 and weekends until 10, a
brasserie menu is served; reservations are not accepted, resulting in long
lines and brisk service. Start with charcuterie or pâté, then choose from
open-faced sandwiches, gourmet salads, and a variety of hot dishes such
as braised beef cheek, roast tuna, and Camdeborde's famed deboned
and breaded pig's trotter. If you don't mind bus fumes, sidewalk tables
make for prime people-watching in summer. Ⓢ *Average main: €22* ⊠ *9
carrefour de l'Odéon, 6e, St-Germain-des-Prés* ☏ *01–44–27–07–50*
⊕ *www.hotel-paris-relais-saint-germain.com* Ⓜ *Odéon* ✛ *4:B3.*

$$　✕ **Le Timbre.** Just when we thought it couldn't get any better, this tiny
BISTRO neighborhood favorite reopened with notable young chef Charles Danet
at the helm, earning enthusiastic acclaim from all quarters. The spare
but constantly changing seasonal menu concentrates on fresh farm-to-
table ingredients, offering meat and seafood dishes and plenty of hearty
vegetables: *filet de boeuf d'Aubrac* (a pedigreed cow from southwest
France) with potato terrine and Pardailhan turnips, scallops with cau-
liflower puree, or sweetbreads with pears and celery. Prices remain very
reasonable for this quality: three-course lunches are €26, four-course
dinners are €43, and five-course tasting dinners are €49. Ⓢ *Average
main: €19* ⊠ *3 rue Ste-Beuve, 6e, St-Germain-des-Prés* ☏ *01–45–49–
10–40* ⊕ *www.restaurantletimbre.com* ⊘ *Closed Sun., Mon., Aug., and
1 wk at Christmas* ⌂ *Reservations essential* Ⓜ *Vavin* ✛ *4:A5.*

$$$$　✕ **Les Bouquinistes.** Expect to hear more English than French in the
BISTRO cheery, contemporary dining room of this bistro, with its closely packed
tables looking out onto the Seine, but the sophisticated seasonal cui-
sine—such as snails and mussels with gnocchi, followed by British Her-
eford beef with squash-stuffed rigatoni and a caramel crème brûlée—is
as authentic as you could hope for. The €36 *menu du marché* (back
from the market) lunch menu seems less imaginative than the pricier
à la carte options—though it does include three courses and a glass
of wine. Ⓢ *Average main: €38* ⊠ *53 quai des Grands-Augustins, 6e,
St-Germain-des-Prés* ☏ *01–43–25–45–94* ⊕ *www.lesbouquinistes.com*
⊘ *Closed Aug.* Ⓜ *St-Michel* ✛ *4:C2.*

$$$ BISTRO Fodor's Choice ★ 🍴 **Semilla.** The duo behind the popular neighborhood bistro Fish and the excellent La Dernière Goutte wineshop have poured their significant expertise into this laid-back bistro in the heart of tony St-Germain-des-Prés. Its sophisticated cuisine, superb wines by the bottle or glass, and total lack of pretension have quickly made Semilla the toast of the town. A lively open kitchen produces a menu of plentiful dishes either raw, roasted, baked, or steamed, with choices that will thrill both carnivores and herbivores. Velvety chestnut soup, beet carpaccio, and the excellent marinated salmon are good choices to start, followed by roasted coquilles St-Jacques with Jerusalem artichoke puree or venison served with celery root and quince. There are also plenty of bistro classics to choose from, like beef tartare or côte de boeuf with roasted potatoes and a fine sauce bordelaise. [$] *Average main: €25* ✉ *54 rue de Seine, 6e, St-Germain-des-Prés* ☎ *01–43–54–34–50* ✍ *Reservations essential* [M] *Odéon, St-Germain-des-Prés* ✥ *4:B3.*

BRINY BLISS

Ever since the first trains from Brittany brought oyster-loving settlers to Montparnasse, the neighborhood has had a proud seafood tradition. The best oysters come from Normandy, Brittany, or Marennes-Oléron on the Atlantic coast. The knobbly shelled *creuses* are more common than the rounder *plates,* which are beloved by connoisseurs. Oysters can be dressed with vinegar and shallots, but a squeeze of lemon—or nothing at all—is probably the best accompaniment. Scoop the raw oyster from its shell with a small fork, slurp the juice, and chew a little before swallowing the taste of the sea.

$$$ JAPANESE 🍴 **Yen.** If you're having what is known in French as a *crise de foie* (liver crisis), the result of overindulging in rich food, this chic Japanese noodle house with a summer terrace and a VIP room upstairs is the perfect antidote. The blond-wood walls soothe the senses, the staff is happy to explain proper slurping technique, and the soba (buckwheat noodles), served in soup or with a restorative broth for dipping, will give you the courage to face another round of caramelized foie gras. The soba noodles are made fresh on the premises every day, showing Parisians that there is more to Japanese cuisine than sushi. [$] *Average main: €31* ✉ *22 rue St-Benoît, 6e, St-Germain-des-Prés* ☎ *01–45–44–11–18* ⏲ *Closed Sun. and 2 wks in Aug.* [M] *St-Germain-des-Prés* ✥ *4:A2.*

MONTPARNASSE

It's hard not to feel part of the café culture in Montparnasse. Along the broad boulevards you can find some of the city's classic brasseries. As storied as they are, many have been bought by chains and drained of the true charm that once attracted artists, politicians, and intellectuals. Though authentic brasseries can still be found—like Le Dôme—some of the area's best food is found at small bistros on narrow side streets.

$$$ BISTRO 🍴 **L'Assiette.** David Rathgeber spent 12 years working for celebrity-chef Alain Ducasse before taking over this landmark restaurant, where he has created his own menu and welcomed a devoted clientele. Expect

bourgeois classics with a subtle modern touch, perhaps white tuna steak with spinach, lemon, capers, and croutons, and crème caramel with salted butter—all executed with the precision you would expect of a Ducasse veteran. The excellent two-course lunch menu is a bargain at €23. Each month, the tea "tasting ateliers" span the globe via the world's great teas, pairing them with French cuisine. [$] *Average main: €27* ✉ *181 rue du Château, 14e, Montparnasse* ☎ *01–43–22–64–86* 🌐 *www.restaurant-lassiette.com* 🕒 *Closed Mon., Tues., Aug., and 1 wk at Christmas* [M] *Pernety, Mouton-Duvernet* ✥ *3:H6.*

$$ BISTRO 🍴 **La Cerisaie.** If you can nab a seat in this unremarkable yellow-and-red dining room (be sure to call ahead), you'll be rewarded with food prepared with such attention to detail that it will restore your faith in humanity. Foie gras makes several appearances on the chalkboard menu, since the chef is from southwest France, but you can also find freshly caught fish and perhaps farmer's pork from Gascony, a rarity in Paris. [$] *Average main: €18* ✉ *70 bd. Edgar Quinet, 14e, Montparnasse* ☎ *01–43–20–98–98* 🌐 *www.restaurantlacerisaie.com* 🕒 *Closed weekends, mid-July–mid-Aug., and 1 wk at Christmas* ✍ *Reservations essential* [M] *Edgar Quinet* ✥ *4:A6.*

$$$ BRASSERIE FAMILY 🍴 **La Coupole.** This world-renowned cavernous spot with Art Deco murals practically defines the term *brasserie*. It's been popular since Jean-Paul Sartre and Simone de Beauvoir were regulars, and it's still great fun. Today it attracts a mix of bourgeois families, tourists, and lone diners treating themselves to a dozen oysters. Recent additions to the classic brasserie menu are a tart of caramelized apple and panfried foie gras, beef fillet flambéed with cognac before your eyes, and profiteroles made with Valrhona chocolate. [$] *Average main: €26* ✉ *102 bd. du Montparnasse, 14e, Montparnasse* ☎ *01–43–20–14–20* 🌐 *www.lacoupole-paris.com* [M] *Vavin* ✥ *4:A6.*

$ MODERN FRENCH FAMILY 🍴 **La Crêperie Josselin.** With lacy curtains, beamed ceilings, and murals, this is the closest you'll get to an authentic Breton crêperie without heading to the coast. Tuck into a hearty buckwheat galette, perfectly crisped on the edges and filled with, perhaps, a classic combo of country ham, egg, cheese, and mushrooms, accompanied by a pitcher of refreshing dry Breton cider. For dessert, the traditional crêpe filled with crème *chataigne* (chestnut) or the sublime *caramel au beurre salé* (salted caramel) is not to be missed. With a two-course lunch *formule* with beverage for €12, this is a great place for a quick, satisfying, and thoroughly French meal. Extra bonus: the kids will love it. [$] *Average main: €10* ✉ *67 rue du Montparnasse, 14e, Montparnasse* ☎ *01–43–20–93–50* 🕒 *Closed Mon., Tues., Aug., and 2 wks in Jan.* 💳 *No credit cards* [M] *Vavin, Edgar Quinet* ✥ *3:H6.*

$$$$ BRASSERIE 🍴 **Le Dôme.** Now a fancy fish brasserie serving seafood delivered fresh from Normandy every day, this restaurant began as a dingy meeting place for exiled artists and intellectuals like Lenin and Picasso. Try the sole meunière or the bouillabaisse, the ingredients of which are on display in their raw form in the restaurant's sparkling fish shop next door. You can still drop by the covered terrace for a cup of coffee or a drink. [$] *Average main: €36* ✉ *108 bd. Montparnasse, 14e, Montparnasse* ☎ *01–43–35–25–81* 🕒 *Closed Sun. and Mon. in July and Aug.* [M] *Vavin* ✥ *4:A6.*

WESTERN PARIS

Change comes slowly to this old bourgeois neighborhood bordering the Bois de Boulogne. It's full of Paris stalwarts, where families have gathered over generations, and you can find some wonderful deeply Parisian bistros and brasseries. Avoid anything looking too chic or polished, where you'll very often pay high prices for mediocre fare.

$$$$ MODERN FRENCH 🍴 **Le Pré Catelan.** Live a Belle Époque fantasy by dining beneath the chestnut trees on the terrace of this fanciful landmark *pavillon* in the Bois de Boulogne. Each of chef Frédéric Anton's dishes is a variation on a theme, such as *l'os à moelle*: bone marrow prepared two ways, one peppered and the other stuffed with porcini and cabbage, both braised in a concentrated meat jus. For a taste of the good life at a (relatively) gentle price, order the €130 lunch menu and soak up the opulent surroundings along with service that's as polished as the silverware. [$] *Average main: €120* ✉ *Rte. de Suresnes, 16e, Western Paris* ☎ *01–44–14–41–14* 🌐 *www.restaurant-precatelan.com* 🕑 *Closed Sun. and Mon., 2 wks in Feb., 3 wks in Aug., and 1 wk in late Oct.–early Nov.* ✍ *Reservations essential* 👔 *Jacket and tie* [M] *Porte Dauphine* ✥ *1:A3.*

WHERE TO EAT
AND STAY IN PARIS

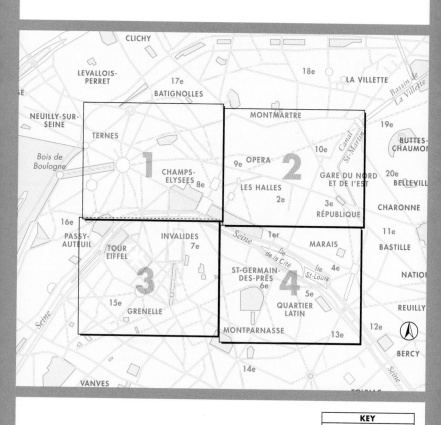

CLICHY

LEVALLOIS-
PERRET

17e

BATIGNOLLES

18e

LA VILLETTE

Bassin de
La Villette

NEUILLY-SUR-
SEINE

TERNES

MONTMARTRE

19e

BUTTES-
CHAUMON

Bois de
Boulogne

1

CHAMPS-
ELYSEES
8e

9e

OPERA

2

10e

Canal St-Martin

GARE DU NORD
ET DE l'EST

20e BELLEVILL

LES HALLES

2e

3e

RÉPUBLIQUE

CHARONNE

16e

PASSY-
AUTEUIL

TOUR
EIFFEL

INVALIDES
7e

1er

Seine
Île
de la Cité

MARAIS

Île
St-Louis

11e

BASTILLE

4e

NATION

3

ST-GERMAIN-
DES-PRÉS
6e

4

5e

REUILLY

15e

GRENELLE

QUARTIER
LATIN

Seine

MONTPARNASSE

13e

12e

BERCY

14e

Seine

VANVES

KEY	
☐	Hotels
◼	Restaurants
◼	Restaurant in Hotel
Ⓜ	Métro Stations

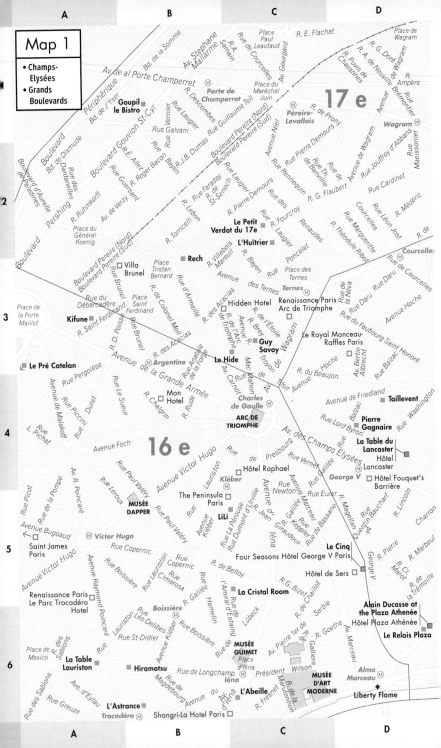

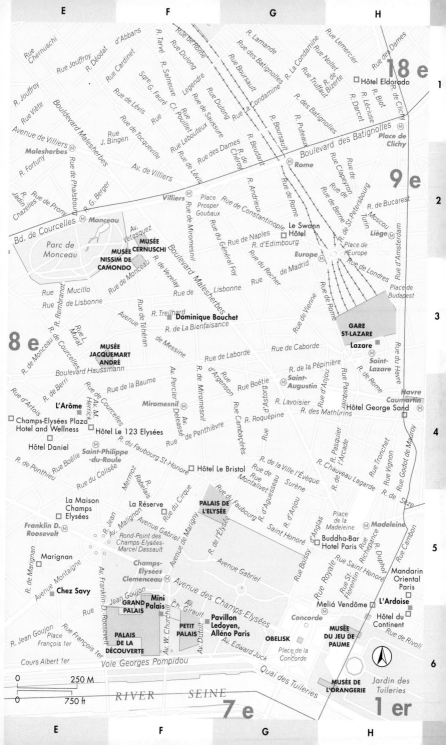

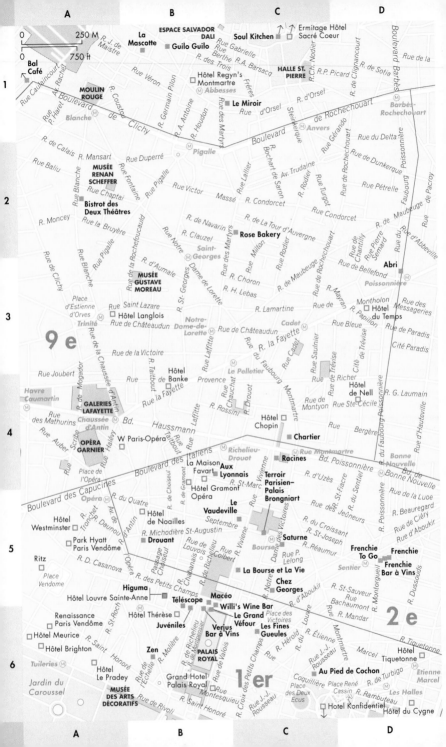

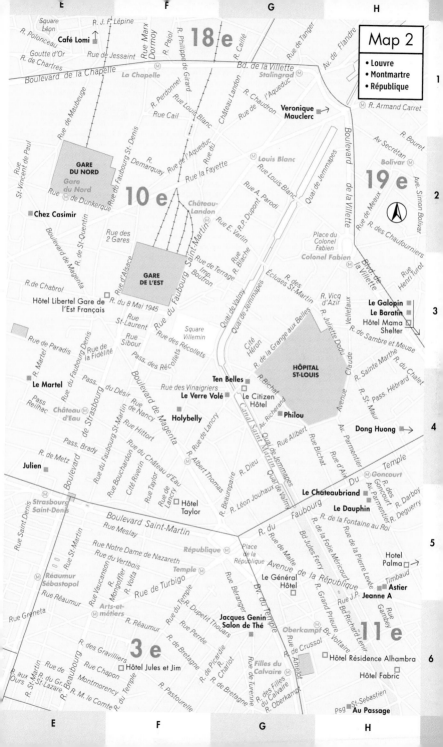

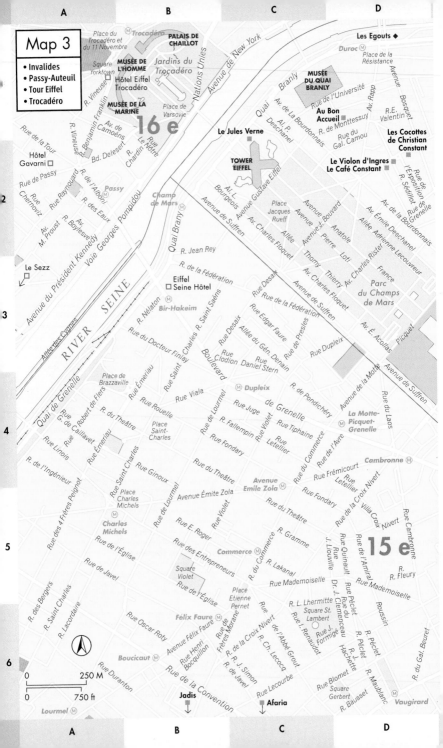

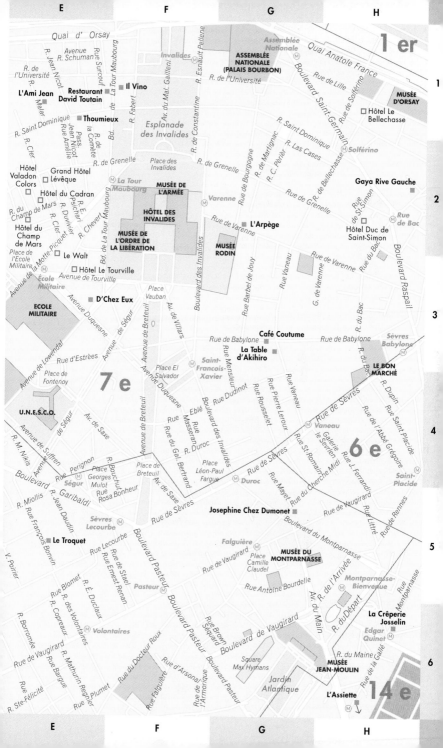

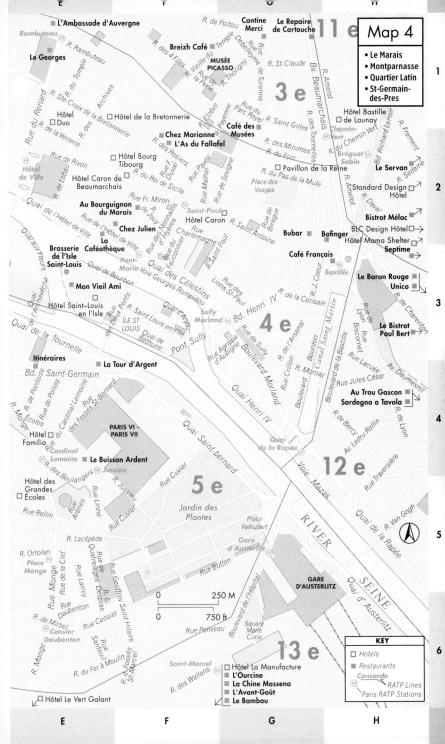

WHERE TO STAY

Updated by Jennifer Ladonne

If your Parisian fantasy involves romantic evenings in a historic hotel, awaking to the aroma of freshly baked croissants and café au lait, here's some good news: you don't have to be French aristocracy to make your dreams come true. With more than 2,000 hotels, the City of Light gives visitors stylish options in all price ranges, and a place with historic charm is practically a given.

In terms of location and price, there are more hotels on the *Rive Droite* (the Right Bank) offering formal luxury with premium service than on the *Rive Gauche* (the Left Bank), where the hotels are frequently smaller and richer in old-fashioned charm. The Rive Droite's 1er, 8e, and 16e arrondissements are still the most exclusive, and the prices there reflect that. Some of these palatial hotels charge more than €1,000 a night for standard rooms, and the high-end competition is heating up. On both sides of the Seine, Paris is in the throes of a lodging renaissance in both established and up-and-coming neighborhoods, with everything from chic new boutique hotels to extravagant five-star palaces. Major landmark luxury hotels are rising to the occasion with lavish renovations. The Shangri-La Hotel Paris and the Hôtel Le Bristol underwent significant refurbishments over the last few years, and the legendary Ritz reopened in 2016 after a four-year facelift. All this is good news for high rollers, especially when you factor in extraordinary new lodgings like the Paris Peninsula and the small but exquisite La Réserve.

But those on a budget should fear not, because less expensive alternatives on the Rive Droite can be found in the fashionable Marais quarter (3e and 4e arrondissements), and a slew of newcomers have laid their cornerstones in the newly chic 9e. A hotbed of stylish hotels are in the Rive Gauche's 6e arrondissement; choices get somewhat cheaper in the 5e and 7e. Everything from excellent budget deals to splendid designer spaces can now be found slightly off the beaten track in the 10e, 13e, and 20e arrondissements. Wherever possible, in the more expensive neighborhoods we've located budget hotels—check out the handful of budget-priced sleeps in the shadow of Notre-Dame, St-Germain-des-Prés, and the Louvre.

As for the environment inside your room, change has been in the air—literally. Enforcement of the no-smoking law is taken very seriously, with few hotels risking the ire of guests well aware of the laws. Amenities have improved, with virtually every hotel now equipped with cable TV (meaning CNN and BBC news in English), high-definition screens, minibars, in-room safes, and free wireless Internet access. Another recent change is the increasing availability of air-conditioning in both hotels and restaurants—a godsend in the *canicules* (dog days) of July and August. One thing that hasn't changed, however, is the lack of elbow room. Indoor spaces—from bed- and bathrooms to elevators—may feel cramped to those not used to life on a European scale. If you're flush and looking for enough room to spread out multiple suitcases, book a suite in one of the city's luxurious palace-like hotels.

PLANNING

BREAKFAST
Almost all Parisian hotels charge extra for breakfast, with per-person prices ranging from €10 to more than €50. If you decide to eat elsewhere, inform the staff so breakfast won't be charged to your bill. Occasionally, Continental breakfast—coffee, baguette, croissant, jam, and butter—will be included in the hotel rate. This is noted as *breakfast* in the meal plan section of each review.

CHECKING IN
Typical check-in and checkout times are 2 pm and noon, respectively, although some properties allow check-in as early as noon and require checkout as early as 10 am. Many flights from North America arrive early in the morning, but having to wait six hours for a room after arriving jet-lagged at 8 am isn't the ideal way to start a vacation. Alert the hotel of your early arrival; while you may not be able to get into your room, you may be able to arrange for baggage storage, especially at the larger establishments.

CHILDREN
Most hotels in Paris allow children under the age of 12 to stay in their parents' room at no charge. Hotel rooms are often on the small side, unable to accommodate cots or cribs, so inquire about connecting rooms, suites, and floors with strategically placed doors to create private corridors for larger families and groups. In the last few years, almost all of the big luxury hotels have gone the extra mile to attract parents with young children, offering child-friendly activities like swimming lessons or playtime, while mom and dad enjoy the spa.

HOTEL FEATURES
Unless stated in the review, hotels usually have elevators, and all guest rooms have air-conditioning, TV, telephone, and a private bathroom. In France, the "first floor" is the floor above the ground floor (*rez-de-chaussée*). The number of rooms listed at the end of each review reflects those with private bathroom (which means they have a shower or a

WHERE SHOULD I STAY?

	Neighborhood Vibe	Pros	Cons
St-Germain and Montparnasse (6e, 14e, 15e)	The center of café culture and the emblem of the Rive Gauche. The mood is leisurely; attractions are easy to access.	A safe, historic area with chic fashion boutiques, famous cafés and brasseries; and lovely side streets; lively all day.	Overdeveloped. Noisy along the main streets; the busy commercial area around the Tour Montparnasse is void of charm.
The Latin Quarter (5e, 6e)	The historic student quarter of the Rive Gauche. Full of narrow, winding streets and major parks and monuments such as the Panthéon.	Plenty of cheap eats and sleeps, discount book and music shops, and noteworthy open-air markets; safe area for walks day and night.	Touristy. No métro stations around the Panthéon; student pubs can be noisy in summer; hotel rooms tend to be smaller.
Marais and Bastille (3e, 4e, 11e)	Museums, chic shops, and bustling bistros line the narrow streets of the Marais, home to Jewish and gay communities. Farther east are stylish cocktail bars and edgy boutiques.	Generally excellent shopping, museum-going, dining, and café culture in the active Marais; bargains aplenty at Bastille hotels; several boutique designer hotels in both areas.	Overcrowded. Marais's narrow sidewalks are always packed, and rooms don't always come cheap; always noisy around the gritty boulevards of Place de la Bastille and Nation.
Montmartre and northeast Paris (18e, 19e, 20e)	The Rive Droite's hilltop district is known for winding streets leading from the racy Pigalle district to the stark-white Sacré-Coeur Basilica.	Amazing views of Paris; romantic cobblestone streets; easy access to Roissy-Charles de Gaulle airport; authentic Parisian neighborhoods.	Inconvenient. Steep staircases are challenging; few métro stations; Pigalle and Barbès area can be unsafe, especially late at night.
Champs-Élysées and Western Paris (8e, 16e, 17e)	The Triangle D'Or (Golden Triangle) and famous avenue are lively 24/7 with nightclubs, cinemas, and shops, all aimed at the moneyed jet set.	Home to most of the city's famous palace-like hotels and haute-couture boutiques, with no shortage of luxurious rooms and designer goods.	Superexpensive. The sky-high prices of this neighborhood, along with its Times Square tendencies, lure pickpockets.
Around the Eiffel Tower (7e, 15e)	The impressive Eiffel Tower and sweeping Champs de Mars sit next to the Seine River.	Safe and quiet, this Rive Gauche area of Paris has picture-perfect views at every turn.	Residential. With few shops and restaurants, this district is quiet at night; long distances between métro stations.
Louvre, Les Halles, Ile de la Cité (1er, 2e, 8e)	The central district around the Tuileries, Louvre, and Place de la Concorde is known for sightseeing and shopping; Les Halles is a buzzing commercial hub.	Convenient for getting around Paris on foot, bus, or métro. Safe, attractive district close to the Seine and shops of all types.	Noisy. The main artery of Rue de Rivoli is loud with traffic during the day; restaurants cater to tourists; a pickpocket's mecca.
Opéra and Grands Boulevards (9e, 10e)	The historic district centered around the Garnier Opera House and Bourse (Stock Exchange) is a popular district for its lively streets and important sites.	Perfect for walking tours, the area has unique Parisian finds, distinct neighborhoods like Canal St-Martin and Belleville, and les Grands Magasins (department stores).	Crowded. Tourists and locals keep districts full of pietons, cars, buses, trucks, taxis, and scooters; be extra alert in areas near major train stations.

tub, but not necessarily both). Tubs don't always have fixed curtains or showerheads; how the French rinse themselves with the handheld nozzle without flooding the entire bathroom remains a cultural mystery. Moderately priced places that expect guests to share toilets or bathrooms are almost extinct, but be sure you know what facilities you are getting when you book a budget hotel.

HOTEL QUALITY

Note that the quality of accommodations can vary from room to room. If you don't like the room you're given, ask to see another. The French star ratings can be misleading: official stars are granted for specific amenities and services rather than for ambience, style, or overall comfort, so you may find that a two-star hotel eclipses a three-star establishment. Many hotels prefer to remain "under-starred" for tax reasons.

LODGING STRATEGY

Where should you stay? With hundreds of Paris hotels, it may seem like a daunting question. But don't worry—our expert writers and editors have done most of the legwork. The 100-plus selections here represent the best and newest properties this city has to offer. Pick an area of town that appeals to you, and find a review quickly in the listings, which are arranged by neighborhood and then alphabetically.

RESERVATIONS

Make reservations as far in advance as possible, especially for May, June, September, and October. Calling directly works, but booking online may be the easiest way to make contact, because hotel staff are more likely to read English than understand it over the phone. Specify arrival and departure dates, room size (single or double), room type (standard, deluxe, or suite), the number of people in your party, and whether you want a bathroom with a shower or bathtub (or both). Double-check if breakfast, Internet, and taxes are included. Ask if a deposit is required and what happens if you cancel. Always request a confirmation number to verify your reservation upon arrival.

WHAT IT COSTS

Often a hotel in a certain price category will have a few less expensive rooms; it's worth asking. In the off-season—late July, August, November, early December, and late January—rates can be considerably lower. Inquire about specials and weekend deals, and whether there are better rates if you're staying a week or longer. There's a nominal city *taxe de séjour* ranging between €0.83 and €4.40 per person, per night, based on the hotel's star rating. Sometimes this tax is included in the room price, sometimes not.

If you're staying in Paris for more than just a few days, you might want to look into the increasingly popular option of renting an apartment. Not only does this often save in nightly costs, but with your own kitchen you can cook some of your own meals.

	WHAT IT COSTS			
	$	$$	$$$	$$$$
FOR TWO PEOPLE	under €121	€121–€175	€176–€250	over €250

Prices in the reviews are the lowest cost of a double standard room in high season.

HOTEL REVIEWS

In alphabetical order by neighborhood. Hotel reviews have been shortened. For full information, visit Fodors.com. Use the coordinate (⊕ 1:B2) at the end of each review to locate a property on the corresponding map at the end of the chapter.

ILE DE LA CITÉ AND ILE ST-LOUIS

Paris's islands give a good representation of the city's long and fascinating history. On Ile de la Cité—home of the glorious 13th-century Sainte-Chapelle and the foreboding Conciergerie, Marie-Antoinette's final home—you'll find some surprising lodging opportunities, including a tiny hotel tucked into the Hôtel Dieu, the city's oldest hospital. Ile St-Louis's elegant streets and leafy riverside walks inspire romance, and so do its small hotels and many elegant, if pricey, rentals.

ILE ST-LOUIS

$$$ HOTEL **Hôtel Saint-Louis en l'Isle.** The location on the exceptionally charming Ile St-Louis is the real draw of this five-story hotel, which retains many of its original 17th-century stone walls and wooden beams. **Pros:** romantic location; ancient architectural details; friendly staff. **Cons:** location is a bit far from the sights; métro stations are not so convenient; small rooms. *Rooms from: €205 ✉ 75 rue St-Louis-en-l'Ile, 4e, Ile St-Louis ☎ 01–46–34–04–80 ⊕ www.saintlouisenlisle.com 20 rooms No meals Ⓜ Pont Marie ⊕ 4:E3.*

AROUND THE EIFFEL TOWER

Hotel rooms with views of Paris's reigning icon come at a premium, but your chances of finding an affordable room with a view are best in this quiet, primarily residential neighborhood. If you don't find one, no worries, there are gorgeous views to be had from every street corner.

$$$ HOTEL FAMILY **Eiffel Seine Hôtel.** This tiny boutique hotel minutes from the Eiffel Tower mixes contemporary amenities and designer furnishings with Art Nouveau flourishes. **Pros:** very close to the Eiffel Tower and Champs de Mars; easy métro access; reasonable rates. **Cons:** long walk from popular sights; minimal space in standard rooms; street noise in some rooms facing river. *Rooms from: €250 ✉ 3 bd. de Grenelle, 15e, Around the Eiffel Tower ☎ 01–45–78–14–81 ⊕ www.hoteleiffelseineparis.com 45 rooms No meals Ⓜ Bir-Hakeim ⊕ 3:B3.*

$$$ ⊞ **Grand Hôtel Lévêque.** Sandwiched between casual cafés, this unob-
HOTEL trusive budget hotel is easy to miss, but its prime location shouldn't
FAMILY be overlooked—the Eiffel Tower and Champs de Mars are around the
corner, and one of the city's finest street markets is literally outside the
front door. **Pros:** in quiet residential district; some balconies with Eiffel
Tower views; free Wi-Fi. **Cons:** air-conditioning only from June to Sep-
tember; faded decor. $ *Rooms from: €199* ⊠ *29 rue Cler, 7e, Around
the Eiffel Tower* ☎ *01–47–05–49–15* ⊕ *www.hotel-leveque.com* ⇶ *50
rooms* ⦿ *No meals* Ⓜ *École Militaire* ✛ *3:E2.*

$$$$ ⊞ **Hôtel du Cadran.** With its display of customized sweets for sale by
HOTEL trendy chocolatier Daniel Mercier, the lobby of the Cadran looks a bit
like a modern chocolate shop. **Pros:** easy walk to Eiffel Tower and Les
Invalides; free Wi-Fi; friendly reception staff. **Cons:** small rooms; pre-
mium prices for district; no restaurant or gym. $ *Rooms from: €270*
⊠ *10 rue du Champ de Mars, 7e, Around the Eiffel Tower* ☎ *01–40–
62–67–00* ⊕ *www.cadranhotel.com* ⇶ *40 rooms, 1 suite* ⦿ *No meals*
Ⓜ *École Militaire* ✛ *3:E2.*

$$ ⊞ **Hôtel du Champ de Mars.** Around the corner from picturesque Rue
HOTEL Cler, this charming, affordable hotel welcomes guests with a Provence-
inspired lobby and huge picture windows overlooking a quiet street.
Pros: good value; walking distance to Eiffel Tower, Les Invalides, and
Rodin Museum; free Wi-Fi. **Cons:** small rooms compared to larger
hotels; no air-conditioning; inconsistent service. $ *Rooms from: €150*
⊠ *7 rue du Champ de Mars, 7e, Around the Eiffel Tower* ☎ *01–45–
51–52–30* ⊕ *www.hotelduchampdemars.com* ⇶ *25 rooms* ⦿ *No meals*
Ⓜ *École Militaire* ✛ *3:E2.*

$$$$ ⊞ **Hôtel Eiffel Trocadéro.** A curious blend of Second Empire and rococo
HOTEL styling awaits guests in this hotel on a quiet corner just off Place Trocadéro. **Pros:** views of Eiffel Tower from upper floors; upscale residential
district convenient to métro; organic breakfast buffet. **Cons:** no full-
service restaurant; long walk to city center; basic rooms feel cramped.
$ *Rooms from: €270* ⊠ *35 rue Benjamin-Franklin, 16e, Around the
Eiffel Tower* ☎ *01–53–70–17–70* ⊕ *www.hoteleiffeltrocadero.com*
⇶ *16 rooms, 1 suite* ⦿ *No meals* Ⓜ *Trocadéro* ✛ *3:A1.*

$$$$ ⊞ **Hôtel Le Bellechasse.** If you like eclectic modern interior design, this
HOTEL tiny boutique hotel right around the corner from the popular Musée
d'Orsay is a good choice for its access to the major sites. **Pros:** central
location near top museums; one-of-a-kind style; helpful staff. **Cons:**
pricey rates; street-facing rooms can be noisy; open bathrooms lack
privacy. $ *Rooms from: €350* ⊠ *8 rue de Bellechasse, 7e, Around
the Eiffel Tower* ☎ *01–45–50–22–31* ⊕ *www.lebellechasse.com* ⇶ *33
rooms* ⦿ *No meals* Ⓜ *Solferino* ✛ *3:H1.*

$$$ ⊞ **Hôtel Le Tourville.** This cozy, contemporary haven near the Eiffel
HOTEL Tower, Champs de Mars, and Invalides is a comfortable base for explor-
ing Paris. **Pros:** convenient location near métro; friendly service; free
Wi-Fi in all rooms. **Cons:** small standard rooms; air-conditioning only
during summer months; no restaurant. $ *Rooms from: €250* ⊠ *16 av.
de Tourville, 7e, Around the Eiffel Tower* ☎ *01–47–05–62–62* ⊕ *www.
paris-hotel-tourville.com* ⇶ *28 rooms, 2 suites* ⦿ *No meals* Ⓜ *École
Militaire* ✛ *3:E3.*

$$$$
HOTEL
🛏 **Hôtel Valadon Colors.** Sharing facilities with its sister hotel, the Cadran, a few steps away, the Hôtel Valadon is a bold experiment in contemporary-chic design that appeals to urban creative types. **Pros:** candy-colored rooms; large closets and windows; convenient to Rue Cler, Eiffel Tower, and Les Invalides. **Cons:** check-in at Hôtel Cadran; lacks traditional Parisian charm; petite bathrooms. $ *Rooms from: €280* ✉ *16 rue Valadon, 7e, Around the Eiffel Tower* 🕾 *01–47–53–89–85* ⊕ *www.hotelvaladon.com* 🛏 *11 rooms, 1 suite* 🍽 *No meals* Ⓜ *École Militaire* ✛ *3:E2.*

$$$$
HOTEL
🛏 **Le Walt.** The convenient location stands out at this boutique hotel in the chic district between the Eiffel Tower and Les Invalides. **Pros:** great location; friendly staff; free Wi-Fi. **Cons:** on a busy street; no hotel restaurant; some complaints about noisy doors in hallways. $ *Rooms from: €320* ✉ *37 av. de la Motte Picquet, 7e, Around the Eiffel Tower* 🕾 *01–45–51–55–83* ⊕ *www.lewaltparis.com* 🛏 *25 rooms* 🍽 *No meals* Ⓜ *École Militaire* ✛ *3:E3.*

$$$$
HOTEL
Fodor's Choice
★
🛏 **Shangri-La Hotel Paris.** Displaying French elegance at its best, this impressively restored 19th-century mansion gazing across the Seine at the Eiffel Tower was once the stately home of Prince Roland Bonaparte, grandnephew of the emperor himself, and his gilded private apartments have been transformed into La Suite Impériale. **Pros:** close to the métro and luxury shopping; varied culinary options; exceptional suites. **Cons:** astronomical rates; pool only open until 9 pm; some obstructed views. $ *Rooms from: €1100* ✉ *10 av. Iéna, 16e, Around the Eiffel Tower* 🕾 *01–53–67–19–98, 01–53–67–19–19* ⊕ *www.shangri-la.com* 🛏 *65 rooms, 36 suites* 🍽 *No meals* Ⓜ *Iéna* ✛ *1:C6.*

CHAMPS-ÉLYSÉES

The land of the palace hotel, the elegant area around the Golden Triangle is catnip for hedge-fund millionaires and international royalty. A good half of Paris's eight palace hotels are clustered here, starting with Le Bristol—a Paris legend—and including the Plaza Athénée, the superb Georges V, and Paris's newest palace, the Peninsula.

$$$$
HOTEL
🛏 **Buddha-Bar Hotel Paris.** True to the sleek and chic DNA of the Buddha-Bar franchise, this glamorous boutique hotel, set in an 18th-century mansion just minutes from prime shopping and museums, is a heady cocktail of stylish Asian design, lavish finishes, and contemporary art. **Pros:** exemplary service; great spa and fitness center; excellent Sunday brunch. **Cons:** decor is not for conservative tastes; pricey. $ *Rooms from: €570* ✉ *4 rue d'Anjou, 8e, Champs-Élysées* 🕾 *01–83–96–88–88* ⊕ *www.buddhabarhotelparis.com* 🛏 *37 rooms, 19 suites* 🍽 *Breakfast* Ⓜ *Madeleine* ✛ *1:H5.*

$$$$
HOTEL
🛏 **Champs-Élysées Plaza Hotel and Wellness.** Discreet, contemporary elegance sums up this graciously renovated seven-story town house steps from the hustle and bustle of the Champs-Élysées. **Pros:** extremely elegant rooms; friendly, attentive service; central location. **Cons:** small spa; gym only has five machines; limited breakfast buffet. $ *Rooms from: €440* ✉ *35 rue de Berri, 8e, Champs-Élysées* 🕾 *01–53–53–20–20*

⊕ *www.champs-elysees-plaza.com* ↰ *9 rooms, 26 suites* ⎮⊘⎮ *No meals* Ⓜ *St-Philippe-du-Roule, George V* ✛ *1:E4.*

$$$$ ▦ **Four Seasons Hôtel George V Paris.** The George V is as poised and pol-
HOTEL ished as on the day it opened in 1928—the original plaster detailing
FAMILY and 17th-century tapestries have been restored, the bas-reliefs regilded,
Fodor's Choice and the marble-floor mosaics rebuilt tile by tile. **Pros:** privileged address
★ near top boutiques; courtyard dining in summer; indoor swimming
pool. **Cons:** several blocks from the nearest métro; extra charge for
ultra-high-speed Wi-Fi; lacks the intimacy of smaller boutique hotels.
Ⓢ *Rooms from: €1100* ✉ *31 av. George V, 8e, Champs-Élysées* ☎ *01-
49-52-70-00* ⊕ *www.fourseasons.com/paris* ↰ *184 rooms, 60 suites*
⎮⊘⎮ *No meals* Ⓜ *George V* ✛ *1:D5.*

$$$$ ▦ **Hidden Hotel.** The rough-hewn-wood facade heralds the eco-friendly
HOTEL theme of this under-the-radar boutique hotel a block from the Arc de
Triomphe, and the interior follows through with handcrafted glass,
wood, stone, and ceramic decor. **Pros:** a block from main métro line and
Champs-Élysées; organic toiletries in recycled packaging; free Wi-Fi.
Cons: rooms on the small side; open-plan bathrooms offer little privacy;
separate entrance and breakfast area for some rooms isn't intimate.
Ⓢ *Rooms from: €270* ✉ *28 rue de l'Arc de Triomphe, 17e, Champs-
Élysées* ☎ *01-40-55-03-57* ⊕ *www.hidden-hotel.com* ↰ *33 rooms, 2
suites* ⎮⊘⎮ *No meals* Ⓜ *Ternes* ✛ *1:B3.*

$$$$ ▦ **Hôtel Daniel.** A contemporary antidote to the minimalist trend, the
HOTEL Daniel is decorated in rich fabrics and antique furnishings from France,
North Africa, and the Far East. **Pros:** intimate atmosphere; luxurious
decor; close to the Champs-Élysées. **Cons:** across from a noisy bar;
expensive rates; inconsistent customer service. Ⓢ *Rooms from: €420*
✉ *8 rue Frédéric Bastiat, 8e, Champs-Élysées* ☎ *01-42-56-17-00*
⊕ *www.hoteldanielparis.com* ↰ *19 rooms, 7 suites* ⎮⊘⎮ *No meals* Ⓜ *St-
Philippe-du-Roule* ✛ *1:E4.*

$$$$ ▦ **Hôtel de Sers.** Built for the Marquis de Sers with a horse-drawn-
HOTEL carriage entrance, inner courtyard, expansive salons, and monumental
staircase, this beautiful structure was transformed into a hotel in 1935.
Pros: convenient central location in the Golden Triangle; many dining
options nearby; soothing Turkish bath and fitness room. **Cons:** basic
rooms a bit small; no formal spa; on the expensive side. Ⓢ *Rooms from:
€500* ✉ *41 av. Pierre 1er de Serbie, 8e, Champs-Élysées* ☎ *01-53-23-
75-75* ⊕ *www.hoteldesers-paris.fr* ↰ *45 rooms, 7 suites* ⎮⊘⎮ *No meals*
Ⓜ *Alma-Marceau, George V* ✛ *1:D5.*

$$$$ ▦ **Hôtel Fouquet's Barrière.** Steps away from one of the world's most
HOTEL famous streets, this luxury hotel adjacent to the legendary Fouquet's
Brasserie at the corner of the Champs-Élysées and Avenue George V is
recognizable by its uniformed valets, parked sports cars, and elegant
Haussmannian entryway. **Pros:** many rooms overlook the Champs-Élysées; very close to métro; beautiful spa and fitness center. **Cons:** very
expensive prices; bar can get overcrowded; corporate events give the
place a business-hotel feel. Ⓢ *Rooms from: €1000* ✉ *46 av. George V,
8e, Champs-Élysées* ☎ *01-40-69-60-00* ⊕ *www.lucienbarriere.com*
↰ *81 rooms, 33 suites* ⎮⊘⎮ *No meals* Ⓜ *George V* ✛ *1:D4.*

$$$$
HOTEL

Hôtel Lancaster. Once a Spanish nobleman's town house, this luxurious retreat dating from 1889 dazzles with its elegant decor, lush courtyard, and international restaurant led by chef Julien Roucheteau. **Pros:** steps away from the Champs-Élysées and five minutes from métro; excellent seasonal menus at La Table du Lancaster. **Cons:** size of rooms varies greatly; decor looks tired. $ *Rooms from: €600* ⊠ *7 rue de Berri, 8e, Champs-Élysées* ☎ *01–40–76–40–76* ⊕ *www.hotel-lancaster.fr* 🔊 *41 rooms, 15 suites* ❄️ *No meals* Ⓜ *George V* ✣ *1:D4.*

$$$$
HOTEL

Hôtel Le 123 Elysées. Italian marble, exposed brick, rough concrete, and sleek wood mix with leather, feathers, Swarovski crystals, and fiber-optic fairy lights to give this boutique hotel a genuinely eclectic atmosphere. **Pros:** chic decor; near luxury shopping; hotel bar open daily. **Cons:** service can be impolite; no on-site restaurant; some rooms quite small for the price. $ *Rooms from: €350* ⊠ *123 rue du Faubourg St-Honoré, 8e, Champs-Élysées* ☎ *01–53–89–01–23* ⊕ *www.astotel. com/hotel/hotel-le-123-elysees/overview* 🔊 *41 rooms* ❄️ *No meals* Ⓜ *St-Philippe du Roule, Franklin-D.-Roosevelt* ✣ *1:E4.*

$$$$
HOTEL
FAMILY
Fodor's Choice
★

Hôtel Le Bristol. The historic Bristol ranks among Paris's most exclusive hotels and has numerous accolades to prove it—and it's even hit the big screen, in Woody Allen's *Midnight in Paris*. **Pros:** rooftop pool with views of Sacré-Coeur; on luxury shopping street; one of the best restaurants in Paris. **Cons:** a few blocks from the nearest métro; old-fashioned atmosphere may not be for everyone; very expensive rates. $ *Rooms from: €1000* ⊠ *112 rue du Faubourg St-Honoré, 8e, Champs-Élysées* ☎ *01–53–43–43–00* ⊕ *www.lebristolparis.com* 🔊 *96 rooms, 92 suites* ❄️ *No meals* Ⓜ *Miromesnil* ✣ *1:F4.*

$$$$
HOTEL
FAMILY
Fodor's Choice
★

Hôtel Plaza Athénée. Distinguished by the scarlet flowers cascading over its elegant facade, this glamorous landmark hotel sits on one of the most expensive avenues in Paris. **Pros:** Eiffel Tower views; special attention to children; Dior Institute spa. **Cons:** some design a bit over-the-top; exorbitant prices. $ *Rooms from: €1100* ⊠ *25 av. Montaigne, 8e, Champs-Élysées* ☎ *01–53–67–66–65* ⊕ *www.dorchestercollection. com/en/paris/hotel-plaza-athenee* 🔊 *154 rooms, 54 suites* ❄️ *No meals* Ⓜ *Alma-Marceau* ✣ *1:D6.*

$$$$
HOTEL
FAMILY

Hôtel Raphael. This discreet palace-like hotel was built in 1925 to cater to travelers spending a season in Paris, so every space is generously sized for long, lavish stays. **Pros:** a block from the Champs-Élysées and Arc de Triomphe; rooftop garden terrace; intimate hotel bar frequented by locals. **Cons:** decor can feel worn and dowdy; some soundproofing issues; neighborhood has a majestic yet cold atmosphere. $ *Rooms from: €650* ⊠ *17 av. Kléber, 16e, Champs-Élysées* ☎ *01–53–64–32–00* ⊕ *www.leshotelsbaverez.com* 🔊 *47 rooms, 36 suites* ❄️ *No meals* Ⓜ *Kléber* ✣ *1:C4.*

$$$$
HOTEL

La Maison Champs Elysées. A 10-minute walk from the city's most famous avenue, this hotel in the heart of the Golden Triangle lures an art-minded crowd with an eclectic twist on a historical Haussmannian *belle demeure*. **Pros:** convenient location close to métro; on quiet street; unique decor. **Cons:** some rooms seem tired; no fitness center; not good for families. $ *Rooms from: €380* ⊠ *8 rue Jean Goujon, 8e, Champs-Élysées*

☏ *01–40–74–64–65* ⊕ *www.lamaisonchampselysees.com* 🛏 *51 rooms, 6 suites* ⦿⦿ *No meals* Ⓜ *Franklin-D.-Roosevelt* ✛ *1:E5.*

$$$$
HOTEL
Fodor'sChoice
★

🛏 **La Réserve.** Set in a splendid 19th-century mansion just steps from the presidential palace and the American Embassy, this aristocratic lodging vies for most elegant small hotel in Paris. **Pros:** top-notch service; splendid views over the Champs-Élysées and Eiffel Tower; excellent dining. **Cons:** very expensive; can be snobby; low on the excitement scale. Ⓢ *Rooms from: €750* ✉ *42 av. Gabriel, 8e, Champs-Élysées* ☏ *01–58–36–60–60* ⊕ *www.lareserve-paris.com* 🛏 *26 rooms, 14 suites* ⦿⦿ *No meals* Ⓜ *Franklin-D.-Roosevelt* ✛ *1:F5.*

$$$$
HOTEL
FAMILY
Fodor'sChoice
★

🛏 **Le Royal Monceau Raffles Paris.** The glamorous Royal Monceau Raffles offers unparalleled luxury along with a hefty dose of cool. **Pros:** ethereal spa and fitness center; art and cooking ateliers for kids; gorgeous terrace garden. **Cons:** prices exceed a king's ransom. Ⓢ *Rooms from: €780* ✉ *37 av. Hoche, 8e, Champs-Élysées* ☏ *01–42–99–88–00* ⊕ *www. leroyalmonceau.com* 🛏 *85 rooms, 64 suites* ⦿⦿ *No meals* Ⓜ *Charles-de-Gaulle-Étoile* ✛ *1:D3.*

$$$$
HOTEL

🛏 **Marignan.** Set smack dab in the middle of Paris's Golden Triangle, just off the Champs-Élysées, this sleek five-star hotel is a paragon of contemporary style. **Pros:** stellar views from upper floors; some rooms have private terraces; great location. **Cons:** a few rooms on the smaller side; not all rooms have great views. Ⓢ *Rooms from: €350* ✉ *12 rue de Marignan, 8e, Champs-Élysées* ☏ *01–40–76–34–56* ⊕ *www.hotel-marignan.com* 🛏 *45 rooms, 5 suites* ⦿⦿ *No meals* Ⓜ *Franklin-D.-Roosevelt* ✛ *1:E5.*

$$$$
HOTEL

🛏 **Mon Hotel.** The contemporary design, modern comforts, and close proximity to the Arc de Triomphe and Champs-Élysées—a 10-minute walk away—are big draws at this stylish boutique hotel. **Pros:** unique contemporary styling; convenient to the métro; quiet residential street. **Cons:** some rooms have limited closet space; no extra beds for children; breakfast costs extra. Ⓢ *Rooms from: €280* ✉ *1–5 rue d'Argentine, 16e, Champs-Élysées* ☏ *01–45–02–76–76* ⊕ *www.monhotel.fr* 🛏 *36 rooms* ⦿⦿ *No meals* Ⓜ *Argentine* ✛ *1:B4.*

$$$$
HOTEL
FAMILY
Fodor'sChoice
★

🛏 **The Peninsula Paris.** After a $900 million renovation that restored the luster of this gem dating from 1908, the lavishly appointed Peninsula raises the bar for luxury hotels in Paris. **Pros:** luxurious touches abound; the city's most beautiful spa; amazing views from higher floors. **Cons:** price out of reach for most mortals; not centrally located; still working out service kinks. Ⓢ *Rooms from: €795* ✉ *19 ave. Kléber, Champs-Élysées* ☏ *01–58–12–28–88* ⊕ *paris.peninsula.com* 🛏 *166 rooms, 34 suites* ⦿⦿ *No meals* Ⓜ *Kléber, Etoile* ✛ *1:C5.*

$$$$
HOTEL

🛏 **Renaissance Paris Arc de Triomphe.** This American-style hotel catering to corporate executives is located in a predominantly business district between the Arc de Triomphe and Place des Ternes. **Pros:** walking distance to métro; spacious rooms; good discounts with Marriott points. **Cons:** neighborhood lacks character; filled with business conferences; rather unfriendly service. Ⓢ *Rooms from: €440* ✉ *39 av. de Wagram, 17e, Champs-Élysées* ☏ *01–55–37–55–37* ⊕ *www.marriott.fr/hotels/travel/parwg-renaissance-paris-arc-de-triomphe-hotel* 🛏 *118 rooms, 20 suites* ⦿⦿ *No meals* Ⓜ *Ternes* ✛ *1:C3.*

$$$
HOTEL
FAMILY
⊡ **Villa Brunel.** On a quiet corner, this small 19th-century building between the Arc de Triomphe and Porte Maillot is an exceptional deal if you don't mind the less-than-convenient location. **Pros:** suites good for families; quiet location; good RER/métro access. **Cons:** a bit off the beaten track; far from most attractions; small bathrooms. $ *Rooms from: €210* ⊠ *46 rue Brunel, 17e, Champs-Élysées* ☎ *01–45–74–74–51* ⊕ *www.villabrunel.com* ⌇ *28 rooms, 4 suites* ⦿⦿ *No meals* Ⓜ *Porte Maillot, Argentine* ✛ *1:B3*.

AROUND THE LOUVRE

Besides a central location starting at Paris's Rive Droite, this neighborhood's many attractions, from the stately Palais Royal gardens to its wealth of fine museums, makes the area around the Louvre a great place to hang your hat. Hotels in the neighborhood run the gamut from stylishly refurbished 18th-century mansions to colorful and reasonably priced boutique hotels.

$$$$
HOTEL
Fodor's Choice
★
⊡ **Grand Hotel Palais Royal.** Just steps from the Palais Royal gardens and a quick walk from the Louvre and Paris's best shopping, this gracious hotel, housed in an 18th-century mansion, is a welcome addition to the neighborhood. **Pros:** stellar service; an island of quiet and calm in a bustling neighborhood. **Cons:** not all rooms come with balconies. $ *Rooms from: €300* ⊠ *4 rue de Valois, 1er, Around the Louvre* ☎ *01–42–96–15–35* ⊕ *www.grandhoteldupalaisroyal.com* ⌇ *57 rooms, 11 suites* ⦿⦿ *No meals* Ⓜ *Palais Royal–Musée du Louvre* ✛ *2:B6*.

$$$$
HOTEL
FAMILY
⊡ **Hôtel Brighton.** A few of the city's most prestigious hotels face the Tuileries or Place de la Concorde, but the 19th-century Brighton occupies the same prime real estate and offers a privileged stay for a fraction of the price. **Pros:** convenient central location; friendly service; breakfast buffet (free for kids under 12). **Cons:** some areas in need of repair; variable quality in decor between rooms; no restaurant for lunch or dinner. $ *Rooms from: €290* ⊠ *218 rue de Rivoli, 1er, Around the Louvre* ☎ *01–47–03–61–61* ⊕ *www.paris-hotel-brighton.com* ⌇ *62 rooms* ⦿⦿ *No meals* Ⓜ *Tuileries* ✛ *2:A6*.

$$$$
HOTEL
⊡ **Hôtel Britannique.** Open since 1861 and a stone's throw from the Louvre, the romantic Britannique blends courteous English service with old-fashioned French elegance near the banks of the Seine. **Pros:** on calm side street; less than a block from the métro/RER station; excellent service from friendly staff. **Cons:** small rooms; soundproofing could be better. $ *Rooms from: €252* ⊠ *20 av. Victoria, 1er, Around the Louvre* ☎ *01–42–33–74–59* ⊕ *www.hotel-britannique.fr* ⌇ *38 rooms, 1 suite* ⦿⦿ *No meals* Ⓜ *Châtelet* ✛ *4:D1*.

$$$
HOTEL
⊡ **Hôtel Crayon.** Managed by artists, this hotel near the Louvre and Palais-Royal distinguishes itself with an eclectic pop-art decor—expect an unusual canvas of local and international guests that's just as colorful. **Pros:** bright decor; very friendly staff; central location. **Cons:** small bathrooms; basement breakfast area; lobby lounge lacks any coziness and warmth. $ *Rooms from: €225* ⊠ *25 rue du Bouloi, 1er, Around the Louvre* ☎ *01–42–36–54–19* ⊕ *www.hotelcrayon.com* ⌇ *26 rooms* ⦿⦿ *No meals* Ⓜ *Louvre* ✛ *4:C1*.

$$ **Hôtel du Continent.** You'd be hard-pressed to find a budget hotel this
HOTEL stylish anywhere in Paris, let alone in an upscale neighborhood close
Fodor's Choice to many of the top attractions. **Pros:** superfriendly staff; all modern
★ amenities; location, location, location. **Cons:** no lobby; tiny bathrooms.
$ *Rooms from: €150* ✉ *30 rue du Mont-Thabor, 1e, Around the Louvre* ☎ *01–42–60–75–32* ⊕ *www.hotelcontinent.com* ⇥ *25 rooms* ⦿ *No meals* Ⓜ *Concord, Tuileries* ✚ *1:H6.*

$$ **Hôtel du Cygne.** Passed down from mother to daughter, "the Swan" is
HOTEL decorated with homey touches like hand-sewn curtains, country quilts,
and interesting flea-market finds. **Pros:** small but comfortable rooms;
central location on a pedestrian street; good value. **Cons:** old building
with small rooms; no elevator; intimidating area after dark. $ *Rooms
from: €125* ✉ *3 rue du Cygne, 1er, Around the Louvre* ☎ *01–42–60–
14–16* ⊕ *www.hotelducygne.fr* ⇥ *18 rooms* ⦿ *No meals* Ⓜ *Étienne
Marcel, Les Halles* ✚ *2:D6.*

$$$$ **Hotel Konfidentiel.** Sleep beneath the preguillotined head of Marie-
HOTEL Antoinette or amid the turmoil of the French Revolution in one of the
FAMILY six individually themed rooms. **Pros:** next to the Louvre; comfortable
rooms; friendly staff. **Cons:** can feel a bit enclosed; showers only in
bathrooms; unreliable Wi-Fi. $ *Rooms from: €379* ✉ *64 rue de l'Arbre
Sec, 1er, Around the Louvre* ☎ *01–55–34–40–40* ⊕ *www.konfidentiel-
paris.com* ⇥ *5 rooms, 1 suite* ⦿ *No meals* Ⓜ *Louvre–Rivoli* ✚ *2:C6.*

$$$$ **Hôtel Le Pradey.** Offering Pierre Marcolini chocolates and Hermès
HOTEL and Nux toiletries, this compact boutique hotel near the Tuileries has
a luxe feel. **Pros:** choice of copious breakfast buffet or quick coffee and
croissant; designer touches throughout; double doors for soundproofing
in suites. **Cons:** smaller rooms lack closet space; rooms vary greatly in
style; nondescript entry and lackluster service results in lukewarm welcome. $ *Rooms from: €390* ✉ *5 rue St-Roch, 1e, Around the Louvre*
☎ *01–42–60–31–70* ⊕ *www.lepradey.com* ⇥ *21 rooms, 7 suites* ⦿ *No
meals* Ⓜ *Tuileries* ✚ *2:A6.*

$$ **Hôtel Louvre Sainte-Anne.** Walk to many major sites from this small,
HOTEL low-key property located between the Opéra and the Louvre. **Pros:** con-
venient location; free Wi-Fi; helpful reception. **Cons:** very small rooms
and dull decor; district can feel very un-Parisian; subterranean breakfast
area slightly claustrophobic. $ *Rooms from: €175* ✉ *32 rue Ste-Anne,
1er, Around the Louvre* ☎ *01–40–20–02–35* ⊕ *www.paris-hotel-louvre.
com* ⇥ *20 rooms* ⦿ *No meals* Ⓜ *Pyramides* ✚ *2:B5.*

$$$$ **Hôtel Meurice.** Since 1835, the Meurice has welcomed royalty and
HOTEL celebrities from the Duchess of Windsor to Salvador Dalí—who both
FAMILY resided in the grande-dame establishment—and Paris's first palace
Fodor's Choice hotel continues to please with service, style, and views. **Pros:** stunning
★ art and architecture; views over the Tuileries gardens; central loca-
tion convenient to métro and major sites. **Cons:** popularity makes the
public areas not very discreet; front-desk service at times unattentive.
$ *Rooms from: €1295* ✉ *228 rue de Rivoli, 1er, Around the Louvre*
☎ *01–44–58–10–09* ⊕ *www.dorchestercollection.com* ⇥ *154 rooms,
54 suites* ⦿ *No meals* Ⓜ *Tuileries, Concorde* ✚ *2:A6.*

$$$ **Hôtel Thérèse.** Tucked away from the traffic and crowds of Avenue de
HOTEL l'Opéra, Hôtel Thérèse, named after the wife of Louis XIV, is a stone's

Apartment Rentals

If you favor extra space plus that special feeling of living like a local, try renting a Paris apartment. Rentals can also offer savings, especially for groups.

Check out the **Paris Tourism Office** website (⊕ *www.parisinfo.com*) for reputable agency listings. Policies differ, but you can expect a minimum required stay from three to seven days; a refundable deposit payable on arrival; possibly an agency fee; and maid and linen service.

The following is a list of property hunters, good-value residence hotels, and apartment services: **Cattalan Johnson** (☎ *01–45–74–87–77* ⊕ *www.cattalanjohnson.com*) is an established French fee-based real estate agent highly specialized in rental properties for more than 25 years. The multilingual staff has a citywide inventory of furnished apartments available for one week to a few years. **Citadines Apert Hotel** (☎ *08–25–33–33–32* ⊕ *www.citadines.fr*) is a chain of apartment-style hotel accommodations. They're somewhat generic, but offer many services and good value for short stays. **Home Rental** (☎ *01–42–25–65–40*

⊕ *www.home-rental.com*) has been in business since 1992 and rents furnished studios to six bedrooms with a one-week minimum stay, short or long term. No agency fees, maid service, cable, and wireless Internet are included. **Lodgis Paris** (☎ *01–70–39–11–11* ⊕ *www.lodgis.com*) has one of the largest selections in Paris; however, the agency fee makes it cheaper per diem to rent for more than one week. **Paris Attitude** (☎ *01–42–96–31–46* ⊕ *www.parisattitude.com*) offers a large selection of furnished rentals of studios to five bedrooms from a week to a year. **Paris Vacation Apartments** (☎ *06–63–60–67–14* ⊕ *www.parisvacationapartments.com*) specializes in luxury rentals, with all-inclusive prices by the week. **Paris-Hospitality** (☎ *01–47–83–75–91* ⊕ *www.parisattitude.com*) lists 350 apartments in prime locations throughout Paris for short- or long-term visits. Concierge services are available. **Rentals in Paris** (☎ *516/874–0474* ⊕ *www.rentals-in-paris.com*) has two dozen centrally located rentals with all-inclusive weekly rates and last-minute special offers.

throw from regal sites like the Louvre, Palais Royal, and the historic Comédie Française theater. **Pros:** excellent location on quiet street; free Wi-Fi; breakfast can be served in room. **Cons:** rooms are relatively small for price; breakfast area located in basement; no restaurant or gym. $ *Rooms from: €210* ⊠ *5/7 rue Thérèse, 1er, Around the Louvre* ☎ *01–42–96–10–01* ⊕ *www.hoteltherese.com* ⇄ *40 rooms* ¶⊙ *No meals* Ⓜ *Pyramides* ✢ *2:B6.*

$ 🛏 **Hôtel Tiquetonne.** Just off the market street of Rue Montorgueil and
HOTEL   a short walk from Les Halles, this is one of the least expensive hotels in the city center. **Pros:** cheap rooms in the center of town; in trendy shopping and nightlife area; some views onto Sacré-Coeur. **Cons:** minimal service and no amenities; noise from the street; decor feels outdated. $ *Rooms from: €80* ⊠ *6 rue Tiquetonne, 2e, Around the Louvre*

☎ *01–42–36–94–58* ⊕ *www.hoteltiquetonne.fr* ⟿ *45 rooms, 33 with bath* ⎢◎⎢ *No meals* Ⓜ *Étienne Marcel* ✛ *2:D6.*

$$$$ ⛫ **Mandarin Oriental Paris.** Of Paris's palace hotels—the highest designa-
HOTEL tion—the Mandarin Oriental is among the most contemporary, with a
soaring marble entryway and a sleek, luxe style that makes a welcome
contrast to the historic grande dames. **Pros:** impressive pool; many rooms
with terraces; child-friendly, with babysitting services. **Cons:** not much
variation in standard rooms; noise from courtyard during special events;
very pricey. Ⓢ *Rooms from: €975* ⊠ *251 rue de St-Honore, 1e, Around
the Louvre* ☎ *01–70–98–78–88* ⊕ *www.mandarinoriental.com/paris*
⟿ *99 rooms, 39 suites* ⎢◎⎢ *No meals* Ⓜ *Tuileries, Concorde* ✛ *1:H5.*

$$$$ ⛫ **Meliá Vendôme.** In a prestigious quarter a few minutes from the Jardin
HOTEL des Tuileries, Place de la Concorde, Opéra Garnier, and the Louvre, the
Meliá Vendôme has handsome and spacious rooms in attractive contemporary tones that exude an understated elegance. **Pros:** outstanding
location in the city center; near world-class shopping; elegant, immaculate rooms. **Cons:** expensive breakfast; no spa or pool; in-room cooling
system unreliable. Ⓢ *Rooms from: €370* ⊠ *8 rue Cambon, 1e, Around
the Louvre* ☎ *01–44–77–54–00* ⊕ *www.melia.com/en/hotels/france/
paris/melia-vendome-boutique-hotel/index.html* ⟿ *78 rooms, 5 suites*
⎢◎⎢ *No meals* Ⓜ *Concorde, Madeleine* ✛ *1:H5.*

$$$$ ⛫ **Renaissance Paris Vendôme.** Hiding behind a classic 19th-century
HOTEL facade is a fresh, contemporary hotel with subtle 1930s influences.
FAMILY **Pros:** posh location; trendy restaurant; full-service spa and fitness room.
Cons: lacks authentic French character; public lounges noisy at times;
packed with business groups. Ⓢ *Rooms from: €620* ⊠ *4 rue du Mont
Thabor, 1er, Around the Louvre* ☎ *01–40–20–20–00* ⊕ *www.marriott.
com* ⟿ *82 rooms, 15 suites* ⎢◎⎢ *No meals* Ⓜ *Tuileries* ✛ *2:A6.*

$$$$ ⛫ **Ritz.** In novels, songs, and common parlance, there's not a word that
HOTEL evokes the romance and luxury of Paris better than the Ritz. **Pros:** spa-
Fodor's Choice cious swimming pool; superlative selection of bars and restaurants; top-
★ notch service. **Cons:** easy to get lost in the vast hotel; paparazzi magnet;
astronomical prices. Ⓢ *Rooms from: €1000* ⊠ *15 pl. Vendôme, 1er,
Around the Louvre* ☎ *01–43–16–30–30* ⊕ *www.ritzparis.com* ⟿ *71
rooms, 72 suites* ⎢◎⎢ *No meals* Ⓜ *Opéra* ✛ *2:A5.*

LES GRANDS BOULEVARDS

This bustling historic district is tops for travelers on a budget. Central
to metro lines, the antiques district, and leafy neighborhoods like Parc
Monceau and Canal St-Martin, there's plenty to explore on foot and a
quick métro ride gets you to most other Paris neighborhoods in a jiffy.

$$$$ ⛫ **Hôtel Banke.** In a stately bank building dating from the early 20th cen-
HOTEL tury, this interesting hotel lies in the heart of the Opéra district, which
is full of shops and theaters. **Pros:** great location; excellent service; free
Internet access. **Cons:** pricey restaurant; cramped gym; several blocks
from the nearest métro. Ⓢ *Rooms from: €290* ⊠ *20 rue LaFayette, 9e,
Les Grands Boulevards* ☎ *01–55–33–22–25* ⊕ *www.hotelbanke.com*
⟿ *80 rooms, 11 suites* ⎢◎⎢ *No meals* Ⓜ *Opéra* ✛ *2:B4.*

$$
HOTEL

Hôtel Chopin. A unique mainstay of the district, the Chopin recalls its 1846 birth date with a creaky-floored lobby and aged woodwork. **Pros:** special location; close to major métro station; great nightlife district. **Cons:** thin walls; single rooms are very small; few amenities. $ *Rooms from: €124* ⊠ *10 bd. Montmartre, 46 passage Jouffroy, 9e, Les Grands Boulevards* ☎ *01–47–70–58–10* ⊕ *www.hotelchopin.fr* ⇕ *36 rooms* ⊙ *No meals* Ⓜ *Grands Boulevards* ✛ *2:C4.*

$$$$
HOTEL
Fodor's Choice
★

Hôtel de Nell. Tucked in a picturesque corner of a chic, up-and-coming neighborhood ripe for exploration, the serenely beautiful Hôtel de Nell offers contemporary luxury with clean lines and uncluttered spaces. **Pros:** great dining and bar on premises; interesting neighborhood to explore. **Cons:** area deserted at night; far from the major Paris attractions. $ *Rooms from: €350* ⊠ *9 rue du Conservatoire, 9e, Les Grands Boulevards* ☎ *01–44–83–83–60* ⊕ *www.hoteldenell.com* ⇕ *33 rooms* ⊙ *No meals* Ⓜ *Bonne Nouvelle* ✛ *2:D4.*

$$$$
HOTEL

Hôtel de Noailles. With a nod to the work of postmodern designers like Putman and Starck, this stylish boutique hotel is both contemporary and cozy. **Pros:** 15- to 20-minute walk to the Louvre and Opéra; a block from the airport bus; free Wi-Fi. **Cons:** no interesting views; some bathrooms in need of renovation; small elevator. $ *Rooms from: €345* ⊠ *9 rue de la Michodière, 2e* ☎ *01–47–42–92–90* ⊕ *www.hotelnoailles. com* ⇕ *56 rooms* ⊙ *No meals* Ⓜ *Opéra* ✛ *2:B5.*

$$$
HOTEL
Fodor's Choice
★

Hôtel du Temps. This stylish new hotel is perfect for visitors looking for bargain lodgings in a crossroads neighborhood ripe for exploration. **Pros:** friendly service; close to métro; terrific neighborhood. **Cons:** tiny bathrooms; rooms facing Rue La Fayette can be noisy. $ *Rooms from: €195* ⊠ *11 rue de Montholon, 9e, Les Grands Boulevards* ☎ *01– 47–70–37–16* ⊕ *hotel-du-temps.fr* ⇕ *23 rooms* ⊙ *No meals* Ⓜ *Cadet, Poissonière* ✛ *2:D3.*

$$$
HOTEL

Hôtel George Sand. This family-run hotel, where the 19th-century writer George Sand once lived, feels fresh and modern while preserving some of its original architectural details. **Pros:** near two famous department stores; historic atmosphere; simple but comfortable rooms. **Cons:** noisy street; can hear métro rumble on lower floors; some rooms are quite small. $ *Rooms from: €250* ⊠ *26 rue des Mathurins, 9e* ☎ *01– 47–42–63–47* ⊕ *www.hotelgeorgesand.com* ⇕ *20 rooms* ⊙ *No meals* Ⓜ *Havre Caumartin* ✛ *1:H4.*

$$$
HOTEL

Hôtel Gramont Opéra. Near the Opéra Garnier and some of the city's best department stores, this family-owned boutique hotel has lots of little extras that make it a great value. **Pros:** good breakfast buffet with eggs to order; personalized and professional service; connecting rooms for families. **Cons:** singles have no desk; small bathrooms; elevator doesn't go to top-floor rooms. $ *Rooms from: €239* ⊠ *22 rue Gramont, 2e, Les Grands Boulevards* ☎ *01–42–96–85–90* ⊕ *www.hotel-gramont-opera.com* ⇕ *25 rooms* ⊙ *No meals* Ⓜ *Quatre-Septembre* ✛ *2:B4.*

$$$
HOTEL

Hôtel Langlois. This darling hotel gained a reputation as one of the most atmospheric budget sleeps in the city, although rates have since crept up. **Pros:** excellent views from the top floor; close to department stores and Opéra Garnier; historic decor. **Cons:** noisy street; off the beaten path; some sagging furniture and worn fabrics. $ *Rooms from: €185* ⊠ *63* *rue St-Lazare, 9e, Les Grands Boulevards* ☎ *01–48–74–78–24* ⊕ *www. hotel-langlois.com* ⇌ *24 rooms, 3 suites* ⎢◎⎢ *No meals* Ⓜ *Trinité* ✛ *2:A3.*

$$$$ ⬚ **Hôtel Westminster.** On one of the most prestigious streets in Paris,
HOTEL between the Opéra and Place Vendôme, this mid-19th-century inn happily retains its old-world feel. **Pros:** prestigious location near major sights; soothing steam room; popular jazz bar. **Cons:** a bit old-fashioned; some rooms overlook an air shaft; poor bathroom plumbing. Ⓢ *Rooms from: €297* ⊠ *13 rue de la Paix, 2e, Les Grands Boulevards* ☎ *01–42–61–57–46* ⊕ *www.warwickhotels.com/westminster* ⇌ *80 rooms, 22 suites* ⎢◎⎢ *No meals* Ⓜ *Opéra* ✛ *2:A5.*

$$$$ ⬚ **La Maison Favart.** An atmospheric indoor pool, relaxing sauna, and
HOTEL around-the-clock concierge are some of the reasons this jewel-box hotel is fast becoming a popular choice for travelers. **Pros:** lovely rooms and interior design; spacious bathrooms; central location within walking distance of the sights. **Cons:** high demand for best rooms; impractical use of space in some rooms and bathrooms; no spa. Ⓢ *Rooms from: €340* ⊠ *5 rue de Marivaux, 2e, Les Grands Boulevards* ☎ *01–42–97– 59–83* ⊕ *www.lamaisonfavart.com* ⇌ *39 rooms* ⎢◎⎢ *No meals* Ⓜ *Quatre-Septembre* ✛ *2:B4.*

$$$ ⬚ **Le Swann Hôtel.** This delightful modern *hôtel littéraire* pays homage
HOTEL to France's greatest literary lion, Marcel Proust. **Pros:** not far from the big department stores; close to public transport; views from some rooms. **Cons:** some street noise; bathrooms are minuscule. Ⓢ *Rooms from: €180* ⊠ *15 rue de Constantinople, 8e, Les Grands Boulevards* ☎ *01–45–22–80–80* ⊕ *www.hotel-leswann.com* ⇌ *81 rooms* ⎢◎⎢ *No meals* Ⓜ *Europe, Villiers, Rome* ✛ *1:G2.*

$$$$ ⬚ **Park Hyatt Paris Vendôme.** Understated luxury with a contemporary
HOTEL Zen vibe differentiates this Hyatt from its more classic neighbors
Fodor's Choice between Place Vendôme and Opéra Garnier. **Pros:** stylish urban-chic
★ design; the latest technology; only in-suite spas in Paris. **Cons:** as part of the Hyatt chain, it can feel anonymous; many corporate events held here; very expensive rates. Ⓢ *Rooms from: €850* ⊠ *3–5 rue de la Paix, 2e, Les Grands Boulevards* ☎ *01–58–71–12–34* ⊕ *www.paris.vendome. hyatt.com* ⇌ *124 rooms, 24 suites* ⎢◎⎢ *No meals* Ⓜ *Concorde, Opéra* ✛ *2:A5.*

$$$$ ⬚ **W Paris-Opéra.** Located near Opéra Garnier, this 91-room hotel—
HOTEL the first W in France—feels part Moulin Rouge, part art gallery, with
Fodor's Choice cheeky and irreverent touches strewn throughout. **Pros:** coveted loca-
★ tion in historic 19th-century building; excellent restaurant; cutting-edge rooms with comfortable beds. **Cons:** fee for Wi-Fi; rooms and public spaces feel claustrophobic; noisy neighborhood. Ⓢ *Rooms from: €450* ⊠ *4 rue Meyerbeer, 9e, Les Grands Boulevards* ☎ *01–77–48– 94–94* ⊕ *www.wparisopera.com* ⇌ *72 rooms, 19 suites* ⎢◎⎢ *No meals* Ⓜ *Chaussée d'Antin–La Fayette* ✛ *2:A4.*

MONTMARTRE

Like a village unto itself, off-the-beaten-path Montmartre and its equally picturesque hotels provide a homey retreat after a day of sightseeing. There's much to explore here, and the old cobbled streets and hidden historic corners harbor lodgings as varied as old, gated mansions and quaint mom-and-pop hotels.

$
HOTEL **Ermitage Hôtel Sacré Coeur.** It's definitely a hike from the nearest métro station, but this family-run hotel in a Napoléon III–era building has a friendly vibe and is filled with mirrored armoires, elegant chandeliers, and other antiques. **Pros:** charming neighborhood; quiet district; warm welcome from staff. **Cons:** no credit cards accepted; no facilities. $ *Rooms from: €120* ⊠ *24 rue Lamarck, 18e, Montmartre* ☎ *01–42–64–79–22* ⊕ *www.ermitagesacrecoeur.fr* ⤶ *5 rooms* ❍| *Breakfast* Ⓜ *Lamarck–Caulaincourt* ✢ *2:C1.*

$
HOTEL **Hôtel Eldorado.** The unpretentious Hôtel Eldorado, just west of Montmartre, is perfect for those who are happy lying low without room phones, satellite TVs, or an elevator. **Pros:** eclectic character; artsy clientele; free Wi-Fi. **Cons:** far from the city center; few amenities; courtyard can be noisy in summer. $ *Rooms from: €90* ⊠ *18 rue des Dames, 17e, Montmartre* ☎ *01–45–22–35–21* ⊕ *www.eldoradohotel.fr* ⤶ *33 rooms, 23 with bath* ❍| *No meals* Ⓜ *Place de Clichy* ✢ *1:H1.*

$$
HOTEL **Hôtel Regyn's Montmartre.** Many travelers book a room in the tiny Hôtel Regyn's Montmartre for its proximity to the Place des Abbesses, one of the most well-known spots in the city thanks to the movie *Amélie.* **Pros:** métro station right outside; great views over Paris; atmospheric locale. **Cons:** no air-conditioning; some street noise; carpets and bathrooms need upgrades. $ *Rooms from: €125* ⊠ *18 pl. des Abbesses, 18e, Montmartre* ☎ *01–42–54–45–21* ⊕ *www.hotel-regyns-paris.com* ⤶ *22 rooms* ❍| *No meals* Ⓜ *Abbesses* ✢ *2:B1.*

THE MARAIS

A major shopping Mecca and the center of gay and Jewish life, the trendy Marais is a vibrant and stylish mosaic in motion. Here elegant grande-dame hotels abut hidden gardens and small boutique hotels harbor chic cocktail bars where guests can blend in with trendsetting locals.

$$$$
HOTEL **Hôtel Bourg Tibourg.** Scented candles and subdued lighting announce the blend of romance and contemplation cultivated by the Hôtel Bourg Tibourg. **Pros:** in the heart of the trendy Marais; moderate prices; great nightlife district. **Cons:** rooms tend to be small and poorly lit; no hotel restaurant; lounge area gets crowded. $ *Rooms from: €290* ⊠ *19 rue du Bourg Tibourg, 4e, Marais* ☎ *01–42–78–47–39* ⊕ *bourgtibourg.com* ⤶ *29 rooms, 1 suite* ❍| *No meals* Ⓜ *Hôtel de Ville* ✢ *4:E2.*

$$$
HOTEL **Hôtel Caron.** On a relatively quiet side street, this contemporary boutique bed-and-breakfast may be petite, but many thoughtful extras make it as accommodating as bigger hotels. **Pros:** excellent location in center of Paris; friendly staff; great amenities. **Cons:** only enough room for small suitcases; no hotel restaurant or bar; tight space in bathrooms. $ *Rooms from: €249* ⊠ *3 rue Caron, 4e, Marais* ☎ *01–40–29–02–94* ⊕ *www.hotelcaron.com* ⤶ *18 rooms* ❍| *No meals* Ⓜ *St-Paul* ✢ *4:G2.*

$$
HOTEL
Fodor's Choice
★ **Hôtel Caron de Beaumarchais.** For that traditional French feeling, book a room at this intimate, affordable, romantic hotel—the theme is the work of former next-door-neighbor Pierre-Augustin Caron de Beaumarchais, a supplier of military aid to American revolutionaries and

the playwright who penned *The Marriage of Figaro* and *The Barber of Seville*. **Pros:** cozy Parisian decor of yesteryear; breakfast in bed served until noon; excellent location within easy walking distance of major monuments. **Cons:** small rooms with few amenities; busy street of bars and cafés can be noisy; may feel old-fashioned for younger crowd. $\boxed{\$}$ *Rooms from: €175* ✉ *12 rue Vieille-du-Temple, 4e, Marais* ☎ *01–42–72–34–12* ⊕ *www.carondebeaumarchais.com* ↘ *19 rooms* ⏸ *No meals* Ⓜ *Hôtel de Ville* ✛ *4:F2.*

$$$ 　**Hôtel de la Bretonnerie.** In a 17th-century *hôtel particulier* (town
HOTEL 　house) on a side street in the Marais, this small hotel with exposed wooden beams and traditional styling sits a few minutes from the Centre Pompidou and the numerous bars and cafés of Rue Vieille du Temple. **Pros:** typical Parisian character; moderate prices; free Wi-Fi access. **Cons:** quality and size of the rooms vary greatly; no air-conditioning; rooms facing street can be noisy. $\boxed{\$}$ *Rooms from: €185* ✉ *22 rue Ste-Croix-de-la-Bretonnerie, 4e, Marais* ☎ *01–48–87–77–63* ⊕ *www.hotelparismaraisbretonnerie.com* ↘ *22 rooms, 7 suites* ⏸ *No meals* Ⓜ *Hôtel de Ville* ✛ *4:E1.*

$$$$ 　**Hôtel Duo.** For this hotel in the heart of the trendy Marais district,
HOTEL 　architect Jean-Philippe Nuel was commissioned to bring things up-to-date with bold colors and dramatic lighting; some rooms still have the original 16th-century beams, but the overall feel is casual urban chic. **Pros:** central location near shops and cafés; walking distance to major monuments; good amenities. **Cons:** noisy neighborhood; service not always delivered with a smile; small standard rooms and bathrooms. $\boxed{\$}$ *Rooms from: €300* ✉ *11 rue du Temple, 4e, Marais* ☎ *01–42–72–72–22* ⊕ *www.duoparis.com* ↘ *58 rooms* ⏸ *No meals* Ⓜ *Hôtel de Ville* ✛ *4:E1.*

$$$ 　**Hôtel Jules & Jim.** In the less-traveled corner of the trendy Marais dis-
HOTEL 　trict, this contemporary boutique hotel feels almost like an art gallery.
Fodor's Choice 　**Pros:** bright and modern; stylish design; close to public transportation.
★ 　**Cons:** the small "Jules" rooms are best for those traveling light or staying just one night; no restaurant. $\boxed{\$}$ *Rooms from: €240* ✉ *11 rue des Gravilliers, 3e, Marais* ☎ *01–44–54–13–13* ⊕ *www.hoteljulesetjim.com* ↘ *22 rooms, 1 duplex* ⏸ *No meals* Ⓜ *Arts et Métiers* ✛ *2:F6.*

$$$$ 　**Pavillon de la Reine.** Hidden off regal Place des Vosges behind a stun-
HOTEL 　ning garden courtyard, this enchanting château has gigantic beams, chunky stone pillars, and a weathered fireplace that speaks to its 1612 origins. **Pros:** historic character; quiet setting; free bicycles for guests. **Cons:** expensive for the area and the size of the rooms; the nearest métro is a few blocks away; no uniform theme in interior design. $\boxed{\$}$ *Rooms from: €440* ✉ *28 pl. des Vosges, 3e, Marais* ☎ *01–40–29–19–19* ⊕ *www.pavillon-de-la-reine.com* ↘ *31 rooms, 23 suites* ⏸ *No meals* Ⓜ *Bastille, St-Paul* ✛ *4:G2.*

EASTERN PARIS

Neighborhoods in the east of Paris—Bastille, République, Oberkampf, and hip Canal St-Martin—are quintessentially young, vibrant, fun, and eclectic. Among the many bars and bistros you'll find everything from stylish boutique hotels to sleek eco-centric sanctuaries. These neighborhoods can be lively at night, so look for lodgings tucked away on a smaller street, especially near the Bastille, or book a courtyard-facing room.

BASTILLE

$$$ HOTEL **BLC Design Hotel.** In the young and trendy area between Bastille and Nation, the BLC pays homage to everything *blanc,* hence the name. **Pros:** cool, contemporary interior; free Wi-Fi access; good location in a lively neighborhood. **Cons:** small spaces; renovations needed in some bathrooms; expensive rates. [$] *Rooms from: €225* ✉ *4 rue Richard Lenoir, 11e, Bastille* ☎ *01–40–09–60–16* 🌐 *www.blcdesign-hotel-paris.com* 🛏 *29 rooms* 🍴 *No meals* [M] *Charonne, Ledru Rollin* ✥ *4:H2.*

$$$ HOTEL **Hôtel Bastille de Launay.** The no-frills decor might seem spartan at first, but this boutique hotel also offers some creature comforts, modern amenities like free Wi-Fi, and a perfect location a few blocks from the regal Place des Vosges. **Pros:** homey proportions; attentive service; reasonably spacious for the neighborhood. **Cons:** tiny elevator; some small rooms; basic bathrooms. [$] *Rooms from: €200* ✉ *42 rue Amelot, 11e, Bastille* ☎ *01–47–00–88–11* 🌐 *www.bastilledelaunay-hotel-paris.com* 🛏 *35 rooms* 🍴 *No meals* [M] *Chemin Vert* ✥ *4:H1.*

$$ HOTEL Fodor's Choice ★ **Hôtel Mama Shelter.** Close to Père-Lachaise in the up-and-coming 20th arrondissement, this large hotel has a fun and funky interior designed by Philippe Starck. **Pros:** trendy design without designer prices; cool vibe; entertainment center in each room. **Cons:** 10-minute walk to métro; nearby club can be noisy. [$] *Rooms from: €159* ✉ *109 rue de Bagnolet, 20e, Bastille* ☎ *01–43–48–48–48* 🌐 *www.mamashelter.com* 🛏 *172 rooms* 🍴 *No meals* [M] *Gambetta* ✥ *2:H3.*

$$$$ HOTEL **Standard Design Hôtel.** For an ultracontemporary hotel in the hipster corner of the Bastille district, the Standard Design is anything but standard. **Pros:** friendly service; personalized gift packs; funky shopping and nightlife district. **Cons:** street noise; some rooms very small; interior design lacks traditional Parisian charm. [$] *Rooms from: €300* ✉ *29 rue des Taillandiers, 11e, Bastille* ☎ *01–48–05–30–97* 🌐 *www.standard-design-hotel-paris.com* 🛏 *37 rooms* 🍴 *No meals* [M] *Bastille* ✥ *4:H2.*

CANAL ST-MARTIN

$$ HOTEL Fodor's Choice ★ **Hôtel Fabric.** This urban-chic hotel tucked away on an old artisan street is fully in tune with the pulse of the lively Oberkampf neighborhood, close to fabulous nightlife, cocktail bars, restaurants, bakeries, and shopping (and the Marais and Canal St-Martin). **Pros:** all-you-can-eat breakfast for €17; lots of great sightseeing within walking distance; warm and helpful staff. **Cons:** rooms can be noisy; very popular so book well in advance. [$] *Rooms from: €153* ✉ *31 rue de la Folie Méricourt, 11e, Canal St-Martin* ☎ *01–43–57–27–00* 🌐 *www.hotelfabric.com* 🛏 *33 rooms* 🍴 *No meals* [M] *Saint-Ambroise, Oberkampf* ✥ *2:H6.*

$$ HOTEL **Hôtel Taylor.** Tucked away on a tiny one-way street between République and Canal St-Martin, the Hôtel Taylor offers spacious rooms at an affordable price in the edgy 10e arrondissement. **Pros:** close to the métro; Wi-Fi available; breakfast can be served in your room. **Cons:** bathrooms and some rooms need refurbishment; street can seem intimidating at night. [$] *Rooms from: €136* ✉ *6 rue Taylor, 10e, Canal*

St-Martin ☎ 01–42–40–11–01 🌐 www.paris-hotel-taylor.com 🛏 54 rooms 🍴 No meals [M] République ⊕ 2:F5.

$$$ HOTEL Fodor's Choice ★ 🏨 **Le Citizen Hôtel.** Boasting direct views over the historic Canal St-Martin and a setting close to the Marais, Le Citizen features a minimalist-chic decor, high-tech touches like loaner iPads, and a cool east-Paris vibe. **Pros:** trendy neighborhood; cool perks; friendly, attentive staff. **Cons:** smallest rooms are best for one person; noisy street; about 20 minutes by métro from the main attractions. [$] *Rooms from: €199 ✉ 96 quai de Jemmapes, 10e, Canal St-Martin ☎ 01–83–62–55–50 🌐 www.lecitizenhotel.com 🛏 12 rooms 🍴 Breakfast [M] Jacques-Bonsergent ⊕ 2:G4.*

RÉPUBLIQUE

$$$ HOTEL 🏨 **Hôtel Libertel Gare de l'Est Français.** This Haussmann-era hotel facing historic Gare de l'Est is two blocks from Gare du Nord and the popular Canal St-Martin district. **Pros:** convenient for Eurostar travelers; smoke-free establishment; friendly multilingual staff. **Cons:** noisy street; unattractive neighborhood; pricey breakfast. [$] *Rooms from: €180 ✉ 13 rue du 8 Mai 1945, 10e, République ☎ 01–40–35–94–14 🌐 www.hotelfrancais.com 🛏 70 rooms 🍴 No meals [M] Gare de l'Est ⊕ 2:E3.*

$$ HOTEL 🏨 **Hôtel Palma.** Down the street from Père-Lachaise Cemetery, this off-the-beaten-path hotel may be far from the action, but the métro is steps away and connects quickly and efficiently to the heart of the city. **Pros:** a block from the Place de Gambetta; breakfast served in room; inexpensive rates. **Cons:** far from city center; lacks Parisian charm. [$] *Rooms from: €135 ✉ Angle 2 rue des Gâtines, 77 av. Gambetta, 20e, République ☎ 01–46–36–13–65 🌐 www.hotelpalma.com 🛏 32 rooms 🍴 No meals [M] Gambetta ⊕ 2:H5.*

$$ HOTEL 🏨 **Hôtel Résidence Alhambra.** The gleaming white facade, enclosed garden, and flower-filled window boxes brighten this hotel in a lesser-known neighborhood between the Marais and Rue Oberkampf. **Pros:** popular nightlife district; friendly service; inexpensive rates. **Cons:** small doubles; a walk to the center of town. [$] *Rooms from: €159 ✉ 13 rue de Malte, 11e, République ☎ 01–47–00–35–52 🌐 www.hotelalhambra.fr 🛏 53 rooms 🍴 No meals [M] Oberkampf ⊕ 2:H6.*

$$$$ HOTEL 🏨 **Le Général Hôtel.** Designer Jean-Philippe Nuel applied his sleek styling to Le Général, one of Paris's first affordable, high-design hotels. **Pros:** friendly service; smart design; in popular nightlife district. **Cons:** noisy neighborhood; not within easy walking distance of major tourist attractions; basic breakfast. [$] *Rooms from: €300 ✉ 5–7 rue Rampon, 11e, République ☎ 01–47–00–41–57 🌐 www.legeneralhotel.com 🛏 43 rooms, 3 suites 🍴 No meals [M] République; Oberkampf ⊕ 2:G5.*

LATIN QUARTER

Leafy and bookish, this quiet *quartier* at the heart of the city retains all the charm of Old Paris, as do its hotels, which tend to be smaller, family-owned establishments or budget chains with character.

$$$$ HOTEL 🏨 **The Five Hôtel.** Small is beautiful at this design hotel on a quiet street near the Rue Mouffetard market and the Latin Quarter. **Pros:** unique design; personalized welcome; quiet side street. **Cons:** most rooms are too small for excessive baggage; the nearest métro is a 15-minute walk;

most rooms only have showers. [$] *Rooms from: €255* ✉ *3 rue Flatters, 5e, Latin Quarter* ☎ *01–43–31–74–21* 🌐 *www.thefivehotel.com* 🛏 *23 rooms, 2 suites* 🍴 *No meals* [M] *Gobelins* ✣ *4:D6.*

$$ HOTEL 🏨 **Hôtel Collège de France.** Exposed stone walls, wooden beams, and medieval artwork echo the style of the Musée Cluny, two blocks from this charming, family-run hotel. **Pros:** walk to Rive Gauche sights; free Wi-Fi; ceiling fans. **Cons:** thin walls between rooms; no air-conditioning. [$] *Rooms from: €140* ✉ *7 rue Thénard, 5e, Latin Quarter* ☎ *01–43–26–78–36* 🌐 *www.hotel-collegedefrance.com* 🛏 *29 rooms* 🍴 *No meals* [M] *Maubert–Mutualité, St-Michel, Cluny–La Sorbonne* ✣ *4:D4.*

$$ HOTEL 🏨 **Hôtel des Grandes Écoles.** Distributed among a trio of three-story buildings, Madame Le Floch's rooms have a distinct grandmotherly vibe because of their flowery wallpaper and lace bedspreads, but they're downright spacious for this part of Paris. **Pros:** close to Latin Quarter nightlife spots; lovely courtyard; good value. **Cons:** uphill walk from the métro; some noisy rooms; few amenities. [$] *Rooms from: €160* ✉ *75 rue du Cardinal Lemoine, 5e, Latin Quarter* ☎ *01–43–26–79–23* 🌐 *www.hotel-grandes-ecoles.com* 🛏 *51 rooms* 🍴 *No meals* [M] *Cardinal Lemoine* ✣ *4:E5.*

$$$$ HOTEL 🏨 **Hôtel des Grands Hommes.** The "great men" this hotel honors with its name rest in peace within the towering Panthéon monument across the street. **Pros:** major Latin Quarter sights within walking distance; comfortable and attractive rooms. **Cons:** closest métro is a 10-minute walk; neighborhood can be loud after dark; high price for this area. [$] *Rooms from: €300* ✉ *17 pl. du Panthéon, 5e, Latin Quarter* ☎ *01–46–34–19–60* 🌐 *www.hoteldesgrandshommes.com* 🛏 *30 rooms* 🍴 *No meals* [M] *RER: Luxembourg* ✣ *4:D4.*

$$$$ HOTEL 🏨 **Hotel Design Sorbonne.** For what French students pay to study at the Sorbonne (tuition is inexpensive), you can stay a few nights next door at this swanky design hotel. **Pros:** centrally located; fun decor; attentive service. **Cons:** tiny rooms for the price; small breakfast room; lacks traditional French flavor. [$] *Rooms from: €280* ✉ *6 rue Victor Cousin, 5e, Latin Quarter* ☎ *01–43–54–01–52* 🌐 *www.hotelsorbonne.com* 🛏 *38 rooms* 🍴 *No meals* [M] *Cluny–La Sorbonne* ✣ *4:C4.*

$$ HOTEL FAMILY 🏨 **Hôtel Familia.** Owners Eric and Sylvie Gaucheron continue to update and improve this popular budget hotel—they've added custom-made wood furniture from Brittany, antique tapestries and prints, and lovely carpeting. **Pros:** attentive, friendly service; great value; lots of character. **Cons:** on a busy street; some rooms are small; some noise between rooms. [$] *Rooms from: €134* ✉ *11 rue des Écoles, 5e, Latin Quarter* ☎ *01–43–54–55–27* 🌐 *www.familiahotel.com* 🛏 *30 rooms* 🍴 *No meals* [M] *Cardinal Lemoine* ✣ *4:E4.*

$$$ HOTEL FAMILY 🏨 **Hôtel Henri IV Rive Gauche.** About 50 paces from Notre-Dame and the Seine, this elegant hotel has identical, impeccable rooms with beige and rose linens and framed prints of architectural drawings. **Pros:** comfortable decor; close to major sights and RER station; friendly reception staff. **Cons:** on a busy street full of late-night bars; single rooms are small; furnishings showing their age. [$] *Rooms from: €230* ✉ *9–11 rue St-Jacques, 5e, Latin Quarter* ☎ *01–46–33–20–20* 🌐 *www.henri-paris-hotel.com* 🛏 *23 rooms* 🍴 *No meals* [M] *St-Michel* ✣ *4:D3.*

$$$ HOTEL 🏨 **Hôtel La Manufacture.** Just behind Place d'Italie and a short stroll from both the Jardin des Plantes and Rue Mouffetard, La Manufacture's lesser-known location makes you feel like a *vrai* (real) Parisian. **Pros:** easy access to major métro and bus lines; safe, nontouristy district; bright breakfast room. **Cons:** street noise; a long stroll to the center of Paris; small rooms. [$] *Rooms from: €180* ✉ *8 rue Philippe de Champagne, 13e, Latin Quarter* ☎ *01–45–35–45–25* 🌐 *www.hotel-la-manufacture.com* 🛏 *57 rooms* 🍴 *No meals* [M] *Place d'Italie* ✣ *4:G6.*

$$ HOTEL FAMILY 🏨 **Hôtel Le Vert Galant.** In a little-known neighborhood west of Place d'Italie you'll find the welcoming Madame Laborde, the proprietress of this plain but proper hotel that encloses a peaceful green garden. **Pros:** quiet location; kitchenettes in some rooms; safe residential district. **Cons:** not very central; no air-conditioning; some noise between rooms. [$] *Rooms from: €160* ✉ *43 rue Croulebarbe, 13e, Latin Quarter* ☎ *01–44–08–83–50* 🌐 *www.vertgalant.com* 🛏 *17 rooms* 🍴 *No meals* [M] *Les Gobelins* ✣ *4:E6.*

$$$$ HOTEL 🏨 **Hôtel Notre Dame.** If you love the quirky and eclectic fashions of Christian Lacroix and don't mind hauling your bags up some steps, this unique boutique hotel overlooking Notre-Dame may be for you. **Pros:** design by Christian Lacroix; views of the river; comfortable beds. **Cons:** stairs can be tricky with large bags; no minibars; some noise from busy street. [$] *Rooms from: €280* ✉ *1 quai Saint-Michel, 5e, Latin Quarter* ☎ *01–43–54–20–43* 🌐 *www.hotelnotredameparis.com* 🛏 *26 rooms* 🍴 *No meals* [M] *St-Michel* ✣ *4:D3.*

$$$ HOTEL 🏨 **Hôtel Relais Saint-Jacques.** Nearly every wall in this Latin Quarter hotel is bedecked with faux-marble and trompe-l'oeil murals. **Pros:** unique Parisian decor; close to Latin Quarter sights; free Wi-Fi. **Cons:** busy street makes it noisy in summer; thin walls between rooms; decor needs refurbishment. [$] *Rooms from: €216* ✉ *35 rue des Écoles, 5e, Latin Quarter* ☎ *01–44–07–45–45* 🌐 *www.hotelrelaissaintjacques.com* 🛏 *38 rooms* 🍴 *No meals* [M] *Maubert–Mutualité* ✣ *4:D4.*

$$$$ HOTEL FAMILY 🏨 **Hôtel Résidence Henri IV.** This small hotel on a quiet cul-de-sac is perfect for travelers—especially those with children—who need a home base where they can kick back, make their own meals, and feel at home. **Pros:** handy kitchenettes; close to Latin Quarter attractions; charming rooms. **Cons:** closest métro is a few blocks away; some rooms on the small side; decor a bit dated. [$] *Rooms from: €299* ✉ *50 rue des Bernadins, 5e, Latin Quarter* ☎ *01–44–41–31–81* 🌐 *www.residencehenri4.com* 🛏 *8 rooms, 5 apartments* 🍴 *No meals* [M] *Maubert–Mutualité* ✣ *4:D4.*

$$$ HOTEL 🏨 **Hotel Seven.** The "seven" refers to the level of heaven you'll find at this extraordinary boutique hotel, where a team of designers and artists has created seven magnificent suites with imaginative themes like Cabaret, Secret Agent, and Marie-Antoinette. **Pros:** fun design elements; copious breakfast buffet; quiet location near Mouffetard market street. **Cons:** small closets; several blocks to closest métro; expensive rates for so few amenities. [$] *Rooms from: €250* ✉ *20 rue Berthollet, 5e, Latin Quarter* ☎ *01–43–31–47–52* 🌐 *www.sevenhotelparis.com* 🛏 *28 rooms, 7 suites* 🍴 *No meals* [M] *Censier–Daubentin* ✣ *4:D6.*

$$$ HOTEL 🏨 **Les Jardins du Luxembourg.** Blessed with a personable staff and a warm ambience, this hotel on a calm cul-de-sac puts you just a block

away from the Jardin du Luxembourg. **Pros:** on a quiet street close to major attractions and transportation; hot buffet breakfast; relaxing sauna. **Cons:** some very small rooms; air-conditioning not very strong. [$] *Rooms from: €199* ✉ *5 impasse Royer-Collard, 5e, Latin Quarter* ☎ *01–40–46–08–88* 🌐 *www.les-jardins-du-luxembourg.com* 🛏 *26 rooms* 🍴 *No meals* [M] *RER: Luxembourg* ✣ *4:C5.*

$ HOTEL 🏨 **Port-Royal Hôtel.** The sparkling rooms and extra-helpful staff at the Port-Royal are well above average for hotels in this price range. **Pros:** excellent value; attentive service; close to two major markets. **Cons:** not very central; on a busy street; no room air-conditioning. [$] *Rooms from: €100* ✉ *8 bd. de Port-Royal, 5e, Latin Quarter* ☎ *01–43–31–70–06* 🌐 *www.port-royal-hotel.fr* 🛏 *46 rooms, 21 with bath* 🍴 *No meals* [M] *Les Gobelins* ✣ *4:C6.*

ST-GERMAIN-DES-PRÉS

True to its Rive Gauche bourgeois-bohemian vibe, lodgings here are an eclectic bunch. You'll find everything from posh L'Hôtel (Oscar Wilde's final dwelling) to smaller hotels with loads of character as well as some good budget options.

$$$$ HOTEL FAMILY 🏨 **Artus Hôtel.** One of the best things about this comfortable six-story hotel is that it's smack in the middle of Rue de Buci in the lively St-Germain-des-Prés district. **Pros:** helpful concierge; excellent location on a market street; kid-friendly vibe. **Cons:** rooms are small and dated for the price; neighborhood is quite busy. [$] *Rooms from: €300* ✉ *34 rue de Buci, 6e, St-Germain-des-Prés* ☎ *01–43–29–07–20* 🌐 *www.artushotel.com* 🛏 *25 rooms, 2 suites* 🍴 *No meals* [M] *Mabillon* ✣ *4:B3.*

$$$$ HOTEL 🏨 **Hôtel Bel Ami.** A short stroll from the famous Café de Flore, the Bel Ami hides its past as an 18th-century textile factory behind low-slung furnishings, computer stations, and flat-screen TVs. **Pros:** central St-Germain-des-Prés location; feels completely up-to-date; spacious fitness center and spa. **Cons:** some guests report loud noise between rooms; pretty pricey; not suitable for families with younger kids. [$] *Rooms from: €590* ✉ *7–11 rue St-Benoît, 6e, St-Germain-des-Prés* ☎ *01–42–61–53–53* 🌐 *www.hotelbelami-paris.com* 🛏 *101 rooms, 7 suites* 🍴 *No meals* [M] *St-Germain-des-Prés* ✣ *4:B2.*

$$ HOTEL FAMILY 🏨 **Hôtel Bonaparte.** The service, amenities, and *petit déjeuner* (breakfast) may be far from luxurious at this unpretentious family-run hotel, but the location in the heart of St-Germain is fabulous. **Pros:** upscale shopping neighborhood; large rooms for the Rive Gauche; welcoming to families. **Cons:** outdated decor; minuscule elevator fits one person; no shower curtains. [$] *Rooms from: €159* ✉ *61 rue Bonaparte, 6e, St-Germain-des-Prés* ☎ *01–43–26–97–37* 🌐 *www.hotelbonaparte.fr* 🛏 *29 rooms* 🍴 *No meals* [M] *St-Sulpice* ✣ *4:B3.*

$$$$ HOTEL FAMILY 🏨 **Hôtel d'Aubusson.** The showpiece at this 17th-century town house in the heart of St-Germain-des-Prés is the stunning front lobby, spanned by massive beams and a gigantic stone fireplace reminiscent of French aristocratic homes of yore. **Pros:** central location near shops and a market street; spacious rooms; staff greets you warmly. **Cons:** some rooms lack character; busy street and bar can be noisy; very touristy.

[$] *Rooms from: €405* ✉ *33 rue Dauphine, 6e, St-Germain-des-Prés* ☎ *01–43–29–43–43* 🌐 *www.hoteldaubusson.com* 🛏 *49 rooms* 🍴 *No meals* [M] *Odéon* ✥ *4:C2.*

$$$$ HOTEL 🏨 **Hôtel de l'Abbaye.** An 18th-century convent, this compact hotel on a tranquil side street near St-Sulpice welcomes you with a cobblestone ante-courtyard. **Pros:** tranquil setting; upscale neighborhood; good value packages. **Cons:** rooms differ greatly in size and style; some bathrooms are quite small; old-fashioned decor a bit somber. [$] *Rooms from: €275* ✉ *10 rue Cassette, 6e, St-Germain-des-Prés* ☎ *01–45–44–38–11* 🌐 *www.hotelabbayeparis.com* 🛏 *35 rooms, 9 suites* 🍴 *Breakfast* [M] *St-Sulpice* ✥ *4:A4.*

$$$$ HOTEL 🏨 **Hôtel Duc de Saint-Simon.** For pure French flavor, including rooms decorated in floral chintz, head to this intimate hotel in a hidden location between Boulevard St-Germain and Rue du Bac. Four of the antiques-filled rooms have spacious terraces overlooking the courtyard. **Pros:** upscale neighborhood close to St-Germain-des-Prés; historic character; friendly service. **Cons:** rooms in the annex are smaller and have no elevator; cramped bathrooms; no room service. [$] *Rooms from: €295* ✉ *14 rue St-Simon, 7e, St-Germain-des-Prés* ☎ *01–44–39–20–20* 🌐 *www.hotelducdesaintsimon.com* 🛏 *29 rooms, 5 suites* 🍴 *No meals* [M] *Rue du Bac* ✥ *3:H2.*

$$$$ HOTEL 🏨 **Hôtel Millésime.** The beautiful stone archway of this 17th-century city mansion in St-Germain-des-Prés was the original entrance to the Saint Germain Abbey—as you enter, you'll feel transported to the sunny south of France. **Pros:** upscale shopping nearby; young, friendly staff; plenty of atmosphere. **Cons:** ground-floor rooms can be noisy; smoke from courtyard when windows are open; some furnishings need repair. [$] *Rooms from: €280* ✉ *15 rue Jacob, 6e, St-Germain-des-Prés* ☎ *01–44–07–97–97* 🌐 *www.millesimehotel.com* 🛏 *19 rooms, 1 suite* 🍴 *No meals* [M] *St-Germain-des-Prés* ✥ *4:B2.*

$$$$ HOTEL 🏨 **Hôtel Odéon Saint-Germain.** Exposed stone walls and original wooden beams give this 16th-century building typical Rive Gauche character, and designer Jacques Garcia's generous use of striped taffeta curtains, velvet upholstery, and plush carpeting imbues it with the distinct luxury of St-Germain-des-Prés. **Pros:** free Internet; luxuriously appointed rooms; in an upscale shopping district near Jardin Luxembourg. **Cons:** small rooms a challenge for those with extra-large suitcases; tiny elevator; prices high for room size and average service. [$] *Rooms from: €260* ✉ *13 rue St-Sulpice, 6e, St-Germain-des-Prés* ☎ *01–43–25–70–11* 🌐 *www.hotelparisodeonsaintgermain.com* 🛏 *24 rooms, 3 junior suites* 🍴 *No meals* [M] *Odéon* ✥ *4:B3.*

$$$$ HOTEL 🏨 **Hôtel Recamier.** This discreet boutique hotel in a quiet corner overlooking Eglise St-Sulpice is perfect if you're seeking a romantic and cozy hideaway in the St-Germain-des-Prés district. **Pros:** peaceful garden courtyard; free Wi-Fi and computer station; well-appointed bathrooms. **Cons:** small closets and bathrooms; room service only until 11 pm; no fitness area, spa, or restaurant. [$] *Rooms from: €290* ✉ *3 bis, pl. St-Sulpice, 6e, St-Germain-des-Prés* ☎ *01–43–26–04–89* 🌐 *www.hotelrecamier.com* 🛏 *24 rooms* 🍴 *No meals* [M] *Mabillon* ✥ *4:B3.*

$$$
HOTEL

⊡ **Hôtel Relais Saint-Sulpice.** Sandwiched between St-Sulpice and the Jardin du Luxembourg, this little hotel wins accolades for its location. **Pros:** chic location; close to two métro stations; bright breakfast room and courtyard. **Cons:** some smallish rooms; noise from the street on weekend evenings; poorly designed lighting. $ *Rooms from: €250* ⊠ *3 rue Garancière, 6e, St-Germain-des-Prés* ☎ *01–46–33–99–00* ⊕ *www. relais-saint-sulpice.com* ↪ *26 rooms* ⑩ *No meals* Ⓜ *St-Germain-des-Prés, St-Sulpice* ✛ *4:B3.*

$$$$
HOTEL

⊡ **Hôtel Verneuil.** Steps away from the Museé d'Orsay and the Louvre sits an intimate and tastefully decorated boutique hotel in the heart of St-Germain. **Pros:** nicely renovated rooms; near-it-all location on Left Bank; welcoming service. **Cons:** sometimes touristy; no restaurant; no gym or spa. $ *Rooms from: €290* ⊠ *8 rue de Verneuil, 7e, St-Germain-des-Prés* ☎ *01–42–60–82–14* ⊕ *www.hotel-verneuil-saint-germain.com* ↪ *26 rooms* ⑩ *No meals* Ⓜ *Rue de Bac* ✛ *4:A2.*

$$$$
HOTEL

⊡ **L'Hôtel.** There's something just a bit naughty in the air at this eccentric and opulent boutique hotel, with its history as an 18th-century *pavillon d'amour* (inn for trysts) and as the place Oscar Wilde died in 1900 (Room 16 to be exact). **Pros:** luxurious decor; elegant bar and restaurant; walking distance to the Musée d'Orsay and the Louvre. **Cons:** some rooms are very small for the price; closest métro station is a few blocks away; eclectic decoration seems mismatched. $ *Rooms from: €325* ⊠ *13 rue des Beaux-Arts, 6e, St-Germain-des-Prés* ☎ *01–44–41–99–00* ⊕ *www.l-hotel.com* ↪ *16 rooms, 4 suites* ⑩ *No meals* Ⓜ *St-Germain-des-Prés* ✛ *4:B2.*

$$$$
HOTEL

⊡ **Relais Christine.** On a quiet street on the Left Bank, this exquisite *hôtel de charme* dates back to the 13th century as a former abbey of the Grands-Augustins and has an impressive stone courtyard and interior garden. **Pros:** quiet address; close to the Latin Quarter; historic character. **Cons:** thin walls in some rooms; no on-site restaurant; a bit touristy. $ *Rooms from: €420* ⊠ *3 rue Christine, 6e, St-Germain-des-Prés* ☎ *01–40–51–60–80* ⊕ *www.relais-christine.com* ↪ *44 rooms, 5 suites* ⑩ *No meals* Ⓜ *Odéon* ✛ *4:C2.*

MONTPARNASSE

Once the famous (or infamous) stomping grounds for the likes of Hemingway, Picasso, Henry Miller, Anaïs Nin, Sartre, etc.—some of whom still remain in the sprawling *cimetière*—Montparnasse has all the trappings of a truly Parisian neighborhood: lively markets, old-fashioned brasseries, and pretty parks. Here you'll find anonymous chain hotels, charming mom-and-pop stops, and everything in between. Focus your search in the more residential areas away from the large boulevards or near the quiet Luxembourg Garden or the Montparnasse cemetery for a real dip into Parisian life.

$$$$
HOTEL

⊡ **Apostrophe Hotel.** Those enamored of the artistic and literary history of Paris's Left Bank will appreciate this whimsical family-run hotel between Montparnasse and Luxembourg Garden. **Pros:** very friendly multilingual staff; quiet street in charming area; close to métro. **Cons:** limited closet space; little privacy with bathrooms opening up directly to rooms; no restaurant or bar. [$] *Rooms from: €260* ✉ *3 rue de Chevreuse, 6e, Montparnasse* ☎ *01–56–54–31–31* ⊕ *www.apostrophe-hotel.com* ⟿ *16 rooms* ⦿ *No meals* Ⓜ *Vavin* ✛ *4:A6.*

$ 🔲 **Hôtel des Bains.** In a charming neighborhood close to Jardin du
HOTEL   Luxembourg and St-Germain-des-Prés, this hidden budget find has tastefully decorated rooms and excellent prices. **Pros:** relaxing garden courtyard; great rates; typical Parisian character. **Cons:** no online booking; streets can be noisy; some rooms and bathrooms very small and worn. [$] *Rooms from: €105* ✉ *33 rue Delambre, 14e, Montparnasse* ☎ *01–43–20–85–27* ⊕ *www.hotel-des-bains-montparnasse.com* ⟿ *34 rooms, 8 suites* ⦿ *No meals* Ⓜ *Vavin, Edgar Quinet* ✛ *4:A6.*

$$$ 🔲 **Hôtel Lenox-Montparnasse.** On a street lined with fish restaurants, this
HOTEL   six-story hotel gets points for its proximity to the Jardin du Luxembourg and good-value amenities like free Wi-Fi access. **Pros:** lively district close to Montparnasse and St-Germain-des-Prés; well-stocked honesty bar; friendly, multilingual staff. **Cons:** standard rooms are small; noisy street; attracts business clientele. [$] *Rooms from: €200* ✉ *15 rue Delambre, 14e, Montparnasse* ☎ *01–43–35–34–50* ⊕ *www.paris-hotel-lenox.com* ⟿ *46 rooms, 6 suites* ⦿ *No meals* Ⓜ *Vavin* ✛ *4:A6.*

$$ 🔲 **Hôtel Raspail-Montparnasse.** Montparnasse was the art capital of the
HOTEL   world in the '20s and '30s, and this affordable hotel captures some of that spirit by naming its rooms after some of the illustrious neighborhood stars—Picasso, Chagall, and Modigliani. **Pros:** convenient to métro and bus; many markets and cafés nearby; friendly staff. **Cons:** traffic noise; some rooms small; dated interiors with worn fabrics. [$] *Rooms from: €170* ✉ *203 bd. Raspail, 14e, Montparnasse* ☎ *01–43–20–62–86* ⊕ *www.hotelraspailmontparnasse.com* ⟿ *38 rooms* ⦿ *No meals* Ⓜ *Vavin* ✛ *4:A6.*

$$$ 🔲 **Hôtel Le Sainte-Beuve.** On a tranquil street between the Jardin du Lux-
HOTEL   embourg and Montparnasse's cafés and brasseries sits this pleasant six-story hotel. **Pros:** stylish decor; good location without the tourist crowds; close to major métro lines. **Cons:** 20-minute walk to the Latin Quarter or St-Germain-des-Prés; small rooms and elevator; unremarkable service. [$] *Rooms from: €200* ✉ *9 rue Ste-Beuve, 6e, Montparnasse* ☎ *01–45–48–20–07* ⊕ *www.hotelsaintebeuve.com* ⟿ *21 rooms, 1 suite* ⦿ *No meals* Ⓜ *Vavin* ✛ *4:A5.*

WESTERN PARIS

Hidden away behind the locked gates and grand Haussmann-era buildings of this leafy enclave bordering the Bois de Boulogne are the well-heeled Parisians—diplomats, low-profile French movie stars, and other Paris aristocracy. Lodgings reflect the more discrete nature of this neighborhood, and what you lose in proximity to central Paris you'll more than gain in elegance and quiet.

$$ 🔲 **Hôtel Gavarni.** Considering the traditional, almost old-fashioned Pari-
HOTEL   sian decor, you may be surprised to learn that this lodging, located in a chic residential neighborhood, is one of the city's first certified eco-friendly hotels. **Pros:** organic breakfast; charming neighborhood; friendly welcome. **Cons:** a few blocks to the nearest métro; standard

15

rooms and bathrooms quite small; few amenities. $ *Rooms from: €160* ✉ *5 rue Gavarni, 16e, Western Paris* ☎ *01–45–24–52–82* ⊕ *www. gavarni.com* ⇥ *21 rooms, 4 suites* |◎| *No meals* ✛ *3:A2.*

$$$$ ⊞ **Le Sezz.** Created by French furniture designer Christophe Pillet in a
HOTEL   chic residential district of Paris, Le Sezz mixes rough stone walls with splashes of tomato red and mustard yellow for the ultimate bachelor-pad feel. **Pros:** trendy designer decor; huge bathtubs; quiet location. **Cons:** close to Eiffel Tower but not much else; limited service for a hotel in this price range; breakfast area feels cold and somber. $ *Rooms from: €270* ✉ *6 av. Frémiet, 16e, Western Paris* ☎ *01–56–75–26–26* ⊕ *www.paris.hotelsezz.com* ⇥ *13 rooms, 13 suites* |◎| *No meals* Ⓜ *Passy* ✛ *3:A3.*

$$$$ ⊞ **Renaissance Paris Le Parc Trocadéro Hotel.** This spacious and historic
HOTEL   urban retreat in an upscale neighborhood, now part of the Marriott
FAMILY   chain, was once the home of Alfred Nobel (who would go on to establish the famous peace prize). **Pros:** near métro stations; 24-hour fitness center and room service; quiet area. **Cons:** hosts large groups; long walk from center of Paris; service and housekeeping could be better. $ *Rooms from: €299* ✉ *55–57 av. Raymond-Poincaré, 16e, Western Paris* ☎ *01–44–05–66–66* ⊕ *www.marriott.com/hotels/travel/ parsp-renaissance-paris-le-parc-trocadero-hotel* ⇥ *100 rooms, 22 suites* |◎| *No meals* Ⓜ *Trocadéro* ✛ *1:A5.*

$$$$ ⊞ **Saint James Paris.** Beyond a stone gateway you'll pass a beautiful
HOTEL   fountain on your way into a grand foyer—this renovated 19th-century mansion feels like a countryside château nestled in the heart of the busy metropolis. **Pros:** beautiful decor and spacious rooms; generous breakfast served in-room; wellness spa. **Cons:** expensive rates; residential area quiet at night; entrance may be difficult to find. $ *Rooms from: €495* ✉ *43 av. Bugeaud, 16e, Western Paris* ☎ *01–44–05–81–81* ⊕ *www. saint-james-paris.com* ⇥ *17 rooms, 32 suites* |◎| *No meals* Ⓜ *Porte Dauphine, Victor Hugo, Rue de la Pompe* ✛ *1:A5.*

SHOPPING

Updated by Jennifer Ladonne

Nothing, but nothing, can push you into the current of Parisian life faster than a few hours of shopping. Follow the lead of locals, who slow to a crawl as their eyes lock on a tempting display. Window-shopping is one of this city's greatest spectator sports; the French call it *lèche-vitrine*—literally, "licking the windows"—which is fitting because many of the displays look good enough to eat.

Store owners here play to sophisticated audiences with voracious appetites for everything from spangly flagship stores to minimalist boutiques to under-the-radar spots in 19th-century glass-roofed *passages*. Parisians know that shopping isn't about the kill, it's about the chase: walking down cobblestone streets looking for items they didn't know they wanted, they're casual yet quick to pounce. They like being seduced by a clever display and relish the performance elements of browsing. Watching them shop can be almost as much fun as shopping yourself.

And nowhere is the infamous Parisian "attitude" more palpable than in the realm of fine shopping—the more *haute* the more hauteur.

Parisians are a proud bunch, and they value decorum. So dress to impress—and remember your manners. You must say *bonjour* upon entering a shop and *merci, au revoir* when leaving, even if it's to no one in particular. Think of it more as announcing your coming and going. Beyond this, protocol becomes less prescribed and more a matter of good judgment. If a salesperson is hovering, there's a reason; let him or her help you. To avoid icy stares, confidence and politeness go a long way.

As for what to buy, the sky's the limit in terms of choices. If your funds aren't limitless, however, take comfort in knowing that treasures can be found on a budget. And if you do decide to indulge, what better place to make that once-in-a-blue-moon splurge? When you get home and friends ask where you got those to-die-for shoes, with a shrug you'll casually say, "These? Oh . . . I bought them in Paris."

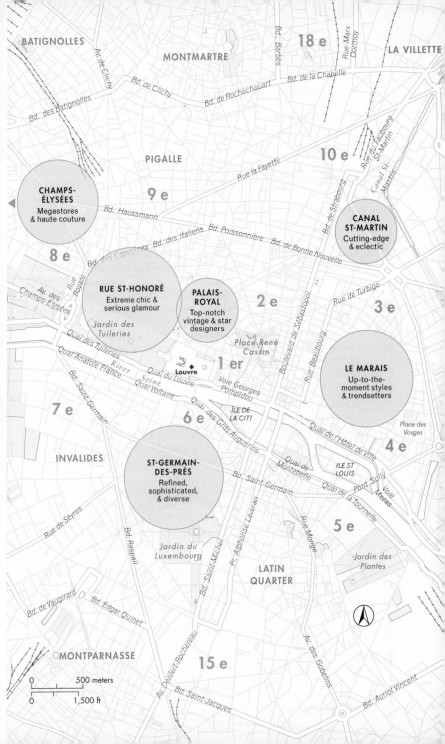

PLANNING

DUTY-FREE

A value-added tax (or T.V.A.) of 20% is imposed on most consumer goods, and the rate can be as high as 33% for certain luxury items. To qualify for a refund, you must have bought more than €175 of goods in the same store on the same day and have stayed three months or less in the EU at the time of purchase. In 2014, the new PABLO reimbursement system was introduced: now, instead of lengthy paper applications, retailers provide computer-generated forms with a barcode and the PABLO logo, which must be scanned in the airport at a designated PABLO terminal before you check in for your outbound flight. Refunds are processed more quickly, and funds are directly credited to your credit card or bank account.

FOOD MARKETS

The city's open-air food markets attract the entire spectrum of Paris society, from the splendid matron with her minuscule dog in tow, to the mustachioed regular picking up his daily baguette. Although some markets are busier than others, there's not one in Paris that doesn't captivate the senses. Each season has its delicacies: *fraises des bois* (wild strawberries) and tender asparagus in spring, squash blossoms and fragrant herbs in summer, saffron-tinted chanterelles in autumn, bergamot oranges in late winter. Year-round you can find pungent *lait cru* (unpasteurized) cheeses, charcuterie, and wild game and fish. Many of the better-known open-air markets are in areas you'd visit for sightseeing. To get a list of market days in your area, ask your concierge or check the markets section on the website ⊕ *www.paris.fr/marches*.

If you're unused to the metric system, it may be helpful to know that *une livre* is French for a pound; *une demi-livre* is a half pound. For cheese or meats, *un morceau* will get you a piece, *une tranche* a slice.

Most markets are open from 8 am to 1 pm three days a week year-round (usually the weekend and one weekday) on a rotating basis.

STORE HOURS

Store hours can be tricky in Paris. Aside from department stores, which keep slightly longer hours and usually shut their doors late on Thursday, shops tend to open around 10 am and close around 7 pm. It's not unusual to find a "back at 3" sign taped on the doors of smaller boutiques at lunchtime. Plan to do most of your foraging between Tuesday and Saturday, as the majority of shops, including department stores, are closed Sunday and some on Monday as well. You can find areas—particularly the Marais and tourist-oriented Champs-Élysées—where stores are open on Sunday. However, if you're making a special trip somewhere, always call ahead to check hours.

■ TIP➔ Galeries Lafayette and Au Printemps each offer 10%-off discount cards to foreign visitors. Some items marked with a red dot, usually designer clothing and sale merchandise, are excluded. To get a card, go to the welcome desk on the main floor of either store. Remember to bring a passport or driver's license.

SHOPPING IN PARIS

Reviews are alphabetical by neighborhood.

CHAMPS-ÉLYSÉES

Step into your Chanel suit, gird your loins, and plunge into Paris's most desirable (and most daunting) hunting grounds, where royals, jet-setters, starlets, and other glitterati converge in pursuit of the high life. This elegant triangle—bordered by Avenues Montaigne, George V, and Champs-Élysées, with Rue François 1er in between—is home to almost all the luxury Goliaths with a few lesser worthies added in.

BEAUTY

Guerlain. This opulent address is a fitting home for Paris's first—and most famous—perfumer. Still the only Paris outlet for legendary perfumes like Shalimar and L'Heure Blue, it has added several new signature scents (including Myrrhe et Délires and Cuir Beluga). Personalized bottles in several sizes can be filled on demand, or, for a mere €30,000, a customized scent can be blended just for you. Sybarites will also appreciate Guerlain's makeup, scented candles, and redesigned spa featuring its much-adored skin-care line. There's an elegant gourmet restaurant for lunch or tea, too. ⊠ *68 av. des Champs-Élysées, 8e, Champs-Élysées* ☎ *01–45–62–52–57* ⊕ *www.guerlain.com* Ⓜ *Franklin-D.-Roosevelt.*

Parfums de Nicolaï. This perfumerie is run by Guerlain family member Patricia de Nicolaï. Children's, women's, and men's scents are on offer (including some unisex), as are sprays for the home and fragrant candles. ⊠ *69 av. Raymond Poincaré, 16e* ☎ *01–44–55–02–00* ⊕ *www.pnicolai.com* Ⓜ *Victor-Hugo.*

CHILDREN'S CLOTHING

Fodor'sChoice ★ **Bonpoint.** Outfit the prince or princess in your life at Bonpoint (yes, royalty *does* shop here). The prices are high, but the quality is exceptional, and the adorable mini-duds couldn't be more stylish: picture a perfect hand-smocked Liberty-print dress, a velvety lambskin vest, or a double-breasted cashmere sweater for Little Lord Fauntleroy. The Avenue Raymond Poincaré boutique is one of more than a dozen citywide. ⊠ *64 av. Raymond Poincaré, 16e, Champs-Élysées* ☎ *01–47–27–60–81* ⊕ *www.bonpoint.com* Ⓜ *Trocadéro.*

FAMILY Fodor'sChoice ★ **Petit Bateau.** Petit Bateau provides a fundamental part of the classic French wardrobe from cradle to teen and beyond. The signature T-shirt—cut close to the body, with smallish shoulders—works equally well with school uniforms or vintage Chanel. Thanks to timeless designs, the high-grade cotton clothes remain wardrobe staples year after year; however, lines in cotton-silk or cotton-cashmere and popular collaborations with chic designers like Carven or Maison Kitsuné mean there's now even more in store. There are boutiques in all the major shopping neighborhoods. Stock up: if you can find this brand back home, the prices are sure to be higher. ⊠ *116 av. des Champs-Élysées, 8e, Champs-Élysées* ☎ *01–40–74–02–03* ⊕ *www.petit-bateau.fr* Ⓜ *George V.*

CLOTHING

Fodor's Choice ★ **Balenciaga.** This venerable Paris house rose to fashion stardom under the brilliant Nicolas Ghesquière, whose abrupt departure in 2012 opened the door for American wunderkind Alexander Wang's brief tenure. Then a frisson of delight rocked the fashion world when it was announced, in late 2015, that Demna Gvasalia, lately of Margiela and the ultra-cool insider label Vetements, would take the helm. Style watchers breathlessly await the results. ✉ *10 av. George V, 8e, Champs-Élysées* ☎ *01–47–20–21–11* ⊕ *www.balenciaga.com* Ⓜ *Alma-Marceau.*

Fodor's Choice ★ **Céline.** Reinvigorated by Michael Kors in the late 1990s, Céline got another much-needed jolt when Phoebe Philo arrived in 2009 and began dazzling the critics with her focused approach. Philo's characteristically refined tailoring and attention to minute details underlie the seeming simplicity of her styles, which veer from flowing pants and long, unstructured jackets to streamlined swing skirts. Along with the ready-to-wear, Céline's exquisite bags and shoes are staples for Paris's fashion cognoscenti. The Avenue Montaigne flagship carries the full line, including eyewear. There's also a St-Germain boutique on Rue de Grenelle. ✉ *53 av. Montaigne, 8e, Champs-Élysées* ☎ *01–40–70–07–03* ⊕ *www.celine.com* Ⓜ *Franklin-D.-Roosevelt.*

Fodor's Choice ★ **Chanel.** Elegant, modern looks with sex appeal and lasting value are Chanel's stock in trade. Although the spectacularly beautiful Avenue Montaigne flagship takes shoppers' breath away, the heart of this revered fashion house—helmed by the one-and-only Karl Lagerfeld—is still the boutique at 31 rue Cambon, where Chanel once perched high up on the mirrored staircase watching audience reactions to her collection debuts. Great investments include all of Coco's favorites: the perfectly tailored suit, a lean soigné dress, or a quilted bag with a gold chain. Handbags, jewelry, shoes, and accessories are all found at the fabulous 42 avenue Montaigne boutique, opposite the flagship store. ✉ *51 av. Montaigne, 8e, Champs-Élysées* ☎ *01–44–50–73–00* ⊕ *www.chanel.com* Ⓜ *Franklin-D.-Roosevelt.*

Fodor's Choice ★ **Christian Dior.** Following John Galliano's inglorious fall from grace in 2012, Raf Simons did a brilliant job of redefining this label, playing with volumes and contrasting geometric forms on fluid, dimensional fabrics for a streamlined yet totally feminine look. But Simons himself decamped in late 2015, leaving Dior once again on the lookout for a creative director capable of taking the illustrious label—second only to Chanel—to even greater heights. ✉ *30 av. Montaigne, 8e, Champs-Élysées* ☎ *01–40–73–73–73* ⊕ *www.dior.com* Ⓜ *Franklin-D.-Roosevelt.*

Dolce & Gabbana. Dolce & Gabbana offers a sexy, young-Italian-widow vibe with a side of moody boyfriend. Svelte silk dresses, sharply tailored suits, and plunging necklines are made for drama. Women's clothes are at the Avenue Montaigne location; men's are at 3 rue Faubourg St-Honoré. ✉ *54 av. Montaigne, 8e, Champs-Élysées* ☎ *01–42–25–68–78* ⊕ *www.dolcegabbana.com* Ⓜ *Alma-Marceau.*

Le66. Finding just the right totally chic, totally black anything is a breeze here. This up-to-the-second concept store, comprised of three boutiques on two levels (including shoes, jewelry, accessories, and men's), lines up all the top names that you know, along with those that you may not but should. Diffusion lines of the major labels mingle with Acne, Marni, Helmut Lang, Rimowa, Alexander Wang, Damir Doma, and nearly 200 others, all hand-picked to ensure fabulousness. If pressed for time, it's a good bet for all-around satisfaction. ⊠ *66 av. des Champs-Élysées, 8e, Champs-Élysées* ☎ *01–53–53–33–80* ⊕ *www.le66.fr* Ⓜ *Franklin-D.-Roosevelt.*

Maison Ullens. A glam Golden Triangle location, a Rem Koolhaas–designed boutique, sumptuous clothes—the Belgian label's first Paris outpost hits all the marks and then some. Founded in 2013, Maison Ullens puts the focus on luxe fabrics and skins in classic-chic designs with plenty of staying power. It has everything you need for après-ski or weekends on Capri. ⊠ *4 rue de Marignan, 8e, Champs-Élysées* ☎ *01–47–20–23–56* ⊕ *www.maisonullens.com* Ⓜ *Franklin-D.-Roosevelt.*

Marni. Marni started out as a little Italian label that put a quirky spin on classic styles, employing retro-ish prints and colors (think citron yellow or seaweed green) and funky fabrics (such as rubberized cotton and filmy silks). Now it has evolved into a major player on the edgy fashion scene. Each season has something new to say—whether it's an inventive take on bold ethnic prints, ingenious knits, or eloquent color schemes. Sought-after shoes and jewelry never make it to sale time. ⊠ *57 av. Montaigne, 8e, Champs-Élysées* ☎ *01–56–88–08–08* ⊕ *www.marni.com* Ⓜ *Franklin-D.-Roosevelt.*

Nina Ricci. Creative director Guillaume Henry, who lately resurrected the venerable Paris label Carven, brings a welcome edginess to this archly feminine line. Ricci's airy white-on-white Avenue Montaigne boutique is one of Paris's dreamiest, and, with the advent of Henry, high on the must-visit list. ⊠ *39 av. Montaigne, 8e, Champs-Élysées* ☎ *01–83–97–72–12* ⊕ *www.ninaricci.com* Ⓜ *Franklin-D.-Roosevelt.*

Prada. Prada spins gold out of fashion straw. Knee-length skirts, peacock colors, cardigan sweaters, geometric prints: the waiting lists cross continents. Shoes, bags, and other accessories for men and women perennially become cult items. ⊠ *10 av. Montaigne, 8e, Champs-Élysées* ☎ *01–53–23–99–40* ⊕ *www.prada.com* Ⓜ *Alma-Marceau.*

Réciproque. Paris's largest, most exclusive consignment store carries everything from furs and jewelry to evening gowns and lingerie. Almost any coveted designer you can think of is represented, and the savings are significant; prices, however, aren't as cheap as you might expect, and there's not much in the way of service or space. The six shops that comprise Réciproque (individually dedicated to women's clothing, menswear, accessories, and the like) are clustered together on Rue de la Pompe; all are closed Sunday and Monday. ⊠ *89, 92, 93, 95, 97, and 101 rue de la Pompe, 16e, Champs-Élysées* ☎ *01–47–04–30–28* ⊕ *www.reciproque.fr* Ⓜ *Rue de la Pompe.*

HOME DECOR

Maison de Baccarat. This museum and crystal store was once the home of Marie-Laure de Noailles, known as the Countess of Bizarre. Philippe Starck revamped the space with his signature cleverness—yes, that's a chandelier floating in an aquarium and, yes, that crystal arm sprouting from the wall alludes to Jean Cocteau (a friend of Noailles). Follow the red carpet to the jewelry room, where crystal baubles hang from bronze figurines, and to the immense table stacked with crystal items for the home. ✉ *11 pl. des États-Unis, 16e, Champs-Élysées* ☎ *01–40–22–11–00* ⊕ *www.baccarat.com* Ⓜ *Iéna.*

JEWELRY AND ACCESSORIES

FodorśChoice
★

Dior Joaillerie. When Victoire de Castellane was signed to create Dior's first line of fine jewelry, she brought a big dollop of wit and panache to the venerable brand. After her romance with death heads, the young designer has returned to what she does best—utterly flamboyant gems in raucous colors, but with a new delicacy and finesse that places her designs at the pinnacle of high jewelry. ✉ *28 av. Montaigne, 8e, Champs-Élysées* ☎ *01–47–23–52–39* ⊕ *www.dior.com* Ⓜ *Franklin-D.-Roosevelt.*

SHOES, HANDBAGS, AND LEATHER GOODS

Berluti. Berluti has been making exquisite and expensive men's shoes for more than a century. "Nothing is too beautiful for feet" is Olga Berluti's motto; she even exposes her creations to the moonlight to give them an extra-special patina. One model is named after Andy Warhol; other famous clients of the past include the Duke of Windsor, Fred Astaire, and James Joyce. ✉ *26 rue Marbeuf, 8e, Champs-Élysées* ☎ *01–53–93–97–97* ⊕ *www.berluti.com* Ⓜ *Franklin-D.-Roosevelt.*

Giuseppe Zanotti Design. Every pair of shoes here is fetish worthy, if not downright dangerous. Mile-high spike heels, buckle stilettos, slinky python booties, and jewel-encrusted black-satin pumps beg to be noticed. More toned-down models, like over-the-knee leather flats, and even sneakers, can be had, too. ✉ *12 av. Montaigne, 8e, Champs-Élysées* ☎ *01–47–20–07–85* ⊕ *www.giuseppezanottidesign. com* Ⓜ *Franklin-D.-Roosevelt.*

Jimmy Choo. This is the place for vampy stilettoes, strappy flats, and butch biker boots. Recent *Belle de Jour*–inspired kitten heels are a nice respite from the famous mile-high styles that put Choo on the map. Beautiful bags, clutches, and small leather items in animal print, reptile, and metallics are deservedly popular. ✉ *34 av. Montaigne, 8e, Champs-Élysées* ☎ *01–47–23–03–39* ⊕ *www.jimmychoo.com* Ⓜ *Franklin-D.-Roosevelt.*

FodorśChoice
★

Louis Vuitton. Louis Vuitton has spawned a voracious fan base from Texas to Tokyo with its mix of classic leather goods and saucy revamped versions orchestrated by Marc Jacobs. His 2013 exit left tall boots to fill, but Nicholas Ghesquière—a daring designer who single-handedly resurrected the Balenciaga label—has done an admirable job. Melding his signature edgy modernism with vintage touches and colors, Ghesquière is taking the legendary luxe label to a glorious new level. ✉ *101 av. des Champs-Élysées, 8e, Champs-Élysées* ☎ *01–53–57–52–00* ⊕ *www.louisvuitton.com* Ⓜ *George V.*

AROUND THE LOUVRE

The flagship stores of big luxury brands rub elbows here with independent boutiques and concept stores notable for their fashion cachet. The fabulous Rue St-Honoré—a bastion of Parisian chic—is the area's retail spine, but the Marché St-Honoré and the Faubourg provide tempting detours. Whatever you do, don't miss the gorgeous Palais-Royal gardens, where flashy fashion stars mix with the discrete purveyors of handmade gloves.

ANTIQUES AND COLLECTIBLES

Astier de Villatte. Come here for tongue-in-chic interpretations of 18th-century table settings and furniture; live out your Baroque or Empire fancies with milk-white china sets and lots of mahogany. Moody candles and incense complete the atmosphere. ✉ *173 rue St-Honoré, 1er* ☎ *01–42–60–74–13* ⊕ *www.astierdevillatte.com* Ⓜ *Tuileries.*

BEAUTY

Anne Sémonin. Anne Sémonin sells skin-care products made out of seaweed and trace elements, as well as essential oils that are popular with fashion models. ✉ *2 rue des Petits-Champs, 2e, Around the Louvre* ☎ *01–42–60–94–66* ⊕ *www.annesemonin.com* Ⓜ *Palais-Royal–Louvre.*

Annick Goutal. Annick Goutal sells its own line of signature scents, which come packaged in gilded gauze purses. Gardenia, Passion, Petite Chérie, and l'Eau d'Hadrien are perennial favorites. ✉ *14 rue de Castiglione, 1er* ☎ *01–42–60–52–82* ⊕ *www.annickgoutal.com* Ⓜ *Concorde.*

By Terry. This small, refined store is the brainchild of Terry de Gunzburg, Yves Saint Laurent's former director of makeup, whose brand of ready-to-wear cosmetics is a favorite of French actresses and socialites. Upstairs, specialists create what de Gunzburg calls *haute couleur*: exclusive made-to-measure makeup tailored for each client (it's very expensive; book far in advance). ✉ *36 Galerie Véro-Dodat, 1er* ☎ *01–44–76–00–76* ⊕ *www.byterry.com* Ⓜ *Palais-Royal–Louvre.*

Ex Nihilo. Find your perfect fragrance from a selection of base perfumes developed by a prominent Paris nose and delivered via a futuristic glass orb. The individual scents—including orange blossom, lychee, peach, and moss—can be worn as originally formulated, or you can pop up to the "sensorial boudoir" to have a customized blend created while you wait. Your precious elixir deserves a handcrafted flacon topped by a lid of onyx, mother of pearl, horn, or leather (diamonds and sapphires are available, too). ✉ *352 rue St-Honoré, 1er, Around the Louvre* ☎ *01–40–15–93–77* ⊕ *www.ex-nihilo-paris.com* Ⓜ *Tuileries.*

Jovoy. Representing 100 artisanal perfumers, Jovoy is not only Paris's largest independent purveyor of fragrances, but also the world's. Owner François Hénin can often be found in the shop expounding on the unique qualities and fascinating histories of the fragrances, some of which date back hundreds of years. Many are exclusive to the boutique. The shop also carries fragrances for the home and a range of beautifully packaged scented candles. ✉ *4 rue de Castiglione, 1er* ☎ *01–40–20–06–19* ⊕ *www.jovoyparis.com* Ⓜ *Tuileries, Concorde.*

CLOSE UP

Notable Neighborhoods, Select Streets

Paris's legendary shopping destinations draw people from the world over, but perhaps a deeper allure lies in lesser-known attractions: the city harbors scores of hidden neighborhoods and shopping streets—some well traveled, others just emerging. Each has a distinct style that reflects the character of the particular quarter. Here are a few of Paris's most satisfying and *très branché* (very trendy) enclaves.

Rue Keller, Rue Charonne (11e). These streets are a haven for young clothing designers. Stylish housewares, jewelry, and art galleries augment the appeal. Start at the end of Rue Keller where it intersects with Rue de la Roquette: walk the length of this short street, then make a right onto Rue Charonne and meander all the way to Rue du Faubourg St-Antoine.

Rue Oberkampf (11e). At the outer edge of the Marais, this street is well known among youthful fashionistas for its eclectic atmosphere and bohemian flavor. High-end jewelry and of-the-minute boutiques are clustered amid stylish wine bars and comfy cafés.

Rue des Abbesses, Rue des Martyrs (18e and 9e). In the shadow of lofty Sacré-Coeur, Rue des Abbesses is studded with shops focused on anything from vintage jewelry and unique clothing to antiques and upscale gardening tools. Turn onto Rue des Martyrs and discover a burgeoning scene, with hot boutiques scattered among inviting cafés, and superb gourmet shops.

Rues Étienne Marcel, du Jour, du Louvre, and Montmartre (2e). Just around the corner from teeming Les Halles, this area is jam-packed with big names (like Yohji Yamamoto

and Agnès b), but it also boasts a multitude of smaller boutiques that are popular with hip young Parisians.

Rue du Bac (7e). After browsing at Le Bon Marché turn the corner at the Grande Epicerie and stroll down this most bountiful of shopping streets. Old and well established, it's where the Paris *beau monde* finds everything from elegant linens and home furnishings to any item of apparel a grownup or child could possibly want.

Rue Vavin (6e). One of Paris's epicenters for outfitting those hopelessly chic Parisian children, this street is lined with boutiques for tots. If you have the kids in tow, follow up with a pony ride at the Luxembourg Gardens (weekends and Wednesday afternoon only). Jewelry stores, clothing stores, and Jean-Paul Hévin (one of Paris's top chocolatiers) give adults plenty to love, too.

Rue Pont Louis Philippe (4e). Known for a plethora of elegant paper and stationery shops, the street also has boutiques selling antiques, musical instruments, artisan jewelry, and classy clothing. It's a great spot for window-shopping en route from the Marais to Ile St-Louis.

Rue Francois Miron (from St-Paul métro to Place St-Gervais, 4e). Many overlook this lovely street at the Marais's Seine-side fringes, but there's plenty to make a wander worthwhile. Parisians in the know head here for spices, top-notch designs for the home, antiques, jewelry, pretty cafés, and much more. Bonus: Two of the oldest houses in Paris are here; they're the medieval half-timbered ones.

Fodor's Choice
★
Les Salons du Palais-Royal Serge Lutens. Every year Shiseido's creative genius, Serge Lutens, dreams up two new fragrances, which are then sold exclusively in this boutique. Each is compellingly original, from the strong *somptueux* scents (often with musk and amber notes) to intense florals (Rose de Nuit). Bottles can be etched and personalized for sumptuous gifts. ⊠ *Jardins du Palais-Royal, 142 Galerie de Valois, 1er* ☎ *01–49–27–09–09* ⊕ *www.sergelutens.com* Ⓜ *Palais-Royal–Louvre.*

Nose. This concept store offers a personalized service to help you find your ideal fragrance. A bilingual specialist takes you through a seven-step diagnostic to identify your olfactory profile—then the smelling begins. With all there is to choose from, one never leaves unsatisfied. Hard-to-locate lines of luxe body lotions, face serums, bath gels, scented candles, and yummy laundry soaps are also stocked. Fans can keep up with promotions and in-store events via the monthly "noseletter." ⊠ *20 rue Bachaumont, 2e, Around the Louvre* ☎ *01–40–26–46–03* ⊕ *nose. fr* Ⓜ *Etienne Marcel.*

BOOKS AND STATIONERY

Librarie Galignani. Dating back to 1520s Venice, this venerable bookstore opened in Paris in 1801 and was the first to specialize in English-language books. Its present location, across from the Tuileries Garden on Rue de Rivoli, opened in 1856, and the wood bookshelves, creaking floors, and hushed interior provide the perfect atmosphere for perusing Paris's best collection of contemporary and classic greats in English and French, plus a huge selection of gorgeous art books. ⊠ *224 rue de Rivoli, 1er* ☎ *01–42–60–76–07* ⊕ *www.galignani.com* Ⓜ *Tuileries.*

W. H. Smith. This bookseller carries a multitude of travel and language books, cookbooks, plus fiction for adults and children. It also has the best selection of foreign magazines and newspapers in Paris (which you're allowed to flip through without interruption—many magazine dealers in France aren't so kind). ⊠ *248 rue de Rivoli, 1er* ☎ *01–44–77–88–99* ⊕ *www.whsmith.fr* Ⓜ *Concorde.*

CLOTHING

& Other Stories. H&M's latest upmarket "style-lab" covers all the major fashion bases while appealing to women of different tastes and ages. Unlike the minimalist COS—another H&M spawn—& Other Stories offers the kind of au courant looks and well-made basics that are beloved by urban sophisticates who wouldn't be caught dead buying the parent brand but still want style on a budget. The shoe collection downstairs is a serious draw all on its own. Accessories, lingerie, and makeup are also available. ⊠ *277 rue St-Honoré, 8e* ☎ *01–53–32–85–05* ⊕ *www.stories.com* Ⓜ *Concorde.*

Fodor's Choice
★
Acne Studios. Justly famous for their sexy, derriere-shaping jeans, the Swedish label for men and women daringly mixes genders and genres in body-hugging or oversized asymmetric styles that rival some of the best catwalk looks. Standout shoes, boots, and accessories—all exhibiting the brand's underplayed cool—are sold here, too. ⊠ *124 Galerie de Valois, 1er* ☎ *01–42–60–16–62* ⊕ *www.acnestudios.com* Ⓜ *Palais-Royal–Louvre.*

16

Agnès b. Agnès b embodies the quintessential French approach to easy but stylish dressing. There are many branches, and the clothes are also sold in department stores, but for the fullest range go to Rue du Jour, where Agnès takes up much of the street (women's and children's wear are at No. 6, menswear at No. 3). For women, classics include sleek black-leather jackets, flattering black jersey separates, and trademark wide-stripe T-shirts. Children love the two-tone T-shirts proclaiming their age. And the stormy-gray velour or corduroy suits you see on those slouchy, scarf-clad men? Agnès b. ⊠ *3 and 6 rue du Jour, 1er, Around the Louvre* ☎ *01–42–33–04–13* ⊕ *europe.agnesb.com* Ⓜ *Châtelet–Les Halles.*

Fodor's Choice ★ **Alexander McQueen.** The first Paris flagship of this lauded label, which won global fame for designing the Duchess of Cambridge's wedding gown, is glorious to behold. The late McQueen's codes—tons of lace, gossamer fabrics, tartans, death's heads, and voluminous silhouettes—are all lavishly on display. But, while staying true to his vision, creative director Sarah Burton isn't as intent on pushing the boundaries as she is on creating her own magic in lavish gowns and dramatic ready-to-wear. Shoes, accessories, and surprisingly affordable jewelry to go with the garments are available as well. ⊠ *372 rue St-Honoré, 1er, Around the Louvre* ☎ *01–70–80–78–00* ⊕ *www.alexandermcqueen. com* Ⓜ *Tuileries.*

Fodor's Choice ★ **Chloé.** Much like the clothes it sells, Chloé's flagship boutique is softly feminine and modern without being stark. Housed in an 18th-century mansion, its creamy-marble floors, gold sconces, and walls in the brand's signature rosy beige are the perfect backdrop for designer Clare Waight Keller's beautifully tailored yet fluid designs. Visitors are met with the kind of sincere attention that is all but extinct in most high-end Paris shops. Whether it's for a handbag or a whole new wardrobe, VIP rooms and professional stylists are available to assist anyone who calls for an appointment. ⊠ *253 rue St-Honoré, 1e* ☎ *01–55–04–03–30* ⊕ *www.chloe.com* Ⓜ *Franklin-D.-Roosevelt.*

Claudie Pierlot. This designer is deservedly lauded for her smart, urban clothes that unite youthful chic with solid designs; they also successfully transition over several seasons. The irresistible combination of classic looks, good tailoring, and affordability keeps loyal fans coming back year after year. ⊠ *1 rue du 29 Juillet, 1er* ☎ *01–42–60–01–19* ⊕ *www. claudiepierlot.com* Ⓜ *Étienne Marcel.*

Colette. This is *the* place for ridiculously cool fashion. So the staff barely deigns to make eye contact—who cares! There are ultramodern trinkets and trifles of all kinds: from Lego-link alarm clocks to snappy iPad cases and tongue-in-chic sportswear—and that's just on the ground floor. The first floor has wearable wares from every internationally known and unknown designer with street cred. The basement has a water bar, plus a small restaurant that's good for a quick bite. ⊠ *213 rue St-Honoré, 1er* ☎ *01–55–35–33–90* ⊕ *www.colette.fr* Ⓜ *Tuileries.*

Cotélac. Cotélac gives feminine shapes a bohemian edge in earthy tones from azure to deep aubergine. The figure-skimming and frillier separates beg to be layered. ✉*284 rue St-Honoré, 1er* ☎*01–47–03–21–14* ⊕*www.cotelac.fr* Ⓜ*Tuileries.*

Didier Ludot. The incredibly charming Didier Ludot inspired a fervent craze for vintage couture, and riffling through his racks of French-made pieces from the '20s to the '80s can yield wonderful Chanel suits, Balenciaga dresses, and Hermès scarves. Ludot has two boutiques in Galerie Montpensier: No. 20 houses his amazing vintage couture collection, while No. 24 has vintage ready-to-wear and accessories. ✉*Jardins du Palais-Royal, 20–24 Galerie Montpensier, 1er* ☎*01–42–96–06–56* ⊕*www.didierludot.fr* Ⓜ*Palais-Royal–Louvre.*

Gabrielle Geppert. Gabrielle Geppert has recently expanded her compact vintage empire under the fashion-forward arcades of the Palais-Royal. At No. 34 you'll find greatest hits from the likes of Dior, Hermès, YSL, Mugler, and Alaïa (picture anything from a 1960s jet-beaded minidress to an '80s disco number). Look for more affordable vintage ready-to-wear at No. 41; Geppert's personal line of vintage-inspired shades, handbags, and jewelry at Nos. 32 and 33; and one-off vintage luxe pieces at No. 31. ✉*31–34 and 41 Galerie de Montpensier, 1er* ☎*01–42–61–53–52* ⊕*www.gabriellegeppert.com* Ⓜ*Palais-Royal–Louvre.*

Jérôme L'Huillier. L'Huillier cut his teeth at the ateliers of Balmain and Givenchy, and it shows. A wizard with silk in all its iterations (the joyously colored prints are L'Huillier's own designs), you can find lively, sexy new interpretations of the wrap dress, along with rainbow-hue blouses, sexy empire-waist dresses, and velvet trench coats in jewel colors. ✉*138–139 Galerie de Valois, 1er* ☎*01–49–26–07–07* ⊕*www.jeromelhuillier.com* Ⓜ*Palais-Royal–Louvre.*

Loris Azzaro. When Azzaro saw his 1970s designs, now collector's items, worn by stars like Nicole Kidman and Liz Hurley, he decided to update his best sellers. He's a master of the dramatic dress: picture floor-length columns with jeweled collars and sheer gowns with strategically placed sequins. ✉*65 rue de Faubourg St-Honoré, 8e* ☎*01–42–66–92–98* ⊕*www.azzaro-couture.com* Ⓜ*Concorde.*

Lucien Pellat-Finet. Lucien Pellat-Finet does cashmere that shakes up the traditional world of cable knits: here, sweaters for men, women, and children come in punchy colors and cheeky motifs. A psychedelic marijuana leaf may bounce across a sky-blue crewneck; a crystal-outlined skull could grin from a sleeveless top. The cashmere is wonderfully soft—and the prices are accordingly high. ✉*231 rue St-Honoré, 1er* ☎*01–42–22–22–77* ⊕*www.lucienpellat-finet.com* Ⓜ*Tuileries.*

Maison Martin Margiela. This famously elusive Belgian designer has earned a devoted following for his avant-garde styling and for his innovative technique, from spiraling seams to deconstructed shirts. Women's fashion is sold at 25 bis, rue de Montpensier, menswear at No. 23 (Passage Potier). Look for Ligne 6—Margiela's cool, secondary line of more casual (and less expensive) clothes for women—in his store at 22 place du Marché St-Honoré. ✉*23 and 25 bis, rue de Montpensier, 1er* ☎*01–40–15–07–55* ⊕*www.maisonmartinmargiela.fr* Ⓜ*Palais-Royal–Louvre.*

Maje. Maje brings a certain ease to looking great. The designs are original, up-to-the-moment, and not wildly expensive—that's why the popular label has expanded exponentially. Seasonal collections include minis in every form; lean, peg-leg trousers in denim and leather; and some of the best outerwear around. ⊠ *267 rue St-Honore, 2e* ☎ *01–42–96–84–93* ⊕ *www.maje.com* Ⓜ *Palais-Royal–Louvre.*

Marc Jacobs. His singular take on 20th-century American classics—from flapper-style (big flowers, unstructured lines, drop waists, flounces) to 1960s prom (empire waists, copious tulle) with a bit of motorcycle chic thrown in—has made Marc Jacobs the darling of American style. Metallics appear in most every collection, as do breezy, feminine fabrics, and lots of layers. Haute couture and ready-to-wear are both here, as is the secondary line, Marc by Marc Jacobs. Bookmarc Paris, Jacob's fun, eclectic mix of everything from art books and stationery to canvas totes and colored markers, is next door at No. 17. ⊠ *19 place du Marché St-Honoré, 1e, Around the Louvre* ☎ *01–40–20–11–30* ⊕ *www.marcjacobs.com* Ⓜ *Tuileries.*

Miu Miu. This Faubourg St-Honoré boutique dispenses with the designer's Modernist ethos in favor of a neo-Baroque sensibility—and it influences everything from the velvet wallpaper to, perhaps, a lavish pair of ruby slippers. Although the shoes and accessories scream glitz, the clothes still have a sleek refinement, with the designer's notorious tension between minimalism and opulence. ⊠ *92 rue du Faubourg St-Honoré, 8e* ☎ *01–58–62–53–20* ⊕ *www.miumiu.com* Ⓜ *Miromesnil.*

Rick Owens. Rick Owens expertly finessed the jump from L.A. rockstar chic to Paris offbeat elegance. Lately defined more by glamour than grunge, his lush fabrics and asymmetrical designs have evolved to a new level of artistry—and wearability. Owens still loves a paradox (shrouding while revealing), and mixes high luxury with a bit of the tooth and the claw. You'll also find shoes, furs, jewelry, and accessories. ⊠ *130–133 Galerie de Valois, 1er* ☎ *01–40–20–42–52* ⊕ *www.rickowens.eu* Ⓜ *Palais-Royal–Louvre.*

Saint Laurent. Yves Saint Laurent revolutionized women's wear in the 1970s, putting pants in couture shows for the first time. His safari jackets, "le smoking" suits, Russian-boho collections, and tailored *Belle de Jour* suits are considered fashion landmarks. Since taking the helm in 2012, Hedi Slimane has managed to stir things up by renaming the brand and nose-tweaking fashion journalists. Despite the controversy, there's no doubt he's returned the brand to its roots, drawing praise for his inspired collections. The menswear shop, at No. 32 rue du Faubourg St-Honoré, features new and sleekly beautiful riffs on Saint Laurent's classic satin-lapel tuxes. ⊠ *38 and 32 rue du Faubourg St-Honoré, 8e* ☎ *01–42–65–74–59* ⊕ *www.ysl.com* Ⓜ *Concorde.*

Stella McCartney. Since launching her own label in 2001, Stella McCartney has steadily built on her success. Season after season, she channels the prevailing mood into innovative takes on classics like the boyfriend blazer, the silk sheath, and the cigarette jean. The clothes flatter real women, and the steep prices can be justified by their staying power (and the fact that nothing was killed in the making). ⊠ *114–121*

Jardin du Palais-Royal

Paris's secret oasis no more. With the arrival of Rick Owens and Stella McCartney, the palace and gardens of the Jardin du Palais-Royal officially joined the ranks of fashion hot spots. Not that it ever lacked allure; those in the know have come here for fabulous shoes, artisanal perfumes, and vintage haute couture for years. Shopping in Paris is no common experience, but shopping at the Palais-Royal—under its neat rows of lime and chestnut trees and vaulted arcades—is almost worship.

Entering the gardens from Rue St-Honoré, you'll see the Colonnes de Buren, a series of sculpted columns, covering the first inner courtyard. Galerie de Montpensier is the long arcade to your left; Galerie de Valois flanks the gardens to your right.

GALERIE DE VALOIS

No. 156: **Pierre Hardy:** head-turning heels that tantalize while they flatter, with some of Paris's best bags to match (☎ 01–42–60–59–75).

No. 142: **Les Salons du Palais-Royal Serge Lutens:** perfumes and exclusive scents from the titular "nose" par excellence are sold in this jewel-like boutique (☎ 01–49–27–09–09).

Nos. 138–139: **Jérôme l'Huillier:** color-saturated silks in sexy, mod

styles, with sleek new takes on the wrap dress (☎ 01–49–26–07–07).

Nos. 130–133: **Rick Owens:** over-the-top rock-star glamour with an avant-garde edge, he makes serious fashion waves worldwide (☎ 01–40–20–42–52).

Nos. 128–129: **Maison Fabre:** proving that practice makes perfect, it's been crafting some of the most beautiful gloves in the world since 1924 (☎ 01–42–60–75–88).

No. 124: **Acne Studios:** Swedish design for men and women who demand it all—style, fit, comfort, and plenty of cool (☎ 01–42–60–16–62).

Nos. 114–121: **Stella McCartney:** McCartney has A-List cred, and her wearable-yet-sexy separates are a must in any well-appointed wardrobe (☎ 01–47–03–03–80).

GALERIE DE MONTPENSIER

Nos. 31–34: **Gabrielle Geppert:** vintage haute couture at its best: why buy a knockoff when you can have the original? Bags, jewelry, and sunglasses, too (☎ 01–42–61–53–52).

Nos. 20–24: **Didier Ludot:** vintage French pieces from the '20s to the '80s—look for couture, ready-to-wear, or tempting accessories. (☎ 01–42–96–06–56).

Galerie de Valois, 1er ☎ *01–47–03–03–80* ⊕ *www.stellamccartney.com* Ⓜ *Palais-Royal–Louvre.*

Tara Jarmon. Tara Jarmon has her bases covered when it comes to that coveted French élan: sleek designs, excellent quality, luxe fabrics, and prices well within the stratosphere. With styles that vie with the high-profile designers, and accessories to match, this label is fast becoming the chic Parisian's wardrobe essential. ✉ *400 rue St-Honoré, 1er* ☎ *01–40–15–02–13* ⊕ *www.tarajarmon.com* Ⓜ *Concorde.*

Vanessa Bruno. Expect a new brew of feminine dressing from Vanessa Bruno: some androgynous pieces (skinny pants) plus delicacy (filmy tops) with a dash of whimsy (lace insets). Separates are coveted for their sleek styling, gorgeous colors, and unerring sexiness. Wardrobe staples include perfectly proportioned cotton tops and sophisticated dresses. Athé, the diffusion line, flies off the racks, so if you see something you love, grab it. Bruno's shoes and accessories are the cherry on the cake: her iconic sequin-striped totes inspired an army of knockoffs. ✉ *12 rue de Castiglione, 1er* ☎ *01–42–61–44–60* ⊕ *www.vanessabruno.com* Ⓜ *Pyramides.*

Ventilo. Ventilo brings cool ethnic style to the city. Where else can you find a bright-fuchsia silk-velvet bolero jacket with sequin appliqué or a modern Mongol leather coat lined in fur? There's also room for classics to mix and match, such as handmade wool turtlenecks and a pleated raincoat that fit perfectly. ✉ *27 bis, rue du Louvre, 2e* ☎ *01–44–76–82–95* ⊕ *www.ventiloparis.tumblr.com* Ⓜ *Étienne Marcel.*

Yohji Yamamoto. A master of the drape, fold, and twist, Yohji Yamamoto made his name in the 1980s. The design legend favors predominantly black clothes that are both functional and edgy. A canny fashion investment, these pieces never go out of style. You'll find ready-to-wear for men and women at the Louvre boutique, along with the Y's casual line. ✉ *25 rue du Louvre, 1er, Around the Louvre* ☎ *01–42–21–42–93* ⊕ *www.yohjiyamamoto.co.jp* Ⓜ *Étienne Marcel.*

DEPARTMENT STORES

BHV. Short for Bazar de l'Hôtel de Ville, BHV houses an enormous basement hardware store that sells everything from doorknobs to cement mixers and has to be seen to be believed. The fashion offerings for men, women, and kids have been totally revamped, with many of the top labels and a fabulous, not-too-crowded lingerie department on the second floor. But BHV is most noteworthy for its high-quality home-decor items, electronics, and office supplies. If you're looking for typically French household goods (like those heavy, gold-rimmed café sets, gorgeous French linens, or Savon de Marseille), this is your ticket. The extensive men's store is across the street at 36 rue de la Verrerie. ✉ *52–64 rue de Rivoli, 4e, Around the Louvre* ☎ *09–77–40–14–00* ⊕ *www.bhv.fr* Ⓜ *Hôtel de Ville.*

FNAC. Parisians flock to FNAC—the high-profile French "cultural" department store—for a huge selection of music and books, as well as photo, TV, and audio equipment. This centrally located branch is among the biggest. ✉ *Forum des Halles, 1er, Around the Louvre* ☎ *08–25–02–00–20* ⊕ *www.fnac.com* Ⓜ *Les Halles.*

FOOD AND TREATS

Jean-Paul Hévin. Forty masterful varieties of chocolate and some of the best pastries in Paris earned Jean-Paul Hévin his world-class chocolatier status. Devotees will be pleased to know that there's also an outpost near the Luxembourg Gardens at 3 rue Vavin. ✉ *231 rue St-Honoré, 1er, Around the Louvre* ☎ *01–55–35–35–96* ⊕ *www.jeanpaulhevin. com* Ⓜ *Tuileries.*

Ladurée. Founded in 1862, Ladurée oozes period atmosphere—even at the big Champs-Élysées branch (No. 75)—but nothing beats the original tearoom on Rue Royale, with its pint-size tables and frescoed ceiling. Ladurée claims a familial link to the invention of the *macaron*, and appropriately, there's a fabulous selection of these lighter-than-air cookies. Classic flavors include pistachio, salted caramel, and coffee; others, like violet–black currant, chestnut, and lime basil, are available seasonally. When you've worked your way through the *macaron* menu, try a cup of the famously rich hot chocolate with a flaky mille-feuille. Ladurée's stylish boxes alone are worth the purchase; filled with sweet treats, they make memorable gifts. ⊠ *16 rue Royale, 8e* ☎ *01–42–60–21–79* ⊕ *www.laduree.com* Ⓜ *Madeleine.*

HOME DECOR

A. Simon. This is where Parisian chefs come for their kitchen needs—from plates and glasses to pans and wooden spoons. The quality is excellent and the prices reasonable. ⊠ *48 rue Montmartre, 2e, Around the Louvre* ☎ *01–42–33–71–65* Ⓜ *Étienne Marcel.*

E. Dehillerin. Never mind the creaky stairs: E. Dehillerin has been around for almost 200 years and clearly knows its business. The huge range of professional cookware in enamel, stainless steel, or fiery copper is gorgeous. During her years in Paris, Julia Child was a regular here. ⊠ *18–20 rue Coquillière, 1er, Around the Louvre* ☎ *01–42–36–53–13* ⊕ *www.e-dehillerin.fr* Ⓜ *Les Halles.*

Gien. Gien has been making fine china since 1821. The faience spans traditional designs—such as those inspired by Italian majolica, blue-and-white delftware, and French toile—as well as contemporary looks. ⊠ *18 rue de l'Arcade, 8e* ☎ *01–42–66–52–32* ⊕ *www.gien.com* Ⓜ *Madeleine.*

La Chalcographie du Louvre. More than 13,000 prints from the Louvre's collection can be had at the museum's own print shop for a relatively minor investment. The most popular images are in stock, easy to view, and can walk right out with you. ⊠ *Louvre museum store, 1er* ☎ *01–40–20–59–35* ⊕ *www.chalcographiedulouvre.com* Ⓜ *Palais-Royal–Louvre.*

JEWELRY AND ACCESSORIES

Fodor's Choice
★ **Cartier.** Cartier flashes its jewels at more than half a dozen boutiques in the city. Longtime favorites such as the Trinity rings and Tank watches compete for attention with the newer Panthère, Love, and Caresse d'Orchidées collections. ⊠ *23 pl. Vendôme, 1er* ☎ *01–44–55–32–20* ⊕ *www.cartier.fr* Ⓜ *Tuileries, Concorde.*

Dary's. This wonderful, family-run cavern teeming with artists, actors, models, and jewelry lovers offers an Ali Baba–ish shopping experience. You'll need to take your time though, because the walls are filled with row upon row of antique jewels from every era, more modern second-hand jewelry, and drawer upon drawer of vintage one-of-a-kinds. ⊠ *362 rue St-Honoré, 1er* ☎ *01–42–60–95–23* ⊕ *www.darys-bijouterie-paris.fr* Ⓜ *Tuileries.*

LINGERIE

Fodor's Choice ★ **Alice Cadolle.** Selling lingerie to Parisians since 1889, Alice Cadolle offers some of the city's most sumptuous couture undergarments. Ready-to-wear bras, corsets, and sleepwear fill the Rue Cambon boutique; made-to-measure service is provided at 255 rue St-Honoré. ⊠ *4 rue Cambon, 1er* ☎ *01–42–60–94–22* ⊕ *www.cadolle.com* Ⓜ *Concorde.*

Fodor's Choice ★ **Chantal Thomass.** The legendary lingerie diva is back with a *Pillow Talk–*meets–Louis XIV–inspired boutique. This is French naughtiness at its best, striking the perfect balance between playful and seductive. Sheer silk negligees edged in Chantilly lace and lascivious bra-and-corset sets punctuate the signature line. ⊠ *211 rue St-Honoré, 1er* ☎ *01–42–60–40–56* ⊕ *www.chantalthomass.fr* Ⓜ *Tuileries.*

Fifi Chachnil. Fifi Chachnil girls are real boudoir babes, with a fondness for quilted-satin bed jackets and lingerie in candy-land colors. The look is cheerfully sexy, with checkered push-up bras, frilled white knickers, and peach-satin corsets. ⊠ *231 rue St-Honoré, 1er* ☎ *01–42–61–21–83* ⊕ *fifichachnil.com* Ⓜ *Tuileries.*

Princesse Tam Tam. Princesse Tam Tam is the go-to for affordable and beguiling bra-and-panty sets that combine sex appeal and playfulness. Designed for mileage as much as allure, the softer-than-soft cotton wrap tops and nighties, lace-edged silk tap pants, camisoles, slips, and adorable separates for the boudoir are comfortable *and* comely. ⊠ *5 rue Montmartre, 1er, Around the Louvre* ☎ *01–45–08–50–69* ⊕ *www.princessetamtam.com* Ⓜ *Les Halles.*

MARKETS

Rue Montorgueil. This old-fashioned market street has evolved into a chic bobo zone; its stalls now thrive amid stylish cafés and the oldest oyster counter in Paris. ⊠ *1er, Around the Louvre* Ⓜ *Châtelet–Les Halles.*

SHOES, HANDBAGS, AND LEATHER GOODS

Causse. This place dates back to a time when the quality of the gloves said it all. Supple python or cherry-lacquered lambskin may not have been the rage in 1892 when this eminent glove maker was founded, but its 125 years in the business add up to unparalleled style and fit. ⊠ *12 rue de Castiglione, 1er* ☎ *01–49–26–91–43* ⊕ *www.causse-gantier.fr* Ⓜ *Tuileries.*

Christian Louboutin. These shoes carry their own red carpet with them, thanks to their trademark crimson soles. Whether tasseled, embroidered, or strappy, in Charvet silk or shiny patent leather, the heels are always perfectly balanced. No wonder they set off such legendary legs as Tina Turner's and Gwyneth Paltrow's. The men's shop is next door at No. 17, and the women's pop-up store (Christian Louboutin Beauté, featuring his cosmetics line) is around the corner at Galerie Véro-Dodat. The glamorous No. 68 rue du Faubourg St-Honoré boutique carries a full line of women's shoes and accessories. ⊠ *19 rue Jean-Jacques Rousseau, 1er, Around the Louvre* ☎ *08–00–94–58–04* ⊕ *www.christianlouboutin.com* Ⓜ *Palais-Royal–Louvre.*

Goyard. These colorful totes are the choice of royals, blue bloods, and the like (clients have included Sir Arthur Conan Doyle, Gregory Peck, and the Duke and Duchess of Windsor). Parisians swear by their durability and longevity; they're copious enough for a mile-long baguette, and durable enough for a magnum of Champagne. What's more, they easily transition into ultrachic beach or diaper bags. ⊠ *233 rue St-Honoré, 1er* ☎ *01–42–60–57–04* ⊕ *www.goyard.com* Ⓜ *Tuileries.*

Hermès. The go-to for those who prefer their logo discrete yet still crave instant recognition, Hermès was established as a saddlery in 1837; then went on to create the eternally chic Kelly (named for Grace Kelly) and Birkin (named for Jane Birkin) handbags. The silk scarves are legendary for their rich colors and intricate designs, which change yearly. Other accessories are also extremely covetable: enamel bracelets, dashing silk-twill ties, and small leather goods. During semiannual sales, in January and July, prices are slashed up to 50%, and the crowds line up for blocks. ⊠ *24 rue du Faubourg St-Honoré, 8e* ☎ *01–40–17–46–00* ⊕ *www.hermes.com* Ⓜ *Concorde.*

Lancaster. A household name in France for 100 years, Lancaster has a reputation for style and craftsmanship. Its bags are chic and sporty, with an emphasis on practicality; and all the classic models are available in this spaceship-modern boutique. Look for the popular cross-body Besace bag (it's made of patent leather or soft cowhide and comes in a rainbow of colors), along with exclusive designs sold only here, some in genuine reptile. Lovely leather covers and bags for every mobile device are here, too. ⊠ *422 rue St-Honoré, 8e* ☎ *01–42–28–88–88* ⊕ *www. lancaster-paris.com* Ⓜ *Concorde.*

Maison Fabre. Until you've eased into an exquisite pair of gloves handcrafted by Fabre, you probably haven't experienced the sensation of having a second skin far superior to your own. Founded in 1924, this is one of Paris's historic *gantiers*. Styles range from classic to haute: picture elbow-length croc leather, coyote-fur mittens, and peccary driving gloves. ⊠ *128–129 Galerie de Valois, 1er* ☎ *01–42–60–75–88* ⊕ *www. maisonfabre.com* Ⓜ *Palais-Royal–Louvre.*

Moynat. Designed to evoke a wheel, as in "we're going places, baby," this gleaming boutique showcases the new Moynat, while evoking the brand's 19th- and early-20th-century glory days, when Pauline Moynat was the queen of luggage design. Women's bags are sleek, expertly engineered, and exceedingly beautiful (the reversible leather tote in either bone/coral or mocha/taupe is an instant classic). Men's briefcases are convex on one side to avoid bumping legs: an ingenious design that harkens back to the advent of automobile travel, when Moynat's trunks were curved to hug a car roof. Crocodile bags, silk scarves, and a thriving bespoke service are cherries on the cake. ⊠ *348 rue St-Honoré, 1er* ☎ *01–47–03–83–90* ⊕ *moynat.com* Ⓜ *Tuileries.*

Perrin. As much as we love a stylish clutch, after a cocktail or two it's likely to end up anywhere. Luckily, this fifth-generation leather goods specialist dispenses with the problem by adding a nifty handhold, in metal, leather, or other luxury skins, to its superchic version. Looking for something larger? The irresistible Baggala hobo bag comes in calf or matte crocodile; and the Bavolet, in red-and-gold python, is a sure showstopper. Gloves, sunglasses, and little leather items are also sold. ⊠ *3 rue d'Alger, 1er, Around the Louvre* ☎ *01–42–36–53–54* ⊕ *perrinparis.com* Ⓜ *Tuileries.*

Pierre Hardy. Pierre Hardy completes the triumvirate (with Vivier and Louboutin) of anointed Paris shoe designers. Armed with a pedigree—Dior, Hermès, Balenciaga—Hardy opened his own boutique in 2003 and made serious waves. Luxe bags are ever popular, and the shoes are unmistakable: sky-scraping platforms and wedges or demure kitten heels double as sculpture with breathtaking details and luscious colors. Movie stars are regularly seen sporting Hardy's popular (and expensive) sneakers. His new jewelry line features sexy, wearable baubles, perfect for a day-to-evening look. ⊠ *Palais-Royal Gardens, 156 Galerie de Valois, 1er* ☏ *01–42–60–59–75* ⊕ *www.pierrehardy.com* Ⓜ *Palais-Royal–Louvre.*

Fodor's Choice
★
Renaud Pellegrino. Just steps away from the Palais-Royal, Renaud Pellegrino is a black-book address for style icons like Catherine Deneuve and Paloma Picasso, who eschew status labels in favor of individuality and staying power. A black lace-over-leather bag or an azure tote with tiny silver grommets brings glamour to daytime looks, and a Mondrianesque patchwork of silk-satin adds magnificence to evening wear. ⊠ *149 rue St-Honoré, 1er* ☏ *01–42–61–75–32* Ⓜ *Palais-Royal–Louvre.*

Roger Vivier. Known for decades for his Pilgrim-buckle shoes and inventive heels, Roger Vivier's name is being resurrected through the creativity of über-Parisienne Inès de la Fressange and the expertise of shoe designer Bruno Frisoni. The results are easily some of the best shoes in town: leather boots that mold to the calf perfectly, towering rhinestone-encrusted or feathered platforms for evening, and vertiginous crocodile pumps. ⊠ *29 rue du Faubourg St-Honoré, 8e* ☏ *01–53–43–00–85* ⊕ *www.rogervivier.com* Ⓜ *Concorde.*

SHOPPING GALLERIES

Galerie Véro-Dodat. Built in 1826, this beautifully restored, glass-ceilinged gallery has painted medallions and copper pillars, plus boutiques selling antiques, contemporary art, accessories, and more. Christian Louboutin is an anchor tenant. At what is now the Café de l'Époque, just at the gallery's entrance, French writer Gérard de Nerval took his last drink before heading to Châtelet to hang himself. ⊠ *19 rue Jean-Jacques Rousseau, 1er* Ⓜ *Palais-Royal–Louvre.*

Fodor's Choice
★
Galerie Vivienne. Located between the Bourse and the Palais-Royal, Galerie Vivienne is the most glorious glass-capped arcade in Paris. The 19th-century beauty is home to an array of interesting boutiques as well as a lovely tearoom (A Priori Thé) and a terrific wineshop called Cave Legrand Filles et Fils. ⊠ *4 rue des Petits-Champs, 2e, Around the Louvre* ⊕ *www.galerie-vivienne.com* Ⓜ *Palais-Royal–Louvre, Bourse.*

Passage du Grand-Cerf. Opened in 1825, this pretty *passage couvert* has regained the interest of Parisians. La Parisette, a small boudoir-pink space at No. 1, sells fun accessories, and Marci Noum, at No. 4, riffs on street fashion. Silk bracelets, crystals, and charms can be nabbed at Eric & Lydie and Satellite. ⊠ *Entrances at 145 rue St-Denis and 8 rue Dussoubs, 2e, Around the Louvre* Ⓜ *Étienne Marcel.*

LES GRANDS BOULEVARDS

From the venerable old boutiques on Rue de la Paix to Paris's great *grands magasins* on Boulevard Haussmann (namely Galeries Lafayette and Au Printemps), there's no shortage of shopping opportunities here. Once you add in the area's elegant covered passages, there is enough to keep you busy for a weekend, if not an entire week.

BARGAIN SHOPPING

Monoprix. With branches throughout the city, this is *the* French dime store par excellence, stocking everyday items like French cosmetics, groceries, toys, kitchen wares, and more. It also has a line of stylish, inexpensive, basic wearables for the whole family—particularly adorable kids' clothes—and isn't a bad place to stock up on French chocolate, jams, or *confit de canard* at reasonable prices. ⊠ *21 av. de l'Opéra, 1er* ☎ *01–42–61–78–08* ⊕ *www.monoprix.fr* Ⓜ *Opéra*.

BEAUTY

Make Up For Ever. Poised at the back of a courtyard, this store is a must-stop for makeup artists, models, actresses, and divas of all stripes. The riotous color selection includes hundreds of hues for foundation, eye shadow, powder, and lipstick. ⊠ *5 rue de la Boétie, 8e, Les Grands Boulevards* ☎ *01–53–05–93–30* ⊕ *www.makeupforever.fr* Ⓜ *St-Augustin*.

CLOTHING

Anouschka. Anouschka has set up shop in her apartment (by appointment only, Monday to Saturday) and has rack upon rack of vintage clothing dating from the 1930s to the '80s. It's the perfect place to find a '50s cocktail dress in mint condition or a mod jacket for him. A former model herself, she calls this a "designer laboratory," and teams from top fashion houses often pop by looking for inspiration. ⊠ *6 av. du Coq, 9e* ☎ *01–48–74–37–00* Ⓜ *St-Lazare, Trinité*.

Charvet. The Parisian equivalent of a Savile Row tailor, Charvet is a conservative, aristocratic institution. It's famed for made-to-measure shirts, exquisite ties, and accessories; for garbing John F. Kennedy, Charles de Gaulle, and the Duke of Windsor; and for its regal address. Although the exquisite silk ties, in hundreds of colors and patterns, and custom-made shirts for men are the biggest draw, refined pieces for women and girls, as well as adorable miniatures for boys, round out the collection. ⊠ *28 pl. Vendôme, 1er* ☎ *01–42–60–30–70* Ⓜ *Opéra*.

Eric Bompard. Eric Bompard provides stylish Parisians with luxury cashmeres in every color, style, and weight; yarns range from light as a feather to a hefty 50-ply for the jaunty caps. The store caters to men and women (there are some kids' models, too). Styles are updated seasonally yet tend toward the classic. ⊠ *75 bd. Haussmann, 8e* ☎ *01–42–68–00–73* ⊕ *www.eric-bompard.com* Ⓜ *Miromesnil*.

DEPARTMENT STORES

Au Printemps. A retail institution, Au Printemps is actually made up of three major stores: Printemps Maison (with home furnishings on four refurbished floors), Printemps Homme (featuring six levels of menswear), and fashion-focused Printemps Mode (which has everything à la mode, from couture to teen trends). Be sure to check out the beauty

16

area, with the Nuxe spa, hair salons, and seemingly every beauty product known to woman under one roof. The luxurious new Printemps Louvre—in the Carrousel du Louvre, at the underground entrance to the museum, across from I.M. Pei's inverted pyramid—carries fine leather goods, accessories, watches, and beauty products; fittingly, it also hosts revolving art exhibitions. ✉ *64 bd. Haussmann, 9e* ☎ *01–42–82–50–00* ⊕ *www.printemps.com* Ⓜ *Havre-Caumartin, St-Lazare.*

Galeries Lafayette. Galeries Lafayette is one of those places that you wander into unawares, leaving hours later a poorer and humbler person. Inside its flagship building at 40 boulevard Haussmann, a Belle Époque stained-glass dome caps the world's largest perfumery. The store bulges with thousands of designers, and free 25-minute fashion shows are held Friday at 3 pm in the upstairs café to showcase their wares (reservations are a must: email *fashionshow@galerieslafayette. com*). Another big draw is the comestibles department, stocked with everything from herbed goat cheese to Iranian caviar. Just across the street at 35 boulevard Haussmann is Galeries Lafayette Maison, which focuses on goods for the fashionable home. The Montparnasse branch is a pale shadow of the Boulevard Haussmann behemoths. ✉ *35–40 bd. Haussmann, 9e* ☎ *01–42–82–34–56* ⊕ *www.galerieslafayette.com* Ⓜ *Chaussée d'Antin, Havre-Caumartin.*

FOOD AND TREATS

À la Mère de Famille. This enchanting shop is well versed in French regional specialties as well as old-fashioned bonbons, chocolates, marzipan, and more. ✉ *35 rue du Faubourg-Montmartre, 9e* ☎ *01–47–70–83–69* ⊕ *www.lameredefamille.com* Ⓜ *Cadet.*

Fauchon. The most iconic of Parisian food stores is expanding globally, but its flagship is still behind the Madeleine church. Established in 1886, Fauchon sells renowned pâté, honey, jelly, tea, and private-label Champagne. Expats come for hard-to-find foreign foods (think U.S. pancake mix or British lemon curd), while those with a sweet tooth make a beeline to the pâtisserie for airy, ganache-filled *macarons*. There's also a café for a quick bite. Be prepared, though: prices can be eye-popping—marzipan fruit for €100 a pound? ✉ *26 pl. de la Madeleine, 8e* ☎ *01–70–39–38–00* ⊕ *www.fauchon.com* Ⓜ *Madeleine.*

Hédiard. Established in 1854, Hédiard gained fame in the 19th century for its high-quality imported spices. These—along with rare teas and beautifully packaged house brands of jam, mustard, and cookies—continue to make excellent gifts. ✉ *21 pl. de la Madeleine, 8e* ☎ *01–43–12–88–88* ⊕ *www.hediard.fr* Ⓜ *Madeleine.*

HOME DECOR

Christofle. Founded in 1830, Christofle has fulfilled all kinds of silver wishes, from a silver service for the Orient Express to a gigantic silver bed. Come for timeless table settings, vases, jewelry boxes, and more. ✉ *24 rue de la Paix, 2e* ☎ *01–42–65–62–43* ⊕ *www.christofle.com* Ⓜ *Opéra.*

JEWELRY AND ACCESSORIES

Alexandre Reza. One of Paris's most exclusive jewelers, Alexandre Reza is first and foremost a gemologist. He travels the world looking for the finest stones and then works them into stunning pieces, many of which are replicas of jewels of historical importance. ✉ *21 pl. Vendôme, 1er* ☎ *01–42–61–51–21* ⊕ *www.alexandrereza.com* Ⓜ *Opéra.*

Chanel Jewelry. Chanel Jewelry feeds off the iconic design elements of the pearl-draped designer: witness the quilting (reimagined for gold rings), camellias (now brooches), and shooting stars (used for her first jewelry collection in 1932, now appearing as diamond rings). ✉ *18 pl. Vendôme, 1er* ☎ *01–40–98–55–55* ⊕ *www.chanel.com* Ⓜ *Tuileries, Opéra.*

Dinh Van. Just around the corner from Place Vendôme's titan jewelers, Dinh Van thumbs its nose at in-your-face opulence. The look here is refreshingly spare. Best sellers include a hammered-gold-orb necklace and leather-cord bracelets joined with geometric shapes in white or yellow gold, some with pavé diamonds. ✉ *16 rue de la Paix, 2e* ☎ *01–42–61–74–49* ⊕ *www.dinhvan.com* Ⓜ *Opéra.*

MARKETS

Rue Lévis. This market, near Parc Monceau, has Alsatian specialties and a terrific cheese shop. It's closed Sunday afternoon and Monday. ✉ *17e, Les Grands Boulevards* Ⓜ *Villiers.*

SHOPPING GALLERIES

Passage des Panoramas. Opened in 1800, Passage des Panoramas is the oldest extant arcade and has become a foodie paradise, with no less than five major gourmet destinations. ✉ *11 bd. Montmartre, 2e, Les Grands Boulevards* Ⓜ *Opéra, Grands Boulevards.*

Passage Jouffroy. Passage Jouffroy is full of eclectic shops selling toys, Asian furnishings, cinema posters, and more. Pain D'épices, at No. 29, specializes in dollhouse decor. ✉ *10–12 bd. Montmartre, 9e, Les Grands Boulevards* Ⓜ *Grands Boulevards.*

Passage Verdeau. Across from Passage Jouffroy, Passage Verdeau has shops carrying antique cameras, comic books, and engravings. Au Bonheur des Dames, at No. 8, has all things embroidery. ✉ *4–6 rue de la Grange Batelière, 9e* Ⓜ *Grands Boulevards.*

TOYS

Fodor'sChoice ★ **Pain d'Epices.** This shop has anything you can imagine for the French home (and garden) in miniature, including Lilliputian croissants, wine decanters, and minuscule instruments in their cases. Build-it-yourself dollhouses include a 17th-century town house and a boulangerie storefront. Upstairs are do-it-yourself teddy-bear kits and classic toys. ✉ *29 Passage Jouffroy, 9e, Les Grands Boulevards* ☎ *01–47–70–08–68* ⊕ *www.paindepices.fr* Ⓜ *Grands Boulevards.*

FAMILY
Fodor'sChoice ★ **Village JouéClub.** Le Passage des Princes—one of the city's historic covered *passages*—is home to Paris's most comprehensive toy store. Part of a large French chain, the two-level Village JouéClub carries all the usual suspects (Barbie, Disney, Hello Kitty, and the like) plus the better traditional European brands, including Vilac, Moulin Roty, and L'Atelier du

Bois. It's made up of more than 10 "shops," each of which is dedicated to a different age group or toy genre. You'll find virtually every kind of plaything here, so be prepared to linger. ⊠ *5 bd. des Italiens, 2e, Les Grands Boulevards* ☎ *01–53–45–41–41* ⊕ *www.villagejoueclub.com* Ⓜ *Richelieu–Drouot.*

WINE

Lavinia. Lavinia has the largest selection of wine in one spot in Europe—more than 6,000 wines and spirits from all over the world, ranging from the simple to the sublime. There are expert English-speaking sommeliers on-site to help you sort it all out, as well as a wine-tasting bar, a bookshop, and a restaurant. ⊠ *3–5 bd. de la Madeleine, 1er* ☎ *01–42–97–20–20* ⊕ *www.lavinia.fr* Ⓜ *St-Augustin.*

Les Caves Augé. One of the best wineshops in Paris, Les Caves Augé has been in operation since 1850. It's just the ticket, whether you're looking for a rare vintage, a select Bordeaux, or a seductive Champagne for a tête-à-tête. English-speaking Marc Sibard is a well-known aficionado and an affable adviser. Check the website for a schedule of tastings—vintners set up on the sidewalk and the wine flows all day. ⊠ *116 bd. Haussmann, 8e* ☎ *01–45–22–16–97* ⊕ *www.cavesauge.com* Ⓜ *St-Augustin.*

MONTMARTRE

To avoid an uphill climb, the Abbesses métro stop on Rue de la Vieuville is a good starting point for serious shoppers. From here, descend picturesque Rue des Martyrs all the way down to Notre-Dame-de-Lorette: the route promises a cornucopia of captivating boutiques that sell everything from chic antiques and offbeat fashion to gourmet food.

CLOTHING

A.P.C. Stock. A.P.C. opened its surplus store steps away from Sacré-Coeur. No need to wait for the sales; funky classics can always be found here for a whopping 50% off. ⊠ *20 rue André del Sarte, 18e, Montmartre* ☎ *01–42–62–10–88* ⊕ *www.apc.fr* Ⓜ *Château Rouge.*

Spree. When Spree first opened, its mission was to give young designers a venue; it has since branched out to include fashion elites like Margiela, Isabel Marant, Golden Goose, and Christian Wijnants. The expertly chosen inventory seems almost curated. A great selection of accessories and jewelry, along with cool furniture and a revolving exhibition of artwork by international artists, complete the gallery feel. ⊠ *16 rue la Vieuville, 18e, Montmartre* ☎ *01–42–23–41–40* ⊕ *www. spree.fr* Ⓜ *Abbesses.*

MARKETS

Fodor'sChoice ★ **Marché aux Puces St-Ouen** (*Clignancourt*). This picturesque market on the city's northern boundary—open weekends 9 to 6, Monday 10 to 5—still lures crowds, but its once-unbeatable prices are now a relic. Packed with antiques booths and *brocante* stalls, the century-old, miles-long labyrinth has been undergoing a mild renaissance lately: witness Village Vintage's recently opened warehouses filled with midcentury-modern pieces at 77 rue des Rosiers, plus other buzzworthy shops and galleries (some of which keep weekend-only hours). Destination eateries—including Philippe Starck's hugely popular Ma Cocotte—are also attracting a hip Paris contingent. Arrive early to pick up the best loot, then linger over an excellent meal or apéro. Be warned, though: if there's one place in Paris where you need to know how to bargain, this is it! If you're arriving by métro, walk under the overpass and take the first left at the Rue de Rosiers to reach the center of the market. Note that stands selling dodgy odds and ends (think designer knockoffs and questionable gadgets) set up around the overpass. These blocks are crowded and gritty; be careful with your valuables. ✉ *18e, Montmartre* ⊕ *www. marcheauxpuces-saintouen.com* Ⓜ *Porte de Clignancourt.*

THE MARAIS

The Marais has stolen the show as the city's hippest shopping destination—and for sheer volume it can't be beat. Rue des Francs Bourgeois and Rue Vieille de Temple form the central retail axis from which the upper and lower Marais branch out. The newest frontier is its northeastern edge (the *haut* Marais), which is known for ultrastylish boutiques, vintage stores, and design ateliers.

ANTIQUES AND COLLECTIBLES

Village St-Paul. This clutch of streets, in the beautiful historic netherworld tucked between the fringes of the Marais and the banks of the Seine, has many antiques shops. ✉ *Enter from Rue St-Paul, 4e, Marais* ⊕ *www.levillagesaintpaul.com* Ⓜ *St-Paul.*

BARGAIN SHOPPING

L'Habilleur. L'Habilleur is a favorite with the fashion press and anyone looking for a deal. For women there's a great selection from designers like Firma, Roberto Collina, and Giorgio Brato. Men can find elegant suits from Paul Smith at slashed prices. ✉ *44 rue de Poitou, 3e, Marais* ☎ *01–48–87–77–12* Ⓜ *St-Sébastien–Froissart.*

FAMILY

Fodor'sChoice

★

Merci. The world's most gorgeous charity shop was put together by the founders of the luxury kids' line Bonpoint. Everything here is high-concept (the designer fashions, furniture, antiques, jewelry, and housewares have been plucked straight from top-tier designers), and it's all offered at a discount. Five percent of the proceeds are earmarked to aid disadvantaged children in Madagascar. The store's three cafés make lingering among Paris's fashion elite a pleasure. ✉ *111 bd. Beaumarchais, 3e, Marais* ☎ *01–42–77–00–33* ⊕ *www.merci-merci.com* Ⓜ *St-Sebastien–Froissart.*

Zadig & Voltaire Stock. Here you'll find new unsold stock from last season. There's a great selection of beautiful cashmere sweaters, silk slip dresses, rocker jeans, and leather jackets, all in their signature luscious colors, for 40%–70% off. ✉ *22 rue Bourg Tibourg, 4e, Marais* ☎ *01–44–59–39–62* ⊕ *www.zadig-et-voltaire.com* Ⓜ *Hôtel de Ville.*

BEAUTY

L'Artisan Parfumeur. L'Artisan Parfumeur is known for its own brand of scents for the home plus perfumes with names like Mûre et Musc (Blackberry and Musk). It also carries sumptuous shower gels, body

16

lotions, and candles in the popular fragrances. ⊠ *32 rue du Bourg Tibourg, 4e, Marais* ☎ *01–48–04–55–66* ⊕ *www.artisanparfumeur. com* Ⓜ *Hôtel de Ville.*

BOOKS AND STATIONERY

Comptoir de l'Image. This is where designers John Galliano, Marc Jacobs, and Emanuel Ungaro stock up on old copies of *Vogue, Harper's Bazaar,* and *The Face.* You'll also find trendy magazines like *Dutch, Purple,* and *Spoon,* plus designer catalogs from the past and rare photo books. Don't go early: whimsical opening hours tend to start after lunch. ⊠ *44 rue de Sévigné, 3e, Marais* ☎ *01–42–72–03–92* Ⓜ *St-Paul.*

CHILDREN'S CLOTHING

FAMILY **Bonton.** Bonton takes the prize for most-coveted duds among those who like to think of children as fashion accessories. (Moms may find some useful wardrobe pointers, too.) Sassy separates in saturated colors layer beautifully, look amazing, and manage to be perfectly kid-friendly. Bonton sells toys and furniture, too. ⊠ *5 bd. des Filles du Calvaire, 3e, Marais* ☎ *01–42–72–34–69* ⊕ *www.bonton.fr* Ⓜ *Filles du Calvaire.*

CLOTHING

Abou d'Abi Bazar. A one-stop outfitter, Abou d'Abi Bazar organizes its collection of up-to-the-moment designers on color-coordinated racks that highlight the asymmetrical design of this opulent boutique. Artsy and bohemian all at once, there is plenty to covet here, from frothy Isabel Marant silk-organza blouses to sumptuous cashmere-blend tunics and satin shirtwaist dresses. Reasonably priced picks make it a desirable destination. ⊠ *125 rue Vieille du Temple, 3e, Marais* ☎ *01–42–71–13–26* ⊕ *www.aboudabibazar.com* Ⓜ *Filles du Calvaire.*

AB33. AB33 is like a sleek boudoir—complete with comfy chair and scented candles—and the clothes here are unabashedly feminine. Separates in luxury fabrics from top designers, irresistible silk lingerie, dainty jewelry, and a selection of accessories celebrate that certain French je ne sais quoi. ⊠ *33 rue Charlot, 3e, Marais* ☎ *01–42–71–02–82* ⊕ *ab33. fr* Ⓜ *Filles du Calvaire.*

Fodor's Choice **Azzedine Alaïa.** Thanks to his perfectly proportioned "king of cling" ★ dresses, Azzedine Alaïa is considered a master at his game. You don't have to be under 20 to look good in his garments. Tina Turner wears them well, as does every other beautiful woman with the courage and the curves. His boutique-workshop-apartment is covered with artwork by Julian Schnabel and is not the kind of place you casually wander into out of curiosity: the sales staff immediately makes you feel awkward in that distinctive Parisian way. Think $3,500 is too much for a dress? The Alaïa stock store (same building, different entrance) takes 40% off last season's styles, samples, and gently worn catwalk items. Access it at 18 rue de la Verrerie. ⊠ *7 rue de Moussy, 4e, Marais* ☎ *01–42–72–30–69* ⊕ *www.alaia.fr* Ⓜ *Hôtel de Ville.*

The Broken Arm. Like the ready-made Duchamp "artwork" for which it is named, The Broken Arm projects a minimalist cool that puts the concept back in concept store. A hypercurated selection of A-list brands for men and women includes vivid separates from the likes of Phillip Lim, Raf Simons, and the sublime Christophe Lemaire. A choice selection of objects and accessories (books, hats, shoes, jewelry, vases, leather goods) elevates the everyday to art. ⊠ *12 rue Perrée, 3e, Marais* ☎ *01–44–61–53–60* ⊕ *www.the-broken-arm.com* Ⓜ *Temple.*

Comptoir des Cotonniers. Comfortable, affordable, au courant clothes make this chain popular. Its reputation is built on smart, wearable styles that stress ease over fussiness. Separates in natural fibers—cotton, silk, and cashmere blends—can be light and breezy or cozy and warm, but they are always soft, flattering, and in a range of beautiful colors. ⊠ *33 rue des Francs-Bourgeois, 4e, Marais* ☎ *01–42–76–95–33* ⊕ *www. comptoirdescotonniers.com* Ⓜ *St-Paul.*

COS. COS—which stands for Collection of Style—is the H&M group's answer to fashion sophisticates, who flock here in droves for high-concept, minimalist designs with serious attention to quality tailoring and fabrics at a reasonable price. Classic accessories and shoes look more expensive than they are. ⊠ *4 rue des Rosiers, 4e, Marais* ☎ *01–44–54– 37–70* ⊕ *www.cosstores.com* Ⓜ *St-Paul.*

Free 'P' Star. Don't let the chaos at Free 'P' Star discourage you—there's gold in them there bins. Determined seekers on a budget can reap heady rewards, at least according to the young hipsters who flock here for anything from a floor-sweeping peasant skirt to a cropped chinchilla cape. A second Marais branch—at 61 rue de la Verrerie—is equally stuffed to the gills. Happy hunting! ⊠ *8 rue Ste-Croix de la Bretonnerie, 4e, Marais* ☎ *01–42–76–03–72* ⊕ *www.freepstar.com* Ⓜ *Hôtel de Ville.*

FrenchTrotters. The flagship store features an understated collection of contemporary French-made classic clothes and accessories for men and women that emphasize quality fabrics, style, and cut over trendiness. You'll also find a handpicked collection of exclusive collaborations with cutting-edge French brands (like sleek leather-and-suede booties by Avril Gau for FrenchTrotters), as well as FrenchTrotters' namesake label, and a limited selection of housewares for chic Parisian apartments. ⊠ *128 rue Vieille du Temple, 3e, Marais* ☎ *01–44–61–00–14* ⊕ *www.frenchtrotters.fr* Ⓜ *St-Sébastien–Froissart, Filles du Calvaire.*

L'Eclaireur. This Rue de Sevigné boutique is Paris's touchstone for edgy, up-to-the-second styles. L'Eclaireur's knack for uncovering new talent and championing established visionaries is legendary—no surprise after 30 years in the business. Hard-to-find geniuses, like leather wizard Isaac Sellam and British prodigy Paul Harnden, cohabit with luxe labels such as Ann Demeulemeester, Haider Ackermann, and Lanvin. ⊠ *40 rue de Sevigné, 3e, Marais* ☎ *01–48–87–10–22* ⊕ *www.leclaireur. com* Ⓜ *St-Paul.*

La Jolie Garde-Robe. Could that minutely pleated, full-length black organdy gown prominently displayed front and center really be a genuine, circa-1955 Madame Grès couture gown? Yes! And a steal at $2,000. There's plenty more to tempt you at this pretty boutique, specializing in ready-to-wear and designer styles from the '30s to the '80s. While the collection isn't huge, it's chosen with a connoisseur's eye. ⊠ *15 rue Commines, 3e, Marais* ☎ *01–42–72–13–90* Ⓜ *Filles du Calvaire.*

16

Majestic Filatures. Wearing a Majestic cashmere-cotton-blend T-shirt, dress, cardigan, or blazer is like spending the day cocooned in your favorite jammies. Fans have been known to buy five pairs of the silky-soft leggings in one go, just to be sure never to run out. The fact that you'll look totally stylish is just gilding the lily. ⊠ *7 rue des Francs Bourgeois, 4e, Marais* ☎ *01–57–40–62–34* ⊕ *www.majesticfilatures. com* Ⓜ *St-Paul.*

Paul & Joe. The brainchild of designer Sophie Albou, Paul & Joe is known for its eclectic, girlish blend of modern trends. There's a retro feel to the diaphanous blouses, A-line jackets with matching short shorts, and swingy felt coats. In summer, she'll mix in a little hippie chic. The men's line, featuring slim, youthful designs, has steadily grown in popularity; and a secondary line, Paul & Joe Sister, has a slouchy, casual edge that attracts a younger clientele. There are eight boutiques across the city. ⊠ *58 rue Vieille du Temple, 3e, Marais* ☎ *01–42–72–42–06* ⊕ *www.paulandjoe.com* Ⓜ *St-Paul.*

Paule Ka. Paule Ka has that movie-star glamour down pat: for daytime, perfectly cut silk shirtdresses with matching coats; for evening, gemstone-studded gowns and furs. Both Hepburns (Audrey and Katherine) could have made this their second home. ⊠ *20 rue Malher, 4e, Marais* ☎ *01–40–29–96–03* ⊕ *pauleka.com* Ⓜ *St-Paul.*

Pretty Box. The owners of Pretty Box have scoured Europe for unique pieces from the '20s through the '80s. Women love the superstylish belts, shoes, and bags—many in reptile—sold here for a fraction of what they'd cost new, along with an eccentric selection of cool separates and Betty Page–era lingerie. The men's collection includes vintage French military coats, sharkskin suits, and a gaggle of riotously patterned shirts. ⊠ *46 rue de Saintonge, 3e, Marais* ☎ *01–48–04–81–71* Ⓜ *St-Sébastien–Froissart.*

Samy Chalon. The inspired shapes and colors at Samy Chalon bring handknits into the 21st century. Updates on the classics are never bulky and ever flattering. Come for form-fitting cashmeres, long mohair wrap coats in deep crimson or indigo, along with light-as-air skirts, and summer dresses made from vintage designer scarves. ⊠ *24 rue Charlot, 3e, Marais* ☎ *01–44–59–39–16* ⊕ *samy-chalon.lexception.com* Ⓜ *Filles du Calvaire.*

Studio W. If you're nostalgic for the days of Studio 54, sashay over to Studio W, where a rare Loris Azzaro gold-chain top or a plunging Guy Laroche beaded couture dress in crimson mousseline has Liza and Bianca written all over them. With plenty of jewelry, shoes, bags, and even gloves to match, this elegant boutique is a must-see for fashion divas who don't mind spending a little more for sublimity. ⊠ *21 rue du Pont aux Choux, 3e, Marais* ☎ *01–44–78–05–02* Ⓜ *St.-Sébastien–Froissart.*

Swildens. Swildens pioneered the haut Marais and has since gained an ardent following of street-smart twenty- and thirtysomethings who insist as much on comfort as they do on cool. Slouchy separates in natural fibers and fetching colors are punctuated by pieces in leather and shearling, along with belted cardigans and long, drapey sweaters that can be worn almost year-round. The clothes accomplish that rare feat of being both of-the-moment and timeless. ✉ *22 rue de Poitou, 3e, Marais* ☎ *01–42–71–19–12* ⊕ *www.swildens.fr* Ⓜ *St-Sébastien–Froissart.*

Vintage Clothing Paris. It's worth a detour to the Marais's outer limits to visit Vintage Clothing Paris, where the racks read like an A-list of designer greats—Yves Saint Laurent, Hermès, Balmain, Valentino, Lagerfeld, and Mugler, just to name a few. Brigitte Petit's minimalist shop is the fashion insider's go-to spot for rare pieces that stand out in a crowd, like a circa-1985 Alaïa suede skirt with peekaboo grommets and a jaunty Yves Saint Laurent Epoch Russe hooded cape. ✉ *10 rue de Crussol, 11e, Marais* ☎ *06–03–00–64–78* ⊕ *www.vintageclothingparis. com* Ⓜ *Filles du Calvaire, Oberkampf.*

Zadig & Voltaire. Zadig & Voltaire rocks the young fashionistas by offering street wear at its best: racy camisoles, cashmere sweaters in gorgeous colors, cropped leather jackets, and form-fitting pants to cosset those tiny French derrieres. Branches abound in every chic corner of Paris. ✉ *42 rue des Francs Bourgeois, 3e, Marais* ☎ *01–44–54–00–60* ⊕ *www. zadig-et-voltaire.com* Ⓜ *St-Paul.*

FOOD AND TREATS

Izraël. This place isn't called the "*épicerie du monde*" for nothing. Izraël is a one-stop shop for any spice under the sun, plus those hard-to-find items you'd otherwise spend days tracking down. Bins overflowing with every variety of candied fruit, nuts, beans, olives, pickles, and preserved fish give this tiny shop the air of an exotic bazaar. You'll also find all manner of canned goods, candies, rare spirits, and baking necessities. ✉ *30 rue François Miron, 4e, Marais* ☎ *01–42–72–66–23* Ⓜ *St-Paul.*

Jacques Genin. Genin offers the essence of great chocolate: not too sweet, with handpicked seasonal ingredients for the velvety ganaches. The tea salon is a great spot to sample one of Genin's masterful takes on classic French pastries and a voluptuous *chocolat chaud.* ✉ *133 rue de Turenne, 3e, Marais* ☎ *01–45–77–29–01* ⊕ *jacquesgenin.fr* Ⓜ *Filles du Calvaire, Oberkampf.*

Le Palais des Thés. White tea, green tea, black tea, tea from China, Japan, Indonesia, South America, and more: you can expect a comprehensive tea experience here. Try one of the flavored varieties such as Hammam, a traditional Turkish recipe with date pulp, orange flower, rose, and red berries. ✉ *64 rue Vieille du Temple, 3e, Marais* ☎ *01–48–87–80–60* ⊕ *www.palaisdesthes.com* Ⓜ *St-Paul.*

Mariage Frères. Mariage Frères, with its colonial *charme* and wooden counters, has 100-plus years of tea purveying behind it. Choose from more than 450 blends from 32 countries, not to mention teapots, teacups, books, and tea-flavor biscuits and candies. High tea and light lunches are served here and at several other Paris locations. ✉ *30 rue du Bourg-Tibourg, 4e, Marais* ☎ *01–42–72–28–11* ⊕ *www.mariagefreres. com* Ⓜ *Hôtel de Ville.*

Méert. The first Paris offshoot of the famous patisserie and tea salon in Lille (one of France's oldest) specializes in the *gauffre,* a delicate waffle handmade in the original 19th-century molds and wrapped in gilt-paper packages. Native to Belgium and northern France, Méert's version is

16

treasured for its light cream center perfumed with Madagascar vanilla. There are also chocolates, pastries, and flavored *guimauves*, the airy French marshmallows. ⊠ *16 rue Elzévir, 3e, Marais* ☎ *01–49–96–56–90* ⊕ *www.meert.fr* Ⓜ *St-Paul.*

HOME DECOR

Kitchen Bazaar. This shop gleams with an astonishing array of culinary essentials for the novice and professional. Don't be surprised if you're struck by the urge to replace every utensil in your kitchen with these cool, contemporary designs. ⊠ *4 rue de Bretagne, 3e, Marais* ☎ *01–44–78–97–04* ⊕ *www.kitchenbazaar.fr* Ⓜ *Filles du Calvaire.*

Le Monde Sauvage. Le Monde Sauvage is a must-visit for home accessories. Expect reversible silk bedspreads in rich colors, velvet throws, hand-quilted bed linens, silk floor cushions, colorful rugs, and the best selection of hand-embroidered curtains in silk, cotton, linen, or velvet. ⊠ *21 rue Sévigné, 4e, Marais* ☎ *01–44–61–02–61* ⊕ *www.lemondesauvage.com* Ⓜ *St-Paul.*

Muji. *Kanketsu* (simplicity) is the guiding philosophy at Muji, and the resulting streamlined designs are all the rage in Europe. Must-haves include a collection of mini-necessities—travel essentials, wee office gizmos, purse-size accoutrements, plus the best notebooks and pens around. They're so useful and adorable you'll want them all. ⊠ *47 rue des Francs Bourgeois, 4e, Marais* ☎ *01–49–96–41–41* ⊕ *www.muji.eu* Ⓜ *St-Paul.*

Sentou. Sentou knocked the Parisian world over the head with its fresh designs. Avant-garde furniture, rugs, and a variety of home accessories line the cool showroom. Look for the April Vase (old test tubes linked together to form different shapes) or the oblong suspended crystal vases and arty tableware. ⊠ *29 rue Francois Miron, 4e, Marais* ☎ *01–42–78–50–60* ⊕ *www.sentou.fr* Ⓜ *St-Paul.*

Van der Straeten. Paris designer Hervé van der Straeten started out creating jewelry for Saint Laurent and Lacroix, designed a perfume bottle for Christian Dior, and then moved on to making rather baroque and often wacky furniture. In his loft gallery-cum-showroom, furniture, lighting, jewelry, and startling mirrors are on display. ⊠ *11 rue Ferdinand Duval, 4e, Marais* ☎ *01–42–78–99–99* ⊕ *www.vanderstraeten.fr* Ⓜ *St-Paul.*

JEWELRY AND ACCESSORIES

Hod. This understated boutique saves the razzle-dazzle for its wares—an outstanding selection of contemporary pieces by Europe's finest young designers. Look for Ileana Makri's delicately bejeweled cat's eye, snake, or winsome feathers; Honorine Jewel's finely wrought golden insect rings, necklaces, and bracelets; and Venessa Arizaga's protection necklaces with a tiny leather purse for your secret lucky charms. Hod has styles for all tastes and budgets. ⊠ *104 rue Vieille du Temple, 3e, Marais* ☎ *09–53–15–83–34* ⊕ *hod-boutique.com* Ⓜ *Filles du Calvaire.*

SHOES, HANDBAGS, AND LEATHER GOODS

K. Jacques. K. Jacques has shod everyone from Brigitte Bardot to Drew Barrymore. The famous St-Tropez–based maker of strappy leather-soled flats has migrated to the big time while still keeping designs classic and comfortable. From gladiator style to lightweight cork platforms, metallics to neutrals, these are perennial favorites. ⊠ *16 rue Pavée, 4e, Marais* ☏ *01–40–27–03–57* ⊕ *www.kjacques.fr* Ⓜ *St-Paul.*

Miguel Lobato. This is a sweet little boutique with accessories for the woman who wants it all. Beautiful high heels by Lanvin, Chloé, and Pierre Hardy and fabulous bags by Martin Margiela, Jil Sander, and Proenza Schouler are just a start. ⊠ *6 rue Malher, 4e, Marais* ☏ *01–48–87–68–14* ⊕ *www.lobato-paris.com* Ⓜ *St-Paul.*

EASTERN PARIS

"Off the beaten track" aptly describes the up-and-coming neighborhoods of eastern Paris, which are dotted with galleries, vintage shops, and funky boutiques. Low-key cool reigns here, so you won't encounter the high-wattage, high-profile designers that vie for attention elsewhere. Instead, local hipster shops ensure a few choice finds that will be seen on you and only you.

BASTILLE

CLOTHING

Isabel Marant. This rising design star is a honeypot of bohemian rock-star style. Her separates skim the body without constricting: layered miniskirts, loose peekaboo sweaters ready to slip from a shoulder, and super fox-fur jackets in lurid colors. Look for the secondary line, Étoile, for a less expensive take. ⊠ *16 rue de Charonne, 11e, Bastille* ☏ *01–49–29–71–55* ⊕ *www.isabelmarant.com* Ⓜ *Ledru-Rollin.*

HOME DECOR

Fodor'sChoice ★ **Borgo delle Tovaglie.** This Naples-based label's soaring new concept store eschews sterile minimalism for an opulence well suited to its lavish Italian linen sheets and pillows. Crafted by hand in yummy colors that change with the seasons, they can be paired with a chic array of dishes, candles, and other treasures for the home. Linger at the stylish bistro—a neighborhood hipster hangout—for an espresso, a glass of wine, or a plate of Italian charcuterie. ⊠ *4 rue du Grand Prieuré, 11e, Oberkampf* ☏ *09–82–33–64–81* ⊕ *www.borgodelletovaglie.com* Ⓜ *Oberkampf.*

Fodor'sChoice ★ **Rose et Marius.** Luxurious perfumed candles from Rose et Marius evoke the romance of Provence. Choose from 40 refillable porcelain tumblers, tipped in real gold or platinum, for a glamorous accent to any room of the house. The fragrances—rose wine, fig tree, and jasmine among them—are also found in a delicious range of soaps, teas, and eaux de toilette. ⊠ *10-12 rue de Charonne, 11e, Bastille* ☏ *09–51–28–48–19* ⊕ *www.roseetmarius.com* Ⓜ *Bastille, Charonne.*

JEWELRY AND ACCESSORIES

Fodor'sChoice ★ **Yves Gratas.** With a knack for pairing gems of varying sizes, brilliance, and texture, Yves Gratas allows each stone to influence the design. Whether it's a spectacular necklace of sapphire beads to be worn long or doubled, or a simple agate sphere tipped in gold and dangling like a tiny planet, these stellar jewels feel like one organic whole. If you're in the Marais, this shop (located just across the "border" in the Oberkampf neighborhood) deserves a detour. ⊠ *9 rue Oberkampf, 11e, Oberkampf* ☏ *01–49–29–00–53* ⊕ *yvesgratas.com* Ⓜ *Filles du Calvaire, Oberkampf.*

16

MARKETS

Marché Bastille. Paris's largest market is as much an event as a place to shop. Blocks of specialized stalls—including ones devoted to rare wines, regional cheeses, game, seafood, and flowers—cater to scores of Parisian chefs and epicures. It's open Thursday and Sunday 7–3. ⊠ *Bd. Richard Lenoir, between Rues Amelot and St-Sabin, 11e, Bastille* Ⓜ *Ledru-Rollin.*

Marché d'Aligre. Arguably the most authentic local market, Marché d'Aligre is open 7:30–1:30 Tuesday through Friday, and 7:30–2:30 on weekends. Don't miss the covered hall on Place d'Aligre, where you can stop by a unique olive-oil boutique for bulk and prebottled oils from top producers. ⊠ *Pl. d'Aligre, 12e, Bastille* Ⓜ *Ledru-Rollin, Bastille.*

CANAL ST-MARTIN
BOOKS AND STATIONERY

Fodor'sChoice
★

Artazart. The best design bookstore in France carries tomes on everything from architecture to tattoo art: there are sections dedicated to photography, fashion, graphic art, typography, illustration, package design, color, and more. ⊠ *83 quai de Valmy, 10e, Canal St-Martin* ☎ *01–40–40–24–00* ⊕ *www.artazart.com* Ⓜ *République.*

CLOTHING

Antoine & Lili. This bright, fuchsia-colored store is packed with an international assortment of eclectic objects and items from Antoine & Lili's own clothing line. There's an ethnic-rummage-sale feel, with old Asian posters, small lanterns, and basket upon basket of inexpensive doodads, baubles, and trinkets for sale. The clothing itself has simple lines, and there are always plenty of raw-silk pieces to pick from. ⊠ *95 quai de Valmy, 10e, Canal St-Martin* ☎ *01–40–37–41–55* ⊕ *www.antoineetlili. com* Ⓜ *Jacques-Bonsergent.*

FAMILY
Fodor'sChoice
★

Centre Commercial. This store's A-list fashion credentials come with a big bonus—everything here is ethically and ecologically sourced. Peruse racks of men's and women's wear from handpicked European and U.S. labels; then head to the stellar shoe department to complete your look. Beneath glass skylights as clear as your conscience, you'll also find a fine selection of natural candles, leather goods, and jewelry. The kids' store just around the corner (22 rue Yves Toudic) is one of the city's best, with toys, decor, and color-coordinated togs that express canal-side cool. ⊠ *2 rue de Marseille, 10e, Canal St-Martin* ☎ *01–42–02–26–08* ⊕ *www.centrecommercial.cc* Ⓜ *Jacques Bonsergent.*

Des Petits Hauts. Des Petits Hauts charmed its way into the local fashion idiom with chic yet beguilingly feminine styles. Fabrics are soft, and styles are casual with a tiny golden star sewn into each garment for good luck. ⊠ *21 rue Beaurepaire, 10e, Canal St-Martin* ☎ *01–75–44–05–83* ⊕ *www.despetitshauts.com* Ⓜ *République.*

Liza Korn. Liza Korn is that rare designer who seems to do it all and do it well. Whether it's rock 'n' roll (grommeted leather baseball or biker jackets), asymmetrical (slant-necked minidresses), or classic (tailored blazers over stovepipe jeans), she raises the bar on eclecticism. Korn's bespoke service optimizes the designer's creativity for a truly one-off look made to your measurements and desires—wedding dresses, too! ⊠ *19 rue Beaurepaire, 10e, Canal St-Martin* ☎ *01–42–01–36–02* ⊕ *www.liza-korn.com* Ⓜ *République.*

HOME DECOR

Idé Co. Little items for the home in a riot of colors are sold at Idé Co. But you'll also find fabulous rubber jewelry and funky stuff for kids big and small. ⊠ *19 rue Beaurepaire, 10e, Canal St-Martin* ☎ *01–42–01–00–11* ⊕ *www.idecoparis.com* Ⓜ *République.*

La Trésorerie. No place outfits chic Canal St-Martin lofts better than this soaring eco-friendly boutique. Housed in a historic treasury, it assembles the crème de la crème of French and European kitchen and dining ware, linens, bath products, small furnishings, hardware, lighting, paint, and more. Local hipsters come to La Trésorerie's bright, Scandinavian-style café for all things fresh, organic, and yummy. ⊠ *11 rue du Château d'Eau, 10e, Canal St-Martin* ☎ *01–40–40–20–46* ⊕ *la-tresorerie.fr* Ⓜ *Jacques Bonsergent.*

JEWELRY AND ACCESSORIES

Médecine Douce. Sculptural pieces that combine leather, suede, rhinestones, agate, or resin with whimsical themes can be found at Médecine Douce. The wildly popular lariat necklace can be looped and dangled according to your mood du jour. ⊠ *10 rue de Marseille, 10e, Canal St-Martin* ☎ *01–82–83–11–53* ⊕ *www.bijouxmedecinedouce.com* Ⓜ *République.*

Viveka Bergström. Viveka Bergström leads the ranks of designers who thumb their noses at the pretensions of traditional costume jewelry—these baubles just want to have fun! Whether it's a bracelet of gigantic rhinestones, a ring of fluorescent pink resin, or a pair of floating angel wings on a necklace, each piece has an acute sense of style while not taking itself too seriously. ⊠ *23 rue de la Grange aux Belles, 10e, Canal St-Martin* ☎ *01–40–03–04–92* ⊕ *viveka-bergstrom.blogspot.fr* Ⓜ *République.*

SHOES, HANDBAGS, AND LEATHER GOODS

Jamin Puech Inventaire. These are last season's models, but no one will guess; savings are 30% to 60%. ⊠ *61 rue d'Hauteville, 10e, Canal St-Martin* ☎ *01–40–22–08–32* ⊕ *www.jamin-puech.com* Ⓜ *Poisonnière.*

LATIN QUARTER

Considering this fabled *quartier* is home to the Sorbonne and historically one of Paris's intellectual-bohemian centers, it's not surprising that it has a rich selection of bookstores—not just for students but for collectors and bargain hunters, too. Gastronomes, meanwhile, flock in to shop at the outstanding charcuteries and fromageries along Rue Mouffetard.

BOOKS AND STATIONERY

Abbey Bookshop. Paris's Canadian bookstore has books on Canadian history as well as new and secondhand Québécois and English-language novels. The Canadian Club of Paris also organizes regular poetry readings and literary conferences here. ⊠ *29 rue de la Parcheminerie, 5e,*

16

Latin Quarter ☎ *01–46–33–16–24* ⊕ *www.abbeybookshop.wordpress. com* Ⓜ *Cluny–La Sorbonne.*

Shakespeare & Company. This sentimental Rive Gauche favorite is named after the bookstore whose American owner, Sylvia Beach, first published James Joyce's *Ulysses.* Nowadays it specializes in expat literature. Although the eccentric and beloved owner, George Whitman, passed away in 2011, his daughter Sylvia has taken up the torch. You can still count on a couple of characters lurking in the stacks, a sometimes spacey staff, the latest titles from British presses, and hidden second-hand treasures in the odd corners and crannies. Check the website for readings and workshops throughout the week. ⊠ *37 rue de la Bûcherie, 5e, Latin Quarter* ☎ *01–43–25–40–93* ⊕ *shakespeareandcompany.com* Ⓜ *St-Michel.*

HOME DECOR

Avant-Scène. Head to Avant-Scène for original, poetic furniture. Owner Elisabeth Delacarte commissions limited-edition pieces from artists like Mark Brazier-Jones, Franck Evennou, Elizabeth Garouste, and Hubert Le Gall. ⊠ *4 pl. de l'Odéon, 6e, Latin Quarter* ☎ *01–46–33–12–40* ⊕ *www.avantscene.fr* Ⓜ *Odéon.*

JEWELRY AND ACCESSORIES

Peggy Kingg. The minimalist accessories designed by former architect Peggy Huynh Kinh include understated totes, shoulder bags, wallets, and belts in the highest-quality leather, as well as a line of picnic bags and elegant office-oriented pieces. Look for them at her streamlined—and recently rebranded—Peggy Kingg boutique. ⊠ *9 rue Coëtlogon, 6e, Latin Quarter* ☎ *01–42–84–83–83* ⊕ *www.peggykingg.com* Ⓜ *St-Sulpice.*

MARKETS

Rue Mouffetard. This colorful market street near the Jardin des Plantes reflects its multicultural neighborhood: vibrant, with a laid-back feel that still smacks of old Paris. It's best on weekends. ⊠ *5e, Latin Quarter* Ⓜ *Monge.*

ST-GERMAIN-DES-PRÉS

Ever since Yves Saint Laurent arrived in the 1960s, the Rive Gauche has been synonymous with iconoclastic style. Trendsetting stores line a jumble of streets in the 6e arrondissement, and exciting boutiques await between Place de l'Odéon and Église St-Sulpice. In the 7e arrondissement, don't miss Rue du Bac and that jewel of a department store, Le Bon Marché.

ANTIQUES AND COLLECTIBLES

Fodor'sChoice ★ **Carré Rive Gauche.** Carré Rive Gauche is where you'll unearth museum-quality pieces. Head to the streets between Rue du Bac, Rue de l'Université, Rue de Lille, and Rue des Sts-Pères to find more than 100 associated shops, marked with a small, blue square banner on their storefronts. ⊠ *Between St-Germain-des-Prés and Musée d'Orsay, 6e, St-Germain-des-Prés* ⊕ *www.carrerivegauche.com* Ⓜ *St-Germain-des-Prés, Rue du Bac.*

FAMILY

Fodor'sChoice

★

Deyrolle. This fascinating 19th-century taxidermist has long been a stop for curiosity seekers. A 2008 fire destroyed what was left of the original shop, but it has been lavishly restored and remains a cabinet of curiosities par excellence. Create your own box of butterflies or metallic beetles from scores of bug-filled drawers or just enjoy the menagerie that includes stuffed zebras, monkeys, lions, bears, and more. Also in stock: collectible shells, corals, and crustaceans, plus a generous library of books and posters that once graced every French schoolroom. There is a line of cool wallpaper murals, too. ⊠ *46 rue du Bac, 7e, St-Germain-des-Prés* ☎ *01–42–22–30–07* ⊕ *www.deyrolle.com* Ⓜ *Rue du Bac.*

BEAUTY

Fodor'sChoice

★

Buly 1803. Although it only opened in 2014, you can be forgiven for thinking Buly 1803 is an antique apothecary—all those jars overflowing with exotic herbs, powders, and elixirs are used to re-create 200-year-old recipes for its skin-care line. The all-natural hand, body, and face products are organic, beautifully packaged, and impossibly chic. ⊠ *6 rue Bonaparte, 6e, St-Germain-des-Prés* ☎ *01–43–29–02–50* ⊕ *www. buly1803.com* Ⓜ *St-Germain-des-Prés.*

Editions de Parfums Frédéric Malle. This perfumerie is based on a simple concept: take the nine most famous noses in France and have them edit singular perfumes. The result? Exceptional, highly concentrated fragrances. Le Parfum de Thérèse, for example, was created by famous Dior nose Edmond Roudnitska for his wife. Monsieur Malle has devised high-tech ways to keep each smelling session unadulterated. At the Rue de Grenelle store, individual scents are released in glass columns—just stick your head in and sniff. A second boutique at 140 avenue Victor Hugo has a glass-fronted "wall of scents," which mists the air with a selected fragrance at the push of a button. ⊠ *37 rue de Grenelle, 7e, St-Germain-des-Prés* ☎ *01–42–22–76–40* ⊕ *www.fredericmalle.com* Ⓜ *Rue du Bac.*

Shu Uemura. Shu Uemura has enhanced those whose faces are their fortune for decades. Models swear by the cleansing oil; free samples are proffered. A huge range of colors, every makeup brush imaginable, and the no-pinch eyelash curler keep fans coming back. ⊠ *176 bd. St-Germain, 6e, St-Germain-des-Prés* ☎ *01–45–48–02–55* ⊕ *www. shuuemura.fr* Ⓜ *St-Germain-des-Prés.*

BOOKS AND STATIONERY

Taschen. Perfect for night owls, Taschen is open until midnight on Friday and Saturday. The Starck-designed shelves and desks hold glam titles on photography, fine art, design, fashion, and fetishes. ⊠ *2 rue de Buci, 6e, St-Germain-des-Prés* ☎ *01–40–51–79–22* ⊕ *www.taschen. com* Ⓜ *Mabillon.*

CHILDREN'S CLOTHING

FAMILY

Pom d'Api. Pom d'Api lines up footwear for babies and preteens in quality leathers and vivid colors. Expect well-made, eye-catching fashion— bright fuchsia sneakers and leopard suede boots, as well as classic Mary Janes in shades of silver, pink, and gold. There are also utility boots for boys and sturdy rain gear. ⊠ *28 rue du Four, 6e, St-Germain-des-Prés* ☎ *01–45–48–39–31* ⊕ *www.pomdapi.fr* Ⓜ *St-Germain-des-Prés.*

16

CLOTHING

Antik Batik. It's hard to resist Antik Batik's wonderful line of ethnically inspired clothes. There are rows of beaded and sequined dresses, Chinese silk tunics, short fur jackets and fur-lined anoraks, flowing organza separates, and some of Paris's most popular sandals and giant scarves. ✉ *26 rue St-Sulpice, 6e, St-Germain-des-Prés* ☎ *01–44–07–68– 53* ⊕ *www.antikbatik.fr* Ⓜ *Odéon, Marais.*

A.P.C. A.P.C. may be antiflash and minimal, but a knowing eye can always pick out its jeans in a crowd. The clothes here are rigorously well made and worth the investment in lasting style. Prime wardrobe pieces include dark indigo and black denim, zip-up cardigans, peacoats, and streamlined ankle boots. ✉ *38 rue Madame, 6e, St-Germain-des-Prés* ☎ *01–42–22–12–77* ⊕ *www.apc.fr* Ⓜ *St-Sulpice.*

Carven. Daringly original designs that are sexy yet wearable account for Carven's steady rise into the fashion stratosphere. Artistic director Guillame Henry's departure in 2014 opened the door to the collaborative efforts of Alexis Martial and Adrien Caillaudaud, who add their own fresh take to the label's meticulous tailoring and up-to-the-minute silhouettes. ✉ *34 rue St-Sulpice, St-Germain-des-Prés* ☎ *09–60–45–47–04* ⊕ *www.carven.com* Ⓜ *St-Sulpice, Odéon.*

Fodor's Choice ★ **Inès de la Fressange.** Paris's number one style icon now brings her legendary chic to an eponymous boutique in the heart of St-Germain-des-Prés. Along with her limited-edition fashions, de la Fressange introduces a line of wearable shoes (including sexy over-the-knee boots and dainty stilettos), plus handbags, accessories, and lingerie. You'll also discover long tables loaded with handpicked housewares and stationery from the tastemaker's favorite French brands. ✉ *24 rue de Grenelle, 7e, St-Germain-des-Prés* ☎ *01–45–48–19–06* ⊕ *www.inesdelafressange.fr* Ⓜ *St-Sulpice, Sèvres-Babylone.*

Karl Lagerfeld. The titular designer's own chiseled profile is a key design element in his St-Germain flagship store. Inside, look for two recently launched lines: Lagerfeld, featuring "everyday" clothes for the urban man, and Karl Lagerfeld Paris (KLP), a ready-to-wear collection for men and women. The latter is aimed at fashion-conscious twenty- and thirtysomethings who want to strut their stuff (think body-slimming jackets, lace-inset tops, and skin-tight jeans, mostly in black, white, and gray). The store also stocks eyewear, accessories, bags, shoes, fragrances, and—you guessed it—Lagerfeld's signature fingerless leather gloves. ✉ *194 bd. St-Germain, 7e, St-Germain-des-Prés* ☎ *01–42–22– 74–99* ⊕ *www.karl.com* Ⓜ *Rue du Bac.*

Maje Stock. This stock store is a prized listing in every chic Parisian's little black book. Shimmy into a pair of leather jeans, don a sheer silk blouse, and top off your outfit with a belted cashmere jacket. Back home, no one will know they're from last season. ✉ *9 rue du Cherche-Midi, 6e, St-Germain-des-Prés* ☎ *01–45–44–21–20* ⊕ *fr.maje.com* Ⓜ *St-Sulpice.*

Sonia Rykiel. Sonia Rykiel has been designing insouciant knitwear since the 1960s. Sweaters drape and cling by turns and her color combinations (she's partial to stripes) are lovely. Opulent silks, furs, accessories dotted with rhinestones, and soft leather bags punctuate the collection.

Sonia by Sonia Rykiel—a smart and playful secondary line that targets a slightly younger crowd—is sold at the 4 rue de Grenelle boutique. ⊠ *175 bd. St-Germain, 6e, St-Germain-des-Prés* ☎ *01–49–54–60–60* ⊕ *www.soniarykiel.com* Ⓜ *St-Germain-des-Prés.*

DEPARTMENT STORES

Fodor's Choice
★

Le Bon Marché. Founded in 1852, Le Bon Marché has emerged as the city's chicest department store. Long a hunting ground for linens and other home items, it has been undergoing a multimillion-euro facelift that brings fashion to the fore. The fact that this department store isn't nearly as crowded as those near the Opéra is an added bonus. On the ground floor of the main building, look for makeup, perfume, and accessories; this is where celebs duck in for essentials while everyone pretends not to notice. On the floor above, you can do laps through labels chichi (Givenchy, Stella McCartney, Lanvin) and überhip (Martin Margiela, Comme des Garçons, Ann Demeulemeester). The next floor up is home to streetwise designers, edgy secondary lines, plus French favorites, including Athé by Vanessa Bruno, Zadig & Voltaire, Tsumori Chisato, Isabel Marant's Étoile, and Majestic. Under the newly restored glass ceiling, the gleaming Le Soulier shoe department assembles the crème de la crème of European shoes. Meanwhile, the refurbished menswear department, Balthazar, has consumed the entire basement level. Across the street, the spanking new home store in the sister building is a great place to stock up on French linens, porcelain, cookware, and luggage, or just relax over tea or a gourmet lunch in the soaring atrium restaurant. Before leaving, be sure to visit the spectacularly renovated La Grande Épicerie and (wine shop): it's the haute couture of grocery stores. Artisanal jams, olive oils, and much more make great gifts, and the luscious pastries, fruit, and huge selection of prepared foods beg to be chosen for a snack. ⊠ *24 rue de Sèvres, 7e, St-Germain-des-Prés* ☎ *01–44–39–80–00* ⊕ *www.lebonmarche.com* Ⓜ *Sèvres-Babylone.*

FOOD AND TREATS

Christian Constant. Christian Constant is deservedly praised for his exquisite ganaches, perfumed with jasmine, ylang-ylang, or verveine. ⊠ *37 rue d'Assas, 6e, St-Germain-des-Prés* ☎ *01–53–63–15–15* ⊕ *www. christianconstant.fr* Ⓜ *St-Placide.*

Debauve & Gallais. The two former chemists who founded Debauve & Gallais in 1800 became the royal chocolate purveyors and were famed for their "health chocolates," made with almond milk. Test the benefits yourself with ganache, truffles, or *pistols* (flavored dark-chocolate disks). ⊠ *30 rue des Sts-Pères, 7e, St-Germain-des-Prés* ☎ *01–45–48–54–67* ⊕ *debauve-et-gallais.fr* Ⓜ *St-Germain-des-Prés.*

Henri Le Roux. The originator of the renowned *caramel au beurre salé*, Henri Le Roux pairs a Breton pedigree with Japanese flair. Brilliant confections result. You can also satisfy your sweet tooth in stores at 52 rue St-Dominique (7e) and 24 rue des Martyrs (9e). ⊠ *1 rue de Bourbon le Château, 6e, St-Germain-des-Prés* ☎ *01–82–28–49–80* ⊕ *www. chocolatleroux.com* Ⓜ *St-Germain-des-Prés.*

Jean-Charles Rouchoux. Rouchoux makes three superb collections of artisanal chocolates: the Ephemeral, with fresh fruit; Made-to-Measure,

The interior of the Galeries Lafayette department store—especially the ceiling—almost outshines the fabulous merchandise.

with animals and figurines; and the Permanent Collection of everyday favorites. ✉ *16 rue d'Assas, 6e, St-Germain-des-Prés* ☎ *01–42–84–29–45* ⊕ *www.jcrochoux.com* Ⓜ *Rennes.*

La Maison du Chocolat. This is chocolate's gold standard. The silky ganaches are renowned for subtlety and flavor. See the website for a full list of locations. ✉ *19 rue de Sèvre, 6e, St-Germain-des-Prés* ☎ *01–45–44–20–40* ⊕ *www.lamaisonduchocolat.fr* Ⓜ *Sèvres-Babylone.*

Patrick Roger. Paris's bad-boy chocolatier likes to shock with provocative shapes and wicked humor. Everything is sinfully good. The Boulevard St-Germain shop is one of six citywide. ✉ *108 bd. St-Germain, 6e, St-Germain-des-Prés* ☎ *01–43–29–38–42* ⊕ *www.patrickroger.com* Ⓜ *Odéon.*

Pierre Hermé. Hermé may be Paris's most renowned pâtissier. Sample the peerless cakes and cookies, or savor the chocolate delights (classic varieties, like the dark-chocolate and orange-rind batons, are perennial favorites). Hermé offers a scrumptious, zesty lemon pound cake pre-boxed and dense enough to survive the trip home. Maybe. There are more than 10 Paris locations. ✉ *72 rue Bonaparte, 6e, St-Germain-des-Prés* ☎ *01–43–54–47–77* ⊕ *www.pierreherme.com* Ⓜ *Odéon.*

Pierre Marcolini. Pierre Marcolini proves it's all in the bean with his specialty *saveurs du monde* collection of Belgian chocolates, made with a single cacao from a single location, such as Madagascar or Ecuador. ✉ *89 rue de Seine, 6e, St-Germain-des-Prés* ☎ *01–44–07–39–07* ⊕ *www.marcolini.com* Ⓜ *Mabillon.*

Richart. How do I love thee? The ways are too numerous to count. At Richart, inspired chocolates dazzle the eye and elevate the palate. In addition to the Boulevard St-Germain boutique, there's another at 27 rue Bonaparte (6e). ⊠ *258 bd. St-Germain, 6e, St-Germain-des-Prés* ☏ *01–45–55–66–00* ⊕ *www.chocolats-richart.com* Ⓜ *St-Germain-des-Prés.*

Tomat's. Tucked into a courtyard, this luxe épicerie carries the full line of Huilerie Artisanale J. Leblanc et Fils oil—15 varieties pressed the old-fashioned way, with a big stone wheel, from olives, hazelnuts, pistachios, or grape seeds. You can also buy aged vinegars, *fleur de sel* (unprocessed sea salt), foie gras, and other regional French delicacies, plus the tools to serve them with. ⊠ *12 rue Jacob, 6e, St-Germain-des-Prés* ☏ *01–44–07–36–58* ⊕ *www.tomats.fr* Ⓜ *Mabillon, St-Germain-des-Prés.*

HOME DECOR

Alexandre Biaggi. Alexandre Biaggi specializes in 20th-century Art Deco and also commissions pieces from such talented designers as Patrick Naggar and Hervé van der Straeten. ⊠ *14 rue de Seine, 6e, St-Germain-des-Prés* ☏ *01–44–07–34–73* ⊕ *alexandrebiaggi.com* Ⓜ *St-Germain-des-Prés.*

Catherine Memmi. This trendsetter in pared-down, tastefully hued housewares also sells lamps, furniture, and home accessories. ⊠ *11 rue St-Sulpice, 6e, St-Germain-des-Prés* ☏ *01–44–07–02–02* ⊕ *www.catherinememmi.com* Ⓜ *St-Sulpice.*

Fodor's Choice ★ **Cire Trudon.** Cire Trudon has illuminated the great palaces and churches of Paris since the 1700s. Nowadays it provides the atmosphere for tony restaurants and exclusive soirées. The all-vegetal, atmospherically scented candles come in elegant black glass, pillars of all sizes, or busts of clients past—like Napoléon and Marie-Antoinette. ⊠ *78 rue de Seine, 6e, St-Germain-des-Prés* ☏ *01–43–26–46–50* ⊕ *www.ciretrudon.com* Ⓜ *Odéon.*

Conran Shop. The brainchild of British entrepreneur Terence Conran, this shop carries expensive contemporary furniture, beautiful bed linens, and items for every other room in the house—all marked by a balance of utility and not-too-sober style. Conran makes even shower curtains fun. ⊠ *117 rue du Bac, 7e, St-Germain-des-Prés* ☏ *01–42–84–10–01* ⊕ *www.conranshop.fr* Ⓜ *Sèvres-Babylone.*

Fodor's Choice ★ **Diptyque.** A Paris mainstay since 1961, Diptyque's flagship shop is famous for its candles, eaux de toilette, and body fragrances in a huge range of sophisticated scents like myrrh, fig tree, wisteria, and quince. They're delightful but not cheap; the candles, for instance, cost nearly $1 per hour of burn time. ⊠ *34 bd. St-Germain, 6e, St-Germain-des-Prés* ☏ *01–43–26–77–44* ⊕ *www.diptyqueparis.fr* Ⓜ *Maubert–Mutualité.*

R&Y Augousti. R&Y Augousti are two Paris-based designers who make furniture and objects for the home from nacre, ostrich, palm wood, and parchment. Also for sale are their hand-tooled leather bags and wallets. ⊠ *103 rue du Bac, 7e, St-Germain-des-Prés* ☏ *01–42–22–22–21* ⊕ *www.augousti.com* Ⓜ *Sèvres-Babylone.*

FAMILY
Fodor's Choice ★ **Zuber.** Have you always wanted to imitate the grand homes of Paris? Here's your chance. Zuber has operated nonstop for more than two centuries as the world's oldest producer of prestige hand-printed

wallpapers, renowned for their magnificent panoramic scenes. Warning: with only one scene produced per year, the wait can be nearly a decade long. Opulent Restoration-era wallpapers (including metallics, silks, velvets, and pressed leather) make modern statements and can be purchased in 32-foot rolls for slightly less than a king's ransom. ⊠ *12 rue des Saints-Pères, 6e, St-Germain-des-Prés* ☏ *01–42–77–95–91* ⊕ *www.zuber.fr* Ⓜ *St-Germain-des-Prés.*

JEWELRY AND ACCESSORIES

Adelline. Entering this jewelry shop is like landing in Ali Baba's cave: each piece is more gorgeous than the last, and the bounty of beautiful shapes and styles satisfies a large range of tastes (and budgets). Cabochon rings can be pebble-size or rock-like, jeweled cuffs sport diamonds in a web of gold, and simple cord-and-gem bracelets cannot fail to make a statement. ⊠ *54 rue Jacob, 6e, St-Germain-des-Prés* ☏ *01–47–03–07–18* ⊕ *www.adelline.com* Ⓜ *St-Germain-des-Prés.*

Agatha. This chain is the perfect place to buy a moderately priced piece of fun jewelry. Agatha's line of earrings, rings, hair accessories, bracelets, necklaces, watches, brooches, and pendants is ultrapopular with Parisians. Styles change quickly, but classics include charm bracelets and fine gold necklaces with whimsical pendants. ⊠ *45 rue Bonaparte, 6e, St-Germain-des-Prés* ☏ *01–46–33–20–00* ⊕ *www. agatha.fr* Ⓜ *St-Germain-des-Prés.*

Alexandra Sojfer. The proprietress of this legendary little store is the queen of walking sticks (the late president François Mitterrand bought his here). Alexandra Sojfer also carries an amazing range of umbrellas, parasols, small leather goods, and other accessories for men and women. ⊠ *218 bd. St-Germain, 7e, St-Germain-des-Prés* ☏ *01–42–22–17–02* ⊕ *www.alexandrasojfer.com* Ⓜ *Rue du Bac.*

Arthus-Bertrand. Dating back to 1803, Arthus-Bertrand has glass showcases full of designer jewelry and numerous objects to celebrate births. ⊠ *54 rue Bonaparte, 6e, St-Germain-des-Prés* ☏ *01–49–54–72–10* ⊕ *www.arthus-bertrand.com* Ⓜ *St-Germain-des-Prés.*

Marie Mercié. Marie Mercié—one of Paris's most fashionable milliners, and one of its last—makes charming hats for every season. Her raffish straw models are masterworks. Husband Anthony Peto, who makes men's headgear, has a store at 56 rue Tiquetonne. ⊠ *23 rue St-Sulpice, 6e, St-Germain-des-Prés* ☏ *01–43–26–45–83* ⊕ *www.mariemercie.com* Ⓜ *Mabillon, St-Sulpice.*

LINGERIE

Fodor'sChoice
★   **Sabbia Rosa.** You could easily walk straight past this discreet, boudoir-like boutique. It is, however, one of the world's finest lingerie stores and the place where actresses Catherine Deneuve and Isabelle Adjani (along with others who might not want to reveal their errand) buy superb French silks. ⊠ *71–73 rue des Sts-Pères, 6e, St-Germain-des-Prés* ☏ *01–45–48–88–37* Ⓜ *St-Germain-des-Prés.*

MARKETS

Boulevard Raspail. The city's major *marché biologique,* or organic market, is on Boulevard Raspail between Rue du Cherche-Midi and Rue de Rennes. Bursting with produce, fish, and eco-friendly products, it's open every Sunday from 9 to 2. The market also operates on Tuesday and Friday, selling nonorganic products from 7 to 2:30. ✉ *6e, St-Germain-des-Prés* Ⓜ *Rennes.*

Rue de Buci. Vendors at this market often tempt you with tastes of their wares: slices of sausage, slivers of peaches. It's closed Sunday afternoon and Monday. ✉ *6e, St-Germain-des-Prés* Ⓜ *Odéon.*

SHOES, HANDBAGS, AND LEATHER GOODS

Fodor's Choice ★ **Avril Gau.** After designing a dozen collections for Chanel, Gau struck out on her own, opening her neo-baroque boutique on the charming Rue des Quatre Vents. Gau takes her inspiration from glamorous French movie icons, dreaming up styles that are elegant and sexy without being trashy. Sleek pumps, wedge booties, ballerina flats, and riding boots (all in the finest quality calf, reptile, and lambskin) are as classy as they come. Bags share the spotlight, with updated riffs on the classics. ✉ *17 rue des Quatre Vents, 6e, St-Germain-des-Prés* ☎ *01–43–29–49–04* ⊕ *www.avrilgau.com* Ⓜ *Odéon.*

Fodor's Choice ★ **Jamin Puech.** Jamin Puech thinks of its bags not just as a necessity, but as jewelry. Nothing's plain Jane here. Beaded bags swing from thin link chains; fringes flutter from dark embossed-leather totes; and small evening purses are covered with shells, oversize sequins, or hand-dyed crochet. The collections fluctuate with the seasons but never fail to be whimsical, imaginative, and highly coveted. ✉ *43 rue Madame, 6e, St-Germain-des-Prés* ☎ *01–45–48–14–85* ⊕ *www.jamin-puech.com* Ⓜ *St-Sulpice.*

Fodor's Choice ★ **Jérôme Dreyfuss.** The newest star in the city's handbag universe has captivated *le tout Paris* with his artsy take on hobo, Birkin, and messenger bags. Unique styles (like the twee-mini) are impossibly cute, and you'll be glad you took out that second mortgage just to tote around a luxe matte-python model. A line of gorgeous, high-heeled footwear is equally chic. ✉ *4 rue Jacob, 6e, St-Germain-des-Prés* ☎ *01–43–54–70–93* ⊕ *www.jerome-dreyfuss.com* Ⓜ *St-Germain-des-Prés.*

Robert Clergerie. Robert Clergerie knows that shoes make the woman. Styles combine visionary design, first-rate craftsmanship, and wearability with rare staying power. Plus, they're still a relative bargain on this side of the Atlantic. ✉ *5 rue du Cherche-Midi, 6e, St-Germain-des-Prés* ☎ *01–45–48–75–47* ⊕ *www.robertclergerie.com* Ⓜ *St-Sulpice.*

Fodor's Choice ★ **Tila March.** Fame came quickly to this ex-fashion editor, whose wildly successful first handbag collection was snatched up by celebs such as Sienna Miller, Kirsten Dunst, and Scarlett Johansson. March uses velvety nubuck in a range of saturated colors—aubergine, olive, brick, taupe, and more—along with sleek matte crocodile to craft everything from large totes (like her handy Daisy bag) to tiny evening bags. With sleekly sophisticated shoes to match, it's not just a boutique—it's a destination. ✉ *24 rue St-Sulpice, 6e, St-Germain-des-Prés* ☎ *01–43–26–69–20* ⊕ *www.tilamarch.com* Ⓜ *Odéon, St-Sulpice.*

Verbreuil. Verbreuil's classic-contemporary handbags are for women whose sense of style transcends any logo. Refined, discrete, and meticulously crafted down to the finest detail, each of the four styles—in calf, crocodile, and shagreen, with luxe variations for evening—will add infinite style and elegance to any outfit. ✉ *4 rue de Fleurus, 6e, St-Germain-des-Prés* ☎ *01–45–49–22–69* ⊕ *www.verbreuil.com* Ⓜ *Vavin, St-Sulpice.*

WINE

La Dernière Goutte. This inviting *cave* (literally wine store or wine cellar) focuses on wines by small French producers. Each is handpicked by the owner, along with a choice selection of estate Champagnes, Armagnac, and the classic Vieille Prune (plum brandy). The friendly English-speaking staff makes browsing a pleasure. Don't miss the Saturday afternoon tastings with the winemakers. ✉ *6 rue de Bourbon le Château, 6e, St-Germain-des-Prés* ☎ *01–46–29–11–62* ⊕ *www.ladernieregoutte.net* Ⓜ *Odéon.*

Ryst-Dupeyron. Ryst-Dupeyron specializes in fine wines and liquors, with Port, Calvados, and Armagnacs that date from 1878. Looking for a great gift idea? Find a bottle from the year of a friend's birth and have it labeled with your friend's name. Personalized bottles can be ordered and delivered on the same day. ✉ *79 rue du Bac, 7e, St-Germain-des-Prés* ☎ *01–45–48–80–93* ⊕ *www.maisonrystdupeyron.com* Ⓜ *Rue du Bac.*

MONTPARNASSE

The legendary Rue d'Alésia alone lands this neighborhood on the Paris shopping radar. If you're willing to dig a little, a thrilling afternoon can be had seeking out the many bargains here—from steeply discounted designer clothes, shoes, and accessories to housewares and kids' togs. Just roll up your sleeves and dive in.

BARGAIN SHOPPING

Rue d'Alésia. This street in the 14e arrondissement is the main place to find stores selling last season's fashions at a discount. Be forewarned: most of them are much more downscale than their elegant sister shops; dressing rooms are not always provided. ✉ *14e, Montparnasse* Ⓜ *Alésia.*

MARKETS

Les Puces des Vanves. This small flea market, on the southern side of the city, is a hit with the fashion and design set. It specializes in easily portable items (like textiles or clothing) and collectible objects that include books, posters, postcards, and glassware. With tables sprawling along both sides of the sidewalk, there's an extravagant selection—just be sure to bargain. It's open on weekends from 8 to 1, but come early for the real deals: good stuff goes fast, and stalls are liable to pack up before noon. ✉ *Av. de le Porte de Vanves and Av. Marc Sangnier, 14e, Montparnasse* Ⓜ *Porte de Vanves.*

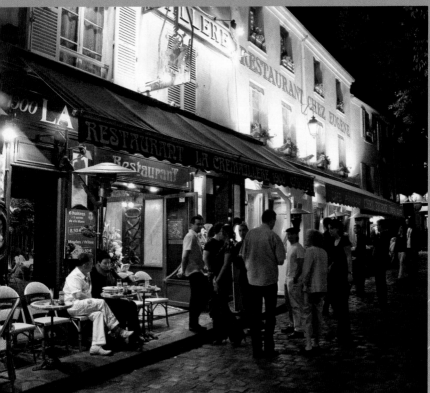

NIGHTLIFE

Updated
by Jennifer
Ladonne

You haven't seen the City of Light until you've seen the city at night. Throngs pour into popular streets, filling the air with the melody of engaged conversation and clinking glasses. This is when locals let down their hair and reveal their true bonhomie, laughing and dancing, flirting and talking. Parisians love to savor life together: they dine out, drink endless espressos, offer innumerable toasts, and are often so reluctant to separate that they party all night.

Parisians go out weekends and weeknights, late and early. They tend to frequent the same places once they've found spots they like: it could be a wine bar, a corner café, a hip music club, or, more and more, a chic cocktail bar in an out-of-the-way neighborhood. A wise way to spend an evening is to pick an area in a neighborhood that interests you, then give yourself time to browse. Parisians also love to bar-hop, and the energy shifts throughout the evening, so be prepared to follow the crowds.

PLANNING

GETTING PAST THE BOUNCER
It shouldn't surprise any nightlife lover that the more *branché* (literally, "plugged-in" or trendy) the spot, the knottier the door-entry issue will be. Most bars aren't a problem, but when it comes to clubbing, don't assume you're going to get in just because you show up. This is particularly true at the hot spots near the Champs-Élysées. Although a limo at your disposal and global fame aren't essential to pass muster, you absolutely must have a cocky yet somehow simultaneously polite attitude and look fabulous. Having a high female quotient in your party definitely helps (models are a particular plus). Solo men—or, worse, groups of men—are going to have a tougher time, unless they are high rollers and have reserved a table (bottle purchase *obligatoire*).

HOURS

Most bars stay open until between midnight and 2 am, with no specific last call; however, wine bars and hotel bars tend to close earlier. Clubs often stay open until 4 am, some until dawn. Many drinking establishments are closed Sunday night, so check before heading out on the town. If you want to hit bars at a relatively quiet hour, go for an apéritif around 6 pm. The more earnest places offer drink specials at this time, and it's also when Parisians congregate to make late-night plans. Do be aware that some spots are better for *apéro* hour than others. Apéritifs are typically sipped while seated at café tables or on a terrace if weather permits.

LATE-NIGHT TRANSPORTATION

The métro runs until 12:40 am Sunday through Thursday; however, there is service on Friday night, Saturday night, and nights before holidays until 2:15 am, when the last train on each line reaches its terminus. After that, you can try a cab, but it can be extremely difficult to find one after midnight or anytime when there's a chance of rain. Taxi stands are plagued with long lines of prospective passengers waiting for a limited number of vehicles, and even calling one on weekends can be a frustrating exercise. Following serious protests by Paris cabbies, the city government has been trying to crack down on smartphone car-hire services, like Uber and its French counterpart Chauffeur Privé, with varying degrees of success. For now, though, these are still thriving; apps can be downloaded at ⊕ *www.uber.com/cities/paris* and ⊕ *www.chauffeur-prive.com* respectively. As long as you're in the Wi-Fi zone, cars usually arrive in less than 10 minutes—and drivers will go anywhere in or outside Paris without sizing you up first and deciding whether they feel like it. Another alternative is the Noctilien, the sometimes rowdy night-bus system. If you stay within biking distance of chosen destinations, Paris's Vélib' bike program is also an option; after a few drinks, though, it may make more sense to just stay out until the métro starts running again at 5:30 am. (⇨ *See the Travel Smart Paris chapter for more on your late-night options.*)

TABLE SERVICE

Some bars have table service; at others (designated by "*Service au Bar*" signs), you must fetch your own drinks. Typically, you will not be permitted to start a tab at the latter unless you are already on friendly terms with the staff.

WHAT TO WEAR

Despite their reputation for flair, Parisians mostly adhere to a conservative-elegant style. Rarely do they deviate from neutrals, and their accessories tend to lean more toward refined chic than all-out bling. Sandals are almost unheard-of for men, and neither sex would ever wear sweatpants on a night out. If you want to blend in (and get into clubs), dress up. Men, you can wear your jeans—designer jeans, that is—but leave the sneakers at your hotel and try adding a blazer. Ladies, dressing up doesn't necessarily mean donning a dress—Parisian girls manage to look like a million bucks in jeans, high-heeled booties, and a stylish top.

BARS

Paris bars run the gamut from the toniest hotel lounge to the tiniest neighborhood *troquet,* where old-timers gather for a chat over their morning *petit blanc.*

Hotel bars were once considered the aristocrats of the genre. Some mix historic pedigrees with a hushed elegance, while others go for a modern, edgy luxe. A few still represent the chicest spots for frequent high-roller visitors to Paris. But breathtaking prices and the fickle Parisian fashion pack ensure that only the latest, highly hyped bars regularly draw in locals.

Cocktail bars, on the other hand, have been steadily gaining popularity and are now grabbing the spotlight in a sophisticated bar scene that was once the domain of a handful of hotels and eminent watering holes. Parisian cocktail bars rival those anywhere in the world, and, as in other places, they focus on mixed drinks—although most offer anything from craft beer to Champagne. Look for libations created with the native spirits, like Calvados or Cognac, that make French cocktail culture unique.

Wine bars are different from regular bars in that they also serve food, from simple snacks (like cheese and charcuterie) to full meals, plus handpicked wines that are often "natural" or *biodynamique.* Wine bars keep mealtime hours and close earlier than proper bars—somewhere between 11 and midnight. Be warned, though: many establishments calling themselves wine bars or *bars à vin* are in fact full-fledged restaurants, with no bar to speak of.

CABARETS

Paris's cabarets range from vintage venues once haunted by Picasso and Piaf to those sinful showplaces where *tableaux vivants* offer acres of bare flesh. Some of these places, like the Lido, are more Vegas than the petticoat vision re-created by Hollywood in Baz Luhrmann's *Moulin Rouge*—but the rebirth of burlesque is making some of the old-school venues more popular. Although you can dine at many cabarets, food isn't the attraction. Prices range from about €50 (admission plus one drink) to more than €200 (dinner plus a show) and can go as high as €300 for the works. At all but a handful of specific cabarets on specific nights, the clientele tends overwhelmingly to be visitors, middle-aged and older, from either the French countryside or abroad.

CLUBS

Paris's hyped *boîtes de nuit*—more often referred to as simply *boîtes* (nightclubs)—tend to be expensive and exclusive. If you're friends with a regular or you've modeled in *Vogue,* you'll have an easier time getting through the door. Cover charges at some can be upwards of €20, with drinks at the bar starting at €10 for a beer. Others are free to enter, but getting past the doorman can still be problematic. Locals looking to dance generally stick to the more laid-back clubs, where the cover ranges from free (usually on slower weekdays) to €20, and the emphasis is on the dancing, music, and offbeat atmosphere (think on a barge or under a bridge). Club popularity depends on the night or event, as Parisians are more loyal to certain DJs than venues and often hit two or three spots before ending up at one of the many after-parties, which can last until noon the next day.

GAY AND LESBIAN BARS AND CLUBS

These bars and clubs—mostly concentrated in the Marais and Les Halles—include some of the hipper addresses in the city. Keep in mind, however, that many of these spots fall in and out of favor at lightning speed. The best way to find out what's hot is by perusing the gay and lesbian magazine *Têtu* (available at newsstands and online at ⊕ *www. tetu.com*) or *2X*, the free "agenda" that can be found in any of the venues listed here. Paris's gay, lesbian, bi, and trans tourist office (⊕ *www. centrelgbtparis.org*) is another good resource, as is the civic-run nightlife website (⊕ *www.parisnightlife.fr/en*).

PUBS

Pubs wooing English-speaking clients with selections of British and Irish beers exist in Paris. They're often good places to watch an important soccer match.

NIGHTLIFE IN PARIS

Reviews are alphabetical by neighborhood.

CHAMPS-ÉLYSÉES

As the sun sets, Paris's most elegant neighborhood comes to life. Join the fashionistas for a *coupe de Champagne* in an opulent hotel bar, spend a night clubbing with the international jet set, or indulge in a bit of over-the-top French "culture" at a cabaret.

BARS

Apicius. Mere steps from the Champs-Élysées, Apicius offers sublime elegance. Wander through the luxe front garden and château restaurant to the sleekly modern black bar where couture cocktails are concocted to suit any cultured taste. Oddly, it's closed Saturday *and* Sunday. ⊠ *20 rue d'Artois, 8e, Champs-Élysées* ☎ *01–43–80–19–66* ⊕ *www.restaurant-apicius.com* Ⓜ *George V.*

Bar Anglais. You might find diplomats and other dignitaries discussing state affairs at this rich red den of masculinity in L'Hôtel Raphael, a stone's throw from the Arc de Triomphe. The hotel's Rooftop Bar, a well-guarded Parisian secret, was voted the best bar in Europe in recent years. ⊠ *17 av. Kléber, 16e, Champs-Élysées* ☎ *01–53–64–32–00* ⊕ *www.leshotelsbaverez.com* Ⓜ *Kléber, Champs-Élysées–Etoile.*

Blind Bar, Maison Champs Elysées. This romantic spot in the ultrachic Maison Champs Elysées offers a wood fire in winter and a quiet terrace in warmer months. Its impressive range of Champagnes and impeccable cocktails is well worth the stellar prices. The separate all-black cigar bar is one of the remaining few in Paris. ⊠ *8 rue Jean Goujon, 8e, Champs-Élysées* ☎ *01–40–74–64–65* ⊕ *www.lamaisonchampselysees. com* Ⓜ *Franklin-D.-Roosevelt, Champs-Elysées–Clémenceau.*

Buddha Bar. While it may be past its prime with Parisians, visitors can't seem to get enough of the high-camp towering gold Buddha that holds court over this bar's giant palm fronds, red satin walls, and colorful chinoiserie. A themed dining room serves pan-Asian fare. ✉ *8 rue Boissy d'Anglas, 8e, Champs-Élysées* ☎ *01–53–05–90–00* ⊕ *www.buddhabar. com* Ⓜ *Concorde.*

Le Bar. The Shangri-La Hotel's glamorous Empire-style bar serves cocktails with a signature Asian touch. La Bauhinia, the hotel's restaurant, has well-attended jazz nights on Friday and Saturday. ✉ *10 av. d'Iéna, 16e, Champs-Élysées* ☎ *01–53–67–19–98* ⊕ *www.shangri-la.com* Ⓜ *Iéna.*

Le Bar at George V. An ultraluxe, clubby hideaway in the Four Seasons Hotel, Le Bar at George V is perfect for stargazing from the plush wine-red armchairs, Cognac in hand. Its charm still lures the glitterati, especially during fashion weeks. Be sure to notice the hotel's signature—and stunning—flower arrangements. ✉ *31 av. George V, 8e, Champs-Élysées* ☎ *01–49–52–70–00* ⊕ *www.fourseasons.com/paris/ dining/lounges/le_bar* Ⓜ *George V.*

Le Bar at the Hôtel Plaza Athénée. Totally refurbished in 2014 by Paris design star Patrick Jouin, this hotel bar *par excellence* has a clubby feel that lures a younger fashion crowd. Lounge in leather chairs under an Yves Klein–blue ceiling installation while sipping stylish cocktails, like the signature Rose Royal (Champagne, raspberry, and a splash of Cognac). Mood lighting and music spun by a live DJ Thursday through Saturday set the tone for a glam late-night rendezvous. ✉ *25 av. Montaigne, 8e, Champs-Élysées* ☎ *01–53–67–66–00* ⊕ *www. dorchestercollection.com* Ⓜ *Alma–Marceau.*

Fodor's Choice ★ **Le Bar du Bristol.** Apparently not satisfied with its usual clientele of the rich and powerful, this sumptuous spot is now vying for the impossibly hip, too. Along with the stellar cocktails dreamed up by award-winning head barman Maxime Hoerth, Le Bar promises exceptional wines plus tapas by superchef Eric Frechon. Weekdays between 7 and 9:30, it showcases curated art videos on its behind-the-bar mirror screen. Chic Paris DJs heat up the scene between 9:30 and 2 on Friday and Saturday. ✉ *112 rue du Faubourg St-Honoré, 8e, Champs-Élysées* ☎ *01–53–43– 43–00* ⊕ *www.lebristolparis.com* Ⓜ *Miromesnil.*

No Comment. Housed in a former swinger's club, this nightclub boasts that it has retained the libertine vibe without the libertine ways. Only the trendiest seem to go—and get in. ✉ *36 rue de Ponthieu, 8e, Champs-Élysées* ☎ *06–88–74–59–86* Ⓜ *Saint-Philippe du Roule.*

Pershing Hall. Pershing Hall has an überstylish lounge with muted colors and minimalist lines, plus an enormous "vertical garden" in the simply stunning indoor courtyard. The chic ambience and hip lounge music make this a popular neighborhood nightspot; starting at 9 pm there's a DJ. Try the signature Lalique cocktail—it comes in an actual Lalique crystal glass. ✉ *49 rue Pierre Charron, 8e, Champs-Élysées* ☎ *01–58– 36–58–00* ⊕ *www.pershinghall.com* Ⓜ *George V.*

Publicis Drugstore. Open daily until 2 am, this bustling, phantasmagorical, multilevel, bar-brasserie–hipster shop is just across the street from the Arc de Triomphe. ✉ *133 av. des Champs-Élysées, 8e, Champs-Élysées* ☎ *01–44–43–79–00* ⊕ *www.publicisdrugstore.com* Ⓜ *Charles de Gaulle–Étoile.*

Fodor's Choice ★ **Saint James Club Paris.** Like a library room out of *Harry Potter,* the bar at the Saint James Club Paris—complete with 5,000 leather-bound volumes and a cozy fireplace—is studiously inviting. It's very French, and open to nonmembers only after 7 pm or during Sunday brunch. The owners are a venerable old Bordeaux family; accordingly, you'll find a respectable selection of Champagnes and wines. ✉ *43 av. Bugeaud, 16e, Champs-Élysées* ☎ *01–44–05–81–81* ⊕ *www.saintjamesclub.com* Ⓜ *Porte Dauphine.*

CABARET

Fodor's Choice ★ **Crazy Horse.** This world-renowned cabaret has elevated the striptease to an art form. Founded in 1951, it's famous for gorgeous dancers and naughty routines characterized by lots of humor and very little clothing. What garments there are have been dazzlingly designed by the likes of Louboutin and Alaïa and shed by top divas (including Dita von Teese). Reserved seats for the show start at €85. ✉ *12 av. George V, 8e, Champs-Élysées* ☎ *01–47–23–32–32* ⊕ *www.lecrazyhorseparis. com* Ⓜ *Alma–Marceau.*

Lido. The legendary Lido celebrated its 70th anniversary in 2016 by launching a new show created by Cirque du Soleil alum Franco Dragone, who adds a modern-day dose of awe-inspiring stage design to the cabaret's trademark style. The 100-minute production—still featuring those beloved Blubell Girls—runs at 9 pm and 11 pm, 365 days a year. Dinner for Two packages for the earlier show include the Soirée Etoile (€165), Soirée Champs-Elysées (€195), and the Soirée Triomphe (€300). If you're on a budget, €115 gets you a ticket plus half a bottle of bubbly. Did we mention these prices are per person? Ah yes, this is Paris nightlife as it's meant to be experienced. Although the Lido holds 1,150, it's best to book your tickets in advance by phone, online, or on-site. ✉ *116 bis, av. des Champs-Élysées, 8e, Champs-Élysées* ☎ *01–40–76–56–10* ⊕ *www.lido.fr* Ⓜ *George V.*

CLUBS

Queen. This mythic gay club of the '90s is not quite as monumental as it once was, but it still packs 'em in and the doors are still difficult to get through, especially—inevitably—on weekends. Proudly hosting a fantastic roster of top DJs, it's known for its campy soirées. These days it attracts a gay-straight mix of international partygoers eager to dance on podiums. ✉ *102 av. des Champs-Élysées, 8e, Champs-Élysées* ☎ *01–53–89–08–90* ⊕ *www.queen.fr* Ⓜ *George V.*

Fodor's Choice ★ **Showcase.** Nestled under the arches of the golden Pont Alexandre III, Showcase takes the gold medal for best location. The sleekly cavernous dance space heats up to a fever pitch after midnight, thanks to the propulsive beats of big-name acts and underground indie groups. Check the website for raucous party nights when international DJs turn up the temperature. ✉ *Pont Alexandre III, Port des Champs-Élysées, 8e, Champs-Élysées* ☎ *01–45–61–25–43* ⊕ *www.showcase.fr* Ⓜ *Champs-Élysées–Clemenceau, Invalides.*

Fodor's Choice ★ **Zig Zag.** One of the city's newer venues, Zig Zag has a state-of-the-art sound system, a glam location, and a riotous dance floor with room for 1,200 revelers. That combination is proving hugely popular.

Join the enthusiastic crowd gyrating to electrobeats from DJs or live bands ensconced on an illuminated stage highlighted by two giant screens, or observe the action from the wraparound balcony. ✉ *32 rue Marbeuf, 8e, Champs-Élysées* ☎ *06–35–25–03–61* ⊕ *zigzagclub. fr* Ⓜ *Franklin-D.-Roosevelt.*

JAZZ CLUBS

Jazz Club Etoile. This moody club at the Méridien Hotel hosts a roster of top-billed international musicians in a classy set of rooms. Check out the Sunday afternoon jazz brunch buffet and the interior garden. ✉ *Méridien Hotel, 81 bd. Gouvion–St-Cyr, 17e, Champs-Élysées* ☎ *01–40–68–30–42* ⊕ *www.jazzclub-paris.com* Ⓜ *Porte Maillot.*

AROUND THE LOUVRE

The cocktail craze has taken off in this atmospheric neighborhood, where dusky speakeasies and cozy hotel bars provide the perfect prelude to an evening of jazz or dancing 'til dawn at hip all-night clubs.

BARS

Fodor'sChoice ★ **Ballroom du Beef Club.** Unmarked black door, basement setting, pressed-tin ceilings, atmospheric lighting—did anyone say speakeasy? All this and luscious libations draw a sophisticated crowd that appreciates the extra touches that make this cocktail bar a standout. ✉ *58 rue Jean-Jacques-Rousseau, 1er, Around the Louvre* ☎ *09–54–37–13–65* Ⓜ *Les Halles, Palais Royal–Musée du Louvre.*

Bar 8. Ever since the monolithic marble bar at the Mandarin Oriental Hotel opened its doors, it has been the "in" game in town. There's an extensive Champagne menu, and the terrace is especially busy during fashion weeks. ✉ *251 rue Saint-Honoré, 1er, Around the Louvre* ☎ *01–70–98–78–88* ⊕ *www.mandarinoriental.com* Ⓜ *Concorde, Tuileries.*

Bar 228. Hôtel Meurice converted its ground-floor Fontainebleau library into the intimate Bar 228, with wood paneling and huge murals depicting the royal hunting forests of Fontainebleau. Its loyal fashion crowd is continually wooed by Philippe Starck's decor updates and lubricated with the bar's famous Bellinis. Try the Meurice Millennium cocktail, made with Champagne, rose liqueur, and Cointreau. ✉ *228 rue de Rivoli, 1er, Around the Louvre* ☎ *01–44–58–10–66* ⊕ *www. dorchestercollection.com* Ⓜ *Tuileries.*

Chacha Club. Behind a nondescript facade you'll find a 1930s-style bar-club-restaurant arranged like a private home, with a series of rooms on three floors—including a special smoking lounge—and lots of corners where the casually stylish cool cats of Paris get cozy until the wee hours. ✉ *47 rue Berger, 1er, Around the Louvre* ☎ *01–40–13–12–12* ⊕ *www. chachaclub.fr* Ⓜ *Louvre–Rivoli.*

Fodor'sChoice ★ **Experimental Cocktail Club.** Fashioned as a speakeasy on a tiny brick-paved street, the Experimental Cocktail Club seems like it should be lighted by gas lamps. The show is all about the *alcool*; colorful, innovative cocktails like the Lemon Drop are mixed with aplomb by friendly (and attractive) bartenders. By 11 pm it's packed with a diverse mix of locals, professionals, and fashionistas, who occasionally dress up like characters from a Toulouse-Lautrec painting on special costume nights. ✉ *37 rue Saint-Sauveur, 2e, Around the Louvre* ☎ *01–45–08–88–09* Ⓜ *Réamur–Sébastopol.*

The Hemingway Bar & the Ritz Bar. Literature lovers, cocktail connoisseurs, and other drink-swilling devotees still flock to the iconic Hemmingway Bar & the Ritz Bar inside the Ritz Hotel, especially after its major four year makeover. ✉ *15 pl. Vendôme, 1er, Around the Louvre* ⊕ *www. ritzparis.com* Ⓜ *Opéra.*

Hôtel Costes. Despite years on the scene, Hôtel Costes still draws big names—and not just during fashion weeks. Expect to cross paths with anyone from Rihanna to Leonardo DiCaprio, as long as you make it past the chilly greeting of the statuesque hostess. Dressing to kill is strongly advised, especially for newcomers; otherwise, expect all the tables to be suddenly reserved. ✉ *239 rue St-Honoré, 1er, Around the Louvre* ☎ *01–42–44–50–50* ⊕ *hotelcostes.com* Ⓜ *Tuileries.*

Jefrey's. A custom-DJ'd music track, enticing love seats, and inventive cocktails make this an easy choice for an intimate evening in sophisticated surroundings. Need further incentive to return? Jefrey's lets you keep your bottle stored on the shelf, with your name on it, for next time. ✉ *14 rue Saint-Sauveur, 2e, Around the Louvre* ☎ *01–42–33–60–77* ⊕ *www.jefreys.fr* Ⓜ *Étienne Marcel.*

L'Assaggio Bar. At this bar, in Chanel's old neighborhood, you can order tea and *macarons* until midnight—in addition to cocktails. ✉ *33–37 rue Cambon, 1e, Around the Louvre* ☎ *01–44–58–44–58* ⊕ *www.castille. com* Ⓜ *Concorde, Madeleine.*

Le Bar O d'Ora Ïto. Slip into a sinuous banquette at Hôtel Odyssey's intimate, stylish bar while you still can. It's an undiscovered gem, ideal for savoring a choice selection of ambrosial cocktails. The Cointreau Fizz—a blend of ginger soda, lemon, and Cointreau, with a split vanilla bean and a hint of rose—is as classy as they come. ✉ *19 rue Herold, 1er, Around the Louvre* ☎ *01–42–36–04–02* ⊕ *www.hotelodysseyparis.com* Ⓜ *Palais Royal–Musée du Louvre, Sentier, Les Halles.*

Le Café Noir. Parisians from *bobos* (bourgeois-bohemians) to *pompiers* (firefighters) are lured to Le Café Noir's elegantly worn digs. In addition to cool drinks and friendly staff, the place features a pipe-smoking papier-mâché fish and a vintage leopard-print-covered motorbike. (The restaurant with the same name is unrelated.) ✉ *65 rue Montmartre, 2e, Around the Louvre* ☎ *01–40–39–07–36* ⊕ *www.cafenoirparis.fr* Ⓜ *Étienne Marcel.*

Le Fumoir. Fashionable neighborhood gallery owners and young professionals meet for late-afternoon wine, early-evening cocktails, or dinner at this oh-so-reliably ultrachic charmer across from the Louvre. It features a superstocked bar in the front, an ample multilingual library in the back, and chessboards for the clientele to use while sipping martinis. ✉ *6 rue de l'Amiral-Coligny, 1er, Around the Louvre* ☎ *01–42–92–00– 24* ⊕ *www.lefumoir.com* Ⓜ *Louvre.*

CLUBS

Kong. Kong is glorious not only for its panoramic skyline views but also for its exquisite manga-inspired decor and kooky, disco-ball-and-kid-sumo-adorned bathrooms. On weekends, top-shelf DJs keep patrons dancing. ⊠ *1 rue du Pont Neuf, 1er, Around the Louvre* ☎ *01–40–39–09–00* ⊕ *www.kong.fr* Ⓜ *Pont Neuf.*

VIP Room. Although it's no longer on the Champs-Élysées, this temple of bling still attracts hot DJs, beautiful people, and—VIPs! Check the website for the latest soirée: usually R&B–hip-hop–Top 40 crowd pleasers. There's a gift shop, a ground-floor café, and a pricey Italian restaurant on the top floor. Dress to impress. ⊠ *188 bis, rue de Rivoli, 1er, Around the Louvre* ☎ *01–58–36–46–00* ⊕ *www.viproom.com* Ⓜ *Palais Royal.*

GAY AND LESBIAN BARS AND CLUBS

Banana Café. Banana Café draws a trendy, scantily clad mixed crowd and offers show tunes in the cellar, where dancing on tables is the norm. A very happy happy hour, lasting from 6 to 11 pm, primes the audience for the incomparable banana "go-go boys" nightly show—ooh la la! ⊠ *13 rue de la Ferronnerie, 1er, Around the Louvre* ☎ *01–42–33–35–31* ⊕ *www.bananacafeparis.com* Ⓜ *Châtelet–Les Halles.*

Club 18. This elegant spot (the oldest gay club in Paris) takes gay pride to the heart of the Louvre district on the weekends. Club 18 boasts a well-earned reputation as a "friendly party scene." ⊠ *18 rue de Beaujolais, 1er, Around the Louvre* ☎ *01–42–97–52–13* ⊕ *www.club18.fr* Ⓜ *Palais Royal.*

Le Dépôt. A cruising bar and club, Le Dépôt has the largest back room in Europe. The ever-popular Gay Tea Dance spices up Sunday afternoon. ⊠ *10 rue aux Ours, 3e, Around the Louvre* ☎ *01–44–54–96–96* ⊕ *www.ledepot-paris.com* Ⓜ *Étienne Marcel.*

Le Duplex. Young tortured-artist types flock here to enjoy the frequent art exhibitions, alternative music, and mood-inspiring ambient lighting. ⊠ *25 rue Michel-Le-Comte, 3e, Around the Louvre* ☎ *01–42–72–80–86* ⊕ *www.leduplex.com* Ⓜ *Rambuteau.*

JAZZ CLUBS

Duc des Lombards. Located in a famously bopping neighborhood, the Duc's cozy interior and top-class jazz acts make it one of the city's most popular small venues. It's best to purchase advance tickets online (go to *bons plans* for discounted tickets). ⊠ *42 rue des Lombards, 1er, Around the Louvre* ☎ *01–42–33–22–88* ⊕ *www.ducdeslombards.com* Ⓜ *Châtelet–Les Halles.*

Le Sunset-Sunside. This two-part club hosts French and American jazz musicians: the Sunside upstairs is devoted mostly to acoustic jazz, while the Sunset downstairs features everything from electronic jazz, fusion, and groove to classic and swing. Jam sessions have been known to last well into the wee hours. ⊠ *60 rue des Lombards, 1er, Around the Louvre* ☎ *01–40–26–46–60* ⊕ *www.sunset-sunside.com* Ⓜ *Châtelet–Les Halles.*

The Paris Cocktail Scene

The cocktail bar is undergoing a renaissance in Paris. In fact, classy concoctions haven't been served up with such flair since the days when the Bloody Mary and the sidecar were introduced at fabled Harry's Bar and martinis were the drink du jour at the Ritz Hotel's Hemingway Bar (the writers and aristocrats who assembled at the latter included the bar's notoriously thirsty namesake).

The new cocktail bars run the gamut from dauntingly elegant hotel lounges to designer dives, and they attract a diverse crowd willing to shell out anywhere from €10 to €26 a pop. Once called barmen, the new curators of cocktails are "mixologists," and the best of the lot garner fame and a following among devoted enthusiasts. Drinks are crafted, ingredients are sourced, the booze is barrel-aged or infused, syrups are house-made, and the ice is artisanal. Many also serve excellent food.

Opening hours tend to be perfect for an apéro (six-o'clock-ish). Closing hours tend to be in sync with average Paris bars (around 2 am); cocktail bars in hotels (which can close as early as 11 pm on weeknights) are an exception. Here are a few standouts:

Ballroom du Beef Club: An unmarked door, a dim interior, and upholstered loveseats add to the speakeasy ambience.

Baton Rouge: A splash of Louisiana and a dash of black magic are making this bar with bayou-inspired decor a new favorite.

Dirty Dick: This destination cocktail club in newly chic Pigalle combines a retro tiki-lounge cheekiness with a serious selection of rum.

Experimental Cocktail Club: Down a dimly lit cobbled street, this is Paris's swankiest speakeasy; the crowds are proof of its popularity.

Glass: Party to the DJ beats at this shrine to urban cool—complete with microbrews and a frozen-drinks machine.

La Conserverie: High-low loft style, a congenial atmosphere, and superlative drinks draw the cocktail cognoscenti.

Le Bar O d'Ora Ïto (Hôtel Odyssey): Sip custom cocktails in a bar that's as sleek and stylish as the hotel that houses it.

L'Entrée des Artistes: It's too moody and dark to read the drinks menu, so just point your finger—it's all good.

Le Mary Celeste: Hipsters come for delicious happy-hour noshes, then stay to linger over craft cocktails and natural wines.

Little Red Door: This tiny trendsetter with atmosphere to spare serves sophisticated choices behind its eponymous door.

Prescription Cocktail Club: Lively and louche, it's just what the doctor ordered—if your doctor is Dorothy Parker.

LES GRANDS BOULEVARDS

An assortment of well-established British-Irish pubs and clubs brings an Anglo-inflected nuance to this many-faceted neighborhood that bustles by day and empties out at night.

BARS

Barramundi. The city's nouveau-riche chill to electro-lounge tunes and world music here, drinking in Barramundi's cool golden ambience as they sip cold tropical drinks at the long copper bar. ⊠ *3 rue Taitbout, 9e, Les Grands Boulevards* ☎ *01–47–70–21–21* ⊕ *www.barramundi.fr* Ⓜ *Richelieu–Drouot.*

> ### APÉRITIFS
>
> For apéritifs French style, try a *pastis*—anise-flavored liquor such as Pernod or Ricard that turns cloudy when water is added; ask for *"un petit jaune, s'il vous plaît."* A *pineau* is Cognac and fruity grape juice. The *kir* (white wine with a dash of black-currant syrup) is a popular drink, too; a *kir royale* is made with Champagne.

Corcoran's Irish Pub. This roomy pub, with several locations in central Paris, has an ample menu, a gorgeous bar, plus old-timey photos and quotations on the walls—such as "He who opens his mouth most is the one who opens his purse least." Conversation turns to dancing at night with a regulated guy-to-girl ratio, so men shouldn't try coming alone. ⊠ *23 bd. Poissonière, 2e, Les Grands Boulevards* ☎ *01–40–39–00–16* ⊕ *www.corcoransirishpub.fr* Ⓜ *Grands Boulevards.*

Fodor's Choice
★
Delaville Café. With its huge, heated sidewalk terrace, Belle Époque mosaic-tile bar, graffitied walls, and swishy lounge, Delaville Café boasts a funky ambience. Hot Paris DJs ignite the scene Thursday to Saturday, so arrive early on weekends if you want a seat. ⊠ *34 bd. Bonne Nouvelle, 10e, Les Grands Boulevards* ☎ *01–48–24–48–09* ⊕ *delavillecafe.com* Ⓜ *Bonne Nouvelle, Grands Boulevards.*

Duke's Bar. A favorite not only for its prestigious location between Opéra and Place Vendôme, but also for its worn-leather chairs and English-private-club feel, the Westminster Hotel's bar offers drinks like the "James Bond" and "Duke's Martini." At times you get the feeling that Mr. Hercule Poirot is lurking just behind that wing chair. ⊠ *13 rue de la Paix, 2e, Les Grands Boulevards* ☎ *01–42–61–55–11* ⊕ *www.leceladon.com* Ⓜ *Opéra.*

Harry's Bar. Also known as Harry's New York Bar, this cozy, wood-paneled hangout decorated with dusty college pennants is popular with expats and American-loving French people who welcome the ghosts of Ernest Hemingway and F. Scott Fitzgerald, who drank themselves unconscious here. Founded in 1911, Gershwin composed *An American in Paris* in the piano bar downstairs and the Bloody Mary is said to have originated on-site. ⊠ *5 rue Daunou, 2e, Les Grands Boulevards* ☎ *01–42–61–71–14* Ⓜ *Opéra.*

Kitty O'Shea's. This ever-popular Irish pub near the Place Vendôme attracts both a posh after-work crowd and salt-of-the-earth types. Authentic trimmings—including stained glass and Gaelic street signs—are decor highlights. A restaurant serves pub standards like

17

CLOSE UP

Jazz Clubs

The French fell hard for jazz during World War I, but the real *coup de foudre*—literally "lightning bolt" or figuratively "love at first sight"—came after the war when Yank sax man Sidney Bechet and 19-year-old song-and-dance vamp Josephine Baker of St. Louis joined a European tour of the Revue Nègre musical. Baker, or the "Black Venus that haunted Baudelaire," as she was known by French critics, instantly became the sweetheart of Paris. Note: a larger-than-life picture of Baker wearing only a smile, a string of pearls, and a thigh-high skirt today adorns a wall of historic photographs along the platform of the Tuileries métro.

By 1934 France had created its own impressive claim to jazz fame, the all-string Quintette du Hot Club de France, which featured Gypsy guitarist Django Reinhardt and his partner, violinist Stéphane Grappelli. They, in turn, influenced string players from country musicians to Carlos Santana. Reinhardt performed throughout much of World War II in the underground French jazz scene. In the 1950s Paris grew to become a major destination of the bebop diaspora, and expat jazz musicians including Bechet, Bud Powell, and Dexter Gordon played the venues along with such jazz greats as Dizzy Gillespie, Charlie Parker, and Miles Davis. France embraced the evolving jazz sound that many Americans were still struggling to accept and provided a worshipful welcome to musicians battling discrimination at home. In Paris, Davis said, he was "treated like a human being."

WANT A NIGHT OF JAZZ?
The French obsession with jazz continues to this day, and travelers seeking

a quintessential Parisian experience have the opportunity to hear jazz artists from all over the world nearly any night of the week. Aficionados can choose anything from traditional jazz to the latest experimental efforts, in clubs ranging from casual to chichi, sedate to hopping. Many venues present a wide spectrum of music. A good option is the double club on Rue des Lombards near Les Halles: Le Sunside specializes in more traditional jazz, and its downstairs sister, Le Sunset, features edgier options.

Names to look for include expat Yank flute-and-sax-man Bobby Rangell and singer Sara Lazarus, and much-loved French musicians like the pianists Alain Jean-Marie and Pierre de Bethman, sax man Didier Malherbe, and Olivier Ker Ourio on the harmonica. For jazz you're less likely to find at home, check out the latest iteration of Gypsy musette (a distinctive, swing-infused interpretation of old Paris dance music) presented by virtuosos like accordionist Richard Galliano, violinist Didier Lockwood, and the guitar-picking Ferre brothers, Boulou and Elios. Look for them inside Duc des Lombards on Rue des Lombards. Alternatively, head to New Morning on Rue des Petites-Ecuries—it's the top spot for experimental and avant-garde jazz.

The best place to find out what's playing and get tickets is at ⊕ *www. infoconcert.com* or on club websites, some of which offer English versions. *Pariscope, Jazz Magazine,* and *Jazz Hot,* available at newsstands, have listings in English and French. Reservations can be critical, especially for leading U.S. jazz musicians. Admission to clubs is rarely more than €20 and often less.

fish-and-chips, and rugby games are shown on the big screen in season. Check the website for guest DJs and concert info. ⊠ *10 rue des Capucines, 2e, Les Grands Boulevards* ☎ *01–40–15–00–30* ⊕ *www. kittyosheas.com* Ⓜ *Opéra.*

Fodor's Choice **La Conserverie.** La Conserverie is a rustic-elegant loft space with exposed
★ ductwork, Aubusson tapestries, comfy sofas, and glass-bottle chandeliers. Skillfully crafted cocktails—for those on and off the wagon—and reliably good food keep the crowd convivial. A smaller downstairs space accommodates romantics. Reserve ahead to be sure of a table. ⊠ *37 bis, rue du Sentier, 2e, Les Grands Boulevards* ☎ *01–40–26–14–94* ⊕ *www. laconserveriebar.com* Ⓜ *Bonne Nouvelle, Sentier.*

Le Bar Long. At the Royal Monceau's innovative bar your mixologist will fix your drink right next to you at the illuminated, Philippe Stark–designed bar. The collection of glasses on the walls isn't just decoration—you may choose which to drink from. A light tapas menu is served between 6 and 11 pm. ⊠ *37 av. Hoche, 8e, Les Grands Boulevards* ☎ *01–42–99–88–00* ⊕ *www.leroyalmonceau.com* Ⓜ *Ternes.*

Le Truskel. What looks, sounds, and feels like an English pub but kicks booty like a punk club? Le Truskel. The basement showcases gigs by the globe's hottest new alternative acts, while a loud, happy Parisian rocker crowd staggers around the roomy bar. ⊠ *12 rue Feydeau, 2e, Les Grands Boulevards* ☎ *01–40–26–59–97* ⊕ *www.truskel.com* Ⓜ *Bourse.*

CABARET

Le Limonaire. This old-world-style wine-and- *chanson* bistro oozes Parisian charm. It serves food until 10 pm Tuesday through Sunday before giving way to the singing of traditional French songs of "expression," with musical accompaniment *bien sûr.* There's no entrance fee; musicians pass the hat. ⊠ *18 cité Bergère, 9e, Les Grands Boulevards* ☎ *01– 45–23–33–33* ⊕ *limonaire.free.fr* Ⓜ *Grands Boulevards.*

CLUBS

Le Rex. Open Wednesday through Sunday, this temple of techno and house is popular with students. One of France's most famous DJs, Laurent Garnier, is sometimes at the turntables. ⊠ *5 bd. Poissonnière, 2e, Les Grands Boulevards* ☎ *01–42–36–10–96* ⊕ *www.rexclub.com* Ⓜ *Grands Boulevards.*

Silencio. David Lynch named his nightclub after a reference in his Oscar-nominated hit, *Mulholland Drive.* Silencio, which hosts concerts, films, and other performances, is open only to members and their guests until midnight; after that everyone is allowed. Guest DJs spin until 4 am Tuesday through Thursday, 6 am on Friday and Saturday. ⊠ *142 rue Montmartre, 2e, Les Grands Boulevards* ☎ *01–40–13–12–33* ⊕ *www. silencio-club.com* Ⓜ *Bourse, Sentier.*

JAZZ CLUBS

Fodor's Choice **New Morning.** At New Morning—the premier spot for serious fans of
★ avant-garde jazz, folk, and world music—the look is spartan, the mood reverential. ⊠ *7 rue des Petites-Ecuries, 10e, Les Grands Boulevards* ☎ *01–45–23–51–41* ⊕ *www.newmorning.com* Ⓜ *Château d'Eau.*

17

MONTMARTRE

Vestiges of this *quartier*'s absinthe-tinged heyday, immortalized by Toulouse-Lautrec and Renoir, still endure in the cabarets and clubs that extend from the heights of Montmartre down to louche Pigalle's newly vibrant cocktail bar and dance scene.

BARS

Fodor'sChoice ★ **Baton Rouge.** This new Louisiana-inspired spot in Pigalle is working its voodoo magic. Cocktails like the Nola Fizz and other creole-inflected nectars summon a time when the livin' was easy; alternately, you can order classic drinks mixed by two of Paris's most revered barmen. A menu of Southern delights (picture Po'Boys, muffaletta sandwiches, and delectable ribs) plus a moody-chic decor add to the bayou vibe. ⊠ *62 rue Notre Dame de Lorette, Montmartre* ⊕ *www.batonrouge. paris* Ⓜ *Notre Dame de Lorette.*

Café la Fourmi. One of Pigalle's trendiest addresses, Café la Fourmi has a funky, spacious bar-café where cool locals party. ⊠ *74 rue des Martyrs, 18e, Montmartre* ☎ *01–42–64–70–35* Ⓜ *Pigalle.*

Fodor'sChoice ★ **Dirty Dick.** An updated version of the classic tiki lounge, this stylish option in the hip Pigalle neighborhood comes complete with lurid lighting, life-size totems, and retro rattan furniture. All the exotic drinks you'd expect at a Polynesian beach hut (or '60s motel lounge) are here—including fruity cocktails, a range of rums, and punch bowls with names like Amazombie. ⊠ *10 rue Frochot, 9e, Montmartre* ☎ *01–48–78–74–58* Ⓜ *Pigalle.*

Fodor'sChoice ★ **Glass.** Masquerading as a dive in Pigalle's rapidly gentrifying red-light district, this dark, candlelighted space is actually a shrine to urban cool. Hipsters party to a DJ while knocking back sophisticated cocktails, artisanal beers, and frosty margaritas from the frozen-drinks machine. It might also be the only place in Paris to find a boilermaker (a beer and a shot). Gourmet hot dogs help fuel the late-night party scene. ⊠ *9 rue Frochot, 9e, Montmartre* ☎ *06–25–16–72–17* ⊕ *www.glassparis. com* Ⓜ *Pigalle.*

Le Rendez-Vous des Amis. This makes an intriguing midway breather if you climb the hill of Montmartre by foot. Le Rendez-Vous des Amis has a jovial staff, eclectic music, and a century's worth of previous patrons immortalized in photos. ⊠ *23 rue Gabrielle, 18e, Montmartre* ☎ *01–46–06–01–60* Ⓜ *Abbesses.*

Le Sancerre. Café by day, Le Sancerre turns into an essential watering hole for Montmartrois and artists at night, with Belgian beers on tap and an impressive list of cocktails. Locals love its traditional old-school vibe. ⊠ *35 rue des Abbesses, 18e, Montmartre* ☎ *01–42–58–08–20* Ⓜ *Abbesses.*

CABARET

Fodor'sChoice ★ **Au Lapin Agile.** An authentic survivor from the 19th century, Au Lapin Agile considers itself the doyen of cabarets. Founded in 1860, it inhabits the same modest house that was a favorite subject of painter Maurice Utrillo. It became the home-away-from-home for Braque, Modigliani, Apollinaire, and Picasso—who once paid for a meal with one of his paintings, then promptly exited and painted another that he named after this place. There are no topless dancers; this is a genuine French cabaret with songs, poetry, and humor (in French) in a pub-like setting. Entry is €28. ✉ *22 rue des Saules, 18e, Montmartre* ☎ *01–46–06–85–87* ⊕ *www.au-lapin-agile.com* Ⓜ *Lamarck–Caulaincourt.*

Michou. The always-decked-out-in-blue owner, Michou, presents an over-the-top show here. It features *tranformiste* men on stage in extravagant drag, performing with high camp for a radically different cabaret experience. Dinner shows are €110 and €140, or you can watch from the bar for €40, which includes a drink. ✉ *80 rue des Martyrs, 18e, Montmartre* ☎ *01–46–06–16–04* ⊕ *www.michou.com* Ⓜ *Pigalle.*

Moulin Rouge. When it opened in 1889, the Moulin Rouge lured Parisians of all social stripes—including, of course, the famous Toulouse-Lautrec, who immortalized the venue and its dancers in his paintings. Although shows are no longer quite so exotic (no elephants or donkey rides for the ladies), you will still see the incomparable French cancan. It's the highlight of what is now a classy version of a Vegas-y revue, starring 100 dancers, acrobats, ventriloquists, and contortionists, and more than 1,000 costumes. Dinner starts at 7, revues at 9 and 11 (arrive 30 minutes early). Men are expected to wear a jacket. Prices range from €112 for just a revue to €210 for a luxe dinner and a show. ✉ *82 bd. de Clichy, 18e, Montmartre* ☎ *01–53–09–82–82* ⊕ *www.moulinrouge. fr* Ⓜ *Blanche.*

17

THE MARAIS

A first-class shopping destination by day, by night this superchic neighborhood draws a diverse and trendy crowd for its *branché* cocktail bars and the city's most vibrant gay and lesbian scene.

BARS

Andy Wahloo. Andy Wahloo has a hip crowd and an Andy Warhol–meets- *Casablanca* decor. Fans of the ginger-rum Wahloo *spéciales* relax on oversize paint-can stools beneath high-kitsch silk-screened Moroccan coffee ads, and listen to funky Arabic Raï remixes. Dancing to DJs starts later in the night. ✉ *69 rue des Gravilliers, 3e, Marais* ☎ *01–42–71–20–38* ⊕ *andywahloo-bar.com* Ⓜ *Arts et Métiers.*

Auld Alliance. You'll feel like an honorary Highlander at Auld Alliance, where Scottish shields adorn the walls and the bar staff (who don kilts for special events) serve 120-plus types of whiskey. Scottish beer and pub grub, including a haggis burger, are also available. It's a great place to catch televised soccer or rugby matches, and, on occasion, live music. ✉ *80 rue François Miron, 4e, Marais* ☎ *01–48–04–30–40* ⊕ *www.theauldalliance.com* Ⓜ *St-Paul.*

Bar at the Hotel Jules & Jim. The look here is something between a chic contemporary Paris apartment and a low-key lounge. Enjoy a cocktail over a good book from the bar library, or relax with a smooth drink in front of the outdoor fireplace. ✉ *11 rue des Gravilliers, 3e, Marais* ☎ *01–44–54–13–13* ⊕ *www.hoteljulesetjim.com* Ⓜ *Arts et Métiers, Rambuteau.*

Candelaria. Steamy Candelaria is a tacqueria by day and a cocktail lounge by night. The tang of tequila hangs in the air at this hip hideaway, where deftly crafted drinks are poured for a contented crowd. ⊠ *52 rue de Saintonge, 3e, Marais* ☎ *01–42–74–41–28* ⊕ *www.candelariaparis. com* Ⓜ *Filles du Calvaire.*

Grazie. Equal parts cocktail bar and gourmet pizzeria, this stylish offspring of the übercool concept store Merci promises top-quality libations and stone-oven-baked pizza. The decor is industrial-rustic, with pressed-tin ceilings and a corrugated-iron bar, all enhanced by mood lighting. It's jam-packed with neighborhood hipsters, so reservations are a must. ⊠ *91 bd. Beaumarchais, 3e, Marais* ☎ *01–42–78–11–96* ⊕ *www.graziegrazie.fr* Ⓜ *Saint-Sébastien–Froissart.*

La Belle Hortense. This spot is heaven for anyone who ever wished they had a book in a bar (or a drink in a bookstore). The *bar litteraire* is the infamous spot where gal-about-town Catherine M. launched her *vie sexuelle* that became a bawdy bestseller. ⊠ *31 rue Vielle-du-Temple, 4e, Marais* ☎ *01–48–04–74–60* Ⓜ *St-Paul.*

La Perle. Straights, gays, and lesbians of all types come to mingle at this bustling, buzzy Marais masterpiece. The crowd makes the place interesting, not the neon lights, diner-style seats, or stripped-down decor. It continues to pack in some of the city's fashion movers and shakers from midafternoon on. ⊠ *78 rue Vielle-du-Temple, 3e, Marais* ☎ *01–42–72–69–93* ⊕ *cafelaperle.com* Ⓜ *Chemin-Vert.*

Le Mary Celeste. Half-price oysters at happy hour (6–7 pm) aren't the only reason this refreshingly unpretentious cocktail bar has been wildly popular since debuting in 2013. One of a trilogy of superhip watering holes (including Candelaria and Glass) opened by a trio of expat restaurateurs, its craft cocktails, microbrews, natural wines, and standout tapas menu deliver the goods and then some. If you're planning to dine, reserve ahead online. ⊠ *1 rue Commines, 3e, Marais* ⊕ *www. lemaryceleste.com* Ⓜ *Saint-Sébastian–Froissart.*

Le Trésor. Located on a tiny street that's a tad separated from the sometimes-madding crowd of the Marais, this large, lively space has mismatched baroque furnishings and a chill vibe. ⊠ *7 rue du Trésor, 4e, Marais* ☎ *01–42–71–35–17* Ⓜ *St-Paul.*

Little Red Door. Behind the red door, you'll discover a dark, cozy lounge that has style, sophistication, and atmosphere without the attitude. Creative cocktails—supplemented by artisanal beers and well-chosen wines by the glass (the last of which aren't always easy to come by in a cocktail bar)—can be enjoyed from a cushy velour barstool or cubbyhole alcove. ⊠ *60 rue Charlot, 3e, Marais* ☎ *01–42–71–19–32* ⊕ *www. lrdparis.com* Ⓜ *Filles du Calvert.*

Max y Jeremy. An almost-too-cool crew can be found in Max y Jeremy's red ember-like interior, drinking cocktails and eating the sultry bite-sized *pintxos* of Basque country. There's a distinct party atmosphere here, which can spill into the street, especially in summer. ⊠ *6 rue Dupuis, 3e, Marais* ☎ *01–42–78–00–68* ⊕ *www.maxyjeremy.com* Ⓜ *Temple.*

Fodor's Choice ★ **Sherry Butt.** On a quiet street close to the Bastille, Sherry Butt's relaxed loftlike atmosphere, imaginative drinks, whiskey flights, and tasty bar menu draw a lively crowd that appreciates meticulously crafted cocktails. A DJ spins on weekends. ✉ *20 rue Beautreillis, 4e, Marais* ☎ *09–83–38–47–80* ⊕ *www.sherrybuttparis.com* Ⓜ *Bastille, Sully-Morland.*

GAY AND LESBIAN BARS AND CLUBS

Café Cox. "Le Cox" is a prime gay pickup joint. Behind the frosted-glass windows of the fire-engine-red hot spot, men appraise the talent. The café is known for its live DJ sets; and the extended Sunday happy hour—from 6 pm to 2 am—is a rollicking good time. ✉ *15 rue des Archives, 4e, Marais* ☎ *01–42–72–08–00* ⊕ *www.cox.fr* Ⓜ *Hôtel de Ville.*

Open Café. Drawing everyone from suits to punks, this spot is less of a gay meat market than neighboring Café Cox. Relaxed and always packed, it has a disco-café vibe. ✉ *17 rue des Archives, 4e, Marais* ☎ *01–42–72–26–18* ⊕ *www.opencafe.fr* Ⓜ *Hôtel de Ville.*

Raidd Bar. The ever-popular Raidd has a darker downstairs bar and potent drinks. The men are hot, and so is the steamy shower show presented after 11 pm—not for timid voyeurs. ✉ *23 rue du Temple, 3e, Marais* ☎ *01–42–77–04–88* ⊕ *www.raiddbar.com* Ⓜ *Hôtel de Ville, St-Paul.*

So What! This happening lesbian bar in the heart of the gay district welcomes all comers (including small groups of men). The DJ in the tiny basement cooks on Friday and Saturday nights. ✉ *30 rue du Roi de Sicile, 4e, Marais* ☎ *01–42–71–24–59* Ⓜ *St-Paul.*

Tango. Carefully safeguarding its dance-hall origins, Tango lures a friendly mixed crowd of gays, lesbians, and "open-minded" heteros. Late-night music is mostly French and American pop, but the DJ plays classic chansons (French torch songs) before midnight—so arrive early to waltz and swing! ✉ *13 rue au Maire, 3e, Marais* ☎ *01–42–72–17–78* ⊕ *www.boite-a-frissons.fr* Ⓜ *Arts et Métiers.*

3W Kafé. 3W, as in "Women With Women," is a pillar of the lesbian scene. ✉ *8 rue des Ecouffes, 4e, Marais* ☎ *01–48–87–39–26* Ⓜ *St-Paul.*

EASTERN PARIS

Young and hip—from the colorful cafés and bars surrounding Place de la Bastille to the newly chic 20e arrondissement, with Oberkampf's artsy cocktail clubs and Canal St-Martin's trendy watering holes in between—there's enough here for a week of stellar nights out.

BASTILLE/NATION

CLUBS

Barrio Latino. Hoping to hear Latin beats in the heart of Paris? Barrio Latino rocks the rafters. The quirky four-story venue has a hacienda-resto, two dance bars, and a top-floor nightclub where devotees shake to salsa and samba all night. The pricey €20 weekend entrance fee includes a drink. ✉ *46–48 rue du Faubourg St-Antoine, 12e, Bastille* ☎ *01–55–78–84–75* ⊕ *www.barrio-latino.com* Ⓜ *Bastille.*

17

Fodor'sChoice **Concrete.** On a barge moored in the Seine, superhip Concrete is one
★ of Paris's preeminent hard-core dance venues. It goes full tilt until the
wee hours on Friday and Saturday nights; it also opens on alternate
Sundays, when you can party from 7 am to 2 am accompanied by live
acts—heavy on the techno—and Paris's hottest DJs. ⊠ *69 port de la
Rapée, Bastille* ☎ *No phone* ⊕ *www.concreteparis.fr* Ⓜ *Gare de Lyon,
Gare d'Austerlitz.*

Le Balajo. A casual dance club in an old ballroom, Le Balajo has been
around since 1936. Latin groove, funk, and R&B disco are the standards, with old-style musette Monday afternoon, salsa on Tuesday and
Thursday nights, and rock on Wednesday night. Friday and Saturday
are ladies' nights, with free entry before 12:30 am. ⊠ *9 rue de Lappe,
11e, Bastille* ☎ *01–47–00–07–87* ⊕ *www.balajo.fr* Ⓜ *Bastille.*

BERCY/TOLBIAC

BARS

Folie en Tête. Folie en Tête or "Lunacy in the Head," is a former mainstay of Paris's '70s punk scene. The comfortable interior is decorated
with percussion instruments, comic books, and old skis. It's known for
world music and jazz, not to mention the traffic light in the toilet that
lets you know when it's safe to enter. ⊠ *33 rue de la Butte aux Cailles,
13e, Eastern Paris* ☎ *01–45–80–65–99* ⊕ *lafolieentete.wix.com/lesite*
Ⓜ *Corvisart, Place d'Italie.*

CLUBS

Le Batofar. An old tugboat refitted as a hip (yet reasonably priced) bar
and concert venue, Le Batofar plays eclectic music, from live world-beat
to electronic and techno. (Stylish) sneakers are recommended on the
slippery deck. ⊠ *Port de la Gare, 13e, Eastern Paris* ☎ *01–53–60–17–00*
⊕ *www.batofar.org* Ⓜ *Bibliothèque.*

Le Djoon. This is not the place to stand around. Le Djoon attracts a
devoted dance crowd, and DJs (inspired by the '80s New York house
scene) mix afro, disco, and funk. It's a taxi-ride away from everywhere,
but a fun diversion from the normally cramped clubs. It's open Friday
and Saturday from 11:30 to 5 am, Thursday from 10 to 1 am. ⊠ *22 bd.
Vincent Auriol, 13e, Eastern Paris* ☎ *01–45–70–83–49* ⊕ *www.djoon.
com* Ⓜ *Quai de la Gare.*

CANAL ST-MARTIN

BARS

Chez Prune. Epitomizing the effortless cool of this arty neighborhood,
Chez Prune is a lively golden getaway. It offers the designers, architects,
and journalists who gather here a prime terrace for gazing out at the
arched footbridges and funkier locals of Canal St-Martin. ⊠ *36 rue
Beaurepaire, 10e, Canal St-Martin* ☎ *01–42–41–30–47* Ⓜ *République,
Jacques Bonsergent.*

Hôtel du Nord. This hotel—which starred in the classic Marcel Carné film
of the same name—has been spiffed up but still maintains its cool with
a vibrant lounge-bar (and restaurant) scene in the buzz-worthy Canal
St-Martin district. ⊠ *102 quai de Jemmapes, 10e, Canal St-Martin*
☎ *01–40–40–78–78* ⊕ *www.hoteldunord.org* Ⓜ *Goncourt.*

La Patache. Among the bars and eateries lining Rue Lancry, you'll find La Patache. It has a wide selection of wines and a retro-inspired ambience fueled by a jukebox and candlelight that illuminates the vintage photos on the wall. ⊠ *60 rue Lancry, 10e, Canal St-Martin* ☎ *01–42–08–14–35* Ⓜ *Jacques-Bonsergent.*

CLUBS

La Java. The spot where Piaf and Chevalier made their names has reinvented itself as a dance club with an emphasis on rock–pop, soul, and electro. It also hosts inexpensive performances by up-and-coming bands. ⊠ *105 rue du Faubourg du Temple, 10e, Canal St-Martin* ☎ *01–42–02–20–52* ⊕ *www.la-java.fr* Ⓜ *Belleville, Goncourt.*

Le Gibus. This is one of Paris's most famous music venues. More than 6,500 concerts (put on by the likes of Iggy Pop, The Clash, and The Police) have packed in fans for 30-plus years. Today the Gibus's cellars are *the* place for electro, techno, and hip-hop. ⊠ *18 rue du Faubourg du Temple, 11e, Canal St-Martin* ☎ *01–47–00–78–88* ⊕ *www.gibus. fr* Ⓜ *République.*

OBERKAMPF

BARS

Café Charbon. Neighborhood bohos are seduced by Café Charbon's warm, wooden, Belle Époque charm and floor-to-soaring-ceiling mirrors. ⊠ *109 rue Oberkampf, 11e, Oberkampf* ☎ *01–43–57–55–13* Ⓜ *Rue St-Maur, Parmentier.*

Favela Chic. This popular Latin cocktail bar took the scene early, forging Oberkampf's hip reputation. Back behind courtyard gates you'll find caipirinhas and mojitos, guest DJs presenting an eclectic mix of samba, soul, and hip-hop, and a nonstop dance scene. ⊠ *18 rue du Faubourg du Temple, 11e, Oberkampf* ☎ *01–40–21–38–14* ⊕ *favelachic. com* Ⓜ *République.*

Fodor'sChoice
★ **L'Entrée des Artistes.** Veterans of some of Paris's best new-generation cocktail clubs, the bar talent here mixes up a few rarified options that will please both amateurs and aficionados. The small, dark bar feels more like an atmospheric neighborhood joint than a magnet for trendy night crawlers. Some very good nibbles and a skillful wine selection are just icing on the cake. ⊠ *8 rue Crussol, 11e, Oberkampf* ☎ *09–50–99–67–11* Ⓜ *Filles du Calvaire, Oberkampf.*

CLUBS

Le Nouveau Casino. You'll find this concert hall and club tucked behind the Café Charbon. Pop and rock concerts prevail during the week, with revelry on Friday and Saturday from midnight until dawn. Hip-hop, house, disco, and techno DJs are the standard. ⊠ *109 rue Oberkampf, 11e, Oberkampf* ☎ *01–43–57–57–40* ⊕ *www.nouveaucasino.net* Ⓜ *Parmentier.*

Pop-In. On a back street just off the Boulevard Beaumarchais (which links the Bastille to République), this dark, hard-partying boho playhouse has a pronounced English-rocker feel. ⊠ *105 rue Amelot, 4e, Oberkampf* ☎ *01–48–05–56–11* ⊕ *popin.fr* Ⓜ *St-Sebastien–Froissart.*

17

PÈRE-LACHAISE

BARS

Mama Shelter. Hip Parisians make the pilgrimage to visit the Island Bar at this hotel, the happeningest spot around. Beautiful people flock in for solid cocktails, foosball, and even an adjacent pizza bar. It's always packed, but lines are out the door Thursday through Saturday, when DJs and other international artists perform. ✉ *109 rue de Bagnolet, 20e, Eastern Paris* ☎ *01–43–48–48–48* ⊕ *www.mamashelter.com* Ⓜ *Alexandre Dumas.*

CLUBS

Flèche d'Or. A bastion of rock concerts and other musical performances, this venue is just across the street from Mama Shelter, in a neighborhood some like to call the Brooklyn of Paris. ✉ *102 bis, rue Bagnolet, 20e, Eastern Paris* ☎ *01–44–64–01–02* ⊕ *www.flechedor.fr* Ⓜ *Alexandre Dumas.*

Le Bellevilloise. This multiuse exhibition space in a hip, up-and-coming neighborhood functions as a bar, dance club, restaurant, and performance venue, with concerts and burlesque shows. ✉ *19–21 rue Boyer, 20e, Eastern Paris* ☎ *01–46–36–07–07* ⊕ *www.labellevilloise.com* Ⓜ *Gambetta, Ménilmontant.*

LATIN QUARTER

The smoke may have cleared from the jazz clubs in the city's historically bohemian quarter, but the atmosphere's still hot—or cool, depending on how you look at it.

BARS

Delmas. This bar-café-resto attracts a buzzing student crowd with its comfy leather couches, exposed brick walls, trompe l'oeil bookcases, and diner-style food. ✉ *2 pl. de la Contrescarpe, 5e, Latin Quarter* ☎ *01–43–26–51–26* ⊕ *www.cafedelmasparis.com* Ⓜ *Cardinal Lemoine.*

Polly Maggoo. This convivial hangout is legendary as the student rioters' unofficial HQ during the May '68 uprising and is named after the satirical French art-house movie about a supermodel. Weekends are wild, with drinks at the wacky tile bar and live Latin music that keeps the party thumping until morning. ✉ *3–5 rue du Petit Pont, 5e, Latin Quarter* ☎ *01–46–33–33–64* Ⓜ *St-Michel.*

CABARET

Paradis Latin. Occupying a building that's attributed to Gustav Eiffel, Paradis Latin peppers its quirky show with acrobatics and eye-popping lighting effects, making this the liveliest and trendiest cabaret on the Left Bank. Prices range from €65 (for the show only) to €190 (with the top-of-line dinner option and wine added in). ✉ *28 rue du Cardinal Lemoine, 5e, Latin Quarter* ☎ *01–43–25–28–28* ⊕ *www.paradislatin. com* Ⓜ *Cardinal Lemoine.*

JAZZ CLUBS

Caveau de la Huchette. One of the few surviving cellar clubs from the 1940s, Caveau de la Huchette boasts the "best boppers" in the city and packs 'em in for swing dancing and Dixieland tunes. It's a killer jazz spot for everyone but claustrophobics. The music continues till dawn Thursday to Saturday. ✉ *5 rue de la Huchette, 5e, Latin Quarter* ☎ *01–43–26–65–05* ⊕ *www.caveaudelahuchette.fr* Ⓜ *St-Michel.*

ST-GERMAIN-DES-PRÉS

Exclusivity is the theme in the bobo (bourgeois-bohème) left bank, where "private" clubs draw celebs and fashionistas, and stylish cocktail bars cater to an urbane mix of students, gallerists, expats, and urban sophisticates.

BARS

Alcazar. Sir Terence Conran's makeover of a 17th-century Parisian *jeu de paume* court features a stylish mezzanine-level bar under a greenhouse-glass roof. DJs and "sound designers" spin mixes into the wee hours Thursday through Saturday. ✉ *62 rue Mazarine, 6e, St-Germain-des-Prés* ☎ *01–53–10–19–99* ⊕ *www.alcazar.fr/en* Ⓜ *Odéon.*

Bar du Marché. Waiters wearing red overalls and revolutionary "Gavroche" hats serve drinks every day of the week at this local institution (they demonstrate particular zeal around happy hour). With bottles of wine at about €25, it draws a quintessential Left Bank mix of expats, fashion-house interns, and even some professional rugby players. Sit outside on the terrace and enjoy the prime corner location. ✉ *75 rue de Seine, 6e, St-Germain-des-Prés* ☎ *01–43–26–55–15* Ⓜ *Mabillon, Odéon.*

Chez Georges. Chez Georges has been serving red wine, pastis, and beer for the past 60-odd years in pretty much the same *caveau* that still packs in devotees today. Older students and locals fill sofas and crowd around tiny, candle-topped tables in the cellar bar before grinding to pulsing world music all night. ✉ *11 rue de Canettes, 6e, St-Germain-des-Prés* ☎ *01–43–26–79–15* Ⓜ *Mabillon.*

Compagnie des Vins Surnaturels. After jump-starting the Paris cocktail bar scene, the partners behind the Experimental Cocktail Club and the Ballroom du Beef Club applied the same winning formula to this hybrid wine bar–nightclub. Plush surroundings, an extensive wine list, and upscale nibbles draw a crowd of hip young Parisians who can hone their wine-tasting skills on classics in every price range. Natural-wine aficionados, get thee to a full-fledged wine bar; though solid, the wine list here does not deliver as promised. ✉ *7 rue Lobineau, 6e, St-Germain-des-Prés* ☎ *06–14–76–81–08* ⊕ *compagniedesvinssurnaturels. com* Ⓜ *Odéon, Mabillon.*

L'Hôtel. The hushed baroque bar at L'Hôtel is ideal for a discreet rendezvous. Designed in typically jaw-dropping Jacques Garcia style, the hideaway evokes the decadent spirit of one-time resident Oscar Wilde. ✉ *13 rue des Beaux-Arts, 6e, St-Germain-des-Prés* ☎ *01–44–41–99–00* ⊕ *www.l-hotel.com* Ⓜ *St-Germain-des-Prés.*

Prescription Cocktail Club. This club is brought to you by the owners of popular cocktail bars in London, New York, and Paris—including the Ballroom du Beef Club and the Experimental Cocktail Club. So rest assured: the atmosphere will be stylish (think upholstered chairs, dim

17

lighting, and vintage touches), the crowd hip, and the drinks tasty. Located in fashionable St-Germain-des-Prés, it's a good after-shopping apéro or dinner option. ✉ *23 rue Mazarine, 6e, St-Germain-des-Prés* ☎ *01–46–34–67–73* ⊕ *www.prescriptioncocktailclub.com* Ⓜ *Odéon.*

CLUBS

Le Montana. It's notoriously difficult to get past the doorman at Le Montana, a sleek club owned by French nightlife king André (Le Baron). A Studio 54 vibe, Vincent Darré decor, and enormous cocktails make it popular among models, actors, artists, and Parisian playboys. ✉ *28 rue St-Benoît, 6e, St-Germain-des-Prés* ☎ *01–44–39–71–00* Ⓜ *St-Germain-des-Prés, Mabillon.*

MONTPARNASSE

Immortalized in the 1920s by the likes of F. Scott Fitzgerald and Pablo Picasso, the cafés and bars in this quiet corner of the city still radiate atmosphere. Whether sipping a sidecar at Hemingway's beloved La Closerie des Lilas or slurping oysters at one of the quarter's storied brasseries, you can't help but fall under Paris's spell here.

BARS

La Closerie des Lilas. La Closerie's swank "American-style" bar lets you drink in the swirling action of the adjacent restaurant and brasserie at a piano bar adorned with plaques honoring former habitués like Man Ray, Jean-Paul Sartre, Samuel Beckett, and Ernest Hemingway, who talks of "the Lilas" in *A Moveable Feast.* ✉ *171 bd. du Montparnasse, 6e, Montparnasse* ☎ *01–40–51–34–50* ⊕ *www.closeriedeslilas. fr* Ⓜ *Montparnasse.*

Le Rosebud. Step through the Art Nouveau front door of Jean-Paul Sartre's one-time haunt and you're instantly immersed in the dark, moody, fourth dimension of Old Montparnasse, where white-jacketed servers and red-lacquered tables transport you into the past. ✉ *11 bis, rue Delambre, 14e, Montparnasse* ☎ *01–43–35–38–54* Ⓜ *Vavin.*

JAZZ CLUBS

Le Petit Journal Montparnasse. This venerable club has long attracted the greats in French and international jazz, with a focus on big band music. Dinner is served from 8 pm to 1 am. A second Le Petit Journal location (at 71 boulevard St-Michel in the Latin Quarter) specializes in Dixieland tunes. ✉ *13 rue du Commandant Mouchotte, 14e, Montparnasse* ☎ *01–43–21–56–70* ⊕ *petitjournalmontparnasse.com* Ⓜ *Montparnasse–Bienvenüe.*

PERFORMING ARTS

Updated by
Nancy Heslin

The performing arts scene in Paris runs the gamut from highbrow to lowbrow, cheap (or free) to break-the-bank expensive. Venues are indoors and outdoors, opulent or spartan, and dress codes vary accordingly. Regardless of the performance you choose, it's probably unlike anything you've seen before. Parisians have an audacious sense of artistic adventure and a stunning eye for scene and staging. An added bonus in this city of classic beauty is that many of the venues themselves—from the opulent interiors of the Opéra Garnier and the Opéra Royal de Versailles to the Art Deco splendor of the Théâtre des Champs-Élysées—are a feast for the eyes.

One thing that sets Paris apart in the arts world is the active participation of the Ministry of Culture, which sponsors numerous concert halls and theaters, like the Comédie Française, that tend to present less commercial, though artistically captivating, productions. Other venues with broader appeal are known for sold-out shows and decade-long runs.

Most performances are in French, although you can find English theater productions. English-language movies are often presented undubbed, with subtitles. Of course, you don't need to speak the language to enjoy opera, classical music, dance, or the circus.

PLANNING

FESTIVALS

The music and theater season generally runs from September to June, but summer is packed with all sorts of performing arts festivals.

Days Off Festival. Held over 10 days in early July at the Philharmonie de Paris, this festival focuses on pop-rock, with some jazz and electro thrown in for good measure. Headliners like Rufus Wainwright and Blur frontman Damon Albarn lure Parisians away from their offices. Tickets can cost as much as €50, but some are *gratis*. ✉ *221 av. Jean-Jaurès, 19e, Eastern Paris* ☎ *01–44–84–44–84* ⊕ *www.daysoff.fr* Ⓜ *Porte de Pantin.*

Festival d'Automne à Paris. Since 1972, the Paris Autumn Festival has featured a packed program that includes contemporary dance, theater, music, the visual arts, and film. From September to December, 100,000 fans attend 50 productions from more than a dozen countries. They're staged in assorted venues in and around the city, and tickets cost €8 to €35. ✉ *Paris* ☎ *01–53–45–17–00* ⊕ *www.festival-automne.com.*

Festival d'Ile de France. In September and October, this fête takes you (and 25,000 other festival goers) to extraordinary venues in Paris and the surrounding region—among them churches, old warehouses, and historical sites. The 30-plus concerts on the program range from world to pop, and Baroque to classical. Tickets cost €6 to €26; they can be purchased online or, depending on availability, 45 minutes before showtime. The festival celebrates its 40th anniversary in 2017. ☎ *01–58–71–01–01* ⊕ *www.festival-idf.fr.*

Jazz à la Villette. The annual Jazz à la Villette Festival is held at various Parc de La Villette venues, including the Philharmonie de Paris and Trabendo, over 10 days in early September. You'll pay €8 to €33 for tickets; check the website for detailed information. ✉ *211 av. Jean Jaurès, 19e, Eastern Paris* ☎ *01–40–03–75–75* ⊕ *www.jazzalavillette. com* Ⓜ *Porte de Pantin.*

Orangerie du Parc de Bagatelle. The Chopin Festival and the Solistes Festival strike musical high notes in the Orangerie du Parc de Bagatelle, one of Paris's most beautiful gardens. The former runs from mid-June through mid-July; the latter is held on three consecutive weekends in September. Tickets will set you back €20 to €34. ✉ *Parc de Bagatelle, Allée de Longchamp, 16e, Western Paris* ☎ *01–53–64–53–80* ⊕ *www.frederic-chopin. com* ⊕ *www.ars-mobilis.com* Ⓜ *Porte Maillot, then Bus 244.*

Parc Floral. Free outdoor classical concerts, staged Saturdays and Sundays at 4 pm from August to mid-September, draw fans to the Parc Floral in Bois de Vincennes (entrance to the park is €6). This is also the spot that hosts the Paris Jazz Festival each weekend in June and July. ✉ *12e, Eastern Paris* ☎ *01–43–28–41–59* ⊕ *www.vincennes.fr* ⊕ *www. parisjazzfestival.fr* Ⓜ *Château de Vincennes.*

Quartier d'Été. Held throughout Paris from mid-July to mid-August, the Quartier d'Été festival attracts international stars of dance, world music, theater, and the circus. Prices for concert tickets typically range from €8 to €20, but half of the performances are free. ✉ *Paris* ☎ *01–44–94–98–00* ⊕ *www.quartierdete.com.*

Rock-en-Seine. This rock festival, which runs each August on the outskirts of Paris, is one of the largest of its kind in France; past headliners include Lana Del Rey, Arcade Fire, and the Foo Fighters. A three-day pass is €119. ✉ *Domaine National de St-Cloud, Parc de St-Cloud, Outside Paris* ⊕ *www.rockenseine.com* Ⓜ *Boulogne-Pont de Saint-Cloud.*

TICKET PRICES AND DISCOUNTS

As anywhere, it's best to buy tickets in advance.

Events range in price from about €5 for standing room at the Opéra Bastille to upward of €180 for an elaborate National Ballet production. Most performances, however, are in the €10 to €35 range. Discounts are often available for limited-visibility seats or for students and senior citizens. Movies cost €6.50 to €11.80, but many cinemas have reduced rates for matinees or for people under a certain age (18 or 26, depending on the venue).

FNAC. FNAC sells tickets online and in its 10 city stores, including one on the Champs-Élysées. ✉ *Galerie du Claridge, 74 av. des Champs-Élysées, 8e, Champs-Élysées* ☎ *08–25–02–00–20 €0.18 per min* ⊕ *www. fnactickets.com* Ⓜ *George V.*

Le Kiosque Théâtre. Half-price tickets for same-day theater performances are available at Le Kiosque Théâtre's Madeleine location. See the website for information on outlets in Place Raoul Dautry (Montparnasse) and Place des Ternes (Les Grands Boulevards). ✉ *Across from 15 pl. de la Madeleine, 7e, Around the Louvre* ⊕ *www.kiosquetheatre.com* Ⓜ *Madeleine.*

Half-price tickets are also obtainable from many theaters during the first week of each new show's run, and inexpensive tickets can often be bought last minute.

WHERE TO GET INFO

Detailed entertainment listings in French can be found in the weekly magazines *Pariscope* and *L'Officiel des Spectacles,* available at newsstands and in bookstores; in the Wednesday entertainment insert *Figaroscope,* in the *Figaro* newspaper (⊕ *evene.lefigaro.fr*); and in the weekly *À Nous Paris,* distributed free in the métro. The webzine *Paris Voice* (⊕ *www.parisvoice.com*) offers superb highlights in English. Most performing arts venues also have their own websites, and many include listings as well as other helpful information in English.

The website of the Paris Tourist Office (⊕ *www.parisinfo.com*) has theater and music listings in English.

ARTS CENTERS

Le Lucernaire. Occupying an abandoned factory, Le Lucernaire wins a standing ovation as far as cultural centers are concerned. With three theaters staging a total of six performances per day, three movie screens, a bookstore, photography exhibitions, a lively restaurant-bar, and the equally lively surrounding neighborhood of Vavin, it caters to young intellectuals. ✉ *53 rue Notre-Dame-des-Champs, 6e, Montparnasse* ☎ *01–45–44–57–34* ⊕ *www.lucernaire.fr* Ⓜ *Notre-Dame-des-Champs.*

Fodor's Choice ★ **Opéra Garnier.** The magnificent, magical former haunt of the Phantom of the Opera, painter Edgar Degas, and any number of legendary opera stars still hosts performances of the Opéra de Paris, along with a fuller calendar of dance performances (the theater is the official home of the Ballet de l'Opéra National de Paris). The grandest opera productions are usually mounted at the Opéra Bastille, whereas the Garnier now presents smaller-scale works such as Mozart's *La Clemenza di Tito* and *Così Fan Tutte*. Gorgeous and intimate though the Garnier is, its tiara-shape theater means that many seats have limited visibility, so it's best to ask specifically what the sight lines are when booking (partial view in French is *visibilité partielle*). The cheaper seats are often those with partial views. Seats generally go on sale at the box office a month before any given show, earlier by phone and online; you must appear in person to buy the cheapest tickets. Last-minute returned or unsold tickets, if available, are offered an hour prior to a performance. The box office is open 11:30–6:30 Monday to Saturday and one hour before curtain call; however, you should get in line up to two hours in advance. You can also check the website at noon on certain Wednesdays for flash sales of sold-out shows. Venue visits (€11) and guided tours in English (€14.50) are available and can be reserved online; check the website for details. (*See Chapter 6, Les Grands Boulevards.*) ✉ *Pl. de l'Opéra, 9e, Les Grands Boulevards* ☎ *08–92–89–90–90 €0.34 per min, 01–71–25–24–23 from outside France* ⊕ *www.operadeparis.fr* ☞ *Box office closed July 17–Aug. 24* Ⓜ *Opéra.*

Fodor'sChoice ★ **Opéra Royal de Versailles.** The most lavish opera house in France (and perhaps in all of Europe) hosts an impressive yearly calendar of major operas, ballets, recitals, and musical theater by world-class French and international performers. The intimate 652-seat theater has excellent acoustics and provides an ideal setting for works by big-name composers, with an emphasis on the Baroque and classical periods. Finished in 1770—just in time for the marriage ceremonies of the young dauphin (later King Louis XVI) and 14-year-old Marie-Antoinette—the structure's stunning neoclassical decor is crafted entirely of gilded and faux-marbled wood. A regular program of smaller concerts is also held in the splendid Hall of Mirrors (Galerie des Glaces) and at the Royal Chapel, where recitals might feature a 300-year-old royal organ. Although it's recommended to buy tickets online one to two months in advance (up to six months ahead for star performers), they can be purchased at the box office on the evening of the performance depending on availability. There are no bad seats at the Royal Opéra, so instead of spending upward of €100 on a ticket, you can get away with something a bit less pricey. For the Hall of Mirrors, you may not see much in the cheap seats, but the sound will still be glorious. (*See Chapter 19, Side Trips from Paris.*) ✉ *Place d'Armes, Versailles* ⊹ *By commuter train (SNCF) from Paris Gare Montparnasse or Paris Gare Saint Lazare to Gare Versailles Chantiers or Rive Droite* ☎ *01–30–83–78–89* ⊕ *www.chateauversailles-spectacles.fr* Ⓜ *RER C: Gare Versailles Rive Gauche.*

Philharmonie de Paris. After a postponement of nearly two decades and an outlay of more than €380 million, the Philharmonie de Paris symphonic concert hall opened in January 2015. Designed by French architect Jean Nouvel, this is one of the world's finest and most expensive auditoriums. It can accommodate 2,400 music lovers, and the adjustable modular seating means you'll be able to see the stage no matter where you sit. Since the hall is home to the Orchestre de Paris, concerts are mostly classical; however, programming includes guest artists and, on weekends, pop, jazz, and world music performances appeal to patrons with more diverse tastes—and smaller budgets. Part of the same complex (formerly known as the Cité de la Musique), **Philharmonie 2** features a 1,000-seat concert hall and a 250-seat amphitheater. Designed by Christian de Portzamparc, they opened in 1995 and present an eclectic range of concerts (some of which are free) in a postmodern setting. The Philharmonie de Paris is a 45-minute métro ride from downtown. If you're driving, there are 600 parking spaces available. ⊠ *221 av. Jean Jaurès, 19e, Eastern Paris* ☎ *01–44–84–44–84* ⊕ *www.philharmoniedeparis. fr* Ⓜ *Porte de Pantin.*

Théâtre des Champs-Élysées. This was the scene of 1913's infamous Battle of the Rite of Spring, when police had to be called in after the audience ripped up seats in outrage at Stravinsky's *Le Sacre du Printemps* score and Nijinsky's choreography. Today Théâtre des Champs-Élysées is elegantly restored and worthy of a visit if only for the architecture (it's one of Paris's most striking examples of Art Deco). The theater also hosts first-rate opera and dance performances, along with orchestral, chamber, and Sunday morning concerts. ⊠ *15 av. Montaigne, 8e, Champs-Élysées* ☎ *01–49–52–50–50* ⊕ *www.theatrechampselysees.fr* Ⓜ *Alma-Marceau.*

CIRCUS

Italian Antonio Franconi helped launch the first Cirque Olympique (considered the start of the modern circus) in Paris in 1783, and the French have been hooked ever since. Circus acts are cherished as high art for all ages here. The city boasts a 19th-century permanent circus theater and sprouts tents in every major park to present spectacles from the sublime to the quirky.

Cirque d'Hiver Bouglione. Cirque d'Hiver Bouglione brings together two famous circus institutions: the beautiful Cirque d'Hiver hall, constructed in 1852, and the Bouglione troupe, known for its rousing assembly of acrobats, jugglers, clowns, trapeze artists, tigers, and house cats that leap through rings of fire. Shows run mid-October to March, with a new production each season. ⊠ *110 rue Amelot, 11e, République* ☎ *01–47–00–28–81* ⊕ *www.cirquedhiver.com* Ⓜ *Filles du Calvaire.*

Cirque National Alexis Gruss. Founded in 1854, Cirque National Alexis Gruss remains true to the *Cirque à l'Ancienne* philosophy, serving up a traditional circus with showy horseback riders, trapeze artists, and clowns. The large-scale production runs mid-October through early January, with performances on Thursday, Friday, and Saturday at 4 or 8 pm, and on Sunday at 4 pm. Tickets cost €20 to €75. ⊠ *Carrefour des cascades, Porte de Passy, 16e, Western Paris* ☎ *01–45–01–71–26* ⊕ *www.alexis-gruss.com* Ⓜ *Ranelagh.*

Espace Chapiteaux. Parc de la Villette is home to Espace Chapiteaux: a circus-tent complex that hosts guest troupes several times a year, as well as students from the National Circus Arts Center. ⊠ *211 av. Jean-Jaurès, 19e, Eastern Paris* ☎ *01–40–03–75–75* ⊕ *www.villette. com* Ⓜ *Porte de Pantin.*

FAMILY **Théâtre Équestre Zingaro.** Ready for a variation on the circus theme? If
FodorśChoice you're lucky enough to be visiting during the two months Zingaro per-
★ forms at home (usually in late fall), you'll have the chance to witness a
truly unique spectacle. Since 1985, France's foremost horse whisperer,
who goes by the name of Bartabas, has created captivating equestrian
shows that mix theater, dance, music, and poetry. The 500-seat theater-
in-the-round on the outskirts of Paris is part of a Gypsy caravan, where
trainers and their families, 45 horses, and Bartabas himself live and
work. The horses perform in close proximity to the audience in astonishing displays of choreography and acrobatic skill. If you can't make
it for Zingaro, there is a consolation prize: in 2003, Bartabas created
the Académie du Spectacle Équestre at the royal stables of Versailles
(Grandes Écuries). Audiences can catch a show there on weekends
(Saturday at 6 pm, Sunday at 3 pm) and on certain weekdays during
school holidays. Expect to pay €21 to €42 for tickets. ⊠ *176 av. Jean
Jaurès, Aubervilliers* ☎ *01–39–02–62–75* ⊕ *www.bartabas.fr* Ⓜ *Fort
d'Aubervilliers.*

CONCERTS

There's something majestic about listening to classical music under the
airy roof of a medieval church, where many free or almost-free lunchtime and evening concerts are performed. Check weekly listings and
flyers posted at the churches for information.

Many museums also host concerts; tickets, affordably priced, are usually sold separately from admission. The Auditorium du Louvre, for
instance, presents chamber music or piano solos on Wednesday evening,
performances by promising new musicians on Thursday afternoon, and
either classic pieces or specially commissioned contemporary ones on
Friday evening. The Musée de Cluny stages medieval music concerts
between September and June, including *l'Heure Musicale* on Sunday at
4 and Monday at 12:30; the Musée d'Orsay, meanwhile, often offers
small-scale concerts in its lower-level auditorium.

FodorśChoice **L'Olympia.** Paris's legendary music hall hosts an eclectic roster of perfor-
★ mances that cover such far-flung genres as gospel, jazz, French *chanson,*
and rock. Edith Piaf rose to fame after a series of Olympia concerts and
Jeff Buckley's famous *Live at the Olympia* was recorded here. Now
everyone from Leonard Cohen to Lady Gaga is in on the action. ⊠ *28
bd. des Capucines, 9e, Les Grands Boulevards* ☎ *08–92–68–33–68*
€0.34 per min ⊕ *en.olympiahall.com* Ⓜ *Madeleine, Opéra.*

FodorśChoice **La Cigale.** What these walls have seen! Artists like Maurice Chevalier
★ and Arletty were once a staple of this small concert hall in the storied
Pigalle neighborhood before cabaret and vaudeville moved in. Today
it's one of Paris's top pop and contemporary music venues, featuring
such acts as Adele and Coldplay. Woody Allen even filmed scenes for
Midnight in Paris here. ⊠ *120 bd. de Rochechouart, 18e, Montmartre*
☎ *01–49–25–89–99* ⊕ *www.lacigale.fr* Ⓜ *Pigalle, Anvers.*

FodorśChoice **Salle Cortot.** This acoustic jewel was built in 1929 by Auguste Perret, who
★ promised to construct "a concert hall that sounds like a Stradivarius."

18

Tickets for the jazz and classical concerts held here can only be bought from the box office 30 minutes beforehand, otherwise go online to ⊕ *www.fnactickets.com* or ⊕ *www.concertclassic.com*. Free student recitals are offered at 12:30 on Tuesday and Thursday from October to April and on some Wednesday afternoons from January to May. ✉ *78 rue Cardinet, 17e, Les Grands Boulevards* ☎ *01–47–63–47–48* ⊕ *www.sallecortot.com* Ⓜ *Malesherbes.*

Salle Gaveau. The 1,020-seat Salle Gaveau is a perfectly appointed gold-and-white hall with remarkable acoustics and a distinctly Parisian allure. It hosts chamber music, orchestral, piano, and vocal recitals. ✉ *45–47 rue la Boétie, 8e, Champs-Élysées* ☎ *01–49–53–05–07* ⊕ *www.sallegaveau.com* Ⓜ *Miromesnil.*

DANCE

Classical ballets are staged in various historic venues, including the gorgeous Opéra Garnier. More avant-garde or up-and-coming choreographers tend to show their works off in the smaller performance spaces of the Bastille and the Marais or in the theaters of nearby suburbs. And of course there's the Centre National de Danse, which aims to make dance accessible to all.

Centre National de la Danse. Occupying a former administrative center in the suburb of Pantin, this space is dedicated to supporting professional dancers by offering classes, rehearsal studios, and a multimedia dance library. A regular program of free and reasonably priced performances, expositions, screenings, and conferences is also open to the public from October to July. ✉ *1 rue Victor Hugo, Pantin* ☎ *01–41–83–98–98* ⊕ *www.cnd.fr* Ⓜ *Hoche; RER: Pantin.*

Maison des Arts de Créteil. This popular dance venue just outside Paris often attracts top-notch international and French companies, such as Blanca Li and Bill T. Jones; it also hosts the cutting-edge EXIT Festival, which runs over 10 days from the end of March. ✉ *1 Pl. Salvador Allende, Creteil* ☎ *01–45–13–19–19* ⊕ *www.maccreteil.com* Ⓜ *Créteil-Préfecture.*

Théâtre de la Bastille. An example of the innovative activity in the Bastille area, Théâtre de la Bastille has an enviable record as a launch pad for tomorrow's modern-dance stars. ✉ *76 rue de la Roquette, 11e, Bastille* ☎ *01–43–57–42–14* ⊕ *www.theatre-bastille.com* Ⓜ *Bastille.*

Théâtre de la Cité Internationale. In the heart of the Cité Internationale Universitaire de Paris, this complex includes three theaters, an international student residence community, and a park. It hosts young, avant-garde companies; however, its future is unclear given the university's proposed budget cuts. ✉ *17 bd. Jourdan, 14e, Montparnasse* ☎ *01–43–13–50–50* ⊕ *www.theatredelacite.com* Ⓜ *RER: Cité Universitaire.*

Théâtre de la Ville. At *the* top spot for contemporary dance, you'll find French and international troupes choreographed by the world's best— like William Forsythe and Anne-Teresa de Keersmaeker's Rosas company. Concerts and theatrical performances are also part of the season.

Book early; shows sell out quickly. ✉ *2 pl. du Châtelet, 4e, Marais* ☎ *01–42–74–22–77* ⊕ *www.theatredelaville-paris.com* Ⓜ *Châtelet.*

FILM

The French call films the *septième art* (seventh art) and discuss the latest releases with the same intensity as they do gallery openings or theatrical debuts. Most theaters run English-language films undubbed, with subtitles, which are indicated with v.o., meaning *version originale*; films that are dubbed are v.f. (*version française*). First-run cinemas are clustered around the principal tourist areas, such as the Champs-Élysées, Boulevard des Italiens near the Opéra, Bastille, Châtelet, and Odéon. For listings online check ⊕ *www.allocine.fr* or ⊕ *www.offi.fr/cinema.*

> ## PUPPET SHOWS
>
> On most Wednesday, Saturday, and Sunday afternoons, the Guignol—the French equivalent of Punch and Judy—can be seen launching their hilarious puppet battles in most of Paris's larger parks. Look for performance spaces called Théâtre de Marionnettes. Entrance is usually €4.50 to €5; performances are in French.

Cinéma des Cinéastes. Catch previews of feature films, as well as documentaries, shorts, children's movies, and rarely shown flicks at Cinéma des Cinéastes. It's an old cabaret transformed into a movie house and wine bar. Tickets for matinées are only €7.50. ✉ *7 av. de Clichy, 17e, Montmartre* ☎ *08–92–68–97–17* *€0.34 per min* ⊕ *www.cinema-des-cineastes.fr* Ⓜ *Place de Clichy.*

Fodor's Choice
★
Cinémathèque Française. This is a mecca for cinephiles brought up on Federico Fellini, Igmar Bergman, and Alain Resnais. Its spectacular home—in the former American Center, designed by Frank Gehry—includes elaborate museum exhibitions plus three cinemas and a video library. ✉ *51 rue de Bercy, 12e, Bastille* ☎ *01–71–19–33–33* ⊕ *www.cinematheque.fr* Ⓜ *Bercy.*

La Géode. It's hard to miss La Géode—a steel globe with a 118-foot diameter in Parc de La Villette. The theater screens wide-angle Omnimax films—including kid-friendly documentaries—on a gigantic spherical surface. ✉ *At Cité des Sciences et de l'Industrie, Parc de La Villette, 26 av. Corentin Cariou, 19e, Eastern Paris* ☎ *01–40–05–79–99* ⊕ *www.lageode.fr* Ⓜ *Porte de La Villette.*

Fodor's Choice
★
La Pagode. Where else but Paris would you find movies shown in an antique pagoda? A Far Eastern fantasy, La Pagode was built in 1896 as a ballroom for the wife of the owner of Le Bon Marché department store. In the 1970s it was slated for demolition but saved by a grassroots wave of support spearheaded by director Louis Malle; in 1990 it was listed as a Historic Monument. Though the fare is standard, the surroundings are enchanting. Come early for tea in the garden (summer only). ✉ *57 bis, rue de Babylone, 7e, Around the Eiffel Tower* ☎ *01–45–55–48–48* Ⓜ *St-François Xavier.*

Le Balzac. Le Balzac often presents directors' talks before film screenings and features live music for silent classics. Every Saturday night, in partnership with the National Conservatory of Music, it hosts a free 20-minute concert before the movie in the main cinema. ⊠ *1 rue Balzac, 8e, Champs-Élysées* ☎ *01–45–61–10–60* ⊕ *www.cinemabalzac.com* Ⓜ *George V.*

Le Desperado. You can watch *version originale* American classics and cult films for €8 on Le Desperado's two screens. ⊠ *23 rue des Écoles, 5e, Latin Quarter* ☎ *01–43–25–72–07* Ⓜ *Maubert-Mutualité.*

Le Forum des Images. The Forum organizes thematic viewings in five state-of-the-art screening rooms, often presenting discussions with directors or film experts beforehand. Archival films and videos, workshops, and lectures are also on the schedule here. Movies cost €6, but roundtables and discussions are free; you can download the Forum app for smartphones. ⊠ *Forum des Halles, 2 rue du Cinéma, Around the Louvre* ☎ *01–44–76–63–00* ⊕ *www.forumdesimages.fr* Ⓜ *Châtelet–Les Halles (St-Eustache exit).*

Fodor's Choice ★ **Le Louxor.** First opened in 1921, Le Louxor reopened in 2013 following a lavish restoration that returned it to its original Egyptian-themed splendor. Now the city's grandest cinema, this Art Deco beauty is gorgeously appointed—all in rich ocher with jewel-tone velvet seating—and shows a roster of contemporary international art films in three cinemas. Have a drink at the top-floor bar or balcony for spectacular views of the neighborhood and Sacré-Coeur. ⊠ *170 bd. Magenta, 10e, Montmartre* ☎ *01–44–63–96–96* ⊕ *www.cinemalouxor.fr* Ⓜ *Barbès-Rochechouart.*

MK2 Bibliothèque. This slick, 20-*salle* cineplex in the shadow of Mitterrand's National Library has trademark scarlet-red chairs—they fit two people without a divider, so the experience is sort of like watching a movie at home on your couch. MK2 Bibliothèque also contains two restaurants, plus shops selling gifts and DVDs. ⊠ *128–162 av. de France, 13e, Eastern Paris* ☎ *08–92–69–84–84* €*0.60 per min* ⊕ *www.mk2.com* Ⓜ *Quai de la Gare, Bibliothèque.*

Parc de La Villette. In July and August, Parc de La Villette shows free open-air movies. Most people pack a picnic; you can also rent deck chairs and blankets for €7 by the entrance. ⊠ *In Prairie du Triangle at Parc de La Villette, 221 av. Jean-Jaurès, 19e, Eastern Paris* ☎ *01–40–03–75–75* ⊕ *www.villette.com* Ⓜ *Porte de Pantin, Porte de La Villette.*

Saint-André des Arts. One of a number of popular cinemas near the Sorbonne, Saint-André des Arts is also one of the best cinemas in Paris. It hosts an annual festival devoted to a single director (like Bergman or Tarkovski) and shows indie films every day at 1 pm. Some of the latter are part of "Les Découvertes de Saint-André" series, which focuses on the work of young filmmakers; these screenings are followed by a discussion (check the website for details). ✉ *30 rue St-André des Arts, 6e, Latin Quarter* ☎ *01–43–26–48–18* ⊕ *cinesaintandre.fr* Ⓜ *St-Michel.*

UGC Ciné-Cité Bercy. This mammoth 18-screen complex is in the Bercy Village shopping area. For sound and seating, it's one of the best. ✉ *2 cour Saint Emilion, 12e, Bastille* ☎ *01–76–64–79–64* ⊕ *www.ugc.fr* Ⓜ *Cour Saint Emilion.*

OPERA

Opéra Bastille. This mammoth ultramodern facility, designed by architect Carlos Ott and inaugurated in 1989, long ago took over the role of Paris's main opera house from the Opéra Garnier (although both operate under the same Opéra de Paris umbrella). Like the building, performances tend to be on the avant-garde side—you're as likely to see a contemporary adaptation of *La Bohème* as you are to hear Kafka set to music. Tickets for Opéra de Paris productions range from €15 to €230 and generally go on sale at the box office a month before shows, earlier by phone and online. Once the doors open, "standing places" can be purchased for €5 from vending machines in the lobby, but you'll need coins or a credit card (no bills) and patience to snag one, as the lines are long. The opera season usually runs September through July; the box office is open Monday through Saturday 11:30–6:30 and one hour before curtain call. If you just want to look around inside, you can also buy tickets for a 90-minute guided tour (€15). (*See Chapter 9, Eastern Paris.*) ✉ *Pl. de la Bastille, 12e, Eastern Paris* ☎ *08–92–89–90–90 €0.34 per minute, 01–71–25–24–23 from outside France, 01–40–01–19–70 Tours* ⊕ *www.operadeparis.fr* ☞ *Box office closed July 17–Aug. 24* Ⓜ *Bastille.*

THEATER

A number of theaters line the Grands Boulevards between the Opéra and République, but there is no Paris equivalent of Broadway or the West End. Shows are mostly in French, with a few rare exceptions. English-language theater groups playing in various venues throughout Paris and its suburbs include the **International Players** (⊕ *www.internationalplayers. co.uk*). Broadway-scale singing-and-dancing musicals are generally staged at either the Palais des Sports or the Palais des Congrès.

Ateliers Berthier. The outlying atelier for the more illustrious Théâtre de l'Odéon is in the 17e, a bit off the beaten path; the upside is that on Sunday it often has a 3 pm matinee in addition to the evening show (usually at 8 pm). ✉ *1 rue André Suarès, 17e, Les Grands Boulevards* ✛ *Corner of Bd. Berthier* ☎ *01–44–85–40–00* ⊕ *www.theatre-odeon. eu* Ⓜ *Porte de Clichy.*

Café de la Gare. This spot offers a fun opportunity to experience a particularly Parisian form of entertainment, the *café-théâtre*—part satire, part variety revue, jazzed up with slapstick humor and performed in a café salon. You'll need a good grasp of French slang and current events to keep up with the jokes. There's no reserved seating; doors open 15 minutes before showtime. ✉ *41 rue du Temple, 4e, Marais* ☎ *01–42–78–52–51* ⊕ *www.cdlg.org* Ⓜ *Hôtel de Ville.*

Casino de Paris. Once a favorite of the immortal Serge Gainsbourg, Casino de Paris has a horseshoe balcony, a cramped but cozy music-hall feel, and performances by everyone from Dora the Explorer to the Scissor Sisters. This is where Josephine Baker performed in the early '30s with her leopard, Chiquita. ✉ *16 rue de Clichy, 9e, Les Grands Boulevards* ☎ *08–92–69–89–26 €0.40 per min* ⊕ *www.casinodeparis. fr* Ⓜ *Trinité.*

Comédie des Champs-Élysées. Next door to the Théâtre des Champs-Élysées, the Comédie des Champs-Élysées offers intriguing productions in its small theater. ✉ *15 av. Montaigne, 8e, Champs-Élysées* ☎ *01–53–23–99–19* ⊕ *www.comediedeschampselysees.com* Ⓜ *Alma-Marceau.*

Comédie Française. Founded in 1680, Comédie Française is the most hallowed institution in French theater. It specializes in splendid classical French plays by the likes of Racine, Molière, and Marivaux. Buy tickets at the box office, by telephone, or online. If the theater is sold out, the Salle Richelieu offers steeply discounted last-minute tickets an hour before the performance. ✉ *Salle Richelieu, Pl. Colette, 1er, Around the Louvre* ☎ *08–25–10–16–80 €0.15 per min* ⊕ *www.comedie-francaise. fr* Ⓜ *Palais-Royal–Musée du Louvre.*

La Cartoucherie. This multitheater complex in a former munitions factory lures cast and spectators into an intimate theatrical world. Go early for a simple meal; actors often help serve "in character." Detailed information for each venue is available at the website. ✉ *In Bois de Vincennes, Rte. du Champ de Manoeuvre, 12e, Eastern Paris* ☎ *01–43–74–24–08 Théâtre du Soleil, 01–43–74–99–61 Théâtre de l'Aquarium, 01–43–28–36–36 Théâtre de la Tempête, 01–48–08–39–74 Théâtre de l'Epée de Bois* ⊕ *www.cartoucherie.fr* Ⓜ *Château de Vincennes, then shuttle bus or Bus 112.*

Le Manoir de Paris. Let yourself be enchanted (and frightened) as 35 talented performers bring Paris legends to life. When you walk through this mansion, the history of the Bloody Baker, the Phantom of the Opera, and Catherine de Medici's hired assassin are acted out—on you! If you're in Paris during Halloween, this is just about the best game in town. On holiday weekends, you could wait hours to get in, but the tour-style performance itself lasts less than 60 minutes. ✉ *18 rue de Paradis, 10e, Eastern Paris* ☎ *06–70–89–35–87* ⊕ *www.lemanoirdeparis. fr* Ⓜ *Poissonniere, Gare de l'Est.*

Odéon–Théâtre de l'Europe. The former home of the Comédie Française now focuses on pan-European theater, offering a variety of European-language productions for no more than €40. ✉ *Pl. de l'Odéon, 6e, St-Germain-des-Prés* ☎ *01–44–85–40–00* ⊕ *www.theatre-odeon.eu* Ⓜ *Odéon.*

Théâtre Darius Milhaud. Théâtre Darius Milhaud stages classics by Camus and Baudelaire, as well as occasional shows for children. ✉ *80 allée Darius Milhaud, 19e, Eastern Paris* ☎ *01–42–01–92–26* ⊕ *www. theatredariusmilhaud.fr* Ⓜ *Porte de Pantin.*

Théâtre de la Huchette. This tiny Rive Gauche venue has been staging the titanic Romanian-French writer Ionesco's *The Bald Soprano* and *The Lesson* since 1957: it holds the world record for a nonstop theater run with 18,200 performances viewed by more than 2 million people. Other productions are also mounted, and for €37 you can see two shows in one day (single tickets cost €25). ⊠ *23 rue de la Huchette, 5e, Latin Quarter* ☎ *01–43–26–38–99* ⊕ *www.theatre-huchette.com* Ⓜ *St-Michel.*

Théâtre de la Renaissance. Belle Époque superstar Sarah Bernhardt (who was the manager from 1893 to 1899) put Théâtre de la Renaissance on the map. Big French stars often perform here. Note that the theater is on the second floor, and there's no elevator. ⊠ *20 bd. Saint-Martin, 10e, Canal St-Martin* ☎ *01–42–02–47–35* ⊕ *www.theatredelarenaissance.com* Ⓜ *Strasbourg–Saint-Denis.*

Théâtre des Abbesses. Part of the Théâtre de la Ville, Théâtre des Abbesses is a 400-seat venue in Montmartre. It features lesser-known theater acts, musicians, and up-and-coming choreographers, who often make it onto the program in the Théâtre de la Ville the following year. ⊠ *31 rue des Abbesses, 18e, Montmartre* ☎ *01–42–74–22–77* ⊕ *www.theatredelaville-paris.com/aux-abbesses* Ⓜ *Abbesses.*

Théâtre des Bouffes du Nord. Welcome to the wonderfully atmospheric, slightly decrepit home of Peter Brook. The renowned British director regularly delights with his quirky experimental productions in French and, sometimes, English. ⊠ *37 bis, bd. de la Chapelle, 10e, Stalingrad/ La Chapelle* ☎ *01–46–07–34–50* ⊕ *www.bouffesdunord.com* Ⓜ *La Chapelle.*

Théâtre du Palais-Royal. Located in the former residence of Cardinal Richelieu, this plush 716-seat, Italian-style theater is bedecked in gold and purple. It specializes in lighter fare, like comedies and theatrical productions aimed at the under-12 set. ⊠ *38 rue de Montpensier, 1er, Around the Louvre* ☎ *01–42–97–40–00* ⊕ *theatrepalaisroyal.com* Ⓜ *Palais-Royal.*

Théâtre Mogador. One of Paris's most sumptuous theaters features musicals and other productions with a pronounced popular appeal (think *Cats* or *Holiday on Ice*). ⊠ *25 rue de Mogador, 9e, Les Grands Boulevards* ☎ *01–53–32–32–32* ⊕ *www.stage-entertainment.fr/theatre-mogador* Ⓜ *Trinité.*

Théâtre National de Chaillot. Housed in an imposing neoclassic building overlooking the Eiffel Tower, Théâtre National de Chaillot has a trio of theaters and a total of 1,600 seats. It's dedicated to experimental, world, and avant-garde drama, dance, and music or a mix of all three. Major names in dance—like the Ballet Royal de Suède and William Forsythe's company—visit regularly. There are programs for children, too. ⊠ *1 pl. du Trocadéro, 16e, Around the Eiffel Tower* ☎ *01–53–65–30–00* ⊕ *theatre-chaillot.fr* Ⓜ *Trocadéro.*

SIDE TRIPS
FROM PARIS

Updated
by Jennifer
Ladonne

With so much to see in Paris, it may seem hard to justify a side trip. But just outside the city lies the rest of the fabled region known as Ile-de-France: there, along with gorgeous countryside and quiet towns, you can find spectacular Versailles, the immense Chartres cathedral, and a little region unto itself where a mouse named Mickey is king.

Plan to spend an entire day (at least) at **Versailles,** perusing the manicured gardens that make up one of the largest parks in Europe, and touring the palace, which includes the Hall of Mirrors and Marie-Antoinette's private retreat in an enclave of the royal park. The charming town of **Chartres** is a lovely day or half-day outing from Paris. Its main attraction is Cathédrale de Chartres, an awe-inspiring Gothic church that looms like a great fantasy ship on the horizon and is world renowned for its stained-glass windows. **Disneyland Paris** arrived in 1992, but the magic was slow to take effect. The resort opened with the uninspiring name of EuroDisney and further baffled the French, for whom no meal is complete without wine, with its ban on alcohol. After the ban was lifted in the park's sit-down restaurants and the site's name was changed, Disneyland Paris became France's leading tourist attraction, drawing sellout crowds of Europeans seeking a kitschy glimpse of the American Dream—and of American families stealing a day from their museum schedule.

PLANNING

Traveling to Chartres, Disneyland Paris, and Versailles from Paris is easy. Although each side trip is within an hour's drive, we *strongly* recommend taking the train from the city rather than renting a car. If Disneyland is your destination and you don't plan to visit Paris, there are shuttle buses that will take you directly from the airports to the park.

The château of Versailles is closed Monday. Disneyland Paris gets extremely crowded on summer weekends, so plan your trip during the week, and early, if possible.

DINING AND LODGING PRICE CATEGORIES (IN EUROS)				
	$	**$$**	**$$$**	**$$$$**
RESTAURANTS	under €18	€18–€24	€25–€32	over €32
HOTELS	under €106	€106–€145	€146–€215	over €215

Restaurant prices are the average cost of a main course at dinner or, if dinner is not served, at lunch. Hotel prices are the lowest cost of a standard double room in high season

VISITOR INFORMATION

Special *forfait* tickets, combining travel and admission, are available for several regional tourist destinations (including Versailles). For general information on the area, check the website of Espace du Tourisme d'Ile-de-France (⊕ *www.visitparisregion.com*), or visit one of its kiosks; you'll find them at the Charles de Gaulle airport, Orly airport, Galeries Lafayette (Homme), Versailles, and Disneyland. Further information on Disneyland can be obtained from the Disneyland Paris reservations office.

VERSAILLES

Fodor'sChoice *16 km (10 miles) west of Paris via A13.*
★

It's hard to tell which is larger at **Château de Versailles**—the world-famous château that housed Louis XIV and 20,000 of his courtiers, or the mass of tour buses and visitors standing in front of it. The grandest palace in France remains one of the marvels of the world. But this edifice was not just home to the Sun King, it was also the new headquarters of the French government (from 1682 to 1789 and again from 1871 to 1879). To accompany the palace, a new city—in fact, a new capital—had to be built from scratch. Tough-thinking town planners took no prisoners, dreaming up vast mansions and avenues broader than the Champs-Élysées.

GETTING HERE AND AROUND

Versailles has three train stations, but its Rive Gauche *gare*—on the RER-C line from Paris, with trains departing from Austerlitz, St-Michel, Invalides, and Champ-de-Mars—provides the easiest access and puts you within a five-minute walk of the château (45 mins, €3.55).

Visitor Information Versailles Tourist Office. ⊠ *2 av. de Paris* ☎ *01–39–24–88–88* ⊕ *www.versailles-tourisme.com.*

EXPLORING

Fodor'sChoice **Château de Versailles.** A two-century spree of indulgence by the consecu-
★   tive reigns of three French kings produced two of the world's most historic landmarks: gloriously, the Palace of Versailles and, momentously, the French Revolution. Less a monument than a world unto itself, Versailles is the king of palaces. The end result of countless francs, 40 years, and 36,000 laborers, it was Louis XIV's monument to himself—the Sun King. In 1661, Louis assembled a dream team consisting of architect Louis Le Vau (and later Jules Hardouin Mansart), landscape designer

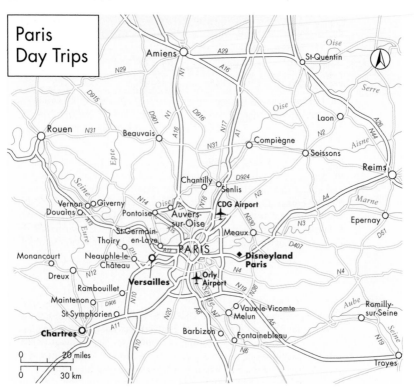

Paris
Day Trips

Amiens · A29 · St-Quentin
N29 · N1 · A16
Oise · Serre
D915 · D901 · D916 · N17 · A1 · Oise · Laon · A26
Rouen · N31 · Beauvais · Compiègne · N2 · Aisne · N44
N31 · Soissons · Reims
Chantilly · D924 · A4 · Marne
Senlis · N2 · Epernay
Vernon · Giverny · N14 · Oise · CDG Airport · N330 · N3 · D61
Douains · Pontoise · Auvers-sur-Oise · Epte
St-Germain-en-Laye · Meaux · D407
Thoiry · PARIS · Disneyland Paris · N4
Monancourt · Neauphle-le-Château · N4
Dreux · N12 · Orly Airport · N19
Rambouillet · Versailles
Maintenon · D906 · N10 · Vaux-le-Vicomte · Aube · Romilly-sur-Seine
St-Symphorien · A11 · Melun · Seine
Chartres · Barbizon · Fontainebleau · N19
· N6 · Troyes

0 — 20 miles
0 — 30 km

André Le Nôtre, and painter Charles Le Brun to give him a palace of the utmost grace and opulence. Construction of the sprawling palace and gardens, which Louis personally and meticulously oversaw, took 40 years to complete. Today the château seems monstrously big, but it wasn't large enough for the army of 20,000 noblemen, servants, and hangers-on who moved in with Louis. A new city—a new capital, in fact—had to be constructed from scratch to accommodate them.

One of the palace highlights is the dazzling **Galerie des Glaces** (Hall of Mirrors). Lavish balls were once held here, as was a later event with much greater world impact: the signing of the Treaty of Versailles, which put an end to World War I on June 28, 1919. **Grands Appartements** (State Apartments) are whipped into a lather of decoration, with painted ceilings, marble walls, parquet floors, and canopy beds topped with ostrich plumes. The **Petits Appartements** (Private Apartments), where the royal family and friends lived, are on a more human scale, lined with 18th-century gold and white rococo boiseries. The **Opéra Royal**, the first oval hall in France, was designed for Louis XV and inaugurated in 1770 for the marriage of 15-year-old Louis XVI to 14-year-old Austrian archduchess Marie-Antoinette. Considered the finest 18th-century opera house in Europe (with acoustics to match), it is now a major venue for world-class performers. Completed in 1701 in the Louis XIV style, the **Appartements du Roi** (King's Apartments) comprise a suite of 15 rooms set in a "U" around the east facade's Marble Court. The **Chambre de la Reine** (Queen's Bed Chamber)—probably the most opulent bedroom in the world—was updated for Marie-Antoinette in the chicest style of the late 18th century. The superb **Salon du Grand Couvert**, antechamber to the Queen's Apartments, is the place where Louis XIV took his supper every evening at 10 o'clock. The sumptuously painted walls and ceilings, tapestries, woodwork, and even the furniture have been returned to their original splendor, making this the only one of the queen's private rooms that can be seen exactly as it was first decorated in the 1670s. The park and gardens outside are a great place to stretch your legs while taking in details of André Le Nôtre's formal landscaping.

Versailles's royal getaways are as impressive in their own right as the main palace. A charmer with the ladies (as Louis's many royal mistresses would attest), the Sun King enjoyed a more relaxed atmosphere in which to conduct his dalliances away from the prying eyes of the court at the **Grand Trianon.** But Versailles's most famous getaway, the **Hameau de la Reine,** was added under the reign of Louis XVI at the request of his relentlessly scrutinized wife, Marie-Antoinette. Seeking to create a simpler "country" life away from the court's endless intrigues, between 1783 and 1787, the queen had her own rustic hamlet built in the image of a charming Normandy village, complete with a mill and dairy, roving livestock, and delightfully natural gardens. The hameau and its grounds have been undergoing extensive renovations since 2014, which will continue into 2018 while remaining open to the public. One of the most visited monuments in the world, Versailles is almost always teeming, especially in the summer months. You may be able to avoid the crowds if you arrive here at 9 am or find a private tour that skirts the lines (there are several). Audioguides are available and frequent guided tours in English visit the private royal apartments. ⊠ *Pl. d'Armes* ☎ *01–30–83–78–00* ⊕ *www.chateauversailles.fr* 🎫 *€18 general admission; €25 all-attractions pass; €10 Marie-Antoinette's Domain; park free (weekend fountain show, €9, Apr.–Oct.). On 1st Sun. of month Nov.–Mar. all palace tours are free* ⊗ *Palace: Apr.–Oct., Tues.–Sun. 9–6:30; Nov.–Mar., Tues.–Sun. 9–5:30. Trianons: Apr.–Oct., Tues.–Sun. noon–6:30; Nov.–Mar., Tues.–Sun. noon–5:30. Garden: Apr.–Oct., daily 8 am–8:30 pm; Nov.–Mar., daily 8–6. Park: Apr.–Oct., daily 7am–8:30 pm; Nov.–Mar., daily 8–6.*

Musée Lambinet. Around the back of Notre-Dame, on Boulevard de la Reine (note the regimented lines of trees), are the elegant Hôtel de Neyret and the Musée Lambinet, a sumptuous mansion from 1751, with collections of paintings, weapons, fans, and porcelain (including the Madame du Barry "Rose"). A tearoom, open Thursday, Saturday, and Sunday afternoons, provides an elegant way to refresh after an intensive round of sightseeing. ⊠ *54 bd. de la Reine* ☎ *01–39–50–30–32* ⊕ *culture-lambinet.versailles.fr* 🎫 *€4* ⊗ *Sat.–Thurs. 2–6.*

Notre-Dame. If you have any energy left after exploring Louis XIV's palace and park, a tour of Versailles—a textbook 18th-century town—offers a telling contrast between the majestic and the domestic. From the front gate of Versailles's palace turn left onto Rue de l'Independence-Américaine and walk over to Rue Carnot past the stately Écuries de la Reine—once the queen's stables, now the regional law courts—to octagonal place Hoche. Down Rue Hoche to the left is the powerful Baroque facade of Notre-Dame, built from 1684 to 1686 by Jules Hardouin-Mansart as the parish church for Louis XIV's new town. ✉ *Versailles* 🌐 *notredameversailles.org.*

Place du Marché-Notre-Dame. This lively square in the heart of the Notre-Dame neighborhood is home to the largest market in the region, far outstripping anything in Paris. Outdoors, stalls offer a veritable cornucopia of fresh fruits, vegetables, herbs, and spices; meanwhile, the four historic halls (dating to the reign of Louis XV and rebuilt in 1841) brim with every gourmet delight—foie gras, fine wines, seafood, game, prepared delicacies, cheese from every corner of France—providing a sensory experience that will overwhelm even the most jaded foodie. The open-air market runs three half-days a week (Tuesday, Friday, and Sunday 7–2), but the covered food halls are open every day except Monday, from early morning until 7:30 pm (closing is at 2 on Sunday). If you're in the mood for more shopping, the town's marvelous antiques district begins at the northwest corner of the market square and extends along the cobbled streets to the charming Passage de la Geôle. ✉ *Versailles.*

WHERE TO EAT

$$$$
MODERN FRENCH
Fodor's Choice ★

🍴 **Gordon Ramsay au Trianon.** Gordon Ramsay—the ebullient "bad boy of *la cuisine Anglaise*"—has amassed a string of restaurants worldwide and maintained a consistent two stars for this one. The dishes here are predictably conversation-worthy: picture exemplary entrées like ravioli of langoustines and lobster cooked in a Riesling bisque with Petrossian caviar and lime consommé, or Périgord foie gras done "2 ways," roasted with a beetroot tart and pressed with green apple and Sauternes. The Trianon's more casual, 60-seat Véranda restaurant is also under Ramsay's sway, and in its black-and-white contemporary setting you can opt for his "light, modern take" on bistro novelties like radicchio and Parmesan risotto with chorizo oil. Teatime provides a delightful (and more reasonable) restorative for weary château-goers, with a French twist on high tea: scones, madeleines, and heavenly *macarons.* [$] *Average main: €55* ✉ *1 bd. de la Reine* ☎ *01–30–84–50–18* 🌐 *www.trianonpalace.fr/savourer/gastronomie/gordon-ramsay-au-trianon* 🕒 *Closed Sun., Mon., and July 27–Aug. 25. No lunch Tues.–Thurs.* ✍ *Reservations essential* 👔 *Jacket required.*

$$$
MODERN FRENCH
Fodor's Choice ★

🍴 **L'Angelique.** Régis Douysset's refined yet unfussy French cuisine attracts the Versailles gourmet crowd. The dining room, in a restored 17th-century town house, is serene and comfortable, with white walls, wood-beam ceilings, dark wood paneling, and tasteful artwork—and the meals served here are among the best in town. A seasonally changing menu offers a good balance of seafood and game: picture a delicate perch fillet with spaghetti *de mer* (in a shellfish bouillon) or venison shoulder with grilled turnips and a spätzle of girolle mushrooms. Desserts alone are worth the Michelin star—the tart *feuilletée*, with candied

peaches, cardamom, and peach sorbet, is ethereal. $ *Average main: €32* ⊠ *27 av. de Saint-Cloud* ☎ *01–30–84–98–85* ⊕ *www.langelique. fr* ☉ *Closed Sun., Mon., 1 wk Christmas, 1 wk Feb., and 2 wks Aug.*

$$$$ ✕ **La Table du 11.** Just steps from the Cathédrale St-Louis, La Table du
MODERN FRENCH   11 has answered the city's dire need for top-quality and well-priced din-
Fodor's Choice   ing with an emphasis on innovative cuisine and small-producer wines.
★   The chic and pleasingly sparse dining room is bright in the day and elegant but cozy at dinnertime. A small menu features the freshest market
dishes: maybe line-caught daurade with candied citrus, Argentine beef
with roasted pumpkin and velvety buratina cheese, and a spectacular
cheese plate for dessert. The two- or three-dish prix-fixe menus are
fairly reasonable for this level of quality. $ *Average main: €34* ⊠ *11
rue Saint-Honoré* ⊕ *www.latabledu11.com* ☉ *Closed Sun. and Mon.*
🍽 *Reservations essential.*

$ ✕ **Lenôtre.** Set in the glamorous Cour des Senteurs, this handsome café
MODERN FRENCH   (a branch of the renowned Paris pastry shop) fills a much-needed gap in
FAMILY   Versailles dining. The warm, English-speaking staff and excellent, well-
Fodor's Choice   priced food—combined with a prime location amid elegant boutiques
★   and beautiful gardens—make it a lovely choice at lunchtime, teatime,
or just about any other time. The outdoor terrace is a fine spot on temperate days. Don't miss the sublime jasmine-scented *macaron,* specially
created for the Cour des Senteurs. $ *Average main: €12* ⊠ *8 rue de la
Chancellerie* ☎ *01–39–02–60–13* ⊕ *www.lenotre.com.*

WHERE TO STAY

$ ▦ **Le Cheval Rouge.** Built in 1676, this unpretentious option is in a cor-
HOTEL   ner of the market square, close to the château and strongly recommended if you plan to explore the town on foot. **Pros:** great setting in
town center; good value for Versailles. **Cons:** bland public areas; some
rooms still need renovating. $ *Rooms from: €94* ⊠ *18 rue André-Ché-
nier* ☎ *01–39–50–03–03* ⊕ *www.chevalrougeversailles.fr* ⇆ *40 rooms*
🍽 *No meals.*

$$$ ▦ **L'Orangerie White-Palacio.** Across a charming garden from the main
B&B/INN   house, this pretty cottage offers two quiet and comfortable suites with
private bathrooms, a common kitchen, and full garden access for meals
or relaxation. **Pros:** friendly, helpful host; very close to main sights.
Cons: cold breakfast; hand-held shower in bath. $ *Rooms from: €165*
⊠ *37 Ave. de Paris, Quartier Saint-Louis* ☎ *09–53–61–07–57* ⊕ *www.l-
orangerie-versailles.fr* ⇆ *2 rooms* 🍽 *Breakfast.*

$$$ ▦ **Trianon Palace Versailles.** Like a modern-day Versailles, this deluxe
HOTEL   turn-of-the-20th-century hotel is a creamy white creation of imposing
size, filled with soaring rooms (including the historic Salle Clemenceau,
site of the 1919 Versailles Peace Conference). **Pros:** palatial glamour;
wonderful setting right by château park; Gordon Ramsay's on-site restaurant. **Cons:** lacks a personal touch; glamourous setting not for everyone. $ *Rooms from: €180* ⊠ *1 bd. de la Reine* ☎ *01–30–84–50–00*
⊕ *www.trianonpalace.fr* ⇆ *176 rooms, 23 suites* 🍽 *No meals.*

NIGHTLIFE AND PERFORMING ARTS

Académie du Spectacle Equestre. On most weekends (and on certain weekdays during school holidays), you can watch 28 elegant white horses and their expert riders perform balletic feats to music in a dazzling hour-long show directed by the great equine choreographer Bartabas. If you can't make it, try catching a morning practice session. Both are held in the converted 17th-century Manège (riding school) at the aptly named Grandes Écuries (grand stables). Located opposite the palace, the structure was built for Louis XIV's royal cavalry. ⊠ *Av. Rockefeller* ☎ *01–39–02–62–75* ⊕ *www.bartabas.fr* ⊙ *Shows €25; morning practice €10.*

Centre de Musique Baroque. An accomplished dancer, Louis XIV was also a great music lover who bankrolled the finest musicians and composers of the day—Lully, Charpentier, Rameau, Marais. So it's only fitting that France's foremost institute for the study and performance of French Baroque music should be based at Versailles. An excellent program of concerts is presented in the château's Opéra Royal and chapel; the latter are free of charge. ⊠ *Versailles* ☎ *01–39–20–78–01* ⊕ *www.cmbv.com.*

Fodor'sChoice **Opéra Royal du Château de Versailles.** One of the most beautiful opera
★ houses in Europe was built for 14-year-old Marie-Antoinette on the occasion of her marriage to Louis XVI, and entering this extravagantly gilded performance hall from the hewn-stone passageway can literally take your breath away. But the beauty is not just skin deep—the intimate 700-seat venue is blessed with rich acoustics. Home to the Royal Opera, it hosts a world-class roster of orchestral and chamber concerts, as well as modern dance and ballet performances. For arts lovers, this spot alone will justify the quick trip from Paris. ⊠ *Château de Versailles* ☎ *01–30–83–78–89* ⊕ *www.chateauversailles-spectacles.fr.*

SHOPPING

19

Aux Colonnes. This charming, highly rated *confiserie* (candy shop) offers a cornucopia of chocolates and traditional French sweets. ⊠ *14 rue Hoche* ⊕ *www.auxcolonnes.com* ⊙ *Closed Mon.*

Fodor'sChoice **La Cour des Senteurs.** At the threshold of Versailles's Old Town, the
★ beautiful Cour des Senteurs—Courtyard of Fragrances—celebrates the town's status as the birthplace of the modern perfumer. Tiny **Maison des Parfums** charmingly recounts the history of perfume with a timeline and interactive displays, while the **Créations Toile de Jouy** boutique features the pretty printed cotton in a range of table linens, handbags, clothing, jewelry, and more. Couture glove maker **Maison Fabre** has a limited-edition perfumed glove in honor of Marie-Antoinette, along with a line of stylish handmade gloves crafted from luxury leathers; and the **Cour des Saveurs** boutique offers inspiration in the art of the French dinner table, with a curated selection of dishes and elegant tableware by established names and young designers, as well as a small épicerie carrying gourmet groceries. ⊠ *8 rue de la Chancellerie* ☎ *01–39–51–17–21* ⊕ *www.parfumsetsenteurs.fr.*

Les Délices du Palais. Everyone heads here to pick up homemade pâté, cold cuts, cheese, salad, and other picnic essentials. ⊠ *4 rue du Maréchal-Foch* ⊕ *www.charcuterie-lesdelicesdupalais.com* ☉ *Closed Mon.*

CHARTRES

39 km (24 miles) southwest of Rambouillet via N10 and A11, 88 km (55 miles) southwest of Paris.

If Versailles is the climax of French secular architecture, Chartres is its religious apogee. All the descriptive prose and poetry that have been lavished on this supreme cathedral can only begin to suggest the glory of its 12th- and 13th-century statuary and stained glass, somehow suffused with burning mysticism and a strange sense of the numinous. Chartres is more than a church—it's a nondenominational spiritual experience. If you arrive in summer from Maintenon across the edge of the Beauce, the richest agrarian plain in France, you can see Chartres's spires rising up from oceans of wheat. The whole town, however, is worth a leisurely exploration. Ancient streets tumble down from the cathedral to the river, lined most weekends with *bouquinistes* selling old books and prints. The streets are especially busy each year on August 15, when pilgrims and tourists flock in for the Procession du Vœu de Louis XIII commemorating the French monarchy's vow to serve the Virgin Mary.

If you need an incentive to linger until dusk, "Chartres en Lumieres" (Chartres's festival of lights) provides it: 28 of the city's most revered monuments, including the glorious Notre-Dame Cathedral, are transformed into vivid light canvases.

GETTING HERE AND AROUND

Both Transilien and main-line (Le Mans–bound) trains leave Paris's Gare Montparnasse for Chartres (50–70 mins, €15). The train station on Place Pierre-Sémard puts you within walking distance of the cathedral.

Visitor Information Chartres Tourist Office. ⊠ *Pl. de la Cathédrale* ☎ *02–37–18–26–26* ⊕ *www.chartres-tourisme.com.*

EXPLORING

Fodor's Choice ★ **Cathédrale Notre-Dame** (*Chartres Cathedral*). Worship on the site of the Cathédrale Notre-Dame, better known as Chartres Cathedral, goes back to before the Gallo-Roman period—the crypt contains a well that was the focus of druid ceremonies. In the late 9th century Charles II (aka "the Bald") presented Chartres with what was believed to be the tunic of the Virgin Mary, a precious relic that went on to attract hordes of pilgrims. The current cathedral, the sixth church on the spot, dates mainly from the 12th and 13th centuries and was erected after the previous building, dating from the 11th century, burned down in 1194. A well-chronicled outburst of religious fervor followed the discovery that the Virgin Mary's relic had miraculously survived unsinged. Motivated by this "miracle," princes and paupers, barons and bourgeoisie gave their money and their labor to build the new cathedral. Ladies of the

manor came to help monks and peasants on the scaffolding in a tremendous resurgence of religious faith that followed the Second Crusade. Just 25 years were needed for Chartres Cathedral to rise again, and it has remained substantially unchanged ever since.

The lower half of the facade survives from the earlier Romanesque church: this can be seen most clearly in the use of round arches rather than pointed Gothic-style ones. The **Royal Portal** is richly sculpted with scenes from the life of Christ—these meticulously detailed figures are among the greatest created during the Middle Ages. The taller of the two spires (380 feet versus 350 feet) was erected at the start of the 16th century, after its predecessor was destroyed by fire; its fanciful Flamboyant intricacy contrasts sharply with the stumpy solemnity of its Romanesque counterpart (access €6, open daily 9:30–noon and 2–4:30). The **rose window** above the main portal dates from the 13th century, and the three windows below it contain some of the finest examples of 12th-century stained-glass artistry in all of France.

As spiritual as Chartres is, the cathedral also had its more-earthbound uses. Look closely and you can see that the main nave floor has a subtle slant. It was designed to provide drainage because this part of the church was often used as a "hostel" by thousands of overnighting pilgrims in medieval times.

Your eyes will need time to adjust to the somber interior. The reward is seeing the gem-like richness of the stained glass, with the famous deep Chartres blue predominating. The oldest window is arguably the most beautiful: **Notre-Dame de la Belle Verrière** (Our Lady of the Lovely Window), in the south choir. The cathedral's windows are gradually being cleaned and repaired—a lengthy, painstaking process—and the contrast with those still covered in the grime of centuries is staggering. It's worth taking a pair of binoculars along with you to pick out the details. If you wish to know more about stained-glass techniques and the motifs used, visit the small exhibit in the gallery opposite the north porch. Since 2008, the cathedral has been undergoing an ambitious €20-million renovation that will continue through 2017. To date, two major chapels (the chapels of the Martyrs and the Apostles) have been completely restored, as have the two bays of the nave and the lower choir and the transept windows. For those who remember these dark recesses before the restoration, the difference is nothing short of miraculous (or alarming, depending on your perspective); an estimated 160,000-square feet of original plasterwork is now visible, and many of the sublime details for which the cathedral is famous have been returned to their 13th-century state. The restoration includes a layer of creamy paint, gilding, and trompe l'oeil marble over the church's entire interior sandstone surface, but changes this sudden and drastic are inevitably accompanied by controversy. For some the transformation is transcendent, for others it's a travesty. It's best to judge for yourself. To help you do this, try to arrange a tour (in English) with local institution Malcolm Miller, whose knowledge of the cathedral's history is formidable. (He leads tours twice a day Monday through Saturday, April–October, and once a day November–March at noon. You can contact him at ☎ *02–37–28–15–58* or at *millerchartres@aol.*

com.) The vast black-and-white labyrinth on the floor of the nave is one of the few to have survived from the Middle Ages; the faithful were expected to travel along its entire length (some 300 yards) on their knees. Guided tours of the **Crypte** start from the Maison de la Crypte opposite the south porch. You can also see a 4th-century Gallo-Roman wall and some 12th-century wall paintings. ⊠ *16 cloître Notre-Dame* ☎ *02–37–21–75–02* ⊕ *www.chartres-tourisme.com* ⊠ *Crypt €3; tours €7.50* ⊙ *Cathedral daily 8:30–7:30; guided tours of crypt Apr.–Oct., daily at 11, 2:15, 3:30, and 4:30; Nov.–Mar., daily at 11 and 4:15.*

Chartres en Lumières. If you need an incentive to linger here until dusk, "Chartres en Lumières" (Chartres's festival of lights) provides it: 28 of the city's most revered monuments, including the glorious Notre-Dame Cathedral, are transformed into vivid light canvases. Thematically based on the history and purpose of each specific site, the animated projections are organized into a city walk that covers a wide swath of the Old Town's cobbled streets and bridges. The spectacle is free and occurs nightly from mid-April through mid-October. A train tour of the illuminated city operates several times a night in summer. ⊠ *Chartres* ⊕ *www.chartresenlumieres.com.*

Musée des Beaux-Arts (*Fine Arts Museum*). Just behind the famed cathedral, the town art museum is housed in a handsome 18th-century building that once served as the bishop's palace. Its varied collection includes Renaissance enamels, a portrait of Erasmus by Holbein, tapestries, armor, and some fine (mainly French) paintings from the 17th, 18th, and 19th centuries. There's also a room devoted to the forceful 20th-century landscapes of Maurice de Vlaminck, who lived in the region. ⊠ *29 cloître Notre-Dame* ☎ *02–37–90–45–80* ⊠ *€3.40* ⊙ *Wed.–Sat. 10–12:30 and 2–6, Sun. 2–5.*

WHERE TO EAT AND STAY

19

$ ✕ **Esprit Gourmand.** On a picturesque street close to the cathedral, this
FRENCH   quaint bistro is a life-saver in a town sorely lacking in quality din-
FAMILY   ing. The traditional French favorites it serves—like roast *poulet* with
Fodor'sChoice   buttery potatoes, sautéed filet of dorade with grilled vegetables, and
★   braised pork that's crisp on the outside and meltingly tender inside—
are perennial crowd pleasers. The dining room, though small, doesn't
feel cramped, and there's a charming garden terrace for outdoor eating in summer. It's wise to reserve ahead, as fine cuisine and excellent
service assure a full house at every meal. $ *Average main: €17* ⊠ *6 rue
du Cheval-Blanc* ☎ *02–37–36–97–84* ⊙ *Closed Mon. and Tues. No
dinner Sun.*

$$ ✕ **Les Feuillantines.** The adventurous cuisine served at Les Feuillantines
FRENCH   (one of Chartres's few gastronomic restaurants) rarely falters and very
Fodor'sChoice   often soars. Try the superb house-made terrine with tangy cornichons
★   to start, followed by duck risotto topped with caramelized shallots
or beef ravioli perfumed with lemongrass and smoked tea. For des-
sert, the copious cheese plate, vanilla-flecked baba à rhum, and divine
melted-chocolate cake all hit the spot. In warmer months, the garden
is an added bonus, as is a good, if slightly unimaginative, wine list.

The location (on a tiny street near the cathedral) is convenient, and in terms of quality for price this cozy spot can't be beat. $ *Average main: €21* ✉ *4 rue du Bourg* ☎ *02–37–30–22–21* ⊘ *Closed Sun. and Mon.* ⩘ *Reservations essential.*

$$ ⛶ **Best Western Le Grand Monarque.** On Chartres's main square, not far HOTEL from the cathedral, this converted coaching inn warmly evokes the 19th century; many guest rooms are outfitted with brick walls, attractive antiques, lush drapes, and modern bathrooms (the best are in a separate turn-of-the-20th-century building overlooking a garden, while the most atmospheric are tucked away in the attic). **Pros:** its old-fashioned charm still works today; the spa and fitness center offers beauty treatments and massage; Michelin-starred restaurant on-site. **Cons:** best rooms are in an annex; uphill walk to cathedral. $ *Rooms from: €145* ✉ *22 pl. des Épars, Chateauneuf-de-Grasse* ☎ *02–37–18–15–15* ⊕ *www.bw-grand-monarque.com* ⇌ *50 rooms, 5 suites* ⟡ *No meals.*

$$$ ⛶ **Château d'Esclimont.** One of France's most spectacular château-hotels HOTEL lies northeast of Chartres in the town of St-Symphorien: with its pointed Fodor'sChoice turrets, moated pools, and checkerboard facade, the 19th-century Escli-★ mont domaine—built by La Rochefoucaulds—is well worth seeking out if you wish to eat and sleep like an aristocrat. **Pros:** the grand style of a country château; wonderful rural setting. **Cons:** service can be pompous; off the beaten path and not easy to find. $ *Rooms from: €200* ✉ *2 rue du Château-d'Esclimont, St-Symphorien-le-Château* ⊕ *24 km (15 miles) northeast of Chartres via N10/D18* ☎ *02–37–31–15–15* ⊕ *www. esclimont.com* ⇌ *48 rooms, 4 suites* ⟡ *No meals.*

DISNEYLAND PARIS

38 km (24 miles) east of Paris via A4.

Disneyland Paris is probably not what you've traveled to France for. But if you have a child in tow, the promise of a day with Mickey might get you through an afternoon at Versailles or Fontainebleau. If you're a dyed-in-the-wool Disney fan, you'll also want to make a beeline here to see how the park has been molded to suit European tastes (Disney's "Imagineers" call it their most lovingly detailed one, and it simultaneously feels both decidedly foreign and eerily familiar). And if you've never experienced this particular form of Disney showmanship before, you may want to put in an appearance simply to find out what all the fuss is about.

GETTING HERE AND AROUND

Take the RER-A from central Paris (stations at Étoile, Auber, Les Halles, Gare de Lyon, and Nation) to Marne-la-Vallée–Chessy—the *gare* there is 100 yards from the Disneyland entrance; trains operate every 10–30 minutes, depending on the time of day (40 mins, €7.50). High-speed TGV train service (⊕ *www.tgv.com*) links Disneyland to Lille, Lyon, Brussels, and London (via Lille and the Channel Tunnel). Disneyland's hotel complex also offers a shuttle bus service connecting it with the Orly and Charles de Gaulle airports; in each case the trip takes about 45 minutes and tickets cost €20.

Visitor Information Disneyland Paris Reservations Office. ☎ *01–60–30–60–90, 407/939-7675 in U.S.* ⊕ *www.disneylandparis.com.*

EXPLORING

FAMILY

Fodor'sChoice

★

Disneyland Paris. A slightly downsized version of its United States counterpart, Disneyland Paris is nevertheless a spectacular sight, created
with an acute attention to detail. **Disneyland Park**, as the original theme
park is styled, consists of five "lands": Main Street U.S.A., Frontierland,
Adventureland, Fantasyland, and Discoveryland. The central theme of
each land is relentlessly echoed in every detail, from attractions to restaurant menus to souvenirs. There's a lot here, so pace yourself: kids can
easily feel overwhelmed by the barrage of stimuli or frustrated by extra-
long waits at the rides (also be aware that there are size restrictions for
some). In **Main Street U.S.A**, tots adore Alice's Curious Labyrinth, Peter
Pan's Flight, and especially the whirling Mad Hatter's Teacups, while
everyone loves the afternoon parades, with huge floats swarming with
all of Disney's most beloved characters—just make sure to stake your
place along Main Street in advance for a good spot.

Top attractions at **Frontierland** are the chilling Phantom Manor,
haunted by holographic spooks, and the thrilling runaway mine train
of Big Thunder Mountain, a roller coaster that plunges wildly through
floods and avalanches in a setting meant to evoke Utah's Monument
Valley. Whiffs of Arabia, Africa, and the Caribbean give **Adventureland**
its exotic cachet; the spicy meals and snacks served here rank among
the best food in the park. Don't miss Pirates of the Caribbean, an exciting *mise-en-scène* populated by lifelike animatronic figures, or Indiana
Jones and the Temple of Doom, a rapid-fire ride that re-creates some
of this hapless hero's most exciting moments.

Fantasyland charms the youngest parkgoers with familiar cartoon
characters from such classic Disney films as *Snow White, Pinocchio,
Dumbo, Alice in Wonderland,* and *Peter Pan.* The focal point of Fantasyland, and indeed Disneyland Paris, is Le Château de la Belle au
Bois Dormant (Sleeping Beauty's Castle), a 140-foot, bubble-gum-pink
structure topped with 16 blue- and gold-tipped turrets. Its design was
allegedly inspired by illustrations from a medieval Book of Hours—if
so, it was by way of Beverly Hills. **Discoveryland** is a high-tech, futuristic eye-popper. Robots on roller skates welcome you on your way to
Star Tours, a pitching, plunging, sense-confounding ride based on the
Star Wars films; and another robot, the staggeringly realistic 9-Eye,
hosts a simulated space journey in Le Visionarium.

The older the child, the more they will enjoy **Walt Disney Studios**, a
cinematically driven area next to the Disneyland Park, where many of
the newer Disney character–themed rides can be found. It's divided into
four "production zones," giving visitors insight into different parts of the
production process, including Animation Couryard, where Disney artists
demonstrate the various phases of character animation, and Production
Courtyard, where you can go on a behind-the-scenes Studio Tram tour of
location sites, movie props, studio interiors, and costumes, ending with
a visit to Catastrophe Canyon in the heart of a film shoot. ⊠ *Marne-la-
Vallée* ☎ *01–64–74–40–00* ⊕ *www.disneylandparis.com* ▨ *€90, or €174
for 3-day Passport; includes admission to all individual attractions within
Disneyland or Walt Disney Studios; tickets for Walt Disney Studios are*

19

also valid for admission to Disneyland during last 3 opening hrs of same day ⏲ Disneyland mid-June–mid-Sept., daily 9 am–10 pm; mid-Sept.–Dec. 19 and Jan. 5–mid-June, weekdays 10–8, weekends 9–8; Dec. 20–Jan. 4, daily 9–8. Walt Disney Studios daily 10–6.

WHERE TO STAY

$$$$ HOTEL ★ **Sequoia Lodge.** Ranging from superluxe to still-a-pretty-penny, Disneyland Paris has 5,000 rooms in five hotels, but your best bet on all counts may be the Sequoia Lodge—a grand re-creation of an American mountain lodge, just a few minutes' walk from the theme park. **Pros:** package deals include admission to theme park; cozy, secluded feel; great pools. **Cons:** restaurants a bit ho-hum; many rooms do not have lake view. [$] *Rooms from: €300* ✉ *Marne-la-Vallée* ☎ *01–60–30–60–90, 407/939–7675 in U.S.* 🌐 *www.disneylandparis.com* 🛏 *1,020 rooms* 🍴 *No meals.*

NIGHTLIFE AND PERFORMING ARTS

Disney Village. Nocturnal entertainment outside the park centers on Disney Village, a vast pleasure mall designed by American architect Frank Gehry. Homesick kids who've had enough of *croque-monsieur* sandwiches will be happy to hear that vintage American-style restaurants—a diner, a deli, and a steak house among them—dominate the food scene here. One highlight within Disney Village is **Buffalo Bill's Wild West Show**, a two-hour dinner extravaganza with a menu of sausage, spareribs, and chili. The entertainment component includes performances by a talented troupe of stunt riders, bronco busters, tribal dancers, and musicians; plus some 50 horses, a dozen buffalo, a bull, and an Annie Oakley–style sharpshooter, with a golden-maned "Buffalo Bill" as emcee. A re-creation of a show that dazzled Parisians 100 years ago, it's corny but great fun. Tickets for shows, which start nightly at 6:30 and 9:30, cost €60 to €77. ✉ *Marne-la-Vallée* 🌐 *www.disneylandparis.com.*

UNDERSTANDING PARIS

BOOKS AND MOVIES

VOCABULARY

BOOKS AND MOVIES

Books

Fiction. Think of writers in Paris, and the romanticized expat figures of the interwar "lost generation" often come to mind: Ernest Hemingway (*The Sun Also Rises*), F. Scott Fitzgerald, Ezra Pound, and Gertrude Stein just to name a few. Further back in time are classics like Charles Dickens's *A Tale of Two Cities,* set during the Revolution, and Henry James's novels *The American* and *The Ambassadors,* both tales of Americans in Europe. The expats of World War II set the scene for future Americans in Paris: James Baldwin's life in the city in the 1950s informed novels such as *Giovanni's Room,* and the denizens of the so-called Beat Hotel (Allen Ginsberg, William Burroughs, and Henry Miller) squeezed in some writing among their less salubrious activities. The Canadian writer Mavis Gallant, who published many stories in *The New Yorker,* also began her tenure in Paris in the '50s; her collection *Paris Stories* is a delight.

Recent best sellers with a Paris setting include, of course, Dan Brown's *The Da Vinci Code,* as well as Diane Johnson's *Le Divorce* and *Le Mariage,* Anita Brookner's *Incidents in the Rue Laugier,* and Patrick Suskind's *Perfume: The Story of a Murderer.* Paul LaFarge's *Haussmann, or the Distinction* spins historical detail about the ambitious city planner into a fascinating period novel. Paula McLain's *The Paris Wife* imagines Hemingway's Paris from the perspective of his first wife, Hadley. For literary snacking, *Paris in Mind* pulls together excerpts from books by American authors.

For Children. Who doesn't remember Miss Clavel and her 12 young students in two straight lines? Ludwig Bemelmans' beloved *Madeleine* series about the namesake heroine is also illustrated with the author's drawings of Paris landmarks such as the Opéra and the Jardins du Luxembourg. *Eloise in Paris,* by Kay Thompson, also has illustrations, these by Hilary Knight (look for his take on Christian Dior). The *Anatole* books by Eve Titus are classics, starring a Gallic mouse. Playful, bright illustrations drive Maira Kalman's *Ooh-la-la (Max in Love);* the singsong language, smattered with French, is perfect for reading aloud. Joan MacPhail Knight wrote a pair of books about an American girl visiting France in the late 1800s: *Charlotte in Giverny* and *Charlotte in Paris.*

History. Recent studies devoted to the capital include Philip Mansel's *Paris Between Empires: Monarchy and Revolution*; Jill Harsin's *Barricades: War on the Streets in Revolutionary Paris*; and Johannes Willms's *Paris: Capital of Europe,* which runs from the Revolution to the Belle Époque. Simon Schama's *Citizens* is a good introduction to the French Revolution. Alistair Horne's *Seven Ages of Paris* skips away from standard historical approaches, breaking the city's past into seven eras and putting a colorful spin on the Renaissance, the Revolution, Napoléon's Empire, and other periods.

Biographies and autobiographies of French luminaries and Paris residents can double as satisfying portraits of the capital during their subjects' lifetimes. Works on Baron Haussmann are especially rich, as the 19th-century prefect so utterly changed the face of the city. For a look at American expatriates in Paris between the wars, pick up *Sylvia Beach and the Lost Generation,* by Noel R. Fitch. Tyler Stovall's *Paris Noir: African-Americans in the City of Light* examines black American artists' affection for Paris during the 20th century; *Harlem in Montmartre,* by William A. Shack, homes in on expat jazz culture. Walter Benjamin's *The Arcades Project* uses the 19th century as a point of intersection for studies on advertising, Baudelaire, the Paris Commune, and other subjects.

Memoirs, Essays, and Observations. Ernest Hemingway's *A Moveable Feast,* the tale of his 1920s expat life in Paris as a struggling writer, grips from its opening lines. Gertrude Stein, one of Hemingway's friends, gave her own version of the era in *The Autobiography of Alice B. Toklas.* In *The Secret Paris of the '30s,* Brassaï put into words the scenes he captured in photographs. Joseph Roth gave an exile's point of view in *Report from a Parisian Paradise.* Art Buchwald's funny yet poignant *I'll Always Have Paris* moves from the postwar GI Bill days through his years as a journalist and adventurer. Stanley Karnow also drew on a reporter's past in *Paris in the Fifties.* Henry Miller's visceral autobiographical works such as *The Tropic of Cancer* reveal a grittier kind of expat life. Janet Flanner's incomparable *Paris Journals* chronicle the city from the 1940s through 1970, and no one has yet matched A.J. Liebling at table, as described in *Between Meals.*

More recent accounts by Americans living in Paris include Edmund White's *Our Paris: Sketches with Memory* (White is also the author of a brief but captivating wander through the city in *The Flâneur*), Alex Karmel's *A Corner in the Marais: Memoir of a Paris Neighborhood,* Thad Carhart's *The Piano Shop on the Left Bank,* and the very funny *Me Talk Pretty One Day,* by David Sedaris. Adam Gopnik, a *New Yorker* writer who lived in Paris in the 1990s, intersperses articles on larger French issues with descriptions of daily life with his wife and son in *Paris to the Moon.* Gopnik also edited the anthology *Americans in Paris,* a collection of observations by everyone from Thomas Jefferson to Cole Porter.

Works in Translation. Many landmarks of French literature have long been claimed as classics in English as well—Victor Hugo's great 19th-century novels, including *The Hunchback of Notre-Dame* and *Les Misérables,* spin elaborate descriptions of Paris. Other 19th-century masterpieces include Gustave Flaubert's *Sentimental Education,* set against the capital's 1848 uprisings, and Honoré de Balzac's *Human Comedy,* a series of dozens of novels, many set in Paris.

Marcel Proust's masterpiece *À la Recherche du Temps Perdu* (*In Search of Lost Time*) describes fin-de-siècle Paris's parks, glittering aristocratic salons, and dread during the Great War. Colette was another great chronicler of the Belle Époque; her short works include *Chéri* and the Claudine stories.

Simone de Beauvoir's *The Prime of Life,* the second book in her autobiographical trilogy, details her relationship with the existentialist philosopher Jean-Paul Sartre in the context of 1930s and '40s Paris, when the Rive Gauche cemented its modern bohemian reputation in its cafés and jazz clubs.

Movies

In English. In 2012, Woody Allen made what many consider to be his best recent film with his playful tribute to the city of love in *Midnight in Paris.* Before that in 2007, French actress Julie Delpy did a sweet cinamatique tale of culture clash in *Two Days in Paris,* and Pixar Studios highlighted Paris' love of fine food in *Ratatouille.* Back in 2006, Sofia Coppola's lavish *Marie Antoinette* focused on the isolation and posh life of France's famous queen; it might not have been a box office hit, but it's an interesting take on life at Versailles. Previous to that, the film version of *The Da Vinci Code* (2006), starring Tom Hanks and Audrey Tautou, was talked about for months preceding its release, although some were disappointed. The heist film *Ronin* (1998) pairs Robert De Niro and Jean Reno with a hyperkinetic chase through the streets of Paris; and in *Frantic* (1987) Harrison Ford plays an American doctor visiting Paris when his wife disappears, and director Roman Polanski shoots the city to build suspense and dread. The Palais-Royal gets an equally tense treatment in the Audrey Hepburn–Cary Grant thriller *Charade* (1963); the 2002 remake, *The Truth About Charlie,* doesn't hold a candle to the original. In *Before Sunset* (2004), Ethan Hawke meets Julie Delpy in Paris in the sequel to *Before Sunrise.*

French Films. One of the biggest hits out of France was *Amélie* (2001), which follows a young woman determined to change people's lives. There's a love angle, *bien sûr,* and the neighborhood of Montmartre is practically a third hero, although Parisians sniffed that it was a sterilized version of the raffish *quartier.*

More recently, Marion Cotillard took home the Oscar for her portrayal of singer Édith Piaf in *La Vie en Rose* (2007), a performance all the more stunning by Cotillard's ability to bring Piaf to the screen in all stages of life.

Jean-Luc Godard's *Breathless* (1960) and François Truffaut's *The 400 Blows* (slang for "raising hell"; 1959) kicked off the New Wave cinema movement. Godard eschewed traditional movie narrative techniques, employing a loose style—including improvised dialogue and handheld camera shots—for his story about a low-level crook (Jean-Paul Belmondo) and his girlfriend (Jean Seberg). Truffaut's film is a masterwork of innocence lost, a semiautobiographical story of a young boy banished to juvenile detention.

Catherine Deneuve is practically a film industry in and of herself. Her movies span the globe; those shot in Paris range from *Belle de Jour* (1967)—Luis Buñuel's study of erotic repression—to *Le Dernier Métro* (1980), a World War II drama.

Classic film noir and contemporary crime dramas are also highlights of French cinema: for a taste, rent *Rififi* (1955), with its excruciatingly tense 33-minute heist scene; *Le Samouraï* (1967), in which Alain Delon plays the ultimate cool assassin; or Robert Bresson's *Pickpocket* (1959). *La Casque d'Or* (1952) looks back to the underworld of the early 1900s, with Simone Signoret as the title irresistible blond. French director Luc Besson introduced a sly female action hero with *La Femme Nikita* (1990), in which Jean Reno chills as the creepy "cleaner" you don't want making house calls.

Filmed during the Occupation, *The Children of Paradise* (1945) became an allegory for the French spirit of resistance: the love story was set in 1840s Paris, thereby getting past the German censors. Other romantic films with memorable takes on Paris include *Cyrano de Bergerac* (1990), with Gérard Depardieu as the large-schnozzed hero; the comedy *When the Cat's Away* (1996); the talk-heavy films of Eric Rohmer; *Camille Claudel* (1988), about the affair between Rodin and fellow sculptor Claudel; and the gritty *The Lovers on the Bridge* (1999), the flaws balanced by the bravado of Juliette Binoche waterskiing on the Seine surrounded by fireworks. *The Red Balloon* (1956) is also a love story of a sort: a children's film of a boy and his faithful balloon.

Musicals. Love in the time of Toulouse-Lautrec? Elton John songs? Baz Luhrmann's *Moulin Rouge* (2001) whirls them together and wins through conviction rather than verisimilitude. John Huston's 1952 film of the same name is also well worth watching. Gene Kelly pursues Leslie Caron through postwar Paris in *An American in Paris* (1951); the Gershwin-fueled film includes a stunning 17-minute dance sequence. Caron reappears as the love interest—this time as a young girl in training to be a courtesan—in *Gigi* (1958). *Funny Face* (1957) stars Fred Astaire and Audrey Hepburn, and there's an unforgettable scene of Hepburn descending the staircase below the *Winged Victory* in the Louvre.

VOCABULARY

One of the trickiest French sounds to pronounce is the nasal final n sound (whether or not the n is actually the last letter of the word). You should try to pronounce it as a sort of nasal grunt—as in "huh." The vowel that precedes the n will govern the vowel sound of the word, and in this list we precede the final n with an h to remind you to be nasal.

Another problem sound is the ubiquitous but untransliterable eu, as in bleu (blue) or deux (two), and the very similar sound in je (I), ce (this), and de (of). The closest equivalent might be the vowel sound in "put," but rounded. The famous rolled r is a glottal sound. Consonants at the ends of words are usually silent; when the following word begins with a vowel, however, the two are run together by sounding the consonant. There are two forms of "you" in French: vous (formal and plural) and tu (a singular, personal form). When addressing an adult you don't know, vous is always best.

ENGLISH	FRENCH	PRONUNCIATION
BASICS		
Yes/no	Oui/non	wee/nohn
Please	S'il vous plaît	seel voo play
Thank you	Merci	mair- **see**
You're welcome	De rien	deh ree- **ehn**
Excuse me, sorry	Pardon	pahr- **don**
Good morning/ afternoon	Bonjour	bohn- **zhoor**
Good evening	Bonsoir	bohn- **swahr**
Good-bye	Au revoir	o ruh- **vwahr**
Mr. (Sir)	Monsieur	muh- **syuh**
Mrs. (Ma'am)	Madame	ma- **dam**
Miss	Mademoiselle	mad-mwa- **zel**
Pleased to meet you	Enchanté(e)	ohn-shahn- **tay**
How are you?	Comment allez-vous?	kuh-mahn-tahl-ay **voo**
Very well, thanks	Très bien, merci	tray bee-ehn, mair- **see**
And you?	Et vous?	ay voo?
NUMBERS		
one	un	uhn
two	deux	deuh
three	trois	twah

ENGLISH	FRENCH	PRONUNCIATION
four	quatre	**kaht**-ruh
five	cinq	sank
six	six	seess
seven	sept	set
eight	huit	wheat
nine	neuf	nuf
ten	dix	deess
eleven	onze	ohnz
twelve	douze	dooz
thirteen	treize	trehz
fourteen	quatorze	kah- **torz**
fifteen	quinze	kanz
sixteen	seize	sez
seventeen	dix-sept	deez- **set**
eighteen	dix-huit	deez- **wheat**
nineteen	dix-neuf	deez- **nuf**
twenty	vingt	vehn
twenty-one	vingt-et-un	vehnt-ay- **uhn**
thirty	trente	trahnt
forty	quarante	ka- **rahnt**
fifty	cinquante	sang- **kahnt**
sixty	soixante	swa- **sahnt**
seventy	soixante-dix	swa-sahnt- **deess**
eighty	quatre-vingts	kaht-ruh- **vehn**
ninety	quatre-vingt-dix	kaht-ruh-vehn- **deess**
one hundred	cent	sahn
one thousand	mille	meel

COLORS

black	noir	nwahr
blue	bleu	bleuh

ENGLISH	FRENCH	PRONUNCIATION
brown	brun/marron	bruhn/mar-**rohn**
green	vert	vair
orange	orange	o-**rahnj**
pink	rose	rose
red	rouge	rouge
violet	violette	vee-o-**let**
white	blanc	blahnk
yellow	jaune	zhone

DAYS OF THE WEEK

Sunday	dimanche	dee-**mahnsh**
Monday	lundi	luhn-**dee**
Tuesday	mardi	mahr-**dee**
Wednesday	mercredi	mair-kruh-**dee**
Thursday	jeudi	zhuh-**dee**
Friday	vendredi	vawn-druh-**dee**
Saturday	samedi	sahm-**dee**

MONTHS

January	janvier	zhahn-vee-**ay**
February	février	feh-vree-**ay**
March	mars	marce
April	avril	a-**vreel**
May	mai	meh
June	juin	zhwehn
July	juillet	zhwee-**ay**
August	août	ah-**oo**
September	septembre	sep-**tahm**-bruh
October	octobre	awk-**to**-bruh
November	novembre	no-**vahm**-bruh
December	décembre	day-**sahm**-bruh

	ENGLISH	FRENCH	PRONUNCIATION

USEFUL PHRASES

ENGLISH	FRENCH	PRONUNCIATION
Do you speak English?	Parlez-vous anglais?	par-lay **voo** ahn- **glay**
I don't speak . . .	Je ne parle pas . . .	zhuh nuh parl pah . . .
French	français	frahn- **say**
I don't understand	Je ne comprends pas	zhuh nuh kohm-**prahn** pah
I understand	Je comprends	zhuh kohm- **prahn**
I don't know	Je ne sais pas	zhuh nuh say **pah**
I'm American/ British	Je suis américain/ anglais	zhuh sweez a-may-ree- **kehn** /ahn- **glay**
What's your name?	Comment vous appelez-vous?	ko-mahn vooz a-pell-ay- **voo**
My name is . . .	Je m'appelle . . .	zhuh ma- **pell** . . .
What time is it?	Quelle heure est-il?	kel air eh- **teel**
How?	Comment?	ko- **mahn**
When?	Quand?	kahn
Yesterday	Hier	yair
Today	Aujourd'hui	o-zhoor- **dwee**
Tomorrow	Demain	duh- **mehn**
Tonight	Ce soir	suh **swahr**
What?	Quoi?	kwah
What is it?	Qu'est-ce que c'est?	kess-kuh- **say**
Why?	Pourquoi?	poor- **kwa**
Who?	Qui?	kee
Where is . . .	Où est . . .	oo ay
the train station?	la gare?	la gar
the subway station?	la station de métro?	la sta- **syon** duh may- **tro**
the bus stop?	l'arrêt de bus?	la-ray duh booss
the post office?	la poste?	la post
the bank?	la banque?	la bahnk

ENGLISH	FRENCH	PRONUNCIATION
the . . . hotel?	l'hôtel . . .?	lo- **tel**
the store?	le magasin?	luh ma-ga- **zehn**
the cashier?	la caisse?	la **kess**
the . . . museum?	le musée . . .?	luh mew- **zay**
the hospital?	l'hôpital?	lo-pee- **tahl**
the elevator?	l'ascenseur?	la-sahn- **seuhr**
the telephone?	le téléphone?	luh tay-lay- **phone**
Where are the . . .	Où sont les . . .	oo sohn lay
restrooms?	toilettes?	twah- **let**
(men/women)	(hommes/femmes)	(**oh**-mm/ **fah**-mm)
Here/there	Ici/là	ee- **see** /la
Left/right	A gauche/à droite	a goash/a draht
Straight ahead	Tout droit	too drwah
Is it near/far?	C'est près/loin?	say pray/lwehn
I'd like . . .	Je voudrais . . .	zhuh voo- **dray**
a room	une chambre	ewn **shahm**-bruh
the key	la clé	la clay
a newspaper	un journal	uhn zhoor- **nahl**
a stamp	un timbre	uhn **tam**-bruh
I'd like to buy . . .	Je voudrais acheter . . .	zhuh voo- **dray** **ahsh**-tay
cigarettes	des cigarettes	day see-ga- **ret**
matches	des allumettes	days a-loo- **met**
soap	du savon	dew sah- **vohn**
city map	un plan de ville	uhn plahn de **veel**
road map	une carte routière	ewn cart roo-tee- **air**
magazine	une revue	ewn reh- **vu**
envelopes	des enveloppes	dayz ahn-veh- **lope**
writing paper	du papier à lettres	dew pa-pee- **ay** a **let**-ruh
postcard	une carte postale	ewn cart pos- **tal**

ENGLISH	FRENCH	PRONUNCIATION
How much is it?	C'est combien?	say comb-bee- **ehn**
A little/a lot	Un peu/beaucoup	uhn peuh/bo- **koo**
More/less	Plus/moins	plu/mwehn
Enough/too (much)	Assez/trop	a-say/tro
I am ill/sick	Je suis malade	zhuh swee ma- **lahd**
Call a . . .	Appelez un . . .	a-play uhn
doctor	docteur	dohk- **tehr**
Help!	Au secours!	o suh- **koor**
Stop!	Arrêtez!	a-reh- **tay**
Fire!	Au feu!	o fuh
Caution!/Look out!	Attention!	a-tahn-see- **ohn**

DINING OUT

A bottle of . . .	une bouteille de . . .	ewn boo- **tay** duh
A cup of . . .	une tasse de . . .	ewn tass duh
A glass of . . .	un verre de . . .	uhn vair duh
Bill/check	l'addition	la-dee-see- **ohn**
Bread	du pain	dew panh
Breakfast	le petit-déjeuner	luh puh- **tee** day-zhuh- **nay**
Butter	du beurre	dew burr
Cheers!	A votre santé!	ah **vo**-truh sahn- **tay**
Cocktail/aperitif	un apéritif	uhn ah-pay-ree- **teef**
Dinner	le dîner	luh dee- **nay**
Dish of the day	le plat du jour	luh plah dew **zhoor**
Enjoy!	Bon appétit!	bohn a-pay- **tee**
Fixed-price menu	le menu	luh may- **new**
Fork	une fourchette	ewn four- **shet**
I am diabetic	Je suis diabétique	zhuh swee dee-ah-bay- **teek**
I am vegetarian	Je suis végétarien(ne)	zhuh swee vay-zhay-ta-ree- **en**

ENGLISH	FRENCH	PRONUNCIATION
I cannot eat . . .	Je ne peux pas manger de . . .	zhuh nuh puh pah mahn- **jay** deh
I'd like to order	Je voudrais commander	zhuh voo- **dray** ko-mahn- **day**
Is service/the tip included?	Est-ce que le service est compris?	ess kuh luh sair- **veess** ay comb- **pree**
It's good/bad	C'est bon/mauvais	say bohn/mo- **vay**
It's hot/cold	C'est chaud/froid	say sho/frwah
Knife	un couteau	uhn koo- **toe**
Lunch	le déjeuner	luh day-zhuh- **nay**
Menu	la carte	la cart
Napkin	une serviette	ewn sair-vee- **et**
Pepper	du poivre	dew **pwah**-vruh
Plate	une assiette	ewn a-see- **et**
Please give me . . .	Donnez-moi . . .	doe-nay- **mwah**
Salt	du sel	dew sell
Spoon	une cuillère	ewn kwee- **air**
Sugar	du sucre	dew **sook**-ruh
Waiter!/Waitress!	Monsieur!/ Mademoiselle!	muh- **syuh** / mad-mwa- **zel**
Wine list	la carte des vins	la cart day vehn

MENU GUIDE

FRENCH	ENGLISH

GENERAL DINING

Entrée	Appetizer/Starter
Garniture au choix	Choice of vegetable side
Plat du jour	Dish of the day
Selon arrivage	When available
Supplément/En sus	Extra charge
Sur commande	Made to order

FRENCH	ENGLISH

PETIT DÉJEUNER (BREAKFAST)

French	English
Confiture	Jam
Miel	Honey
Oeuf à la coque	Boiled egg
Oeufs sur le plat	Fried eggs
Oeufs brouillés	Scrambled eggs
Tartine	Bread with butter

POISSONS/FRUITS DE MER (FISH/SEAFOOD)

French	English
Anchois	Anchovies
Bar	Bass
Brandade de morue	Creamed salt cod
Brochet	Pike
Cabillaud/Morue	Fresh cod
Calmar	Squid
Coquilles St-Jacques	Scallops
Crevettes	Shrimp
Daurade	Sea bream
Ecrevisses	Prawns/Crayfish
Harengs	Herring
Homard	Lobster
Huîtres	Oysters
Langoustine	Prawn/Lobster
Lotte	Monkfish
Moules	Mussels
Palourdes	Clams
Saumon	Salmon
Thon	Tuna
Truite	Trout

FRENCH	ENGLISH

VIANDE (MEAT)

Agneau	Lamb
Boeuf	Beef
Boudin	Sausage
Boulettes de viande	Meatballs
Brochettes	Kebabs
Cassoulet	Casserole of white beans, meat
Cervelle	Brains
Chateaubriand	Double fillet steak
Choucroute garnie	Sausages with sauerkraut
Côtelettes	Chops
Côte/Côte de boeuf	Rib/T-bone steak
Cuisses de grenouilles	Frogs' legs
Entrecôte	Rib or rib-eye steak
Épaule	Shoulder
Escalope	Cutlet
Foie	Liver
Gigot	Leg
Porc	Pork
Ris de veau	Veal sweetbreads
Rognons	Kidneys
Saucisses	Sausages
Selle	Saddle
Tournedos	Tenderloin of T-bone steak
Veau	Veal

METHODS OF PREPARATION

A point	Medium
A l'étouffée	Stewed
Au four	Baked
Ballotine	Boned, stuffed, and rolled

FRENCH	ENGLISH
Bien cuit	Well-done
Bleu	Very rare
Frit	Fried
Grillé	Grilled
Rôti	Roast
Saignant	Rare

VOLAILLES/GIBIER (POULTRY/GAME)

Blanc de volaille	Chicken breast
Canard/Caneton	Duck/Duckling
Cerf/Chevreuil	Venison (red/roe)
Coq au vin	Chicken stewed in red wine
Dinde/Dindonneau	Turkey/Young turkey
Faisan	Pheasant
Lapin/Lièvre	Rabbit/Wild hare
Oie	Goose
Pintade/Pintadeau	Guinea fowl/Young guinea fowl
Poulet/Poussin	Chicken/Spring chicken

LÉGUMES (VEGETABLES)

Artichaut	Artichoke
Asperge	Asparagus
Aubergine	Eggplant
Carottes	Carrots
Champignons	Mushrooms
Chou-fleur	Cauliflower
Chou (rouge)	Cabbage (red)
Laitue	Lettuce
Oignons	Onions
Petits pois	Peas
Pomme de terre	Potato
Tomates	Tomatoes

FRENCH	ENGLISH

FRUITS/NOIX (FRUITS/NUTS)

Abricot	Apricot
Amandes	Almonds
Ananas	Pineapple
Cassis	Black currants
Cerises	Cherries
Citron/Citron vert	Lemon/Lime
Fraises	Strawberries
Framboises	Raspberries
Pamplemousse	Grapefruit
Pêche	Peach
Poire	Pear
Pomme	Apple
Prunes/Pruneaux	Plums/Prunes
Raisins/Raisins secs	Grapes/Raisins

DESSERTS

Coupe (glacée)	Sundae
Crème Chantilly	Whipped cream
Gâteau au chocolat	Chocolate cake
Glace	Ice cream
Tarte tatin	Caramelized apple tart
Tourte	Layer cake

DRINKS

A l'eau	With water
Avec des glaçons	On the rocks
Bière	Beer
Blonde/brune	Light/dark
Café noir/crème	Black coffee/with steamed milk
Chocolat chaud	Hot chocolate
Eau-de-vie	Brandy

FRENCH	ENGLISH
Eau minérale	Mineral water
Gazeuse/non gazeuse	Carbonated/still
Jus de . . .	. . . juice
Lait	Milk
Sec	Straight or dry
Thé	Tea
Au lait/au citron	With milk/lemon
Vin	Wine
Blanc	White
Doux	Sweet
Léger	Light
Brut	Very dry
Rouge	Red

TRAVEL SMART
PARIS

GETTING HERE AND AROUND

Addresses in Paris are fairly straightforward: there's the number, the street name, and the zip code designating one of Paris's 20 *arrondissements* (districts); for instance, in Paris 75010, the last two digits ("10") indicate that the address is in the 10e. The large 16e arrondissement has two numbers assigned to it: 75016 and 75116. ⇨ *For the layout of Paris's arrondissements, see the What's Where map in the Experience chapter.*

The arrondissements are laid out in a spiral, beginning from the area around the Louvre (1er arrondissement), then moving clockwise through the Marais, the Latin Quarter, St-Germain, and then out from the city center to the outskirts to Ménilmontant/Père-Lachaise (20e arrondissement). Occasionally you may see an address with a number plus *bis*—for instance, 20 bis, rue Vavin. This indicates the next entrance or door down from 20 rue Vavin. Note that in France you enter a building on the ground floor, or *rez-de-chaussée* (RC or 0), and go up one floor to the first floor, or *premier étage*. General address terms used in this book are *av.* (avenue), *bd.* (boulevard), *carrefour* (crossway), *cours* (promenade), *passage* (passageway), *pl.* (place), *quai* (quay/wharf/pier), *rue* (street), and *sq.* (square).

▌ AIR TRAVEL

Flying time to Paris is about 7 hours from New York, 8 hours from Chicago, and 11 hours from Los Angeles. Flying time from London to Paris is 1½ hours.

The French are notoriously stringent about security, particularly for international flights. Don't be surprised by the armed security officers patrolling the airports, and be prepared for very long check-in lines. Peak travel times in France are between mid-July and September, during the Christmas–New Year's holidays in late December and early January,

and during the February school break. Through these periods airports are especially crowded, so allow plenty of extra time. Never leave your luggage unattended, even for a moment. Unattended bags are considered a security risk and may be destroyed.

Airline and Airport Links.com. Airline and Airport Links.com has links to many of the world's airlines and airports. ⊕ *www. airlineandairportlinks.com.*

Airline Security Issues Transportation Security Administration. ⊕ *www.tsa.gov.*

AIRPORTS

The major airports are Charles de Gaulle (CDG, also known as Roissy), 26 km (16 miles) northeast of Paris, and Orly (ORY), 16 km (10 miles) south of Paris. Both are easily accessible from the city. Whether you take a car or bus to travel from Paris to the airport on your departure, always allot an extra hour because of the often horrendous traffic tie-ups in the airports themselves (especially in peak seasons and at peak times). Free light-rail connections (Orlyval and CDGval), available between the major terminals, are one option for avoiding some of the traffic mess, but still give yourself enough time to navigate these busy airports.

Airport Information Charles de Gaulle/ Roissy and Orly. ☎ 3950 (press "0" for service in English) €0.35 per minute, 0033/1–70–36–39–50 outside of France ⊕ *www.adp.fr.*

GROUND TRANSPORTATION

By bus from CDG/Roissy: Roissybus, operated by the RATP (Paris Transit Authority), runs between Charles de Gaulle (T1 and T3) and the Opéra every 15 minutes from 6 am to 8:45 pm and then every 20 minutes until 12:30 am; the cost is €11. The trip takes about 60 minutes in regular traffic, about 90 minutes at rush hour.

By shuttle from CDG/Roissy: The Air France shuttle service is a comfortable option, and you don't need to have flown the carrier to use it. Line 2 goes from the airport to Paris's Charles de Gaulle–Étoile and Porte Maillot métro stations from 5:45 am to 11 pm. It leaves every 30 minutes until 9:45 pm, with two further services at 10:20 pm and 11 pm. Tickets cost €17 one way when bought onboard (it's marginally cheaper if you book online or buy a return ticket). Line 4 goes to Montparnasse and the Gare de Lyon from 6 am to 10 pm. Buses run every 30 minutes and cost €17.50. Passengers arriving in Terminal 1 need to take Exit 32; Terminals 2A and 2C go to Exit C10; 2B and 2D take Exit B1; 2E and 2F go to the Arrivals-level bus station between the two terminals. There's a 15% discount on any of these buses for parties of four or more.

A number of van companies, such as SuperShuttle Paris, serve both Charles de Gaulle and Orly airports. Prices are set, so there are no surprises even if traffic is a snail-pace nightmare. To make a reservation, call or reserve online at least one week in advance, and an air-conditioned van with a bilingual chauffeur will be waiting for you. Confirm the day before. The shared van service costs a third of their exclusive non-stop option but picks up other passengers, which adds at least 20 minutes to the trip.

By taxi from CDG/Roissy: Taxis are generally the least desirable mode of transportation into the city. If you're traveling at peak hours, journey times—and, by extension, prices—are unpredictable. At best, the ride takes 30 minutes, but it can be as long as an hour; fares can range from €50 to €70. Wecab, a subsidiary of Taxis G7 (*see Taxi Travel, below*) offers a special shared taxi service between CDG and Paris that costs 40% less than a regular cab. Taxis G7 also offers Familycabs with baby car seats and boosters. ParisGreenCar is an eco-friendly alternative; it operates an energy-efficient fleet of hybrid taxis and makes a €0.50 charitable donation for every booking. Whatever company you choose, only take an official taxi from designated areas outside the terminal; these cabs have both an illuminated roof sign and a meter.

By train from CDG/Roissy: The cheapest—and arguably the fastest—way into Paris from CDG is via the RER-B Line, the suburban express train, which runs from 5 am to 11 pm daily. The free CDGVal lightrail connects each airport terminal (except 2G) to the Roissypôle RER station in 6 minutes. For Terminal 2G, take the free N2 "navette" shuttle bus outside Terminal 2F. Trains to central Paris (Les Halles, Gare du Nord, St-Michel, Luxembourg) depart every 10 to 20 minutes. The fare (including métro connection) is €10, and journey time is usually about 30 minutes.

By bus from Orly: RATP's Orlybus leaves every 10 to 20 minutes for the Denfert-Rochereau métro station in Montparnasse from Exit C in Orly South and Exit D in Orly West. The cost is €7.70. The cheapest bus is the RATP city bus 183, which shuttles you from métro Porte de Choisy (Line 7) to Orly South (Gate C, stop 4) or West (Gate D/G at Arrivals) for just €2. It departs every 30 to 40 minutes from 6 am to 12:20 am (frequency may be reduced on Sundays and holidays); travel time is approximately 50 minutes.

By shuttle from Orly: Air France's Line 1 shuttle bus runs from Orly to Les Invalides, Étoile, and Montparnasse every 20 to 30 minutes from 6 am to 11:40 pm. (You need not have flown on Air France to use this service.) The fare is €12.50, and journey time is between 45 and 60 minutes, depending on traffic. To find the bus, take Exit K from Orly South or Exit D from Orly West. Private van companies also provide shuttle service.

By taxi from Orly: You'll find taxi stands at Orly South as you exit the baggage claim area at "M" and at Orly West by Arrivals "B" (look for icons indicating taxis ahead). A cab downtown will cost €40 to €55 and take at least 25 minutes if traffic is light.

By train from Orly: The cheapest way to get into Paris by train is to take the shuttle bus ("*Paris par le train*") from Exit F at Orly South or Exit G at Orly West to the station RER-C Pont de Rungis–Aéroport d'Orly. Trains to Paris leave every 15 to 20 minutes. The fare is €2.50 (shuttle) plus €4.35 (RER), and journey time is about 35 minutes. Another slightly faster option is to take RATP's monorail service, Orlyval, which runs between the Antony RER-B station and Orly Airport daily every 8 to 15 minutes from 6 am to 11 pm. Passengers arriving in the South Terminal should use the Orlyval counter between Exits K and J; take Exit A if you've arrived in the West Terminal. The fare to downtown Paris is €12.05 and includes the RER transfer.

■ TIP➜ **A Paris-Visite pass allows you unlimited public transportation over 1, 2, 3, or 5 consecutive days and includes airport travel. Prices start at €11.15**

TRAVEL TO CENTRAL PARIS		
Via	CDG	Orly
Taxi	30 mins–60 mins; €50–€70	25 mins–45 mins; €40–€55
Bus	60 mins–90 mins; €11	45 mins–60 mins; €2–€7.50
Airport Shuttle	1 hr–2 hrs; €17–€45	45 mins–90 mins; €12.50–€45
RER	30 mins; €10	35 mins; €6.85–€12.05

TRANSFERS BETWEEN AIRPORTS
To travel between Paris's airports, there are several options. *See the "By Train" options above:* The RER-B goes from CDG to Paris St-Michel–Notre Dame where you transfer to the RER-C to Orly West. Travel time is about 60 to 80 minutes, and tickets cost €16.15. Air France's Line 3 shuttle bus also runs between the airports for €21 one way, every 30 minutes; the trip takes about 70 minutes.

Taxis are available but expensive: from €70 to €90, depending on traffic.

Contacts Air France Bus. ☎ 08-92-35-08-20 *(recorded information in English) €0.34 per min* ⊕ *en.lescarsairfrance.com.* **Paris-GreenCar.** ☎ 01-82-28-38-70 ⊕ *www.parisgreencar.com.* **RATP.** ☎ 3246 €0.30 per min ⊕ *www.ratp.fr.* **SuperShuttle Paris.** ☎ 08-11-70-78-12 €0.06 per min. ⊕ *www.supershuttle.fr.*

FLIGHTS

As one of the premier destinations in the world, Paris is serviced by a great many international carriers and a surprisingly large number of U.S.-based airlines. Air France (which partners with Delta) is the French flag carrier and offers numerous direct flights (often several per day) between Paris's Charles de Gaulle Airport and New York City's JFK Airport; Newark, New Jersey; Washington's Dulles Airport; and the cities of Boston, Atlanta, Miami, Chicago, Houston, Seattle, San Francisco, and Los Angeles. Most other North American cities are served through Air France's partnership with Delta via connecting flights. American-based carriers are usually less expensive but offer, on the whole, fewer nonstop direct flights. United Airlines has nonstop flights to Paris from Chicago, New York, and San Francisco. American Airlines offers nonstop service from numerous cities, including New York City's JFK, Boston, Chicago, Dallas/Fort Worth, and Miami. In Canada, Air France and Air Canada are the leading choices for travel from Toronto and Montréal (in peak season departures are often daily); Air Transat also serves these destinations in summer. From London, Air France and British Airways offer up to 15 flights per day in peak season. In addition, direct routes link Manchester, Edinburgh, and Southampton with Paris. Ryanair, easyJet, CityJet, Flybe, and Aer Lingus offer direct service from Paris to Dublin, Birmingham, London, Glasgow, Zurich, Copenhagen, Madrid, Marrakech, Prague, Brussels, and other cities. Tickets are available online only and need to be booked well in advance to get the best prices—a one-way ticket from Paris to Dublin could cost a mere €45, for example. But with the low-cost airlines you must be mindful of auxiliary charges that could set you back about €40 for a single piece of checked luggage.

▐ BOAT TRAVEL

Ferries linking France and the United Kingdom cross the Channel in about 90 minutes; popular routes connect Boulogne and Folkestone, Le Havre, and Portsmouth, and—the most booked passage—Calais and Dover. P&O European Ferries alone has 23 sailings a day between Calais and Dover. A company called Direct Ferries groups the websites for several operators to make reservations more streamlined.

The driving distance from Calais to Paris is 290 km (180 miles). The fastest routes to Paris from each port are via N43, A26, and A1 from Calais and the Channel Tunnel; and via N1 from Boulogne.

Information Direct Ferries. ☎ *08–92–23– 08–58 €0.45 per min* ⊕ *www.directferries.fr.* **P&O European Ferries.** ☎ *03-66-74-03-25* ⊕ *www.poferries.com.*

▐ BUS TRAVEL

ARRIVING AND
DEPARTING PARIS

The excellent national train service in France means that long-distance bus service in the country is practically nonexistent; regional buses are found where train service is spotty. Local bus information to the rare rural areas where trains do not go can be obtained from the SNCF *(see Train Travel, below).*

The largest international bus operator here is Eurolines, whose main terminal is in the Parisian suburb of Bagnolet (a ½-hour métro ride from central Paris, at the end of métro Line 3). It runs to more than 600 cities in Europe. In general, the price of a round-trip bus ticket is 50% less than that

of a plane ticket and 25% less than that of a train ticket, so if you have the time and the energy, this is a good way to cut the cost of travel.

Eurolines provides bus service from London's Victoria Coach Station, via the Dover–Calais ferry, to Paris's Porte de Bagnolet. There's an 8 am departure that arrives in Paris at 5 pm, an 11 am departure that arrives at 8:30 pm, and a 1:30 pm departure that arrives at 10:15 pm, plus three overnight trips with departures at 8 pm, 10 pm, and 11:30 pm that pull into Paris between 7:15 am and 9 am. Fares are €35–€55 round-trip. The company also offers a 15-day (€225–€320) or 30-day (€340–€425) pass if you're planning on doing the grand European tour. Ask about one of the Circle tours that leave from Paris (for example, via London, Amsterdam, then back to Paris again). Check the Eurolines website for special discounts or incentives, and avoid buying your ticket at the last minute, when prices are highest. Reservations for international bus trips are essential.

IN PARIS

With dedicated bus lanes now in place throughout the city—allowing buses and taxis to whiz past other traffic mired in tedious jams—taking the bus is an appealing option. Although nothing can beat the métro for speed, buses offer great city views, and the newer ones are equipped with air-conditioning—a real perk on those sweltering August days.

Paris buses are green and white; the route number and destination are marked in front, major stopping places along the sides. Glass-covered bus shelters contain timetables and route maps; note that buses must be hailed at these larger bus shelters, as they service multiple lines and routes. Smaller stops are designated simply by a pole bearing bus numbers.

Today 347 bus routes thread throughout Paris, reaching virtually every nook and cranny of the city. On weekdays and Saturday, buses run every 5 to 10 minutes, but you'll have to wait 15 to 20 minutes on Sunday and holidays. One ticket will take you anywhere within the city and is valid for one bus transfer within 90 minutes.

Most routes operate from 7 am to 8 pm; some continue until midnight. After midnight you must take either the métro (which shuts down at 12:40 am Sunday through Thursday and 2:15 am on Friday, Saturday, and the night before holidays) or one of the Noctilien lines (indicated by a separate signal at bus stops). Using the same tickets as the métro and regular buses, 47 Noctilien buses operate every 10 to 60 minutes (12:30 am–5:30 am) between Châtelet, major train stations, and various nearby suburbs; you can hail them at any point on their route.

A map of the bus system is on the flip side of every métro map, in all métro stations, and at all bus stops. Maps are also found in each bus; a free map is available at RER stations and tourist offices. A recorded message and onboard electronic display announce the name of the next stop. To get off, press one of the red buttons mounted on the silver poles that run the length of the bus, and the *arrêt demandé* (stop requested) light directly behind the driver will light up. Use the middle or rear door to exit.

The Balabus—an orange-and-white public bus that runs on Sunday and holidays from 1:30 pm to 8:30 pm, April through September—gives an eye-catching 50-minute tour around the major sights. You can use your Paris-Visite or Mobilis pass (*see Métro Travel*), or one to three bus tickets, depending on how far you ride. The route runs from La Défense to the Gare de Lyon.

The city also has expanded its tram system with the opening of new lines: T-5 (St-Denis to Garges-Sarcelles); T-6 (Châtillon to Viroflay); and T-7 (Ville-juif to Athis-Mons). T-8 (St-Denis to Épinay-Villetanuese) opened in part in late 2014, with underground access available in mid-2016. Designed more to serve locals getting into and around the city, these lines operate in the suburbs, with T-3 trams running along Paris's entire southern edge. One ticket is good for the whole line.

Trams and buses take the same tickets as the métro. When buying tickets, your best bet is a *carnet* of 10 tickets, available for €14.10 at any métro station. A single ticket can be bought onboard for €1.80 (exact change appreciated). If you have individual tickets or Paris-Visite passes, you should be prepared to validate your ticket in the gray machines at the entrance of the vehicle. You can also buy tickets in most bar–tabac stores displaying the lime-green métro symbol above their street signs.

Bus Information Eurolines. ☎ 08–92–89–90–91 €0.34 per min, 0033/141–862–421 from abroad ⊕ www.eurolines.fr ⊕ www.eurolines-pass.eu. **Noctilien.** ⊕ vianavigo.com. **RATP.** ☎ 3246 €0.30 per min ⊕ www.ratp.fr.

▌ CAR TRAVEL

We can't say it too many times: unless you have a special, compelling reason, do yourself a favor and **avoid driving in Paris.** But if you've decided to do it anyway, there are some things to know. France's roads are classified into five types; they are numbered and have letter prefixes: *A* (*autoroute*, expressways), *N* (*route natio-nale*), *D* (*route départmentale*), and the smaller *C* or *V*. There are excellent links between Paris and most French cities. When trying to get around Ile-de-France, it's often difficult to avoid Paris—just try to steer clear of rush hours (7–9:30 and 4:30–7:30). A *péage* (toll) must be paid on most expressways outside Ile-de-France: the rate varies but can be steep. Certain booths allow you to pay with a credit card.

The major ring road encircling Paris is called the *périphérique,* with the *péri-phérique intérieur* going counterclock-wise around the city, and the *périphérique extérieur,* or the outside ring, going clockwise; maximum speed is 70 kph (43 mph). Up to five lanes wide, the périphérique is a major highway from which 30 *portes* (gates) connect Paris to the major highways of France. The names of these highways function on the same principle as the métro, with the final destination as the determining point in the direction you must take.

Heading north, look for Porte de la Chapelle (direction Lille and Charles de Gaulle Airport); east, for Porte de Bagnolet (direction Metz and Nancy); south, for Porte d'Orléans (direction Lyon and Bordeaux); and west, for Porte d'Auteuil (direction Rouen and Chartres) or Porte de St-Cloud (Boulogne-Billancourt).

GASOLINE

There are gas stations throughout the city, but they can be difficult to spot; you will often find them in the underground tunnels that cross the city and in larger parking garages. Gas is expensive and prices vary enormously, ranging from about €1.38 to €1.87 per liter. If you're on your way out of Paris, save money by waiting until you've left the city to fill up. All gas stations accept credit cards.

PARKING

Finding parking in Paris is tough. Both meters and parking-ticket machines use parking cards (*cartes de stationnement–"Paris Carte"*), which you can purchase at any café posting the red "Tabac" sign. They're sold in two denominations: €15 and €40. Metered parking in the capital costs €2.40 to €4 per hour, depending on the arrondissement, and is payable Monday to Saturday from 9 am to 8 pm, with a two-hour limit. Insert your card into the nearest meter (they do not accept coins), choose the approximate amount of time you expect to stay, and receive a green receipt. Place it on the dashboard on the passenger side, making sure the receipt is clearly visible to the meter patrol. Parking tickets are expensive, and there's no shortage of blue-uniformed parking police. Parking lots, indicated by a blue sign with a white "P," are usually underground; they generally charge around €2.50 per hour or €19 to €30 per day (outside of the city center you'll pay €10 to €15 per day). One bright spot: you can park for free on Sunday, national holidays, and in certain residential areas in August. Parking meters with yellow circles indicate the free-parking zone during August. Before walking away, double-check that the car doors are locked and that any valuables are out of sight, either in the glove compartment or the trunk.

ROAD CONDITIONS

Chaotic traffic is a way of life in Paris. Some streets in the city center can seem impossibly narrow; street signs are often hard to spot; jaded city drivers often make erratic, last-minute maneuvers without signaling; and motorcycles often weave around traffic. Priority is given to drivers coming from the right, so watch for drivers barreling out of small streets on your right. When the speed limit is 30 kph (18.5 mph) cyclists can travel against traffic on one-way streets, so keep an eye open for them as well. Traffic lights are placed to the left and right of crosswalks, not above, so they may be blocked from view by vehicles ahead of you.

There are a few major roundabouts at the most congested intersections, notably at L'Étoile (around the Arc de Triomphe), Place de la Bastille, and Place de la Concorde. Watch oncoming cars carefully and stick to the outer lane to make your exit. The *périphériques* (ring roads) are generally easier to use, and the quays that parallel the Seine can be a downright pleasure to drive when there's no traffic. Electronic signs on the périphériques and highways post traffic conditions: *fluide* (clear) or *bouchon* (jammed).

Some important traffic terms and signs to note: *sortie* (exit), *sens unique* (one way), *stationnement interdit* (no parking), *impasse* (dead end). Blue rectangular signs indicate a highway; triangles carry illustrations of a particular traffic hazard;

speed limits are indicated in a circle, with the maximum speed circled in red.

RULES OF THE ROAD

You must always carry vehicle registration documents and your personal identification. The French police are entitled to stop you at will to verify your ID and your car—such spot checks are frequent, especially at peak holiday times. In France you drive on the right and give priority to drivers coming from the right (this rule is called *priorité à droite*).

The driver and all passengers in vehicles must wear seat belts, and children under 12 may not travel in the front seat. Children under 10 need to be in a car seat or specific child-restraining device, always in the back seat. Speed limits are designated by the type of road you're driving on: 130 kph (80 mph) or 110 kph (70 mph) on expressways (*autoroutes*), 90 kph (55 mph) on divided roads (*routes nationales*), 50 kph (30 mph) on departmental roads (*routes*), and 35 kph (22 mph) in some cities and towns (*villes et villages*). These limits are reduced by 10 kph (6 mph) in rainy, snowy, and foggy conditions. Drivers are expected to know these limits, so signs are generally posted only when there are exceptions to the rules. Right-hand turns are not allowed on a red light.

The use of headsets and handheld cellular phones while driving is forbidden (even if you are only holding them); the penalty is a €135 fine. Alcohol laws are also quite tough—there is a 0.05% blood alcohol limit (a lower limit than in the United States), which drops to 0.02% for drivers who've been licensed for fewer than three years.

▌ MÉTRO TRAVEL

Taking the métro is the most efficient way to get around Paris. Métro stations are recognizable either by a large yellow "M" within a circle or by the distinctive curly green Art Nouveau railings and archway bearing the full title (*Métropolitain*).

Sixteen métro and five RER (Réseau Express Régional, or the Regional Express Network) lines crisscross Paris and the suburbs, and you are seldom more than 500 yards from the nearest station. The métro network connects at several points in Paris with the RER, the commuter trains that go from the city center to the suburbs. RER trains crossing Paris on their way from suburb to suburb can be great time-savers because they make only a few stops in the city (you can use the same tickets for the métro and the RER within Paris).

It's essential to know the name of the last station on the line you take, as this name appears on all signs. A connection (you can make as many as you like on one ticket) is called a *correspondance*. At junction stations, illuminated orange signs bearing the name of the line terminus appear over the correct corridors for each correspondence. Illuminated blue signs marked *sortie* indicate the station exit. Note that tickets are valid only inside the gates, or *limites*.

Access to métro and RER platforms is through an automatic ticket barrier. Slide your ticket in and pick it up as it pops out. **Keep your ticket during your journey**; you'll need it to leave the RER system and in case you run into any green-clad ticket inspectors, who will impose a hefty fine if you can't produce your ticket (they even accept credit cards!).

Métro service starts at 5:30 am and continues until 12:40 am Sunday through Thursday, and until 2:15 am on Friday, Saturday, and nights before holidays, when the last train on each line reaches its terminus. Some lines and stations in Paris are a bit risky at night, in particular Lines 2 and 13, and the mazelike stations at Les Halles and République. But in general, the métro is relatively safe throughout, providing you don't travel alone late at night or walk around with your wallet hanging out of your back pocket.

All métro tickets and passes are valid not only for the métro but also for all RER, tram, and bus travel within Paris. Métro tickets cost €1.80 each; a *carnet* (10 tickets for €14.10) is a better value. The *Carte Navigo* system is the monthly and weekly subscription plan, with reusable cards available at most ticket windows; as of September 2015, there is one rate for all five zones. Receive a Pass Navigo Découverte for €5 plus the subscription for weekly (€21.25, valid Monday–Sunday) or monthly (€70, beginning the first of the month) service. Be sure to immediately attach a passport-size photo and sign your name. This magnetic swipe card allows you to zoom through the turnstiles and can be kept for years; just recharge it at any purple kiosk in the métro stations. Visitors can also purchase the one-day (Mobilis) and one- to five-day (Paris-Visite) passes for unlimited travel on the entire RATP network; both are valid starting any day of the week. Mobilis costs €7. Paris-Visite—which also gives you discounts on a few museums and attractions—costs €11.15 (one day), €18.15 (two days), €24.80 (three days), or €35.70 (five days).

■ TIP→ RATP, which runs the city's public transport system, launched a dozen apps in late 2015, including "monRERA." It provides up-to-the-minute info on delays and travel times and can even tell you which end of the métro platform to stand on to facilitate the exit at your destination.

RATP. ☎ 3246 €0.30 per min ⊕ www.ratp.fr.

TICKET/PASS	PRICE
Single Fare	€1.80 (not valid for métro transfer if purchased on a bus)
Daily Mobilis Pass	€7
Paris-Visite One-Day Pass	€11.15
10-Ticket Carnet	€14.10
Paris-Visite Two-Day Pass	€18.15
Paris-Visite Three-Day Pass	€24.80
Paris-Visite Five-Day Pass	€35.70
Pass Navigo Découverte Weekly	€21.25
Pass Navigo Découverte Monthly	€70

■ TAXI TRAVEL

Taxi rates are based on location and time. Monday to Saturday, daytime rates (10 am–5 pm) within Paris are €1.05 per km (½ mile); nighttime rates (5 pm–10 am) are €1.27 per km. On Sunday, you'll pay €1.56 per km from midnight to 7 am and €1.27 from 7 am to midnight within Paris. Rates to suburban zones and airports are usually a flat €1.56 per km. There's a basic hire charge of €2.60 for all rides, and a €1 supplement per piece of luggage (stroller, skis, etc.). Waiting time is charged at €32 to €38 per hour. The easiest way to get a taxi is to ask your hotel or a restaurant to call one for you, or go to the nearest taxi stand (you can find one every couple of blocks)—they're marked by a square, dark-blue sign with a white "T" in the middle. ■ TIP→ People waiting for cabs often form a line, but will jump at any available taxi; be firm and don't let people cut in front of you. A taxi is available when the entire sign is lighted green and taken when it's lighted red. They'll accept a fourth passenger for an average supplement of € 3. It's customary to tip the driver up to 5% *(See Tipping in Essentials.).*

Taxi Companies Alpha Taxis. ☎ 01-45-85-85-85 ⊕ www.alphataxis.fr. **Taxis Bleus.** ☎ 3609 €0.35 per min, ⊕ www.taxis-bleus.com. **Taxis G7.** ☎ 01-41-27-66-99 for service in English, 3607 €0.15 per min ⊕ www.taxisg7.fr.

■ TRAIN TRAVEL

The SNCF, France's rail system, is fast, punctual, comfortable, and comprehensive—when it's not on strike. There are various options: local trains, overnight trains with sleeping accommodations, and the high-speed TGVs (or Trains à Grande Vitesse), which average 255 kph (160 mph) on the Lyon/southeast line and 320 kph (200 mph) on the Lille and Bordeaux/ southwest lines.

The TGVs, the fastest way to get around the country, operate between Paris and Lille/Calais, Paris and Lyon/Switzerland/ Provence, Paris and Angers/Nantes, Paris and Tours/Poitiers/Bordeaux, Paris and Brussels, and Paris and Amsterdam. TGVs also go direct to Avignon, Marseille, and Nice. As with other mainline trains, a small supplement may be assessed at peak hours.

Paris has six international rail stations: Gare du Nord (northern France, northern Europe, and England via Calais or Boulogne); Gare St-Lazare (Normandy, and England via Dieppe); Gare de l'Est (Strasbourg, Luxembourg, Basel, southern Germany, and central Europe); Gare de Lyon (Lyon, Marseille, Provence, Geneva, and Italy); Gare d'Austerlitz (Loire Valley, central France, and overnight to Nice and Spain); and Gare Montparnasse (Brittany, Aquitaine, TGV-Atlantique service to the west and southwest of France, Spain). Smoking is prohibited on all trains in France.

The country has two classes of train service: *première* (first class) or *deuxième* (second). First-class seats have 50% more legroom and nicer upholstery than those in second class, and the first-class cars tend to be quieter. First-class seats on the TGV also have power sockets for computer connections and individual reading lights, but fares cost nearly twice as much as those for second-class seats.

Fares are cheaper if you avoid traveling at peak times (around holidays and weekends), purchase tickets at least 15 days in advance (look for *billet Prem's*), or find your destination among the last-minute offers online every Tuesday. For the lowest possible fares on soon-to-depart trains, check the SNCF website's "Les Petits Prix Train" section; twice a year, SNCF also has early-bird prices for travel in France.

You can call for train information or reserve tickets in any Paris station, irrespective of destination, and you can access the multilingual computerized schedule information network at any Paris station. You can also make reservations and buy your ticket while at the computer. Go to the Grandes Lignes counter for travel within France and to the Billets Internationaux desk if you're heading out of the country.

If you plan to travel outside Paris by train, consider purchasing a France Rail Pass through Rail Europe; it allows for one, two, three, four, five, six, seven, eight, nine, or fifteen days of unlimited train travel in a one-month period. If you travel solo for three days, first class will run you $265 and second class $215; you can add up to six days on this pass for $37 a day for first class, $30 a day for second class. For two people traveling together on a Saver Pass, the first-class cost is $252 per person, and in second class it's $204.

France is one of 28 countries where you can use Eurail passes, which provide unlimited train travel for a set amount of time. If you plan to rack up the miles, get a Global Pass; it's valid for first-class rail travel in all member nations for periods ranging from five days ($518) to three months ($1,815). The Regional Pass, which covers rail travel in and between pairs of bordering countries over a two-month period, is an alternative. Unlike most Eurail passes, Regional Passes are available for first- or second-class travel; prices begin at $353 (first class) and $283 (second class) for four days of travel; up to six extra days can be purchased.

In addition to standard Eurail passes, there is the Eurail youth pass (for those under age 26, with second-class travel), the Eurail Saver Pass (which gives a discount for two to five people traveling together), and the Eurail flexi pass (which allows a certain number of travel days within a flexible period). ■TIP➔ A select few European train stations sell Eurail passes—but only some are available, and they cost more. So it's best to buy yours at home before leaving for France. Passes can be purchased through the Eurail website or through travel agents.

Another option is to buy one of the discount rail passes available for sale only in France from SNCF. You can, for instance, save up to 50% by purchasing a discount Railcard.

Reduced fares are available for senior citizens (over 60), and for children under 12 and up to four accompanying adults. If you purchase an individual ticket from SNCF in France and you're under 28, you also get an automatic 25% reduction (a valid ID such as an ISIC card or your passport is necessary).

If you're going to be using the train quite a bit during your stay in France and if you're under 28, consider buying the Carte 12–27 (€50), which offers unlimited 50% reductions for one year on TER and intercity trains without reservations (provided that there's space available at that price; otherwise, you'll just get the standard 25% discount).

If you don't benefit from any of these reductions and you plan on traveling at least 200 km (132 miles) round-trip and don't mind staying over a Saturday night, look into the Carte Week-end. This ticket also gives you a 25% reduction.

■TIP➔ A rail pass does not guarantee you a seat on the train you wish to ride. You need to book seats ahead even if you have a pass.

Seat reservations (available at a minimal fee) are required on TGVs and are a good idea on trains that may be crowded—particularly in summer and during holidays on popular routes. You also need a reservation for sleeping accommodations.

Train Information Rail Europe. ☎ 800/622–8600 in the U.S. and Canada, 847/916–1028 ⊕ www.raileurope.com. **SNCF.** ☎ 3635 €0.40 per min ⊕ www.voyages-sncf.com. **TGV.** ☎ 3635 €0.40 per min ⊕ www.tgv.com.

THE CHANNEL TUNNEL

Short of flying, taking the Channel Tunnel is the fastest way to cross the English Channel: 35 minutes from Folkestone to Calais, 60 minutes from motorway to motorway, or two hours and 15 minutes from London's St. Pancras Station to Paris's Gare du Nord, with stops in Ebbsfleet (UK), Ashford (UK), Calais, and Lille. The Belgian border is just a short drive northeast of Calais. High-speed Eurostar trains use the same tunnels to connect London's St. Pancras Station directly with Midi Station in Brussels in around two hours.

There's a vast range of prices for Eurostar—round-trip tickets range from €620 for first class (with access to the Philippe Starck–designed Première Class lounge and a three-course Raymond Blanc meal) to €114 for second class, depending on when you travel.

It's a good idea to make a reservation if you're traveling with your car on a Chunnel train; vehicles without reservations, if they can get on at all, are charged 20% extra.

Channel Tunnel Information Eurostar.
☎ 08–92–35–35–39 €0.40 per min ⊕ www.
eurostar.co.uk. Eurotunnel. ☎ 08–10–63–03–
04 €0.06 per min ⊕ www.eurotunnel.com.

▍ VÉLIB' BICYCLE TRAVEL

Cycling is a wonderful way to get a different view of Paris while working off all those extra calories you've consumed—and Vélib', a self-service bike-rental program launched by the city in 2007, makes it easy. More than 20,000 bikes are available 24/7 at some 1,800 docking stations citywide. To take advantage of the service, you must first buy a pass (1- and 7-day versions can be purchased online for €1.70 and €8, respectively). Then you simply release a bike from any station, pedal away, and return it to any station when you're done. Individual rides lasting less than 30 minutes are free; for longer ones, minimal user fees apply.

Information Vélib'. ☎ 01–30–79–79–30
⊕ en.velib.paris.fr.

ESSENTIALS

■ COMMUNICATIONS

INTERNET AND WI-FI

Getting online here is rarely a problem because free or pay-as-you-go Wi-Fi (pronounced *wee-fee*) is widely available. Many hotels have business services with Internet access or high-speed wireless access; and these days most accommodations offer in-room Wi-Fi as well, sometimes at an extra cost. Moreover, Paris has made a big push in going wireless in recent years, so Wi-Fi is now offered in 296 public places, including parks, squares, and civic centers (like the Centre Pompidou) as well as many libraries; look for the "Paris Wi-Fi" logo. Access is free and unlimited for anyone (you just need to select the "Orange" network, and then launch your browser); however, network speed may not be as fast as you are used to back home. Cafés will usually have a Wi-Fi sticker on their window if there is wireless available, but verify before ordering a drink. McDonald's also has free Wi-Fi spaces (sometimes disabled during peak dining hours), as do the 40-odd Starbucks outlets. Note that you may pick up a signal for "Free Wi-Fi," but this is the name of a French Internet provider, and its network is open only to paying clients. If you're traveling with a laptop, carry a spare battery and an adapter to use with European-style plugs. Never plug your computer into any socket before asking about surge protection.

PHONES

The good news is that with Wi-Fi more and more available—although not always reliable—you should be able to Skype or Facetime for free (just make sure to turn off your Data Roaming). This means you can avoid using the phone in your hotel, which is almost always the most expensive option due to the huge surcharges hotels add to all calls, particularly international ones. If you do want to use the phone, calling cards can keep costs low, but only if you buy them locally. Mobile phones (*below*), which are sometimes more prevalent than landlines, are another alternative; as expensive as mobile phone calls can be, they are still usually much cheaper than calls from your hotel.

The country code for France is 33. The first two digits of French numbers are a prefix determined by zone: Paris and Ile-de-France, 01; the northwest, 02; the northeast, 03; the southeast, 04; and the southwest, 05. Note that it's often cheaper to call between 9 pm and 9 am. Pay close attention to numbers beginning with 08: some—but not all—are toll-free (when you dial one with a fee attached, a recorded message will tell you how much it will cost to proceed with the call, usually €0.15 to €0.40 per minute). Numbers beginning with 09, connected to DSL and Internet lines, are generally free when calling in France. Numbers that begin with 06 and 07 are reserved for cell phones.

When dialing France from abroad, you should drop the initial 0 from the telephone number (all numbers listed in this book include the initial 0, which is used for calling *from within* France). To call a number in Paris from the United States, dial 00–33 plus the phone number, but minus the initial 0 listed for the specific number in Paris. In other words, the local number for the Louvre is 01–40–20–51–51. To call this number from New York City, dial 00–33–1–40–20–51–51. To call this number from within Paris, dial 01–40–20–51–51.

CALLING CARDS

French phone booths will be phased out by 2018, and, as of February 2016, French pay phones no longer accept *télécartes* (phone cards); however, 72% of them will accept a *ticket téléphone,* a prepaid calling card, which can be purchased through Orange boutiques. These work on any phone (including your hotel phone); to use one, you dial a free number, and then punch in a code indicated on the back of the card.

CALLING OUTSIDE FRANCE

If you use a prepaid cell phone bought in France, calls to the United States and Canada cost around €1 per minute, and nearly double that to the rest of the world, depending on the provider; incoming calls are usually at no cost. Foreign cell phones used in France to call the United States or Canada will generally be more costly; it's best to check with your carrier to know your options. Note that most telecom operators in France offer an all-in-one service, with Internet, free local and international calls, and French TV, for an amazing monthly rate of about €35; hence, many landlines feature free international calling to most countries. But if you're staying in a rental apartment with a phone, ask first before you start calling abroad.

To make a direct international call out of France, dial 00 and wait for the tone; then dial the country code (1 for the United States and Canada, 44 for the United Kingdom) and the area code (minus any initial 0) and number.

To call with the help of an operator, dial the toll-free number 08–00–99–00 plus the last two digits of the country code. Dial 08–00–99–00–11 for the United States and Canada, 08–00–99–00–44 for the United Kingdom.

CALLING WITHIN FRANCE

For telephone information in France, you need to call one of the dozen or so six-digit *renseignement* numbers that begin with 118. (For Les Pages Jaunes—the French Yellow Pages—you dial 118–008.) The average price for one of these calls is €0.40 per minute.

Since all local numbers in Paris and the Ile-de-France begin with a 01, you must dial the full 10-digit number, including the initial 0.

MOBILE PHONES

Cell phones are called *portables* in France, and most Parisians have one. If you own a multiband cell phone (some countries use different frequencies than the United States) and your service provider uses the world-standard GSM network (as do T-Mobile and AT&T), you can probably use it while you're here. International travel plans are increasingly attractive; however, roaming fees can be steep— $1.29 a minute is considered reasonable. And overseas you normally pay the toll charges for incoming calls. It's almost always cheaper to send a text message than to make a call, since these have a very low set fee (often less than 5¢).

If you just want to make local calls, consider buying a new SIM card (your provider may have to unlock your phone for you to use it) plus a prepaid service plan that will cover your destination (this will usually include free incoming calls and texts). You'll then have a local number and can make local calls at local rates. When comparison shopping, check out Lycamobile; it carries SIM cards and has convenient pay-as-you-go plans with lower calling rates than Orange.

■TIP➔ **If you travel internationally frequently, save one of your old mobile phones or buy a cheap one online; ask your cell-phone company to unlock it for you, and take it with you as a travel phone, buying a new SIM card with pay-as-you-go service in each destination.**

Cellular Abroad rents cell phones packaged with prepaid SIM cards that give you a French cell-phone number and calling rates (you can also use your own phone or tablet with their SIM cards). Mobal sells GSM phones that will operate in 190 countries. Planetfone rents GSM phones, which can be used in more than 150 countries, but the per-minute rates are expensive. You can also buy a disposable "BIC" prepaid phone (available from Orange outlets, tabacs, magazine kiosks, and some supermarkets). Calls to the United States made with Le French Mobile—a

LOCAL DO'S AND TABOOS

CUSTOMS OF THE COUNTRY

The French like to look at people (that's half the point of cafés and fashion), so you might as well get used to it—it's as natural here as breathing. They'll look at your shoes or your watch, check out what you're wearing or reading. What they will not do is maintain steady eye contact or smile. If a stranger of the opposite sex smiles at you, it's best to do as the French do and return only a blank look before turning away. If you smile back, you might find yourself in a Pepé Le Pew–type situation.

Visitors' exuberance—and accompanying loud voices—may cause discreet Parisians to raise their eyebrows or give a deep chesty sigh. They're not being rude, but they're telling you that they think you are. Be aware of your surroundings and lower your voice accordingly, especially in churches, museums, restaurants, theaters, cinemas, and the métro.

When entering and leaving a shop, greet and say good-bye to the staff. A simple *bonjour, monsieur/madame*, and *au revoir, merci* are considered a virtual necessity for politeness. Other basic pleasantries in French include *bonne journée* (have a nice day); *bonne soirée* (have a nice evening); *enchanté* (nice to meet you); *s'il vous plaît* (please); and *je vous en prie* (you're welcome). When asking for directions or other help, be sure to preface your request with a polite phrase such as *excusez-moi, madame/monsieur* (excuse me, ma'am/sir).

GREETINGS

When meeting someone for the first time, whether in a social or a professional setting, it's appropriate to shake hands. Other than that, the French like to kiss. For the Parisians, it's two *bisous*, which are more like air kisses with your cheeks touching lightly—don't actually smack your lips onto the person's face!

OUT ON THE TOWN

When visiting a French home, don't expect to be invited into the kitchen or taken on a house tour. The French have a very definite sense of personal space, and you'll be escorted to what are considered the guest areas. If you're invited to dinner, be sure to bring a gift, such as wine, flowers, or chocolates.

Table manners are often considered a litmus test of your character or upbringing. When dining out, note that the French fill wineglasses only half full—it's considered bad manners to fill it to the brim. They never serve themselves before serving the rest of the table. During a meal, keep both hands above the table, and keep your elbows off the table. Bread is broken, never cut, and is placed next to the plate, never on the plate. When slicing a cheese, don't cut off the point (or "nose"). Coffee or tea is ordered after dessert, not with dessert. (In fact, coffee and tea usually aren't ordered with any courses during meals, except breakfast.) Eating on the street is generally frowned on—though with the onslaught of Starbucks you can sometimes see people drinking coffee on the go.

LANGUAGE

One of the best ways to avoid being an Ugly American is to learn a bit of the local language. Parisians may appear prickly at first to English-speaking visitors, but it usually helps if you make an effort to speak some French. A simple, friendly *bonjour* will do, as will asking if the person you're greeting speaks English (*parlez-vous anglais?*).

service catering to English-speaking visitors—can be costly, but it offers a range of plans without the obligation of long-term contracts.

Contacts Cellular Abroad. ☎ *00800/36–23–33–33 in France, 800/287–5072 in the U.S. and Canada* ⊕ *www.cellularabroad.com.* **Le French Mobile.** ☎ *01–74–95–95–00* ⊕ *www. lefrenchmobile.com.* **Lycamobile.** ☎ *866/277–3221 in the U.S. and Canada* ⊕ *www. lycamobile.us.* **Mobal.** ☎ *888/888–9162 in the U.S. and Canada* ⊕ *www.mobal.com.* **Orange.** ☎ *09–69–36–39–00 English helpline in France* ⊕ *www.orange.fr.* **Planet Fone.** ☎ *888/988–4777 in the U.S.* ⊕ *www.planetfone.com.*

▌ CUSTOMS AND DUTIES

You're always allowed to bring goods of a certain value back home without having to pay any duty or import tax. But there's a limit on the amount of tobacco and liquor you can return with duty-free, and some countries have separate limits for perfumes; for exact quotas, check with your customs department. The values of so-called duty-free goods are included in these amounts. When you shop abroad, save all your receipts, as customs inspectors may ask to see them as well as the items you purchased. If the total value of your goods is more than the duty-free limit, you'll have to pay a tax (most often a flat percentage) on the value of everything beyond that limit.

If you're coming from outside the European Union (EU), you may import the following duty-free: (1) 200 cigarettes or 100 cigars or 50 grams of tobacco; (2) 2 liters of wine and, in addition, (a) 1 liter of alcohol over 22% volume (most spirits) or (b) 2 liters of alcohol under 22% volume (fortified or sparkling wine) or (c) 4 more liters of table wine; (3) perfume, coffee, tea, and other goods to the value of about €430 (€150 for ages 14 and under).

If you're arriving from an EU country, you may be required to declare all goods and prove that anything over the standard limit is for personal consumption. But there is no limit or customs tariff imposed on goods carried within the EU except on tobacco (800 cigarettes, 200 cigars, or 1 kilogram of tobacco) and alcohol (10 liters of spirits, 90 liters of wine, with a maximum of 60 liters of sparkling wine, or 110 liters of beer).

PETS

Any pet coming to France must have recent rabies shots (no less than 21 days before departure), all standard vaccinations, and either a microchip or a tattoo. Be sure to have all paperwork on hand at the airport—including the bilingual *"Certificat Vétérinaire vers l'UE"* (EU veterinary certificate), as customs officials will inspect the animal in question. The form can be downloaded from the Animal and Plant Health Inspection Service website (⊕ *www.aphis.usda.gov*).

Information in Paris Direction des Douanes. ☎ *08–11–20–44–44 €0.06 per minute, 0033/01–72–40–78–50 from the U.S.* ⊕ *www.douane.gouv.fr.*

U.S. Information U.S. Customs and Border Protection. ⊕ *www.cbp.gov.*

▌ ELECTRICITY

The electrical current in Paris is 220 volts, 50 cycles alternating current (AC); and electrical outlets take Continental-type plugs, with two round prongs. So you may need to use both an adapter (which enables you to plug your appliance into the different style of socket) and a converter (which allows it to run on the different voltage). Most laptops and mobile phone chargers are dual voltage (i.e., they operate equally well on 110 and 220 volts), so require only an adapter. These days the same is true of many small appliances, though be wary of hair dryers. Always check labels and manufacturer instructions to be sure. Don't use 110-volt outlets marked "For Shavers Only" for high-wattage appliances such as hair dryers.

▌EMERGENCIES

The French National Health Care system (*la Sécu*) has been organized to provide fully equipped, fully staffed hospitals within 30 minutes of every resident in Paris. A sign of a white cross in a blue box appears on all hospitals. This book does not list the major Paris hospitals, as the French government prefers that an emergency operator assign you the best and most convenient option. Note that if you're able to walk into a hospital emergency room by yourself, you are often considered "low priority," and the wait can be interminable (but nowhere near as long as at an ER stateside). So if time is of the essence, it's best to call 112—the French equivalent of 911. Be sure to check with your insurance company before going abroad to verify that you are covered for medical care in other countries.

In a less urgent situation, do what the French do and call SOS Médecins or SOS Dentaire services; like magic, in less than an hour, a certified, experienced doctor or dentist arrives at the door, armed with an old leather case filled with the essentials for diagnosis and treatment (at an average cost of €65). The doctor or dentist may or may not be bilingual, but, at worst, will have a rudimentary understanding of English. This is a very helpful 24-hour service to use for common symptoms of benign illnesses that need to be treated quickly for comfort, such as high fever, toothache, or upset stomachs (a late-night digestive consequence of eating like the French).

The American Hospital (which also has a dental unit) and the Institut Hospitalier Franco-Britannique (formerly the Hertford British Hospital) both have 24-hour emergency hotlines with bilingual doctors and nurses who can provide advice. For small problems, go to a pharmacy, marked by a green neon cross. Pharmacists are authorized to administer first aid and recommend over-the-counter drugs,

and they can be very helpful in advising you in English or sending you to the nearest English-speaking pharmacist.

Call the police (112 or 17) if there has been a crime or an act of violence. On the street, some French phrases that may be needed in an emergency are *Au secours!* (Help!), *urgence* (emergency), *samu* (ambulance), *pompiers* (firemen), *poste de police* (police station), *médecin* (doctor), and *hôpital* (hospital). A hotline of note is SOS Help for English-language crisis information, open daily 3 pm–11 pm.

Doctor and Dentist Referrals SOS Dentaire. ☏ *01–43–37–51–00.* **SOS Médecin.** ☏ *01–47–07–77–77, 3624 €0.15 per min* ⊕ *www. sosmedecins.com.*

Foreign Embassies U.S. Embassy Consular Section. ✉ *4 av. Gabriel, 8e, Champs-Élysées* ☏ *01–43–12–22–22, appointments required (online form) except for lost or stolen passports and emergencies, in which case press "0" when you hear the automated message* ⊕ *france.usembassy.gov* Ⓜ *Concorde.*

General Emergency Contacts Ambulance. ☏ *15.* **Fire Department.** ☏ *18.* **General emergency services for police, fire, and ambulance (like 911).** ☏ *112.* **Police.** ☏ *112, 17.*

Hospitals and Clinics The American Hospital. ✉ *63 bd. Victor-Hugo, Neuilly-sur-Seine* ☏ *01–46–41–25–25* ⊕ *www.american-hospital. org.* **Institut Hospitalier Franco-Britannique.** ✉ *3 rue Barbès, or 4 rue Kléber, Levallois-Perret* ☏ *01–47–59–59–59* ⊕ *www.ihfb.org/en.*

Hotline SOS Help. ☏ *01–46–21–46–46* ⊕ *www.soshelpline.org.*

Pharmacies Pharmacie des Arts. ✉ *106 bd. Montparnasse, 14e, Montparnasse* ☏ *01–43–35–44–88.* **Pharmacie Internationale.** ✉ *5 pl. Pigalle, 9e, Montmartre* ☏ *01–48–78–38–12* ⊕ *pharmacieinternationale.pharminfo.fr.* **Pharmacie du Drugstore des Champs-Elysées.** ✉ *Galerie des Champs, 133 av. des Champs-Élysées, 8e, Champs-Élysées*

☎ *01–47–20–39–25.* **Pharmacie Matignon.**
✉ *1 av. Matignon, at Rond-Point des Champs-Élysées, 8e, Champs-Élysées* ☎ *01–43–59–86–55* ⊕ *www.pharmaciematignon.com.*

▌ HOLIDAYS

With 11 national holidays (*jours feriés*) and five weeks of paid vacation, the French have their share of repose. In May there's a holiday nearly every week, so be prepared for stores, banks, and the post office to shut their doors for days at a time. If a holiday falls on a Tuesday or Thursday, many businesses *font le pont* (make the bridge) and close on that Monday or Friday as well. Some exchange booths in tourist areas, small grocery stores, restaurants, cafés, and bakeries usually remain open. Bastille Day (July 14) is observed in true French form. Celebrations begin on the evening of the 13th, when city firefighters open the doors to their stations, often classed as historical monuments, to host their much-acclaimed all-night balls and finish the next day with the annual military parade and air show.

Note that these dates are for the calendar year 2017: January 1 (New Year's Day); April 16–17 (Easter Sunday–Monday); May 1 (Labor Day); May 8 (VE Day); May 25 (Ascension Day); June 5 (Pentecost Monday); July 14 (Bastille Day); August 15 (Assumption Day); November 1 (All Saints' Day); November 11 (Armistice Day); December 25 (Christmas).

▌ HOURS OF OPERATION

On weekdays banks are generally open 9–5, with a lunchtime closure from 12:30 to 2 (note that the Banque de France is an exception, operating 9:30–12:30 and 2–4); some banks are also open Saturday 9–5. In general, government offices and businesses are open 9–5. *See Mail, below, for post office hours.*

Most museums are closed one day a week (typically Monday or Tuesday) and on a handful of national holidays. Generally, museums and national monuments are open from 10 to 5 or 6. A few close for lunch (noon–2) and are open only in the afternoon on Sunday. Many of the large museums have one *nocturne* (nighttime) opening per week, when they welcome visitors until 9:30 or 10. Pharmacies are generally open Monday to Saturday 8:30–8. Nearby pharmacies that stay open late, for 24 hours, or on Sunday, are listed on the door.

Generally, large shops are open from 9 or 10 to 7 or 8 Monday to Saturday and remain open through lunchtime. Many of the large department stores stay open later on Thursday. Smaller shops and many supermarkets often open earlier (8 am) but take a lengthy lunch break (1–3) and generally close around 8 pm; small food shops are often open Sunday morning 9–1. There is typically a small corner grocery store that stays open late, usually until 11, if you're in a bind for basic necessities like diapers, bread, cheese, or fruit. Note that prices are substantially higher in such outlets than in the larger supermarkets. Not all stores stay open on Sunday, except in the Marais, where shops that stand side by side on Rue des Francs Bourgeois, from antiques dealers to chic little designers, open their doors to hordes of Sunday browsers. The Bastille, the Quartier Latin, the Champs-Élysées, Ile St-Louis, and the Ile de la Cité also have shops that open Sunday. Keep in mind, though, that many small shops close from mid-July to the end of August.

▌ MAIL

Post offices, or PTT, are scattered throughout every arrondissement and are recognizable by a yellow "La Poste" sign. They're usually open weekdays 8–7 and Saturday 8–noon. Airmail (*prioritaire*) letters or postcards usually take at least four days to reach North America. If you have questions, you can chat live with a customer service representative in English via ⊕ *www.laposte.fr/particulier.* When shipping home antiques or art, request assistance from the dealer, who can usually handle the customs paperwork for you or recommend a licensed shipping company.

Airmail letters and postcards to the United States and Canada cost €1.20 for 20 grams, €2.10 for 50 grams, and €2.60 for 100 grams. Stamps can be bought in post offices and cafés displaying a red "Tabac" sign.

SHIPPING PACKAGES

Sending overnight mail from Paris is relatively easy. Besides DHL, Federal Express, and UPS, the French post office has an overnight mail service called Chronopost that has special prepaid boxes for international use (and also boxes specifically made to mail wine). All agencies listed can be used as drop-off points, and all have information in English.

Express Services DHL. ☒ *23 rue Feydeau, 2e, Les Grands Boulevards* ☎ *08–25–10–00–80 customer service, €0.18 per min* ⊕ *www.dhl. com.* **Federal Express.** ☒ *63 bd. Haussmann, 8e, Around the Louvre* ☎ *01–40–85–56–60* ⊕ *www.fedex.com/fr.* **UPS.** ☒ *Office Depot, 168 rue du Faubourg St-Honoré, 8e, Les Grands Boulevards* ☎ *08–21–23–38–77 €0.12 per min* ⊕ *www.ups.com.*

▌ MONEY

Although a stay in Paris is far from cheap, you can find plenty of affordable places to eat and shop, particularly if you avoid the obvious tourist traps. Prices tend to reflect the standing of an area in the eyes of Parisians; the touristy area where value is most difficult to find is the 8e arrondissement, on and around the Champs-Élysées. Places where you can generally be certain to shop, eat, and stay without overpaying include the St-Michel/Sorbonne area on the Rive Gauche; the mazelike streets around Les Halles and Le Marais in central Paris; in Montparnasse south of the boulevard; and in the Bastille, République, and Belleville areas of eastern Paris.

In cafés, bars, and some restaurants you can save money by eating or drinking at the counter instead of sitting at a table. Two prices are listed—*au comptoir* (at the counter) and *à salle* (at a table)—and sometimes a third for the terrace. A cup of coffee, standing at a bar, costs from €2; if you sit, it will cost €2.50 to €7. A glass of beer costs from €3 standing and from €4 to €7 sitting; a soft drink costs between €3 and €5. A ham sandwich will cost between €3.50 and €6.

Expect to pay €8 to €15 for a short taxi ride. Museum entry is usually between €7 and €12, though there are hours or days of the week when admission is reduced or free. If you plan on museum hopping, it might be better value to pick up a Paris Museum Pass valid for two, four, or six consecutive days; these cost €42, €56, and €69 respectively.

Prices throughout this guide are given for adults. Substantially reduced fees are almost always available for children, students, and senior citizens.

ATMS AND BANKS

Your own bank will probably charge a fee for using ATMs (*guichets*) abroad; the foreign bank you use may also charge a fee. Nevertheless, you can usually get a better exchange rate at ATMs than at currency-exchange offices, which are a disappearing breed. And extracting funds as you need them is a safer option than carrying around a large amount of cash. Be sure to know your withdrawal limit before taking out cash, and note that French ATMs sometimes restrict how much money you can take out, regardless of your bank balance.

Although ATMs are plentiful, you may have to hunt around for Cirrus and Plus locations (they can be looked up online at ⊕ *www.mastercard.ca/atm-locator. html* and ⊕ *www.visa.com/atmlocator*, respectively). Note, too, that you may have better luck with ATMs if you're using a debit card that doubles as a Visa or MasterCard.

The largest bank in France, BNP Paribas, has agreements with both Barclay's and Bank of America, among others, that allow no-fee withdrawals between affiliated ATMs, typically a savings of $5 per transaction. Check with your local bank to see if it has an agreement with a French bank.

■ TIP→ To get cash at ATMs in Paris, your PIN must be four digits long. If yours has five or more, remember to change it before you leave. If you're having trouble remembering your PIN, do not try more than twice, because at the third attempt the machine will eat your card, and you will have to go back when the bank is open to retrieve it.

CREDIT CARDS

It's a good idea to inform your credit-card company before you travel, especially if you don't go abroad very often. Otherwise, the credit-card company might put a hold on your card owing to unusual activity—not a good thing halfway through your trip. Record all your credit-card numbers, plus the phone numbers to call if your cards are lost or stolen, in a safe place (but not your wallet or purse!), so you're prepared should something go wrong. Some travelers also like to leave a USB key with this information plus scanned passport pages with a trusted family member back home. Both MasterCard and Visa have general numbers you can call if your card is lost, but you're better off dialing the number of your issuing bank, since MasterCard and Visa generally just transfer you to your bank anyway; your bank's number is usually printed on your card. Take note: American Express is less widely accepted in France, so it's wise to have a back-up card.

If you plan to use your credit card for cash advances, you'll need to apply for a PIN at least two weeks before your trip. Although it's usually cheaper (and safer) to use a credit card abroad for large purchases (so you can cancel payments or be reimbursed if there's a problem), some credit-card companies *and* the banks that issue them add substantial percentages to all foreign transactions, whether they're in a foreign currency or not. Check on these fees before leaving home, so there won't be any surprises when you get the bill.

■ TIP→ Before you charge something, ask the merchant whether he or she plans to do a dynamic currency conversion (DCC). In such a transaction the credit-card processor (shop, restaurant, or hotel, not Visa or MasterCard) converts the currency and charges you in dollars. In most cases you'll pay the merchant a 3% fee for this service in addition to any credit-card company and issuing-bank foreign-transaction surcharges.

Reporting Lost Cards American Express.
☎ 800/528–4800 in the U.S. and Canada, 01–47–77–70–00 ⊕ www.americanexpress. com. **MasterCard.** ☎ 800/627–8372 in the U.S. and Canada, 08–00–90–13–87 ⊕ www. mastercard.com. **Visa.** ☎ 800/847–2911 in the U.S. and Canada, 08–00–90–11–79 ⊕ www. visa.com.

CURRENCY AND EXCHANGE

In 2002 the single European Union (EU) currency—the euro—became the official currency of the 12 (now 19) countries participating in the controversial European Monetary Union (with the notable exceptions of Great Britain, Denmark, and Sweden). The euro system has eight coins: 1 and 2 euros, plus 1, 2, 5, 10, 20, and 50 cents. All coins have one side that has the value of the euro on it, whereas the opposite side is adorned with each country's own unique national symbol. (Be aware that, because of their high nickel content, euro coins can pose problems for people with an allergic sensitivity to the metal.) There are also seven colorful notes: 5, 10, 20, 50, 100, 200, and 500 euros. Notes have the principal architectural styles from antiquity onward on one side and the map and the flag of Europe on the other and are the same for all countries. If you happen to have brought some rumpled old francs from home on this trip, you may as well frame them and hang them on the wall for posterity, not prosperity: the Banque de France stopped exchanging francs in 2012.

At this writing, €1 equaled approximately US$1.09 and $1.44 Canadian.

The easiest way to get euros is through ATMs; you can find them in airports, train stations, and throughout the city. ATM rates are excellent because they are based on wholesale rates offered only by major banks. Whenever possible, it's best to use machines that are protected by a door and not directly on the street; don't speak to people in line, and always cover your hand when entering your code in case there is a hidden camera. ■ TIP→ It's a good idea to bring some euros with you from home so you don't have to wait in line at the airport. At exchange booths always confirm the rate with the teller before changing money. You won't do as well at exchange booths in airports or rail and bus stations, in hotels, in restaurants, or in stores. French banks only exchange the money of their own clients.

▌ PACKING

You'll notice it right away: in Paris the women dress well to go shopping, to go to the cinema, to have a drink; the men look good when they're fixing their cars. Admittedly you may see them wearing sweats now, even when they're not doing something *sportif*—but we're not talking gray hoodies. Embroidered designs, quilted materials, animal prints, sparkles: leave it to the French to create a style that's comfy chic. If you want to blend in, don't wear shorts, traditional sweats, or sneakers. Good food in good settings especially deserves good clothing—not necessarily a suit and tie, but a long-sleeved shirt and pants for him, something nice for her.

Be sure to bring rain gear, a comfortable pair of walking shoes, and a sweater or pashmina for cool churches and museums. You can never tell about the weather, so it's prudent to have a small, foldable umbrella. If you'd like to scrutinize the stained glass in churches, bring a pair of small binoculars. A small package of tissues is always a good idea for the occasional rustic bathroom in cafés, airports, and train stations. An additional note: if you're the kind of person who likes a washcloth in the bathroom, bring your own; they're not something you'll find in Paris hotels.

▌ PASSPORTS AND VISAS

All citizens of Canada and the United States, even infants, need a valid passport to enter France for stays of up to 90 days. If you lose your passport, call the nearest embassy or consulate and the local police immediately.

▌ RESTROOMS

Use of public toilet facilities in cafés and bars is usually reserved for customers, so you may need to buy a little something first. Bathrooms are often downstairs and can be unisex, which may mean walking by a men's urinal to reach the cubicle. Turkish-style toilets—holes in the ground with porcelain pads for your feet—are now fortunately scarce. Stand as far away as possible when you press the flushing mechanism to avoid water damage to your shoes. In certain cafés the lights will not come on in the bathroom until the cubicle door is locked. These lights work on a three-minute timer to save electricity. Simply press the button again if the lights go out. Clean public toilets are available in fast-food chains, department stores, and public parks. Paris also has 400 *sanisettes,* or public toilet units, located around the city; most are open from 6 am to 10 pm, but about a quarter of them remain open until 1 am, and 20 operate 24/7. They are free and generally as proper as one could expect, because they self-clean after every use. Elsewhere in the city, you may have to pay €0.50 to €1.50—irksome yes, but when you gotta go, you gotta pay.

There are restroom attendants in train and métro stations, so always bring some coins to the bathroom. Attendants in restaurants and clubs are in charge of cleaning the bathrooms and perhaps handing you a clean towel; slip some small change into the prominently placed saucer.

▌SAFETY

Paris is as safe as any big city can be, but you should always remain streetwise and alert. Certain neighborhoods are more seedy than dangerous, thanks to the night trade that goes on around Les Halles and St-Denis and on Boulevard de Clichy in Pigalle. Some off-the-beaten-path neighborhoods (particularly the outlying suburban communities) may warrant extra precaution. When in doubt, stick to the boulevards and well-lighted, populated streets; keep in mind, however, that the Champs-Élysées, Notre-Dame, and Louvre areas are a haven for pickpockets.

The métro is quite safe overall, though some lines and stations, in particular Lines 2 and 13, get dodgy late at night, so try not to travel alone, memorize the time of the last métro train to your station, ride in the first car by the conductor, and just use common sense. If you're worried, spend the money on a taxi. Pickpocketing is the main problem, day or night. Be wary of anyone crowding you unnecessarily, distracting you, or leaning into you. As much as possible, try to blend in and speak softly (as the French do). Pickpockets often work in groups—and they move fast; on the métro they usually strike just before a stop so that they can leap off the train as it pulls into the station. Be especially careful if taking the RER from Charles de Gaulle/Roissy airport into town; disoriented or jet-lagged travelers are vulnerable to sticky fingers.

Pickpockets love bling and won't miss the opportunity to yank off a necklace or follow a tourist wearing a flashy girl's-best-friend on her finger. They often target purses and laptop bags, so keep your valuables on your person. It's also wise to distribute your cash, credit cards, IDs, and other valuables between a deep front pocket, an inside jacket or vest pocket, and a hidden money pouch. Don't reach for the money pouch once you're in public. If someone holding a map, even a well-dressed woman, asks for directions, go against your helpful American nature and keep walking. Also be wary of the "ring trick" when a passerby suddenly stops in front of you to pick a gold ring off the ground and then offers to sell it to you.

A tremendous number of protest demonstrations are held in Paris—scarcely a week goes by without some kind of march or public gathering. Most are peaceful, but it's best to avoid them. The CRS (French riot police) carefully guard all major demonstrations, directing traffic and preventing violence. They are armed and use tear gas when and if they see fit.

Report any thefts or other problems to the police as soon as possible (note that *officiers* wear a badge indicating what languages they speak). There are three or four police stations in every arrondissement in Paris and one police station in every train station; go to the one in the area where the event occurred. In the case of pickpocketing or other theft, the police will give you a *Déclaration de Perte ou de Vol* (receipt for theft or loss). Police reports must be made in person, and the process is helped along by the S.A.V.E. assistance system for foreign victims—a multilingual software program that files your complaint (and provides you with a receipt) in English. You can also pre-file an incident of theft report in French online at ⊕ *www.pre-plainte-en-ligne. gouv.fr*; this saves time on the paperwork, although a visit in person to the police station will still be necessary. Valuables are usually unrecoverable, but identity documents have been known to resurface. You may need your receipt of theft or loss to replace stolen train and plane tickets or passports; the receipts may also be useful for filing insurance claims.

Although women traveling alone sometimes encounter troublesome comments and the like, *dragueurs* (men who persistently profess their undying love to hapless female passersby) are a dying breed in this increasingly politically correct world. Note that smiling automatically out of politeness is not part of French culture and can be quickly misinterpreted. If you encounter a problem, don't be afraid to show your irritation. Completely ignoring the dragueur should be discouragement enough; if the hassling doesn't let up, don't hesitate to move quickly away.

■TIP→ A few words of advice: leave your jewelry at home, and make sure that smartphones and tablets stay out of sight. Don't talk to strangers. If someone approaches asking you to take a photo, sign a petition, or provide directions, just keep walking.

▌ TAXES

Taxes must be included in affixed prices in France. Prices in restaurants and hotels must by law include taxes and service charges. ■TIP→ If these appear as additional items on your bill, you should complain. There is, however, one exception: don't be shocked to find the *taxe de séjour* (tourist tax) on your hotel tab when you check out. Ranging from €0.20 to €4.40 per person per day, it is applied to all types of lodging. Even if you prepaid your accommodation online through a third-party travel website, you'll still have to cough up the coins.

The standard rate of the V.A.T. (value-added tax, known in France as T.V.A.) is now 20%. A lower rate applies to restaurant food (10%), but it can be as high as 33% for certain luxury items. The V.A.T. for services (restaurants, theaters, etc.) is not refundable, but foreigners are often entitled to a V.A.T. refund on goods they buy. To qualify for one, you must have bought more than €175 worth on the same day in the same participating store (look for the "Tax-Free" sticker on the door) and have stayed three months or less in the EU at the time of purchase.

■TIP→ A new procedure for obtaining this refund—the PABLO system—was launched in 2014. Participating retailers will provide you with a computer-generated PABLO Value-Added Tax (V.A.T.) refund form containing a barcode and the PABLO logo. You then scan the code before checking in at the airport for your outbound flight. The PABLO machines at CDG and Orly provide service in English and can credit the refunded amount directly to your bank account.

At the airport, be sure to have your passport, your ticket, and your PABLO form for items purchased. Go to the La Détaxe/ tax refund machine, scan the form's barcode and you'll receive a message *"OK bordereau validé"* ("OK, form valid") with a green screen (a red screen will give further instructions). An electronic confirmation will be sent directly to the retailer for your reimbursement to be processed. Remember, this must be done BEFORE checking-in your luggage.

▌ TIME

The time difference between New York and Paris is six hours (so when it's 1 pm in New York, it's 7 pm in Paris). The time difference between London and Paris is one hour (so 1 pm in London is 2 pm in Paris). Note that Daylight Saving Time is different in Europe and North America: European clocks change one week earlier in the fall and three weeks later in the spring.

The European format for abbreviating dates is day/month/year, so 7/5/06 means May 7, not July 5.

▌ TIPPING

While Americans may have been voted the world's worst tourists, they are the heavyweight champions when it comes to tipping. In France, this is not a cultural norm. Bills in bars and restaurants must by law include service (despite what entrepreneurial servers may tell you), so tipping isn't required. Waiters are paid well; it is polite, however, to round your bill with small change unless you're dissatisfied. The amount varies—from €0.20 for a beer to €1–€3 after a meal. In expensive restaurants, it's common to leave an additional 5%–10% on the table.

With taxi drivers, round up for shorter trips and add up to 5% of the tab for longer ones. Tip hairdressers 10%. In some theaters and hotels cloakroom attendants may expect nothing (watch for signs that say *pourboire interdit*—tipping forbidden; otherwise, give them €1).

If you stay more than two or three days in a hotel, leave something for the chambermaid—about €1–€2 per day; if the chambermaid also does pressing or laundering for you, give her an extra €1.50–€2 on top of the bill. Expect to pay €2 (€1 in a moderately priced hotel) to the person who carries your bags or hails a taxi for you. In hotels providing room service, give €1–€2 to the waiter (unless breakfast is routinely served in your room). If the concierge has been helpful, leave a tip of €5–€20 depending on the service.

Museum guides should get €1–€1.50 after a tour. For other kinds of tours, tip the guide or leader 10% of the tour cost. It's standard practice to tip long-distance bus drivers about €2 after an excursion, too.

TIPPING GUIDELINES FOR PARIS	
Bellhop	€1–€2, depending on the level of the hotel
Hotel Concierge	€5–€20 if he or she performs a service for you
Hotel Doorman	€1–€2 if he helps you get a cab
Hotel Maid	€1–€2 a day (either daily or at the end of your stay, in cash)
Hotel Room-Service Waiter	€1–€2 per delivery, even if a service charge has been added
Taxi Driver	5% is considered a good tip
Tour Guide	10% of the cost of the tour
Valet Parking Attendant	€1–€2, but only when you get your car
Waiter	Round up for small bills, €1–€3 for meals, 5%–10% in expensive restaurants
Restroom Attendant	Restroom attendants in more expensive restaurants expect small change or €1

▌ TOURS

Guided tours are a good option when you don't want to do it all yourself. And not all are an if-it's-Tuesday-this-must-be-Belgium experience. A knowledgeable guide can take you places that you might never discover on your own, and you may be pushed to see more than you would have otherwise. Tours aren't for everyone, but they can be just the thing for trips to places where making travel arrangements is difficult or time-consuming (particularly when you don't speak the language). Whenever you book a guided tour, find out what's included and what isn't. In most cases prices in tour brochures don't include fees and taxes, plus you'll be expected to tip your guide (in cash) at the end of the tour.

BIKE AND SEGWAY TOURS

A number of companies organize bike tours around Paris and its environs (Versailles, Chantilly, and Fontainebleau);

these always include bikes, helmets, and an English-speaking guide. Costs start at around €35 for a half day; reservations are recommended.

Fat Tire Bike Tours is the best-known Anglophone group; in addition to a general-orientation bike tour, it organizes a nighttime cycling trip that includes a boat cruise on the Seine; Segway tours are also available. Paris à Vélo, C'est Sympa offers tours that take pedal pushers through the heart of Paris or around outlying arrondissements.

Information Fat Tire Bike Tours. ✉ *24 rue Edgar Faure, 15e* ☎ *01-82-88-80-96, 866/614-6218 in the U.S. and Canada* ⊕ *www. fattirebiketoursparis.com.* **Paris à Vélo, C'est Sympa.** ✉ *22 rue Alphonse Baudin, 11e* ☎ *01-48-87-60-01* ⊕ *www.parisvelosympa.com.*

BOAT TOURS

Several boat-tour companies operate Seine cruises that include sightseeing and, in some cases, dining. Batobus offers a convenient way to travel between all major sites along the river, including Notre-Dame, the Louvre, and the Eiffel Tower. A ticket for one day of unlimited hop-on/hop-off travel costs €16. One-hour Bateaux Parisiens sightseeing cruises cost €14 and depart from the Eiffel Tower every 30 minutes from 10 to 10, April to September; themed dinner and lunch cruises start at €40 and €33 respectively. Canauxrama organizes leisurely tours year-round in flat-bottom barges along the Canal St-Martin in eastern Paris. There are four daily departures from April to October (less during the rest of the year); trips cost €18 and last about 2½ hours, with commentary in French and English. Compagnie des Bateaux-Mouches runs a tight ship 12 months of the year. Tickets for the 70-minute Seine tour cost €13.50; lunch cruises are €55, and dinner cruises start at €75. Other year-round operators include Paris Canal, which offers 2½-hour trips with live bilingual commentary between the Musée d'Orsay and the Parc de La Villette (€14), and Yachts de

Paris, which organizes romantic 2½-hour "gourmand cruises" that include a three-course dinner (from €205, drinks extra).

Information Bateaux Parisiens. ✉ *Port de la Bourdonnais, 7e* ☎ *08-25-01-01-01* ⊕ *www. bateauxparisiens.com.* **Batobus.** ✉ *Port de la Bourdonnais, 7e* ☎ *08-25-05-01-01 €0.15 per min* ⊕ *www.batobus.com.* **Canauxrama.** ✉ *Bassin de la Villette, 13 quai de la Loire, 19e* ☎ *01-42-39-15-00* ⊕ *www.canauxrama.com.* **Compagnie des Bateaux-Mouches.** ✉ *Port de la Conférence, 8e* ☎ *01-42-25-96-10* ⊕ *www.bateaux-mouches.fr.* **Paris Canal.** ✉ *Paris Canal, Bassin de la Villette, 21 quai de la Loire, 19e* ☎ *01-42-40-96-97* ⊕ *www. pariscanal.com.* **Yachts de Paris.** ✉ *Port Henri IV, 4e* ☎ *01-44-54-14-70* ⊕ *entreprises. yachtsdeparis.fr.*

BUS TOURS

Pariscityvision.com runs a broad assortment of tours and day trips starting at €21. Buses are equipped with headsets that provide commentary in more than a dozen languages, and there are special recordings for children. Paris L'Open Tour offers hop-on/hop-off tours in a London-style double-decker bus with English or French commentary, again given via individual headsets; you can catch one at any of the 50 pickup points on its four lines. Passes cost €32 (1 day), €36 (2 days), or €40 (3 days). More hop-on/hop-off tours aboard double-decker buses are available through Big Bus Tours Paris; these feature 10 stops, and a ticket good for two consecutive days costs €32. Low-cost Foxity has two main departures, from Notre-Dame and Opéra; a two-hour outing with headphone commentary costs €17. By day or night, Foxity takes visitors around most of central Paris and offers rare handicap access. For an inexpensive, commentary-free alternative, try a regular Parisian bus. The Montmartrobus (€1.80) runs from the Anvers métro station to the top of Montmartre's winding streets. April through September on Sunday and holidays, the RATP's Balabus runs from Gare de Lyon to the Grande Arche de la Défense, passing by dozens of major sights on the way; tickets are €1.80 each, with one to three tickets required, depending on how far you travel.

Information Big Bus Tours. ⊠ *17 quai de Grenelle, 15e* ☎ *01-53-95-39-53* ⊕ *eng. bigbustours.com/paris/home.html.* **Foxity.** ⊠ *3 rue de la Chaussée d'Antin, 9e* ☎ *01-40-17-09-22* ⊕ *www.foxity.com.* **Paris L'Open Tour.** ⊠ *13 rue Auber, 9e* ☎ *01-42-66-56-56* ⊕ *www.paris. opentour.com/en.* **Pariscityvision.com.** ⊠ *2 rue des Pyramides, 1er* ☎ *01-44-55-61-00* ⊕ *www. pariscityvision.com.* **RATP.** ☎ *3246 €0.30 per min* ⊕ *www.ratp.fr.*

MINIBUS AND CAR TOURS

Pariscityvision.com runs minibus excursions with a multilingual guide to places like Mont St-Michel and the Loire Valley (check the website for promos and prices). Paris Trip and Paris Major Limousine organize tours of Paris and environs by limousine, Mercedes, or minibus (for 4–15 passengers) for a minimum of four hours. Chauffeurs are bilingual. Prices range from €68 to €999, depending on the type of vehicle and the distance covered. Another four-wheel option is 4 Roues sous 1 Parapluie: take the Unknown Paris tour (90 minutes, €60) and discover the city's best-kept secrets in an old-school Citroën 2CV (France's answer to the Volkswagen Beetle), or try a ride around the Champs-Élysées (45 minutes, €30). With 20-odd options available in this iconic car, you can leave the driving to others and just enjoy being a tourist.

Information 4 Rues sous 1 Parapluie. ⊠ *22 rue Bernard Dimey, 18e* ☎ *01-58-59-27-82* ⊕ *www.4roues-sous-1parapluie.com.* **Paris Major Limousine.** ⊠ *199 bd. Malesherbes, 17e* ☎ *01-44-52-50-00* ⊕ *www.1st-limousine-services.com.* **Paris Trip.** ⊠ *2 Cité de Pusy, 17e* ☎ *01-56-79-05-23* ⊕ *www.paristrip.com.* **Pariscityvision.com.** ⊠ *2 rue des Pyramides, 1er* ☎ *01-44-55-61-00* ⊕ *www. pariscityvision.com.*

SPECIAL-INTEREST AND WALKING TOURS

Has it been a while since Art History 101? Paris Muse can help guide you through the city's museums; with its staff of art historians (all native English-speakers) you can crack the da Vinci code or gain a new understanding of hell in front of Rodin's sculpted gates. Rates start at €80, including museum admission.

If you'd like a bit of guidance flexing your own artistic muscles, take a themed photography tour with Paris Photo Tours. Run by Randy Harris, these relaxed excursions are perfect for first-time visitors and anyone hoping to improve their photographic skills. Expect to pay $165 for a daytime tour, $275 for the evening version.

Sign up with Chic Shopping Paris to smoothly navigate the city's retail scene. Tours, which start at €100, include Chic Consignment (focusing on vintage–secondhand places), Très Teens, and Unique Boutiques; itineraries can also be tailor-made to fit your interests.

Edible Paris, the brainchild of food writer Rosa Jackson, is a customized service for vacationing gastronomes. Submit a wish list of your interests and guidelines for your tastes, and you'll receive a personalized itinerary, maps, and restaurant reservations on request. Prices start around €125 per half day.

Paris by Mouth—the most popular English-language website about eating and drinking in the city—offers tasting tours led by local food writers. Three-hour outings, which run every day of the week, are available for two to six people (€95 per person). Private tours and larger group tours are available upon request; you can also add on a wine tasting, shared lunch, or baguette-making class.

Paris Walks offers a wide selection of tours, some year-round, that range from neighborhood visits and museum jaunts to themed tours such as Writers of the Left Bank. The guides are knowledgeable, taking you into less trammeled streets and divulging interesting stories about even the most unprepossessing spots. A two-hour group tour costs €12, and you don't have to reserve.

For a more intimate experience, Context Paris offers specialized in-depth tours of the city's art and architecture led by English-speaking architects and art historians; tours aimed at foodies are also available. Prices range from €88 per person for a three-hour group tour to around €380 per party for a full day of custom touring (maximum five people).

Black Paris Tours explores the places made famous by African American musicians, writers, artists, and political exiles. Options include a 5½-hour walking-bus-métro tour (€75) that provides first-time visitors with a city orientation and a primer on the history of African Americans in Paris.

Interesting walking tours are also available from the Centre des Monuments Nationaux; you can find a list in the weekly magazine *L'Officiel des Spectacles*, which covers them under the heading "Conférences" (most tours are in French, unless otherwise noted).

If you are as interested in the locals as in the sights per se, you can't go wrong with Paris Greeters (*Parisien d'un Jour*). English-speaking resident volunteers take groups of up to six visitors out for a stroll, providing an insider's look at Parisian life along the way. Best of all, the experience is free, though donations are always welcome.

Information Black Paris Tours. ☎ 01–46–37–03–96, 972/325–8516 U.S. Office ⊕ www.blackparistour.com. **Centre des monuments nationaux.** ✉ Bureau des Visites/Conférences, Hôtel de Sully, 62 rue St-Antoine, 4e ☎ 01–44–61–20–00 ⊕ www.monuments-nationaux.fr. **Chic Shopping Paris.** ☎ 573/355–9777 U.S. Office ⊕ www.chicshoppingparis.com. **Context Paris.** ☎ 800/691–6036 U.S. Office ⊕ www.contexttravel.com. **Edible Paris.** ⊕ www.

edible-paris.com. **Paris by Mouth.** ⊕ www.parisbymouth.com. **Paris Greeters.** ⊕ www.greeters.paris. **Paris Muse.** ☎ 06–73–77–33–52 ⊕ www.parismuse.com. **Paris Photo Tours.** ☎ 425/281–4649 U.S. office ⊕ www.parisphototours.com. **Paris Walks.** ✉ 12 passage Meunier, St Denis ☎ 01–48–09–21–40 ⊕ www.paris-walks.com.

▮ VISITOR INFORMATION

The regional tourism board—with multiple Arrivals-level kiosks at both Charles de Gaulle and Orly airports—can provide you with maps, brochures, and more the moment you touch down. Once you're in Paris, you can turn to the civic tourist information office. The main one is centrally located on Rue des Pyramides (near the Opéra), and four branch offices are stationed at the city's most popular tourist sights. Most are open daily; the Gare de Lyon and Gare de l'Est branches, however, are open Monday through Saturday only. These tourism bureaus have friendly, efficient, multilingual staff. You can gather info on special events, local transit, hotels, tours, excursions, and discount passes. You can also purchase museum passes and the coveted passports for Versailles, which enable you to avoid additional lines at the château. Extra kiosks pop up in the summer by Notre-Dame, Hotel de Ville, the Champs-Élysées, and Bastille.

Local Tourism Information Office du Tourisme de la Ville de Paris Anvers. ✉ Across from 72 bd. Rochechouart, 18e, Montmartre ⊕ www.parisinfo.com Ⓜ Anvers. **Office du Tourisme de la Ville de Paris Gare de l'Est.** ✉ Facing platform 1 and 2, Pl. du 11 novembre 1918, 10e, Canal St-Martin ⊕ www.parisinfo.com Ⓜ Gare de l'Est. **Office du Tourisme de la Ville de Paris Gare de Lyon.** ✉ Hall 1, facing L & M platforms, 20 bd. Diderot, 12e, Bastille ⊕ www.parisinfo.com Ⓜ Gare de Lyon. **Office du Tourisme de la Ville de Paris Gare du Nord.** ✉ Under glass ceiling at Ile de France section, 18 rue de Dunkerque, 10e, Stalingrad/La Chapelle ⊕ www.parisinfo.com Ⓜ Gare *du Nord.* **Office du Tourisme de la Ville de Paris Pyramides.** ✉ *25 rue des Pyramides, 1er, Around the Louvre* ⊕ *www.parisinfo.com* Ⓜ *Pyramides.* **Visit Paris Region.** ⊕ *www.visitparisregion.com.*

ONLINE RESOURCES

Besides the official tourist office websites ⊕ *en.parisinfo.com* and ⊕ *www.visitparisregion.com*, there are several other helpful government-sponsored sites. The Paris mayor's office site, ⊕ *www.paris.fr*, covers all kinds of public cultural attractions, student resources, parks, markets, and more. On the French Ministry of Culture's site, ⊕ *www.culture.fr*, you can search by theme (contemporary art, cinema, music, theater, etc.) or by region (Paris is in the Ile-de-France). The Réunion des Musées Nationaux hosts a group site, ⊕ *www.rmn.fr*, that provides visitor info and exhibition updates for 20 member museums; most are in Paris proper, including the Louvre, the Musée Rodin, and the Musée d'Orsay.

A useful website for checking Paris addresses is the phone and address directory, Les Pages Jaunes (⊕ *www.pagesjaunes.fr*). Input a specific address, and you get not just a street map but a photo as well.

The team at Paris by Mouth (⊕ *parisbymouth.com*) dishes on the local food scene with help from expat writers like Alexander Lobrano. Also check Lobrano's site (⊕ *www.hungryforparis.com*) for his latest Hungry for Paris & France dining reviews and favorite Paris food links. Secrets of Paris (⊕ *www.secretsofparis.com*) has a free online newsletter with tips on dining, nightlife, accommodations, and sightseeing off the beaten path. Though not entirely dedicated to Paris, France Today (⊕ *www.francetoday.com*) and The Local (⊕ *www.thelocal.fr*) often cover Paris-related news, arts events, and restaurants.

There are all sorts of Paris-related blogs that can be great sources of information and travel inspiration. Some of our faves are Do it in Paris (⊕ *www.doitinparis.com*), a bilingual site focused on fashion, shopping, dining, and fun activities; and the Hip Paris Blog (⊕ *hipparis.com*), which combines a trendy array of Parisian pics with insight into food, arts, and local living. Professional pastry-chef-turned-author David Lebovitz left California to live (and write exquisitely about) the sweet life in Paris on his blog at ⊕ *www.davidlebovitz.com*. French Word-a-Day (⊕ *www.french-word-a-day.typepad.com*) is an engaging slice of life, with a vocabulary bonus.

INDEX

PHOTO CREDITS

Cover Photos: Front cover: Bildagentur Huber/Kremer Susanne/Fototeca 9x12 [Description: Eiffel Tower, Trocadero]. Back cover (from left to right): Tom Nance/iStockphoto; Madeleine Openshaw/ Shutterstock; Samot / Shutterstock. Spine: Ferenc Cegledi/Shutterstock. 1, Sam Gillespie/Alamy. 2, Matthew Dixon / Shutterstock. Chapter 1: Experience: 8-9, Bildarchiv Monheim/age fotostock. 16 (left), Paris Tourist Office / Stéphane Querbes. 16 (top center), Bryan Busovicki/Shutterstock. 16 (bottom center), Bensliman/Shutterstock. 16 (top right), Jan Kranendonk/Shutterstock. 16 (bottom right), Ferenc Cegledi/Shutterstock. 17 (top left), wikipedia.org. 17 (bottom left), José Fuste Raga/age fotostock. 17 (top center), Jan Kranendonk/Shutterstock. 17 (bottom center), Joanne Rosensweig. 17 (right), travelstock44/Alamy. Chapter 2: Ile de la Cité and Ile St-Louis: 29, Jonathan Larsen/Shutterstock. 31, ImageGap/Alamy. 32, David Noton/Alamy. 34, Zoom-zoom | Dreamstime.com. Chapter 3: Around the Eiffel Tower: 39, John Kellerman / Alamy. 41, Patrick Hermans/Shutterstock. 42, Cristina CIO-CHINA/Shutterstock. 43, Directphoto.org/Alamy. 45, tkachuk/Shutterstock. Chapter 4: The Champs-Elysées: 49, Art Kowalsky/Alamy. 51, Clay McLachlan/Aurora Photos. 52, dalbera/Flickr. 55, fabio chironi/age fotostock. Chapter 5: Around the Louvre: 61, blickwinkel/Alamy. 63, Sylvain Grandadam/ age fotostock. 64, David A. Barnes/Alamy. 66, Travel Pix Collection/age fotostock. 69, Dennis_dolkens | Dreamstime.com. Chapter 6: Les Grand Boulevards: 75, Kevin George/Alamy. 77, Tristan Deschamps/ Alamy. 78, Kiev.Victor / Shutterstock. Chapter 7: Montmartre: 85, Hemis/Alamy. 87, Matthew Bergheiser/Shutterstock. 88, Jon Arnold Images/Alamy. 91, rfx/Shutterstock. 92, Brian Jannsen / age fotostock. Chapter 8: Le Marais: 97, Oliver Knight/Alamy. 99, Berndt Fischer/age fotostock. 100, Halie Cousineau/ Fodor's Travel. 106, Claude Valette/Flickr, [CC BY-ND 2.0]. Chapter 9: Eastern Paris: 111, Bob Handelman/Alamy. 113, Berndt Fischer/age fotostock. 114, f1 online/Alamy. 117, M&G Therin-Weise / age fotostock. 118, Emile Lombard/Flickr, [CC BY-ND 2.0]. Chapter 10: The Latin Quarter: 125, Danita Delimont/Alamy. 127, AA World Travel Library/Alamy. 128, Renaud Visage/age fotostock. 132, Aschaf/Flickr. Chapter 11: St-Germain-des-Pres: 137, Robert Harding Picture Library Ltd/Alamy. 139, Robert Harding Picture Library Ltd/Alamy. 140, Ian Dagnall/Alamy. 142, David Noton Photography/Alamy. 144, Mark Edward Smith/age fotostock. Chapter 12: Montparnasse: 147, Berndt Fischer/ age fotostock. 149 and 150, Berndt Fischer/age fotostock. Chapter 13: Western Paris: 155, Iwan Baan for Fondation Louis Vuitton/Gehry Partners LLP. 157, Brian Yarvin/age fotostock. 158, tbkmedia.de/ Alamy. Chapter 14: Where to Eat: 163, Adam Wasilewski / Alamy. 164, Halie Cousineau/ Fodor's Travel. 165 (bottom), Pitrs10 | Dreamstime.com. 165 (top), Benbdprod | Dreamstime.com. 166, Dana Ward/Shutterstock. Chapter 15: Where to Stay: 227, Four Seasons Hotels and Resorts. 228, The Leading Hotels of the World. Chapter 16: Shopping: 255, Directphoto / age fotostock. 256, Croixboisee, Fodors.com member. 292, Walter Bibikow / age fotostock. Chapter 17: Nightlife: 297, David R. Frazier Photolibrary, Inc. / Alamy. 298, cgo2/Flickr. Chapter 18: Performing Arts: 321 and 322, Directphoto.org/Alamy. 333, Jose Fuste Raga / age fotostock. Chapter 19: Side Trips from Paris: 335, Wojtek Buss/age fotostock. 336, Photodisc. 341, AM Corporation/Alamy. 345, José Ignacio Soto/Shutterstock About Our Writers: All photos are courtesy of the writers except for the following: Linda Hervieux, courtesy of Michael Honegger.

NOTES

NOTES

NOTES

NOTES

NOTES

NOTES

NOTES

NOTES

NOTES

NOTES

ABOUT OUR WRITERS

 Nancy Heslin is the editor in chief of the English-language *Riviera Reporter* magazine and a professor at the École de Journalisme in Nice. Since swapping Canada for the Côte d'Azur in 2001, she's distinguished herself as a go-to authority on the region, being interviewed by the likes of CBS, BBC, and APF. She has taken the TGV with Tom Cruise to Marseille, lunched with Prince Albert in Monaco, and sipped Champagne with Paris Hilton in St-Tropez as a staffer for some leading celebrity magazines. Nancy became a French citizen in 2010; she works her baguette butt off with endurance sports like the Nice Ironman (no, she didn't win). For this edition, she updated the Experience Paris, Travel Smart Paris, and Performing Arts chapters.

 Journalist and photographer Linda Hervieux has explored most corners of Paris since moving to the City of Light in 2004. Her writing has appeared in the *New York Times,* the *International Herald Tribune,* and the *New York Daily News,* among others. For Fodor's she has scoped out more than 100 museums and galleries and spent countless hours in her favorite: the mighty Musée du Louvre, where she studied art history. Her website is ⊕ *www.lindahervieux.com.* She updated the Around the Louvre chapter this edition.

 When writer-editor Jennifer Ladonne decided it was time to leave her longtime home of Manhattan, there was only one place to go: Paris. Her insatiable curiosity—which earned her a reputation in New York for knowing just the right place to go for just the right anything—has found the perfect home in the inexhaustible streets of Paris. An avid cook and wine lover, she's a frequent contributor on food, culture, and travel

and a monthly columnist for the magazine *France Today*. Whether you're looking for the best neighborhood bistros or the perfect little black dress, she's the person to ask, as we did for our Where to Eat, Shopping, Where to Stay, Nightlife, and Side Trips From Paris chapters.

 A life-long urban explorer, journalist and photo editor Virginia Power has been strolling the streets of Paris for the past 25 years. She has written and reported on a variety of subjects—culture, politics, sports, social issues—for *Newsweek*, *Paris* Magazine, and other publications. Writing for Fodor's has brought her back to doing what she does best: wandering, discovering, and enjoying what Paris has to offer. This edition, she updated the Montparnasse and St-Germain-des-Prés neighborhood chapters.

 Jack Vermee is a Canadian university lecturer, film critic, screenwriter, film festival programmer, and freelance writer/editor who happily exchanged nature for culture by moving from Vancouver to Paris six years ago. Starting in the pre-video days of the early 1980s, when he first visited the city to watch classic films at the old Cinémathèque Française, he has carried on a shameless love affair with *la ville-lumière* and its innumerable charms. He suspects the love affair will never run its course—with 6,100 city streets to explore and new adventures just around the next corner, how could it? Jack brought his knowledge to the following neighborhood chapters: Les Grands Boulevards, Montmartre, the Marais, Eastern Paris, Western Paris, Around the Eiffel Tower, Champs-Élysées, Ile St-Lous and Ile de la Cité, and the Latin Quarter. You can reach him at *jvermee@gmail.com.*

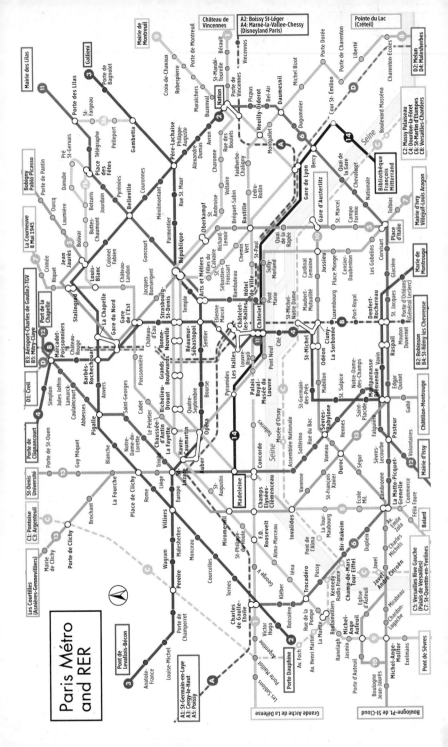